THE REIGN

LIFE IN ELIZABETH'S BRITAIN

Also by Matthew Engel

That's The Way It Crumbles
Engel's England
Eleven Minutes Late
Extracts from the Red Notebooks
Tickle the Public

THE REIGN

LIFE IN ELIZABETH'S BRITAIN

Part 1: The Way It Was, 1952–79

Matthew Engel

Atlantic Books
London

Published in hardback in Great Britain in 2022 by Atlantic Books,
an imprint of Atlantic Books Ltd.

Copyright © Matthew Engel, 2022

10 9 8 7 6 5 4 3 2

A CIP catalogue record for this book is available from the British Library.

Hardback ISBN: 978-1-78649-667-6
E-book ISBN: 978-1-78649-668-3

Front endpaper: Piccadilly Circus, London, 1952 (© *Illustrated London News Ltd/
Mary Evans*)
Back endpaper: Piccadilly Circus, London, 1979 (*Archive Photos/Getty Images*)

Printed and bound by CPI Group (UK) Ltd, Croydon CR0 4YY

Atlantic Books
An imprint of Atlantic Books Ltd
Ormond House
26–27 Boswell Street
London
WC1N 3JZ

For all those we have loved and lost.

When, two days previously, the news of the approaching end had been made public, astonished grief had swept over the country. It appeared as if some monstrous reversal of the course of nature was about to take place. The vast majority of her subjects had never known a time when Queen Victoria had not been reigning over them. She had become an indissoluble part of their whole scheme of things, and that they were about to lose her appeared a scarcely possible thought.

Lytton Strachey, *Queen Victoria*

CONTENTS

AUTHOR'S NOTE

By 6 February 2022, the seventieth anniversary of Queen Elizabeth II's accession to the throne, only about one-seventh of the British population had been alive on the fateful day her father, George VI, died.

I am a member of that elite, but a very junior one. I was just shy of eight months old by then and, despite taking an interest in the news from an early age, my memory does not stretch to 6 February 1952 – nor to the Coronation, which came just before my second birthday. So, like the other six-sevenths of today's Britain, the Queen for me has always been the Queen.

Meanwhile, as for the rest of the one-seventh, almost everyone who might have cooed over my cot or my old-fashioned pram has now passed out of my life. And yet – from 1952 to 2022 – the Queen has been a constant presence at the nation's heart, ageing only imperceptibly: a reign that has turned into something quite extraordinary yet taken entirely for granted. In that time Britain and the world have altered beyond recognition.

This is not another book about the monarchy. It is the story of how different Britain has become in the years of Elizabeth II. This first part takes the story from 1952 to the political turning point of 1979. Subject to my own health and sanity, and the continued existence of the planet, Part Two will take the story from there to wherever it leads to complete the journey: from bowler hats to baseball caps, conscription to cancel culture, Wakes weeks to woke. Please sit back and enjoy the ride.

Matthew Engel, Herefordshire
July 2022

For those who might find some of the contents far-fetched, a bibliography and a full set of references can be found on my website, matthewengel.co.uk

PROLOGUE

O N NEW YEAR'S DAY 1951, THE BBC LIGHT PROGRAMME tentatively scheduled a new 'serial play of country life' to be broadcast in fifteen-minute chunks every weekday.

The field was crowded, there being already two well-established daily serials: *Mrs Dale's Diary*, the saga of a suburban doctor's wife, and *Dick Barton – Special Agent*, a prototype James Bond without the sex or the dry martinis. One was aimed at housewives; the other mainly at prepubescent schoolboys.

The new idea was credited to a Lincolnshire farmer who had remarked at a meeting with the BBC: 'What we need is a farming Dick Barton!' And the same scriptwriters were called in to work on the new programme: *The Archers*. But it was not clear who they thought the audience might actually be.

The programme's early tone was palatable, if a touch pedantic and preachy. This was in tune with the earnest, optimistic house style of both the early BBC and Clement Attlee's post-war Labour government, then drawing wearily towards its close. Part of the initial aim was to convey sugared messages from Whitehall to the farmers – although the 11.45 a.m. slot was not the most obvious time to attract them. They did not then have radios in their tractors; indeed, they did not necessarily have tractors. On that level, the programme never really worked.

But another purpose was for the countryside to speak to the

town. And, in that, *The Archers* succeeded triumphantly. By luck or judgment it spoke to something very profound within the British – or more specifically the English – character: the melancholic craving of a thoroughly urban populace for an idealized rustic past. Within four months, Dick Barton, who had seen off every villain on the planet, was himself history: ejected from his prime early-evening slot by Dan and Doris Archer of Brookfield Farm in the imaginary Midland village of Ambridge. Mrs Dale would last until 1969. But to last that long, the programme had to be rebranded (as *The Dales*), recast and even relocated – to an imaginary East Anglian new town.*

The Archers was totally rooted to its own spot, and as the decades passed, the programme became a living history of rural England. The old farmhand characters and smallholders faded away, to be replaced by machines, agribusiness and dozens of urban transplants, bringing their attitudes to Ambridge along with their packing cases. And the scripts, as in all English villages, became more worldly. Storylines that in the early 1950s would be well hidden – a gay son here, a nasty case of domestic violence there – became common. These were nearly always handled with more taste and delicacy than would be attempted by the television versions of what came to be called soap operas. In fact, the TV soaps were never the appropriate comparison. There is another one.

Since 1951, three couples have presided over Brookfield Farm: Dan and Doris; their son Phil and his wife Jill; and in their turn, their son David and his wife Ruth. Since February 1952 to date, only one has presided over the United Kingdom: Elizabeth and, until 2021, Philip.

The fundamental principle of both operations is that dynasty is everything. The marriage of the central characters must be fundamentally solid. The farm – or as the royal family say in private, the firm – must be passed on without blemish. This is not preordained:

---

* In 1963 the actress who played the original Mrs Dale, Ellis Powell, was summarily dismissed after fifteen years – 'chucked out like an old sock,' she said – to be replaced by the better-known Jessie Matthews. Powell died barely two months later, on the dole and very bitter. In her will, her net fortune was £15.

Ruth Archer once had a little dalliance, but evidently stopped short of full-scale infidelity; rumours of Prince Philip's affairs were around since at least the late 1950s, though it is hard to cast doubt on a marriage that lasted nearly seventy-four years.

Yet around that central core, anything goes. The peripheral characters have to be flawed and mischievous, or there is no soap opera to sustain public interest. And on the whole the Windsors have been more imaginative and creative in producing storylines than the Archers. All the way from Princess Margaret and Peter Townsend, through Chas and Di, to Randy Andy and Harry and Meghan. Certainly no BBC hierarch would have allowed anyone to be written out of the script with such horrific implausibility as Princess Di was. It often seems that Ambridge is a far more realistic embodiment of the nation's aspirations than Buckingham Palace.

The Archers has had its own moments of unreality. There is a suspicion that Walter Gabriel, the programme's best-loved yokel, was meant to be 70 at the start. The character died thirty-eight years later, having just celebrated his 92nd birthday, as though a used car dealer had nipped into the studio and turned back the clock. One minor figure, Mrs Turvey, was said to have died three times over.

The number of unnatural deaths over the years has been suspiciously high for a small village – seven times the normal rate, according to research in 2011. That was the year which began with Nigel Pargetter's fatal fall from the roof of his reasonably substantial country house – but with a scream, it was calculated, of a length more appropriate to a fall from the roof of York Minster. That was the uncharacteristically crass way *The Archers* chose to celebrate its diamond jubilee. The Queen, celebrating her own in 2012, led a year of national celebration.

And in 2020, a year when life turned out to be stranger than fiction, the monarchy again proved stronger. The social distancing rules prevented *The Archers* being recorded in the usual way and, after a hiatus, the normally zippy scripts were replaced by tedious monologues.

Meanwhile, the Queen, having outlived Walter Gabriel, delivered two majestic broadcasts perfectly calibrated to rally the nation. It is one contention of this book that the Queen's longevity, steadfastness, bearing and careful judgment have played an underrated role in British history since 1952.

Very few British institutions have come through all those years of astonishing change and drama with their integrity not just intact but enhanced. The monarchy (if not always the royal family) is one of them. The Queen is the motif for this book. But the story that follows is not about her – and still less about *The Archers*. It is about the British.

THE
1950s

1

GOD SAVE THE . . .

TUESDAY, 5 FEBRUARY 1952, WAS HIS IDEA OF A PERFECT DAY. He was at Sandringham, the favourite among his homes. A shooting party, no fuss, a few friends and locals: tenants, game-keepers, policemen. He killed nine hares and a pigeon, apparently: his last shot being a bull's eye on a hare at top speed. He had dinner with his wife and younger daughter, Margaret; the two grandchildren, Charles and Anne, aged three and eighteen months respectively, were already tucked up. Then he went to bed, alone, around 10.30.

At midnight, a watchman saw him fiddling with the window latch, so the date of his death is known, if not the time. At 7.30 the next morning his valet found him, as he brought a cup of tea. The first hint to the outside world was the sight of the doctor from nearby Wolferton, heading towards the estate, driving fast, coat – according to some reports – over his pyjamas. There was nothing he could do. The king was 56, too young for his death to be accepted as timely, but not as young as we would think it now. The official code word for this eventuality was 'Hyde Park Corner'.

On the previous Thursday, King George VI had been at newly opened London Airport to see off his elder daughter, Elizabeth, and her dashing husband Philip. They were flying to Nairobi to start a five-month tour of the Empire which her father and mother had been due to undertake before the King became ill. 'The King, looking well, stood bareheaded in the chill wind that for some hours had scourged the waiting crowd,' said the *Manchester Guardian*. The MP and diarist 'Chips' Channon, one of the few with access to television, saw things differently when the newsreel footage was shown, in the leisurely way of the early fifties, on the Saturday. He described the King as looking 'cross, almost mad-looking',* and noted his plan to go shooting the following week. 'Suicide,' said Channon.

The king had been ill, on and off, for almost four years. A great many long words were used in print to describe his condition and what was being done to alleviate it. One word was not used. Cancer was still subject to an ancient taboo, partly because it was perceived as almost invariably fatal and partly because it was associated with taint – that it was somehow the patient's fault.† The secrecy often applied most stringently to the person who had most right to know: the patient. No matter who it was. In September 1951, Lord Moran, Winston Churchill's personal physician during the war, explained the King's situation to his most famous patient. 'Why are they talking about "structural changes"?' Churchill asked. 'Because they were anxious to avoid talking about cancer,' replied Moran.

Shortly after that, Churchill, who was then Leader of the Opposition, had a letter from the King's private secretary, Sir Alan 'Tommy' Lascelles, who also knew the truth, and remarked to Moran: 'The King did not know that Lascelles was writing to me. Poor fellow, he does not know what it means.' Thus the man who reigned over the greatest empire the world has ever seen, who was ex officio privy to Churchill's wartime secrets, was not to be told what was ravaging his own frail body.

Dr John Marks, later chairman of the British Medical Association and a young doctor at the time, told me this was quite normal. 'People didn't talk about health the way we do now,' he reflected in 2018. 'It was moaned about but patients wouldn't go into details. They probably wouldn't even know the details. God Has Spoken.'

---

*   Which might be attributed to the pan-stick he had taken to wearing in public.

†   Since the King had lung cancer and was a heavy smoker, that might be the historical judgment too. But Richard Doll's ground-breaking report linking the disease to tobacco was not published until 1950 and was not yet considered definitive.

He meant the doctor-God rather than any other God. 'Those were the good old days,' he chuckled.*

———·———

By the time the King died, Churchill, now 77, was again prime minister, after leading the Conservatives to a narrow majority over Labour in October 1951. Now he was actually entitled to be among the first to know. His earlier clandestine briefing did not make him any more prepared for the reality, however. The Downing Street private secretary, Jock Colville, found him in tears. Colville tried to reassure him by saying how well he and the Queen would get on, but Churchill just replied that he did not know her and that 'she was only a child'.

Word reached Fleet Street at 10.45, and across London the news was chalked up on the news-sellers' boards while they waited for the capital's three evening papers to thunder off the presses. The BBC interrupted their radio programmes half an hour later (having waited for *Mrs Dale's Diary* to finish), and then decided to close down completely between the 1 p.m. and 6 p.m. editions of the news, a decision seen as ludicrous at the time.

By lunchtime, anyone in Britain who was not alone would almost certainly have heard. The person who most needed to know had not. But the 25-year-old woman who left Britain as Princess Elizabeth was not well placed: she and Philip had spent the night in upcountry Kenya at the famous (and from that moment, much more famous) Treetops Hotel, watching animals at the waterhole below. At the moment she became Queen, she was, depending who was doing the guessing, on an aerial platform entranced by baboons, hippos, rhinos or lions. Unless, most charmingly, it was the moment an eagle hovered over her head.

She heard fourth-hand. Philip, when told by his aide Mike Parker, 'looked as if you'd dropped half the world on him'. When

* The doctors had known the King's condition was terminal since they operated on him in 1951. Astonishingly, the operation took place in Buckingham Palace rather than a properly equipped hospital.

he took his wife aside to break the news to her, she immediately slipped on the cloak of composure she would wear the rest of her life. If she cried, it was in the deepest privacy.

———.———

For those less directly affected, it was a big moment. But not *that* big a moment. Not everyone can remember precisely how they heard, the way those alive in 1939 remembered Neville Chamberlain's declaration of war on Germany, or those later would recall the assassination of President Kennedy and the events of 9/11.* Interestingly, those who were at school in 1952 often have more vivid memories of that day than those who were already adults. But then, as Elizabeth became Queen, Britain's 51-year-olds found themselves living under their sixth monarch: kings and queens came and went, and God was eternal. (By 2022 God had become an optional extra and the Queen seemingly eternal.)

David McKie was a sixth-former at Christ's Hospital in Sussex, a very traditional school which had a daily prayer mentioning the church and the King. McKie reminded the boy doing the prayer that he now had to say 'the Queen'. The boy looked doubtful. A master was called. The master looked aghast: 'But this is the form we've always used.' He was finally persuaded that you couldn't talk about the King if there wasn't one.

My brother Anthony, aged eight, was called to a school assembly where the announcement was enlivened by a boy who kept laughing. The boy later explained he thought the head had said 'The cane is dead' – the cane being a far more pervasive presence for 1950s schoolboys than some distant monarch. Peter Overstall, seven, remembers going home to hear his mother say: 'It was so unfair on him. He never wanted to be king.' Rose Williams, six, just lay on the floor screaming because there was no *Listen with Mother* on the radio.

Those who actually served the King could be the most blasé.

———————————

* News of a comparable 'where were you when . . .' bombshell – Princess Diana's fatal car crash in 1997 – broke while Britain slept, in the early hours of a Sunday.

Neal Ascherson was a marine commando at an outstation in the Malayan jungle. 'Everyone was shocked when we heard but I don't remember anyone doing anything about it, holding a memorial parade, anything like that. It seemed very far away and it didn't seem very relevant to us.' In Richard Vinen's history of National Service, he tells of another platoon commander in Malaya who was told by his radio operator 'King's dead' and assumed this was a reference to a Sergeant King, which would have been far more alarming.

Nicholas Faith was in an artillery barracks in Shropshire: 'I remember a squaddie responding with "What useless fuckers the Royal family are." That's always stuck with me.' Brian Hough from Manchester had been looking forward to his last night of freedom with his mates before reporting for his call-up the next morning: 'But bugger me all the pubs were closed. I wasn't chuffed about that.'

Petra Green was working as a filing clerk at Harrods, and that was very different. 'The supervisor knocked on her desk and called us all over, about twenty of us. She was a real martinet and we all thought, "What have we done now?" "Girls," she said. "The king has died." She then said she didn't know what to do, so some of us stood there and some sat down. Then after a while she said it was lunchtime and that we could go.

'So I walked along Knightsbridge with a friend. I saw a lot of men with homburg hats and umbrellas and they were just standing there as if to attention, with tears down their faces. It was the start of a terrible time. All the window displays were changed. Everything was black or purple, mostly black. Or there were huge wreath arrangements. It was as if the world had died. It was so depressing.'

And the focus now was very much on London. The BBC summoned up the courage to begin broadcasting again, expunging any hints of levity. The new Queen and consort began a fraught journey home, with a two-hour delay caused by a storm at Entebbe Airport and then a nineteen-hour flight. They arrived just before the dusk of a wintry Thursday to be greeted by her prime minister. That evening, Ruth Raven was waiting for a 28 bus on Kensington High Street –

on her way to an evening class – when two black cars flashed by heading towards town. She realized who one of them must contain. The bus queue was so surprised they began talking to each other.

That night, the prime minister made a radio address to the nation. By now he had recovered all his zest, reaching a magnificent crescendo: 'I, whose youth was passed in the august, unchallenged and tranquil glories of the Victorian era, may well feel a thrill in invoking once more the prayer and the anthem: GOD SAVE THE QUEEN.'

Everyone had to get used to that. Barristers were again Queen's Counsel,* and people rode the Queen's Highway and spoke the Queen's English (perhaps); malefactors would now serve their time at *Her* Majesty's Pleasure. His Majesty's Theatre in Haymarket changed its name, as it had done for Victoria and again when she died. After his abandoned night at the pub, Brian Hough (pronounced *Huff*, 'Huffy' to his mates) had to report to the Ladysmith Barracks in Ashton-under-Lyne, a fourpenny bus ride from home; this also annoyed him – he had been hoping for somewhere more exotic. His friends were being sent far away, like Scotland or the south-west: 'I thought that'd be great. I'd never been further than Rhyl.' But he was among the first soldiers in fifty-one years to swear allegiance to the Queen, and he was quite chuffed by that.

In Whitehall, civil servants at the Treasury were still wiping their bottoms with hard, abrasive, old-fashioned toilet paper marked ON HIS MAJESTY'S SERVICE. When it was time to restock, it was thought indelicate to change this wording to HER MAJESTY. The next batch just said GOVERNMENT PROPERTY.

---

* Two of them were old enough to have been Queen's Counsel fifty-one years earlier.

2

THE STATE OF HER
REALM, 1952

I N 1952, AS NOW, ANYONE LOOKING FOR – OR EVEN FANTASIZING
about – a substantial country house without being fixated on a
particular location would turn to the pages of *Country Life*. In the
week the King died, they would have found the following:

Attractive Late Georgian: 6 beds, 20 acres and cottage   £10,000
16th century country house, Suffolk   £9,250
Bucks manor house and duck pond   £8,500
Queen Anne house near Norwich, tennis court, bowling
green, rose gardens   £7,500

Even allowing for seventy years' worth of inflation, these delightful-
sounding old houses were indeed bargains: £7,500 in 1952 equals
£200,000 in 2022, which would hardly buy a log cabin in any
village in south-east England. But few people then wanted an old
country house, however charming. They were icy, draughty, run-
down, difficult to restore, extravagant to maintain and considered a
worse investment than the stock market.

True, the British were used to discomfort. A reconnaissance
visit to the Queen Anne house might involve an overnight stay
in Norwich. The only hotels in the city with even three stars from
the AA were the Maid's Head and the Royal, both less than £1 a
night even for the best room. In these two, all rooms had a basin

with hot and cold water, which was a rare luxury, though the toilet or bathroom would entail a trudge down a frigid landing. The modern usage of *en suite* was as yet unrecorded in the *Oxford English Dictionary*.

Even in a city like Norwich, dinner would be problematic: meat was still rationed and Britain's worldwide reputation for terrible cooking was at its absolute peak. But there was the odd green shoot. Raymond Postgate was a pacifist and socialist but also a bon viveur and the founder of the Good Food Club, whose members became the volunteer reviewers for the first ever *Good Food Guide*.

The inaugural edition, dated 1951–52, was a slim volume which encouraged readers to praise good food when they got it and denounce it when they didn't. Postgate advised restaurant-goers, especially in the provinces, to 'concentrate on meals the British do well', i.e. breakfast ('but avoid the sausages') and high tea. With roast meat still in short supply, he said, it could be safely eaten only in the countryside and specialist restaurants – and certainly not in Soho.

In some places, the food sounds positively appetizing despite the difficulties: poached salmon with red wine sauce and red berry caviar (The Bell at Aston Clinton); 'duckling which really is duckling and not an ancient drake' (Dixon Arms at Chelford, Cheshire); and excellent trout 'in grim and drab surroundings' at the Windsor Hotel, Cardiff Docks. The Friary Hotel, Derby, even had 'iced water at need', which was most un-British. At the White Hart, Burton, 'a soup of real stock' followed by jugged hare was served to a lunch guest who arrived *after two o'clock*, which was almost unimaginable. There were even touches of exoticism. At the Ring O' Bells, Chagford, Colonel Davies's speciality was 'a full-dress Indian curry' – but, the *Guide* warned, 'this must of course be ordered in advance'.

Well, of course. But it might not have been easy, although in 1952 all rural numbers and many urban ones were easy enough to memorize. Indeed, they often sounded more like the football results. Very few people had phones, which is not surprising since it cost as much to make a five-minute daytime call from London to Manchester as to stay at the Maid's Head. In Shropshire you could phone Major Foster on Ryton 4 or Lieutenant-Colonel Head on Yockleton 3. In Wales, the Reverend Griff-Preston was on Aberangell 2 and the Gladestry Call Office was Gladestry 1, which may still have been the only phone in the village. Even in a fair-sized and reasonably moneyed town, the two AA-listed hotels in Marlborough, the Ailesbury Arms and the Castle & Ball, were 1 and 2, which must have been galling for the Castle & Ball. Many calls and all long-distance ones were still made through the operator – particularly in the country. A friendly set-up, though not conducive to privacy, like the party lines that had to be shared with neighbours.

The roads were tortuous and the accident rate was high. The trains were dirty, clapped-out and slower than in the 1930s. In July 1952, the last London tram disappeared into the heavenly depot for a long sleep, hardly mourned. Within ten years they had vanished from everywhere in Britain except Blackpool seafront. The transports of necessity were buses and bicycles, associated with men in grubby macs wearing bicycle clips. The transports of aspiration included motorbikes, which carried both risk and a certain élan – except for the versions that had sidecars, which shared the risk and diminished the élan. The ultimate desire was of course a car: ownership doubled from about 15 per cent of households to 30 per cent over the decade.

Villages began emptying as farm labourers left the land for the plentiful and more lucrative jobs in town. No one wanted quaintness. They wanted the future they saw when they went to the cinema in vast numbers to see Hollywood films. They wanted cars. They wanted phones. They wanted sofas, washing machines, fridges, gas cookers and, certainly from 1953, televisions. They wanted *warmth*. They wanted *cleanliness*. They wanted *food*. They wanted *ease*.

Everyone had suffered since at least the summer of 1940, when the war became serious. Many, but by no means all, had suffered through the 1930s as well. In wartime, grumbling was muted, but by 1952 the war had been over for longer than it had lasted. Labour had been voted into power in 1945 by a massive majority, to the astonishment of practically everyone, including the protagonists,

Churchill and Attlee, and, reputedly, a woman lunching at the Savoy Hotel as the results came through who announced: 'But this is terrible – they've elected a Labour government, and the country will never stand for that.' A little-known operation, the Gallup Poll, had been predicting precisely this result since 1943 by using new-fangled sampling techniques. It had been ignored.

The woman at the Savoy was not wholly wrong. The country wanted Labour to introduce its policies of egalitarianism, fairness, welfare and even nationalization. People had no nostalgia for the selective poverty of the 1930s. But they grew weary of the general drudgery and dreariness of the 1940s and the downside of every Labour government – a tendency towards fussiness and bossiness. Attlee wanted to end rationing, but he was not obsessive about it. In 1950 Churchill neatly christened Attlee's Britain 'Queuetopia', and the long lines for routine items helped account for the swing against Labour, especially among women voters.

Labour's plans to pierce the gloom were thwarted by the outbreak of the Korean War in June 1950, which at the time looked like a potential World War Three, the more so when newly Communist China joined in less than four months later. It was essentially a war of Communist aggression, started by a North Korean invasion of the non-Communist – though far from democratic – South. But the response was an American show under United Nations flags (Stalin was boycotting the Security Council when the vote was taken). Britain could not honourably demur and once again had to divert its now fragile resources towards defence – although after April 1951, when President Truman sacked his commander General MacArthur, who was tempted to start nuking, it faded into something more distant, limited and local.

That was too late for Labour. At the election of 1950 its parliamentary majority had already slumped from 148 to 5. In October 1951 it was forced to face the country again: the Labour vote went up to what remains an all-time high: nearly 14 million, more than the Conservatives. But the lingering Liberal vote collapsed, giving the Tories a narrow but workable majority of 17. Even what was then the *Manchester Guardian*, torturing itself, turned away from its radical roots and suggested that a little spell of Tory government might be best: 'the Left will only rediscover its soul in a spell of political adversity'.

Before that, Attlee's Britain offered one final hurrah. There had been longstanding plans to mark the centenary of Prince Albert's memorable Great Exhibition in 1851. And these came to pass: in summer 1951 the Festival of Britain was staged on the South Bank of the Thames, centred on the futuristic architecture of the Festival Hall and the Skylon, a 300-foot steel structure built on a frame: the joke went that it represented modern Britain – no visible means of support. It was more respectfully described as a luminous exclamation mark or a cigar. To modern eyes it might look more like a very generous helping of wacky baccy.

The Festival was mainly a hymn to modernity – to the new industries that would power Britain into the future. One of the most popular sights was that of the giant Bristol Brabazon, the great hope for transatlantic aviation dominance, flying overhead. Churchill called the whole event 'three-dimensional socialist propaganda'. The Festival was actually very popular – there were more than 8 million visitors – with enough plain fun to balance the earnestness. The writer Michael Frayn beautifully categorized it as the creation of what we would later think of as *Guardian* readers: 'the radical middle-classes . . . the Herbivores, or gentle ruminants, who look out from the lush pastures which are their natural station in life with eyes full of sorrow for less fortunate creatures, guiltily conscious of their advantages, though not usually ceasing to eat the grass'.

As the leaves of summer 1951 fell, the Carnivores took charge again. Churchill's new Minister of Works, David Eccles, paid a brief, vengeful visit to instruct the Festival's director, Sir Gerald Barry, what must be torn down. It was, in Frayn's words, 'like a dictator's henchman picking out prisoners for execution'. The hit list encompassed practically everything except the Festival Hall. With special venom, Skylon was sold for scrap. The site lay derelict for ten years.

In the popular imagination, the 1950s in Britain was a black-and-white decade, or at least a grey one. The historical record is extensive but almost none of it is in colour: not the few surviving TV programmes, not the newspapers; it was still far from the norm in the cinema, and the women's magazines did have a few pages, primarily for adverts. The art of black-and-white photography – best exemplified in Britain by the magazine *Picture Post*, which died young in 1957 – reached its apogee in the early part of the decade. But our own less artful photographs are the most significant: those long-ago weddings, holidays, picnics and outings are still lodged in people's minds, but colourlessly.

This is not just a retrospective judgment. 'The aftermath of war was perceived and later remembered through a register of greys: the colours of bombed ruins and rubble, the hue of fatigue and austerity, of ongoing rationing and uncertainty,' as the art historian Lynda Nead put it. Once some of the rubble was cleared, the bomb sites did acquire some colour, even if that colour was brown – usually a muddy brown – relieved in season by the pinky red of rosebay and the yellow of ragwort. And as they awaited their future, usually an ugly one, these sites, thousands of them, acquired new life as adventure playgrounds, all the more enticing for being every bit as unofficial as the flowers; and furthermore, impromptu, mysterious and a touch dangerous. Not all the bombs had exploded – yet.

The great buildings of the cities, whatever their original colour, had turned close to black, the effect of decades of soot. It was not just that the soot made the buildings look ugly; before settling on the stonework like an airborne fungus, it blocked the sun. Between 1960 and 1990, after the first Clean Air Act but before obvious climate change, the sunshine figures for Central London were 20 per cent higher than they were before 1950.

The lack of colour was not just an outdoor phenomenon, nor did it go away quickly – colour TV, after all, did not take over Britain until the early 1970s. The designers commissioned by the Festival of Britain made merry with the palette, and by the mid-1950s paint companies were offering over a thousand shades, but – except for the cars and the three-piece suites – the objects of desire in the 1950s tended to be white (washing machines, cookers, fridges), black (telephones), or black, white and grey, surrounded by walnut (TVs). The French historian Michel Pastoureau attributes the tradition of black-and-whiteness to the stern Protestantism of the early industrialists. There was no technical reason why people could not have pink fridges.

In 1952, the population of Britain was overwhelmingly the colour generally known as white, though a colour chart might then have described the average British skin tone as 'pasty' or 'mashed potato'. Most of the population were so used to the greyness, cold, drizzle, fog and smoke they were long past noticing. But the newest Britons, who had started to arrive from the Caribbean in numbers from the late 1940s, noticed it all acutely.

Many early West Indian migrants were fascinated and baffled by the smoke that came out of the terraced streets of the cities, and assumed that every home was a tiny factory. Mike Phillips from Guyana wrote of the smell: 'sharp, almost chemical, like tar melting to a liquid in the sun . . . After a while it got so that you didn't notice it any more . . . the first sign of autumn was this smell, coming from nowhere, until you looked up and saw the thin plumes of smoke growing out of the chimneys.'

On the plus side, Britain was at peace with itself in that crime figures were low – as they had been in the 1930s – and falling. Crime statistics always come with a health warning because they depend on whether (a) victims think the case worth reporting, and (b) the police think it worth recording. But there is no reason to query the historian Peter Hennessy's judgment that Britain was 'almost certainly at its most lawful and orderly ever'. This must have been connected with the fact that the country had also sobered up: the per capita consumption of beer in 1951–52 was less than half the level prior to 1914.

And the country was pious, or appeared to be. In the ten years after the war, organized Christianity – as measured by church membership, Sunday school enrolment and confirmations – saw a growth unseen since the eighteenth century. Marriage rates were exceptionally high; divorce rates, after a post-war spike when men came home and sometimes found things had changed, were very low. Necessity often trumped romance at the altar: one estimate is that up to a third of all weddings were of the shotgun variety. 'Living in sin' and single motherhood were both serious taboos. And some of the statistics have rather ungodly explanations: actual attendance at church was not that huge – only 15 per cent said they went every week – and we will come to the question of why children went to Sunday school later.

Still, it was also a trusting country: the appearance of an unbidden stranger at the front door was not automatically perceived as a threat. Tradesmen came by all the time. In a largely carless society, there were multiple deliveries. There might be the baker's van; the butcher's boy on a bike; and the milkman, famous in folklore for stopping off at an especially welcoming house for an extra helping of cream; there was the insurance man, usually the ever-reliable Prudential representative, the Man from the Pru; and, less welcome, the rent man. Often there would be door-to-door salesmen, sometimes even selling stuff one might want. In villages and poorer districts it was quite normal to leave doors unlocked, even when out or away. 'Nothing to steal,' people would say.

Street beggars were rare,* but in country areas especially there were tramps: mostly, one realizes now, old soldiers, their brains perhaps a little scrambled by what was later classified as post-traumatic stress, usually grateful for a little food or an odd job or two, conveying their appreciation or otherwise to their fellow travellers with a coded sign on the garden wall – a sort of prototype Tripadvisor.

The scriptwriter and broadcaster Denis Norden put the trust down to a national sense of solidarity built up in the war. 'The whole country was still possessed by a sense of relief,' he said. 'We weren't going to get bombed any more. It was never expressed in words. It was a national unity that was more or less one hundred per cent, not affected by class or faith or anything like that.

---

* I never saw one until I first went to France, aged 14, and was shocked.

It has never happened since and it's unthinkable now. There was a common experience. You didn't embrace. You didn't have to talk about it. But you were absolutely aware that other people were feeling the same.'

Of course, there was still a hierarchy, although by the early fifties it was less rigid than it had been before the war, because the rich were less rich and the poor were less poor. And there remains an academic debate as to which Britain was dominant: the communitarian model, typified by nipping next door for a cup of sugar and by the Cockney knees-up at the boozer round the old joanna; or the suspicious face at the window, peering round the net curtains.

There is a telling guide to the level of trust. The big cities were long past single-digit telephone numbers, and by 1952 the phone system – run by the Post Office – allowed most London subscribers to dial local calls themselves: the first three letters of the exchange, then the four-figure number. These exchanges often had evocative names: cultural (BYRon, ELGar, WORdsworth), the heroically naval (CUNningham, FRObisher, RODney) and the improbably rural (ACOrn, PRImrose, SPEedwell, LABurnum).

What is really interesting is to look at the old telephone directories: they were amazingly inclusive. Until his death in 1949 you could have called radio's biggest comedy star, Tommy Handley, on PADdington 8584; and in 1952 there was still a whole troupe of other celebrities available: the actress Hermione Gingold (SLOane 5921), the writer Ivy Compton-Burnett (WEStern 2025) and the broadcaster Franklin Engelmann (EDGware 4896). Outside London you could call Mrs Max Mallowan (aka Agatha Christie) on Wallingford 2248.* And before he died in April, Sir Stafford Cripps, lately Chancellor of the Exchequer, might well have been available at his Gloucestershire retreat on Frampton Mansell 66. Addresses were also given: as late as 1959 you could call the next prime minister but one, Harold Wilson MP, at his home, 12 Southway, NW11, on MEAdway 2626. A trawl of the latest *Who's Who* would yield an even richer haul.

---

* The three-letter codes only applied in London and five other big cities.

There was even a London phone book listing for Winston Churchill, though this one sold cycles and radios. Britain's leading fascist, Sir Oswald Mosley, however, cheerfully gave away his notional whereabouts, though in 1952 he was spending most of his time in Ireland. Most amazingly of all, you could call any one of London's eight telephone area managers and ask for them by name.

Not their first name. These were men who, for public consumption, were identified by initials and surname.* The etiquette about names remained strict, very similar to the rules that govern the French use of *tu* and *vous*. First names were for primary-school children, close friends and familiar inferiors. Teachers called older children, certainly males and most especially public-school males, by their surnames; and often boys would follow suit among themselves, a habit which might persist into later life. The armed forces reinforced these conventions.

In the 1950s, Britain was a society defined by war: most adult males had seen service, many in one of the two world wars, a few in both. There were still a fair number alive who had served in the Boer War. And Portsmouth-born Harry Figg, said to have been in the Ashanti War of 1873, was still alive in Sydney, aged about 97. The overwhelming majority of 18-year-old males were heading for National Service, some being sent to Korea. The number of conscientious objectors was vanishingly small: most felt it would disgrace their father and alienate their friends.

The armed forces represented the most extreme version of hierarchy, and hierarchy begets conformity. And this, when added to the British tendency towards diffidence, made Britain in the early fifties a very conformist place indeed. Maisie Griffith worked in Greenlands, a long-gone upmarket department store in Hereford: 'Everyone above us was addressed formally: Miss Luscombe, Miss Herbert, Mr Burrows.'

---

* Like the writer C. S. Lewis, the cricket commentator E. W. Swanton, the philosopher and broadcaster C. E. M. Joad and the historian A. J. P. Taylor. It was very much a male affectation.

Victor de Waal, who later took up a very different career, started work in a shipping office. 'However hot it was you did not take your jacket off in the office. In the summer you could have the window open but then within ten minutes a blank sheet of paper would be covered with soot.' Even in the normally liberal world of journalism, rules could trump efficiency and common sense. Long before air conditioning, Joe Haines took his jacket off on a warm summer's day while working as a sub-editor on the *Glasgow Herald*: 'I was told immediately to put it back on again.' Later, when promoted to work at Westminster, Haines was reprimanded by a senior colleague for wearing suede shoes.

Robert Armstrong (later Lord Armstrong) was a junior official at the Treasury, which was considered one of the more egalitarian branches of government. 'It would have been unheard of not to wear a suit to work, a dark suit. We also worked on Saturday mornings. We still wore a jacket and tie but then it could be a sports jacket.' Heading towards the office, a hat was de rigueur. 'Some of us wore bowler hats and some of us homburgs. I would sometimes wear a bowler and cut through the Horse Guards Arch. If the soldier on duty saw someone with a bowler hat and a rolled umbrella he might think you were an officer and salute you. I rather liked that.'

Lowly clerks in provincial bank branches might be marked down as unambitious simply for wearing a subversive soft collar rather than a traditional stiff one. Even students would mimic these norms. Roy Hattersley was an undergraduate at Hull. 'I wore a tie most of the time,' he recalled. 'I'm sure I went to lectures in ties. I've still got a picture of me at university. It wasn't a special day but I was wearing not just a tie but a double-breasted suit.'

The outward respectability often concealed a great deal of domestic squalor. In Greater London alone, about 111,000 houses had been destroyed in the war. Conditions in those that remained were often Edwardian. In the old London County Council area – what's now called inner London – in 1952 only a third of households could tick off all four basic essentials of modern living: a fitted bath, toilet, kitchen sink, cooker. Fridges were extreme luxuries, freezers unheard of. Nearly half the households had no fitted bath at all, and many more had to share.* More than a third had to share a toilet.

Aspiring actor Edward Barnes came down from Wigan with wife and toddler in 1953, renting a basement from a vicar for £1 a week: 'There was no kitchen, just a gas cooker under the stairs. There was a bathroom but no hot water. We didn't think, "These are awful conditions." They were the conditions we lived in.' In the north and the countryside, outside toilets were common. It was a good place to catch up on current affairs, because the newspapers were often cut up for lavatorial purposes – not much harsher in texture than the Izal and Bronco rolls sold for the purpose. Billy Connolly, brought up in Glasgow tenements, summed up the terror of the dark, cold night-time pees:

> *Oh dear, what can the matter be?*
> *Ah'm scaird tae go tae the lavat'ry.*
> *Ah've nae been since two weeks last Saturday.*
> *I know who's hidin' in there!*

Even the rich had their problems: the bigger the house, the colder it was likely to be. And the tax system was justifiably harsh/self-defeatingly penal (delete to taste) on the highest earners. In 1951, anyone earning £15,000 a year (against an average of £344) would keep only a third of it, and according to the Inland Revenue only seventy people were known to net more than £6,000. There would have been criminal and quasi-legal exceptions, of course, but stiff exchange control meant the Revenue knew a great deal more than they would later.

The rich eventually found ways to get richer; the ghosts in the privy stayed outdoors when the toilets moved in; problems of housing changed but never went away. Some other wartime

---

* In Northampton, my parents and my two older brothers shared a bathroom in the late 1940s with an actor from the local Repertory Theatre. 'He did spend an awful lot of time in there,' my mother recalled.

embuggerances proved more tractable. Due to more reliable supplies (luck) and greater willingness to let prices find their own level (judgment), the Conservatives were able to chip away at the rationing system. In October 1952, tea was freed. In 1953, the Coronation year, came sugar, sweets and chocolate. Sweets had already been derationed once under Labour, before overwhelming demand forced a clampdown four months later. In February 1953 sweets returned to the free market, this time for ever; a solitary sherbet lemon would never taste quite so scrumptious again.

In May 1954, butter, cheese, margarine and cooking fat followed, and finally, two months later, in the midst of England's coldest and gloomiest summer of the century, meat came off and it was all over. Everything was still rationed in a sense, but only by price.

----·----

The notion of a new age was helped by the new Queen's name and by the return of the gnarled old lion to Downing Street. Churchill talked of 'the grandeur and genius of the Elizabethan Age' in his broadcast the day after the King's death, and had the skill to do it without sounding trite. Soon enough it became a cliché; then the whole 'New Elizabethanism' notion fell out of fashion. But the country did have a sense of adventure. One suspects part of it was a leftover from the war for the type of man who never settled easily back into civilian life, or felt guilty about his own marginal contribution or about being too young to serve.

Some of the daredevilry was deliciously eccentric. Six weeks into the new reign, the 2nd Baron Noel-Buxton – invalided out of his officer cadet training unit in 1940 – decided to walk across the Thames at Westminster in pursuit of his theory that the Romans had forded the river there. At 9 a.m., low water on an early spring morning, with the conformists still crossing the bridge in their bowlers, he put on a sweater, flannel trousers and rubber-soled shoes, and began wading. His lordship was six-foot-three; he calculated that the maximum depth would be a foot shorter. It did not quite work out: he had to swim most of the way. But he insisted, 'The ford is undoubtedly there. I feel I have proved my point.'

The same spirit extended right down the age range. A month later, Richard and James Norris, aged 13 and 9, were found in St James's Park having been missing from their Stepney home for a week. They had bought food by getting the deposit back on lemonade bottles they found, and had been sleeping in the back of an abandoned lorry full of old clothes. Richard said he did not like playing in the streets: 'I want to live in the country.' Later that summer, Patricia and Lawrence Mayhew from Kingsbury, Middlesex, aged 13 and 12, left church one Sunday and went to Euston 'to see the trains'. Then they played hopping in and out of them. They finally hopped off at Inverness.

For most children, playing in the streets – or the bomb sites – was excitement enough. And it was an excitement open to all children not long after they could walk. The right to roam was sacred. A child's life was governed predominantly by peer pressure, and play derived from the collective imagination. Jane Gerson was a fifties child from middle-class Finchley: 'We didn't think about men who could be dangerous. From the age of four I used to go to my best friend's house up the road and play in what we called the wilderness. "Don't accept sweets from strangers and don't get into anyone's car." That's all you needed to know.'

Which is exactly what I was told too. It is absolutely false that paedophilia did not exist, though the word was not in regular use. My mum referred to 'funny men'. These certainly existed, and occasionally the idyll of freedom would produce ghastly casualties. In the late 1940s the Criminal Lunatic Asylum at Broadmoor in Berkshire had been renamed more delicately as the Broadmoor Institution and, in keeping with progressive thinking, placed under the control of the Department of Health rather than the stern old Home Office.

In 1951, John Straffen, 21, was sent to Broadmoor for murdering two small girls in Bath, having escaped hanging because of insanity. But in April 1952 he exploited a gap in the security system, and jumped from a shed roof to freedom. Straffen was out for four hours, in which time he reached the nearby village of Farley Hill, where a woman was trusting enough to offer him a cup of tea but alarmed enough by his conversation to ring Broadmoor the moment he left. That night, a five-year-old girl in Farley Hill was reported missing. Linda Bowyer had been riding round the quiet village on her bike. Her body was found the next morning, in a bluebell wood. There was actually some lingering doubt both about Straffen's sanity and, on this occasion, his guilt: he had admitted to the previous murders but not this one, and there were some pieces of evidence that did not quite fit. But the coincidence was too over-whelming to dissuade a jury. The upshot was that he spent the next fifty-five years in maximum security prisons, a British record, there being no asylum deemed safe enough to hold him.

Broadmoor was forced to install sirens to warn the neighbours of future escapes. And Linda's parents had to endure their own living death. What no one ever suggested was any reason why a five-year-old should not be allowed to ride her bike round a small, tucked-away village on an April afternoon.

Children everywhere, boys mainly, were getting into scrapes, and some of these also had catastrophic consequences. They were reported phlegmatically in the press, without immediate demands for retribution. Some of the 1952 cases were bafflingly horrendous (a 13-year-old in Birmingham shot dead playing Cowboys and Indians); some involved recklessness (an 11-year-old savaged at a Glasgow zoo after deciding to pat the leopards); some were examples of the stoicism that made Britain great (13-year-old Raymond Wilson of Hackney sat through lessons for two hours after a classmate shot him in the leg with a heavy Luger).

This stoicism extended to major disasters as well. Death was commonplace in war, and Britain was still on a war footing; health and safety was hardly even a concept, let alone a cliché. And the second half of 1952 was full of public disasters, including the Lynmouth floods in Devon (thirty-four dead) and the worst train crash since 1915 (112 dead) – a three-train pile-up at Harrow and Wealdstone that could have been avoided by the use of a simple safety mechanism in use elsewhere on the network for decades, but not on the main line to Euston.

The railways did not feel like the future. Britain's eyes were on the skies. And test pilots were among the great heroes of the era, the perfect exemplars of the New Elizabethans. Among them was John Derry of de Havilland. On 6 September he climbed into a prototype DH.110 jet fighter to show off its tricks at the Farnborough Airshow in Hampshire. The plane disintegrated in mid-air, killing Derry, his observer and twenty-nine spectators. The *Daily Mail* leader the next day robustly called it 'the cruel price exacted by a pitiless Fate for the pride we all feel in our latest aircraft. Every one of those tens of thousands of people who packed the ground must have known there was an element of risk.' They obviously did know: the second day went ahead as planned, with another huge crowd.

At the other end of Britain, another trailblazer was on Loch Ness, also going for glory. John Cobb was a former wartime pilot like Derry, and a racing driver before that. He already held the world land speed record, and was now aiming to recapture the water speed record from the Americans, breaking the 200-mph barrier into the bargain in his jet-propelled speedboat *Crusader*.

Throughout September, starting before the Farnborough crash, the *Mail* headlines tracked his preparations:

Sep 4 COBB TOUCHES OVER 100
Sep 5 THE CRUSADER DOES 130
Sep 19 COBB IS READY FOR SPEED BID
Sep 20 WEATHER HOLDS UP JOHN COBB
Sep 23 TOO ROUGH FOR COBB BID
Sep 29 COBB TRIES AGAIN
Sep 30 'BLEW UP LIKE CONFETTI'

To a modern eye, he looked older than his 52 years, as 52-year-olds did in those days. He averaged 206 mph over the measured mile. Then, after passing the mile marker – according to eyewitnesses – he struck three waves, and *Crusader* disintegrated. His body was found soon afterwards.

Cobb's record did not count because the rules demanded two runs, though the official arbiters, the Motor Marine Association, accepted that he was the fastest. 'The glories he had won during his lifetime were not for himself,' proclaimed the Pathé News voiceover, 'but for his country. For John Cobb was, above all, a great Englishman.' Maybe so, though that was perhaps not the most tactful way to describe a Briton's death on a Scottish loch.

Patriotic self-regard was not confined to newsreel announcers. British war films – in the mind's eye, if not reality – typically starring jut-jawed Jack Hawkins and discreetly handsome Kenneth More smoking pipes and bashing Jerry, hurtled through the studios into the cinemas, somewhat sanitized by being in black-and-white. There was little sense that any other countries took part in the conflict, nor of the horrors the Nazis unleashed on them. *The Diary of Anne Frank* was first published in Britain in 1952 by an obscure firm called Constellation Books. It was turned down by larger companies; Secker and Warburg declared that 'the English reading public would avert their eyes from so painful a story'. No Jack Hawkins, no Kenneth More, no interest. It was well reviewed in the literate papers, but Secker's judgment looked sound enough until it was put on stage four years later. Traditional discreet British anti-Semitism continued unabated: nothing ever said out loud until the regretful letter arrived responding to an application to join the golf club.

Patriotic Englishmen (and women and Scotsmen and Welshmen and, especially, Protestant Ulstermen) were proud of what they had achieved in the war. And most were proud of the fairer Britain that was taking shape. The newspapers were whipping up hopes for the future, particularly in the air. Now the opposition was not Germany but a country that was both less malevolent and more formidable. And even that one was nervous.

'The year 1952 promises to be a critical one for the American air transport industry', reported *The New York Times* on 4 May, 'which is to say the operators and the makers of the planes and engines which since the war have dominated the field. That domination is seriously threatened by the British.'

The nervousness was caused by the world's first commercial jet airliner, a de Havilland Comet flown by the old British Overseas Airways Corporation (BOAC) which the previous day had managed to reach Johannesburg inside twenty-four hours with only five stops – considered quite something. In July, the Comet got to Tokyo. By August it was clipping thirteen hours off the usual time to Ceylon. Later that month, the American First World War air ace Eddie Rickenbacker was in London in his capacity as president of Eastern Airlines – and he was shopping. De Havilland's designers were already working on not just a Mark 2 Comet but a Mark 3, which would seat seventy-five passengers, and Rickenbacker wanted between thirty and fifty of them.

Unfortunately, he wanted them by 1955, and de Havilland was talking of 1957. 'That is not good at all,' Rickenbacker declared. 'I must have them quickly.' This was not language British manufacturers traditionally understood. He may have done some light shopping at Harrods, but he left without committing himself to buying anything from de Havilland. 'Wonderful plane . . . slow production,' he said. *The New York Times* had given up nervousness and moved to smugness. 'The problem was that, while the British had the "know how",' it summed up, 'there was some doubt whether they had the "can do".' This was not the first or last time Americans would take this view of Britain.

The British press was still determined not to hear a word against the Comet. In October the plane met its first mishap when a flight failed to take off in Rome and ploughed into rough ground at the end of the runway. The plane was a write-off but no one was badly hurt. Not exactly a good news story – except in the *Daily Mail*. PLANE SHOWS ITS SAFETY, said a headline: 'The record breaking Comet did not catch fire, thus adding to its reputation as the safest plane in the world. "It just bumped a bit," said a passenger.'

———·———

The spirit of Pollyanna did not extend to one subject that might have been a source of pride: the low crime rate. For the popular press 1952 was the Year of the Cosh, a word now almost gone from the language except for being 'under the cosh', usually meaning hard-pressed at work. A cosh was an unofficial version of a police truncheon; in expert hands, even a scrunched-up newspaper filled with heavy old pre-decimal pennies might do the job. It was a nasty way of whacking someone, but better than shooting.

The crime of the year was the Eastcastle Street mailbag robbery, when £300,000 (£10 million at 2022 prices) was stolen from a mail van in the West End. It was planned and executed as a classic military occupation and ultimately credited, once he got a taste for self-publicity rather than self-effacement, to the 'King of the Underworld', Billy Hill. No one was tried, never mind convicted, though the police threw everything at the case and Churchill demanded daily bulletins. One guard was badly coshed, which ruined the jollity. But since the losers had no human face, the public were relatively unperturbed.

Robbing Her Majesty's mails was a favoured activity in 1952. Other villains specialized in removing the fur coats and jewellery of the wealthy, possibly getting their addresses from the telephone directory, though more often – it was said – via the pages of *Country Life* or *Tatler*. There were occasional cases of women being coshed in the street for small amounts of money, but these seemed to be very occasional. Nonetheless, the middle classes were presented as being in a state of panic. 'People say today in Surrey that they dare not leave their houses to go to the pictures,' Sir Tom Eastham QC, deputy chairman of Surrey Quarter Sessions, said as he jailed three housebreakers. There was a solution and the *Daily Mail* knew what it was: the restoration of corporal punishment, abolished as an option for the courts in 1948. It still existed in prisons, and at home and most certainly in schools. The *Mail* called for the return of not just the birch but that old and vicious naval favourite, the cat o' nine tails: 'We believe the first thing is to restore the "cat". Let the statisticians juggle the figures. The country knows that the great increase in crime has coincided with the Soft Age.' Later the letters poured in and the paper summed up: 'Almost without exception they call for flogging . . .'

———•———

A much greater menace was being almost wholly ignored: Britain's filthy air. It was a menace understood by a forgotten hero called

Arnold Marsh, who had identified it by the 1920s, began banging on about it and eventually became secretary of the National Smoke Abatement Society. One might have guessed that the smog (smoke + fog) in Britain's cities was caused by the industrial chimneys belching into the skies of urban Britain. Or maybe the quarter-billion or so cigarettes that the populace smoked every day. But the main culprit was more like 15 million domestic fires, burning what was then considered the country's main natural resource for about three-quarters of the year from those tiny faux-factories identified by the early West Indian immigrants.

It was here, in Britain's homes – otherwise unheated, often unplumbed; damp, tatty from years of war and want, without labour-saving gadgets or home entertainment beyond the wireless – that the greatest danger lay. And not just in the cities. In the 1930s Marsh told of how he had seen a baby and pram covered with soot after an hour in a farmyard in beautiful Borrowdale, and how Manx sheep darkened whenever an easterly blew in from Manchester. In the 1940s he was described, not affectionately, as a 'red-hot zealot' by a reviewer for, of all things, *Nature* magazine. All his published comments were in fact reasoned and understanding. He said he found it relatively easy to get industry to alleviate problems, but he understood that, in a country where almost everyone had coal fires and almost no one had central heating, domestic change would be a long process.

But in the meantime, it was a vicious circle – each home's smoke helping wreck the environment for those around it: 'Black sombre buildings, dirty windows,' Marsh had told a meeting in Manchester in 1929, 'Darkening paintwork, filthy streets and dark skies must all have their insidious effects on us which, coupled with the physiological effects of curtailed supply of sunlight, must necessarily influence our happiness, our attitude towards our fellows – indeed our whole outlook on life.'

It could be much worse than that. In late November 1952, with the weather already turning snowy, the National Coal Board placed adverts announcing that 'nutty slack' would be available off the ration – pointing out that it was cheaper than ordinary coal.

Behind the humorous name was something much smaller than regular coal (the largest lumps being as big as two matchboxes), less useful and more polluting. But, the adverts insisted, 'it burns brightly and warmly if you mix it sensibly with your ordinary house coal'. Underneath, there were some rather gratuitous 'you need us' statistics, pointing out that 98 per cent of British families had coal fires in their main living room and 85 per cent had no other means of heating that room.

A week later, an anticyclone settled over England, keeping it dry. On the south coast that made it cold and bright. Further inland it was foggy. In London it was something else: with almost every fire in the metropolis alight, the high pressure pushed the smoke downwards. This was what the Victorians had called a 'London particular', not a clean white fog but something browny-yellow and acrid. And this was the mother of all London particulars. It lasted four days.

At the time, much of the reporting concentrated on the disruption to traffic, a certain amount of opportunist crime, the postponement of football matches, and the oddities like people in the Isle of Dogs claiming they could not see their feet. The following month the Minister of Health, Iain Macleod, accepted in the Commons that 2,851 more people had died in London that week than in the corresponding week the year before.

Colonel Marcus Lipton, the Labour MP for Brixton, talked of 6,000 excess deaths in five weeks and used the phrase 'mass extermination'. Eventually, 4,000 became the most quoted figure, a death toll in a finite period due to a single cause that would not be surpassed in the UK until the Covid epidemic, equivalent to thirty-six Harrow train crashes, but with far less publicity. The word *smog*, though it had been around since at least 1905, was not mentioned as a cause by *The Times* until the following October, and even then it appeared in inverted commas, as though its very existence was in doubt.

The casualties also included an unspecified number of cattle at the Smithfield Show and a huge number of plants at Kew Gardens. The soot lay so thick on the plants that did survive they had to be cleaned with hydrochloric acid, which according to the Met Office was itself one of the components of the smog that had proved so fatal, along with 800 tons of sulphuric acid.

When the National Smoke Abatement Society met in Glasgow for its 1953 conference, Arnold Marsh sensed that it finally had people's attention. 'This fear of another similar smog is not such a bad thing,' he said, 'for government action only follows public demand.' And London's medical officer of health, Dr J. A. Scott, had no doubt about the guiltiest culprit: 'that abomination – nutty slack'.

————◆————

So this was the realm the Queen had inherited: dirty, dingy and dangerous, with a people and government oblivious to much that should have been obvious. But there was also a sense of relief – no one was bombing them; the threat of the Korean War spreading seemed more remote; there was more food around. And there was a sense that their own lives were starting to get better.

What about the standing of the country, the fate of the greatest empire the world had seen, Britain's ability to compete at everything with the rest of the world? Perhaps best not to dwell too much on that. In July, the new ocean liner SS *United States* smashed the record time for Atlantic crossings that had been held since 1938 by the *Queen Mary* to win what was known as the Blue Riband. On her maiden voyage she steamed from Ambrose Light in New York Bay to Bishop Rock off the Scillies in three and a half days, compared to the old record of just under four, and did the same on the way back.

On another journey, less than two months later, the captain of the *United States*, Commodore John Anderson, found that he was fast approaching and about to overtake the *Queen Mary*'s newer, bigger sister, the *Queen Elizabeth*. There was a haze over the ocean and he immediately issued instructions to veer far enough off course to become invisible. It was an act of chivalry. He did not want to humiliate his British counterpart in front of the *Queen Elizabeth*'s passengers. 'I'm sure any Cunard captain in the same position would have done the same thing,' Anderson said later.

We shall never know. The rise of air travel meant that the old Blue Riband became obsolete and has remained with the SS *United States* ever since. And poor old Britain no longer ruled the waves, even symbolically.

3

THE CROWNING GLORY

THE DAY THE KING DIED, THE UP-AND-COMING COMEDIAN Kenneth Williams wrote in his diary: 'The atmosphere in the city is heavy with grief, for the King was loved by so many.' Two days later the diarist had other preoccupations: 'Got *The Listener*. Terrible photograph of me, really appalling. Livid.'

One suspects that here Williams spoke for England, which was not his normal role in life. When a public figure dies suddenly, there is always an initial shock. But for those without a personal connection, the sadness soon wears off and their lives resume. Shallow mourning.

Throughout that February there was a great deal of outward show: more than three-quarters of the shops on Kensington High Street had a sombre display. More than 300,000 people filed past the coffin in Westminster Hall. But then the public always relishes the chance to take part in a royal event, however humbly.

Even the BBC lightened up a little and allowed minor concessions to the listeners during the ten days before the funeral. The two and a half radio networks (Home Service, Light Programme and the part-time, highbrow Third Programme) were merged into one, and Mrs Dale and Dan Archer were allowed back. But mostly it was heavy-duty stuff with no laughs. The single infant television channel, by now in over half a million homes, was even drabber. The brief Sunday offering was children's TV, newsreels and concertos. On

Saturday there was a dose of Jane Austen. Even the Catholic Bishop of Leeds (and future cardinal), John Heenan, attacked the BBC's output as 'organized gloom . . . sombre and mirthless . . . unrelieved by almost any sign of hope'. The day after the burial, *The Goon Show* was allowed back. It seems unlikely that Bluebottle was allowed to say 'You rotten swine, you! You have deaded me!'

The funeral comprised a procession from Westminster Hall via a circuitous route to St James's Palace. The gun carriage carrying the coffin was then taken less ceremoniously to Paddington station and then by train to Windsor for the actual funeral. Michael Griffith from Herefordshire, doing National Service in the Royal Army Medical Corps, was part of a stretcher party in Horse Guards in case anyone collapsed: 'We had no business at all, and as soon as the cortege went by we could go. I was due for some leave and managed to get to Paddington for a train home before the King.' The two processions were televised, but distantly, and without sticking in the national consciousness; the funeral itself was not televised at all.

———◆———

Six days later Winston Churchill rang his doctor, Lord Moran, in the early evening and asked him to come at once. Moran found the prime minister in bed at Number 10 wearing his boiler suit. 'I took up the telephone when I woke an hour ago,' said the PM, 'and I couldn't think of the words I wanted . . . This went on for three or four minutes . . . What does it mean, Charles? Am I going to have a stroke?' He did not get a clear answer. The next day, Moran, who loved intrigue, busied himself not with the medical ramifications but the political ones, initiating discussions at the most rarefied levels of the Cabinet and Palace, about whether Churchill might have to step down.

At the time, the Conservative Party did not have anything quite so vulgar as a procedure for electing its leaders. In case of vacancy, a successor emerged by a mysterious process less like modern democracy than the methods employed in eleventh-century Scotland or the medieval papacy.

The process of getting rid of a failing leader was also mysterious, though the Conservatives, unlike Labour, have always been
good at it. But this was Churchill. Who was going to tell him? The
monarch, perhaps? The question got as far as Lascelles, the
monarch's private secretary. 'The King might have done it,' he said,
'but he is gone.' It all came to nothing anyway. Five days after
the scare, Churchill had to go to the Commons to defend himself
against an opposition censure motion. He was on top form, and the
opposition was routed.

It is sometimes said Churchill was losing the plot throughout
his second term in office. In 1954, Joe Haines had just graduated
to become a parliamentary correspondent: 'I was the youngest
member of the Press Gallery and had a seat above the prime minister
when he spoke. They talk of Churchill being ga-ga but there
wasn't any sign of that when I was there. He was still sharp and
good at it.'

The whole truth is surely that the autumn of life is like any other
autumn. There are sunny days and drab days, and sometimes the
weather will perk up before the frost takes over. One faculty or
other is first to go and in Churchill's case it was his hearing, which
inevitably made him more withdrawn when he was not doing
the talking. In any case, every ache, pain and fumble gets magnified
if you are self-obsessed (which Churchill certainly was) and have
your own personal physician who is plotting to cash in with a
book about your health. There would be more mini-crises over
the next three years, the most serious being a real stroke in the
summer of 1953, which was hushed up. But he bounced back even
from that. He would keep contemplating retirement, then find a
reason to stay.

The first reason was the Queen herself. All his initial horror
had melted away: he was in raptures about her. 'Lovely, inspiring.
All the film people in the world, if they had scoured the globe,
could not have found anyone so suited to the part,' he told Moran.
He was revelling in reprising the role of Lord Melbourne with
the young Victoria, and there were hints that Elizabeth enjoyed
his company too. Their audiences were long ones. 'What do you

talk about?' someone once asked. 'Horse racing mostly,' he said blithely. Neither the monarch nor the prime minister had had much formal education: perhaps that's why they proved such good learners.

Had the King's death come a bit earlier or the election a bit later, the new Queen would have had the taciturn Attlee instead. The transition would have been met with less historic sweep and fewer golden cadences; for the Queen, it might have been less fun. On the other hand, Attlee might have emboldened her to confront the this-is-the-way-we-always-do-it-ism of the powerful Lascelles.

The sway of the Cabinet over this monarch would never be as great again, and Churchill made some crucial early decisions. One was to ensure that the Coronation did not take place for sixteen months, until June 1953, which gave him another excuse not to give up.

———◆———

As had become customary, the details of the newly elected parliament and government were collated in a book published soon afterwards by *The Times*. The size of the Conservative majorities in the Home Counties and the Labour majorities in the mining ones are of merely academic interest. But the 1951 book also provides a fascinating snapshot, or rather 625 snapshots. There is a head-and-shoulders photo of every MP: black-and-white, though in another sense all white, of course, but mainly grey.

Only seventeen of them were women, the lowest figure at any post-war election, though the numbers would not increase significantly until the 1990s. There were a lot of horn-rimmed spectacles. About sixty of the men had moustaches, some fierce, some caddish; the moustache-men included one past prime minister (Attlee) and three future ones (Eden, Macmillan and Wilson – who wisely got rid of his). There were no beards at all. These were very rare in the 1950s, except among the curious alliance of sailors, beatniks and rabbis. A reporter spotted one under a top hat in the Royal Enclosure at Ascot in 1952, and thought it worthy of mention. A few MPs still wore wing collars, in the manner of Chamberlain at Munich, and you could hardly be more out of fashion than that. Most of the Tories and some of the starchier Labour members wore a uniform of short black coat, striped trousers and dark tie.

Several dozen of them – overwhelmingly Conservative – still proclaimed their military rank, lieutenant-colonels being the most numerous. This group included Walter Bromley-Davenport, a former army boxing champion, whose political career peaked as an opposition whip – his role until the night he thought he saw a backbencher walking away from the House before the 10 p.m. vote, moved swiftly towards him and kicked him hard up the arse. The arse turned out to belong to the Belgian ambassador.

There were very few Sirs, though these would increase greatly in the long period of Tory government to come, when the party could revive its practice of knighting backbenchers to keep them voting as instructed. In due course, following Belgium's failure to invade vengefully, there was even Sir Walter Bromley-Davenport.

The small majority government they maintained in office for three and a half years had one overriding objective: Churchill, like Charles II, did not want to go on his travels again. It was understood that there would be no wholesale dismantling of the welfare state or the newly nationalized industries (except steel, as a gesture). And as Minister of Labour Churchill appointed Sir Walter Monckton, an almost apolitical barrister whose emollient charm helped him obey his instructions: keep the peace. This was achieved largely by giving trade unions what they wanted. The number of strikes averted at the last minute – especially on the railways – made him very popular, though hindsight has been less kind, certainly in his own party.

Labour had devalued the pound in 1949 from around $4* to $2.80. The new Chancellor, R. A. 'Rab' Butler,† toyed with following Labour's 1949 devaluation by letting the pound float, which was code for allowing it to sink further. The Cabinet rebelled

---

* My father always referred to the half-crown coin (now 12½ p) as 'half a dollar', which for much of his life it had been.

† Richard Austen Butler, hence Rab.

and Butler's tenure became best known for 'Butskellism', which referred to the similarities in policy of Butler and his Labour predecessor, Hugh Gaitskell. Butler hated the word.

Provided ministers caused no controversy, Churchill was happy to let them get on with it. He knew his limitations, particularly when it came to economics. However, the PM was his own Minister of Defence, and was full of zest when Anthony Eden became seriously ill in April 1953 and he could be his own Foreign Secretary as well.

He did want one last Churchillian achievement: to win the peace, as he had won the war. Just before Eden's illness, Stalin had died, to be replaced by a leadership that was more collective and less obviously murderous. Another reason to keep going. Then the Queen and Philip went off for nearly six months to resume their aborted Commonwealth tour, and constitutional proprieties prevented an unnecessary resignation in her absence. That took him into 1954.

———•———

The monarchy also required his attention, even over matters that every other couple in the land would decide for themselves. The first storm blew up with the King hardly buried. Old Queen Mary, George V's widow, frail but sharp, heard word that Earl Mountbatten of Burma, Philip's uncle, had boasted at a dinner party that the House of Mountbatten now reigned over Britain. But the Cabinet refused to countenance the claim: Windsor, it was; Windsor it would remain. The case was not helped by the fact that many in the Establishment regarded Mountbatten as a bumptious braggart. For Philip, this issue would be a long-running sore. 'I am the only man in the country not allowed to give his name to his children,' he told friends.

The royal couple did not want to leave their well-loved home at Clarence House to go to Buckingham Palace; the Queen's mother and sister did not want to swap homes. The government insisted that's where the monarch had to live, which was fair enough, though there might perhaps have been a room or two among the

Palace's 775 for the extended family. The main problem was perhaps not so much the house as a home, but sharing it with the entire sprawling HQ of the monarchy and the sense that Lascelles controlled it all.

The Queen herself was winning everyone's hearts: at her first state opening of parliament she far outshone the performances of her stumbling father. But Philip was perceived as a problem, chafing in a new, undefined role for which he was ill prepared. In soap opera terms, he did find a niche: as the blunt, slightly more demotic, forward-thinking, occasionally irreverent counterpart to the Queen's faultless but bland persona. He often walked a tightrope, but did not fall off that much.

The notion of New Elizabethanism was still flourishing. In 1953 *The Elizabethan*, a new non-stop train from King's Cross to Edinburgh, did the trip in a record six and three-quarter hours. British European Airways appropriated the name 'Elizabethan' for its new short-haul plane, which had left the factory as the Airspeed Ambassador. The plane was not hopeless, and it was useful for flights round the UK and the near Continent for most of the 1950s. But it had an old-fashioned piston engine and moved into obsolescence quite quickly. Much the same happened to the whole Elizabethan concept.

Perhaps the term fell out of favour because it was too quickly appropriated for purposes of exhortation. 'What we want in this Elizabethan era is for manufacturers to wake up and get some of the old Elizabethan spirit in their bones,' said the Labour politician Alf Robens. Dame Caroline Haslett told a conference of business-women: 'The new Elizabethan age can be a good age for women if only we work hard for it.' The once-socialist historian A. L. Rowse, giving a talk called 'A New Elizabethan Age?' called for more artistic achievement and less 'carping, denigrating criticism – particularly from the Left intellectuals'. There was even a children's comic called *The Young Elizabethan*. This was rather worthy and did not live long, though it is credited with introducing the world to the obstreperous schoolboy Nigel Molesworth. The mild post-Goon subversiveness of St Custard's was more in tune with the mood than the worthiness was. The British were suffering from exhortation exhaustion.

The last manifestation of New Elizabethanism may well have been on the chin of the actor (and later TV executive) Edward Barnes, whose response to the accession was to pronounce himself a New Elizabethan before cultivating a very Drakean beard. He shaved it off once for an acting role. Otherwise it remained into the 2020s, having faded gently from brown to grey.

One historian saw a deeper meaning in the harking-back. 'The media wrote excitedly about a new Elizabethan age,' wrote Sir Michael Howard, adding that they were more accurate than they knew. 'Once again we were, as we had been then, a power of the second rank, teetering on the verge of bankruptcy and punching far beyond our weight in international affairs.'

———·———

Part of the 'keep Philip happy' campaign was giving him notional charge of the Coronation arrangements as chairman of the Coronation Commission. It was not a sinecure, but the power lay elsewhere – mainly with the Earl Marshal, a title that had made successive Dukes of Norfolk the nation's hereditary impresario since 1672. The duties now rested with Bernard, the 16th Duke, who had done the same job for George VI's Coronation in 1937, when he was only 28. The experience added to his authority, as did his rather splendid bearing. Also involved was David Eccles, the Minister of Works – traditionally the drabbest job in government, though not when there was a festival site to obliterate or a Coronation to run – plus anyone who could successfully purport to represent the Queen's wishes, which might or might not include Philip.

One of the most crucial decisions had been taken even before she was proclaimed queen: her official title. Times had changed since her father's day:

His Majesty George the Sixth, by the Grace of God, of Great Britain, Ireland and the British Dominions beyond the Seas, King, Defender of the Faith, Emperor of India morphed into

Her Majesty Elizabeth the Second, by the Grace of God
Queen of this Realm and of Her other Realms and Territories,
Head of the Commonwealth, Defender of the Faith

which is a miniature history lesson in itself. The judicious changes
did nothing to placate the Scots; as far as they were concerned this
was their first Elizabeth, as the Scottish and English crowns were
united only on Elizabeth I's death. Their cavils were ignored, but it
was a lingering sore for some. There was one other complainant: a
young and eccentric MP who was offended by the absence of
'British' before 'Commonwealth'. The MP's name was Enoch
Powell. Her 'other Realms' were allowed to adapt the title to their
own tastes, which was far-sighted.

The next decision was the choice of date – 2 June 1953, a Tuesday
– apparently after advice from the Meteorological Office, who said
the date had an excellent record for sunshine. The really difficult
issue involved the uppity new medium of television. In October
1952, a gruff statement from the Earl Marshal announced that live
coverage from Westminster Abbey would be restricted to 'west of
the organ screen', which meant that her people could see the Queen
entering and leaving the Abbey, but the sacred mysteries enacted
east of the screen were off limits. There was, however, a bizarre
inconsistency. Film cameras, still photography and radio commentary would all be allowed in the forbidden area, and the BBC
could show the film later.

The provenance of the edict was not entirely clear. Churchill had
a visceral fear and hatred of TV, the natural reaction of the elderly
to new technology. The Archbishop of Canterbury had told
American journalists only a few weeks earlier: 'The world would
have been a happier place if television had never been discovered.'
(The erratic pronouncements of 'Flogger' Fisher, a nickname from
his eighteen years as headmaster of Repton, punctuated the decade.)

The Queen was clearly nervous too – her first Christmas broadcast was sound only – and the Establishment was collectively

anxious for her welfare on the big day under what were perceived as intrusive cameras and hot lights. However, the response to the original ruling was much hotter. 'A bad and reactionary decision', said the *Daily Express*. 'A monumental piece of misjudgment', said the *Daily Mirror*'s star columnist, Bill Connor, who used the pen name 'Cassandra'. Meanwhile, the case for the defence was led by the *Daily Telegraph*'s leader writer, in a tone more suited to the enthronement of Charles I: 'It is most discreditable that a partisan and demagogic agitation should be raised against the "favoured few in the Abbey", that is to say Her Majesty's invited guests, in order to support the supposed rights of the favoured few who own television sets.' But Churchill – who wanted the Coronation to be a Tory-led triumph to lick Labour's Festival of Britain – had by now switched sides, and told Norfolk to rethink.

The BBC sensed the wind had changed after Peter Dimmock, the suave executive in charge of Coronation coverage, organized a trial run to show the lights would not be a problem. Afterwards he went to the loo and found himself next to Norfolk. 'Come on, Bernard. Say yes,' he remarked mid-pee. The answering grunt sounded like assent. Archbishop Fisher was perhaps the last holdout, telling Churchill: 'But these television sets are everywhere. If the service is televised it will be seen not only by people in their homes but in public houses.' The argument was lost. There were two main conditions: the most sacred moments, the anointment and communion, were not to be filmed by anyone. And no close-ups of her.

And so the nation moved on to other preparations. The makers of souvenir trinkets were already in business, submitting their designs to a Central Souvenirs Committee for approval: decorative Staffordshire pottery, reserved for export since the war; a scarlet pennant with the Royal cipher for cyclists; and crown-embroidered panties (this last rejected). Strange figures like Rouge Dragon, Portcullis Pursuivant and the Lord High Constable began to be mentioned in the papers. Potential American tourists, bearing precious dollars, were horrified to be told they could indeed get a hotel room with a view of the procession for just over £1,000 a week – three years' wages for the average British worker. Hoteliers responded by saying this figure was 'fantastic', though it is not clear which meaning of *fantastic* they had in mind.

More nervous than the Queen herself were those hopeful but uncertain of their place in the Abbey. The upper reaches were beside themselves. 'Conversation has taken on a Gilbert and Sullivan quality,' Chips Channon wrote in his diary more than six months in advance, after a luncheon with duchesses and countesses. 'Coaches and robes, tiaras and decorations.' And even the Cabinet found itself discussing who might and might not wear velvet court dress, white kerseymere breeches and the levée dress of a Privy Counsellor.

Lesser mortals took longer to get excited. But it got to them eventually, partly because 'the favoured few who own television sets' were now becoming less few and would prove generally hospitable admitting the less favoured. And just before the sup-posedly reliably balmy day of 2 June, thousands gravitated towards London to be greeted by a cruel north wind and sharp showers with hints of sleet – weather that failed to improve much.

Ruth Patrick had come up to the Mall with a group from her teachers' training college in Eltham to stay the night on the pavement (written parental permission required). 'We must have had coats but we just lay down on the pavement. I don't think any of us slept. We sat there singing songs, slightly naughty I think, but not naughty like they would be now. Late in the evening came the news that Everest had been climbed and you could hear the cheering gradually move down the Mall as it was passed on.

'At 4.30 in the morning, the police came by and moved us forward so more people could come in behind us. We cheered everyone who came along, including the road sweepers. Then we cheered the soldiers. Of course then it rained. And we cheered everyone in the procession going to the Abbey, especially the Queen of Tonga who was the only one in an open-top carriage. She must have got drenched. Then we cheered them on the way back to the Palace . . .' 'And then you went home?' 'Ooh, no. We went down to the Palace to see them on the balcony. Some of the girls were so exhausted that on the train back they slept right past Eltham and ended up in Dartford.'

Murray Hedgcock, a young journalist newly arrived from Melbourne, won a seat in the ballot for a place in the stand by the Dorchester Hotel reserved for Australians, and took his own 8-mm cine film. 'The seat cost £4 and I was only earning £7 a week. I filmed the Australian prime minister and the Queen of Tonga in the rain. But just as the royal coach came by, my film began to run out, so in my version the Queen was decorated with sprocket holes.'

David McKie, still at school in Sussex, came up with a coachload and stood outside St James's Palace. 'We waited for hours and hours in the rain and saw the Queen for about twenty seconds. The rain actually made it better because there was great camaraderie in the crowd and everyone was so full of friendship.' The newspapers were passed around, including the *Daily Express*, with its famous front page headline: ALL THIS – AND EVEREST TOO!

And next to that, separated by an 'exclusive' drawing of the Queen's Coronation dress, was BRITON ON ROOF OF THE WORLD. Actually it was Edmund Hillary, 'a 34-year-old 6ft 4in New Zealand beekeeper'. But in 1953 'Briton' was close enough – for the New Zealanders as well as the British. And the cold can only have increased the crowd's empathy for the distant hero.

Meanwhile, Douglas Wright was at prep school near Newbury. 'The head was a sort of 1950s geek. He had rigged up a twelve-inch TV so we were all very excited by that. He liked new kit – reel-to-reel tape recorders and ride-on mowers – and he didn't like kids interfering with them.'

Some schoolboys were not remotely excited. In Leeds, Ian Lee's parents had adamantly refused to have a TV until his father won one in a raffle: a nine-inch Alba. The whole family and half the street crammed into their living room. Ian opted out. 'I rang my friend Andrew and we walked through the empty streets. It was terribly quiet.' Eleven-year-old John O'Sullivan was doing much the same, across the Pennines: 'A boy called Simon Hayes and I wandered round deserted Crosby kicking stones. We just thought it would be boring.' It is surprising these places were not clogged with boys, bored witless. There were younger dissenters too. 'I spent the whole Coronation sitting under the table reading a *Reader's Digest*

story about Siamese twins,' said Laura Frank, aged six. 'I had no
interest in the Coronation whatever.'

There were places where television did not yet reach, but it was
a holiday across the country. Twelve-year-old Inky Thomson grew
up in the Yorkshire mining village of Bolton upon Dearne. 'The
bunting was up and they did a house-to-house collection to pay for
a street party. They used the money for fish and chips. I wasn't into
royalty. I *was* interested in fish and chips.'

And there were places where electricity did not reach, so TV
was not even a remote option. One was the Golden Valley in
Herefordshire. The posh major who ran the New Inn at Longtown
organized a sports day for the villagers. 'It was a helluva bloody
cold day,' recalled Sam Williams. 'We had football, drinking
and falling over. The old boy in goal had a job to stand before
the game.'

'Did he let many in?'

'He didn't stop any.'

———————•———————

One young man had a totally different experience. The Mancunian
National Serviceman Brian Hough had got his wish to go further
than a fourpenny bus ride. He was in the King's Regiment
(Liverpool), which did not change its name under Queen Anne or
Queen Victoria, and did not change it now. That made him not an
ordinary private but, by regimental tradition, 'Kingsman Hough',
which he liked, though he was not much of a monarchist. The army
took him first to Salisbury and then to Hong Kong, for intensive
battle training, and then to Korea.

He was a week short of 19 when they landed in Pusan in the late
summer of 1952. 'When we sailed into Pusan Harbour the smell
was awful,' he recalled. 'I thought it was just the harbour itself
but it was the whole country. I thought I knew about poor people
from Manchester but believe me I didn't. We ended up giving our
food to Korean children. They weren't begging, they just stood
there looking at us.'

By this time, the Korean War had become much like the First

World War: two lines of trenches, sometimes a thousand yards apart, sometimes two hundred. And there Huffy stayed, except for a period when he was invalided out to Japan, having been near slaughtered by rat-borne fleas. 'Mostly it was night patrol. Listening for the Chinese. About four men on patrol, and you'd just lie there all night, listening. If the Chinese did attack you'd be the first to cop it. And you'd also do fighting patrols, when you'd be looking for trouble.

'That winter, cold wasn't the word. We didn't have the equipment. We wore two pairs of socks, long johns and fleecy trousers over them, then our uniform. We were given parkas but they were stamped US ARMY. The worst day was when Jack Goulding got hit. He was called up the same day as me. He was a printer on the *Daily Express* in Manchester. He was courting. When we embarked at Liverpool, he said he had got married the day before.

'We were on patrol and we just walked into the Chinese. First thing was just madness, noise. Then Jack was down. I gave covering fire and when things got quieter, we could see he still had some movement and we did eventually manage to drag him back. You could see he was never going to survive. He was airlifted out to Japan but we knew it was hopeless.'

The Kingsmen were entrenched near the Hook, a ridge that commanded the route to Seoul and was crucial to the Communists' hopes of capturing the South Korean capital for a third and final time. Six days before the Coronation, while Britain put out the bunting, the Chinese infantry rained a thousand shells on the mostly British forces, with the Duke of Wellington's Regiment ('the Dukes') taking the brunt.

'They said there was more blood spilt on that hill than anywhere else in Korea,' Hough recalled. 'Late afternoon the assault started and it went on all night and all day. I was firing back from a machine gun pit. Some of the Chinese got into the trenches and there was hand-to-hand fighting and our company was moved along to join battle in the Duke of Wellington's positions. There was a young Chinese guy hanging on the barbed wire, staring at me. Wherever I was, his eyes followed me all day. But we couldn't do anything about it because occasionally the Chinese would booby-trap the dead. I can see him now, poor bugger.'

Eventually all the attacks were repulsed. Twenty-eight British soldiers were killed. 'After the Hook it went peaceful,' said Hough. 'Coronation Day was a beautiful, sunny day. We could have been on a hill in the Peak District, rambling up Kinder Scout.'

At midday – around dawn in London – a present from the Queen arrived in the trenches: a bottle of beer each. 'Then there was a rumble of tanks, *our tanks*, and they started firing. Not live rounds but red, white and blue smoke shells. The Chinese didn't take kindly to that so the rest of the day they knocked seven sorts of shit out of us. So when I think of Coronation Day you can stick it where the sun don't shine.'

———

Back in cold, damp London, the sun did not shine but the day was a triumph. Despite – maybe even because of – the weather. The Queen came on to the balcony of Buckingham Palace six times to greet the crowds below, the last appearance at midnight. Never had the monarchy's reputation stood so high, and not just in Britain. The beauty, the poise and the dignity of the young Queen entranced the world.

The other great winner was the originally unwanted guest. 'As Elizabeth II came down the aisle after being crowned, she looked Byzantine, a holy idol,' wrote the royal biographer Robert Lacey. 'The camera kept focusing on her. Her face grew bigger and bigger in the frame as she approached. The cameraman held this view on her, transfixed, knowing that rules risked being broken, but not willing to swing away until he got the order. It never came. The image was compelling . . . It transcended the old rules and created a new rule of its own. Keep close. Get intimate. Television had no boundaries but the power of its picture.'

The front page of the following day's *Express* had the splash headline THIS GLEAMING LADY. On page two, the old world of newspapers paid tribute to the medium that had just come of age: TV MILLIONS SAW MORE THAN THE ABBEY PEERS.

But there were crises coming along for both the young monarch of the country and the new monarch of the media. In an anteroom at the Abbey a journalist happened to spot the Queen's sister Princess Margaret softly brushing the lapel of a Palace official, Group Captain Peter Townsend, 'with a tender hand'. This is not a service normally provided by princesses for courtiers, and it was reported in some New York papers the next day. The British papers, constrained by old proprieties as well as old proprietors concerned for their place in the highest social circles, held off. For the moment.

Meanwhile, the BBC was about to face an existential crisis.

4

WHAT'S ON TONIGHT?

F ROM 1951, WHEN ABOUT 3 PER CENT OF BRITISH HOUSEHOLDS had television sets, to 1963, when the figure was about 80 per cent, the BBC had one sure-fire way to ensnare most of them. It was a gentle panel game, *What's My Line?*, hosted by Eamonn Andrews, an engaging and versatile Dubliner.

A member of the public would appear and do a short and usually confusing mime to depict what they did for a living. The four panellists would then have to guess what it was by asking yes/no questions. If they reached ten noes, the contestant was deemed to have won and would depart – thanks to the BBC's famous munificence – with a certificate. The best-remembered guest was a saggar maker's bottom knocker, a genuine job in the pottery industry.

It ran for 413 programmes,* most often with its regular panellists: David Nixon, an amiable magician; Lady Isobel Barnett, charming and elegant; Barbara Kelly, a mildly abrasive Canadian; plus the undoubted star of the show, Gilbert Harding, whose penchant for explosive outbursts (mostly just irritable on screen, sometimes appallingly rude off) were often the next morning's headlines. 'I have been dragged along to this third-rate place to a third-rate

---

* And was occasionally revived, mainly on ITV, at various times in the following decades.

dinner for third-rate people,' he once announced as he began a speaking engagement at a magistrates' dinner in Hounslow.

For much of the 1950s Harding was just about the best-known man in the country. But he seems to have been in a permanent state of self-disgust. 'He was frustrated, among other things, by what he felt to be the waste of his talents, and looked upon himself as a don *manqué*,' wrote his friend Sir Denis Brogan. He had no known attachments, and his contemporaries assumed he was homosexual. If so, that could also have been frustrating. It is hard to imagine how he could have conducted any such relationship in the 1950s. As the much-loved curmudgeon of the masses, it would have been instant career death.

Almost every trace of *What's My Line?* has been wiped – victim of both primitive TV technology and the BBC's early scorched-earth policy towards their old programmes. An episode does survive, from 1957. Watching it is like drinking distilled essence of fifties-ness. It is formal: the guests are addressed as Mr Hall or Mrs Rowlands, not Charles (let alone 'Charlie') or Barbara. Mr Hall is in a double-breasted suit and looks like a high-ranking civil servant. The chairman and male panellists are in dinner jackets, handkerchiefs in top pockets. The women look like their dazzling companions.

Throughout the programme wisps of smoke waft across the screen from David Nixon's invisible ashtray. There is an implicit suggestion that men and women do different things and have different needs: 'Could this product be used by me?' Barbara Kelly asks Mrs Rowlands, who is a diamond setter. 'No.' These are industrial diamonds, you see. 'Could this be used by men?' So yes.

One feature of the programme was the mystery guest, who would habitually disguise their voice while the panellists, blindfolded, grope for clues. This time it is the cricketer Denis Compton, one of Harding's few rivals in celebrity status. 'Are you a coloured person?' Harding enquires, the polite formulation at the time. He is not.

Then there are the mimes performed by the contestants. It is noted that Mr Hall looks as though he is pushing a wheelbarrow. From this, the panellists eventually divine that he works in a hotel. 'If you were years younger I'd say you were one of the gorgeous little pages,' declares Lady Barnett. And indeed he is a 'head page boy', even though he looks about sixty.

It is the mimes that make one realize *What's My Line?* would be unthinkable in the twenty-first century. Saggar maker's bottom knockers apparently still exist, but thousands of old crafts and skills have gone. And the vast majority of the mimes would now involve someone tapping a keyboard.

———◆———

Exactly a week after the Coronation, on 9 June 1953, when the fuss was slowly dying away, what did Britain's only TV channel have to offer? There was more royal stuff in the morning – a thanksgiving service from St Paul's. Then it closed down until *For Women: Leisure and Pleasure* at 3.15 p.m. (a country walk in Monmouthshire, Mexican folk songs, and part four of a course on oil painting), straight after *Woman's Hour* on the radio, and followed by *Watch with Mother*. It being Tuesday, that was *Andy Pandy*.*

Then the set would have another little snooze before the children's serial *The Heir of Skipton*, which was followed by a two-hour-long hiatus known as the 'Toddlers' Truce', supposedly allowing the children to be put to bed without tears on either side. At 7.30 was the newsreel before the evening's entertainment began: a musical pageant by Ralph Reader, put on by the Boy Scouts, followed by a more adult variety show staged for the armed forces, and then a documentary about the workings of a typical London magistrates' court. At 10.20 came the weather forecast, the news (sound only) and that was it.

That might not sound terribly exciting. And the TV that night would be partially outshone by the BBC's own radio commentary on Randolph Turpin from Leamington fighting for the world middleweight title. But Scouting was big in the fifties, and the local variety nights they put on – 'gang shows' – were hugely popular.

---

* The schedule that evolved also had *Picture Book* on Monday, *Bill and Ben* on Wednesday, *Rag, Tag and Bobtail* on Thursday and *The Woodentops* on Friday. Some of us will remember this when everything else fades.

And Reader, who devised the concept, was a gifted songwriter. The show for the forces was introduced by the rising star Benny Hill, and the programme on the courts, hackneyed though such formats would later become, was ground-breaking at the time. The BBC's monopoly enticed people to watch and enjoy what they did not know they wanted. It broadened horizons.

Seventeen years after the first flickering pictures, those horizons finally belonged to a fast-growing portion of the British public. The Coronation was not the only factor. A month earlier, the televised coverage of the dramatic 1953 FA Cup final, starring 38-year-old Stanley Matthews, also brought neighbours into the nearest house sporting an aerial. The social historian Joe Moran says the real boom did not come until hire purchase restrictions were eased in July 1954, which allowed people to buy a set for £6 down or perhaps no deposit at all.

But, just over two years after its great triumph in the Abbey, the BBC's imperium would all be over: from insignificant beginnings, the enemy had gathered its forces. In the early 1950s television was still an obscure backwater within the mighty BBC and the corporation's own publications, the *Radio Times* and *The Listener*, were still aptly named – in the schedules TV was an afterthought, compared to, say, the regional variations on the Home Service. There was no mention of broadcasting at all in the 1951 Tory manifesto. Churchill's dislike of television extended to calling it the '*tee-vee*', with exaggerated emphasis for extra contempt.

But a number of the newer, more business-minded MPs were interested, including two young go-getters, John Profumo and Ian Harvey. In March 1952 Churchill put the northern businessman Lord Woolton (who had made his name as the wartime Minister of Food) in charge of broadcasting policy, and in a White Paper two months later the Cabinet allowed Woolton to float the idea of 'some element of competition' in television.

Opponents immediately christened this 'sponsored broadcasting' along the lines of American TV, something that sent shudders down the spine of opponents – Conservative backbenchers included, some of whom had seen for themselves the prevailing transatlantic

crassness and preferred the genteel paternalism of the BBC. There
was little interest even in the City. And of course, in 1952 the vast
majority of the British public had never seen any kind of television
at all, except perhaps in a shop window.

The most vehement opponent was Lord Reith, founding father
of the BBC but out of it since 1938 and, still only 62, long-term
underemployed and bitter, especially against Churchill. 'Somebody
introduced dog-racing into England,' he told the House of Lords.
'And somebody introduced Christianity and printing and the uses
of electricity. And somebody introduced smallpox, bubonic plague
and the Black Death. Somebody is minded now to introduce
sponsored broadcasting into this country.' He was greeted by
cheers, as well as laughter. Later he accused the government of
introducing 'a maggot – a quite unnecessary maggot – into the body
politic of England'.

The driving force behind the maggot was Norman Collins, a
former BBC executive who had been passed over for the job of
Director of Television in 1950 and now exacted exquisite revenge.
He was perhaps as influential in his new mission as Reith had been
a generation earlier. After the Coronation, when the growing
salience of TV and Britain's improving economic outlook made the
White Paper's plans more relevant, the antis gained a new ally,
though he did not volunteer for the role and said not a word. His
name was J. Fred Muggs, and he was a chimpanzee.

Muggs, who appeared in a turtleneck pullover and rubber
trousers, was the mascot and co-star of the American breakfast
show *Today*, which was on air as the Coronation was taking place.
There was huge interest in the event in the US, and the network was
showing grainy telegraphed still pictures – the nearest thing to live
transatlantic TV then available – accompanied by John Snagge's
commentary from the BBC World Service.

Whenever Snagge's short-wave words began to fade, as they
did, the NBC network's anchorman filled in by interviewing his
resident royal expert, Muggs. This drew a furious response in
the British press, and helped galvanize opposition to Collins's
plans on the basis that this was exactly the kind of outrage one

could expect at home in future. The Labour MP Christopher Mayhew brought along a chimp to a public debate in Windsor to make the point. 'Chimpanzees cannot read, write, act or sing but they have one great value for commercial television: publicity value,' said Mayhew.*

To quell the unease of their more traditionalist backbenchers, the government was forced to promise that the new station 'will not vulgarise the Queen'. By the time the Television Act 1954 had been passed, there were heavy restrictions on advertising time, and rules governing the amount of British programmes, public service programmes and political balance. The new operation was also split into separate regions, with their own local commitments. And 'sponsored television' was barred – even the term 'commercial television' was sanitized in favour of 'independent television' under the control of an Independent Television Authority, whose chairman was to be the thoroughly Establishment figure of the aesthete Kenneth Clark.† This did not appease everyone; when Clark set foot, as a guest, in the Athenaeum – the most intellectual of the West End gentlemen's clubs – he was booed.

By the time the new channel opened for business, it looked, to the untutored eye, disarmingly like the BBC. 'The British,' said an American observer, 'have decided to paint the gaudy thing a sombre grey to blend in with the general fog.'

This was not quite true: ITV actually did something wonderful. The sombre grey hemmed it in so it could not explore the most savage shores of commercialism. Whether the owners liked it or not, there had to be serious news, current affairs and drama. But the new network was still less hidebound than its rival, and it yanked the BBC away from its smug monopolism and improved it greatly. The upshot was that, for the next thirty-five years at least, Britain

---

* Mayhew called his chimp J. Fred Muggeridge, after Malcolm, the pundit and controversialist. The original Muggs was reported to be still alive and living in Florida in 2018, aged 66, outliving all the other main protagonists in the 'sponsored television' argument. Perhaps only his constitutional ineligibility – he was born in Africa, not the US – stopped him being elected president.

† In the sixties, Clark would present the series *Civilisation*, the BBC's first great triumph – intellectually and in ratings terms – of the colour TV era.

had what was often called – in a phrase popularized and perhaps invented by the critic Milton Shulman – 'the least worst television in the world'.

The first sign of this came on ITV's first night, 22 September 1955. Just over half an hour before its grand launch, Grace Archer, the new bride of Phil, son and heir of Dan and Doris in *The Archers*, rushed into a blazing barn to save a horse – to the consternation of an audience estimated at around 9 million. Grace did not survive. The timing was shrugged off as a complete coincidence by the BBC, which was a forgivable fib.

It was, in reality, a magnificent act of guerrilla warfare, approved by the corporate hierarchy. But there appears to have been another purpose too, which had nothing to do with Grace and everything to do with the actress who played her, Ysanne Churchman. It was revealed by Godfrey Baseley, *The Archers*' creator, forty years later: 'She was trying to get the actors to join a trade union, so I killed her off.'

ITV's tanks would lay waste to much BBC territory in the years to come. But the Ambridge fire was a signal that the corporation itself was not dead, dying or obsolete. And nor was its precious, original outlet: steam radio.

———•———

However, television was now turning rapidly from a luxury item to an essential. In 1949, some people reportedly put TV aerials on their roof to make jealousy-prone neighbours think they had a set, which became problematic if the licence detector vans passed by. By the mid-fifties there was a certain snobbery, mostly among intellectuals, about *not* owning one. But the reservoir of holdouts was drying up. Henceforth, the British increasingly lived up to their reputation of preferring home and hearth to anything else: the hearth belching out smoke to poison anyone sufficiently nonconformist to be passing by during *Sunday Night at the London Palladium*.

The 'baby boom' (a term disavowed by the Office for National Statistics in 2018) is a protean concept originally applied to the frantic nesting after the war, and later on to the whole period between the mid-forties and mid-sixties. The actual figures show a peak close to 900,000 live births in 1945, gently falling to a plateau around 700,000 ten years later. It then rose again steadily almost to the same peak over the next ten years.*

And no wonder. If couples were staying in of an evening, snuggled up on the sofa, what else might they do *après*-telly? Especially as there were usually only two warm places in Britain's cold homes – fireside and bed. There is also a perceived link between fertility and optimism. In the late forties, nesting often took place in conditions even a pair of sparrows might consider constrained. By 1955 there was growing prosperity; there was indeed optimism, which had been bruised in the harsh times after the war, and life was increasingly home-centred. Wives were mainly based there and, at first anyway, most seemed to be content that way. But they wanted *things* – even before hire purchase ('the never-never') and ITV's advertisements came along to beckon them towards domestic Nirvana.

A survey by Mass Observation in 1956 showed that housewives worked a fifteen-hour day (slightly less on Sundays) and they wanted those hours reduced. The first requirement for that purpose was a vacuum cleaner, which was now in half of Britain's homes, followed by a washing machine. 'Look at mummy's washing doing itself,' said an ad in *Good Housekeeping* showing two toddlers transfixed by the glass door and the swirling clothes. 'It's child's play with a Bendix.' In a new home, certainly, plastics were also part of the solution. Formica worktops and tables, along with stainless-steel sinks, were crucial. Plastic doilies were in: 'She doesn't have to search for uncrumpled doilies. She chooses plastic, dainty as lace; uses them again and again and again.' And everyone wanted one of those increasingly sophisticated cookers – the nationalized gas and electricity boards competed with each other. Fridges, at this stage, were an optional extra, along with more rarefied objects of desire

---

* The baby boom is now held to have included anyone born up to the mid-sixties. It is used here in its original sense, born to couples remaking their lives in the early years of peace.

like a liquidizer, a Russell Hobbs kettle ('the world's only self-watching kettle'), a toaster and, in the far distance for most, a dishwasher or tumble dryer.

Every home had its own priorities. 'For us, the phone came first,' said the radio critic Gillian Reynolds, who grew up on a council estate in Liverpool, 'and then the three-piece suite, dark green, my mother's pride and joy. But we didn't have a washing machine for ages and we never had a fridge. We had a north-facing larder with a marble shelf. That did.' Two armchairs and a sofa were generally high on the fifties wish list, and were becoming more affordable thanks to the new polyurethane filling – and the never-never. Three-quarters of all furniture was bought on credit. Someone who had paid for their own furniture, rather than inheriting it, was regarded with contempt by the old aristocracy. Now everyone was at it.

Many of the hobbies that grew in the 1950s were also home-centred. Joe Moran has said that one traditionally female pursuit grew in popularity because it was just about possible to watch TV and knit simultaneously – and be satisfied you were not wasting time. However, the telly-knitters preferred using lighter yarns: a Fair Isle sweater, for instance, needed much more concentration.

Then there was the 'do it yourself' craze. This predated mass-audience TV: in March 1953 the *Daily Express* noticed how builders' merchants and paint makers were increasingly selling direct to householders rather than to professionals. The demand was for smaller tins of quick-drying paints. However, this would then be stimulated by TV – in this case not so much by the advertising as by the BBC's DIY expert Barry Bucknell.

At the peak of his fame, in 1962, when he renovated an entire house on screen, Bucknell was said to get up to 40,000 letters a week. Bucknell had a cheery, self-deprecating style and was a bit unexpected in real life – like the gourmet Raymond Postgate, he had been a wartime pacifist and also a Labour councillor. But his idea of redecoration was distinctly aggressive and, from the mid-fifties, millions watched as 'such unappealing features as Victorian fire-places, panelled doors and cornices give way to plywood, melamine and headache-inducing wall coverings'. He fitted the fifties.

Bucknell's outdoor equivalent was Percy Thrower, another avuncular character – right down to the pipe and Labrador, in his case. Gardening was already well established as Britain's No. 1 male hobby. But Thrower enhanced its appeal on BBC programmes like *Gardening Club* and *Gardeners' World*. Much of his advice, however, was such that it would now risk the setting up of a war crimes tribunal: 'DDT,' he once said, 'that's not too dangerous.' *Silent Spring*, the book that exposed the lethality of DDT and other pesticides, was not published until 1962, and a 1950s greenhouse was more like a chemistry lab.

'Percy was a man of his time,' said the modern-day gardening expert Professor Stefan Buczacki. 'Fumigating greenhouses, killing off the mites and whitefly, by setting fire to flakes of nicotine was standard. There was mercurous chloride, sold as calomel, which was used to treat clubroot in brassicas and was really terrible stuff. You dipped the roots in calomel and got it all over your fingers and no one bothered. Sodium chlorate was used as a weedkiller. It lasted for ever and it crept through the soil.

'This wasn't just in gardening. There was Flit spray to kill flies and that was DDT-based. It was even used on head lice in children. People who had been through the war were used to taking risks but they just didn't know how dangerous it was.'

It was certainly not just Percy. Arthur Hellyer, who wrote over a hundred gardening books, was still recommending DDT in a volume published as late as 1968: to deal with everything from ants, apple sawfly and asparagus beetles to weevils, whitefly and woodlice.

All this was of a piece with washing machines and plastic doilies. Many people had been through not just one world war, but two, plus a worldwide depression and a huge dollop of post-war austerity. They not only wanted life to be easier, they craved modernity; they wanted simple solutions and they trusted science to provide them. It was an attitude that changed only when the generations changed.

5

WOMEN AND CHILDREN

Bᴜᴛ ᴛʜᴇ ɢᴏᴏᴅ ʟɪꜰᴇ ᴄᴏᴜʟᴅ ʙᴇ ᴇʟᴜꜱɪᴠᴇ, ᴇxᴄᴇᴘᴛ ꜰᴏʀ ᴛʜᴇ ʏᴏᴜɴɢ housewives in the adverts, who all looked vaguely like the young monarch. For some, there was the donkey stone . . .

'I had to be out washing my doorstep every Thursday morning,' recalled Eileen Cook, from the Lancashire mill town of Colne. 'If you weren't doing it by quarter past nine people thought you must be ill, they'd be knocking on the door asking if you were all right.

'There were a lot of old women living up my street and they were traditionalists. They'd soon pull you up if you weren't out first thing, you couldn't have a lie-in. They'd say that they were a respectable street. You'd be out there with your bucket and brushes scrubbing and swilling, then you donkey-stoned your step.'

The donkey stone was a particularly northern invention, a scouring aid designed to brighten the front steps of terraced houses. The tradition had been fading, like any stone left unscoured, even in the 1930s, but was revived in the war because the shine was a useful guide to getting home in the blackout. And Colne was a place where the old ways died hard. Mrs Cook was expected to do her windows, her front door and her letter box – and then start on the inside. It was a kind of communal activity, enforced by peer-group pressure – and it might have helped to avoid the loneliness that was noticeably setting in among wives in less traditional communities by the late 1950s.

However much domestic bliss housewives had before childbirth (and the older neighbours could always count up to nine months), conformity then set in quickly. Home births were slowly going out of fashion but the maternity hospitals could be very strict. That forgotten usage, *confinement*, still applied.

'You had to stay in bed in the nursing home, sometimes for more than a week,' said Dorothy Cooke, who married an airline pilot and moved from the Welsh border to Buckinghamshire. 'They wouldn't let you out until the baby got its birth weight back.'

'I stayed for ten days,' said the former Ruth Patrick (now Mrs Borrill). 'The baby was taken into the nursery and brought to me to be fed every four hours. They might get a bottle in the night but otherwise they could cry and cry and they soon learned it didn't do any good, didn't they? When I got home I remember the health visitor came once and that was it. Gran came over to look after Christopher [her older child] when Marion was born, but as soon as I came out she went back. We had neighbours. I didn't think I was hard done by.'

Dorothy Cooke had four children, evenly spaced at two-year intervals. 'So we sometimes had two loads of nappies hanging on the line,' she recalled. 'And in cold weather they'd turn to chunks of ice. If you dropped them they'd break. I put the children to bed at six, when I used to play "Goodnight Children, Everywhere" on the piano. There was no advice from anyone. You just did what your mother had done. We didn't have advertisements to lead us on.'

Beyond the reach of the nurses and, in some cases, old-fashioned grandmothers, it was possible for mothers to use their own intuition and instincts in looking after their babies. They were encouraged to do this by the American Dr Benjamin Spock's massive bestseller *The Common Sense Book of Baby and Child Care*, which told millions of mothers what they wanted to hear, which was essentially 'Don't panic'. In particular, he told them that if a baby is crying, feeding is a sensible response instead of having to wait until the precise hour has struck.

Then, in the spring of 1953, came a British counterpart, *Child*

Care and the Growth of Love by the child psychologist John Bowlby. This achieved nothing like the audience of Spock's but was one of a series of books that were lastingly influential in Bowlby's own field. He found a direct correlation between deprivation of maternal affection on the one hand and future delinquency and mental difficulties on the other. This became known as 'attachment theory'. Bowlby counselled against parents taking even quite short holidays away from their small children. The near-six-month post-Coronation royal tour – hugely successful on its own terms – would have horrified Bowlby: Charles was five, Anne three. Bowlby thought that mothers with children of that age would do better not to work at all.

Another 1953 book, Vera Brittain's *Lady Into Woman*, a history of women since Victoria's time, emphasized what had been achieved: 'The idea that women were all semi-invalids, incapacitated in varying degrees by menstruation, pregnancy, and the menopause, began to change in the nineteen-twenties.' Most modern men, she said, now saw their wives not as a dependent or a servant but as an 'intelligent, independent companion'. And it is certainly true that up and down the country, strong women, like those in Colne, had a power base inside their homes and took no nonsense from anyone, least of all their husbands.

But for those who wanted independence beyond their marriage, the road was still rocky. The percentage of women in the workforce rose very marginally between the 1951 and 1961 censuses, from 31 to 33, and a very high proportion of those jobs would have been low-paid, dreary and part-time. Renée Gerson (née Cohen) was considered a misfit in her own family, where she was tarnished by the dread insult *bluestocking*. She won a place at University College London just after the war but was bumped by a government directive giving priority to demobbed servicemen. So she went to evening classes at Birkbeck College and did an 'intermediate BA', which was not a full degree, got married and had children.

In 1957 she went in for the 'state scholarship': twelve university places were available for 3,000 applicants. She was in the lucky dozen . . . but that only provided funding. She still had to find a place. One condition was that the course must *not* be useful, i.e. not career-oriented like law or medicine. She wanted to do history, but UCL this time was less inviting. 'I think we did have a married woman once, didn't we?' murmured one of the interviewing panel, suggesting it was not something to be repeated. The London School of Economics initially assumed she was applying for a secretarial job. She thought their embarrassment made them guilty enough to let her in.

Revel Guest had all the qualifications to become a Conservative MP in the 1950s, in the footsteps of father, grandfather and three uncles. There was one small problem: being *her* not *him*. She had studied at the LSE, worked in the Commons and at the United Nations, was full of vigour and spark – and had been blooded in the hopeless seat of Swansea East in 1955. 'I was interested in changing the world. I went to about twenty-six selection committees. They wouldn't have me, either because I was a woman or because I hadn't got any money. They wanted someone who would be generous in the constituency. They just didn't think women were serious people. They were seen as only talking about babies and nail polish.' She later became a pioneering TV and film producer.

Another Conservative woman of that generation sought selection at Maidstone. The area agent reported back to the party's central office that she had been asked how she would cope with her two young twins: 'I do not think her reply did her a lot of good. She spoke of having an excellent nanny.' She tried for another seat, where the choice, the retiring MP complained, was 'between a bloody woman and a bloody Jew'. This time the bloody woman won, and thus, in 1959, Margaret Thatcher became MP for Finchley.

Around that time, an aspiring journalist called Katharine Whitehorn got a maternity relief job as an assistant editor on the magazine *Woman's Own*, which, naturally, was run by men. It had the normal unchallenging columns of the time: a medical column by 'Dr Roderick Wimpole', actually a woman with a medical diction- ary who had once lived for six months with a gynaecologist; knitting, which mattered ('*You* make a mistake,' the knitting editor told Whitehorn, 'and all you have to do is apologise. *I* make a mistake, and cardigans have one sleeve longer than the other all over Britain'); cooking, clothes, home decorating; and of course an advice column, written under the fireside-cosy pseudonym of 'Evelyn Home'.

The ethos was clear, as Whitehorn recalled in her autobiography: 'It was supposed to reinforce women in their role as wives and mothers, cheer them up and enable them to carry on.' If a woman complained of a wandering husband, the answer was simple: 'It must, surely, be your fault: you haven't been loving enough, you haven't responded to his needs, you've been coming down to breakfast in your curlers.' The aim was to make the readers avoid the same pitfalls. And there is one crucial piece of evidence, suggesting that women themselves were a force for societal conservatism: they voted that way. Polling data suggests that if women had not had the vote, Labour would have been in power throughout the 1950s – and beyond.

The world of work, however, might well have turned women bolshie. It was the age of the typing pool, which had replaced the grim Victorian world of male secretaries, high desks and quill pens – changing sex and becoming hardly less grim. Barbara Hosking had her first job in the typing pool at the HQ of the Rank cinema chain. Men could smoke in the office; women could not. Men did not have to clock in; women did. Conversation and laughter was discouraged. When she was promoted and escaped these rules, she sensed: 'I wasn't a senior woman, I was an honorary man.'

There was also the risk of unwanted bottom-pats, and more besides. Revel Guest, who herself had a stint in the huge typing pool at Westminster Hall, concluded: 'The women who did succeed knew how to handle a man who put his hands where they shouldn't.'

And some women proved themselves decidedly robust. Barbara MacArthur joined the Cardiff City Police in the early 1950s. Her beat included the Tiger Bay docks area, and she patrolled alone, protected only by a felt cap, a heavy rubber torch – WPCs not being allowed helmets or truncheons – and a pair of oversized, chest-high, navy-blue knickers. She was grateful for these in a scuffle, since trousers were banned. The wandering hands keenest on investigating the knickers came from a burly sergeant; she finally saw him off by a strategy of aggressive tickling. She loved her job.

The public sector was relatively advanced about employing women – the Civil Service and teaching adopted equal pay in 1955, twenty years before it became at least notionally compulsory; the BBC even offered maternity leave. But there was not just a glass ceiling; if women took even a couple of steps up they would usually bash their heads. The Foreign Office began employing women in 1946, but, for them, marriage was an expulsion offence and female ambassadors were a long way off. In Vera Brittain's words, 'Most women still occupy positions as substitute-delegates, vice-chairmen, sub-editors and assistant-secretaries.'

This was not entirely due to the unreasoning prejudice of male employers. In this strange outlier of a decade, girls had become so fixated on marriage that for most a career was not even an aspiration. High-school heads complained that girls were leaving early to concentrate on husband-hunting, and the women's secretary of the University Appointments Committee at Oxford (i.e. the job-finders for graduates) said she should have studied geography: the girls kept telling her they had to live near their fiancé's job. One major department store, with a long-established managerial training scheme, banned women from it because they kept dropping out.

But there were pockets of British society that were utterly outrageous. On the eve of the St Leger Stakes, the final classic of the flat racing season, run at Doncaster, the town's mayor traditionally hosted a banquet for the major figures involved. In 1956 the mayor, Councillor Elizabeth Dougal Callander, was barred from her own event. 'Of course it is all wrong,' she said. 'I was told it might be embarrassing for me. But I have been to many functions when I was the only woman present.'

This was a poignant coincidence. Four months earlier, the opening colts' classic – the 2,000 Guineas at Newmarket – had been won by 50–1 shot Gilles de Retz, officially trained by an obscure figure called Charles Jerdein. The real trainer, as everyone in racing knew, was Helen Johnson Houghton, who was not allowed to have a training licence because . . .

'Bloody maddening,' she said more than half a century later (she lived to be 102). 'It seems so ridiculous in this day and age, doesn't it? Beyond belief. But that's all in the past, and I no longer agonise over it.' It took ten years and a much less phlegmatic woman, Florence Nagle, to take the Jockey Club – racing's antique ruling body – to court and force them to end the fiction that only men could train horses. It seems a pity Gilles de Retz did not run in the St Leger. The mayor and trainer could have dined together. The Queen, who did have a horse in the race, might even have joined them.

———◆———

If the married women of the 1950s were indeed trapped in a domestic cage of their own making, their children had a freedom that might now appear quite extraordinary. These two facts are directly related.

Perhaps the most vivid of all evocations of 1950s boyhoods is the Rob Reiner film *Stand By Me* (from a Stephen King novella) about a group of twelve-year-olds – made in 1986, set in 1959. The adults are distant, almost spectral, figures with their own preoccupations; the girls are almost non-existent; boundaries are unpoliced, leading to limitless adventure with an undertow of cruelty. It is endless summer.

It is a Hollywood film, set in small-town Oregon, and nothing in Oldham or Oswestry was the same as that, although, as it happens, the English summer of 1959 did a fair impression of an American one. By that time, after four years of ITV, which was obsessed with westerns, British kids' imaginations were highly Americanized: Cowboys and Indians dominated boys' playground games, surpassing even Cops and Robbers; the Indians were allowed to whoop but not normally to win. Yet there was still an eternal rhythm to the playground year: snowball fights, skating (frozen ponds, not ice rinks), football, tree climbing, cricket, conkers – interspersed with ever-changing crazes, from trainspotting to the hula hoop.

If the 1950s marked the beginnings of a new era of Spock- and Bowlby-influenced childcare – kinder, gentler, more responsive – it was also a last hurrah for a previous era of notionally stricter, but in practice more distant, discipline: adults had to find out what you had done, which was not always easy. Even in a well-functioning family, fathers might play little part in one's life except for occasional treats or retribution ('Just you wait till your father gets home'); teachers did their job, well or badly, quite often violently. But childhood was a condition essentially cured by other children.

From an early age, it was quite usual for kids to wander off and play with friends, siblings, neighbouring kids, any kids. Christian Wolmar, growing up in West London, would just go off to Holland Park and wait to be invited into the endless, informal, communal game of football. Anthony Powers, whose mother was a worrier, was wandering round London, no questions asked, aged about ten.* In Oldham, Richard Price not merely caught the bus to school aged seven on his own, he changed buses halfway. These experiences were normal. There were obviously huge variations between circumstances: town and country; slum and suburb; back alley and big garden. But the general pattern was that children could be left to their own devices, not electronic ones.

One of Bowlby's most quoted lines was: 'Life is best organized as a series of daring ventures from a secure base.' And it is precisely that secure base that made a fifties childhood possible. Firstly and crucially, mothers were generally at home but very happy to get the kids out of the house and their hair. They could set vague rules about strangers and crossing roads. And they would normally be there for mealtimes – and provide comfort if disaster struck, whether a badly cut knee or a falling-out of friends.

Secondly, if mums went out, there was normally a support network of neighbours and/or extended family. This could be extreme in the terraced streets of the big cities. 'It was "Go to your Aunt Lill's or Aunt Kit's, while I go to work",'† recalled a woman

---

* At a similar age, as a non-Londoner, I would come down to stay with my grandmother in Golders Green. 'Bye, darling,' she would say, and the metropolis was all mine.

† The aunts were not necessarily real aunts. *Aunt* and *uncle* were often used as honorifics for parental friends.

who grew up in prelapsarian Stepney. 'They'd look after you, and the next day Mum would take them down their dinner or scrub their steps. She couldn't afford to pay them, you see.' Above toddler-age, 'looking after' did not mean constant supervision, just their reliable presence.

Thirdly, there was less traffic. Away from main roads, a car was mostly a rarity. Fourthly, there was more open space: from the bombsites in the inner cities to the slagheaps of the mining villages (technically forbidden as playgrounds but still universally used) to the empty plots in suburbia to the miles of open fields around, say, the tiny Buckinghamshire village of Milton Keynes. Fifthly, television was not yet ubiquitous, and programmes were limited.

All these factors would change, and those changes were happening even before the grand summer of 1959. There were, however, about 750 designated play streets in Britain where through traffic was banned for much of the day. Which may have been very convenient for at least 0.01 per cent of the nation's children.

Still, there were plenty of adventures to be had. Ysenda Maxtone Graham, who mined the memories of dozens of mid-century children for her book on summer holidays, came to see their existence as that of cats, coming in and going out as they pleased, rather than dogs, who had to be taken for walks. One of her interviewees was sent to the corner shop for sugar at two and a half (though mum did see her across the road first). Four, she concluded, was the normal age for freedom. As they grew, 'games were physical, violent, cruel, dangerous, varied and long-drawn-out. Everyone was being dramatically and brutally toughened up . . . This was Beanpole Britain: a nation of children who had not an ounce of fat on them because they were running around in the same place all day.'

Two weeks after Hillary and Tenzing climbed Everest, eight-year-old Craig Mackie of Brixton climbed forty feet up a church tower before getting stuck. He was not pleased with himself: 'I've been up much higher on trees,' he said. And, the *Daily Express* reported, he was spanked by Mum.

Michael Krohn, 14, and his 8-year-old sister, Vivienne, set out from the beach in Dawlish in a dinghy they found by the water's edge. 'We won't be long,' shouted Vivienne. They were found by a rescue plane, calmer than their parents, thirty-two hours later. Seven-year-old Jim Brennan of County Durham was sent on an errand by bus to his uncle's house two miles away. He did the first part as instructed, but just missed the bus home. So he got into his uncle's van and drove that for a mile and a half until crashing into, of all places, a police station. The cumulative offences involved could have led to fifteen months in jail. Instead, he got spanked, and the promise of a new bike was withdrawn.

Joan and Alan Hewitt from Yorkshire (12 and 8) wanted to see the circus in London. So Joan secretly withdrew £5 from the Post Office, took the train, saw the circus and booked them into a hotel. Five-year-old Richard Brown from Brixton, playing truant with his seven-year-old brother, Peter, fell between the wheels of the *Golden Arrow*, the Pullman train to the Continent. The passengers were delayed half an hour; the foreman collapsed with shock; Richard was a bit frightened. Why did the boys play truant? Said Peter: 'We had to do take-away sums. They are too hard.'

And so on. Even three-year-olds joined in. Barry Barnett's tricycle was abandoned on the pavement near his home in Stoke Newington, with no sign of Barry. He was found, many frantic hours later, licking an ice cream on the far side of London, at Sydenham. He had jumped on a 171 bus and had 'a lovely ride'.

In Hampshire, a five-year-old, Carol Bodman, was thrown off a bus by a busy main road because she did not have the penny-ha'penny fare. All the opprobrium – from passengers, press and the bus company spokesman – fell on the conductor, who was convinced the child must have spent the money on sweets. No one thought it odd that a five-year-old should be on a bus alone. And no one seems to have raised the alarm about three-year-old Barry either. Just before the Hampshire story, two separate murderers had been sentenced in highly publicized cases for killing children they did not know.

And, even without encountering a murderer, many fifties adventures ended tragically. Cowboys and Indians produced at least two more shootings after 1952 – one fatal, when somehow a cap gun was replaced by a real one – and a seven-year-old was burned at the stake all too realistically in Lancashire. Unexploded wartime bombs were picked up, with terrible results; Bonfire Night delivered annual carnage; railways constantly caused casualties, especially in the south-east where the live rail was in use; in zoos, big cats and gorillas exerted a sometimes-fatal fascination.

Sometimes the death toll reached staggering proportions. On the last weekend of January 1954, twenty-two people – twenty boys, a girl, and a father trying to rescue his son – died *in Lancashire alone* while ice-skating on ponds and canals that were starting to thaw when the sun came out and the temperature rose above freezing. The toll included four brothers from Wigan. Even from this distance, it is heartbreaking to read the reports.

Did no one care? Of course they did. The police tried desperately to warn people off the ice, using loudspeaker vans and messages broadcast on the radio, at cinemas and at football matches. Are children better off now that no parent would dream of letting them go skating outside an artificial ice rink unsupervised, or more likely at all? That is a more complicated question.

———•———

Even before television, children did not spend every moment out of doors. This one adored *Children's Favourites* on a Saturday morning, introduced by Derek McCulloch, 'Uncle Mac', who was ubiquitous on children's radio. But I never quite cared for this self-appointed uncle: he sounded rather in pain working through the delightful if rather static playlist – 'The Happy Wanderer', 'Beep Beep', 'Gilly Gilly Ossenfeffer', etc. He probably *was* in pain: he lost an eye in the First World War and later lost a leg in a car crash – and the pain levels may have increased when the audience started asking for pop songs. He never even sounded as though he liked children much, which might, as time went by, make one wonder why he was doing this for a living . . .

6

THE MORAL TONE

I N 1952, VICTOR DE WAAL BECAME ASSISTANT CURATE OF THE
Church of England parish of St Mary the Virgin, Isleworth, near
the once-remote hamlet of Heath Row. Reverend de Waal had a
stipend of £250 – nothing so secular as a salary. More than half of
this went on his keep, but there was enough money left for occasional
trips to London. This was, after all, an era when £1 bought you a
dozen trips to the cinema, ninety-six stamps, about eighty bus rides
and a six months' supply of the *Daily Express*.

It was a working-class parish covering a population of about
8,000, with a brand-new, rather American-looking church and a
hall, which was astonishingly vibrant. 'There were lots of children
and Sunday schools and scouts and guides and camps and youth
clubs and entertainments in the church hall – skiffle groups, I
remember,' de Waal told me.

Under a law dating back exactly 400 years, to 1552, Sunday
church attendance was technically compulsory.* But, although the
early 1950s had a reputation for enforcing conformity, it did not
extend that far. Attendance, de Waal said, was 'about a hundred or
so'. But hundreds of children went to the Sunday schools, as was
still common across the country.

'My understanding,' I began to say cautiously, 'is that the main

---

* It remained so until a tidy-up of antiquated laws in 1969.

point of sending them to Sunday school was that it was the only time of the week when weary parents in small houses could safely . . .'

'Oh, we all knew *that*,' he replied.

The figure of 15 per cent as weekly churchgoers came from a survey by the sociologist Geoffrey Gorer. One may assume this was a question where respondents might have been inclined to exaggerate rather than understate, and de Waal's estimate suggests a much lower percentage – though that seems reasonable in a new church serving young families on new estates.

But belief persisted in the 1950s, or so people told callers with clipboards: different surveys showed half the population believing in the afterlife and nearly three-quarters regarding Jesus as the Son of God. And the British did cling close to the churches for the rites of passage. Nearly three-quarters of marriages took place in church and 60 per cent of English babies were baptized into the good old C of E.

When a Labour MP, John Parker, tried to loosen the Sunday trading laws to allow more entertainment in 1953, his private member's bill was rejected in the Commons by a six-to-one majority, and the Noes were backed up by opinion polls. This was the laughing-stock Sunday dissected in both one of the most famous episodes of *Hancock's Half Hour* ('Ah dear, dear . . . ah, dear me . . . What's the time?' 'Two o'clock.' 'Is that all?') and John Osborne's *Look Back in Anger* ('Why do I do this every Sunday? Even the book reviews seem to be the same as last week's') in a country regulated by the Shops Act 1950, which allowed the sale of pin-up magazines on the Sabbath but not the Bible. The then-powerful Lord's Day Observance Society was supported by some trade unions and, perhaps, all those couples who valued their kid-free Sunday opportunity.

————·————

There was one astonishing explosion of religious feeling in the 1950s that suggested a country that was not just static, modernist and materialistic but looking for *something* less tangible, even if they had no idea what. In the spring of 1954 the American evangelist

Billy Graham spent three months in London. The initial response from the Anglican establishment was cool, but he began to draw five-figure crowds to the Harringay Arena, outdrawing the greyhound track next door, which was an achievement in those days. And it became a kind of craze. Everyone wanted to see and hear this latest star turn from the States.

It helped that, unlike the Danny Kaye show, which had been a sensation at the London Palladium six years earlier, admission was free. And it helped that Graham was only 35 and a brilliant preacher, without the fixed smile of the classic American purveyor of snake-oil religion, and not a crook nor a phoney nor a political extremist. He charmed the *Daily Mirror*'s Cassandra by inviting him to lunch – and, eventually, the Queen. By the time of his grand finale at Wembley, even the Archbishop of Canterbury – who, like Cassandra, had been snotty at the start – turned up, along with about 120,000 others, and offered a blessing. Nearly 2 million heard his 'crusade',* and another million-plus in Scotland a year later. 'I think that he is a good man,' Cassandra concluded. 'He has been welcomed with an exuberance that almost makes us blush behind our precious Anglo-Saxon reserve.'

But what was the upshot? At the end of each London rally, people were asked to 'come forward' and make 'decisions for Christ' or for spiritual counselling. Their data was then harvested: 36,431 came forward over the three months, 2 per cent of the attendance. Most were under 19. There were undoubtedly some young men who were inspired to become priests, presumably on the evangelical wing of the C of E, which was to become increasingly significant. 'An element of something close to ecstasy was starting to be admitted to a place that had been very dry and stony,' Andrew Brown and Linda Woodhead wrote half a century later, in *That Was the Church That Was*. Other than that . . . there were more lasting crazes ahead. And the dry and stony wing did not go away.

A few months later, in January 1955, the BBC Home Service

---

* A word Graham diplomatically abandoned in favour of *mission* after 9/11, shortly before he retired.

commissioned Margaret Knight, a lecturer in psychology at Aberdeen University and a humanist, to give a pair of talks called *Morals without Religion*. She suggested uncoupling moral education from religious education; it was possible to impart Christ's moral philosophy without insisting on the absolute truth of the virgin birth, the resurrection, and humanity's dependence on the will of God. The *Manchester Guardian*'s initial report said there had been very few complaints about these 'deeply serious' talks.

But the Home Service included regional opt-outs, and most of the regional controllers, like birds sensing the approaching thunderclouds well before the farmer, exercised their rights. So most of the country did not hear Mrs Knight. The Bishop of Coventry, Neville Gorton, thought the world should know, and complained – very loudly – to the *Daily Express*. He called her 'this brusque, so-competent, bossy female' and described her words as 'pernicious'.

The next day he rowed back from some of the personal insults, but otherwise set about acting as Mrs Knight's unpaid publicist in a full-scale article for the *Express*: 'I take strong objection to this particular broadcast. The BBC gives the weight of its authority to an unknown, irresponsible woman . . . as a means of getting over her own particular destructive propaganda.'

The furore was a nine-day wonder, though it may help explain why to this day humanists are banned from Radio 4's *Thought for the Day*. Some of the bishop's supporters were even more intemperate: 'More suitable to Radio Moscow,' Mrs R. S. Brown of New Malden told the *Express*. Even the *Guardian*'s postbag was mixed: the Church Council of St Augustine's, Highbury, was 'shocked and horrified beyond anything words can express that the . . . BBC should dare to violate all the laws of decency and Christian conduct by broadcasting the pagan views of Mrs Knight.' However shaky the faith of the average Briton, the reaction of the committed certainly explains what happened later that year.

———·———

It took almost a fortnight for the most consequential bit of fluff in British history, the one Princess Margaret removed from Peter Townsend's lapel on Coronation Day, to find its way into the British press.

Townsend was a genuine, much-decorated war hero, who shot down at least eleven enemy aircraft before, during and after the Battle of Britain. He was responsible for the first German plane shot down on English soil,* and visited the survivors in hospital. He came through it all, minus a big toe, and became a group captain (equivalent to colonel). In 1944, Air Chief Marshal Sir Charles Portal called him in and offered him a three-month secondment – 'if you don't find the idea particularly revolting' – to be an equerry to the King. Since Townsend was sensitive, charming, handsome, competent, conventional and easy to have around, the royals resisted all the air force's attempts to reclaim him.

His duties included the three-month royal tour to South Africa in 1947, and on his return he found that distance had not lent enchantment to a difficult marriage. Divorce followed, and he was, in the essential phrase of the time, 'the innocent party', which was not merely an idiotic way to describe the complexities of marital breakdown but often involved role play for public consumption. Innocent parties were still welcome in the royal presence, including the Royal Enclosure at Ascot; guilty ones were not. Some sources believe his *tendresse* with Margaret dated back to South Africa, when she was 16 and he was twice her age. And even by 1953, it was only seventeen years since the abdication crisis, when the prospect of Edward VIII marrying the twice-divorced Wallis Simpson forced him from the throne. It very rapidly became clear that a controversial marriage was now definitely on the agenda again.

As with everything else involving Buckingham Palace, the precise manoeuvrings are hidden in a fog thicker than a London pea-souper. It is thought that Townsend had declared his love to Margaret just after her father's death, which she had taken far more obviously to heart than her sister, who suddenly had little time for emotion. It is

---

* A Heinkel near Whitby, in February 1940.

thought that the Queen, Queen Mother and the prime minister were all initially sympathetic, though not Mrs Churchill and certainly not the mighty Tommy Lascelles.

History was not quite repeating itself. With Charles and Anne around, Margaret was most unlikely to become Queen. Mrs Simpson, now Duchess of Windsor, was regarded by just about everyone apart from her besotted husband as – that splendid old euphemism – 'a piece of work'; Townsend was much liked. But the feeling grew, in that inner circle, that he had crossed an uncrossable line – and, as the much older of the two, had behaved like rather a shit.

No one was as seared by the abdication or hated Mrs Simpson more than the Queen Mother. However, she and Margaret were both on a visit to Rhodesia when Lascelles and the government seized the moment to have Townsend exiled to Brussels for two years in the rather insulting post of air attaché; by the time that ended the princess would be twenty-five. Until then, under a 1772 Act, she needed the monarch's permission to marry. After that, she would be free at least to marry, though there could still be constraints. Or, with luck, the romance would have cooled off. Or Townsend might have choked on a bowl of *moules-frites*.

Before the fuss died away for the duration, the *Mirror*, Britain's biggest-selling daily, ran a readers' poll: of more than 70,000 votes, just under 97 per cent said they should be allowed to marry. Donald Zec* was one of the paper's star writers at the time. I put it to him that kind of figure sounded suspiciously North Korean. Was it rigged? He shook his head: 'The readership were very B-picture in their emotions.'

Halfway through Townsend's exile, in the autumn of 1954, it was announced that the automatic ban on 'guilty parties' in divorce cases would no longer apply in the Royal Enclosure, which suggested a softening in Palace attitudes on this point. However, there was a catch. There would now be a new inner sanctum, the Queen's Lawn,

---

* Donald Zec was the oldest person I interviewed for this book, still lucid and funny close to his 100th birthday. He died, aged 102, in 2021.

for a few hundred 'personal friends of the Queen'. And there the ban would remain.

The following year, the most anticipated twenty-fifth birthday in history arrived. Margaret, following family tradition, was at Balmoral. So were about 300 hacks and snappers: an unprecedented royal doorstepping. By October, Townsend, back from banishment, was regularly seeing Margaret inside different houses, with vast murmurations of journalists outside. Their speculation and the weight of opinion polls were both very much for wedding bells.

For Peter and Margaret, the bells never did ring. A series of forces overwhelmed them: the subtle, perhaps entirely tacit, 'do you really have to' attitude of her mother and sister; the overt displeasure of the Archbishop of Canterbury, suppurating with unction, and *The Times*, whose firm editorial pronouncement, it is said, was decisive in convincing the couple that the game was up.

The government was in a tricky position. Anthony Eden (now Sir Anthony), who had finally replaced Churchill, was himself divorced, as were two other men in the Cabinet – with two more about to join them. But the very influential Marquess of Salisbury represented the old guard. He had his own private chapel at Hatfield House which he attended daily, possibly giving instructions to God. He rallied the Cabinet into outright opposition.

And then, on Halloween, Margaret said goodbye to her lover and made a brief statement beginning: 'Mindful of the Church's teachings that Christian marriage is indissoluble . . .' Margaret had told the archbishop the news first: 'What a wonderful person the Holy Spirit is!' he responded. Three days later, the archbishop lied on TV: 'There had been no pressure from church or state.' And that was that. Three years later, with the Queen's back turned, they had what looked like a brief old-flame fling. A year after that, Townsend married the daughter of some Belgian friends, and lived discreetly ever after, in France.

It was the last great victory for Britain's unofficial religion of the early fifties, façade-ism: the belief that nothing matters more than keeping up appearances. There could have been another solution. The couple could have been cut quietly adrift, given a nice house in the Cotswolds, settled down, had children and Labradors, and waited for the times (and *The Times*) to change before a consensual return to the fold. But, being Margaret, she would probably have run out screaming.

'She wanted the apple and to eat it,' said Donald Zec. 'She wanted all the dances, all the boyfriends, but they in turn had to treat her like royalty. I think she got over Townsend fairly quickly. She liked being the tragic princess but it didn't stop her dancing.' As far as the royal soap opera went, this was a much better storyline and she played her role beautifully over the years: the bitter, crabby and imperious counterpoint to her too-perfect sister.

But even that perfection was starting to look frayed. As the fuss was fading, on a wintry day in Stoke-on-Trent, the Queen and Duke of Edinburgh went to see 2,500 children dressed in shorts and singlets give a gymnastic display. Having waited twenty-five minutes in a cold rain, fifty of them collapsed. It seemed another sign that the Palace was losing its empathy with the people.

7

THE IMMORAL TONE

ONE DAY IN THE FIFTIES, THE COMIC WRITER DENIS NORDEN got the dread letter calling him for jury service, and he was obliged to spend a week at the London Sessions dealing with a variety of small cases. He soon discovered they were richer in humorous potential than anything one dared invent.

In his first case, a youth was charged with indecent behaviour, which involved him being in the cinema, sitting next to a girl with whom he was only slightly acquainted and moving to what might have been the second stage of sexual activity had things not gone drastically wrong: she rushed out, sobbing, to call the police.

The constable involved read out the boy's statement: 'She let me keep my hand on her tit for more than ten minutes so I thought it would be all right.' The boy's barrister, as callow as his client if less worldly, honed in on one word: 'I put it to you, constable, my client did not use the word *tit*, he said *breast*.'

'He said *tit*,' insisted the copper. And this *breast–tit* back-and-forth went on for some time until the judge finally interrupted: 'You're not going to ask him that again, are you?'

'It goes to character, Your Honour. The sort of boy who customarily uses the word *tit* is altogether different in character and behaviour from one who refers to that part of the body as . . .'

'Oh, do give over,' the judge said.

There is more in that anecdote about Britain in the 1950s than

you might find in a whole bookshelf of learned tomes: the notion
that class and character were somehow connected; the furtive nature
of sex in general and youthful sex in particular; the lingering
usefulness of the cinema – as TV cut dramatically into its business
– as a darkened room where members of the opposite sex could
consort before marriage; the prissiness of most discourse . . . but
also, in the judge's response, an underlying robustness.

The general British embarrassment about just about everything,
but sex in particular, was well-attested. It was summed up by one
of the decade's more risqué cabaret performers, Paddy Roberts:

> *Oh the Englishman could not be called romantic*
> *His technique is not particularly good*
> *All the French and the Italians*
> *Chase their women round like stallions*
> *But the Englishman's a suet pud.*

There is evidence that sexual intercourse did take place in the early
1950s, even between one's parents, gross as that idea seemed. It
even took place outside the marriage bed, as the number of brides
with bumps attested. Yet the British attitude to sex remained a
matter of startling paradoxes.

In the fading music halls, the master of comic timing Max Miller
was still doing his star turn:

> *When roses are red, they're ready for pluckin'*
> *When a girl is sixteen, she's ready for . . .*

Then he would point disapprovingly at the audience: *"Ere, 'ere.'* He
even performed at the 1950 Royal Variety Performance, the jokes
toned down a bit. Yet the authorities were clamping down on the
saucy seaside postcards of Donald McGill.

In the *Daily Mirror*, the cartoon heroine Jane would strip to her
frilly undies at every opportunity. But if the popular papers began
to discuss sex seriously, preachers would begin denouncing them
from the pulpit. The *News of the World* highlighted minor court

cases too salacious for the local papers, using code words like *intimacy* (sex) and *impropriety* (adulterous sex) and *offences* (unmentionable goings-on). The paper was read every Sunday in almost half the homes in Britain – many of which must have been inhabited by both children and churchgoers.

On many London streets, prostitution was both rife and overt, indeed blatant. But the city's teenagers were expected to learn about sex by a kind of osmosis, to avoid parental embarrassment. 'You found out the little you knew from your girlfriends. Mum would never mention anything about sex to me,' a woman from South London later told a researcher.

Some of these paradoxes can be attributed to the ancient British (more specifically English) vices of secrecy and hypocrisy, which were honed to perfection in the Victorian era. But sexual attitudes in the 1950s were not just a continuation of the past: they acquired a fierce quality of their own, like the darkness before the dawn. The war may have been a factor in this. There was much reticence about what really happened: on the battlefield and in bed. Some of that was modesty, some of it shame. So much was left unsaid.

In some respects, there was more candour than before. The first Kinsey Report, on the sexual behaviour of the American male, was generally ignored in Britain when it appeared in 1948. Five years later, its author, Dr Alfred Kinsey, turned to the American female, and the *Daily Mirror* splashed on the story.* It announced in bold type that nearly half of the married women Kinsey surveyed had had sex before their wedding; more than a quarter had been unfaithful after it; and two-thirds of marriages ran into difficulties over sex, mainly because of men's misunderstanding of the female libido. The *News of the World*'s great rival, *The People*, conducted a poll of British women, and announced that only one in nine had been unfaithful – which, it said proudly, meant they were less promiscuous than the Americans. Or more secretive, maybe? But

---

* It overwhelmed the news of both the overthrow of General Mossadeq's radical government in Iran, an event which still has reverberations for British foreign policy nearly seventy years later, and England's recapture of the Ashes.

this was at least a more mature response than that provided by *The Times*, who did not mention the name Alfred Kinsey in his lifetime.*

Kinsey also suggested that heavy petting before marriage was likely to secure a relationship. Mary Brown, then the *Mirror*'s agony aunt, was stern about this: 'I assert that "petting to the limit" can be harmful. I may sound old-fashioned, but Nature is old-fashioned too . . . And the boy and girl who rouse each other to the edge of delirium and then stop short of release are doing themselves psychological and spiritual harm.' The modern answer would be to take the train all the way to the terminus. But that was a bad idea in 1953, partly because it would have been too daring even for the *Mirror*, and partly because there were serious practical objections.

———·———

Bryan Magee was at Oxford in the early 1950s, having already done his National Service. Even for a relatively mature student, the rules and etiquette governing romance were complex, as he recalled nearly sixty years later: 'There was a process of courtship which in most cases would last weeks. Most of the ex-soldiers went through the process. You then had sex in your bed in the afternoon. There was no problem with that. What you couldn't actually do is spend the night together. The penalty for doing that was quite draconian. You couldn't spend the night with a girl. You could spend it with a man, but only from the same college.'

The colleges were all single-sex, and the handful of Oxbridge women's colleges were run on a basis that was something like a conventional boarding school but with a strong dollop of St Trinian's. 'I thought Oxford was wonderful,' said Marigold Johnson (née Hunt). 'I'd never had any contact, even as childhood friends, with boys ever.' In 1952 she was confined to the college for half a term, having being seen in a ballgown at 8 a.m. after going to the summer commemoration ball with the athlete Roger Bannister. 'Did they stick to it?' 'Oh yes, but it was easy to climb in and out.'

---

* The first reference came on his death in 1956, when he merited one sentence. He was described as 'the biologist who turned to the study of social anthropology'.

Johnson said alcohol was banned at her college, Lady Margaret Hall, until the arrival of Prince Astrid of Norway, who told them: 'I must have beer because that's what I use for my hair.' Because so few were admitted, Oxbridge girls benefited because boys were six or seven a penny. The consequences of this, however, could be dire. One of David McKie's contemporaries got his girlfriend pregnant: 'She got sent down instantly. He didn't. That's the way it happened. Not him. Her.'

Even amidst the dreaming spires, the students of the early fifties had some privations. The living arrangements were often medieval. Rationing was still in force. Gillian Reynolds (née Morton) remembers putting a butter dish outside her room to get her weekly four ounces. However, suffering was not shared evenly. 'I remember one girl saying "I couldn't get along without my granny's £1,000 a year." My mother used to send me a pound note every week.'

Reynolds had to jump through nerve-wracking hoops from her state school in Liverpool to get to Oxford. The future MP Julian Critchley, from Shrewsbury School, recalled that nobody cared what kind of A levels he got: 'They just wanted my As to be long not short.'

Outside Oxbridge colleges, relatively few young people had a room of their own, and certainly not one offering privacy. Even fewer had cars. Otherwise, as the historian of British sex Paul Ferris put it, there were 'walls in back lanes for knee-tremblers, grass in parks, and sofas for five minutes when a parent had gone to the shops'. Another practical difficulty for the male was the nature of women's underwear. 'The nylon stocking was still suspended from a constricting girdle of unyielding firmness,' wrote Peter Lewis in his history of the decade, 'a fortification virtually impossible to bypass without active collusion, and preferably plenty of time . . . Unpremeditated impulses were often frustrated by such hurdles.'*

There was also the question of consequences. The condoms available at the time were disliked, distrusted, and unlikely to be

---

* Though the upside was an extra frisson, like the pleasure of opening a nicely wrapped Christmas present.

available on a whim. Intrauterine devices (IUDs) were rare. The Family Planning Association offered clinics, though not everywhere, and it lived up to its name. It gave advice and offered cervical caps to women who were married or (from 1952) about to be. 'Clients had to sit in a row with their stockings round their ankles, waiting to see a doctor,' wrote Ferris. 'As usual with sex, those who indulged in it were expected to suffer a little.'

If sex did take place with unwanted success, then abortion was an option, for both rich and poor. The rich always knew someone who knew someone who knew a doctor somewhere close to Harley Street who would deal with the situation, at a price. The legality of this was fuzzy and best not investigated.

For the poor, there was always someone nearby who, for a much smaller fee, just wanted to help. They were nearly always the maternal types. In Kate Thompson's East End memoir, *The Stepney Doorstep Society*, it was 'Denise's mum, Polly',* a mother of seven. 'She only ever helped girls up to a certain stage. Her chosen method was a crochet hook. She used the kitchen table, laying down a rubber sheet. If the pregnancy had been advanced enough and the foetus intact, Polly would wash it and bury it in the churchyard opposite . . . Over the years, dozens of girls in the same predicament traipsed through their doors, pale-faced and terrified.' Denise never knew whether money changed hands, but she knew how grateful many were. She did not know how many of these makeshift operations might have gone wrong.

Or, of course, they might let the baby live. Lorna Sage became pregnant, aged 15, in 1958, and gave birth in a grim, remote ex-workhouse turned NHS hospital in Shropshire. 'Over it hung an air of grudging public charity . . . unmarried mothers had the worst of it, but being married didn't improve your status much,' Sage wrote in her memoir *Bad Blood*. She endured one of those long fifties confinements; visiting hours were brief, it was almost impossible to reach the hospital by bus, and telephone calls were out of the question.

---

*   Not their real names.

'The regime was rigid . . . hair-washing was strictly forbidden, even if you were well enough to walk to the bathroom; bathing was rationed and make-up was frowned upon.' The babies were segregated from their mothers and brought out for four-hourly breastfeeds during the day. Sage was about to get a lecture for her latest offence when Matron was diverted by a new outrage. 'She'd spotted down the ward an enormity, a woman with red nails. Marching smartly to the bedside she picked up the woman's hand and flung it back at her with disgust: "We don't feed our babies on nail varnish!" she announced, looking around her in triumph, and sailed through the swing doors.'

Even masturbation did not constitute entirely safe sex. Aside from the usual oblique lectures from dried-up old dominies about the subject, the boys of Uppingham School could be further discouraged by having their trouser pockets sewn up.*

Just mentioning the word *masturbation* was problematic. The Mary Grant column in *Woman's Own* would have occasional mysterious footnotes to readers saying simply: 'What you describe is not unusual and few would consider it wrong.' Any clarity would risk complaints from the readers and an outright ban from the censors in Ireland, a country whose sexual attitudes made British life seem very relaxed.

But Britain was not relaxed at all, even by its own historic standards. In the early fifties, a coalition of extremists decided to Do Something about Britain's supposedly declining morals, and did so under the aegis of Churchill's generally complaisant government. It was spearheaded by Sir David Maxwell Fyfe, a well-regarded and in many ways progressive barrister who had made his name crushing Hermann Goering in cross-examination at the Nuremberg trials and helped father the European Convention on Human Rights. He was not the last politician to trash his own reputation after being

---

* The atypical Old Uppinghamian Stephen Fry, uncharacteristically spoiling a good story, believes the sewn-up pockets were merely intended as a deterrent to slouching and slovenliness. Any other consequence was a by-product. Generally, hands in pockets were a grave affront to the public school ethos of the era, except apparently at Eton, where the boys were too grand to take much notice of the masters.

appointed Home Secretary, but he did so with unusual relish on more than one front.

The first was a clampdown on anything that might assist the masturbatory urges of the British male, which Maxwell Fyfe led with the zestful backing of platoons of chief constables, battalions of judges and regiments of magistrates. The police were said to have been influenced by a report from Interpol linking crime and pornography. Their response was undiscerning: 167,000 books and magazines went to the furnace in 1954, the year of the blazing book, compared to 900 in 1935.

The US had replaced the traditionally filthy French as the main purveyors of what was often very soft porn, and the flames consumed many copies of pre-*Playboy* offerings such as *Wink* and *Flirt* ('bevies of high-heel beauties'). Caught in the sniper fire were Donald McGill's lavishly coloured drawings of curvaceous women, put-upon husbands, shocked vicars, randy milkmen and other British stereotypes. These had been on sale as postcards at seaside resorts since the 1930s, selling in their millions without much complaint. They were rich in music-hall innuendo:

> *Cook*: 'Oh, Professor! I'm afraid I ate it. I thought it was a pickled gherkin.'
> *Woman at upstairs window*: 'I say, milkman, have you got the time?' *Milkman*: 'Yes, I've got the time. But 'oo's going to look after my 'orse?'
> *Girl to soldier*: 'How long's your furlough?'
> *Old maid to burglar*: 'If you're not out of my bedroom in 24 hours I'll phone the police!'

McGill was a quiet, intellectually inclined man who never made much money from his art and was wistful about being pigeon-holed. When he was summonsed, aged almost 80, to appear in court at Lincoln, he was mainly worried about the neighbours finding out how naive he had been about his worth. He was fined £50, which was hefty. The purge was nationwide; thousands of postcards were destroyed.

Sometimes the campaign touched the confines of lunacy. In June 1954, Swindon magistrates ordered the destruction of an illustrated copy of *The Decameron*, J. M. Rigg's 1903 translation of Boccaccio's fourteenth-century masterpiece, which was found in Elsie Foulds's shop on Commercial Road. 'The work in question deals very considerably with sexual gratification,' explained the prosecution. 'There was nothing in there which you would not see in any art gallery in the land,' said the defence. The decision was reversed on appeal. It was a rare victory: the works of Jean Genet were also seized (for keeps, this time) by customs in 1956 before the puritans began to calm down.

This might not have spared the 223 (approximately) works of 'Hank Janson', pseudonymous author of Chicago tough-guy novels with sexy covers and mildly lubricious text. These were the staple diet of adolescent boys who had grown out of Biggles. 'Raymond Chandler and Dashiell Hammett had elevated the hard-boiled 'tec story into something like poetry,' reminisced Colin Dunne in the *Daily Mail* sixty years on, 'but Hank turned up the violence and the sex and took it back downmarket. Right down.' Dunne said the trick was to remove the cover to avoid drawing parental attention to the text.

The books were mass-produced almost monthly between 1946 and 1968 with titles like *When Dames Get Tough, Gun Moll for Hire* and *Hotsy You'll Be Chilled*. The author of most, if not all, these works of Americana was of course British, and in real life had the less butch-sounding name of Stephen Frances. He had enough nous and royalties to head to Spain, where there was no extradition treaty, before 1954 when the two directors of the publishers were fined £2,000 each and jailed for six months. The judge at the Old Bailey, passing sentence, talked of 'literary pollution', 'an abyss of filth' and 'a veritable pool of depravity'. The defence unavailingly pointed out that among the biggest customers was Her Majesty's government, which bought the books and distributed them to the armed forces.

London. A cold and misty November evening. The junior minister had been to dinner at the Polish Embassy. He had been drinking but, he insisted, was not drunk. He was heading back to his West End bedsit just as the pubs were chucking out and the Coldstream guardsmen were returning to their barracks. So he wandered into St James's Park; a guardsman went past him, but slowly; they had both done this before, in the minister's case for many years.

The embassy kirsch, he reflected later, must have dulled his senses. He knew the place they had chosen was patrolled before midnight . . . On the way to the police station he briefly tried to make a run for it. Later he gave a false name, then immediately relented and accepted his fate. In theory, it was a £5 fine for gross indecency and breaking park regulations. In practice, he was sentenced to living death.

Ian Harvey had all the attributes: Fettes College, Christ Church, Oxford, president of the Union and a lieutenant-colonel; he married money (Colman's Mustard), had two daughters, made a name for himself in the up-and-coming trades of advertising and PR, then found a safe-ish Tory seat near London. At 44, in a more gerontocratic age, he was at the Foreign Office and advancing nicely. He was regarded as a good egg.

It was chance that, when he needed a pad in town for late-night sittings, he took one near the park and began to notice the discreet encounters taking place below. He had known the sexual yearnings of his inner self for many years – but, it seems, no one else did, except the anonymous soldiers he began to meet cautiously in the park late at night. He had hurt no one.

The day before the court case was the Varsity rugby match at Twickenham, a regular social event on his calendar. Many of his Commons friends were there, as usual. 'They obviously did not know whether to wish me luck or to say good-bye. So they solved the problem by not saying anything,' he wrote in his autobiography. All very British. He paid a final courtesy call on the Foreign Office to say good luck to his successor, John Profumo, went to the country and gave up writing his diary: 'There was nothing of interest to write.'

He was by no means the first. This was late 1958, and the Wolfenden Committee had already recommended, though not achieved, the legalization of homosexual acts between consenting adult males. He was not the last, either. Homosexuality had been subject to prohibitions and taboos throughout recorded history. There was an obvious reason for this: heterosexuality was considered essential to the continued existence of the species*; homosexuality was a potential distraction from that basic societal objective. In some cultures, in some periods, most famously in ancient Greece and Rome, it was tolerated as an adjunct to the norms of marriage and procreation. In others, it was not.

Buggery was a capital crime in England from Henry VIII's reign to Victoria's. The last hangings for the offence were in 1835, but the 1861 Offences Against the Person Act allowed suspected homosexuals to be strip-searched for signs of anal penetration. This was not easy to prove, and remained theoretical until the infamous Labouchère Amendment of 1885 which created the completely undefined offence of 'gross indecency' between men.† It came to mean whatever the police wanted it to mean.

Quite why Maxwell Fyfe marshalled the forces of law and order so vigorously to suppress it in the early 1950s remains bewildering. There had never been a time when the British were so committed to conventional sexuality. This was already enforced zealously by parental and peer-group pressure. Which is why a man like Harvey drifted towards conformity, and then found himself satisfying his most pressing sexual need in a royal park on a cold November night.

Maxwell Fyfe told the Commons in 1953: 'Homosexuals, in general, are exhibitionists and proselytizers and a danger to others, especially the young,' a remark Harvey may have heard with a shudder. He may also have heard that the number of homosexual

---

* The first successful artificial insemination in humans is believed to have been conducted in Philadelphia in 1884. But the technique was little known in Britain until the 1980s and unregulated until 1990.

† Lesbianism has never been a crime in Britain. The delightful suggestion that this was because Queen Victoria believed it impossible appears to be unsubstantiated.

offences known to the police had multiplied fivefold in fifteen years. Of course they had – the police had been ordered to forget genuine crime and shine torches into bushes. This was also the year a Labour MP, Bill Field, was forced out of public life after what looked like a clear case of entrapment. The year before, the northern comedian George Williams was sentenced to two years in jail and, unofficially, ten years without work. The year after came the dreadful case of Alan Turing, the brilliant mathematician and codebreaker, who reported a petty theft, which led the police to his low-life sexual partner – and Turing to a course of chemical castration, the loss of his security clearance and, ultimately, suicide.

The most publicized case was that of the upmarket trio of Lord Montagu of Beaulieu, his cousin Michael Pitt-Rivers and the *Daily Mail*'s diplomatic correspondent Peter Wildeblood, arrested in January 1954 and jailed after being betrayed by a pair of unscrupulous RAF men. The most interesting aspect of this case were the reports of the crowd booing outside the court in Winchester. They did not boo the defendants; they booed their two accusers.

Meanwhile, the Admiralty responded with an order insisting that naval officers 'stamp out the evil . . . of unnatural vice'. It was suggested that officers should inspect jars of Vaseline and gel for pubic hairs. Which was particularly funny if you knew the rumours, as much of London did, that the man shortly to become First Sea Lord, Earl Mountbatten, was over-fond of young boys.*

One arrest in 1953, not at all funny at the time, has assumed a certain comic resonance at a distance. It concerned the actor John Gielgud, knighted earlier in the year, an honour greeted with great joy not just because of his professional brilliance but because of his benign, scatty nature. After a long day rehearsing a new play, *A Day by the Sea*, he was tempted to visit a toilet in Chelsea, well known as a 'cottaging' site, and clumsily propositioned a police decoy. He had been warned before by a friendly copper not to say who he really was, so the daft old thing said he was 'Arthur Gielgud',

---

* This assertion has been subsequently reinforced by many sources, including FBI files.

his real name. He got a second chance the next morning when the desk sergeant managed to rush him through court before the official start time, which would have been fine if a reporter had not passed the courtroom door and heard an unmistakable voice . . .

By the time Gielgud had been fined £10 and reached the rehearsal room, the *Evening Standard* carrying the story was already being passed round. 'Well, John,' said Sybil Thorndike, 'what a very silly bugger you have been.' On the first night, Thorndike had to lead him on stage, trembling. There was an immediate standing ovation. On the other hand, when the actress Greer Garson gave a talk the following month and mentioned his name, it was booed by, of all improbable illiberals, the students of Manchester University. These really were strange times. Gielgud himself was mortified and took much time to recover his confidence fully. As he wrote to his friend, Cecil Beaton: 'It's so hard to say what I feel – to have let down the whole side – the theatre, my friends, myself and my family – and all for the most idiotic and momentary impulse.'

Even the medical profession had trouble keeping an even keel on this subject. A Cambridge graduate followed convention and got married, but worried that he fantasized about men not women. The doctor reassured him, saying, 'If you're not an artist and you're not effeminate, you can't be homosexual.'*

It was quite possible to escape the primeval oppression and inhumanity, certainly for the well-heeled. The rich, like Noël Coward and Somerset Maugham, acquired homes in places where the climate was friendlier – meteorologically as well as sexually. Discretion helped. Terence Rattigan told his lover, Adrian Brown, not to answer the telephone.† But it was possible to survive. Power helped. 'Binkie' Beaumont, the leading manager and producer in West End theatre at the time, ran an outrageous salon at his home in Lord North Street, where he would hold auditions, 'reclining in

---

* On the other hand, Sir Michael Howard (the military historian, not the politician) went to a Harley Street consultant soon after the war because he feared he was homosexual. 'And what,' said the consultant impatiently, 'makes you think there is anything wrong with *that*?' And Howard lived gaily ever after.
† Rattigan was mostly worried that his mother might call.

pastel pyjamas on black silk bed sheets, while young men would hopefully camp it up around him in search of a role'. Later in the decade, the future interior designer Nicky Haslam, then a handsome young Old Etonian and, shall we say, a man's man about town, revelled in it all: 'Its illegality and the necessity for camouflage did make homosexuality more interesting and, I hate to say it, fun.'

There was a protective ring round the artistic subcultures, especially the stage. Even in politics there were plenty of men whose illegal tastes were known to everyone except their constituents. When one, the left-winger Tom Driberg, was elected in 1942, another, the Tory Chips Channon, showed him round the toilets: 'the most important rooms,' said Channon. Driberg was a flagrant risk-taker, keenest on rough trade, yet he survived unscathed in the Commons for twenty-eight years. 'If anything, I became more promiscuous after my election to Parliament, relying on my new status to get me out of tight corners.' For non-public figures who shunned conformity but maintained discretion, the risk was minimal, especially if they had a stable relationship and cared nothing for neighbourhood gossip: the police patrolled parks and public toilets, not suburban bedrooms. But someone like Ian Harvey, trying to have it all – fame, furtiveness, family and façade – ended with nothing. His autobiography was called *To Fall Like Lucifer*.

A very few big-city pubs were known to be *gay*, a code word that had not even spread into the newsrooms of Fleet Street, since it was used constantly in headlines to denote innocent happiness. There it was possible to lapse into Polari, the camp argot which at that stage was an almost infallible indicator of whether the other person was on the same sexual wavelength. If one proceeded cautiously, such a pub could offer more chance of a warm bed than a cold cell. In a small town, the situation might be far more dangerous, and there was much localized persecution of alleged networks. From 1953, the press began to report these cases more freely than before, which added to the moral panic.

But why did they bother? Obviously, there was long-standing animus and fear: the well-informed Australian writer Donald Horne wrote that Washington was pressuring London to weed out homosexuals from important jobs as 'hopeless security risks'. This would link the mania to the then unexplained disappearance of the presumed Foreign Office spies Guy Burgess and Donald Maclean in 1951. But it also makes it more bizarre: homosexuals were risks because they were blackmailable; they were blackmailable primarily because of the illegality.

Before he left office, Maxwell Fyfe surprisingly proposed to the Cabinet an inquiry into the laws on both homosexuality and prostitution. Another surprise, to those in the know, might have been the choice of chairman: Sir John Wolfenden, a former head-master of Uppingham School, home of the sewn-up trouser pockets, and at this point vice-chancellor of Reading University. Piquantly, perversely, Wolfenden was appointed although his son Jeremy was not only homosexual but flamboyant about it. When appointed, father reportedly wrote to son: 'I have only two requests to make of you at the moment. One, that we stay out of each other's way for the time being and two, that you wear rather less make-up.'

Perhaps going to extremes offered a kind of protection. In 1954, a startling announcement emanated from a Spitfire pilot, racing driver and father-of-two, formerly known as Robert Cowell, revealing a different identity: Roberta Cowell – 'Betty' to her friends, to whom this was old news. 'Since 18 May 1951, I have been Roberta Cowell, female', as she put it later. 'I have become a woman physically, psychologically, glandularly and legally.'

This was unprecedented in Britain, on the outer edges of what was both possible and lawful. But the authorities took medical advice in re-registering her identity. And the press coverage was uncensorious, if a little baffled. She went back to motor racing and in 1957 won the long-established Shelsley Walsh Hill Climb in Worcestershire, setting a women's record. Everyone seemed delighted for her. One paper called it 'an outstanding triumph by British surgeons'.

8

LET HIM HAVE IT, GODDARD

SIR DAVID MAXWELL FYFE HAD ONE FURTHER CONTRIBUTION TO make to British history, more lasting than his attempts to wipe out personal sexual preferences. He put paid to the fine old English tradition of hanging, which dated back at least 1,600 years. This was the reverse of his intention, and it took twelve years for events to run their course, but just before 11 p.m. on 27 January 1953 he finalized a decision that would kill capital punishment as surely as it would kill the man whose death he confirmed.

A few hours earlier he had met a deputation of MPs, led by Aneurin Bevan, who pleaded with him to use his power as Home Secretary to exercise the royal prerogative of mercy and commute the sentence of Derek Bentley from death to life imprisonment. He wrote back and politely declined. Ten hours later, Bentley was hanged in Wandsworth Prison.

Judges in a murder case had no discretion: if the jury found the defendant guilty, they had to put on the black cap and ritually pronounce the death sentence. In the early fifties, executions came at a steady clip, just over one a month. But so did reprieves: almost half the men convicted had their sentence commuted – from death to life – and almost all the women. By yet another ancient tradition, the Home Secretary never gave his reasons.

The hangings rarely rated more than a paragraph or two in the papers: the death of Alfred Moore, convicted of killing two policemen in Yorkshire, was the eleventh item in a news-in-brief column in the *Daily Telegraph*. That was an extreme case of indifference, since George VI had died the same morning and the press was understandably preoccupied. But it was not all that extreme.

The Bentley case was different, from the very first splash *Daily Mail* headline: CHICAGO GUN BATTLE IN LONDON. Bentley was 19, illiterate, low-functioning ('a three-quarter wit,' said one MP, kindly) and easily led. His accomplice, Christopher Craig, was 16, near-illiterate – dyslexic, most likely – but sharp, obsessed with guns and deeply angry after his older brother was jailed, perhaps unjustly, for armed robbery. Craig led Bentley to raid, of all childish things, a confectionery warehouse. He handed Bentley a spiked knuckleduster; Craig himself had a loaded Colt .45. They were so inept they were spotted from her bedroom window by a little girl, whose parents called the police. Bentley, cornered on the roof, surrendered at once and made no attempt to escape. Craig wounded one policeman and then shot PC Sidney Miles in the forehead with instant effect. When Craig ran out of bullets he jumped and landed, on a greenhouse roof, badly injuring himself.

One can lose oneself for ever in the intricacies of this case, but the relevant facts are simple. Craig, being under 18, could not be executed; Bentley could, and on the legal principle of 'joint enterprise' was liable since he admitted knowing that Craig had a gun. This was potentially negated by the fact that he was in police custody when the fatal shot was fired. But, against that, police evidence was that he had encouraged Craig by uttering five words: 'Let him have it, Chris.' In the folklore surrounding Bentley, these words are held to be ambiguous – potentially meaning that he should hand over the gun. But this was no part of the defence, because neither Bentley nor Craig remembered those words being uttered.

Most of the Lord Chief Justices of England and Wales since 1958 would be remembered easily only by judges and barristers. Rayner Goddard, who held the job for the twelve years before that, was different. In 1946, the Attlee government, having no suitable quasi-political figure in mind, had allowed the judges the chance to pick one of their own. They seemed to have no doubt: his colleagues were in awe of Goddard and many remained so; he had a quick mind, a formidable knowledge of the law, and forthright opinions.

'A great man . . . the very embodiment of the common law,' wrote his colleague Lord Denning. 'He rarely read the [court] papers beforehand . . . he brooked no delay . . . he dominated the Court . . . I have known him not to bother to ask them [his colleagues, when he sat with others on the bench] but to take their assent for granted and deliver judgment forthwith . . . He usually gave judgment *extempore* – straight off the reel. Occasionally in a difficult case he would take time to consider it.'

Well, that was jolly decent of him. He certainly got through cases swiftly, which pleases everyone in court except perhaps the defendant. And, though famously stern, he was unpredictable and sometimes surprisingly lenient. By January 1953, however, he was almost 76, and his self-confidence had turned to arrogance and was approaching egomania. He was already leading a campaign to bring the use of the birch back into the sentencing armoury, to curb the imaginary rise in crime – though, as a judge, that was not really his business. One of the perks of his job was the right to take charge of any case he wanted. He picked the Craig–Bentley trial, like a plum.

It was all over in three days. All judges have the right to interrupt; most do so sparingly. Goddard did like to make his own ejaculations during a trial and he did so on this occasion 250 times, which would constitute one about every three minutes.* His aim was clear, and his summing-up, far from being the customary précis of the evidence, reads more like the statement of a prosecutor. Both defendants were found guilty.

The appeal was brief and absurd, which is unsurprising, given that the three judges were in effect junior to the judge they were judging; the House of Lords was not involved. The Home Secretary

---

* Malicious rumours circulated at the time that when Goddard pronounced the death penalty it induced another kind of ejaculation.

was the Bentley family's one hope; even Goddard said privately he thought Bentley would be reprieved – the jury had recommended mercy, as was their right. Maxwell Fyfe never offered a clue to his thinking, even in his dull memoirs. This is perhaps understandable, because he was responsible for the police; they expected his protection, and coppers on the beat would have seen a reprieve as allowing Bentley to get away with murder. Yet another tradition was always to hang police killers.

Even when he was in opposition, Maxwell Fyfe had insisted that a wrongful verdict in a murder case was impossible. 'I do not believe that the chances of error in a murder case . . . constitute a factor which we must consider, any more than we must consider the danger of death in crossing a street . . . There is no practical possibility,' he said in a Commons debate on hanging in 1948. It is amazing he was never run over.

And he was not a reliable witness. In his memoirs, he even gets wrong the crucial quote, which he renders as 'Give it him, Chris.' But perhaps that is understandable too. Reading the court transcript, it seemed incredible that the words were ever heard and remembered so precisely by three separate police officers from those traumatic and terrible moments, let alone by the Home Secretary. It seems to me overwhelmingly likely that, stricken by the loss of their colleague and deeply aware that Craig would never hang, they wanted to ensure that someone paid the price.

There is corroboration for this: there were other policemen present who were never called to court; one of them, Claude Pain, unburdened himself aged 80 and insisted the words were never said; John Parris, Craig's barrister, later found that a very similar phrase had been used to hang a man called William Appleby in 1940; members of both families insisted that Bentley never called Craig 'Chris' but always 'Kit' (or 'Kid'). But everything happened too quickly, too intimidatingly, in Goddard's court for any of this to come out.

On a cold morning, about 500 people turned up to stand outside Wandsworth Prison at the appointed hour of Bentley's death. They included one of the great characters of the era, Mrs Violet Van der

Elst, a wealthy widow who devoted her time and money to bringing an end to the death penalty. She knocked on the prison gate crying, 'This boy is being murdered,' then led her supporters in funereal hymns. Not everyone in the crowd agreed: some talked volubly about 'cosh boys'. But the general mood was sorrowful: the fact that the killer lived and the far less guilty accomplice died offended Britain's sense of fair play.*

Two months later, something else happened. Beresford Brown, one of the Jamaican migrants who were starting to colonize parts of West London, was attempting a bit of home improvement when he found an unexpectedly hollow bit of wall. His shock when he peeled away a bit of wallpaper to reveal a naked female body was nothing to the shock the police felt when he told them the address.

———•———

In November 1949, a strange fellow who, like Derek Bentley, would have been written off as 'sub-normal', had walked into a police station in Wales and gave them a confused account of the death of his wife, Beryl. His name was Timothy Evans, of 10 Rillington Place, Notting Hill.

Evans was sub-literate, suggestible and no stranger to petty theft. He was also very frightened. Before sentencing him to death for murder a mere six weeks later, Mr Justice Lewis said he had 'lied and lied and lied'. And he had. But with increasing certainty, he began to tell the truth, too late. He started to accuse his downstairs neighbour John Christie, who had, speaking softly but compellingly, given evidence against him. Evans was duly hanged.

The truth was that Beryl – already the mother of a toddler, Geraldine – had become pregnant. The pair were both broke and hopeless, and could not cope with another child. Christie said he knew what to do, and offered to perform an illegal abortion. Later, he sorrowfully told Evans the abortion had gone wrong, that Beryl had died, that Geraldine was safe with friends and

---

*   Craig was released in 1963 and is believed to have led a quiet and blameless life thereafter, as a plumber in Buckinghamshire.

advised him to stay with his Welsh relatives because he was also implicated. In fact, both mother and child had been strangled, as the police found when they searched the property. The jury took forty minutes to find Evans guilty of murdering his daughter. From what they had heard, they could do little else: the defence barrister's belated attempt to accuse the self-assured Christie seemed to them desperate.

What the police failed to find, because they did not look, were the two bodies of women already in shallow graves in the tiny garden. Nor did they notice the human thighbone propping up a fence; it did not have CLUE written on it in large letters. Even more glaringly than with Bentley, the police appeared to have doctored the facts – in this case Evans's uncharacteristically coherent confession. Goddard, this time hearing the appeal, was as brisk as ever.*

Evans's last-known words, to his mother and sister, were 'Christie done it'. But no one thought any more about that until Beresford Brown began messing about in the downstairs kitchen.

———◆———

By this point Christie had already moved away after fraudulently sub-letting his flat. He had checked into a hostel at King's Cross, and then rapidly out again when he saw the headlines. He was now the object of a major manhunt. The hiding place discovered by Brown contained three female bodies. The remains of Mrs Ethel Christie, not seen for several months, were hidden under the floorboards. These four murders took place after Evans was hanged; the two bodies in the garden predated Evans's arrival at Rillington Place. Most of the victims had been raped and strangled. On 31 March, Christie was arrested, wandering by the Thames.

Events kept jostling each other in 1953. Stalin had died earlier that month. The new revelations at Rillington Place coincided with

---

* Evans was charged with both murders but only Geraldine's death was put to the jury, a common procedure at the time. At the appeal, Goddard, astonishingly, was sitting alongside Mr Justice Humphreys, whose son Christmas had been the prosecuting barrister. But perhaps Goddard never asked his opinion.

the death of Queen Mary, the new Queen's grandmother. On April Fool's Day, Murray Hedgcock, the young Aussie journalist – still wide-eyed about being in Britain – went to Windsor to see all the flowers in her honour. He would always associate that visit with the cries of the evening-paper sellers: 'CHRISTIE IN THE DOCK! CHRISTIE IN THE DOCK!'

In late June – Everest climbed; the new Queen crowned; Churchill seriously but secretly ill after his stroke – Christie's trial began. He was accused only of murdering his wife, but confessed to having committed the others as well, except that of little Geraldine. This jury took a full eighty-five minutes to reject his one half-serious line of defence (insanity). While they were out, Christie insouciantly asked if anyone knew the Test score. Then the black cap came out again. After he was taken down to the cells, his defence barristers went down to see him. Derek Curtis-Bennett QC asked how he felt about another man being hanged for a murder he had committed. Christie replied that he felt terrible. He had always been against the death penalty.

———•———

Evans was a poor fool, not quite holy. Christie was a serial strangler – like Stalin, a monster of depravity, a repulsive mutant variation of humanity. He admitted responsibility for all the corpses found at Rillington Place except that of little Geraldine; maybe he had murdered others, he couldn't remember. But now the British Establishment followed their own basest instincts. There could be no admission of fault. Sir Lionel Heald, the attorney general, undertook the prosecution himself and quickly got to the nub: 'It is most important that nothing avoidable should be said in Court which might cast an unjustified reflection on the administration of justice.' In other words, the plan was to keep pretending that Christie really had not murdered Geraldine and that Evans had been rightly hanged.

Heald would have liked to keep MPs silent in the same way, but that was a little harder because Labour MPs and some Conservatives were getting very cross indeed. As the justice campaigner Bob

Woffinden later summed up, the government's position meant that: 1) two stranglers, using the same trademark methods, were by chance living in the same little house; 2) Evans just happened, at his trial, to accuse the only other person in London strangling people that way; and 3) Christie kept lying at Evans's trial just for fun.

The ineffable Maxwell Fyfe half bowed to pressure for a public inquiry into the handling of the Evans case. He asked a QC, John Scott Henderson, to review the facts in private – a 'preposterous' decision, said the *Express*. Henderson understood the mission, a whitewash job, but poured it on so hurriedly and ineptly it only increased the pressure. Maxwell Fyfe, asked to delay Christie's execution to give him the chance to tell the truth, refused, explaining (when it was too late) that it would be 'an inhuman thing to do'. He did ask Scott Henderson to have a second look at the evidence. More whitewash. More anger.

In 1955 there was a further trial that caught the public imagination. This was the case of Ruth Ellis, who fired four shots into her unfaithful lover, David Blakely, outside a Hampstead pub. Her guilt was never in doubt, and she played no role in trying to save her own life. But she was 28 and blonde and attractive and troubled and enigmatic. Mind you, her blonde came from peroxide, she was promiscuous herself and the relationship was mutually abusive. But Blakely, a louche representative of the metropolitan motor-racing set, was obviously a rat. So a Bentley-style campaign to reprieve her began.

By now Maxwell Fyfe was Lord Chancellor, hiding in the House of Lords under an assumed name (the Earl of Kilmuir). His successor at the Home Office was Gwilym Lloyd George, son of the more famous David. It was put to him that she should be reprieved because this was a *crime passionel*. But that was a tricky concept for both English law and English temperament. And though Lloyd George was a Welshman, he was much less passionate than his father. Ellis was duly hanged, the last woman to suffer the supreme punishment in the UK. And though there were still forty men to follow, this has given her a sort of eternal fame, and the martyrdom myth persists. It adds to Donald Zec's point about the Peter

Townsend situation: the B-picture emotions of the British public.

There were far more unjustifiable executions in that era – among them George Kelly of Liverpool (hanged 1950, conviction declared unsafe 2003); Mahmood Hussein Mattan of Cardiff (hanged 1952, pardoned 1998); and Styllou Christofi, the second-last woman to die (hanged 1954, quite likely insane), whose case troubled even her executioner, Albert Pierrepoint. Kelly was a locally well-known criminal, arrested as a usual suspect; the conviction of Mattan, a Somali man with a loyal and loving family, was a racist disgrace; Christofi, who strangled her daughter-in-law in their home on the very same Hampstead street where Ellis would shoot Blakely barely eight months later, was middle-aged, unattractive and spoke little English. One way and another, hardly anyone cared about her.

Despite all this, the crime of the early to mid-1950s often had a certain period charm, shading into Ealing comedy. Most people still had little worth stealing; and the things they were acquiring or coveted were a little hard to lift or unload. Furs, jewellery, large amounts of cash were the major targets and were unlikely to be found in the average British home.

There were heaps of guns around – mostly left over from the war – but they were rarely used. Instead, feuding gangs happily slashed each other with razors, which was fine; occasionally a bank guard got coshed during a robbery, and this seemed not quite cricket. The crime historian Duncan Campbell told me that the inside man, who kept the villains informed, often got the bashing, to confuse the police. All art involves some suffering.

The Messina clan from Malta, who ran Soho at the start of the decade, were broken up not so much by the police but by Duncan Webb, the eccentric, self-promoting, slightly mad crime reporter of *The People*, whose desk was shielded by bulletproof glass and who reputedly lived behind a door with eight locks. The Messinas specialized in vice, a thrilling fifties word that encompassed everything to do with sex.

The Maltese never entirely went away but were partly replaced by two rival gangs, the Montagues and Capulets of their era – led by the Godfatherish Jack Spot (speciality: protection rackets) and the chirpy Bogart-lookalike Billy Hill (big heists and gambling scams).

Hill, in particular, was very PR-minded and got Webb to ghost his autobiography, *Boss of Britain's Underworld*, though he was always careful to add that he had now retired (which he had not). This book was launched in 1955 with a magnificent Soho party, attended by Bert Hardy, the star photographer of *Picture Post*. The caption beneath the team photo of battered, happy, dinner-jacketed gangsters read: 'From left: Soho Ted, Bugsy, Groin Frankie, Billy Hill, Ruby Sparks, Razor Frankie, College Harry, Frany the Spaniel, Cherry Bill, Johnny Ricco, a female journalist and Russian Ted.'

Spot's counterblast, *Jack Spot: The Man of a Thousand Cuts*, came in 1958, after he had got into a couple of street fights and had some whopping cuts inflicted on him. He lived more quietly thereafter.

———•———

Beyond walking distance from Soho, Hill and Spot were just minor celebrities. Other gangs had appeared, far more visible, more bewildering and less discriminate in their violence. And no one at first knew what to make of them, because of their bizarre dress code. They looked like groups of fifth-form Etonians, granted an exeat after a hard day's Latin and hoping to be served an illicit bitter shandy. They were thus, at first sight, rather easy to tease.

Which is why, on a July night in 1953, three other youths on a bench on Clapham Common decided to stretch out their legs and block the path of one of these phony Etonians, 15-year-old Ronald Coleman, who was passing by with his girlfriend. The phrase 'Go round the other way, you flash cunt' was murmured. Coleman went to fetch his mates. Shortly afterwards, one of the bench boys, John Beckley, lay dying after being stabbed six times.

And thus Britain became acquainted with what were first called Edwardians, shortened that autumn to Teddy Boys and then to Teds. It was a youth cult of a type never seen before, and the father (or maybe the deranged uncle) of all those that followed. It derived from a late-forties fashion for the clothes of Edwardian dandies, started by Savile Row tailors and lapped up by the West End bucks, whose fathers would have worn them.*

And then this St James style jumped on the Bakerloo line and got out – ten minutes and a whole world away – at Elephant & Castle and some of the roughest districts of London. Here it became more expressive and individual. The basics were the long Edwardian jacket, tight-fitting trousers and waistcoats. Optional extras included ornate socks, soft-soled brothel-creeper shoes, and a Tony Curtis or DA (duck's arse) haircut. Later, Wild West influences crept in, as they were inclined to do in the fifties, like bootlace ties, as worn by saloon gunslingers. It was a look, not a uniform.

But if you dolled yourself up like that in South London in that very judgmental era, you had to be tough. Press coverage of the Teds was almost invariably censorious because they were implicated in many more serious incidents throughout the decade, including the Notting Hill race riots. Occasionally, someone would study them more carefully.

'The least confident young men do not reach contentment with their ordinary selves and continue anxiously to impress others with a false super-self,' a psychiatrist wrote in *Picture Post*. 'The Edwardian clothes are at once a shield against the world and a shield to hide inner vulnerability.' One social worker thought this cohort of urban children, infants in wartime, were particularly traumatized by absent fathers, bombing and/or evacuation.

After the incident on Clapham Common, Ronald Coleman was accused of murder. But when mobs are involved, this is devilish hard to prove; he was acquitted but, considered too dangerous for borstal, jailed for assault. However, Mickey Davies – at 20, much older than most of the others – was convicted and sentenced

---

* This in turn was a male response to the female New Look, started by Christian Dior in 1947, which emphasized the figure but not the legs – transgressive in its own way, by using more material for long skirts in those austere times.

to hang. The evidence against Davies was very flaky indeed, and after much prevarication, even Maxwell Fyfe reprieved him. Lord Pakenham, who in his later incarnation as the Earl of Longford would become Britain's patron saint of unpopular causes, fought for a pardon that never came, but Davies was released after just seven years, which suggested a governmental guilty conscience. He came out, started cleaning windows and was forgotten. Had he been hanged, he could have been as famous as Evans, Bentley and Ellis.

By the time Davies emerged from prison, the mayhem was finally fading. But in 1958 a guard on a late-night service from Waterloo to Windsor reported that a dozen Teds, in fancy waistcoats, were causing trouble by continually opening and slamming doors with the train travelling at speed. Police were called and took their names. They turned out to be Etonians, returning to school after a night at the theatre.

9

SHOULDERS BACK!

WHETHER OR NOT THE TED GENERATION HAD ALREADY BEEN traumatized, they were nearly all about to face another trauma. Every male teenager in Britain, as they reached their eighteenth birthday, had to register for National Service, a continuation of wartime conscription. Almost every male teenager then had to spend two years doing it.*

There were means of escape: an essential job, which did not cover many 18-year-olds; disability or piety; flat feet or bedwetting; homosexuality, though officers would often brush the notion aside, saying that a bit of discipline could soon cure that. The tiny proportion of young men who then went to university could get a deferment, but there were pluses and minuses to that. Avoidance for most was unthinkable; their fathers and grandfathers had been to war and they would do their duty too, in less dangerous times. Less than 1 in 200 declared themselves conscientious objectors, a brave choice because 'conshies' were never popular, and they still had to fulfil a non-combatant role.

Three-quarters were assigned to the Army, and the best way to nick a place in the less drill-minded RAF or Royal Navy was to plan ahead and join the air or sea cadets at school. It was also possible

---

* The stint was originally eighteen months, but was lengthened during the Korean War.

to apply for officer training, though – and who would have thought it in Britain, of all places? – the public schoolboys were the ones who just kept being chosen.

There was at least some logic in this: as happens in prison, those who spent their childhoods in either rough slums or posh boarding schools adapted best, especially in the terrifying early weeks of being woken long before official reveille by sadistic sergeants and corporals bellowing 'Hands off cocks and on socks!' and similar cheery greetings. Many had never slept away from home and cried the first night and sometimes beyond. Perhaps the greatest initial terror was the fear of being unveiled as the only virgin in the room, not knowing that about three-quarters were thinking the same thing. Many were still virginal two years later. Girls knew conscripts were a poor catch because the pay was pathetic.

The first two months of initial training were designed to be tough. After that, it either became much easier, even cushy, or – as with Brian Hough in Korea – very tough indeed. Between 1945 and 1963, 2.3 million conscripts served in the forces; and, though Britain kept finding wars to fight even after Korea, only 395 (less than one in 5,000) were killed in action. Rather more died in accidents and bar-room brawls. One died from 'a surfeit of cream cake'.

By the late fifties, the Army became far more interested in training specialists for a career instead of acting as the nation's finishing school. The system withered away: by a fluke, the last cohort called up were those born in September 1939, the first month of the war. The survivors are now all over 80. Unlucky? The strange thing is that everyone I have spoken to who went through this long-obsolete rite of passage regards their time in the forces with an affection that is something more than the rosy glow of youth. Some of them are the least bellicose men one could meet.

Neil Barnes from Portsmouth spent his time moving model aircraft round a board in an RAF control room, the pre-computer way of keeping tabs on what was up there. It was far more interesting than working in an insurance office. 'It got me out of a job I disliked,' he said. 'I met people I would never otherwise have met who became lifelong friends. And the government were very keen on us being educated. I spent much of my time going on courses. I would never have gone to university otherwise.'

Ian Mayes from Northampton, also in the RAF, was posted to Germany. 'It was wonderful. I saw it as a huge opportunity to meet Germans. When other people were messing about in the NAAFI at the weekend I would take a train to Cologne or Düsseldorf and forced myself to learn German.'

David McKie was commissioned in the Royal Army Service Corps and sent to the disputed city of Trieste, where there had been fighting but was now calm. 'We spent a lot of time drinking coffee and lying on the beach. Sometimes we'd drive to Venice for dinner. All paid for by the Queen. I thought there was a lot to be said for National Service. Less so when we were sent to Salisbury Plain.'

Leslie Fielding from London also became an officer, in the Royal Artillery, despite being from a state school. He never left Britain, never fired a shot in anger, went to Cambridge and then joined the Foreign Office. Just over a decade later, he was sent to Cambodia as chargé d'affaires just after a government-directed mob had burned down the embassy: 'The Army stretched me. When I was put into Phnom Penh, almost alone, the embassy ruined and chaos all around, I had total confidence.'

Andreas Whittam Smith, who grew up in Birkenhead, mucked up officer-selection by offending the brigadier in charge. (He did better in later life.) The Army sent him to Berlin and he spent his time guarding the only prisoner in Spandau jail, whom he never glimpsed. 'I am proud to say that in my period on guard Rudolf Hess did not escape. And I'm glad I did it. The test was "Can you get on with all types?" And I can.'

And these reflections contrast with those who did not go. Adam Fergusson, later an MEP, was ruled out by asthma. 'I couldn't have done it but I felt I missed an important experience,' he said. The future journalist Stephen Fay won a scholarship to university in Canada, and by the time he was back conscription had been abolished. 'At the time I was very pleased to avoid it,' he told me. 'But about ten years later I began to feel I had missed out.'

Some of those called up were already famous, and not all of

them complied. The daredevil racing driver Mike Hawthorn kept skittering round Europe to avoid being served with his call-up papers, which brought much bad publicity. The cricketer Colin Cowdrey served twenty-six days in the RAF in 1955 before being discharged for flat feet, which caused some adverse comment: he scored a thousand runs that summer. Most of the public soon forgot; some of his cricketing contemporaries did not. None of those I interviewed who did serve felt impelled to stay on in the forces, though Fielding thought about it. 'We used to count the days,' said Whittam Smith. 'Hark, the herald angels shout! Fifty-four days and we'll be out.'

There were also incidents that pointed up the extent to which the forces perpetuated the class system by compulsion. Later in 1955, other RAF men were ordered to attend an all-night party to serve officers and their wives, wearing 'silver wigs, lace cravats, green velvet frock coats, knickerbockers, white silk stockings, and buckled shoes'. They were not happy. The actor Johnny Briggs (Mike Baldwin in *Coronation Street*) recalled driving his CO to a gymkhana in Germany. 'There were three entrances. The first said "Officers and Ladies", the next "NCOs and Wives" and the third "Other Ranks and Women".'

Did Britain shower gratitude on the minority who endured the sharp end? Brian Hough was still in Korea when the ceasefire came. He went out into no man's land to help recover the bodies – 'Some had been there eighteen months. It was a horrible job.'

Huffy's ship docked at Southampton in January 1954. 'We got a packet of cheese sandwiches, a ticket back to Manchester and half a crown. When we got to Euston someone said "Are you coming for a pint?" So we had two and then I had sixpence left. I got to Manchester. We'd docked early so no one was expecting us but someone gave me a lift home from the station. The family had no idea who was at the door. The next Monday we all went to the barracks at Ashton-under-Lyne. There was this poor lieutenant there and he had no idea who we were. We hadn't been paid but he raced around and found us two weeks' money. That was the hero's welcome.'

One old soldier did become a kind of hero. The man with the

largest, loudest, most frightening voice in the Army, Sergeant-Major
Ronald Brittain retired in 1954 after thirty-seven years, mostly
spent terrifying virgin soldiers on the parade ground. And then he
made himself into a novelty act – cameo roles in war films, voiceovers
for adverts, a member of the Society of Toastmasters – as though
National Service, as many conscripts suspected, had been some
kind of cosmic joke all along.

———·———

Another incident of Brian Hough's eventful military service was
being called in to see an officer while on the voyage out, and asked
his opinion of Korea. Shrewdly, he asked the reason for the question.
   'Because you were a member of the Labour Party Young
Socialists.'
   'Hang on,' said Hough. 'It was the Labour Party who took us
into Korea. If you doubt my loyalty . . .'
   'None of that, Hough,' the officer replied. And that was the end
of the matter.
   Now that the Communists were the enemy, Conservative Britain
had trouble accepting Labour patriotism. 'Is your father a Labour
MP? Is your father a Bevanite?' an officer selection board asked one
conscript, Marine J. K. Baird. The answer to both was 'Yes'. The
boy was turned down. Nothing to do with politics, a junior minister
insisted when questioned in the Commons (not by the father). Perish
the thought.
   The difference between the legitimate and illegitimate Left was
neatly summed up when Stalin died in 1953. 'His purpose was
evil and his methods unspeakable,' wrote the *Mirror* columnist
Cassandra. 'Never have I met anyone so kindly and considerate,'
said the British Communist leader Harry Pollitt. Serving in Korea
was not a recipe for inspiring British servicemen with Communist
zeal. Only one Briton captured by the Chinese, Marine Andrew
Condron, opted to stay there after the Armistice, and he wisely
opted to come back before the Cultural Revolution.
   It was later alleged that in at least one Midlands industrial town,
the town clerk was instructed, even in the mid-1960s, to keep all

the supposedly secret ballots cast for Communists in local elections. This made it possible to check the numbers against the counterfoils and then the electoral roll; the names were then forwarded to Special Branch.* Elsewhere, anonymous men in macs would write down the names of those who signed the Communists' nomination papers.†

They were of course looking in the wrong place. The traitors were not in the industrial towns or left-wing meetings. They were hiding in plain sight, in the Foreign Office and security services. Guy Burgess (Eton and Cambridge) and Donald Maclean (Gresham's School and Cambridge) had already vanished in 1951, to reappear in Moscow five years later; Kim Philby (Westminster School and Cambridge) was suspected but still at large. In the end they were all punished severely, by a life sentence without parole, living in the Soviet Union.

In the meantime, there was huge embarrassment in London and the Americans were livid. 'Burgess and Maclean had the effect of shattering the entire culture of the FO,' wrote one senior official, John Henniker. 'It appeared that men who had been at the centre of events and with apparently impeccable backgrounds and believed to be gentlemen were totally unreliable. It was a complete shock to the [personnel] department and the FO itself.' Henniker was promptly appointed head of personnel and, in his words, 'demystified the processes of promotion'.

Meanwhile, the Reds were replacing Jerry as the villains in the British imagination. Ian Fleming's first James Bond novel, *Casino Royale*, made its debut in 1953 with the Russians as the enemy, rather than a cat-stroking megalomaniac. Bond became and remains the world's most famous secret agent, though in real life fame is not the object of the exercise. However, one former head of MI6 told Peter Hennessy that Bond was a great aid to recruiting informants overseas. Presumably they thought the lifestyle was included.

Many National Service boys had their view of the enemy formed

---

* This is still possible, though illegal.
† This is legal, though sinister.

more by another fictional character, James Bigglesworth. The First World War pilot Captain W. E. Johns spent the fifties producing twenty-nine of his (gulp) ninety-eight Biggles books. And for Biggles there were definitely new battles to fight: his wartime antagonist Erich von Stalhein was now working for the Russians, the swine.* James Bigglesworth is a less sexy name than James Bond, and indeed Biggles never had much of a sex life. This may help explain why Bond lives on and on in the cinema and the Biggles books are period pieces.

In real life, Anglo-Russian relations in the early fifties were conducted by means of an endless quadrille between Eisenhower, Churchill, Stalin and then his heirs, and whoever happened to be French prime minister that week.† This largely involved Churchill interposing himself between the two remaining great powers in the hope of achieving his last great ambition of making peace.

The most promising development came in April 1956, a year after Eden replaced Churchill. The two Russian leaders, Nikita Khrushchev and Marshal Nikolai Bulganin,‡ arrived in Britain for a ten-day visit on the Soviet cruiser *Ordzhonikidze*. They had a celebrity welcome and a very full programme (If it's Monday, this must be Birmingham). Professor Sergey Radchenko has retrospectively billed it as 'Khrushchev's charm offensive', though both sides sometimes set aside the charm and became offensive.

There was much talk but little agreement. The British banged on about freedoms. The Soviet response was to mention Britain's colonies. The British then threw in Russian control of the Eastern Bloc. 'No analogy,' said Khrushchev. 'Relations with these countries . . . are based on equality and respect of national sovereignty.' Dinner with the Labour Party was really bad-tempered and Khrushchev said he preferred the Conservatives, which might not have been wholly unpleasing to Labour.

---

* Though in the 1958 book *Biggles Buries a Hatchet*, Biggles discovers that Stalhein has been imprisoned by his new masters and smuggles him to London and safety.
† The job changed hands seventeen times in the 1950s.
‡ Cheerily billed by the press as B&K, though it soon became clear K&B was the correct pecking order.

There was also the unfortunate business with Commander Buster Crabb, the naval diver evidently sent by MI6, at the Navy's behest, to investigate certain underwater features of the *Ordzhonikidze*. This was a fairly obvious breach of hospitality. And no one bothered to mention the escapade to Eden, which was a breach of common sense. Crabb was never seen again: the mystery persists. And a few months later, such a goodwill visit would be impossible anyway. Both countries were by then in disgrace.

10

SUMMONED BY BUZZERS

AFTER LEAVING UNIVERSITY, THE FUTURE LABOUR CABINET minister Roy Hattersley went to work for Daniel Doncaster & Sons of Sheffield, Makers of High Quality Steel, Pressings, Stampings and Forgings, founded 1778. It was meant to be high-quality too: the output included propeller blades for aircraft and submarines. Hattersley was appointed assistant to Richard Doncaster – known as Mr Richard in the traditional style of old family firms; there could only be one Mr Doncaster at a time.

'It was a very hierarchical organization,' Hattersley recalled. 'There was a staff canteen, for the managers, and a works canteen. But there was a strict hierarchy within the staff canteen. There was a dais with a top table where the directors and senior management sat, a step up from everyone else.' It was also rather hidebound. 'I had to put "And oblige" at the end of every letter. I asked if we had to do it even if there was no obliging involved. Mr Richard said the company had been putting "And oblige" at the end of letters for more than 150 years and that we weren't going to stop now.'

Nor was it, in Hattersley's memory, scrupulously efficient. One of his jobs involved doing a graph showing how long each stage of a complicated process would take. He spent days doing this and submitted his work to a senior manager.

'No,' he was told. 'That's wrong.'

'I'm sure I've done it right.'

'It's not the answer I *wanted*,' the manager replied, picking up a pen to redraw it. 'I want the answer to prove *this*.'

Hattersley found a more agreeable job working for the health service soon enough, before edging into politics. But his time at the company left him with a lasting sense of the realities of mid-fifties Britain. 'As a country, we were lost. That phrase "lost an empire and not found a role" was very true. We had a huge amount of pride about what we had achieved in the war but we were also very conscious that the economy was struggling. This combination of physical, economic and political impotence and moral superiority made us very confused.'

The scale of industry in Britain was still awesome. The rail marshalling yard at Toton in Nottinghamshire, the biggest in Europe, handled a million loaded sixteen-ton coal wagons a year. In Yorkshire, the Dearne Valley alone had sixteen coal mines within a few miles of each other. 'I could practically spit at five of them,' said Inky Thomson, who began work as an apprentice engineer at Goldthorpe Colliery when he left school in 1955. The National Coal Board employed nearly 700,000 people.

The banks of the Tyne and the Clyde were still lined with bustling shipyards. In Barrow, Vickers's naval dockyard dominated the compact town. Four times a day a cycle-borne army, many thousands strong, poured in and out, governed by a buzzer heard all over Barrow, at 7.30 a.m., then again for lunch at 12, the end of lunch at 1, then home again for working-class teatime (i.e. middle-class dinner). It was not advisable to get in the cyclists' way. Barrow has always been a place where peace is bad for business, and the Cold War kept it throbbing.

Towns based on non-bellicose industries were already starting to give off distress signals. In the Pennine weaving town of Barnoldswick (pronounced *Bar-lick*), the fourteen big mills of 1914 had dwindled to four by 1950. The disruptions of war had reinforced the logic of processing cotton where it was grown, especially where labour was cheap, as in Asia. 'The industry had to be seen as going downhill,' according to the town's historian Stanley Graham. 'If you had a shed with a thousand looms, the cost of the machinery all written off, you could still make a profit. But there was no point in modernizing.'

Weaving was women's work, which required no strength but, on the old machines, great skill. The top workers would be on ten looms at once and they had to pay constant attention to avoid running out of weft. And the sheds were horrendously noisy. Everyone who worked there ended up at least slightly deaf. 'I've seen people who visited a weaving shed come out and be physically sick because of the noise,' said Graham. 'You couldn't hear someone next to you unless they stood next to your ear and shouted into it. You could always spot anyone who worked in a weaving shed because they had exaggerated lip movements from doing mee-maw [a form of lip reading]. If anyone from outside needed to pass on a message you'd tell the person nearest the door and it'd be all round the shed in minutes.'

Since the women might be working up to fourteen hours a day, it made the social structure very different from somewhere like Barrow. I asked Graham if it meant a more equal society. 'Well, it might. Some men did help out. Others didn't. And the one thing men wouldn't do is hang out the washing. They'd be called a Mary Ann.'

Some industries were still expanding. Take ICI – which, as everyone knew, stood for Imperial Chemical Industries. Nearly all its products – plastics, synthetic fibres, pharmaceuticals, fertilizer, paint – were booming in the fifties. 'The priority for ICI, as for its counterparts in Germany and the US, was to ensure that manufacturing capacity kept pace with demand,' wrote the economic historian Geoffrey Owen.

And whole cities were still given over to the specialities that built them. 'The place stank. But if you grew up with it, it was Chanel,' recalled the Hull-born theatre director Barrie Rutter. 'When the sluice gate opened at the fishmeal plant it just sat over the city. Acrid. All the lasses wore white wellies and white turbans. When they came out it was a mass of white walking home. But they had yellow hands from dying the smoked haddock until rubber gloves came in.'

The Hessle Road, heading landwards, was completely given over to fish. 'Not just fishermen but the bobbers who landed the fish, the women making nets, thousands of them,' said Ken Knox. This was a place whose traditional life made the coal industry look soft. Knox made his first trip on a trawler as a galley boy on the *St Keverne* in 1951.

'Fifteen,' he said. 'You'd just left your school desk. Next you were on a ship for three weeks with twenty hardcore fishermen. And you'd be suffering from seasickness, homesickness and every other sickness. On my first trip I sat peeling potatoes in what I called my misery corner. That's when you make your decision.' Knox chose to stick at it.

'Plenty of fish in the sea,' mums used to tell teenagers if they had just been dumped by a boy or girlfriend. Plenty of coal in the seams. Plenty of cotton to be spun. Plenty of ships to be built . . .

———•———

For many years the dominant explanation of British decline has rested on what one might call the Sir Hughe Knatchbull-Hugessen theory of history. Knatchbull-Hugessen was Britain's wartime ambassador to neutral Turkey, best remembered not for his outlandish name but for failing to notice that his valet was a Nazi spy. In 1939, one story goes, a British businessman was sent out by Whitehall to buy up strategic Turkish products and deny them to the Germans. The ambassador refused to help: 'Don't speak to me of commerce and finance, sir. It goes in one ear and out the other.'

Later in this book, this theme will become more dominant: the banks' reluctance to finance entrepreneurs; the clubbiness of the City; the intellectual contempt for business, not just from old-school diplomats but from an elite that accorded more honour to William Morris the Arts and Crafts pioneer than William Morris the motor magnate; and so on.

In the 1950s, rising living standards were a more significant fact of life than industrial decline. But there were already some signs. The working lives of Yorkshire miners, Hull fishwives, Lancashire cotton weavers and the buzzer-driven men of Barrow were tough and often repetitive (though alleviated in some industries by frequent strikes). But the lifestyle of the unloved men who ran the businesses seemed not just hierarchical and self-serving, as Roy Hattersley intuited from his stint at Doncaster's, but also less than strenuous. A clue to this might be gauged from the railway timetables.

In 1958, E. W. D. Tennant of Ugley, near Bishop's Stortford, complained to *The Times* that the carriages in the morning rush hour were being 'invaded by ladies, with the result that business-men holding season tickets are crowded out and forced to stand in the corridors'.

'Which is the more important,' he asked, 'that the regular workers should be able to read their newspapers and keep abreast of world affairs and arrive fresh for their business or that the seats should be filled by women travelling to London to have their hair permed and to shop?' One can ignore the tone as the routine husbandly banter of the era. What is significant here is the time. The complaint was specifically about trains leaving 'between 8.30 and 9.30'. Commuting from Bishop's Stortford, that suggests some men were getting down to business in London just before 11. They did not necessarily stay late either.

The generic morning train seems to have been the 8.15. THE 8.15 IS BACK AGAIN, said an *Express* headline when a seventeen-day rail strike ended in 1955. This might have been a bit early for the man actually in charge of the trains. General Sir Brian Robertson, the head of the British Transport Commission, had rushed from his home in Stroud, Gloucestershire, to London to avert a previous rail strike just before Christmas 1953. He took the 8.42, which, with luck, would have got him in the office for a late-morning coffee, or an early lunch.

---·---

Robertson did avert that strike under government instruction, in the then customary give-'em-the-money manner. Rab Butler, the Chancellor, who had been excluded from negotiations to stop him playing Scrooge, got a late-night call from Churchill to tell him it was settled. 'On what terms?' Butler asked, warily. 'Theirs, old cock!'

To be fair, a Christmas train strike was no small inconvenience before mass motoring, and there was a sense that the grievances in this case had some merit. But throughout the decade industrial relations grew more tetchy, the workers' demands more insistent and the bourgeoisie less sympathetic. Middle England's most influential newspapers, the *Express* (which far outsold the *Mail* in that era) and the *Telegraph*, gleefully fed their outrage.

The forties union leaders – 'salt-of-the-earth types with silver hair and watch chains' – played the game. But the hierarchy was changing, typified by the giant Transport and General Workers' Union (T&G): its long-time leader Arthur Deakin and his anointed heir Jock Tiffin died within months of each other in 1955, paving the way for the younger and less biddable Frank Cousins. That year, unemployment hit the floor: in July only 185,000 people in Great Britain were out of work, less than 1 per cent of the working population.*

And the leaders themselves were finding it harder to control their members. *Differential* was declared the 1955 Word of the Year by the *Express*, as workers responded to any pay rise from a group behind them in the pecking order by insisting that the differential be restored. *Demarcation* might have been another contender. There was a six-month dispute at the Cammell Laird shipyard in Birkenhead ('the screwy strike') between the wood-workers and the shipwrights, about who should 'drill the holes for the screws joining plastic material to metal in the insulated holds of fruit ships'.

The screwy strike dragged on from 1955 into 1956. The shipwrights won in the end, but maybe no one did. Or no one in Britain. Eleven years after its surrender, Japan overtook Britain to become the world's leading shipbuilders. And it was all downhill from there. However, Geoffrey Owen, a former editor of the *Financial Times*, concluded that labour relations were not the major cause in the decline of any British industry – including shipbuilding,

---

* Great Britain does not include the very different case of Ulster, where it was above 5 per cent.

one of the first where the sinking process became obvious. Basically, the management misunderstood the changing market.

The shop floor was often far from united. A third of the working class habitually voted Tory, out of deference or individuality. Some of these disapproved of strikes but went along quietly. Those who did stand out against strikes were often forcibly quietened by being 'sent to Coventry'.* Sometimes this could have dreadful results: a train driver in Essex who worked during the 1955 strike committed suicide; a blind radio and TV engineer in Hertfordshire dependent on his colleagues found the goodwill dwindling away – even the woman who normally walked him home refused; a crane driver in Derbyshire who declined to join a one-day strike *because his own union told him not to*, had no conversations at work for more than a year. Sometimes it could be quite comical. Maintenance engineers who worked through a strike at several sites owned by the food company J. Lyons were able to ride out their ostracism. 'We can talk among ourselves,' explained one worker. 'There are sixty-six of us.'

Some found themselves fined by their unions. One cutter at a Burtons tailoring factory in Lancashire was ordered to cough up for producing forty-eight suits in a week rather than the maximum forty-six. On the other hand, in an era when the main protection against preposterous dismissal was a shortage of replacements, employers were quite capable of petty vindictiveness of their own.

After his daughter and baby grandson were killed in a tube crash, Bill Grant took two days off work: one after the disaster, the other for the double funeral. So he was docked two days' pay by his employers, British Railways. These matters 'are dealt with quite impersonally', said a spokesman. Four men employed by the Co-op in Oldham were told their wives could not own private businesses 'in competition with the society'. Three of the women were hairdressers, the other had taken over an off-licence.

The merest whiff of alcohol could have repercussions. A nurse in

---

* A phase of unknown origin dating back to at least the early eighteenth century.

Suffolk was dismissed because she nipped into a pub after her shift to buy cigarettes. It seems to have been the uniform and the pub that were the issue, not the smoking. 'It was a breach of a well-known unwritten rule,' said an official. And in Cardiff a tax clerk was sacked by the Inland Revenue when Whitehall noticed his address: the Butchers Arms, Llandaff. Asked if he worked there, he said he occasionally helped his mum behind the bar, unpaid. Out. Bad publicity made the Revenue relent but he had already found something better; it was not hard in the fifties. Interestingly, none of these employers were capitalists.

———•———

It was unfortunate for the reputation of British businessmen that the most prominent of them was quite possibly the worst. His name was Sir Bernard Docker, chairman and managing director of the Birmingham Small Arms Company (BSA) – though it was his wife who was more famous.

He was the only child of Dudley Docker, a hard-driving old-school Black Country businessman, and effectively inherited the old man's BSA job and his directorship of the Midland Bank. The old man did not live to meet his son's twice-widowed second wife, Norah.

Lady Docker was synonymous with the fifties while having nothing in common with the era. She was a car salesman's daughter who became a nightclub hostess with a gift for marrying money, and a publicity maniac famous for being famous, cutting a figure about halfway between mid-life Princess Margaret and Dame Edna Everage. In a later age she would have danced the TV tango before zipping off to eat insects in the jungle. Instead, she pranced around dressed to the nines in a succession of custom-made Daimlers – the most famous being gold-plated – played marbles with miners, consorted with gangsters and sometimes got pissed, which on one occasion ended in her being banned from Monte Carlo, thus ending her own reign as the queen of Eurotrash. And much else besides, usually watched benignly by her husband, and even more lovingly by the press.

Meanwhile, BSA was starting to creak. The company was founded in 1861, and originally did what its name implied – indeed, early in the Hitler war no one else in Britain could supply rifles. But it had long since diversified, first into bicycles, then into motorbikes and cars – buying the infant Daimler company in 1910, a deal masterminded by Dudley Docker. However, in the long decline of British manufacturing, motorbikes were the first to topple over. The Japanese, as with shipbuilding, were starting to operate with awesome scale and efficiency; and the British failed to take the nifty Italian Vespas and Lambrettas seriously enough. On top of that, in Geoffrey Owen's words, 'BSA had been badly run for years'.

The Midland kicked Docker junior off the board in 1953; it took another three years for his fellow BSA directors to pluck up the courage and enough votes to follow suit. What emerged was horrendous. In his last full year he received £33,000 in pay and pension contributions, which might have been fair enough.* Much more startling were his £11,000 expenses. These did not include the five special Daimlers the firm paid for. Nor the £2,000 it cost to fly two of the cars to Monaco. Nor the £8,000, which his colleagues rejected, for Lady Docker's outfits ('sapphire mink bolero £2,500'). Although they were never destitute, the Dockers had to sell the yacht and endure a long, sad twilight.

The same went for BSA, which sold off both Daimler and the cycle business but still expired in 1973, before either of the Dockers. The collapse of the motorcycle industry can hardly be pinned wholly on Sir Bernard. The trouble with all British motorbikes in the late fifties, one expert reflected later, was that they were either boring or the engines were unreliable and vibrated unpleasantly, and either way they leaked oil. The Japanese machines were just better. The designers knew this; the bosses failed to listen.

---

* For rough 2020s values, multiply figures by about twenty. Even profligate bosses were restrained in salary terms by post-1980 standards, and much more stringently taxed.

In 1955, before Sir Bernard's fall, the *Daily Express* thought it would be a good wheeze to set up a lunch between Docker and docker, i.e. between never-say-no Norah and the leader of the increasingly militant dockworkers' union, Arthur Horner. It was 1955, the year unemployment went close to zero. 'Why are you always striking and upsetting business?' Lady Docker demanded. 'We're in business too,' Horner replied. 'Our business is selling labour. Like any other business, we want to get the best price for it. So we get a good price for it when other people need it most.'

The *Express* was always stern editorially about union excesses. One day Donald Zec was within earshot when the proprietor Lord Beaverbrook arrived at his office to be confronted by a picket line of print workers.

'What do they want?' he asked a subordinate.

'More money.'

'Give it to 'em,' replied Beaverbrook.

At the more realistic end of commerce, Michael Griffith from Herefordshire came out of the Army after his appearance at the King's funeral. Just before getting married in 1953, he and his bride, Maisie, found a chemist's shop for sale in the village of Ewyas Harold: a run-down, old-fashioned place: loads of wooden drawers marked with the names of drugs. He was not actually a pharmacist himself, not liking exams, but his father was – so he was able to take the prescriptions up to Dad's shop in Hereford and get them done overnight for a still largely carless clientele in the countryside.

Michael was obliging and energetic, and rebuilt the trade in the village: 'When people asked for something I hadn't got, I'd say, "I'll get that." And we expanded into pet food and veterinary stuff.' In 1956 he moved into bigger premises and needed £2,000, which he scraped together with loans from the bank and his parents. For the Griffiths, like many other young couples, the fifties were a time of forward strides. And the story of that shop offers a series of snapshots of the changes in Britain over the next forty years.

11

YEARS OF LIVING DANGEROUSLY

RETROSPECTIVELY, PEOPLE WERE INCLINED TO SAY THAT LADY Docker had brightened a grey country in a grey decade, or some such. No one in the fifties could match Lady Docker for brass neck, tin ear and gold accessories, but mere eccentricity was never rationed.

But the males who stood out were mostly daredevils. Some were old enough to know better. There was still Lord Noel-Buxton, who followed his earlier feat of not-quite-walking across the Thames by making it across the Humber ('unexpectedly easy') and then the Severn, which is seriously dangerous – low tide is followed by the onrushing Severn Bore. Wearing a golfing jacket and shorts, he clambered out as the Bore swirled around his ankles, and announced his retirement.

And then there was the Mad Major. He was not rich; indeed he was out of work, which was his excuse for what he did beyond seeking attention and a thrill. His name was Christopher Draper, who had flown in both wars without ever finding much purpose in peace. In 1931 he had caused a sensation by flying under Tower and Westminster bridges and was warned not to do it again. He didn't. Twenty-two years later, aged 61, he skipped Tower Bridge and flew under fifteen others instead, all the way to Kew. No one seemed very perturbed this time. He got a job, a conditional discharge and a short suspension of his pilot's licence. Then he kept flying until he was 72, and lived to be 86.

Draper was a precursor of a recognizable fifties type: the fighter-pilot *manqué* without a war big enough to crave his attention. Not all were British: at an air show in Liverpool in 1956, more than 100,000 watched as the French birdman Léo Valentin jumped from 9,000 feet wearing balsa-wood wings; the aim was to glide and then open the parachute to land. But he did not glide; one wing had apparently clipped the plane. And the parachute never opened. He landed in a cornfield and the French buried him with military honours.

But the extreme obsession with the war was distinctly British, as it remains. It was already being fed by the films. And the young men for whom the war ended too damn quickly had to satisfy their lust for danger elsewhere. They were epitomized by the test pilots, racing drivers, jockeys and, ye gods, the crazed riders of the Manx TT course. In racing, the steeplechase jockeys were always the most at risk but their counterparts on the flat did not even wear head protectors until 1956. That did not save one star jockey, Emmanuel ('Manny') Mercer, three years later, when he was thrown before the start and kicked in the head at Ascot. The news was announced to the crowd with a sentence that sums up the worst of the 1950s: 'The stewards regret to announce that the last race has been abandoned as E. Mercer has been killed.' Note the terseness, the cold formality of the initial, and the fact that the stewards were expressing regret for the loss of the race, not the rider.

In some fields, it is miraculous that anyone ever got through to nightfall. In 1953 Jaguar asked their chief test driver Norman Dewis to get back the 'flying mile' record for production models which had just been lost to a Spanish sports car. He was despatched to a closed stretch of Belgian motorway (Britain had no motorways) and shut in an airless space created out of an XK120 with no seat, never mind a seat belt – no nothing – and went like hell. He broke the record with 174 mph. Dewis did stuff like that all the time. Most amazingly, he lived to be 98.

The face of the decade was the beautiful one given to the

Hollywood actor James Dean. He was in his silver Porsche Spyder
on his way to drive in a road race when he collided with a clunky
Ford Tudor turning left across his path, and died on a California
highway, aged 24, which only enhanced his celebrity.* He still
stares at us hauntingly from myriad images. He was 'half in love
with death, obsessed with men who risked it in war, in the bull ring,
on the motor racing circuit', wrote Peter Lewis.

The same might go for the whole decade. But in Britain, a
country suffering from severe emotional constipation, families often
never spoke of those they lost, including – or perhaps especially –
their children.

———•———

In countries facing existential crises – war, civil strife, pandemic,
starvation – the less immediate problems of life attract little
attention. Embattled Third World states do not devote many
resources to environmental improvements or curbing tobacco use
or health and safety. Britain's own embattlement dwindled only
slowly, and the disasters kept coming.

The various carnages of 1952[†] were followed swiftly by the
North Sea storm and tidal surge that drowned more than 300
people on the east coast of England (and nearly 2,000 in the
Netherlands) plus thousands of other mammals and millions of
earthworms. That same night, the Stranraer–Larne ferry sank and
133 died. Deaths came on the railways: there were three collisions
on the British rail network in forty hours just before Christmas
1955. 'These things go in cycles,' said the transport minister, Harold
Watkinson, with staggering nonchalance, after the third. 'I was half
expecting another one.'

They came on the increasingly crowded roads: 5,000 died in
1950; almost 7,000 in 1960. They came in the home: the coal gas

---

* Logically, the Ford driver, a student called Donald Turnupseed, was mainly to
blame, since he crossed Dean's path. But Dean's speed is unknown – estimates vary
from 55 to 85 mph – and the inquest made no judgment. His innocence would
hardly fit the legend. Turnupseed died in 1995.
† See pp. 27–9, 32–4.

then used for domestic consumption contained carbon monoxide and many died – often by accident, sometimes through suicide, sometimes as a by-product of criminal intent. Five people in Southport and four children under seven in Dagenham were said to have died after the pipes had been fixed to bypass the meter and thus avoid payment.* Chip pans burned down houses; nighties caught light, often when girls looked in mirrors above open fires just before bedtime; and people smoked in bed, the post-coital fag being the most satisfying and the one most likely to provoke somnolence and thus incineration.

Indeed, people smoked everywhere, including the non-smoking portions of trains. Until the mid-sixties, it was normal for carriages to be divided into compartments seating six or eight (sometimes with no corridor). The non-smoking compartments were clearly marked, but the etiquette was that you could smoke in them if no one objected. It was polite to ask, 'Anyone mind if I smoke?'; silence was deemed to convey consent. The answer 'Yes, I do mind' was considered most unsporting.

Danger even lurked in the tiles that all the zealous new DIY-ers craved for their fireplaces and bathrooms. A doctor at Derbyshire Royal Infirmary discovered by chance that orange tiles were radioactive – way beyond the limits allowed in atomic labs. Green tiles were also affected, but not as badly. The problem was due to the pre-war use of uranium in the colouring. It was all of a piece with the poison in the potting shed.

———◆———

However, even chain-smoking in a flammable nightie while leaning against an orange-tiled fireplace was nothing like as terrifying as one means of transport. Yes, it was admitted, flying had had its teething problems. But now Britain's new jet airliner, the de Havilland Comet, was the nation's pride, as the patriotic press kept saying, even if the pathetic Americans shied away from buying

---

* North Sea gas, which was much safer, came on stream in 1966, and covered the whole of Great Britain by 1977 and Northern Ireland by 1987.

them. True, there had been a couple of hiccups: in the plane's first year, two crashed on take-off, the British plane in Rome and a Canadian one. Everyone survived the first; none the second. Pilot error, it was suggested before a wing defect was identified.

Then, in May 1953, a year almost to the day since the plane's triumphant maiden commercial flight, a BOAC Comet fell out of the sky near Calcutta. All forty-three aboard dead. 'Freak weather', insisted the *Telegraph*. *The Times* gravely agreed. The *Express* insisted that whatever went wrong, it was not the plane's fault. BOAC's chairman, Sir Miles Thomas, refused to ground the Comets. 'It is certain that his decision was not based on expediency,' said the paper's leader column. 'It was based on knowledge and confidence. Now let that confidence be backed by the nation. For the Comet must not fail. It bears on its wings Britain's hope of world supremacy in the air-faring age.' The column was headed FLY ON, FLY ON TO GLORY.

Eight months later, in January 1954, another BOAC version crashed into the sea near Elba. Thirty-five dead.* There was no obvious reason, although there was a quiet fear that there was a structural issue and the planes were grounded. 'Unfounded – the Comet is all right,' declared the *Express* air correspondent, after dozens of modifications were made, none of them relevant. The public believed this; every seat was filled on the first flight after the hiatus. Three months later a South African Airways Comet went down near Naples. Twenty-one dead, and with them all the hopes of Britain's aviation industry. As *The Guardian* later put it: 'The nation, already mourning the dead of the accidents, went into mourning for itself.'

It was at this point that Arnold Hall, director of the Royal Aircraft Establishment at Farnborough, took charge. He authorized an experiment whereby an entire Comet fuselage was placed in a giant water tank; the fuselage was itself filled with water and sealed; and then the interior pressure was increased and decreased at three-

---

* Some of the bodies were spotted by a passing BEA pilot called Stanley Key, whose name will appear again later.

minute intervals to simulate, at high speed, a normal aircraft's way of life.

Then suddenly it happened – after the equivalent of a mere year in the air: the fuselage split. Hall, then still short of 40, went on to become a revered figure in aeronautics, industry and education. The surviving Comets never carried another passenger; nor did the planned successors, the Comets 2 and 3. The Comet 4 appeared in 1958, without the square windows deemed to have exacerbated the stress in the early models. It led a relatively blameless and obscure life. By then the US had seized the advantage: the Comet 4's more capacious contemporary, the Boeing 707, had nearly a thousand sales; the Comet less than a hundred.

At the official inquiry into the original disasters, Hall was rock-solid and impressive. But there was one witness who reduced everyone to silence. He was 70-year-old Lord Brabazon of Tara, the father-figure of British aviation and the chairman of the board that had allowed the Comet to fly again after the second crash. He told the tribunal chairman, Lord Cohen, that if you grounded every aircraft that had an unexplained crash there would be scarcely a plane in the sky. He went on: 'You and I know the cause of this accident. It is due to the adventurous pioneering spirit of our race . . . We all went into it with our eyes wide open . . . I cannot believe that this court, or our country, will censure us because we ventured . . . You, my Lord, would not have the aeronautical people in this country . . . in craven fear lest they be censured in such a court as this for trying to lead the world.'

Had Brab not had so many other skills, he might have made a fine columnist in the *Express* or the *Mail*. But most of the people who died did not seek to lead the world. They were not Peter Twiss or John 'Cat's Eyes' Cunningham.* They did not want to jump out of planes wearing balsa-wood wings or fly under the Thames bridges. They wanted to land safely. And far too many did not.

---

* In 1956, Twiss flew at 1,132 mph over Hampshire, infuriating a nurseryman who claimed his giant greenhouse had been smashed by the sonic boom. Cunningham was de Havilland's chief test pilot, innocently flying the Comet 1 when it was at its least dangerous. Twiss lived to be 90, Cunningham 84.

———·———

Throughout the 1950s, planes fell out of the sky with staggering regularity. Accident records list 480 serious incidents to British-registered aircraft in the 1950s, with 1,621 fatalities – not counting combat planes. This compares to 351 and 2,131 for the next six decades *combined*.

Limiting the figures to 'scheduled revenue flights' only, there were thirty-five such cases in the 1950s with 392 fatalities. In the sixty years from 1960 to 2019, the figures are fifty-four and 651. Excluding the Comets, BOAC had five crashes in the fifties with at least nine dead, and its short-haul counterpart BEA had six crashes in the decade with more than twenty dead – including the most resonant of them all, at Munich in 1958, with eight Manchester United players among the victims. There was so much plane wreckage in the Mediterranean that the search party hunting for the Comet lost off Elba in January 1954 found part of the fuselage of a Lockheed Lodestar that had vanished five years earlier.

Smaller planes, and above all RAF planes, crashed all the time. In 1956, six out of eight RAF Hunter jets on an exercise in Norfolk crashed after being caught in fog. One pilot died; another parachuted to safety and had lamb chops for lunch at a house nearby. Two weeks earlier a Gloster Meteor night fighter had crashed into a bungalow in the middle of Wadhurst, Sussex, killing two on the ground as well as the two aboard. The pilot was thought to have been larking about to impress his parents who lived nearby, though not in the bungalow he hit.

The Meteor (aka the Meatbox) was the only Allied jet to see combat in the war, and afterwards became notorious within the RAF for killing its pilots, most regularly because they were unable to maintain control in cloud. The most authoritative figure is that a total of 890 Meteors were lost in RAF service, killing 450 pilots – 145 of these crashes occurred in 1953 alone. This seems to have gone largely unnoticed by the public; no one even thought it odd in September 1953 when two pilots were killed in Meteors on the same day at two different air shows.

Half a century later, in a long-running thread on this subject on an old pilots' website, comments included:

> 'Such things in those days were not appalling but just what happened in aviation.'
> 'The students were all more scared of being suspected of LMF* than they were of the aircraft.'
> 'Oh, for the days when flying was dangerous and sex was safe!'

The future Conservative Cabinet minister Norman Tebbit flew Meteors in the fifties, and said they were basically good planes but had specific problems involving the artificial horizon in bad weather and a propensity to run out of fuel. Safety was not a priority. 'It was like World War Two. The thinking was World War Two. The senior officers had all been in World War Two.'

It was not necessarily that much safer in any kind of plane. Tebbit later became a BOAC pilot and in 1958 was assigned to the airline's new round-the-world route, flying 707s west via the US to Tokyo. There were no satellites or computers; inertial navigation, the technology that preceded GPS, had not yet arrived. At night, they flew by the stars.

'It was ten hours from Honolulu to Tokyo, which was a bit worrying,' Tebbit recalled. 'We were marginal on range, and there were no navigation aids and very poorly forecast winds because there was only one weather ship in that whole part of the Pacific. And if you were in cloud a lot, it did make things rather hairy. You could be absolutely certain that where you thought you were, you weren't because you didn't know the strength of the wind. And engines were much less reliable.'

'Was there a sense of danger?' I asked him.

'Oh, inevitably. Occasionally even the passengers could see one of the engines had stopped.'

Tebbit would later become famous as an anti-trade-union

---

* Lack of moral fibre.

politician, although paradoxically much of his political grounding came as an official of the pilots' union, BALPA. He says his aim in the union was to improve safety, which he felt was further compromised by the rostering system. 'You were falling asleep all the time,' he said. 'I remember waking up one night and looking around the flight deck. There were four of us. There was the captain, asleep, the first officer, asleep, the radio officer, asleep. This was solely because of the ridiculous hours.'

———•———

There was one Englishman who embodied everything about this side of 1950s Britain. He was tall, blond, brilliant, and angelically handsome in the manner of James Dean. His name was Mike Hawthorn, he was Britain's first world motor racing champion and he was born to the breed.

His father was a racer, killed on the roads in 1954, obliging his son to take over his performance-car dealership in Surrey. Hawthorn began racing at 21, moved to Formula 1 in 1952, won his first Grand Prix in 1953; in 1955 he was party to the infamous crash at Le Mans which killed eighty-three spectators, then won the race; in 1958 his fellow roisterer and Ferrari teammate Peter Collins was killed in the German Grand Prix; two months later Hawthorn was world champion, a single point ahead of his fellow Briton Stirling Moss. He immediately announced his retirement. Three months after that, Hawthorn was dead, aged 29.

Much of Hawthorn's life is even more enigmatic than Dean's. And nothing was more enigmatic than his death. It occurred on the Guildford bypass, and would have been rather banal had it been less mysterious. It was rumoured all along that he had been racing his Jaguar against a Mercedes driven by a mate of his, Rob Walker. Before his death, Walker talked on condition that nothing was printed until he died. And, yes, he said, 'We were having a bit of a dice.' He said that at the time to a policeman, who told him to keep quiet about it. Walker told the coroner he had just gone into top gear, without mentioning that top gear for him meant 100 mph.

This still does not explain why the world's top racing driver wrote himself off after a meat-and-drink skid on a fast road without even a Donald Turnupseed in sight. There have been theories – the tyres, the throttle, the wet road, he was shot, he had a blackout caused by kidney disease, which was rumoured to be incurable and may have made him even more reckless. But he had just got engaged – no time to die. Stirling Moss lived to be Sir Stirling, and died aged 90, part of the language: 'Oo do you think you are? Stirling Moss?' As a plant, moss is a survivor, but the hawthorn flower never lasts beyond springtime.

12

THE REIGN OF ERROR

THE NAME WAS BRETHERTON, RUSSELL BRETHERTON. ANOTHER name not to match Bond, James Bond. The kind of name a comedy scriptwriter might choose to depict a luckless civil servant being given a job for which he is totally unfit. Which is exactly what did happen to Russell Bretherton.

He was an under-secretary at the Department of Trade, quite high up the pecking order, and looked the part too: neatly parted hair, clipped moustache, chalk-stripe suit, waistcoat. He was not a fool: he had been a much-admired economics tutor at Oxford.* But he was also not a senior political figure with clout, to put it mildly.

Bretherton was sent to Brussels in the autumn of 1955 to attend a series of meetings with the six countries of what was then the European Coal and Steel Community, the precursor of the European Economic Community which mutated into the European Community and then the European Union and maybe – one day – the United States of Europe, something advocated in 1930 by Winston Churchill.

The Coal and Steel Community had been proposed by the French foreign minister Robert Schuman in 1950. It meant taking away control over two crucial raw materials from governments

---

* He was also an expert on lepidopterology and discovered a hitherto-unnoticed breed of moth which he named for his wife: *Zygaena lonicerae jocelyne*.

and handing them to a new supranational body. It was attractive to France as a means of limiting Germany's ability to make war, and to the Germans as a means of easing their readmission to civilized society. It had no appeal to Britain: Clement Attlee, still the prime minister at the time, called it 'utterly undemocratic and . . . responsible to nobody'.

This was a template for British attitudes for the next seven years; you might say the next seventy. Whatever Churchill thought in 1930, uniting Europe was not a priority by the fifties. And the fact that the Continentals themselves were arranging this made it ridiculous. Who were these people? Britain had just saved Europe from tyranny (with a little help). Britain was the leading power in Europe, so Britain should lead Europe. But Britain did not want to lead Europe; it just expected Europe to follow. Jean Monnet, the EU's founding father, described this attitude as 'the price of victory – the illusion that you could maintain what you had, without change'.

Anthony Eden put it another way in a speech in New York in 1952, when he talked about 'the frequent suggestions' that the UK might join a European federation. Then he crushed them: 'This is something which we know, in our bones, we cannot do.' But four other countries – Italy, Belgium, the Netherlands and Luxembourg – did join up with France and Germany and sign up for coal and steel, and it worked well enough for the group of six to acquire further ambitions. They met in the Sicilian city of Messina in 1955 to plan the next step: negotiations in Brussels to refine the details of a common market. And they invited Britain, like social climbers hoping the lord of the manor might grace their little soireé. Instead, Britain humiliated them by sending a servant. A civil servant, but a servant nonetheless.

In hindsight, this was the last chance for the British to shape the new Europe to their own ends, politically and economically. Bretherton himself seems to have sensed it. But he had no agency. His instructions were 'to co-operate, to be helpful, but to enter into no commitment'. One version has it that he eventually walked out, which is improbable. He said later he was told to leave because

Britain's presence served no further purpose. The six signed the Treaty of Rome on 25 March 1957.

———·———

The banishment of Bretherton took place in November 1955, seven months after Churchill retired. Almost Eden's first act as prime minister was to hold and win an election, partly by using the new-fangled television with charm and skill. With a big majority, and the country increasingly comfortable and fully employed, the only person who appeared to have nothing useful to do was Eden. He had little domestic agenda of his own, though he was said to be passionate about technical education. He might more profitably have concentrated on that, because no one else ever did, to Britain's lasting detriment. Instead he kept trying to micromanage his foreign secretary, Harold Macmillan.

Already some were sensing a certain brittleness of character. In his previous incarnation, when he was at the Foreign Office and inclined to bother Churchill, his conversations with the Number 10 private office often ended: 'And tell Winston that I am at the end of my tether.' It became an in-joke among Churchill's aides: 'The Foreign Secretary's at the E of his T again.' On his last night in Downing Street, in April 1955, after he had hosted a farewell dinner with the Queen as guest of honour, Churchill muttered to his private secretary, 'I don't believe Anthony can do it.'

In the autumn the economy became more troubled, and by January 1956 criticism was growing; even the loyal *Telegraph* joined in: 'lost prestige and reputation . . . anti-climax . . . wavering . . . half-measures'. What people wanted, said Middle England's tablet of stone, was 'the smack of firm government'. Then Eden found the purpose that would define his premiership for ever.

Britain's imperial involvement in the Middle East is largely forgotten at home, though it was long, tortuous and frequently malign. In 1953, Eden had persuaded both Churchill and the US to help overthrow the popular and radical Iranian leader Mohammad Mosaddegh, who had nationalized the oil industry, in favour of the Shah – bitterly remembered as if it were yesterday in Tehran. In

Egypt, Britain had effectively controlled the country during the reign of repulsive King Farouk – 'gourmand, libertine, kleptomaniac, drug-trafficker and buffoon', as the historian Piers Brendon put it, not unkindly. Farouk was overthrown by his own army in 1952, and the original coup leader, General Neguib, was soon superseded by the most forceful of his subordinates, Colonel Gamal Nasser.

As Foreign Secretary, Eden played this cleverly at first, successfully negotiating the removal of Britain's 70,000 troops from the Suez Canal Zone, to the delight of the Treasury, the new Egyptian regime and, above all, the British squaddies. For them it was the posting from hell – hot, dusty, filthy, boring, disease-ridden and, often enough, murderous. Britain and the US also agreed to supply some arms and to finance Nasser's great project: the Aswan Dam on the Nile. Part of the deal was that troops could return to protect the canal in the event of war. This mattered to Britain, and to France, since – unlike the Americans – they depended on the canal for oil.

Nasser, however, was not content to be a more puritanical Farouk. Though no democrat, he was not without idealism. He saw himself as an Egyptian nationalist, a pan-Arabist, an anti-colonialist. He kept tweaking Western noses and, anxious for more arms, also did business with the Soviet bloc. This infuriated the Americans who, in July 1956, withdrew their support for the dam. Whereupon the Egyptians nationalized the Suez Canal Company, French-run with much British investment.

There is no greater error in statecraft than assuming that what was true in one crisis will be true in another. Eden had forged his reputation as an anti-appeaser in 1938 and was judged to be right. Now he knew who Nasser was – he was Hitler all over again, and had to be stopped. Firm government, they wanted. 'This act of plunder,' Eden warned the nation, 'must not succeed.'

But it was not plunder: the canal was due to revert to Egypt in twelve years anyway; the shareholders would be compensated and the canal would stay open. How would the British feel if Egypt controlled the Thames? The Americans, with their own ambivalence towards British imperialism, half recognized this and backed away from intervention – an attitude not unconnected to the imminence of the US election, with President Eisenhower seeking a second term. Also, they had other ways to get oil.

But Eden was in too deep. It was not just him obsessing. If he did nothing, he would be perceived as weak. Where would that leave Britain's faltering influence in the Middle East? What might Winston say? What would all the still-dedicated imperialists on the backbenches say? What would the *Telegraph* say about the 'smack of firm government'?

The Times was already calling the nation to seize the moment, like a 1914 recruiting sergeant: 'Doubtless it is good to have a flourishing tourist trade, to win Test matches, and to be regaled by photographs of Miss Diana Dors being pushed into a swimming pool,' it editorialized. 'But nations do not live by circuses alone. The people, in their silent way, know this better than the critics. They still want Britain great.'

The Times did not speak for many of those commanded to maintain the greatness. The government invoked the small print in the National Service rules and recalled 20,000 old squaddies and matelots who thought they had done their bit. Many just ignored the summons; there were mini mutinies as men waited in camps, being given the full 'orrible-little-man treatment all over again. They were mostly in their mid-twenties and married now, they weren't having it, and the top brass told the sergeant-majors to go easy. And Eden had never thought of the consequences for their families. One woman in Middlesbrough, left without her husband and his wages, was hauled into court for breaking into her gas meter to feed her children.

Meanwhile, far from real life, there was an autumn of mutual threats and occasional negotiation, but no acceptable solution. Then finally a rather odd coalition of the willing emerged. It involved Israel, anxious to get their retaliation in first before Egypt's Soviet arms arrived. It involved France, convinced that Nasser was arming and inciting the rebels against French rule in Algeria. And it involved Britain, which was desperate to do *something*, as long as no one knew about this new alliance.

And thus the cover-up began before the crime. The Israelis would invade Egypt, and their allies would intervene and take control of the canal in the guise of peacekeepers. The British insisted on utter secrecy about this arrangement. They even destroyed their copy of the agreement between the three sides signed at Sèvres near Paris (the French merely lost theirs). After the French generals visited Eden at Chequers, the page they signed in the visitors' book was torn out.* Most of the Cabinet were not told. Foreign Office officials were not told. Eisenhower was not told. The need to maintain the pretence meant the British flotilla could not leave Malta until after the Israelis had started marching, and had to proceed at the pace of the slowest landing craft. What could go wrong?

The fighting went quite well, considering. The Israelis raced through Sinai; the British and French bombed the Egyptian bases, gave Port Said a bashing and got a fair distance down the canal before the politics and economics became impossible. This spared the invaders from having to cope with the crisis that would have followed success: if Nasser – popular at home – was overthrown, they had no way of governing the country.

And the timing was terrible. Eisenhower was livid about the distraction from his election week. Much worse, it coincided with, and gave cover to, Moscow's brutal invasion of its rebellious quasi-colony, Hungary. This was the final proof that Stalin was no aberration and that Soviet Communism was irredeemable. Never again would starry-eyed Western radicals look to Russia for inspiration. This should have been, in its bleak way, a great moment for liberal democracy. Instead, both systems looked as bad as each other.

During the week of combat the UK government's popularity rose as the nation briefly thrilled to the drumbeat of war. That faded more slowly than it might have done, even as the US refused to prop up Britain's financial reserves and Eden had to call a halt. The

---

* In 1966, Sir Hugh Carleton Greene, the director-general of the BBC, was talking about Suez to Lord Normanbrook, who (as Sir Norman Brook) had been the Cabinet secretary during Suez. Green said that he expected the whole truth would emerge some day. Lord Normanbrook replied: 'Damned good care has been taken to see that the whole truth never does emerge.'

deception was still not a proven fact: on December 20, six weeks after the ceasefire, Eden still denied to the Commons the existence of 'some dishonourable conspiracy' – which did leave open the possibility that it was an honourable conspiracy. But suspicion soon hardened into fact. Eden was humiliated; broken in health, spirit and reputation. Three weeks after that, he was history.

It was not the last time Britain got involved in an ill-judged foreign war; it was the last time it would do so without the Americans. It had become an incipient dementia patient being grounded by the family after one crackpot adventure too many. But, in a strange way, Suez did have to happen. The imperialist Right had to be chastened and neutralized or it would have happened somewhere else when the natives got restless, probably more bloodily. In the context of the decade, the price of twenty-two British dead (compared to about 2,000 Egyptians) was, from the British perspective, surprisingly cheap.

13

THE YOUNG ONES

IN MAY 1956, LITERARY LONDON WAS TRANSFIXED BY A NEW hero. His name was Colin Wilson, and he had just published his first book, *The Outsider*. The anonymous literary critic of *The Listener* called it 'the most remarkable book upon which the reviewer has ever had to pass judgment'.

Cyril Connolly of the *Sunday Times* merely called it 'one of the most remarkable first books I have read for a long time' and Philip Toynbee of *The Observer* 'a most impressive study, of a kind which is too rare in England . . . a real contribution to our understanding'. By August the gleeful publisher, Victor Gollancz, had reprinted the work eight times. It was a phenomenon.

That summer Wilson had turned 25. He came from a working-class family in Leicester, had done menial work in a warehouse, a lab and a morgue, had lived in a sleeping bag on Hampstead Heath and written an unpublished million-word novel. The following year he added to his CV the experience of having his girlfriend's father burst in on them brandishing a whip and shouting, 'The game's up, Wilson.' In a sense, he was right because, by then, Wilsonmania was already over.

It is a little hard to explain *The Outsider* or to judge it fairly: the names dropped in the first chapter include Henri Barbusse, Villiers de l'Isle-Adam, Professor Whitehead, Schopenhauer, Spengler, Boehme, Guido Ruggiero and Sardou, and soon the reader might begin to feel a craving for either an Agatha Christie or lunch. Even Connolly later admitted he had not read it properly. It is a work that combines literary criticism, philosophy and psychology, and its status as a bestseller was quite clearly the product of a hysteria epidemic.

It is difficult to craft grand theories from complex situations, which was perhaps Wilson's mistake. His second book, *Religion and the Rebel*, was monstered, and most of the 119 (approx.) books he produced subsequently were ignored except by a small but faithful following. He was later said to have irritated people by believing his own publicity. But 1956 seemed to be a particular moment in history. There was a craving for new sensation, and the notion of a voracious autodidact whose dad worked in a shoe factory was a perfect fit. Had he gone to Oxford, no one would have noticed.

Already that month, the play *Look Back in Anger* had opened at the Royal Court. Its author, John Osborne, was another non-silver-spooner. But he got none of the unanimous acclaim enjoyed by Wilson:

'altogether inadequate' – *The Times*
'the most putrid bosh' – *Evening News*
'self-pitying snivel' – *Evening Standard*

On the other hand:

'a play of extraordinary importance' – *Financial Times*
'outstanding promise' – *Sunday Times*
'I doubt if I could love anyone who did not wish to see Look Back in Anger' – *The Observer*

This last from Kenneth Tynan, a critic never knowingly understated. Those who disagreed were marooned on the wrong side of history, like the Munich appeasers and the Suez zealots. Jimmy Porter, Osborne's central character, is indeed a man, young and angry, though Kenneth Allsop neatly defined his unfocused anger as 'neurological masturbation'. And so Osborne and Wilson and at least a dozen other up-and-coming male playwrights and novelists (most frequently, Kingsley Amis and John Braine) were all categorized as 'angry young men', though at the time they generally only got angry when they were lumped together so glibly. Mostly, they were rather pleased with themselves. Who wouldn't be, if lionized for one's brilliance while still the right side of thirty?

But they did tend to have certain things in common. Most were indeed outsiders who had been nowhere near university (except Amis), were grittily provincial (though not Amis nor Harold Pinter), lustily heterosexual – in contrast to much of the ruling clique in the theatre – and impatiently anti-establishment. Osborne and Pinter, between them, redefined the concept of the play, previously stultified by the need to appeal to the all-too-real theatregoer Terence Rattigan called 'Aunt Edna': Osborne, with glorious risk-taking versatility; Pinter with his dogged insistence on bleak realism. In the list of Britain's triumphs since 1952, drama must be near the top.*

In later life, the Angries mostly did get grumpy, and in many cases (not Pinter) decidedly right-wing. Perhaps the least grumpy of them all turned out to be Wilson. Stung by the way London turned on him, he retreated to Cornwall with the whip-cracker's daughter, began his polymathic production line of books focusing on true crime, the occult and existentialism for his niche readers, and became a genial host to those he trusted, and 'a kind, mostly serene man'.

————◆————

'Suez and the coming of rock-and-roll divide twentieth-century British history,' according to the historian Eric Hobsbawm. But even before that there were stirrings, little green shoots above the wintry soil that could later be identified as the first hints of the spring-like exuberance known as 'The Sixties'.

As early as 1953 there was a hint of what was to come. The

---

* Perhaps the most original talent of all was the working-class Salford playwright Shelagh Delaney whose hit *A Taste of Honey* smashed various taboos in 1958. The difference between her and the young men, said the programme for the Joan Littlewood production, was that 'she knows what she is angry about'.

American 'sob singer' Johnnie Ray was carried, allegedly semi-conscious, to his car to save him from screaming girls after a concert in Manchester. Ray was a fragile, troubled figure and rather deaf, making him an altogether unlikely precursor of a loud and feral historical movement. But he touched a previously undiscovered nerve with the public.

Then came the Teds, and in November 1955 a very different development: a young woman called Mary Quant started designing, selling and eventually making clothes that took her fancy instead of following the dictates of Paris fashion houses. The old orthodoxy had been embodied in Britain by a model called Barbara Goalen, who claimed 'vital statistics'* (a very fifties phrase) of 33–18–31. These figures were as unattainable to the average woman as Len Hutton's batting average to a man or Japanese productivity growth to a less-focused nation.

In her first shop in Chelsea, Quant sold what she wanted to wear. 'One day I pulled on an eight-year-old boy's sweater for fun. I was enchanted with the result. And, in six months, all the birds were wearing the skinny-ribs that resulted. It was the same thing with string tops. As a joke, I put a man's string vest over the dark dress I was wearing. The effect was electric.'

It certainly was. As she put it in her first autobiography: 'Rightly or wrongly, I have been credited with the Lolita Look, the Schoolgirl Look, the Wet Weather Look, the Kinky Look, the Good Girl Look and lots of others and it is said that I was first with knickerbockers, gilt chains, shoulder-strap bags and high boots. I like being given the credit for such things.' But she was not arrogant about it. There was just something in the air: 'The clothes I made happened to fit in exactly with the teenage trend, with pop records and espresso bars and jazz clubs.'

Britain's first coffee craze, in the eighteenth century, was vaguely Oriental in origin, and the twenty-first century iteration would be emphatically American. The 1950s boom was wholly Italian. The

---

* 'Charlies-waist-hips', as she nicely put it. Goalen's appearance was rather forbidding, but she sounded fun.

credit is given to a dental supplies salesman called Pino Riservato, who had been traipsing round England trying to find not just receptive dentists but, more hopelessly, a decent cup of coffee.* A relation was a director of the Milan-based Gaggia company, which had created a machine that gleamed, spewed steam and chuffed and puffed like the *Flying Scotsman* and somehow thus brought forth espresso.

Riservato tried to interest café-owners but failed, so he started his own outlet, the Moka coffee bar, in Soho in 1953. Then everyone wanted a Gaggia. There were 500 espresso bars in London by 1960. Hipper than the old milk bars, more welcoming to kids than the pubs, they incubated the British version of beatnikery, usually involving duffel coats, fishermen's jumpers that might have warmed Colin Wilson on Hampstead Heath, and maybe a wispy teenage beard that the Army would shave off gleefully on Day 1 of National Service.

The music that would change the world, however, was indeed American. And at first it cloaked its revolutionary intentions in heavy disguise. Bill Haley & His Comets, who fired the first gunshots with 'Rock Around the Clock', looked precisely the kind of band that might safely be employed to provide foxtrots and quicksteps at an early fifties student hop or Young Conservative annual ball.

Indeed, 'Rock Around the Clock' was originally listed in the Decca catalogue as a foxtrot and issued as a B-side to a forgotten song called 'Thirteen Women (and Only One Man in Town)', which reached No. 23 in the US. It was rescued first by being used in the 1955 film *Blackboard Jungle*, and then went top of the bill by getting its own plot-light, rock-heavy movie named after the song.

Some kids had apparently cottoned on after *Blackboard Jungle*. 'People were saying "Didya hear that music, man?"' recalled one music-mad pre-teen in South-East London. 'Because in England we'd never heard anything – the BBC controls it and won't play that sort of music.' The boy's name was Keith Richards.

---

* But then, just try to find a decent pot of tea in Italy.

And then came word of another American phenomenon, one who blazed much brighter and longer than Bill Haley, though not as long as Richards and his schoolmate Mick Jagger. He even came to the notice of the senior mistress at a North London comprehensive school, who walked into the staffroom and announced sternly: 'I must speak to a boy called EP because he's carved his name on every desk in the school.'

In May 1956, the big-band leader Ted Heath (not the future prime minister) came back from a tour of the US. He was interviewed by the *Daily Express* record critic Cyril Stapleton, a man in his forties who doubled as a bandleader himself. Heath was in his fifties. Stapleton mentioned rock and roll. 'Do you think it will catch on in Britain?'

'It's primarily music for coloured folk,' said Heath, 'played by coloured bands. It includes a great deal of jumping up and down and crazy antics, which I do not feel would be acceptable here . . . I don't think it will find any place in my programmes.'

'Sorry, I can't agree with you, Ted,' wrote Stapleton. 'A young man named Elvis Presley . . . is just getting under way. His record of "Heartbreak Hotel" should be appearing in the best sellers soon – despite the fact you can't understand a word he's singing about.'

Before the month was out, Stapleton was proved right and six more Elvis numbers would hit the charts before 1956 was done. But Stapleton was a rarity. 'If this is singing, then I give up,' said Geoffrey Everitt in the *New Musical Express*. No reference to Presley can be found in any of Britain's quality papers that summer. When *The Times* first mentioned his name in September, it was in a dispatch from Washington headed U.S. SCENES RECALL 'JUNGLE BIRD HOUSE AT THE ZOO' which was long enough to merit four sub-headings, which were: HOODLUM ELEMENTS; A PASSING FAD; NATIONAL CRAZE; WEEPING AND MOANING.

In total it was every bit as perceptive as the paper's leader on Diana Dors and Suez. But Presley, far away and largely invisible, was mostly playing the dance halls of the segregated Southern states, where the idea of a white man playing 'coloured music' was

IN SORROW
AND IN GLORY

The royal gamekeepers guard
George's VI's coffin in the church
at Sandringham, February 1952.

A London street party for
Elizabeth II's coronation,
June 1953.

A LESS INSULAR NATION

Jamaican immigrants arriving in Britain, 1954.

The manager of a pioneering London Chinese restaurant, the Hong Kong, teaches the writer Olga Noble-Mathews of *Good Housekeeping* how to use chopsticks, 1952.

THE TELLY TAKEOVER: (*top left*) Janice Isaacs of Wembley hugs host Michael Miles after a big win on ITV's top-rated game show, *Take Your Pick*, 1955; (*top right*) Gilbert Harding, the curmudgeonly star of BBC's *What's My Line*, tackles his massive mailbag; (*below*) in a village near Pontypridd, a Welsh family pays homage to the deity of the decade, 1959.

FORMALITY RULES

The Welsh golfer
Dai Rees, tie neatly
knotted, plays an iron
off the fairway in a
tournament at
Sunningdale, 1955.

Oxford University
students, almost in
uniform, pay attention,
1958.

CASUALTIES

John Cobb sets out on his fatal attempt to break the water speed world record at Loch Ness, 1952.

Mike Hawthorn in a Ferrari at the British Grand Prix at Aintree, 1957, eighteen months before his death on the Guildford bypass.

Britain's top model, the hourglass-shaped Barbara Goalen, prepares for a shoot, 1953.

The flamboyant Lady Docker entertains a group of coal miners on her yacht, 1954.

Catching tiddlers in the River Wye, Hereford, 1955.

Before he was famous, the film-maker Ken Russell took still photos, notably a series of shots of kids on the London bomb sites-turned-makeshift playgrounds in 1954. 'They did what they liked, and then went home for their tea,' he said.

A grocer in Tottenham, 1958

Ploughing, somewhere in England, 1952.

highly significant. The British adults who did notice him picked up the raw sexuality and completely missed the unique voice, talent and sheer range. A London schoolboy asked a young teacher what he thought of Elvis. 'Disgusting,' was the reply. This boy's name was Roger Daltrey.

The newspapers, in their dying days as the nation's chief news medium, did pick up on what began to happen in the cinemas, which were dying even faster as the nation's chief entertainment medium. *Rock Around the Clock* opened in cinemas in late summer. And that was the moment when teenage culture erupted in Britain. Its lava would engulf the feeble defences erected by adults: mild reprisal, censure and disdain.

As the film spread from the West End to the suburbs and then to the benighted provinces, the idea grew among teenagers that they should get up and jive to the music, a forbidden practice even in some dance halls. In a few places, seats were ripped out. Cinema managers, in a failing business because the adults were now home watching TV, called the police. A more sensible idea would have been to remove some of the seats themselves, to create space and show the film for months. The odd fracas ensued, notably outside the Trocadero cinema in Elephant & Castle, home of the Teds. 'It seems to have been a mild sort of riot,' said Peter Lewis. 'Nine arrests, two policemen injured, some cups and saucers thrown about the streets and one or two £1 fines awarded.'

Full moral panic took over. The Gaumont chain stopped Sunday showings: 'Sunday is the worst night for rowdyism,' said a spokesman. The film was cancelled in Blackpool, and banned by councils in quaint and unfrequented villages like Birmingham and Brighton. Following the Elephant 'riot', *Rock Around the Clock* was replaced at the Trocadero by something far more demure and suitable: *Gun Fury*. And Sir Malcolm Sargent, then permanent master of the revels at the Last Night of the Proms, fleeing the country for the peace of Johannesburg, offered his considered judgment on the rock and roll phenomenon: 'primitive tomtom thumping'.

There was, however, silent but expressive appreciation from an unexpected source. The Queen asked for a copy of the film to be sent to Balmoral. Later the title track was played at the Duke of Kent's twenty-first party in Buckinghamshire, where a (no doubt weary) reporter noted, Her Majesty stayed until 3.12 a.m.

---·---

The *Daily Telegraph*, very precise on the monarch's bedtime, was vaguer on other matters, describing rock and roll as 'an extravagant jazz', a description that would have offended everyone. The jazz crowd were generally older and better educated; the fierce urgency of the response to Bill Haley was surely connected to the fact that the 18-year-old males were about to be carted off for freshers' weeks less beguiling than those offered to future generations. On the other hand (except while on National Service), they had far more cash than previous generations.

Briefly, linked to both these streams and what would later become the folk scene, was skiffle, a very British genre (though with some American roots) full of British make-do and self-deprecation and involving such sophisticated instruments as the washboard, the tea chest and the paper and comb. John Lennon was an early exponent. It was big at the 2i's coffee bar in Soho, where Tommy Steele, Cliff Richard, Adam Faith, what would become The Shadows, and many others all honed their skills; and again on *Six-Five Special*, the BBC's first attempt at coolness, which began in February 1957.

Things were moving on quickly. Tommy Steele, Britain's first home-grown rock star, had hit No. 1 with his version of 'Singing the Blues' the previous month. But still disapproval lurked. In July, Steele was expelled from his suite at the Majestic Hotel, Lytham St Annes, for playing the xylophone at 2 a.m.

By now, it was possible to glimpse the beginnings of something that would create ongoing moral panics on a much greater scale. In 1956, Farnham magistrates heard the case against a 21-year-old soldier caught smoking 'Indian hemp', aka cannabis. The soldier was discharged after giving the police the names and addresses of his suppliers and being told by the chairman to give up 'this messy Eastern habit'.

At that stage, he could lawfully have switched to another drug.

Heroin was not made illegal in the UK until 1964. In 1955 the law was due to be changed, but *The Times* had a leader arguing – and this is truly mind-blowing – that it should remain legal. It pointed out that Britain had a grand total of forty-seven heroin addicts and that 'there is no efficient substitute for heroin in relieving pain in the terminal stages of cancer in some patients or for relieving certain forms of chronic cough'. It was also prescribed for diarrhoea and even colds.

In fact, there was a technical problem with the bill, and the government had to back away. Eventually, heroin did join cannabis as illegal, and since that time no one at all in the UK has ever attempted to indulge in either of these messy habits, now have they?

14

THE NEWCOMERS

IN THE SUMMER OF 1948, A 14,000-TON GERMAN-BUILT SHIP with a chequered past behind it and a bitter end to come was ploughing its way through the Atlantic, returning to England from Australia the back way. It was far from full so, when it stopped in Kingston, Jamaica, to pick up some returning British servicemen, the captain authorized adverts in the local press offering cheap passage.

As this was happening, a new British Nationality Bill was approaching the closing stages of its passage through Westminster. It was mostly technical, taking account of the way the British Empire was becoming the Commonwealth and creating new descriptions – 'Citizen of the UK and Colonies' and 'Commonwealth Citizen' – to run alongside the old 'British Subject' and pave the way for more countries to follow the subcontinent to independence.

These two designations were to be equivalent: Mother England would still welcome all her children, even if they no longer depended on her bosom. For the opposition Conservatives, the future Home Secretary Sir David Maxwell Fyfe expressed his approval: 'We must maintain our great metropolitan tradition of hospitality to everyone from every part of our Empire.'

Between four and eight hundred Jamaicans embarked at Kingston – on what started life as the German passenger ship *Monte Rosa* and was now the British *Empire Windrush* – to test this tradition.

They had been educated the British way – some well, some less so
– and thought they knew something about their destination. They
did not, however, understand the nuances: that just because a
member of the British ruling class says, 'Oh, you *must* pop round
sometime,' it does not mean you just turn up for tea. And that even
if you do have a specific invitation, the hospitality wears thin after
midnight and certainly after a long weekend. And conversely, no
one in parliament had thought to ask what the consequences might
be from extending an unconditional welcome to half a billion
people, mostly poor – ten times the existing population of Britain.

The ship was given what was described as an 'official welcome',
and the bomb shelter by Clapham South station was reopened for
those without offers of accommodation or jobs. When eleven
Labour MPs wrote to the PM to complain about the new arrivals,
they received a bland reply. But privately the government was
already unnerved: this had not been foreseen. It was too late for the
bill to be discreetly amended.

This was not the first set of arrivals from the West Indies,* but it
was the first to be widely noticed. Official welcomes were not the
norm. Instead there were cursory checks (mainly to catch stow-
aways) and then nothing – often no aftercare at all. In the strange
mixture of pernickitiness and nonchalance that characterized
Britain in the era, this was perhaps the strangest case of all. New
immigrants were received off the ships with hardly any more
bureaucracy than if they had arrived at Southampton or Tilbury
from Waterloo or Fenchurch Street.†

It would take three more prime ministers and fourteen years to
pass any legislation that would change that, and even then the issues
raised refused to go away; they are yet to do so. The casualness
finally exploded into full-blown scandal *seventy years* after the ship
docked. Even Professor David Olusoga, a harsh critic of white

---

* The *Ormonde* and *Almanzora* had carried a smaller number, mainly ex-servicemen,
in 1947.
† Hence the difficulty of pinning down the numbers who came on the *Windrush* –
the ship's records, recently examined, suggest 663 were most recently resident in
the Caribbean.

attitudes, describes the arrangements as 'incredibly liberal'. In the nineteenth century, the historian Sir John Seeley famously said Britain 'conquered half the world in a fit of absence of mind'. It became a multi-ethnic country in the same way.

The word *racist* was rarely used in Britain in the 1950s. The preferred term was *racialist*, which was already being used to condemn the segregationist policies of the deep south of both the US and Africa. The home-based British were not especially racialist; most had had minimal or zero experience of non-whites (there were barely 20,000 in Britain after the GIs left in 1945). They just did not trust anyone or anything foreign and unfamiliar, whether that meant Pakistanis or pasta.

When Italian men came to Bedfordshire to do perhaps the nastiest job in Britain, working in the kilns of the brickworks, their wives faced complaints about the cooking smells. At Bullcroft Colliery in Doncaster, the men refused to work with Italians, calling them 'lazy, dirty, quarrelsome and unpleasant'. The situation was not helped when a Tory MP said the miners' attitude was due to the Italians' 'sex appeal to the miners' wives and daughters'.

Despite all that was by then known about the Nazis, the brochure for the Stanmore Hotel in Margate still had a discreet line in 1954 saying: 'The management respectfully advise that they reserve the right to refuse accommodation to members of the Hebrew faith, whether booked or not.' (I do admire the chutzpah of the word *respectfully*.) The tennis player Angela Buxton, who was Jewish despite her English-rose name, was refused admission to club after club and had to practise on the private court owned by Sir Simon Marks, chairman of Marks & Spencer. In 1956 she reached the final of the singles at Wimbledon and won the doubles – playing with another pariah, the black American Althea Gibson. Buxton was still barred from the traditional Wimbledon ball, until her mother threatened to raise hell. And she was never invited to join the All England Club, though she lived until 2020.

Meanwhile, a British airman based in Hong Kong was in 1953

refused permission to marry a Eurasian girl, and was promptly posted to Colombo instead. He gave way and did as he was told.

So that was the background. And on top of all that, the West Indians – unlike the Italians – had not been actively sought. The vast majority came lawfully and legitimately, but not personally invited to fill a gap. There was some specific recruitment in the early 1950s from London Transport and, to a lesser extent, British Railways, but not at this stage the NHS. Essentially they came as what would be later known, sneeringly, as 'economic migrants'. They were mostly facing poverty back home but not an immediate humanitarian disaster or political persecution. They wanted to better themselves and help their families.

That led them to two or maybe three points of conflict. Though Britain had very little unemployment, workers still feared competition from migrants who might work for less and undermine their hard-won prosperity. Occasionally there would be male angst about sexual competition.

But the third point was by far the most crucial. Britain was already facing an intractable housing crisis, with young families living in insanitary slums or inadequate lodgings or with their own parents. Now here were hundreds more needing homes. And soon there would be thousands and thousands. The numbers were still small before 1951 but then came two significant events: that year, Jamaica was hit by Hurricane Charlie, its worst storm since 1903; the next year, the US clamped down on West Indian migration. Then the numbers really rose: by 1955, 42,000 arrived. And not many went back; their families needed their money.

For most of those years, Maxwell Fyfe, who hanged Derek Bentley but championed 'metropolitan hospitality', was Home Secretary. He and his colleagues could have channelled investment to the Caribbean. Or they could have admitted what they already knew: that the notion of hospitality could not be infinite – what if all 400 million Indians and Pakistanis turned up? – and that a queue was essential for everyone's sake. Jamaica did not admit the British without question: proof of sufficient funds was required. Every country which depended on immigration had its own criteria for who they wanted: Israel wanted more Jews to fight the Arabs; Australia had a whites-only policy; the US rejected the sick, the destitute, Communists, anarchists and bigamists, and, after 1952, all but a hundred Jamaicans a year.

But Britain had a genuine dilemma. If a new law was overtly race-based it would destroy the remnant of the imperial happy-family myth. But if a single Canadian or Australian wartime pilot was detained at London Airport, the Right – and most especially the *Express* newspapers, owned by the Empire-obsessed Lord Beaverbrook – would go berserk. So the government dithered, as did the opposition: Labour MPs found themselves torn between their own instincts and the opinions of their voters. Was Britain a nation like any other, or the hub of an empire? Until it made up its mind, immigration officers were not allowed even to ask British subjects on arrival what their plans might be.

It was hard for those early migrants. 'Everything you touched was cold,' said Bernie Grant, later a Labour MP. 'The food was cold, the furniture was cold, the table was cold.' Sometimes the cold was the first thing they noticed. One group of 146 arrived at Victoria Station from Barbados via Genoa, Calais, the Channel ferry and Dover. It was 10.30 p.m. on the night of London's heaviest snowfall in seven years. An *Express* reporter watched them arrive:

Pop-eyed piccaninnies being tagged along, slithering and splashing their plimsolled feet. Strong, brown workers from the plantations, in their baseball caps and battered trilbies. Ebony mammas with hats perched on top of the bandanas they wore wound round their heads. Men in sheepskin; women wearing feather boas; children in sandals. Where would they spend this, their first night in the alien snow? Half had friends, and the friends had spare beds. The other half, friendless, shuffled off into the night. Why did they come? Herbert Bennet, from Barbados, answered typically: 'My father, a carpenter, is unemployed. And I have four brothers and two sisters.'

Not all the words would be acceptable in a modern British news-paper, but the tone conveyed the sympathetic helplessness of a war correspondent watching a line of refugees. And there was also a metaphorical chill. 'Every time you went out was like walking into a freezing day with a cold wind blowing needle sharp bits of ice right in your face,' wrote Mike Phillips, '. . . the inevitable question: "Why don't you go back where you came from?"'

Phillips was a Guyanese teenager transplanted to Islington. At night, going home from the cinema, it was much worse. 'I moved like a cat, every sense tuned up, taking a different route every time. One night a group of boys erupted out of an alleyway, yelling and waving chains, but I was fast . . .' He leapt on a bus, pulling away from a stop, and clung to the pole. God bless those old Routemasters.

But the biggest shock to the newcomers was the sight of 'ordinary white people doing ordinary work'. On arrival, a white porter would often carry their luggage, speaking an English they had never heard before and barely understood. The only whites they had known were colonial officials and missionaries. It was also a warning: maybe it was not so easy to find a job.

———•———

The workplace would prove a major battleground, though it was not always easy to tell the difference between prejudice and the fear of being undercut: in particular, the bus companies in provincial cities danced a delicate quadrille involving the existing workers, their unions, the employers and potential recruits. The middle two, especially the unions, might take different stances in different places but they rarely encouraged the newcomers. Even mental hospitals, where recruitment is always problematic, could be unwelcoming – though when nurses in Swansea voted against accepting six trainees from Barbados, three other hospitals immediately offered to snap them up.

Some of the stories of prejudice were indeed outrageous. Carmel Jones, an Anglican from Jamaica, arrived in 1955, went to church and was greeted by the vicar: 'Thank you for coming, but I would be delighted if you didn't come back. My congregation is uncomfortable in the company of black people.' It was a common experience, said Jones, especially with the Church of England. He later became chief executive of the Pentecostal Churches, who moved into the C-of-E-sized gap. In Newcastle, Francis Dove, the five-year-old son of a West African dentist, was rejected by three private prep schools. The fear was that other parents would withdraw their own children.

But this was not the whole story. In 1955, Jamaica's chief minister, Norman Manley, sent his sociologist son Douglas to Britain to give him a full report on conditions. Manley junior concluded there was a lot of prejudice but also a 'large reservoir of goodwill'. He was most concerned about the loss of Jamaica's own bravest and brightest. After all, a remittance economy is no way to build a nation. And the West Indians were rarely using the experience to go back. The theft of other countries' talent has never bothered the liberal classes most enthusiastic about immigration to Britain.

The goodwill was real too. In 1950 the West Indian cricketers had won their first Test series in England, and the charm of their play and the attendant calypsos created far more delight than angst. Aspirant Caribbean writers in London also found themselves briefly fashionable. 'Reviewers sought in West Indian fiction what was apparently absent in post-war Britain: colour, gaiety, innocence, virility,' said the Guyanese writer David Dabydeen. 'Such poignant desire for the characteristics of the Noble Savage ensured that West Indian writing was eagerly received by the literati, even as the real thing – the nigger – was being hunted down and hounded out of the neighbourhood.'

The trouble was that the indigenous people thought it was *their* neighbourhood. And 'gaiety' (old meaning) was not necessarily what they wanted next door late at night. Aside from unreasonable hatreds, there was a rational dislike of some West Indian neighbours – particularly in the early days when they were mainly single men. No one had prepared the elderly white couples, living in decaying terraces with net curtains, for the loud parties, music and laughter that now often came from next door.

Demand pushed the rents up, if landlords would let to immigrants at all. Those rents could only be paid if the tenants sublet, to cram in more migrants; and overcrowding meant parties spilling on to the street. Bad landlords were wildly overcharging for bad, unsanitary houses to people seen as bad neighbours. If the new drove out the old, so much the better. The landlords could buy further houses for buttons and let them to yet more desperate migrants.

The councils began to yell to the government. In 1955, Lambeth said there was 'no hope whatever' of housing the 3,500 West Indians crowded into Brixton. Birmingham, which prided itself on being a 'no colour bar city', had 60,000 on its council-house waiting list, and sent a deputation to Whitehall. 'Birmingham can always promise a welcome, but the time is with us when it simply cannot offer a home,' said Alderman William Bowen. Hammersmith sent a pleading letter to the Ministry of Housing: 'The problem is a national one with which local authorities cannot be expected to cope.' The government was otherwise occupied.

Finally it happened, first in Nottingham and then in London, around Notting Hill, as a wet summer turned to a suddenly sultry autumn in 1958. No one died in Britain's only significant modern inter-race riots; other countries have seen much worse. But they did galvanize both government and public opinion.

Both events appear to have been started as a reaction to the sight of a white woman arm in arm with a black man. In both cases there has never been any serious doubt that white youths – many of them Teds – were overwhelmingly responsible for the violence. This was exacerbated in London by the stirring of neo-Fascists. Mr Justice Salmon certainly had no doubts. He told nine white youths who armed themselves with iron bars and attacked random black men that they had 'filled the whole nation with horror, indignation, and disgust', and jailed them for four years, way beyond expectations.

The disgust was real, and so was the sympathy for the victims. Nonetheless, polls started showing 80 per cent support for immigration controls, and the signals from Westminster suggested, if not urgency, then at least a shuffling of papers. David Olusoga, while maintaining that the victims were in effect being punished, offers two theories on this development: 1) the government was now catching up with public opinion; 2) the public was now catching up with a governmental class that had always been conspiring to restrict immigration. No reasonable interpretation of history can support the second notion. As Maxwell Fyfe told the Cabinet in 1954, rejecting even the setting-up of a committee: 'I think that the question is not yet sufficiently acute and we should not, therefore, add to our difficulties.' Cock-up, not conspiracy.

Meanwhile, things were happening from the other direction. Although the number of West Indian migrants apparently fell after 1955 (no one could be sure, because even now no one was counting), incomers began arriving from South Asia. This took many different forms. The textile industry in the north of England believed itself desperate for labour, especially to work the unpopular night and weekend shifts. So they advertised in Indian and, especially, Pakistani newspapers, and then used their early recruits to spread the word: the 'Ali-get-Ali scheme'. But the mills were doomed, and by 1958 unemployment was rising generally, especially among the unskilled. By this time, a quarter of Pakistanis in both Bradford and Sheffield were already out of work, with bleak prospects for new arrivals.

There were happier stories further south. A single company was largely responsible for Southall's transformation from a nondescript patch of Middlesex to the Sikh capital of Britain. The R. Woolf rubber factory in nearby Hayes had a manager who had served with Sikh soldiers in the war and admired their work ethic. He was delighted to employ them. By 1960 there were a thousand Sikhs in Southall – almost all male, living maybe twenty to a house. They were served by what may have been Britain's first Asian corner shop, run by Pritam Singh Sangha, who sent his daughter round with the news whenever a new consignment of spices and lentils arrived from India. Southall was also handy for expanding London Airport, which offered (a) jobs and (b) flights – in case, so Sangha liked to say, they all got kicked out and had to fly home.

It was a kind of joke. But there were reasons to be uneasy. On a May night in 1959, death did come to the edge of Notting Hill. An Antiguan carpenter called Kelso Cochrane was walking home after midnight; he had been to hospital after breaking his thumb at work. He was set upon by three white youths and stabbed to death. The police insisted the motive was robbery, which was probably what might be called a white lie – to prevent a repeat of the previous year's riots. The police strategy was successful to that extent, but not in other ways: no one was ever charged.

Upmarket racialism had not gone away either. In July 1958 three American women – a doctor's wife, a librarian and a social worker – arrived at the reception desk of the much-lauded Goring Hotel in Victoria on their luxury trip round Europe. Asked what they wanted, they said they had reservations. 'There must be a mistake, there must be,' said the receptionist. She fetched the manager, who told them it was a strict rule: 'No coloured people.'

London was crowded because the world's Anglican bishops were in town for the decennial Lambeth Conference: at least twenty of them were in the hotel. The women waited four hours before new rooms were found, across London in Bloomsbury. There was a later report that the bishops were definitely discussing the incident and might just say or do something, but nothing to suggest they actually said or did anything.

The following week, the Labour MP John Baird introduced a parliamentary bill to ban such discrimination. It had no chance of immediate success but it was the first shot in a long and ultimately successful battle. He mentioned the case of the Scala Ballroom in Wolverhampton: it had had its licence renewed despite displaying a sign saying 'No coloured person will be admitted here', which was at least honest. And he did have the pleasure of describing the Goring as 'a common lodging house'.*

Early in 1954, a British troopship left Yokohama in Japan bound for Southampton. It was a long and trouble-plagued voyage, but the

---

* John Baird was father of the boy turned down for officer training, after questions about his father's politics. The hotel is still owned by the heirs of Otto Goring. It was an old favourite of the Queen, her mother and Mrs Thatcher.

ship reached Port Said safely and was finally heading home, almost full. Many of the passengers were soldiers wounded in Korea, some of them survivors from the Third Battle of the Hook, where Brian Hough had fought – and 160 women and children. Then, off the coast of Algeria, fire broke out in the engine room. Within two hours the flames had swept through the vessel. Many jumped from the blazing decks into the sea, some naked. Most waited calmly for the lifeboats: as if, said a survivor, they were in a slow cinema queue.

It was just after dawn, the sea was calm, several ships were nearby and responded rapidly; the ship stayed afloat until the following day. Apart from four men killed in the initial blaze, everyone else survived. It was a miracle, even though the vessel was completely in breach of fire regulations. The evacuation was everything that of the *Titanic* was not: a masterpiece of efficiency. The inquiry exonerated the captain and everyone else aboard. In Britain, the name of the ship is now almost as famous as the *Titanic*, yet it meant nothing at all at the time except in the context of its final hours. It was the *Empire Windrush*.

15

REACH FOR THE SKY

Through the decades, British politicians have become obsessed with a new statistic, fetishized it for a few years and then forgotten about it: the balance of payments had its day, as did inflation, unemployment, the money supply (though hardly anyone understood what that meant), the deficit, and then inflation again. In the 1950s it was the housing figures.

In the Ministry of Housing there was a kind of a cricket scoreboard showing the number of homes completed towards the government's election-led target – not a promise – of building 300,000 a year. The Tories' first post-war housing minister, Harold Macmillan, used the cricket analogy, and said how much he enjoyed seeing the runs accumulate. And in 1953, the Conservatives' second year back in government, they met the target, to warm applause.

One pertinent fact about cricket is that it can be more satisfying to score an elegant single than an ugly four, but the four still counts four times as much. Macmillan, in his house-building strategy, was not averse to ugly. And, for his purposes, a house was certainly a home, but a home was not necessarily a house.

The Attlee government, forever associated with austerity, was far more concerned about quality than the Tories. Aneurin Bevan, as Minister of Health, had authority over housing and wanted 'spacious homes fitted with all the labour-saving appliances invented by domestic science'. He even insisted on downstairs loos, as well as bathrooms for families used to neither. These were council houses: in the private sector, building and even repairs were severely restricted. But there were too many different ministries and local authorities involved. Under Labour, supply chains often failed to work: there would be bricks without bricklayers, bricklayers without bricks, and a lot of half-finished buildings. Macmillan sorted all that.

Churchill gave him full control and Macmillan immediately appointed a businessman, Percy Mills, to circumvent the Civil Service and solve the problems, and an MP called Ernest Marples as his junior minister. Marples was by temperament a 1980s Tory, born a generation too soon: self-made, self-aggrandizing, dynamic, corner-cutting. Together they scored the runs. But.

The surprise hit of 1940s building had been the supposedly temporary 'prefabs' – bungalows that were quick and cheap to build, but cosy, sanitary and with generous gardens. Built-in fridges, even. Most of the tenants loved them ('a place of wonder', said Neil Kinnock, who grew up in one) and a few of them – both houses and occupants – may yet celebrate their centenaries. There might be a lesson in that.

The classic sociological text of the 1950s was *Family and Kinship in East London*, a study of the old-established working-class community of Bethnal Green, many of whose inhabitants had already been decanted to the new council estate at Debden, twenty-five minutes further out on the Central line. The authors, Michael Young and Peter Willmott, lovingly described the old East End with its history of 'matrilocality'* and the small village-like 'turnings', each with its one or two pubs, its two or three shops, and its own runner employed by the local illegal bookmaker. Plus its own street parties and sometimes its own war memorial.

Young and Willmott contrasted this mostly favourably with

---

* i.e. Most couples lived near the wife's mother. And often with her, especially at first.

Debden, with its bathrooms and gardens but lack of shops, pubs and personality. 'Women feel the lack of friends, as of kin, more keenly than their menfolk.' Revisionists have accused Young and Willmott of over-sentimentalizing the old ways and ignoring the tensions and feuds; Professor Jon Lawrence has suggested that their findings even contradict Young's own notes. He also says that the population stability they idealized was itself a relatively new phenomenon, caused by rent controls being imposed on unbroken tenancies after the First World War – making mobility expensive.

Nonetheless, it is clear that the new towns and new estates did not live up to their billing. Bevan's 900-square-foot minimum for a family-of-five council house was changed by Macmillan into a maximum; the downstairs loos were junked. This was not just a case of government cutbacks, the phrase that rings – sometimes loud, sometimes muffled – throughout modern British history. The Tories wanted owner-occupiers, not mollycoddled and subsidized council tenants. These had, said the future Tory MP Charles Curran, 'the freedom of an adult . . . combined with the carefree security of a child'. He did not approve.

Promised amenities on the new estates rarely got built: nursery schools, playgrounds, community and health centres. In the new town of Newton Aycliffe in County Durham, housing densities were soon increased from eight to fourteen per acre, shortly after Lord Beveridge, founding father of the welfare state, retired as chairman of the town's corporation. The editor of the town's monthly newsletter complained: 'The village green community is being replaced by elongated terraces in rows upon rows like barracks, with no privacy, no refinement and very little green to break them up.'

But Macmillan's career was heading skywards and so was housing policy. In 1956 his successor as Minister of Housing, Duncan Sandys, slashed council-house subsidies to cut out just about everyone except the elderly and people displaced by the slum clearance that was now getting under way in earnest. Some of these houses were beyond saving; some not. Sandys made another change in funding to make it advantageous for councils to build higher blocks. 'The old system was inequitable,' Sandys told the Commons, adding: 'This has unintentionally influenced local authorities to concentrate on building blocks of three, four and five storeys, which, I believe, many honourable members will agree are most monotonous.' The reference to monotony fitted with the powerful and fashionable attack by the architectural critic Ian Nairn on the unvarying new suburbs that he christened 'Subtopia' in the *Architectural Review* in 1955.

Many of the tenants of the smallish blocks did not care for them either, like Mrs Lennon of the Bell Green estate in Coventry: 'I have a small baby. I can't get her outside at all unless I push her right round the back of the flats, where I can leave the pram under the window.' But Mrs Lennon's solution – a house and garden – was not the one favoured by Sandys.

There were good reasons to be tempted by high-rise. Britain does not have infinite amounts of land. The British do not regard countryside as empty space, as Americans do. By the mid-fifties, 150 acres of farmland were said to be disappearing every day. Green belts were being ordained around several cities but, especially in the south-east, houses just leapfrogged the barrier. And the new towns and new estates were starting to be seen as soulless and lonely as well as land-gobbling. Reaching for the sky spoke loudly to Macmillan, en route to Downing Street and still in search of quick runs. And even louder to a generation of architects in love with Le Corbusier and concrete and brutalism and, it has to be said, their own egos.

By 1957, London County Council was covering vast swathes of the East End with tower blocks 'some of them eighteen or nineteen storeys high', as the *Telegraph* reported in a tone of child-like wonder. And, that spring, work was beginning on the Park Hill estate in Sheffield. This incorporated the idea, pioneered by the power couple of British architecture, Peter and Alison Smithson, of 'streets in the sky' that were supposed to recreate the joy of neighbourliness fourteen floors up. The *Manchester Guardian* put it even more enticingly: 'All kinds of domestic supplies will be carried by elevators from the ground to verandas around each storey.' Lovely word, *veranda* – conjuring up gin and tonic and tropical sunsets. Perhaps the elevators would bring the ice and lemon.

————·————

Even the villages were changing. Lorna Sage grew up in Hanmer, just inside Wales near Wrexham. Early in the decade, her parents moved into a new council house: 'designed for the model family of the 1950s ads: man at work, wife home-making, children (two, one of each) sporty and clean and extrovert'. It was a major change: 'In Hanmer, up until then, your house came with your livelihood, more or less, and most roles had been passed on through generations.'

But those roles were disappearing. Farm workers were leaving the land at a rate of 20,000 a year, and later in the decade neither council houses nor anything else were being built in the villages.* Most farmers just replaced the men, and the horses, with tractors and combines and increased their output.† In the corn and potato lands of Lincolnshire, the migrant workers arrived at harvest time: Poles, Germans and Italians.

The local boys either commuted to urban jobs by car, bike or bus, or moved into the towns and cities, where the gin and tonics might just await them on their verandas.

---

* I saw it with a child's eyes in Northamptonshire: the empty stone cottage next-door-but-one gradually crumbled.

† In 1950, horses on farms outnumbered tractors by six to one.

16

OF DUKES AND DEBS

THE DAY THE BRITISH ARISTOCRACY CHANGED FOR EVER WAS 11 October 1953. That was when the body of the 12th Duke of Bedford was found in deep woodland on his Devon estate. There was a single shotgun wound to the head. In the wonderful film *Kind Hearts and Coronets*, released four years earlier, the fictional 8th Duke of Chalfont is found dead in very similar circumstances, having been murdered by the kinsman plotting to become the next duke.

It is highly unlikely that life was actually imitating art. True, the 13th Duke of Bedford had little love for his father, and vice versa. Against that, he had a cast-iron alibi, being at his fruit farm near Cape Town at the time; he was happy there and had no wish to become duke – and even if these facts were fake, it would have been far more profitable to wait a year, which would have avoided nearly £5 million in death duties. Only the government had a motive. The coroner quickly concluded it was an accident: it was the old duke's custom to go out shooting hawks who threatened his prize budgerigars.

So the new Duke of Bedford came back to the ancestral home, Woburn Abbey in Bedfordshire – a hopeless mess due to wartime decay and his father's neglect – found a few just about liveable rooms and wondered what to do next. Two traits ran through his lineage: there was more than a touch of insanity – his father had been a pro-Nazi evangelical Christian ('unusual views', said the *Telegraph*) – and the 9th Duke had shot himself in a fit of madness. But the 11th Duke, though 'forbidding, aloof and autocratic', clearly also had some flair for showmanship – he was closely involved with the foundation of Whipsnade Zoo. And No. 13 certainly had that gene.

There were twenty-seven non-royal dukes in the 1950s. Three dukedoms (Leeds, Newcastle and Portland) have since become extinct, not widely mourned. But in a country that steers clear of revolution, the dukes have mostly been rich and virile enough to avoid the great risks that can bring down a dynasty: war, Labour governments and infertility. Woburn was not the first stately home to be commodified, and even Blenheim Palace was already open to the public. But the new Bedford turned himself into a self-publicist surpassed in that era only by Lady Docker, and his park into a palace of varieties with everything from a petting zoo to occasional nudist weekends. The Duke of Marlborough, the master of Blenheim, denounced him as 'a cad'.

After the death, just after the Queen was crowned in 1953, of the formidable, philandering, fascist-leaning 'Bendor', the 2nd Duke of Westminster, the Inland Revenue set up a special sub-department to collect £20 million worth of death duties, which could then have paid for twenty coronations.

Lower down the scale of nobility, times were much harder. Costs, staff shortages, taxes and death duties made stately homes liabilities rather than assets, and, as the prices in *Country Life* showed, no one wanted to live in them. At least 400 historic country houses were demolished in the ten years after the war, and the peak came as late as 1955; empty ones were regularly destroyed by mysterious fires, as happens so often to unwanted but well-insured buildings. 'A national tragedy, indeed, a national scandal, is taking place before our eyes,' said Lord Crawford.

Some found new uses: schools, offices, training centres, even nunneries. As land values rose through the decade, those who clung on could survive, and when their daughters reached 18 they would aim to present them to the Queen as debutantes and give them their own 'coming out'* party, to announce their arrival on the social scene and the nuptial market. However, for some parents, maintaining the front was still a struggle. Phyllida Barstow, who chronicled this world, wrote that weekend guests might be told airily to put their shoes outside the bedroom door if they needed cleaning and the gardener's boy would see to them. But, she added, if you tactlessly opened the door at the sound of shoes being dropped, you would probably come face to face with your host. Men in grey top hats were seen travelling by bus to attend the Eton v. Harrow match at Lord's; and in 1955 *The Economist* estimated that three-quarters of the men wearing morning dress at Ascot had begged, borrowed or rented it.

———◦———

But the uppermost part of the upper class was untouched by the travails of those far down the order of precedence. Exempt from income tax, death duties and even the TV licence, the monarch's wealth now towered over even the richest dukes. The throne was also above criticism to an extent unknown in the two previous centuries – especially in those magical early years of Elizabeth II. The highest peak of celebrity was probably reached when she arrived at Sydney Harbour to be greeted by what was officially estimated as a million onlookers, more than half the city's population. And thus it went on almost throughout her two months in Australia.

Deep below the surface, there were rustlings. Even that rock-star reception had to be muted in Western Australia due to a polio epidemic: mostly the Queen self-isolated aboard SS *Gothic*; when the Queen stepped ashore, no one could come within six feet of her and there were no handshakes, a regime that would be echoed sixty-six years later. Bouquets from children were thrown in dustbins. Some felt it could have been handled more tactfully.

There was also the problem of her husband, who was still having trouble adjusting to life in his gilded cage. Most British people will

---

* A phrase that would acquire a very different meaning.

know nothing of their neighbours' sex lives (unless the walls are thin), yet they are all experts on the royal consort's alleged infidelities. And in the winter of 1956–57, the Duke of Edinburgh disappeared on a solo journey – entourage and crew excepted – on the royal yacht to the southern hemisphere, with royal duties of course, but a lot of down time as well. There were rumours of goings-on which peaked on the return journey when news broke that his friend, shipmate and equerry Mike Parker had broken up with his wife.

Rumours swirled about the duke himself and broke cover, as was then customary, in the American press: 'Queen, Duke in Rift Over Party Girl'. And it gathered momentum after the Palace denied it. Since the denial came from the permanently aloof and contemptuous Palace press office, the assumption was there was indeed a rift.

There was, however, a happy ending. Shortly afterwards, the Queen and her new prime minister, Harold Macmillan, agreed to give the duke the title 'Prince Philip' – a fetching love token, gratefully received. Two years later it was decided that their descendants without grander titles would bear the surname Mountbatten-Windsor, which salved the prince's self-esteem, even if it did not blind his roving eye. Whatever, they stayed married longer than only a handful of the Queen's subjects. And the dynasty was on both their minds: in 1959, after a ten-year gap, the Queen was pregnant again.

But as some issues receded, others took their place. In 1956, a young freelance photographer called Ray Bellisario had come across the Queen under an umbrella on a soaking-wet official visit to Cornwall. He sold the snap to several papers. Intrusive, said the Palace. Thus was launched a career for him and dozens of less durable imitators, and the start of an eternal irritation to the royal family.

The paparazzi would be one more headache in a job that was full of them. The Queen was young, ill-educated, with minimal experience of real life, beset by cobwebbed courtiers yet shielded from broader truths. She was ever-conscious of her uncle David, Edward VIII, who wanted everything his way and had paid with his throne. As a result, she may have erred on the side of stasis. Her subjects, wrote the politician Douglas Hurd in his royal biography, 'expect the Queen to move but not to be seen moving'.

By the mid-fifties, there was chuntering about her style from the cheeky chappies at the *Daily Mirror* and the licensed contrarian Malcolm Muggeridge. But in 1957 a single article hit home. It appeared in an obscure and otherwise-forgotten magazine called *The National and English Review*, and was written by the editor, John Grigg, who had recently and reluctantly acquired his late father's peerage as Lord Altrincham. It was moderate, guarded, loyal, constructive and sensible: he suggested that courtiers should be drawn from a wider social circle, the Queen should occasionally risk speaking more spontaneously, and that the 'grotesque' habit of presenting debutantes – from a narrow social circle – to the Queen should be abolished. How dare he?

'It will give widespread and justified offence,' said the London *Daily Telegraph*. 'Vulgar,' said papers as vulgar as the *Daily Express* and the Sydney *Daily Telegraph*.* 'He's a very silly man,' said the Archbishop of Canterbury. Altrincham had his face slapped in the street by a member of the (loopy) League of Empire Loyalists, and even the magistrate fining his assailant said that 95 per cent of people were disgusted by the article. And Altrincham Borough Council issued a statement dissociating themselves from their notional lord. Whether any of his critics had read the article remained unclear. As did the reason it caused so much fuss. But it was August, when news can be scarce; it came from a peer, which gave it cachet; above all, it hit a nerve. Three months later, the Palace quietly announced that the debs' presentations would cease after the following year. It was said that the Queen was bored witless by the whole ritual and glad to be shot of it; the prince even more so, pretty faces notwithstanding.

——·——

---

*   An enduringly rumbustious right-wing tabloid, now owned by Rupert Murdoch, unrelated to its British namesake.

And so, on a cold March afternoon in 1958, nearly 500 girls in chiffon and flimsy silk calf-length dresses (mostly pale blue that year) lined up outside the Palace railings to be briefly presented to the Queen and consort. Nearly all had been trained in the curtsey and attendant arts by a 'genteel sergeant-major' called Madame Vacani in a studio close to Harrods. A record 1,400 girls had applied, or their mothers had, so there would be two more days of this, as the royals may have glumly noted.

The presentation, and the season of parties and balls that would follow, was theoretically a means of preserving the purity of the human stud book. In theory, only girls whose mothers had themselves been presented were eligible, but increasingly there were ways round this. 'We had to put a stop to it,' Princess Margaret supposedly said later. 'Every tart in London was getting in.'

Fiona MacCarthy was one of that last cohort and later recorded the scene. 'What made that wait outside the palace so peculiarly memorable,' she said, 'was not just the savage weather assailing the poor debs . . . It was the deeper certainty that this whole old world of privilege and upper-class frivolity was doomed.' A small crowd watched this moment in history. 'It isn't the sight it used to be,' one elderly man told a *Times* reporter. 'In the old days, they wore tiaras and jewels and feathers. It was really something to see.'

———◆———

But the old ways were not necessarily dead. Around the same time, a lieutenant in the Life Guards – very possibly what was called a 'debs' delight' himself – went into the officers' mess wearing a dinner jacket. Asked where he was going, he said he was taking a girl to the opera. The following day he received a reprimand: he was informed that, while it was acceptable for a Life Guards officer to wear a black tie to the theatre, a white tie was obligatory at the opera.

17

SO GOOD

THE PHRASE THAT DEFINED A DECADE WAS APPARENTLY UTTERED at The Eyrie, the home of Bedford Town Football Club, in July 1957. It was an event unimaginable in modern times. A complex set-piece political speech that drew a crowd of 3,000 on a summer Saturday afternoon. All-comers admitted, including hecklers who were answered back, not bundled out. A light-hearted passage that required some familiarity with *The Pilgrim's Progress*. And security arrangements that were unobtrusive, close to non-existent.

Harold Macmillan had been prime minister for six months when he came to Bedford. Did he actually say 'You've Never Had It So Good'? What he said in the speech was 'most of our people have never had it so good', which was true. But that seemed to be part of a passage warning that this was now threatened by inflation.

However, with Macmillan, what you heard, or thought you heard, was not necessarily what you got. Some political commentators thought he was saying the reverse: that his own Chancellor, Peter Thorneycroft, was exaggerating the risks of inflation and was threatening prosperity. Macmillan later claimed that he *did* say '*You*'ve never had it so good', in response to a young boiler-suited heckler, contrasting his fortunes with those of pensioners. Anyway, both he and his Labour opponents fell in love with the phrase and were bandying it around in the Commons five days later and for years afterwards.

After Sir Anthony Eden's implosion at Suez, Macmillan had come through on the rails ahead of the more obvious Rab Butler. Again the mysterious Conservative process of 'consultations' came into play. These had been a formality two years earlier when Eden was Churchill's acknowledged heir.

On this occasion, and not for the last time, the pundits were wrong-footed. The Cabinet was near-unanimously for Mac, as were most of the backbenchers, their view shoved along by the normally aloof Butler's sudden appearances in the Commons smoking room as soon as the game was afoot. Butler was efficient and respected. But he was tainted by never having been a soldier (too young for the first war, a minister in the second), and above all by his role, as a junior minister, in Chamberlain's fateful talks with Hitler at Munich. 'I *had* to defend it,' he said many years later, adding that umbrellas had such horrible associations for him he had never carried one since. 'He was an appeaser *after* the war started,' said Joe Haines. 'He wasn't trusted.'

Macmillan was not exactly trusted either. His own equivocal role during Suez ('first in, first out,' it was said) left a legacy of bitterness on the Right. But there was something majestic in his slipperiness. He presented himself somewhere between a philosopher king and an aristocratic old fogey: 'Would you like to join my shooting party?' he asked prospective Cabinet ministers while embarking on a campaign of relentless modernization. He replaced Eden's manic energy with an air of calm, while in fact giving the government a sense of clear purpose it had lacked since Labour ran out of steam in the late 1940s.

Harold Wilson, the rising star of the Labour front bench, spotted what was happening: 'Macmillan is a genius. He is holding up the banner of Suez for the party to follow and is leading the party away from Suez.' He was leading the party away from all their totems. Without repudiating Eden, he hustled things along: a few months after the debacle he was having a pally summit with Eisenhower, quietly accepting Nasser's terms for using the canal and starting to extricate Britain from its ridiculous situation in Cyprus. Here the majority Greeks (who wanted union with Greece) had been distracted from their inclination to massacre the minority Turks (who wanted partition) by the opportunity of murdering British troops instead. The British retaliated with exemplary executions and discreet acts of torture.

Macmillan broke the deadlock by releasing the Greek Cypriot leader Archbishop Makarios from exile on the Seychelles. This had the added benefit of inciting the resignation of Lord Salisbury, who had become a nuisance. Salisbury had been seen as a necessary presence, a guardian of sound Tory principles. Macmillan thought the electorate were not interested in that. What they wanted, as the historian Professor Simon Ball put it, was 'peace, nest eggs and white goods'.

In May, Britain exploded a primitive hydrogen bomb over Christmas Island in the Pacific, where clearly no one of importance lived. This was useful cover for Macmillan, implying that Britain was still a major player, while behind the wisps of mushroom cloud he planned to almost halve the British Army's manpower and abolish National Service. And early in 1958 Macmillan finally clarified what he had meant at Bedford. Thorneycroft and his two junior Treasury ministers, Nigel Birch and Enoch Powell, wanted to maintain fiscal discipline and curb social spending; Macmillan believed in Keynesian economics and winning the next election. Macmillan prevailed, and the trio resigned in a huff. He shrugged such matters off as 'little local difficulties', and then flew off to tour the Commonwealth. A year on from Suez – and Elvis – it was possible to discern a new era. One might almost call it the 1960s.

———•———

By late 1957, seven in eight households were still without a fridge, four-fifths had no phone and three-quarters no washing machine. About one in fifty had central heating. But more than half now had a television, and most of them, most of the time, were watching ITV rather than the BBC. The adverts fed the nation's increasing acquisitiveness.

And so did the programmes. A fridge or washing machine might well be 'tonight's star prize' on *Take Your Pick!* with Michael Miles on a Friday night; winning the £1,000 Treasure Trail jackpot on Hughie Green's *Double Your Money* on Thursday would buy both – and several of the newly available Continental package holidays thrown in. Green, with the mid-Atlantic accent of a Radio Luxembourg disc jockey and the self-promoting smarm of Ernest Marples, was the very embodiment of early ITV.

But the real stars were the adverts. Though the programmes were largely American, the ads were not. Much of the commercial content on US TV comprised bored hosts forced to recite 'a word from our sponsors' – far too many words quite often. But with sponsored programmes banned in Britain and advertising time restricted, thirty-second slots rapidly developed in Britain into an art form that spread worldwide.

'Spot ads did exist in the States but the advertising was pre-dominately anchorman-led,' recalled the advertising legend Jeremy Bullmore, who joined J. Walter Thompson in 1954. 'I remember thinking, "How can anyone do anything in thirty seconds?" But within a few years great skills had developed in economy of communication and little of that was learned from the States. But we clearly did influence the US.'

And the stars of the commercial breaks were the jingles. One jingle-writer alone, a former singer called Johnny Johnston, was said to be responsible for the chords, and sometimes the words, of 4,500 of them:

> 'Rael-Brook Toplin – the shirt you don't iron.'
> 'Now hands that do dishes can be soft as your face, with mild green Fairy Liquid.'
> 'This is the luxury you can afford. Buy Cyril Lord.' [carpets]
> 'Keep going well, keep going well, you're going well with Shell, Shell, Shell.'

And, above all:

> 'A million housewives every day pick up a can of beans and say: Beanz meanz Heinz.'

Names fade from the mind, faces fade, children of the fifties can no longer remember why they have just opened the fridge, but those jingles never fade.

After 1956, the main cost-of-living index was changed to reflect the changing realities: out went candles, rabbits and turnips; in came soda water, dog food, nylons, camera films and second-hand cars. At first, ITV did not share the nation's growing prosperity. Three months after the network's launch in 1955, the *Daily Express*, whose owner Lord Beaverbrook had rejected the chance to invest in it, gleefully ran the headline ITV: STAGGERING LOSSES. The controllers panicked, cut back on news and banished the contractual-obligation cultural content to the margins.

Beaverbrook's rival, the *Daily Mail* – whose owner Lord Rothermere had said yes – lasted two years, lost nearly £3 million and sold out, just before the turn. By 1959 the London weekday station Associated-Rediffusion was making over £7 million a year, profits then regarded as obscene. Roy Thomson, the Canadian who bought *The Times* and *Sunday Times* thanks to the profits he made from Scottish TV, said an ITV franchise was 'a licence to print your own money', a comment he may have regretted.

But though ITV was dominating the ratings, the BBC was not lying doggo. Grace Archer's fiery death on opening night was a harbinger. The director-general for most of the fifties was Sir Ian Jacob, normally described dismissively as 'an old soldier', a cipher between the starchy William Haley (emphatically not to be confused with Bill Haley) and the very sixties figure of Hugh Carleton Greene (equally not to be confused with Hughie Green).

The journalist Nicholas Faith argued persuasively that the snazzed-up BBC had put down roots much earlier – that Jacob was the true reformer and Greene his protégé. On Jacob's watch came ground-breaking programmes like the nightly current affairs show *Tonight*, the potent interviews of *Face to Face* and the entrenchment of the BBC's sporting dominance. Meanwhile, ITV was besotted with very watchable Americo-trash. Jacob's big failing, Faith admitted, was to be too slow in reforming the dreary news department while the combative Robin Day was bringing tough modern interview techniques to ITV. But Jacob did face down Eden during Suez when the government demanded propaganda.

Meanwhile, Bernard Levin, commissioned by the *Manchester Guardian* to tell its then fastidious readers about ITV, heroically lasted more than two years before running out screaming. 'The overwhelming majority of programmes on ITV are, always have been, and, as far as I can see, always will be, beneath contempt,' he concluded. 'Besides, I have other ways to spend an evening.'

Macmillan actually lost a by-election to the Liberals in early 1958, which was like being savaged by a presumed-dead sheep. One complication for him was the triumphant return to power of the unbiddable General de Gaulle in France after years of weak, rotating governments. Out of office, de Gaulle had opposed the Common Market. Inside, he embraced and sought to dominate the new body.

But by mid-year, with the meanie ministers out of the Treasury, the polls turned favourable for the Tories. In 1959 the new Chancellor, Derick Heathcoat-Amory, produced a giveaway budget on cue. Average wage-earners gained a few quid; the tiny number on £100,000 gained nearly £4,000 – but they were still paying £85,000 in tax. The British kept spending, or at least acquiring debt, by buying their big wants on the never-never. Also on cue for the prime minister came one of the finest summers of the century. Suez was long forgotten. As summer turned to autumn, the grateful voters duly handed Macmillan an increased majority.

It was a prototype modern election, with both TV channels playing a major role and the Conservatives craftily targeting the *nouveau*-not-so-*pauvre*. Peter Hennessy thought Britain had a choice between two class acts: the skill of Macmillan and the 'fierce straightness' of the Labour leader, Hugh Gaitskell. They have had no such choice since. *The Times* was not impressed. Grudgingly recommending a Tory majority, the leader column saw 'no conviction or fire . . . It is not thus that a great people are summoned to yet another session in their endless appointment with history.'

Or perhaps it was a sign of a people feeling more contentment and optimism and unity than they had known before or ever
would again.

———·———

In 1957 a new cartoon strip appeared in the northern edition of the
Daily Mirror. It was drawn by Reg Smythe from Hartlepool, and it
was obviously set thereabouts. Its central figure wore a cloth cap,
indoors and out; had a permanent fag-end (look-no-hands) between
his lips, drank pints every night, thumped his wife regularly, got
into a tin bath by the fire irregularly and worked hardly at all.

Within a year Andy Capp had spread to the *Mirror*'s London
edition. Soon after that, quite astonishingly, it began being syndica-
ted to vast numbers of newspapers, big and small, across the US.
Apart from the Queen, Churchill, London fog, Sherlock Holmes
and, eventually, The Beatles, he was probably the sum total of
small-town America's knowledge of Britain. He was not quite what
the Conservative Party had in mind when it put out a poster before
the 1959 election showing a man in a cloth cap captioned 'You're
Looking at a Conservative'.

But who knew who was what any more? The Labour-supporting
Mirror had run the vaguely Soviet slogan 'Forward with the
People' on its front page since 1945; four days after the 1959
election, it disappeared.

At least Labour could be sure of its status as the only alternative.
The Liberals made no progress, though a bright young chappie
called Jeremy Thorpe captured North Devon. The nationalist votes
in Scotland and Wales were derisory, and in Scotland the Tories
lost seats, a tiny cloud. All twelve of the Northern Ireland seats
were won as usual by Ulster Unionists, reliable Tory allies. They
had no coherent moderate opposition; Sinn Féin, the political wing
of the Irish Republican Army, contested every seat, without much
campaigning since most of the candidates were locked up for their
part in the low-level and futile IRA resistance of the time.

Ulster was run by the Protestants for the Protestants, with its
own prime minister and cabinet, and no one in London cared. Its

government was led, lackadaisically – for twenty years – by the grandee Lord Brookeborough who, on first joining the Ulster Cabinet in 1933, had marked the occasion by firing 125 of his estate workers, i.e. every single Catholic he employed. 'He was good company and a good raconteur,' said the man who would eventually succeed him, Terence O'Neill. 'Those who met him imagined he was relaxing away from his desk. What they didn't realize was that there was no desk.'

18

KEEP GOING WELL

ALONG WITH THE SOUND OF THE JINGLES, A SINGLE SMELL OF the fifties lingers. It is the whiff of an old-fashioned grocer's shop. Every child of that generation seems to remember it; hardly anyone can describe it. 'A mixture of sliced ham, sliced cheese and the starch of the shopkeeper's coat' was the most succinct version I heard. Some think broken biscuits and a mound of butter on a marble-top table come into it.

My mum, a non-driver, would take me into Northampton on the bus and I would imbibe that smell in Kingham's, Civil's or James Bros or the old-fashioned Sainsbury's, airier than the local shops with an enormous slab of marble as a worktop, but still not self-service. Even a substantial town with a huge outdoor market had no actual supermarket and only a handful of national chains, like M&S, Boots and Mac Fisheries (with its own unforgettable smell).

There were still callers. The Liverpudlian Oxford graduate Gillian Reynolds's mum bought her first vacuum cleaner from a door-to-door salesman. Others came bearing brushes, pots and pans or their own paintings. In our village in Northamptonshire there would always be Mr Clifton the baker and Mr Toms the greengrocer, and the odd tramp. Mr Clifton found us our cairn terrier. In the Metroland suburb of Kingsbury, the Frank family became friendly with their dustman, James Hanratty – always Mr

Hanratty. His pleasant if not very bright son, also James, helped them build their garage.

———•———

Ball games aside, Cowboys and Indians dominated boys' play more than ever, as though this was some eternal verity of boyhood rather than a reflection of Hollywood's and now ITV's reliance on westerns. There was still Cops and Robbers, but the BBC was sending us a strangely pacific message. In 1955 it began showing *Dixon of Dock Green*, which soon settled into a family viewing slot early on a Saturday evening.

The premise of the series required a suspension of belief from the start since it centred round the same character and actor (PC George Dixon, played by Jack Warner) who had been shot dead five years earlier in a hit film, *The Blue Lamp*. And again, as time went on, with Dixon still in uniform and Warner reaching 80, it became both ridiculous and anachronistic as more abrasive and violent police dramas took hold.

In the mid-fifties, though, Dixon fitted the middle-class perception of its police force: unimpeachable, gentle souls who might just give a young scamp the proverbial clip round the ear'ole for scrumping a few apples from a neighbour's orchard, but would never dream of inventing evidence to get someone hanged. Almost simultaneously, and one assumes coincidentally, British crime figures began an upward trend that would last almost forty years. Oddly, though, the popular press seemed rather less hysterical about crime in the late fifties than in the heyday of the cosh boys and Teds a few years earlier.

One long-forgotten case did attract attention, and it focused on an aspect of policing far removed from gentle George Dixon. It happened in mainland Britain's most northerly town, Thurso – isolated, chilly and, especially for teenagers, dull. In December 1957, two policemen came into a cafe at 10.30 on a Saturday night to an unfriendly reception from a group of youths, one of whom, John Waters, ended up being taken down an alleyway and thumped by one of the coppers – which was probably happening in dull towns from Thurso to the Scillies (Dock Green excepted) on a regular basis.

But the Waters family made a fuss. The other copper offered them a bribe to keep quiet. And the 'Thurso Boy' shemozzle ended with questions in parliament, prime-ministerial intervention and a public tribunal, which sided with the boy, whereupon the Caithness Constabulary had to decide on the action they would take against the policemen . . . which was nothing. And everyone in Thurso lived more quietly ever after.

Meanwhile, the ultimate penalty was becoming rarer. Twice since the war the Commons had voted to abolish hanging; twice the Lords had thrown it out. In 1957 the government forced through a compromise. Murder would be a capital offence only for serial killings, shootings, explosions, murders in the course of theft or while escaping or resisting arrest – or for the murder of a police or prison officer. The number of hangings was cut by two-thirds to about four a year. It was a compromise that pleased no one except the genteel poisoners and stranglers who were now spared.

And it did not stop controversy. In 1959 Ronald Marwood was convicted of stabbing a policeman in a drunken brawl outside a North London dance hall. It was a messy case. He was hitherto a solid citizen; he gave himself up; the evidence was not clear-cut. It might have been manslaughter; he might have been reprieved. But the Home Secretary, now Rab Butler, honoured the custom that police killers had to hang.

———◆———

Another hugely popular TV programme of the era was a comedy, though it was perhaps more realistic than Dixon. ITV's National Service sitcom, *The Army Game*, shown from 1957 to 1961, showed a group of stock-character conscripts – the gormless one, the skiving one, the tubby one, the effete one, the crafty corporal – all battling against the sergeant-major and the general nonsenses of military life. Production values were primitive but it was gloriously written and acted, and spoke directly to the nation's menfolk who had been through it all and the womenfolk who had done so vicariously.

The series began two months after the announcement that National Service was ending. Even though the Army wanted fewer people, it now had to compete with other employers to get more suitable ones. And that produced a tragi-comic situation no scriptwriter would have dared invent.

In January 1959, Rifleman Terence Williams, born ten months too early to escape the call-up, was inducted into the Green Jackets, accompanied by a large media contingent shepherded by army officers with apparent expertise in the infant art of public relations. 'We are sure his joining the Army will help recruiting,' said one of them. They had the wrong man. Terence Williams was better known as Terry Dene, one of the wave of young British pop stars who surfaced in Elvis's wake. And Elvis was the template for this exercise. He had already been drafted and was serving as a hunky GI – a conscientious one too. The great man refused a cushy number and mucked in, acquiring skills in marksmanship, karate and, less happily, amphetamine use. Dene was a more fragile character. Within two days he was in a psychiatric ward. Within eight days he was recommended for discharge.

On his first night back on stage in Derby, he was met by competing factions, some chanting 'We love you, Terry' and others 'Left-right, left-right'. He had a very public marriage break-up and sought refuge in the gentler world of gospel singing. Shortly afterwards, another incipient rock star, Marty Wilde, failed his medical due to 'corns'. In the Commons, MPs lumped together Dene, Wilde and the Thurso Boy, in a general denunciation of youth's diminishing moral fibre.

———•———

The BBC's gently nostalgic series glorifying Scottish country doctors, *Dr Finlay's Casebook*, did not arrive until 1962; it ran for nine years, televisual balm for those who found the decade too unnerving. But there were real-life rural equivalents across the country. Denys Brierley qualified as a doctor in 1948, just as the National Health Service began; like most of his contemporaries he did not like the idea much; unlike many of them, who took refuge in the US or the White Dominions, he stayed, and in 1954 moved to a general

practice in the Golden Valley in Herefordshire, a community so
rural it was still a decade away from electricity. That was no
problem: 'We had paraffin: the heaters were warmer than a two-bar
electric fire and the lamps were as strong as a hundred-watt bulb.'

And he eventually came to realize he was also living in a golden
age: medical advance was making the hopeless cases curable and
the difficult routine. 'In the fifties it was marvellous,' Dr Brierley
recalled. 'You got antibiotics which changed everything. They had
to be used intelligently, which a lot of GPs didn't do. But before
then, people came with sore throats, got tonsillitis and were ill for a
month. That's why tonsils came out. Or you could get rheumatic
fever and it could spread to the heart. They'd get St Vitus's dance.
And for TB, streptomycin came in and at first it really did work.'

His enthusiasm was echoed by Dr John Marks, who also started
as a GP in 1954, in the very different surroundings of Hertfordshire,
serving the new council estate at Borehamwood. 'When I qualified,
hip treatment was science fiction and a heart transplant ridiculous.
Polio was just starting to drop away, along with diphtheria, smallpox, whooping cough, tetanus.* So there was more attention for
previous untreated symptoms, like prolapses and male ruptures.
Before that, people either wore a truss or put up with it.'

Getting out of bed for house calls was part of the job. But Brierley
would know it must be serious. 'There was a culture that you just
got on with things. I think that was true everywhere but more so in
a farming community. If you got an illness you just threw it off.
This had pluses and minuses. Sometimes they would have serious
symptoms and leave it too late.'

Bureaucracy was invisible. One day a doctor they had never met
came out and asked to have lunch with Brierley and his partners. 'I
suppose he was inspecting us but he never let on. We never had any
interference.' And doctors certainly did not have to worry about
their patients' opinions.

---

* Polio, which could develop into 'infantile paralysis' and permanent disability, was
a major scourge of children until the development of a vaccine in the 1950s. Britain
has had no confirmed case of paralysis since 1984.

When Kay Kendall, actress wife of actor Rex Harrison, died of leukaemia in 1959 aged just 32, the *Daily Mirror* headline was THE SECRET THEY ALL KEPT FROM KAY. She was treated like the late King. 'We all knew, as she did not, that she was critically ill,' wrote Donald Zec, now the *Mirror*'s showbiz columnist. 'Harrison, told before anyone how grave it was, played out his role superbly.' In the *Express*, Anne Scott-James questioned the strategy: 'I think she would have liked to have been treated like a brave adult instead of a tender child.' This viewpoint would eventually win the argument.

———•———

Perhaps TV medical dramas were responsible for changing the doctor-as-God syndrome. By the end of the fifties the new medium's tentacles had reached into every corner of British life. And the mighty cinema industry was under threat: 26 million filmgoers a week in 1952 had dwindled to 11 million by 1959. In 1956, the Rank Organisation, the UK's leading film company (whose Rank starlets, mostly busty, had epitomized the golden years), began closing cinemas en masse. By 1959 it was starting to convert its Odeons and Gaumonts into bowling alleys and then bingo halls.

Even so, Britain was still Hollywood's most important overseas market. Zec, travelling to Los Angeles regularly for Britain's top-selling daily, got the benefit of that. 'Americans like numbers,' he explained. 'Five million sales meant fourteen million readers. So in one week I interviewed Gary Cooper, Henry Fonda, Humphrey Bogart and Kirk Douglas. Not for my pretty face.' Once, Bogart called him as soon as he had checked in and ordered him to report to his yacht on Saturday morning for a weekend's sailing. He flew first-class, often in Seat 1A.

The theatre was also experiencing headwinds. Both cinema and the stage understandably bitched about entertainment tax, which comprised a quarter to a half of the cost of a ticket. 'If theatres continue to close,' said Dame Edith Evans, 'we would become in due course a nation of inarticulate morons.'*

---

* I like to think of her saying this in her Lady Bracknell voice.

Pubs were also in trouble. In Norfolk, landlords won the right to open later to attract drinkers after TV shut down. And in Heanor, Derbyshire, a quarter of the district's forty publicans were said to have taken other jobs and deputed their wives to run the bar. And another great British institution was in its death throes. A deal to sell Collins Music Hall on Islington Green fell through early in 1958; it was conveniently damaged by fire a few months later and never re-opened.

That left only three theatres in London still showing regular weekly variety – but even they mostly preferred TV stars and pop singers to the old-fashioned turns. Still, the young Australian Barry Humphries, newly arrived in London in 1959, was in time to catch the Metropolitan on the Edgware Road: 'You could sit up there in the gods and you were in a picture by Sickert. You could smoke, of course, and sip a pint of old and mild, and lean over the brass rail and there, way down there on the stage, was Hetty King in her mariner's suit, smoking her pipe and singing "All the Nice Girls Love a Sailor".' Or Randolph Sutton. Or G. H. Elliott. All of that, and all of them, would be gone soon enough.

Nationwide, more than a hundred music halls had closed since the war. The old ways lingered in resorts like Blackpool, where the impresario gave a special dispensation to allow a single nightly use of *bloody* for a bit of shock value.

And there were still the old repertory theatres, just about. Edward Barnes worked in several doing weekly rep, as actor and stage manager: 'You'd do a dress rehearsal on the Monday, then the day after the play opened, you'd start rehearsing the next production. Playing twice nightly quite often.' One of his stints was at the Theatre Royal, St Helens. On top of the normal punishing regime, they had an extra wrinkle. 'A special Friday night melodrama, only two performances – nothing to do with the other play they were doing all week, except that it had the same actors,' he recalled. 'On Friday you'd go in knowing you wouldn't know it but hoping you'd get away with it. As long as you had an approximation of what you were doing and got down to the cue at the end it was OK. We had full houses on Friday and Saturday. I was very happy there.'

In 1950, Northampton (population: 100,000) had ten cinemas; it went down to six in the sixties, then two, then, when the population was close to doubling, to a single screen, before multiplexes changed the dynamic. The town also had two theatres, one of them the New Theatre, opened in 1912 – a handsome building that for forty years held its own at the bottom end of what was known as 'the No. 1 circuit', the theatres who could attract big names for variety or more challenging plays.

But TV did for all that. The New Theatre closed in 1958. The shows towards the end included *We've Nothing On To-night*, *Sexciting*, *The Naughtiest Girl of All*, *We Never Clothed*, *My Bare Lady* and *Strip! Strip! Hooray!* The Newd Theatre, they called it at the end. And after that there really was nothing on tonight.*

Some theatres rebranded themselves by adding the word *Continental* to their title, which meant they ripped out the stalls, put in tables and chairs, and served food – 'famous continental dishes, like pie and chips', as the comedian Roy Hudd put it. That was even less successful than the strippers. But the last great music-hall comic was still standing, just about. Max Miller, the Cheeky Chappie, had played the Metropolitan often enough and was in the West End, and getting good reviews, in 1959. One of his gifts was knowing just how far he could take the cheek and the double entendres, all based on his instinctive feel of a live audience.

'I never know till halfway through one gag what the next one is going to be,' Miller told his biographer. 'I must have a free hand. I'm a solo turn, first, foremost and for ever. I don't want production, thank you. Nobody, not God Almighty, can tell me how to perform. Television – that's the thing of the future, but it's not for me.' His last stage appearance came the following year, and he died in 1963, aged 68. There'll never be another, as he used to say.

There was not a lot Miller or anyone else could say on the BBC: 'God, Good God, My God, Blast, Hell, Damn, Bloody, Gorblimey,

---

* Aged six, I attended (and adored) the New Theatre's last Christmas panto, Cyril Fletcher in *Sleeping Beauty*. There was no suggestion that I might go to any of the other productions round that time.

Ruddy etc. etc.' were all specifically banned from all light entertainment shows by the *BBC Variety Programmes Policy Guide* of
1949, which held sway well into the 1950s. – the 'etc. etc.' presumably covering words that were too indelicate even to put in the
policy guide. That must have included *bastard*, since even *basket* –
the traditional euphemism – was itself banned.

Jokes about 'lavatories, effeminacy in men and immorality of
any kind' were taboo, as were references to 'honeymoon couples,
chambermaids, fig leaves, prostitution, ladies' underwear e.g. winter
draws on, animal habits e.g. rabbits, lodgers and commercial
travellers' – the last three all being regarded in folklore as particularly
promiscuous, though the list curiously omits milkmen.* Eventually,
the BBC allowed people to laugh about the policy guide.

———•———

Football crowds also went down during the fifties, though its
theatres were not demolished, they merely decayed. Average
attendances in the top division, the First, dropped from a peak of
nearly 39,000 in 1949 to under 32,000. The clubs were primarily
local, mainly run by muck-and-brass businessmen – not necessarily
all that rich themselves but a great deal richer than their players.
They were running a slavery racket.

By the end of the 1950s, players' wages had increased to £20 a
week: that was not an average, nor the minimum, it was the
maximum (and it was lower in the summer). The greatest players in
the country – Stanley Matthews, Tom Finney, Johnny Haynes – all
got the same, a figure somewhat above the average man's wages,
but not by much. If they objected, well, fine, they could do something
else for a living, but not football, anywhere: the club would refuse
to release their registration.

There were ways round it, but not many. Matthews, acting as

---

* There may have been some significance to the guide's distribution in 1949, the year
  Max Miller finished serving a five-year ban from the airwaves for telling an
  unscripted joke so gloriously filthy that it would not have been approved in any era
  of the BBC's existence. Somewhat ahead of its time, the guide banned the word
  nigger but made a specific exemption for *nigger minstrels*.

his own agent, charged £100 for personal appearances; Finney thought about moving from Preston after a big offer from Italy which was blocked by his club's chairman. Instead, England's greatest outside-left made pocket money by practising his other trade – plumbing. Others spent summers on building sites. For less lustrous stars, there was the amateur football of the north-east, *amateur* being a splendid example of the era's discreet hypocrisy: in the words of the County Durham journalist Mike Amos, 'even an average player would find a lot more than a leather tongue in his boot'.

Footballers' solidarity was enhanced by homogeneity. They were, almost to a man, working-class, Anglo-Saxon or Celt, tough and unpretentious. They had lived through the war, done National Service, and most might have ended up in a factory. What was there to complain about? They lived in their communities and waited at bus stops with everyone else. Exotics were rare: most famously Manchester City had the goalkeeper Bert Trautmann, an ex-German PoW who won them the 1956 FA Cup with some spectacular saves while obviously injured. The problem was later diagnosed as a broken neck. He probably did more for Anglo-German relations than any diplomat.

True, with the top rate of tax above 80 per cent, it was an egalitarian era. But Max Miller was not paid £20 a week, and nor was Tommy Trinder, the original host of *Sunday Night at the London Palladium*, the top-rated TV show of the late fifties – and also Johnny Haynes's boss as chairman of Fulham.

Other sports stars existed even more precariously. Rugby union players were not paid at all, unless they headed north to play professional rugby league, in which case they were banished for ever from the boozy camaraderie of their old clubhouses – though the idea of north-eastern-style boot money is thought to have just about arrived in the Welsh game before 1960.

Cricket comprised a mixture of poorly paid professionals and amateurs who were assumed not to need paying, though sinecures might be found to help them out. Money was never really discussed until Denis Compton, the most charismatic player of his generation, opened a huge suitcase of unopened mail which he assumed were requests for autographs. One letter was a huge offer of £2,000 a year to write a newspaper column; another, dated six months later, withdrew it for lack of response. Compton then met the businessman Bagenal Harvey, who took over his affairs and thus became Britain's first sports agent. He made Compton, among much else, the face of Brylcreem, the male hair goo, which was responsible for the shiny, straight hair of most of the nation's sportsmen, Teddy Boys and much smaller boys.

The most famous cricketing feat of the decade was the Ashes-winning performance of Jim Laker, who took nineteen wickets in the 1956 Manchester Test match, then had to make the long pre-motorway journey to London to play for Surrey the next day. He stopped for a beer in a pub that was showing the news, and Laker watched his still-unmatched feat on a tiny TV on the bar with the other customers. No one recognized him. In one version, the barman remarked on the uselessness of the Aussie batting. 'Too right,' said Jim, downing his pint.

Tennis players were amateur unless they joined Jack Kramer's American pro tour, which was good sense but considered poor form; they tried to win Wimbledon before signing, since they were banned thereafter. Professional golf was considered legitimate and the first prize at the Open Championship – £100 in 1939 – had reached £1,000 in 1959. Some of the golfers still played wearing ties.

Sport mattered but then again it didn't. Yards from winning the 1956 Grand National, the Queen Mother's horse Devon Loch jumped an imaginary fence and slithered to the ground. The owner left her box and went straight to comfort the jockey, trainer and stable lads. 'It was the most perfect display of dignity I have ever witnessed,' said the Duke of Devonshire afterwards.

In 1954, on a damp cinder track in Oxford and having trained only very part-time, Roger Bannister became the first man to run a mile in under four minutes. That night he and his friends and pacemakers, the Chrisses – Chataway and Brasher – walked up Harrow Hill and looked down on the lights of London. 'We didn't have anything to say to each other,' Bannister recalled later. 'We all knew that the world was at our feet and that we could do anything we wanted in life.' What Bannister wanted to do was give up running, which he did less than six months later, to concentrate on his career as a neurologist, at which he also excelled.

Twenty-three days after the run that made Bannister world-famous, on more wet cinders, this time in Birmingham, another barrier in the history of the mile was broken. A local girl called Diane Leather became the first woman to run it in less than five minutes. She received somewhat less fanfare than Bannister; indeed her time was not even officially treated as a world record. After six women had collapsed at the end of the 800 metres at the 1928 Olympics, the idea of them racing any distance longer than 200 metres was seen as unladylike and dangerous. Leather did, however, have tea with the Lord Mayor of Birmingham. She became a social worker, a Samaritan and a mother of four, and bore no resentment whatever. To her too, sport was just sport.

————◦————

In 1957, the Wolfenden Report on prostitution and homosexuality was published. The government gratefully accepted its recommendations on the first aspect – to take it indoors in keeping with traditional British discretion – and in time duly legislated.

On the second, it was less welcoming. The report proposed the legalization of sexual relations between consenting male adults (21 and over). It was received with applause from surprising quarters, including the Archbishop of Canterbury (who still thought it a sin) and the *Daily Express*. It was condemned by the *Daily Mail* ('. . . would certainly encourage an increase in perversion'), and the *Sunday Express* columnist John Gordon, who called the report 'a pansies' charter'. A *Daily Mirror* poll found readers narrowly against reform. The government stuck with the status quo and did nothing.

This was probably wise. For a start, no change in the law was likely to get past such Tory MPs as James Dance of Bromsgrove, who blamed 'unnatural vice' for the fall of both the Roman Empire

and Nazi Germany. According to the modern gayfinder-general
Michael Bloch, of the three Tory prime ministers of the decade
(Churchill, Eden and Macmillan), 'none was a stranger to homosexuality'. Mostly youthful, even if true. But perhaps there were
reasons for discretion.

The most surprisingly discreet aspect of the report's aftermath
was the behaviour of the press. Sir John Wolfenden's fears that
his position as chairman might be compromised by his son Jeremy's
blatant homosexuality proved unfounded. Not a word was
printed about this, even though dozens of London journalists must
have known.

And though the practice was illegal and would remain so until
1967, the campery associated with it was a staple of British comedy,
from pantomime to the piers and even on air. Homosexuality could
be inferred but never imputed or admitted. No one was higher-
camp than the American pianist/entertainer/show-off Liberace, who
arrived in Britain in 1956 to be met by hordes of adoring women
and a tirade of adjectives from the *Mirror* columnist Cassandra,
who called him a 'deadly, winking, sniggering, chromium-plated,
scent-impregnated, luminous, quivering, giggling, fruit-flavoured,
mincing, ice-covered heap of Mother Love'.

Even his colleague Donald Zec thought he had overdone it: 'a
huge artillery barrage aimed at demolishing a meringue'. It was
adjective No. 9 that proved fatal – *fruit* implying Liberace was
homosexual. He told the libel jury he was not. He lied. He won,
and won big: £8,000 in damages, enough to pay almost the entire
annual wage bill of any football team in the land. 'I cried all the way
to the bank,' he said afterwards.

———•———

An earthly decade is merely a random grouping of ten rotations of
the sun, which somehow helps us construct some kind of sense from
our messy lives. Was there a single event in Britain, as the 1950s
gave way, that foreshadowed some kind of a new era?

Perhaps it came just before Christmas 1959, with an exhibition
at County Hall in London called *High Buildings* showing the new

skyscraper office blocks planned for the banks of the Thames: the Shell Centre and what would become known as Millbank Tower. 'Tall blocks provide architectural distinction in the skyline,' said Hubert Bennett, the London County Council's chief architect. 'It is considered unlikely that buildings higher than these two will be put up in London,' predicted the *Daily Telegraph*.

Perhaps it had come at the start of 1959, inside the still low-rise offices of the actual City of London. A cosy deal, engineered by Establishment bankers, to sell British Aluminium to an American rival Alcoa was upended by a German Jewish refugee called Siegmund Warburg, who put together a rival consortium. This brief skirmish turned into a rout of the old guard, to the immense benefit of British Aluminium's shareholders. 'Business in the square mile would never be the same,' reflected *Management Today* decades later.

Perhaps it was the new Obscene Publications Act in 1959, piloted by a young Labour MP Roy Jenkins, which allowed 'literary merit' to be used as a defence against Cromwellian chief constables and magistrates. Perhaps it was the government's decision, two weeks after being re-elected in October 1959, to abolish all restrictions on spending money for holidays overseas, enabling people to take expensive foreign holidays as well as cheap ones.

Perhaps it was the death that spring of the Dowager Marchioness of Londonderry, the great society hostess of the 1930s. Perhaps it was the upper-class riot staged on the Circle line in March, when a couple of hundred posh hell-raisers commandeered a train for a party. Lord Valentine Thynne, younger son of the Marquess of Bath, was to the fore, showing the Teds that yobbery was thoroughly egalitarian.

Or perhaps it came with an unnoticed moment in the lives of two entirely unknown people: when a West London landlord tried to set himself up for the sixties by acquiring an ambitious teenager as his mistress. His name was Peter Rachman; hers was Christine Keeler.

But the old world maundered on. There was still smog; there were still terrible and avoidable accidents. Sometimes one caused the other: ninety were killed in a train crash in smog at Lewisham just before Christmas 1957. There was still Lady Docker, just about, who announced in March 1959 that £100,000 worth of jewellery had been stolen from her Rolls-Royce while she was opening a hairdressing salon in Southampton. The other great fifties character Billy Hill visited her at home and offered to help find them, free of charge.

And there was still Archbishop Fisher, getting ever odder. In November 1959 he suggested that adultery might be made a criminal offence. The *Church Times* gently pointed out that this did not quite square with his previously expressed support for legalizing homosexuality – and that there might be a problem housing the prisoners.

The world did not feel exactly safe. The launch of the first Sputnik in 1957 created extreme unease – especially in the US, fearful that the Soviet Union was ahead in both exploration of space and weaponry for use on Earth. In Britain, intellectual opinion inclined to the view that nuclear bombs should be abolished; and the Campaign for Nuclear Disarmament began annual marches between the Atomic Weapons Research Establishment in Aldermaston, Berkshire, and Trafalgar Square. Its aims were never achieved, but the sense of comradeship engendered by the marches, and the accompanying music and the snuggling together in sleeping bags, created a template for much that followed.

Yet day to day, the United Kingdom managed to feel secure and satisfied, bordering on smug. The Conservative victory in the 1959 election indicated that. And in that last long lovely summer of the fifties, there were moments when it seemed life might go on every bit as placidly for ever. It was an illusion, of course. Even in Ambridge the *Archers* scriptwriters were allowed to try for a younger audience by getting one of the farmhands to form a skiffle group. And in Buckingham Palace, Elizabeth and Philip were expecting a new bundle of joy, who would be called Andrew.

THE 1960s

1

WIVES AND SERVANTS

O N NEW YEAR'S DAY 1960, A YOUNG MAN CALLED JOHN 'HOPPY' Hopkins arrived in London to make a new start. He was 22 and a graduate of Cambridge, where he had studied general science, jazz, drugs and sex, not necessarily in that order. For a while, he worked as a technician for the Atomic Energy Authority at Harwell before taking a holiday at a Communist youth festival and, not surprisingly, losing his security clearance.

He brought his camera and soon found a job as an assistant to a commercial photographer. 'It was heaven,' he said. He also found himself welcome in the scattered pockets of louche sub-versiveness that were starting to emerge in the run-down areas of West London.

Photographers had little status in the 1950s. At a function, one dared to approach Betty Kenward, the absurd figure whose 'Jennifer's Diary' column in *Tatler* (and then *Queen*) fawningly chronicled upper-crust social life. 'My photographers never speak to me at parties,' she snapped imperiously. In February 1960 this upstart, Jones or something, became engaged to Princess Margaret. In the springtime they were married in Westminster Abbey amid full palaver, complete with Richard Dimbleby TV commentary, and

Antony Armstrong-Jones went on to become Earl of Snowdon.*

The marriage, by chance, resembled a medieval dynastic alliance. It linked the royal family with Bohemia, or at least the London versions of it like Fitzrovia, Notting Hillia (now up-and-coming) and Rotherhithia, where Armstrong-Jones rented his bachelor flat.

And thus indirectly with John Hopkins. Photographers were about to join the elite. Snowdon was to be closely associated with the pioneering *Sunday Times* magazine, launched in 1962; Hopkins took much-admired photos of the rock scene and the capital's underbelly. He also became a major figure in what would become aggrandized as Britain's counterculture, and for a while was what the music producer Joe Boyd called 'the closest thing the movement ever had to a leader'.

That was about five years away, which was a long, long time in the 1960s. There is still endless debate about when the sixties, as a concept, began. Any date between 1956 and 1963 might be defensible. But 1 January 1960, and Hoppy's arrival, is at least one possibility.

The counterculture as such comprised a tiny fraction of the population. For many millions of Britons – Kenward on the one hand, Tyneside shipworkers on the other – the events were not much more than a rumour. But it was a revolutionary time, when new sensations came so frequently that the world seemed to be spiralling out of control. And it was also a war, a cultural war, between the attitudes of old and new. And though, by the end of the decade, the new had captured once-unimaginable terrain, not every victory would be permanent, not every victory could be justified, not every victory was cheered by those one might think would be cheering it.

---

* Kenward never quite left the fifties, though her columns persisted until 1991. She was said to have spent the day the engagement was announced kicking the office wastepaper basket in fury. She refused to mention the groom's name, whatever it was; her columns referred to 'Princess Margaret and her husband'. Even her *Daily Telegraph* obituary called her 'insufferably snobbish and crotchety'.

The *News of the World* – 'the Screws' – was a British institution that had changed not at all over the previous decade, except that – like its chief rival for the nation's attention on a Sunday morning, the church – its audience had been drifting slowly downwards: from a staggering sale of 8.5 million in 1950 to a mere 6.5 million.*

Its discreetly Delphic messages about the week's more lubricious court cases still reached far more than those of its godly opposition. But its owners, the Carr family, were getting nervous, and on the last day of the decade it was announced that Stafford Somerfield was taking over as editor. He had an agenda, was given a budget to fulfil it, and immediately paid £35,000 for a series of ghostwritten articles under the byline of the sexy actress Diana Dors, whose semi-private life was more daring than her film roles.

And over the opening weeks of the 1960s, she delivered what Somerfield wanted: 'There were no half measures at my parties. Off came the sweaters, bras and panties. In fact it was a case of off with everything – except the lights . . .' This was the first, if not the most typical, example of the new brazenness. And circulation did perk up for a while.

Before Dors had even removed her coat in print, never mind her panties, there came more portentous news. Penguin Books had decided to publish an unexpurgated paperback of *Lady Chatterley's Lover*, the D. H. Lawrence novel that had lain, officially unpublished in Britain, for more than thirty years. Penguin's founder, Sir Allen Lane, was emboldened by a court overturning its prohibition in the US – and even more by the 1.5 million copies sold as a result. Lawrence's explicit depictions of the affair between Lady Constance Chatterley and her husband's gamekeeper, and the even more explicit language used in the process, was set up to be the first test case for the new, more flexible Obscene Publications Act.

Though it turned out not to be quite the first. Frederick Shaw, reinventing a tradition that dated back to Charles II's day, published

---

* Since many copies were read by more than one person, almost half the British population, children included, must have regularly read, skimmed or glimpsed the paper in 1950.

a book – the *Ladies' Directory* – giving contact details for London prostitutes, a useful service for potential customers since touting for business had been taken away from public view under another 1959 law, the Street Offences Act. The courts did not think it useful, however. Shaw got nine months for 'conspiracy to corrupt public morals', and henceforth the ladies concerned were obliged to post coded messages in newsagents' windows: FRENCH LESSONS GIVEN or LARGE CHEST FOR SALE. Later they would slip cards into phone boxes. Love does not always find a way, as Princess Margaret had discovered some years earlier, but sex does.

The Chatterley case came to trial in October 1960. In folklore it was lost the moment the prosecution counsel, Mervyn Griffith-Jones, asked the jury – twelve property-owning but otherwise fairly random Londoners – in his opening speech to consider: 'Would you approve of your young sons, young daughters – because girls can read as well as boys – reading this book? Is it a book that you would have lying around in your own house? Is it a book that you would even wish your wife or your servants to read?' And several onlookers noticed the jurors suppress titters at that moment. Griffith-Jones also reminded them that *phallus* meant penis, 'for those of you who have forgotten your Greek'.

The case may have been lost even before that. The defence called thirty-five expert witnesses to assert the book's literary value, with more in reserve; the prosecution had none. This was not a cunning plan or arrogance or even a technical legal decision, as the government claimed at the time; the Home Office could not find a single reputable figure to speak against Lady C. Some observers felt Griffith-Jones had not properly read the book, though he had painstakingly counted the thirty uses of *fuck* or *fucking*, the fourteen *cunts* and so on, down to the three *pisses*. All the witnesses had read it, even though the book was banned.

Yet Griffith-Jones had reason to be confident. The judge, Mr Justice Byrne, had been carefully chosen. He was 64, sitting for the final time, a conservative Catholic with close government connections, and in his summing-up he did his best to help. Weirdly, his wife sat beside him every day, and if the judge's face was not expressive enough during the trial, hers was. And after the 'not guilty' verdict came in, he omitted the customary thank-you to the jurors and just glared at them.

Eight days later, on 10 November, Lady C was legally sold in Britain at last. Penguin did not match the sales of the much bigger American market, it surpassed them, reaching 2 million in the seven weeks remaining of 1960. The judge harrumphed into retirement, but Griffith-Jones lived to fight more wrong-headed battles on behalf of the state, one of which would have tragic consequences.

Most opinion appeared to back the judgment. The right-wing *Daily Express*, the left-wing *Daily Herald* and the Methodist preacher Donald Soper all gave nuanced approval. And *The Guardian** marked the occasion by printing, in a quote from the trial, the word *fuck*, believed to be a British-newspaper first (rogue insertions by mischievous printers excepted). One Tory MP called for the paper to be prosecuted for obscene libel.

About the book, some peers were even more hysterical. The 6th Earl of Craven was travelling north on the M1 on publication day and stopped at the newly opened Newport Pagnell service station. He later told the House of Lords what he saw: 'At every serving counter sat a snigger of youths. Every one of them had a copy of this book held up to his face with one hand while he forked nourishment into his open mouth with the other. They held the seeds of suggestive lust.'

The earl was quite a young fogey: he was 43 at the time. It apparently never occurred to him that if the case had not been brought, and Lady C had been published normally, it would have sold well without making much impact on sniggers of youths. Not every peer was that daft. One of them was asked if he minded his daughter reading the book. Certainly not, he said, but he had the strongest objection to it being read by his gamekeeper.

———◆———

* The old *Manchester Guardian* had changed its name in 1959 as part of a slow move southwards.

Mostly, 1960 did a remarkably accurate impersonation of the 1950s, as would 1961 and 1962. There were a few straws in the wind, though. At the Old Vic, Franco Zeffirelli directed John Stride and Judi Dench as Romeo and Juliet and told Stride to play the part 'like a puppy dog seeing a bitch for the first time'. He did. 'Everything is up – his ears, his tail, his nose,' said Zeffirelli, approvingly. Old-guard critics were bemused, but Kenneth Tynan in *The Observer* said the production was 'a revelation, even perhaps a revolution', and Stride pronounced himself 'exhilarated'. Dench said she was 'exhausted'.

The Easter ban-the-bomb protest was the biggest yet, the organizers having realized the previous year that if they marched from the weapons base at Aldermaston to London rather than the reverse, as before, they would gain numbers instead of seeing people peel off. 'There was no doubt this was the largest demonstration London has seen this century,' said the BBC, estimating between sixty to a hundred thousand in Trafalgar Square. It was almost totally peaceful.

In the last month of 1959, Barbara Moore, a Russian-born engineer, walked from Edinburgh to London inside a week, which attracted some attention, the trains being only a little faster. She wore a blue boiler-suit, a red headscarf and, at least part of the time, slippers. She then had a couple of days in hospital (septic blister) and a fortnight's break, before making her way to John o'Groats to start the 1960s by doing what is now considered the obvious thing to do when you get there: head south and keep going. By the time she reached Penzance twenty-three days later, at least 10,000 were walking with her – as if from Aldermaston – and her arrival at Land's End, just before midnight, dominated the next day's front pages.

Why on earth did she attract so much attention? She was certainly treated as a crank: vegetarian, almost vegan (then a little-known variant and, if known, regarded as dangerous). Indeed, she ate very little at all. She claimed that, without drinking, smoking and sex, she could live to 150, or maybe 200. Above all, she was 57 and female. And women – whatever their age – did not do this sort of thing. She did, and indeed trebled down: her next trick was to walk across America, which she did in eighty-five days.

More conventional women in Britain turned in 1960 to the Tupperware party, whereby they invited friends round for tea to hear a spiel about the glories of airtight plastic containers, and wouldn't they like to buy some too. Market research had suggested British housewives would be too 'shy and retiring' to stoop to such brash American techniques. In the first two years, a hundred thousand such parties were reportedly held in Britain, 'several at the homes of titled women'.

Also in 1960, the Football Association ended its ancient taboo on Sunday soccer, which reached down to every level of the organized game.* Perhaps there was something much broader happening here. In October, the *Radio Times* altered its publishing schedules: instead of each issue printing the programmes from Sunday to Saturday, they ran from Saturday to Friday. What this seemingly minor change suggested was that the weekend was no longer something that belonged only to those invited to country-house parties but to telly-watchers too. Previously, many people had to work Saturday mornings, and Sunday was a day of obligations and prohibitions. Now, as church authority diminished and union power grew, the two days were starting to merge into interchangeable twins.

Some aspects of the world to come met setbacks. Foxes, embarking on their long march to take over London and assume supreme power, were sighted in the Kentish suburbs. Twenty were shot by Ministry of Agriculture officials near Chislehurst. An experimental Post Office–run carphone service in Lancashire flopped: too expensive and too vulnerable to eavesdroppers. There was also a spate of thefts of cash from the mail vans of trains, one of them headlined by the *Daily Express* – three years prematurely – as THE GREAT TRAIN ROBBERY. This one yielded £8,000. The craze might have taught the police, Post Office and railways some timely lessons.

---

* Northamptonshire folklore had it that, while the ban persisted, the secretary of the county FA got wind of an illicit Sunday match and was so angry he went along and stood sternly in the centre circle. The disrespectful wretches just played round him.

It didn't. In this case, a pathetic blanketed figure in a wheelchair was being carried in the guard's van of an evening train out of Waterloo, there being no other disabled facilities. Just after Clapham Junction, the invalid and his carer got to work on the mailbags, and on the lonely stretch by Wandsworth Cemetery they handed the bags over to accomplices, who had fixed the signal at red, and leapt off. Some inventive and railway-savvy villains called Bob Welch, Tommy Wisbey and Roger Cordrey were rumoured to be involved in these capers. We shall hear of them again.

———•———

The sixties were only ten weeks old when a *Daily Mail* columnist, Eve Perrick, went off on one about that only recently discovered sub-group of society: the teenager. 'Teenmania,' she began, 'has its own language and customs (both rather slovenly), no constitution except that of complete conformity to its self-styled non-conformist citizens, no rulers other than the temporary dictators of style and approach who emerge from time to time from the film studios and gramophone record companies.'

The vocabulary was to blame, thought Perrick. 'Without the word teenager to wear like a badge of office, young people would have been just like anyone else, only younger . . .' If she was this agitated in March 1960, when Michael Holliday and Anthony Newley were vying with each other at the top of what was still called the hit parade, she was going to face a long, hard decade.

2

C'MON, LITTLE MISS, LET'S DO THE TWIST

I N THE SUMMER OF 1961 THE TRANSISTOR RADIO BECAME VERY popular in Britain. And very unpopular. For the first time, music was now easily portable, but it was not yet personal. No matter how deep the forest or high the mountain, tranquillity was at risk. Columnists and letter-writers were understandably agitated: 'Fiendish invention ... mechanical midgets ... little horrors ... oasis of peace ... inferno of noise,' said a *Times* leader.

London buses were especially problematic because it was sometimes the conductors who had the radio. Or they would take the radio-owner's side. 'Don't be so miserable,' one complainant was told. 'If you don't like it, take a taxi.' Eastbourne threatened offenders with £5 fines. One woman said she was assailed on the beach by six different radios, apparently tuned to six different stations. It is hard to imagine this being true; Britain didn't have six stations, and not even one playing solid pop.

Radio music was strictly limited on the BBC because of a punitive agreement with the Musicians' Union restricting 'needle time'. This meant the Light Programme, the only possible outlet for pop, was infested with bland cover versions of hits, performed by in-house singers and musicians. Otherwise, there was Brian Matthew's *Saturday Club* and *Pick of the Pops*, mainly associated with Alan

Freeman ('Hi, there, pop-pickers!'), and that was about it outside
Housewives' Choice. Sir Tim Rice remembers that *Record Retailer*
magazine used to list the number of plays the current hits received
on the BBC: 'The No. 1 would have about eleven or twelve a week.'
Radio Luxembourg, evenings only, and to some extent the American
Forces Network were the only widely available alternatives, but
reception was patchy.

   Home-grown male singers continued to emerge, mainly from the
Soho scene. Many were discovered and nurtured by Larry Parnes
(nicknamed 'Parnes, shillings and pence'), whose first step was to
change their names to something he thought suited them, as if they
were a litter of puppies. Tommy Hicks had already found fame as
Tommy Steele. He was followed by other names, all newly minted,
like Marty Wilde, Vince Eager, Georgie Fame and, Parnes's special
favourite, a handsome Scouse docker unpromisingly called Ron
Wycherley, who was transformed instantly into Billy Fury. Parnes
was more insistent than that: the boys would be professionally
coiffed, beautified and kitted out before being unleashed. Simon
Napier-Bell, a next-generation pop manager, compared the process
to a sultan grooming new recruits for the harem.

   There were certainly homoerotic undercurrents here, though it
was said Parnes avoided mixing business and pleasure. He did much
else for his boys, though they struggled to crack the land of milk and
honey that lay beyond the Statue of Liberty. British pop was stifled
by the twin hegemony of the BBC and the United States. Occasionally, there were messengers from those distant shores. There
was a cohort of working-class lads, known as the Cunard Yanks,
with jobs on the transatlantic liners. They would return from New
York bearing amazing records, clothes and stories to their wide-
eyed mates. It is no coincidence that their home port was Liverpool.
One of them sold the teenage George Harrison a Gretsch guitar.

   But the early sixties were a thin time musically even in the US.
Rock and roll was missing, presumed dead. Bill Haley was history;
Elvis, demobbed from his stint in the Army, was frittering away his
talent making third-rate movies; Jerry Lee Lewis had married his
13-year-old cousin which was only marginally OK in Louisiana and

not at all in Luton; exuberant Little Richard had retreated into religion; and our very own Cliff Richard was starting the long retreat from his brief incarnation as edgy. The sensation of the early 1960s was a dance craze: the twist. And very strange it was, because, as one pop historian said, 'it was the least sexual dance craze in forty years'. There was not a hint of bodily contact. It was popularized in the US by a teenager from Philadelphia called Chubby Checker in 1960 but it took another eighteen months to make much impact in Europe; even the Cunard Yanks may have missed it.

Some British dance halls banned the twist for no obvious reason. It was theoretically as prescriptive as the foxtrot, but then mutated into various spin-offs like the Madison, Watusi, the Frug and the Mashed Potato, and eventually no one knew what they were meant to be doing and so did what they felt like. Which is, I suppose, the evolution of modern disco-dancing.

And indeed in 1961 London did get its first discotheque. Helene Cordet, a French-Greek actress and childhood friend of Prince Philip, opened the Saddle Room off Park Lane, and brought with her the word for this new phenomenon. The décor was baronial, the clientele wealthy; and the males probably had a lordly insouciance about the *après-disco* that was a long way from the fretful fumblings of the provincial dance hall.

———•———

On a cool summer's day in July 1962, a young middle-class couple called Edward Mayhew and Florence Ponting were married in Oxford and drove down to begin their honeymoon by the Dorset coast. The wedding itself was conventional in an era when convention was still followed rigorously.

What happened on the wedding night, however, departed from the norm. It was what did *not* happen that was so unusual. Through a combination of gaucheness on Edward's part, naivety on Florence's and an excess of English reticence from them both, they failed to complete the physical procedure that customarily follows a marriage, with devastating consequences.

Edward and Florence (born circa 1940) did not actually exist.

They were the creations of Ian McEwan, the central figures of his much-admired short novel *On Chesil Beach* (2007), which is how we know the precise sequence of events on this private occasion. A few years ago, while writing a magazine article, I phoned McEwan to ask him why he had set the book in 1962. He seemed quite pleased that someone had noticed.

'I have often thought "Could I write that novel and set it now?"' he said. 'I don't think it would be entirely impossible, but it would have to be two young Muslims, perhaps someone marrying a cousin he hasn't met from a remote village in Bangladesh. My Chesil Beach couple were almost the last of a line. A few years later and it would have been unlikely.'

Disastrous wedding nights are probably common even now – it can be a stressful day, after all. And that would have been more true in an era when couples were expected to hit top form at once without any match practice. Sometimes sexual innocence could last indefinitely. In the fifties the country doctor Denys Brierley was called out to a remote farm cottage and a woman who was bleeding profusely. When he arrived, he saw the problem at once. 'She's having a miscarriage,' he explained to the husband. 'But we don't do anything like that,' the husband said in a shocked tone. Dr Brierley backtracked: 'Well, it could just be a very heavy period.' She was taken to hospital, and Brierley warned the nurse to say nothing about miscarrying. 'I think the wife knew all right,' he said. 'But it was very 1950s.'

In midsummer 1962, around the time of the imaginary Ponting wedding, the *Daily Mirror* trumpeted a blockbuster series for the following week by star writer Audrey Whiting, THE NO-BABY PILL: 'Whiting answers the questions every married woman – and man – is asking today.' And it was indeed a classic *Mirror* series of the sixties: boldly presented, accessibly written, earnestly researched – and dealing seriously with the fears of long-term side effects (which would turn out to have some justification). Whiting weighed the evidence and concluded 'as a married woman' that she would be willing to take the pill as a calculated risk. But she dodged any mention of single women.

Around this time, the former Christ's Hospital boy David McKie was in a pub in Surbiton when a man came in with a briefcase and started chatting. 'He opened it up and showed us a pill box. He said "Look at this. It's going to transform our lives." And it did.' It rescued working-class women from being baby machines – much less essential now that infants were far more likely to survive. It gave them the chance to plan the family they wanted and to have a career as well.

It also transformed unmarried lives – but that was problematic, because the rules were changing more slowly than the realities. The normal way to get the pill was through your doctor or the Family Planning Association, neither of whom could be relied on for discreet sympathy. At the FPA, women had to fill in a form asking how often they had sex. If the answer was more than three times a week, a husband was liable to be called in for a talking-to. And there did have to be a husband, or the FPA would have nothing to do with you. The upshot was, as with medical abortions, that the rich might find a back door where the poor would struggle.

In 1963, *Which?* magazine, founded in 1957 to help housewives choose between washing machines and the like, broke new ground in its consumer reporting by testing contraceptives – twenty-seven different types of sheath, eight of them made by the market leader, Durex. This was sold as a separate and expensive (ten shillings) members-only supplement, to avoid frightening their squeamish readers or delighting sniggers of youths in motorway caffs. The conclusions might have frightened them too. *Which?* concluded that all twenty-seven would be in breach of the proposed British Standard, which allowed a failure rate of 1 per cent; Durex were livid. One foreign sheath had a rate of 20 per cent.

And in the *Mirror*, even the progressive columnist Marjorie Proops could not resist a moralizing conclusion. 'One thing about the report which pleases me: it may make those "unofficial" users of contraceptives, the unmarrieds who slink into rubber goods shops, think twice before taking a chance. According to *Which?*, the risk was considerable.' But condoms did improve, and Durex had already introduced lubricated versions. And their huge sales were also helped by schoolboys who carried them in their wallets on the off-chance, or to impress their mates, a process helped if you chucked away one of the packet of three, used or not.

For women, this was a more serious matter. In 1952 a woman called Helen Brook had been asked to help out at the FPA's Islington clinic, where the volunteers were known as *the ladies* and the clients as *the women*. She then moved on to take over a clinic previously run by the late pioneer of contraception, Marie Stopes, where she began giving discreet advice to the unwed. When her bosses got nervous, she went her own way and opened the first Brook Advisory Centre, in South London; and, with a deep breath, began giving advice not just to the unwed but the under-16s. The Charity Commission threatened to remove its charitable status but the centres survived. Brook did not believe in permissiveness, wrote her journalist niece Nikki Knewstub: 'She cared desperately for the ruined lives of teenage girls made mothers for the want of sex education.'

In time, readily available contraception would indeed touch all human lives – while, of course, preventing the creation of other lives. The Anglican Communion had already approved contraception's role in 'family life', and there were hints the Vatican might follow. Once even the bishops had accepted that sex could be recreational without being procreational, that might also be considered a philosophical lifeline to the still-outlawed homosexuals. Anyway, it would turn out that people did still want children, but when it suited them and less of them than before.

In the meantime, even the slightest deviation from the old values remained risky for public figures. In July 1963, Dr Peter Henderson Bryce, the chief medical officer to the Ministry of Education, mentioned to a conference of teachers that he saw no harm in engaged couples having sex. The moralistic minority of MPs rose in righteous fury, and might have made much more of it had his comment not coincided with the start of the summer recess.

Now and again there were signs that the country was lightening up. At the start of 1962, Liz Mayo, 21, was forced to resign as chairman* of Chesham Young Conservatives after staging a striptease at their New Year's Eve party. The fact she did it offstage and all the audience saw was a hand throwing items from the wings did not save her. A year later, she was re-elected unanimously.

And in Cambridge there was a fuss about five girls from Girton College either appearing topless or being pressurized not to appear topless in a student production of the musical *Expresso Bongo*. What happened in the end seems lost in the mists, even for the play's producer, Stephen Frears. 'I vaguely remember something about curtains and possibly gauze,' he said. 'I do remember the show being a big success. It was iconoclastic and a popular musical. It was the populism that was so subversive of Cambridge.' Frears went on to become a famous film director; his lead actor, Richard Eyre, became the artistic director of the National Theatre. The girls? They probably became Cabinet ministers.

---

*   As the job was always called then, even in the Women's Institutes.

3

GOODBYE TO ALL THAT

HAROLD MACMILLAN'S CAREER AS PRIME MINISTER REACHED its apogee in the opening weeks of 1960. It came with a parliamentary speech – but not in the House of Commons. It was delivered 6,000 miles away in Cape Town, in the House of Assembly, a body chosen – with fig-leaf exceptions – by the South African white minority, a situation the Assembly had no intention of altering.

It became known as the 'Wind of Change' speech, in which Macmillan told South Africa it had to adapt and accommodate the rise of African nationalism. The genius of it was that he sugared the message with so many expressions of support, friendship and admiration that the audience of politicians – almost entirely split between extreme white supremacists and less extreme white supremacists – applauded him. And white crowds cheered him at the dockside as he boarded his ship home.

But his counterpart, Hendrik Verwoerd, understood Macmillan's message all right. His government took no notice: indeed, its oppression, systematized under the alleged separate but equal doctrine of apartheid, took a new turn the following month, when the South African police killed sixty-nine protesters in the township of Sharpeville, with a number shot in the back. Sharpeville had a galvanic effect on world opinion, leading rapidly to Resolution 134 at the UN Security Council – which initiated the long cold war between South Africa and the world (Britain abstained) – and, a year later, to Verwoerd flouncing out of the Commonwealth. None of which had much short- or medium-term effect on life in South Africa, which carried on in its own bitter way for another thirty years. Calls for boycotts of South African produce were so effective that Britain's imports of Cape apples doubled.

Macmillan, however, was not primarily concerned with South Africa. He was distancing himself from its regime to facilitate the more-or-less honourable dissolution of the British Empire. He had no illusions. In old age Macmillan would remember the advice given to him earlier on his Africa trip by Sir James Robertson, an old colonial hand then serving as governor-general of Nigeria. 'Are these people ready for self-government?' he asked. 'Of course not,' Robertson replied, suggesting twenty years would be right. But then he added they should have it at once – because otherwise all the potential leaders would turn into rebels and there would be twenty years of repression and bloodshed. Macmillan thought this very wise. Iain Macleod, his Colonial Secretary, told him the same thing.

The process had started three years earlier, in Ghana, which had seemed like low-hanging fruit. It was compact, pacific, relatively prosperous – its cocoa beans provided half the world's chocolate – with a strong black bourgeoisie, good schools and hospitals, and an obvious popular leader, Kwame Nkrumah, who was already effectively functioning as prime minister. Unfortunately, Nkrumah was high-handed before independence; afterwards came the descent towards egomania, kleptomania and anti-Western tendencies ended only by an army coup which restarted the process with similar results, leading to general impoverishment.

Thus it would go across Africa, with differing degrees of dreadfulness, to the smug delight of the white South Africans and their many sympathizers in Britain. But, crucially, the problems would no longer be the responsibility of a small and distant country with troubles of its own. And so the offloading process continued. West Africa was the easiest because there were so few white settlers to get in the way. Elsewhere, it was a three-way dispute. The Mau Mau campaign against whites in Kenya, which had gone on throughout the 1950s, led to war crimes all round. This included a British atrocity against black detainees in 1959, when eleven were clubbed to death (and many more maimed) at Hola Camp. It was denounced most eloquently in the Commons by a Conservative backbencher, Enoch Powell.

In central Africa, there was a short-lived federation of Rhodesia and Nyasaland – designed to stave off independence with benign white rule. It was dominated by a hulking great man called Roy Welensky: half Jewish, half Afrikaner, born in a dosshouse run by his dirt-poor parents. He was one of fourteen children and became an engine driver, Rhodesia's heavyweight boxing champion and a trade unionist, gaining a reputation as a wily negotiator. Until he met Macmillan.

Northern Rhodesia and Nyasaland were given majority-rule independence as Zambia and Malawi. With South Africa wholly detached from Britain, that left only Southern Rhodesia.* Job almost done then.

The independence ceremonies became a ritualized staple of the early sixties. Britain would send royalty and a minister (both usually minor) for the ceremony of handing over authority to someone they had often just released from jail. Sierra Leone was an early recipient, in April 1961. The run-up was marked by the arrest of eighteen opposition leaders and a few bloodless explosions. The formalities were delayed because the not-quite-finished parliament had been flooded by a thunderstorm the previous night. In the absence of other materials, some of the new flags were used for the mopping-up.

But otherwise all went smoothly. There were always gifts. Britain gave Sierra Leone a selection of rose bowls, silver salvers and bon-bon dishes; the more practical Americans sent two mobile medical units. The duty royal, the young Duke of Kent, impressed everyone with his own speech, his message of goodwill from Her Majesty and his dancing with the prime minister's daughter at the independence ball. At midnight the Union Jack was lowered, a pristine replacement

---

* Which became known as Rhodesia, and ultimately Zimbabwe.

run up, and the British went home and largely forgot that they ever had anything to do with the place.

Sierra Leone was somewhat atypical because its new leader, Sir Milton Margai, ruled cautiously, benignly and inclusively. He sent whisky and brandy to his prisoners on independence day, released them soon afterwards, and took care to keep the opposition onside for the three years of power before his death. It was left to his successor, his brother Albert, to start down the road to perdition, corruption, dictatorship and civil war.

———·———

If Macmillan had died three years after taking office – perhaps, prematurely but picturesquely, on the *Capetown Castle* en route home from South Africa – he would have been remembered as a hugely successful prime minister, certainly by those not inclined to delve too deep into economic minutiae. As it was, he had not quite reached half-time as prime minister, and very soon he would find himself playing upwind with the opposition getting rougher and the crowd starting to howl abuse. And there were also, in a phrase coined by Macmillan when asked the greatest problem about being prime minister: 'Events, dear boy, events.'

According to Macmillan's biographer, D. R. Thorpe: 'A distinct change of mood came over Britain in 1960 . . . people began to observe not how well Britain was doing, but how other countries seemed to be doing much better.' In the spring of 1960 there was the embarrassment of having to scrap Blue Streak, the home-grown missile launcher supposed to carry Britain's very own hydrogen bomb. It was turning out to be ruinously expensive, and vulnerable to attack. But the events, dear boy, were also global. Two weeks later, an American U-2 spy plane was shot down over Russia, which wrecked a planned summit in Paris and restored hard frost to the Cold War.

In the prime-ministerial head, thoughts came together towards a simple conclusion: Britain needed more friends, and there was only one place to turn. A Civil Service report to the Cabinet noted that Europe might become a bloc comparable to the US and the Soviet

Union: 'If that happens and if we remain outside, our relative position in the world is bound to decline.' Thus, in July, the Cabinet decided in principle to start talks with what were then known as 'The Six'. A year later, it became official. Macmillan sent his most zealous European, Ted Heath, to negotiate, and five of the six were pleased to have such a distinguished supplicant. The French president, General Charles de Gaulle, thought differently.

By the autumn of 1960 Britain had strikes galore and deteriorating trade figures; by the following July, things were so dire that the Chancellor, Selwyn Lloyd, had to produce an emergency budget to stop the public having it so good, raising purchase tax and the lending rate and instituting a 'pay pause' to curb inflation. The next month, Labour went ahead in the Gallup poll for the first time since the previous election, never to be dislodged until after the next one.

There was also a succession of British spy scandals, a very sensitive business in the Cold War. Early in 1961, five people – three real Commies and two greedy stooges – were arrested and given long sentences for stealing whatever secrets might have lurked in the naval warfare base at Portland. Then, after a court hearing held almost wholly behind closed doors, a former MI6 operative, George Blake, was jailed for forty-two years by Rayner Goddard's successor as Lord Chief Justice, Lord Parker. Blake's crimes were particularly galling, as he effectively handed over many British agents to the Russians and heaven knows what fate. Parker was perceived as doing the government's bidding in imposing such a sentence, but even the prime minister described it as 'savage' in his diary. And, after Macmillan left office, Blake would have the last laugh.

Due to the secrecy, Blake's case made far less of a splash than the next – the arrest and trial of John Vassall, an Admiralty clerk and, not incidentally, a homosexual, who was posted to Moscow, got entwined in a honeytrap set by the KGB and was threatened with exposure unless he started stealing secrets. Which he did, and which he carried on doing when back in London and working in the private office of the Admiralty's No. 2 minister, a courtly gentleman called Tam Galbraith. Vassall's work sometimes included delivering sensitive material to Galbraith's country home, and communicating about office furniture and the like. In the late 1950s this involved writing letters. And Galbraith sometimes began his letters 'My dear Vassall', which in the febrile mood of the time was taken to mean Galbraith was homosexual too. He felt obliged to resign but was quickly rehabilitated by Macmillan. Vassall got eighteen years.

Amid all this, Macmillan, previously the apotheosis of calm, had felt sufficiently rattled that July to sack a third of his Cabinet, without noticeably refreshing it, an occasion immortalized by one of the great political one-liners: 'Greater love hath no man than this,' said the young Liberal MP Jeremy Thorpe, channelling John 15:13, 'that he lay down his friends for his life.'

And then suddenly, on the day Vassall was sentenced, came the news that we might all be facing the death penalty. It was the day the Cuban Missile Crisis began.

———◆———

It was a completely normal week, yet abnormal; nervous yet phlegmatic. The post-war generation had grown up with the knowledge that there had already been two world wars that century, that there was likely to be another one, that it would probably be nuclear and we would all die. We absorbed this subconsciously, as children have always had to absorb the notion of death. There being no rolling news nor even hourly bulletins, there was no point obsessing. As Ian McEwan, away at boarding school, put it: 'I remember being pretty sure it was going to happen but kept writing my weekly letter home with the sports scores.' And, once it was over, we never again felt threatened so collectively and so imminently.*

In a way, the crisis found Britain more impotent than ever: President Kennedy's initial response did not involve consulting with allies. But he began making midnight calls to Downing Street (midnight in Washington, 5 a.m. in London, i.e. more convenient

---

* At my own boarding school, we were called to an unheard-of mid-afternoon assembly. It turned out to be nothing to do with Cuba but to announce the sudden death of a popular, sporty fellow pupil. This was an early lesson in how one death can be far more upsetting than the fate of millions.

for Kennedy), using Macmillan as a father confessor or psychotherapist to give him guidance and reassurance – rather as wise
prime ministers might use the monarch. Which was pretty much the
role Macmillan wanted to play.

But a few weeks after the crisis, the doyen of American foreign
policy Dean Acheson attacked Britain with his own most memorable
line: 'Great Britain has lost an Empire and has not yet found a role.'
In context it was even crueller than that. Acheson went on: 'The
attempt to play a separate role – that is a role apart from Europe
. . . this role is about to be played out.' And he added that Britain's
policies were as weak as its military power.

The following sequence of events then took place in December
1962 and January 1963:

1. Britain went incandescent over Acheson: 'a stab in the
   back' – *Daily Express*; 'a calculated insult' – the Institute of
   Directors; and, after much thought, 'Mr Acheson has fallen
   into an error which has been made by quite a lot of people
   in the past four hundred years, including Philip of Spain,
   Louis XIV, Napoleon, the Kaiser and Hitler' – Harold
   Macmillan.

2. After the Blue Streak fiasco, Britain agreed to buy the
   American equivalent, Skybolt. But then Washington
   decided to cancel that without telling Macmillan; not even
   a 'by the way . . .' on those 5 a.m. phone calls. Now a third
   name came into play – the US's new model, Polaris. (All
   these missile launchers sounded either like racehorses or
   varieties of carrot.) But the US were refusing to sell: they
   wanted it under the control of a multilateral NATO force.
   The fallout, Macmillan thought, could scupper his
   government.

3. Kennedy and Macmillan held a summit in the Bahamas,
   planned during their warm chats during the Cuba crisis as
   a relaxed statesmanly *tour d'horizon* in the sunshine. In
   fact, it was dominated by Skybolt and Polaris. Here loomed
   real humiliation. Macmillan launched into a series of

speeches which could hardly have been matched by Pericles or Atticus Finch, and the Americans gave way, partly through exhaustion. And on favourable terms. Britain *had* found a role: that of pretending to be a global power. Now it could maintain that pretence.

4. The triumph crumbled to dust. De Gaulle had already hinted to Macmillan what was going to happen. Nassau sealed it. The French were not going to get the same deal on Polaris, and anyway did not have the submarines to fire them. With Britain in the Common Market, he told a press conference that 'it would seem like a colossal Atlantic community under American dependence and direction'. So, he would veto Britain's application.

And what were the British doing to Macmillan? They were laughing at him.

———————————

On 11 May 1961, the hard-to-please Bernard Levin, then working as theatre critic of the *Daily Express*, used the following adjectives in a single sentence of his review: 'brilliant, adult, hard-boiled, accurate, merciless, witty, unexpected, alive, exhilarating, cleansing, right, true, and good'. He was writing about *Beyond the Fringe*, a series of sketches which had opened the night before, starring four young humorists, at the little Fortune Theatre.

In fact, Levin's laughter in the front stalls was so screechingly loud it was said that the cast had an interval discussion to consider whether they could do anything about it. The show had proved a phenomenon at the Edinburgh Festival the year before, but it had also had a trial run in Brighton at which the audience had marched out en masse, also noisily (a surprising insight into local social history). Yet Britain, if not Brighton, was ready for this.

John Cleese, then an undergraduate, was awestruck by it all and said all four were 'near-genius level', which was no exaggeration. They also complemented each other: the languid Peter Cook, so naturally funny that he could have audiences in fits just by saying

'Good evening'; the polymath Jonathan Miller; Alan Bennett, northern and understated; and Dudley Moore, put-upon and lame but a musical virtuoso.

The *Fringe* generation had not fought the war and were ready for a little gentle mockery of the jut-jawed genre of fifties films – and of the war itself. And they had been brought up on the wild subversion of the Goons rather than the down-to-earth humour of Tommy Handley. They could also face seeing the prime minister mocked. In one of the sketches Cook as Macmillan talked about his meeting with Kennedy and Britain's attempt to be an honest broker: 'I agreed with him when he said no nation could be more honest, and he agreed with me . . . no nation could be broker.' They even touched on everyone's deepest fears: 'Now, we shall receive four minutes' warning of any impending nuclear attack,' said Peter Cook, as a civil defence official. 'Some people have said, "Oh my goodness me – four minutes? – that's not a very long time!" Well, I would remind those doubters that some people in this great country of ours can run *a mile* in four minutes.'

Whether this was satire or comedy was a matter of semantics. The material is still funny even now, which suggests it was comedy, and it was gentle enough to get little attention from the Lord Chamberlain, the official theatre censor. But it was seen universally as the start of the 'satire boom': a dramatic springtime for humour, and the onset of autumn for the values of Brighton's Aunt Ednas. Even Macmillan turned up one night, which was game of him.

In October, two new lambs were born. One was the Establishment club in Soho, founded by Cook, which – as a private club – was immune from censorship. The name came from a coinage popularized by the journalist Henry Fairlie, which he defined as not just official power but 'the whole matrix of official and social relations within which power is exercised'. It was the Establishment who formed the audience on opening night. According to John Wells, who was onstage: 'Rich girls in lovely diaphanous dresses wriggled and squealed in the crowd, their rock-jawed escorts bellowing above the din. "Hello, Jeremy! You going to Antonia's thrash on Thursday?"' Next to the Fortune Theatre it became *the* place to go.

That same month came the other lamb, seemingly much more fragile and sickly. It was the direct descendant of a magazine that Christopher Booker, Richard Ingrams, Paul Foot and Willie Rushton – another contrasting but complementary quartet – had produced at Shrewsbury School. After much discussion (*The Yellow Press? Finger? The Bladder?*) it was named *Private Eye*. And it looked like a school magazine, though not an official one. The ever-fertile Cook was livid: he'd wanted to do something similar himself. After ten issues, when the lambkin was beginning to suckle and grow, the original backer Andrew Osmond pulled out and Cook, flush with money, and his business partner Nick Luard bought it. The rest is living history.

For the next year, satire remained a rumour to at least 99 per cent of the British population, barring those who crammed its West End citadels or read the *Eye*. But in 1962 something extraordinary happened: it found a place on what was then the BBC's only TV channel. In what was surely the greatest leap in British television history, the corporation announced 'an entertainment for late on Saturday night' called *That Was the Week That Was*. The effect was staggering: suddenly, in an era when TV was seen live or not at all, the in place to be on a Saturday night was *in*.

Whether *TW3* – as it soon became known – was a leap forward or into the abyss was a matter for anxious discussion among BBC executives. It might have been strangled at birth had they not had word that ITV was planning something similar. An instruction came down from a jumpy executive: 'The word "satire" will not appear in the programme or be used in connection with it in the publicity.' On opening night there was a song with the chorus:

> *Sex before Marriage*
> *Sex before Marriage*
> *Goes on everywhere from Hull to Harwich*

Except that 'sex' was censored and replaced with 'love', rendering it ridiculous.

But somehow it all just worked. The producer and master of the revels, Ned Sherrin, chose as his presenter an unknown called David Frost – a contemporary of Cook in the Cambridge Footlights. Frost was considered, in that glittering company, untalented but indefatigable. But when the camera swung towards him, he just exuded calm and charm. Otherwise, the whole thing was like a tightrope walk. The material had to be fresh-minted every week and put together at high speed. It was rough-edged, sometimes sloppy, amateur-looking. It was also audacious, insolent and thrilling.*

It pushed BBC guidelines to the limits and beyond. The prime minister thought it best to keep out of the way. After the first edition, Reginald Bevins – as Postmaster General the responsible minister – was asked if he was going to do something about the programme. 'Yes, I will,' he said. A note came through from Macmillan: 'Oh no, you won't.'

TW3 flew through the firmament like a shooting star. In the early days, the BBC's director-general, Hugh Carleton Greene, would drop by for drinks afterwards. 'Very good! Very good!' he said on one occasion, possibly after he had one or two. 'Not dirty enough!' There were only thirty-seven episodes, spread over thirteen months. The show was on a summer break while the Profumo scandal, of which more shortly, was at its peak in 1963. This was perhaps a blessing: the mixture was over-rich already.

By October, both main parties had changed leaders: Macmillan and the late Hugh Gaitskell having been replaced by Sir Alec Douglas-Home and Harold Wilson. The show did a consumer review, finishing with Frost saying the choice was 'Dull Alec versus Smart Alec', a very fair summary. Complaints, muted in the early days, were loud about that. Generally, the governors harassed the once-supportive Carleton Greene; his minions harassed Sherrin. Finally it was decided that *TW3* would be taken off for 1964, which was certain to be an election year. It never returned.

There were successors in due course: *Not So Much a Programme,*

---

*   As an 11-year-old I was allowed to stay up to watch it during the school holidays. I might not have got every joke, but the sense that schoolboy impertinence was now legal made it very exciting.

More a Way of Life (with Frost) and *BBC-3* (hosted by Robert Robinson). They had their moments and produced new stars, like John Bird. The glory had departed, although the legacy of energy infused by *TW3* would sustain BBC comedy for at least two decades. *Beyond the Fringe* went to Broadway and was a huge hit there. The Establishment hit its high spot in 1962 when it brought over the magnificently outrageous US comic Lenny Bruce and had a huge *succès de scandale*. They tried to repeat the trick a year later, and this time Bruce was denied entry to Britain. The upshot was that the club, who had paid Bruce up front, went bust and fell briefly into the hands of gangsters before closing. That was the satire boom that was.

If there was any doubt, it ended in January 1966. The great iconoclast David Frost gave a breakfast party (kidneys, bacon and egg, caviar with sour cream) for twenty people including the prime minister (by then Harold Wilson), the Bishop of Woolwich and Lord Longford. 'This was a private party,' said Frost, 'and I hope a chance for a few friends who don't always meet to gather and chat.' Beyond satire really. But Britain would never be quite the same again.

4

READ ALL ABOUT IT!

THE SATIRISTS WERE VERY SOFT ON THE ROYALS. *TW3* DID HAVE an item about Richard Dimbleby commentating on the Royal Barge sinking on the Thames: 'And now the Queen, smiling radiantly, is swimming for her life. Her Majesty is wearing a silk ensemble in canary yellow . . .' Every comical young writer in London was sending in gags, and this was a reheated Footlights sketch written by one Ian Lang, who would later become a member of John Major's Cabinet.

Amid the churn of the 1960s, the monarchy was hardly an issue. The Queen was no longer the world's No. 1 rock star. There were many more real rock stars, and even among heads of state she was already old hat. All the attention in the early sixties focused on President Kennedy and his wife, Jackie. He was actually older than either the Queen or Prince Philip, but he oozed youth, informality and (bogus) good health.

Traditionally, the national anthem was still played in cinemas at the end of the evening showing, but the rush to escape beforehand to catch last orders or the last bus was turning into a national joke. In 1961 it was reported from Glasgow that the only man to stay behind to pay his respects to Her Majesty found himself locked in for the night. This was not a localized phenomenon. In response, G. Atkinson of Islington complained: 'I myself have been jostled, winded, and even injured severely by a stiletto heel in the stampede to escape.'* By 1964 the ABC chain of cinemas was experimenting with playing the anthem before the film started, but this never caught on and the whole custom just withered away. The return to reverence has yet to arrive.

The Queen was certainly not unpopular, but there was not much melodrama. There were two new babies: Prince Andrew in 1960 and Edward four years later. It was said she was a more accessible and doting mother to these two than to Charles and Anne, that the Queen and Philip were unusually settled and to-gether in those years, and that the Palace, with the younger boys whooping round the endless corridors, suddenly had a 'cheerful family feel'.

And who was there to create scandal? Princess Margaret was newly married, and the storm clouds were not yet visible from a distance. The Queen's cousin, the Earl of Harewood, got divorced after fathering an illegitimate child, but no one much cared about him. The Queen's children were too young for major mischief. But the papers took what they could get. In June 1963, Prince Charles was a 14-year-old serving a lengthy sentence at Gordonstoun, the ferocious Scottish school beloved by his father and which Charles called 'Colditz in kilts'. He was on a training ketch berthed in the Hebrides, and wandered into a hotel bar. Uncertain what to do next, he ordered a cherry brandy, a customary introduction to adult drinking but illegal for under-18s. There were only a couple of people in the bar. Alas for him, one of them was an ambitious young freelance journalist.

And that was as bad as things got. The Queen was no longer new to the job: the balance of power between her and the courtiers had changed; she knew what she had to do. And she also knew what she wanted to do: after the first ten years or so, her annual cycle of events already seemed as though it had been engraved in stone by

---

* My friend Jeremy Bugler, on an early date with a new girlfriend, began to rise for the anthem – then noticed his companion very firmly staying seated. He quickly sat down again. Good move. Jerry and Sue celebrated their golden wedding some time ago.

Edward the Confessor. But there was no reason for her to attend every day of Royal Ascot while boycotting football and tennis for decades on end, except that she enjoyed one and not the others.

Sometimes she could still wow everyone. In 1961 she battled the politicians not to cancel a visit to Ghana – where things were rapidly going pear-shaped under Nkrumah – even though there was unrest, violence and obvious risk. The *Telegraph* called the tour 'a triumphal success'. Macmillan said the week was 'one of the most trying of my life'. In June 1964 she went to Aberdeen, which had been beset by a high-profile typhoid outbreak caused by contaminated tins of South American corned beef. Only three people died, but more than 400 fell ill; potential visitors shunned Aberdeen, and the rest of Britain shunned the products of Fray Bentos. When she got there, 50,000 cheered the Queen, who effectively declared the crisis over simply by turning up. And, twenty years on from the war, she was greeted in Germany with, according to Ben Pimlott, 'an almost embarrassing degree of delight'.

Other visits were more problematic. In India, Prince Philip went on a tiger shoot – the Maharaja of Jaipur *insisted* – and bagged a lame tigress, just as he was helping set up the World Wildlife Fund; the Queen's inhibitions led her not to make the *Namaste* salutation when meeting dignitaries. At that time, in that place, the second error mattered more than the first. Even the couple's return to the Antipodes in 1963 was a disappointment. It would have been fine but for comparisons with their unrepeatable first visit; and Britain's dalliance with Europe was a factor. Still, the royals noticed, and it would affect their thinking later in the sixties.

Beneath the royal summit, on the upper slopes of British aristocracy, chill winds were also blowing. Weeks before the Beeching Report that would dismember British Railways, the 10th Duke of Beaufort began a campaign to save his ancestral privilege that four trains a day must stop at Badminton, his local station on the Great Western main line. 'The Duke wants to preserve his rights,' said his agent, which was not the most diplomatic way of phrasing it in the iconoclastic sixties as a response to the railways' unsentimental new businessman boss, Dr Richard Beeching.

The duke did have a case, dating back to the railway being built on his land, and on this he certainly had the support of the local peasantry. But a junior minister, John Hay – a Tory at that – swept him aside, pointing out that a hundred families had similar claims on the Western Region alone. Hay also mentioned the Meyrick family of Hinton Admiral in Hampshire, who were still in the habit of ringing up, as if for a taxi, to command the attention of the Bournemouth–London express. All this, said Hay, was 'a potential obstacle to the carrying out of the policy of the railways in modern times' – meaning they wanted to close all these annoying country stations.

Still, the kerfuffle kept Badminton open until 1968, seven years longer than any of its neighbours. And the government did keep its promise of providing alternative transport links. Unfortunately, in this case it was the M4 motorway, which went smack through the territory of the Duke of Beaufort's Hunt. 'The greatest nightmare,' said the duke.

Still, Beaufort got by with his 50,000 acres. The Duke of Rutland was flush enough to invite 600 guests to his daughter's coming-out party at Belvoir Castle. But even the Duchy of Westminster had some tricky years after the death of Bendor, the mighty 2nd Duke, who despite his legendary sexual energy left no male heir; in 1953 his title passed for ten years to an ageing cousin kept sequestered after suffering brain damage at birth. But, with large chunks of London in the portfolio, the family came through it all very nicely.

For real nightmares among the twenty-six dukes, the 11th Duke of Argyll would be the most convincing claimant, when his third marriage (of four) disintegrated in a blaze of spectacular publicity. The duke won a divorce decree against the duchess in a Scottish court: 'Her attitude towards the sanctity of marriage was what moderns would call enlightened,' said the judge. That was the only understatement associated with this case.

Margaret Whigham was a Scottish millionaire's daughter brought up in New York who rapidly transfixed the rich young males of two continents. She opted for a presentable and upmarket American called Charles Sweeny, and they were married in 1933 in one of those London society weddings that drew huge crowds of gawpers in the pre-TV era. When Cole Porter's *Anything Goes* came to London in 1935, P. G. Wodehouse had the job of de-Americanizing the lyrics of the hit song 'You're the Top!' which contained dozens of lovers' gushing superlatives. Wodehouse slipped in the rhyme 'You're Mussolini, you're Mrs Sweeny' – an ill-starred coupling, though not an impossible one given the numbers they both notched up.

And she did not stay Mrs Sweeny that long; in 1951 she became the Duchess of Argyll, a promotion that unfortunately required her to marry the duke, a duty she did not carry out entirely in the spirit of the fifties' women's magazines. Before the decade was done, the duke, suspiciously rifling through his wife's desk, had found the names of eighty-eight apparent lovers and two interesting photographs, taken with a Polaroid instant camera in the mirrored bathroom of her Mayfair flat. One showed a naked man masturbating and the other the duchess performing fellatio. She was not naked; she was wearing three strands of pearls. In both pictures, the man's head was out of shot.

Practically everyone whose name had ever been linked with the duchess was suggested as 'the headless man' except for her husband and Mussolini, who had an alibi after being strung up on a lamp post. Two names were most persistent: those of Duncan Sandys, Churchill's son-in-law, and the actor Douglas Fairbanks Jr.

Shortly after Fairbanks's death in 2000, Channel 4 showed a documentary stating convincingly that he was the self-pleasurer because there were messages in his writing on the back of the print. However, it concluded that the one performing *à deux* had to be Sandys, the man largely responsible for tower blocks but at the time in question the defence minister. Polaroid cameras had long been around in the US but were not marketed in Britain until 1961. The only one in Britain was said to belong to the Ministry of Defence.

Years later, the socialite Lady Colin Campbell insisted the man concerned was an American airline executive called Bill Lyons, who might well have had a Polaroid, though that was a boring answer. In any case, even this story would soon be eclipsed, because headless men were soon to be replaced by an entire Establishment of headless chickens.

———

Even without the goings-on, there was plenty going on. Just before Christmas 1962, *That Was The Week That Was* ran a sketch making fun of 'Cross-Bencher', the anonymous column of bland political chit-chat that appeared in the *Sunday Express* every week. The column had had a bad run recently, in that its predictions kept on being wrong. This is not the sort of thing readers were inclined to notice, certainly not *Express* readers, unless it involved the racing tipster. But Hugh Cudlipp, boss of the rival *Mirror*, did notice, and mischievously had it fed as an item to *TW3*.

So the actors read out all the duff forecasts and mocked them, and then handed over to David Frost, who opened the early edition of the next day's paper and read: 'Despite his mysterious minor illness, Hugh Gaitskell is well on the way to recovery.' Frost then shook his head and sighed: 'Sorry, Hugh.'

Gaitskell was the leader of the Labour Party, who by now, with Macmillan floundering in the polls, looked to be on the path to victory in the next election. He was 56, respected, vigorous and increasingly commanding. He was thought to have had a nasty bout of the flu, bad enough to merit a stay in hospital. But he came out before Christmas. Then he went back in, and deteriorated mysteriously and rapidly. On 17 January 1963, he died.

The death was attributed to lupus, which remains a mysterious, protean and unpredictable condition. More excitable elements of MI5 suspected that Gaitskell might have been poisoned by the KGB; in December he had been to the embassy to collect a visa for a planned Moscow trip that never happened and, as a VIP, was offered coffee and biscuits.

Though no one expected a vacancy for Labour leader, the leading contender was Harold Wilson, who had made many trips to Moscow over the years and was vaguely associated with the left of the Labour Party. So – QED for MI5 – he was obviously a Russian agent. And indeed Gaitskell's doctor did approach MI5 to discuss whether he might have been murdered.

A senior spook, Peter Wright – later to become famous for his revelatory book *Spycatcher* – was despatched to see the chemical defence boffins* at Porton Down. He was told there was very little information about lupus, and what there was suggested a fatal dose would need more than coffee and biscuits. But maybe the Russians had come up with a refinement. However, Dr Ladell, a senior figure at Porton known as 'The Sorcerer', said it would take too much work to investigate and they were already overloaded. And that was that. One might have thought that the murder/ Wilson-the-spy theory was a mad fantasy – and with hindsight completely disproved by Wilson's actions as prime minister. But one might also have thought it was a potential national disaster. Either way, ignoring it because Ladell's department was short-staffed was clearly absurd.

Wilfred Sendall, the journalist who was writing 'Cross-Bencher' at that time, knew who was responsible for Gaitskell's death: he blamed himself.

———◆———

Most of the country also had more urgent priorities. The previous winter, 1961–62, had been cold, especially around Christmas time, when the barrister Lord Birkett wrote a paean in *The Times* to the delights of reading in bed. Later came a response to Birkett from Sidney Morris of Birmingham, a member of the shivering majority rather than the 3 per cent who had central heating: 'It would be a great service to those of us who do not enjoy central heating if he, or any kind reader, could suggest how this can be done without hands and shoulders becoming numb with cold.' The summer of 1962 was also fairly dismal. And then, on Boxing Day 1962, it started to snow.

The winter of '63, as it is known to everyone who lived through

---

* All scientists were known as 'boffins' in that era, especially in the popular newspapers.

it, was the first – though far from the last – sensational event of that year. Day after day, the temperatures would match the coldest day of an averagely miserable winter, but Britain's meteorological fickleness went AWOL and stayed away for seventy days before the snowdrifts were replaced by their traditional tail-gunners, the floods.

Over New Year, the South had its heaviest snowfall in eighty-two years. For weeks, getting stuck in snowdrifts was a potential hazard of any journey, by road or rail. Domestic water pipes froze, forcing people to queue at the ancient standpipes in the street – the original parish pump; sometimes bonfires had to be lit to prevent these freezing too. Helicopters had to rescue hundreds of staff from the Fylingdales early-warning radar station on the Yorkshire Moors, not once but twice.

Swaddled babies died in the bitter bedrooms, or were gassed when the pipes cracked. Two thousand ponies were buried by blizzards on Dartmoor; sheep starved on the fells. The sea froze along the south coast. In rural Herefordshire, recalled farm worker Sam Williams, they had the benefit of snowploughs, which had not been available in the other really bad post-war winter of 1947: 'The trouble was the drivers couldn't tell where the hedgerows were so they weren't any use.'

Fuel was not as desperately short as it had been in that wretched 'are you sure we won the war?' winter, though power-station workers did their best to make it so by staging a work-to-rule. Domestic coal supplies held out, but only just. Sport almost ground to a halt, and the football pools, then by far the country's most ubiquitous form of gambling, set up a panel of experts to predict results. 'It puts it on a level with ludo,' snorted Norman Banks, a director of Bolton Wanderers. What else could they do? The Scottish Cup tie between Airdrie and Stranraer was postponed *thirty-three* times.

Some people were happy. The Herefordshire country doctor Denys Brierley found that he could get round the lanes well enough in his Volkswagen. 'People were absolutely fine,' he said. 'There was no increase in illness. In fact they were better. They mixed less and the air was cold, so they got fewer germs.' The future *Telegraph* editor Charles Moore, aged six in Sussex, recalled: 'We sledged incessantly on snow that grew icier and therefore thrillingly faster as the weeks passed . . . For me, this was an enchanted time which I passionately did not want to end.'*

Others, with a different concept of passion, perhaps looked back to sunny days gone by. Maybe that hot day two summers before, when a government minister, staying with Lord Astor at his home at Cliveden, heard delighted squeals coming from the swimming pool and came across a 19-year-old missing her swimsuit and trying desperately to cover herself . . .

On 15 March 1963, shortly after the snowfields started to disappear and revealed swathes of dead grass, the *Daily Express* had a puzzling front page. The headline story said that a minister had offered his resignation 'for personal reasons' and the prime minister had asked him to stay. Adjacent to that was a story, with picture, about a 'model' who had gone missing when she was meant to be a witness in the trial of a man accused of trying to murder her. Most *Express* readers might have been a little bored or baffled by the prominence given to these two stories, though the girl was pretty enough. In the bars of Fleet Street and Westminster, however, the coded message would have been understood.

The minister at the pool and in the *Express* story was John Profumo, Minister for War, which was not even a Cabinet job. Still, he was on the up. He was 48, descended from Italian aristocracy – rich family, Harrow, Oxford, good war, very charming (charm is never to be confused with niceness), inclined to arrogance. His marriage to the actress Valerie Hobson, then starring in *The King and I* in Drury Lane was the wedding of the year in 1954. 'Miss

---

* My take, aged 11, was very different. At boarding school, football was abolished and we were forced to run endless cross-countries along the roads. Early in the morning I would torture myself by listening to the Test match commentaries from Australia under my pillow, where they talked about England's dropped catches and the heat. I passionately wanted to be there not here.

Hobson will abandon her acting career,' he said at the time. 'That is her own idea as well as mine.'

The girl at the pool – and the 'model' – was Christine Keeler. She was now 21, brought up in a converted railway carriage, almost totally uneducated but knowing, with a natural poise and bewitching beauty. At the pool, she cast an instant spell on Profumo.

They were introduced by Stephen Ward. He was aged 50 and a character who was hard to categorize in Britain's stratified society. He was an osteopath, a craft then regarded with disdain by the medical profession (never much interested in bad backs), yet became so highly regarded that he built a celebrity clientele. He was also a gifted artist. Personally, though clearly heterosexual, Ward had less interest in the customary activities of naked bodies than either Profumo or Keeler. He did like having girls around his house in Wimpole Mews, which is why both Keeler and her friend Mandy Rice-Davies lodged there for a while. He loved company, conversation, social climbing, convention-breaking and intrigue. He was undeniably louche, which turned out to be a capital offence.

Ward's friends included Yevgeny Ivanov, who was a Russian spy – one evidently tolerated under unofficial Cold War rules that allowed a certain amount of fair spying all round. There was also Lord Astor, so grateful for Ward's osteopathic skills (and keen to have him around for impromptu sessions), that he allowed him and his eclectic crowd of friends unlimited use of a Thames-side cottage on the Cliveden estate, and use of the pool. The big-house guests would mingle with the cottage guests, who that fateful weekend included Ivanov; fateful because the minister asked for Christine's phone number.

There is one incontrovertible fact about the Profumo affair. There was an affair, though hardly one of grand passion. Profumo did have sex with Christine Keeler, perhaps more often than he ever admitted, and once in his marital bed when the family were on holiday – 'an especially intimate betrayal,' wrote his son David, 'which my mother always found hard to forgive'.

'I simply thought that she was a very beautiful little girl who seemed to like sexual intercourse,' Profumo reflected to David. 'She

knew absolutely nothing. She had never read a book . . . All she
knew was about make-up and hair, and about gramophone records
and a little about nightclubs.'

The justification for this routine piece of adultery – which should
have concerned only three people – becoming a national, indeed
global, obsession for six months rested on one other fact and two
connected suppositions.* Profumo lied to the House of Commons.
It happened the week after the puzzling *Express* front page, as the
whispers grew louder about the minister and the missing model,
whose disappearance had nothing to do with Profumo and
everything to do with her instinct to run from trouble.

The Tory hierarchy recalled Profumo from a holiday in Italy
and, having taken a couple of sleeping pills, he was woken to explain
himself to a hastily convened 3 a.m. star chamber of senior
colleagues. The crucial question was said to have come from Iain
Macleod, the chairman of the Conservative Party: 'C'mon, Jack.
Did you fuck her or not?' Profumo gave his answer groggily then
and much more suavely to the Commons later: 'Miss Keeler and I
were on friendly terms. There was no impropriety whatever.'

It was June before the story unravelled. Keeler had found a
manager who was anxious for her to monetize her bombshell.
The single truth was wrapped in what was probably a bodyguard
of her own lies, and Profumo disappeared from parliament and
public life with astonishing finality. He fucked her and lied,
but why did that matter to anyone except his wife? Eden had led
Britain to war on falsehoods; so later did Tony Blair. Why did this
lie matter?

It was said there was a security risk, because Keeler had slept
with the war minister and the spy Ivanov. Profumo might have told
her military secrets which she then spilled to Ivanov. But the most
reliable guides to this tangled mess do not believe Keeler ever did
sleep with Ivanov; he was married, a professional spy in an

---

* There was also a great deal of extraneous noise about e.g. Ward's dealings with
MI5 and the violent feuds involving some of Keeler's other lovers. These matters
all help obscure the real iniquity.

unfriendly country and inherently wary of entrapment. If she did, the most likely timing was that first weekend, before Profumo had got to her. And anyway, as he said, it is absurd to imagine that Profumo was reckless enough to start chattering to Keeler about defence secrets. It was not a meeting of minds. If they spoke at all, said Noel Howard-Jones, a close friend of Ward, she would have talked about herself. 'The idea she could ever have discussed anything serious in bed is quite preposterous. You only have to know Christine to know that's true.'

But someone had a vested interest in playing up the security aspect. After Hugh Gaitskell's death, enough of the party's MPs put aside their wariness about the wily and wriggly Harold Wilson and voted for him ahead of his impulsive, unreliable and regularly drunken rival, George Brown. For the new leader, Profumo was gold dust. After the multiple spy scandals, here was another Tory-bashing stick for Wilson, and also a chance to finesse any of the tendentious whispers about his own patriotism.

Had Gaitskell lived, Labour's approach might have been much softer. His general air of priggish rectitude would not have been suited to the murky depths of this business. And in any case, it was well known at Westminster that Gaitskell had been engaged in an extramarital affair of his own – with, of all people, Ann Fleming, wife of James Bond's creator Ian.

———•———

That word *model* played a curious role in this business. It was widely understood to mean that both Keeler and Rice-Davies were prostitutes – or the more upmarket version, call girls. But was this true? 'They weren't call girls, by any means,' insisted the journalist Donald Zec. 'They were good-time girls. Besotted by the idea of being discovered or getting a small part in the Rank Organisation charm school. Or a job in the Embassy Club, being taken out by well-known people, hitting the high spots.'

One might say that all heterosexual mating rituals from the advent of reliable contraception to the rebalancing of gender relationships in the twenty-first century had an element of prostitution to them. Men nearly always had more money than women and paid for a first date. It was understood that the possibility of sex was, if not an immediate contractual obligation, then at least on offer just over the horizon, long before anyone contemplated marriage.

When the coupling involved the likes of Christine and Mandy and the rich men to whom they gravitated, it was more blatant. They both had a stint as the live-in lovers of the property racketeer Peter Rachman – not a great catch in terms of looks or, reputedly, sexual technique. But he lavished expensive gifts on them. Profumo handed Christine £20, a significant amount then, to give to her mum. She also slept with the property and retail tycoon Charles Clore, who gave her £50. He could have given her a mink coat instead, but he was a busy man: buildings to knock down, chain stores to buy. These were certainly not transactions as such. So where was that £50 on the scale that lies between a prostitute's fee and a token of undying romantic love?

A group of different men were convinced they knew what was going on, and set in motion a train of events that ended in a death. This was the real scandal. Four days after Profumo's original denial, four men met under the aegis of the inept Home Secretary Henry Brooke. They had identified the villain, Stephen Ward. All they needed to do was to find a crime. Sir Roger Hollis, the head of MI5, ruled out using the Official Secrets Act. The other three – Brooke, his domineering chief civil servant Sir Charles Cunningham, and the stressed commissioner of the increasingly out-of-control Metropolitan Police, Sir Joseph Simpson – knew what to do.

'Girls whom Ward knew seemed conveniently available for his male acquaintances,' wrote Richard Davenport-Hines in his fine account of the scandal, 'and it was unthinkable to the official mind that they might be sexually independent young women capable of making their own choices.' Obviously, he was pimping. 'Living off immoral earnings' – that was the way to get him. What everyone with any knowledge of the Ward ménage knew was that the girls scrounged off him. But this was no time for inconvenient facts.

Whether Brooke was motivated by political imperatives (Ward

had been blabbing to contacts in the Labour Party) or moral outrage is a matter of conjecture, but the Met could hardly have put in more resources if they thought Gaitskell *had* been assassinated. By the time of Profumo's undenial in early June, Britain was in the grip of hysteria. WHAT THE HELL IS GOING ON IN THIS COUNTRY? screeched the *Daily Mirror* the next day. No one knew, certainly not the prime minister. He was found one day fretting about a rumour that eight High Court judges had been involved in an orgy. 'One,' he said, 'perhaps two conceivably. But eight – I just can't believe it.' But he sort of did. 'Anything was possible and only the worst was to be believed,' reflected Christopher Booker, the first editor of *Private Eye*. There was even a new incarnation of the Headless Man, the mysterious Man in the Mask.*

Only one man was silent, the henceforth cloistered Profumo; only one was calm, Ward, who even after he was arrested on the pimping charge maintained a touching faith in truth, justice and above all his friends. But they melted away like the snow: cowardly and/or intimidated by the police. Instead, he was met in court by the barrister who came back from the reputational grave. Mervyn Griffith-Jones, practically laughed out of court for his wife-and-servants remark at the Lady Chatterley trial, stormed out of his corner slugging hard. He called Ward 'a thoroughly filthy fellow', and this jury, perhaps imagining there was a Thoroughly Filthy Fellows (Eradication) Act, took him seriously. Ward's barrister was completely over-matched. Griffith-Jones told them it was 'in the highest public interest to do your duty and return a verdict of guilty'. It was a pimping case, for heaven's sake. What the hell was going on in this country?

Mr Justice Marshall's summing-up, according to Ludovic Kennedy, who was in court, was biased not in content but emphasis and intonation; there was anecdotal evidence that Marshall had been given informal instructions about the required result. Certainly

---

* Mandy claimed at one point that she had been at a dinner party where a masked naked man acted as waiter. He had a mask on because he was so well known. If he existed.

the jury was prevented – probably by the Lord Chief Justice – from hearing evidence from the Appeal Court that Ward's main accuser, Keeler, had lied in another case involving the feuding lovers. For those lies she was later jailed. Neither she nor Rice-Davies was jailed for lying about Ward to protect their contracts with newspapers for their stories monstering him.

Ward got the message. He had a brief word with Tom Mangold of the *Daily Express* afterwards: 'This is a political revenge trial,' he said. 'Someone had to be sacrificed and that someone was me.' Before the judge had finished his summing-up, he went home, wrote some letters, took a vast quantity of Nembutal and died, after the guilty verdict, without regaining consciousness. There were six mourners at his funeral.

The official report into the Profumo affair appeared in September. It was written, single-handed, by Lord Denning, Master of the Rolls. Denning was a very popular judge: he looked and sounded like a Hampshire farmer, spoke and wrote in plain English, was known as 'Tom' and generally made *simpatico* judgments.

The report was written racily, with even racier sub-headings. It read like an old judge's first attempt at a bestselling novel. The original typescript was stamped TOP SECRET twice on every page. The finished product sold 100,000. Denning knew little of the subjects he wrote about, but he knew his duty. Everyone who still mattered (i.e. not Profumo or Ward) was exonerated. Surprise, surprise.

5

THEY LOVE US, YEAH, YEAH, YEAH

IN JANUARY 1963, BRITAIN'S LEADING SINGING STAR CLIFF Richard had to miss the premiere of his own new film, *Summer Holiday*, after 3,000 screaming fans broke through a police cordon in Leicester Square and mobbed his car. After two unsuccessful attempts to reach the cinema, police advised him to turn back. Cliff was said to be 'terribly upset'.

A month later, the chart-topping teenage chanteuse Helen Shapiro was heading the bill on a tour that had reached Carlisle. She had returned to the hotel after the show with the other touring artistes. Dinner after 10 p.m. was impossible almost anywhere in Britain beyond walking distance from Leicester Square, but someone invited them in to the Carlisle Golf Club's annual ball where the remnants of the buffet were still available. So they scoffed some food and Shapiro began twisting. Then a committee member asked them to leave. 'Some of her friends were wearing leather jackets at what was after all a private ball,' a guest told the *Daily Express*, which incidentally identified the friends as 'the vocal-instrumental group, the Four Beatles', before concentrating again on Shapiro's embarrassment.

A few weeks later the pecking order changed somewhat, and the screamers had changed their allegiance. The Beatles were the bill-toppers now. By the autumn, they had overhauled Profumo and Keeler and were challenging the royals as the most famous people in Britain. By early 1964, with President Kennedy dead, they may have been the most famous people in the world. Even the committee of Carlisle Golf Club had some vague idea who they were.

There are no analogies for the speed and extent with which Beatlemania swept the world, apart from Spanish flu and Covid. Before the 1960s, word travelled too slowly. Afterwards, cultural tastes splintered again. Forty years later, the Harry Potter books provided a similar if more limited phenomenon: equally unforeseen, equally hard to explain in terms of its scale. But J. K. Rowling shared two virtues with John, Paul, George and Ringo: an appeal that went beyond the original target age group, and that other helpful but not essential ingredient – being damn good.

Some commentators have tried to see the rise of The Beatles as being somehow connected to the Profumo affair – the disgrace of the old being cleansed by the exuberance of the young – or even the harsh winter. But that cannot explain the universality of their fame. They represented above all the resumption of the revolutionary fervour spearheaded by Bill Haley and Elvis before them. Their early hits, which are hard to see as great works of art, generated surges of electricity that had been missing from the charts for five years.

But there was a national dimension. They represented a kind of Britishness previously uncelebrated in their own land: working-class (or close enough), cheeky, quick-witted; not just northern but scouse, a concept hardly known in southern England never mind overseas,* where Englishness was considered synonymous with Sherlock Holmes, fog, bowler hats, stiff upper lips and not much else.

They had just the right degree of rebelliousness: hair a little longer than the militaristic male norm; jackets a little outré but still smart (they had not forsaken ties completely even in 1966). If you had taken a Beatle home for supper in 1963, mum and dad might have eyed them suspiciously, but they would have been won over well before pudding. And they were authentic: edgy John, cutesy

---

* *The Times* used the words *scouse* or *scouser* just twice between 1900 and 1965.

Paul, enigmatic George and zany Ringo. Other pop singers, before and after, had images created by their managers; The Beatles were pretty much what they seemed.

And they had learned their trade. Prototype versions of the group had played the YMCAs and awesome venues like Finch Lane bus depot and Litherland Town Hall. They had been the Quarrymen, John and the Moondogs, the Beat Brothers, the Silver Beetles. Above all they went to Hamburg, which was the pop music equivalent of basic training for the marines. They did all-night shifts: one hour onstage, one hour off from 6 p.m. to 6 a.m. 'We would never have developed as much if we'd stayed at home,' John Lennon reflected later. 'We played what we liked best. The Germans liked it, as long as it was loud. But it was only back in Liverpool that we realized the difference and saw what had happened. Everyone else was playing Cliff Richard shit.'

Lennon, Paul McCartney, George Harrison and the then-drummer Pete Best came back from their second stint in Hamburg in 1961 and began playing regularly in a sweaty Liverpool hole called the Cavern Club. They became a local cult and drew the attention of the young man who managed the city's leading record store, a rather lost soul working in his father's business. Thus Brian Epstein came into their lives as manager. He smartened them up, smoothed out some rough edges, made the operation business-like and hawked them around seeking recording contracts, undaunted by the rejections that, in all good stories, must precede success. Epstein persevered, and George Martin of Parlophone said yes.

What Epstein did not do was interfere with their music. He was obliged to do the dirty work by reluctantly sacking Best, one of the great nearly men of history, but it was not his choice. Martin's musical judgment combined with the other three's sense that Ringo Starr, who had filled in for Best occasionally, was more of a team player. They did not even stop to say sorry when they sacked him; the clattering train was already moving too fast.

At the end of October 1962, just after the Cuba crisis, The Beatles' debut single 'Love Me Do' crept into the lower reaches of the charts. The New Musical Express used to run a short feature called 'New to the Charts', a profile of any fresh artistes in that week's Top Thirty. The headline was LIVERPOOL'S BEATLES WROTE THEIR OWN HIT, something considered as novel as a talking dog.

The week before the Carlisle incident, word of The Beatles had reached London. The Liverpudlian Gillian Reynolds, back from Oxford and preoccupied with motherhood, told a university friend, Maureen Cleave – now writing for the London *Evening Standard* – to come up to the Cavern: something extraordinary was happening. Cleave came, saw and was bowled over: she noted the girls queuing for two and a half hours to see the band; she noted the group's 'self-confidence and professional polish' and their charm and their onstage patter, which she compared to Max Miller, slightly bawdy but conscious of not going too far. She did not say much about the music but she noted its effect. It was Gillian who fed her the best line: 'Their physical appearance inspires frenzy. They look beat-up and depraved in the nicest possible way.'

In January the boys had played a concert in Dingwall in the Highlands to an audience of 'about twenty'. In February, a few days after the Carlisle incident, their second release 'Please Please Me' had reached No. 2. In May they had their first undisputed No. 1, 'From Me to You'. By June they were so popular they were forced to race away from fans after a concert at New Brighton, whereupon Paul got nicked for speeding.

By August, the emblematic early Beatles song 'She Loves You' had sold a quarter of a million copies before release. In September, hundreds of girls rushed the stage of the Royal Albert Hall 'hurling litter' the moment The Beatles appeared and had to be repelled by a wall of commissionaires. One report explained that the litter was an expression of delight not disapproval, but did not state whether the detritus included knickers. In October, girls broke a back door and stormed the theatre as the group rehearsed for their star turn on *Sunday Night at the London Palladium*. Others climbed on to the roof. In November, they were the overwhelming centre of attention at the Royal Variety Show, even though Marlene Dietrich was top of the bill. That was the night when Lennon introduced 'Twist and Shout' by announcing: 'Will the people in the cheaper seats clap your hands? All the rest of you, if you'll just rattle your jewellery.'

In February 1964, they touched down in New York: 3,000 teenagers ran wild, hurling themselves at the 150 policemen at the start of the group's first brief tour, which culminated in their appearance on the *Ed Sullivan Show*, the American equivalent of the Palladium. Seventy million tuned in. By then it was time for the Carlisle Golf Club ball again. One wonders what they talked about.

———·———

In the early stages of The Beatles' escape from earthly gravity into outer space, they still had some contractual commitments not associated with superstars. The most unusual was at Stowe, a Buckinghamshire public school with mildly liberal tendencies where a Liverpudlian pupil, David Moores,* successfully negotiated with Brian Epstein to organize a concert. It was not just the setting that was unusual: Stowe had not yet embraced co-education, so the audience was overwhelmingly male – and also restrained by school rules. They did not scream; they listened.

Beatlemania encompassed primarily the response of younger teenage and preteen girls to the Fab Four. If The Beatles were not around, the groups who followed behind them would do instead. The music did not matter much, since they were screaming too loud to hear it. And the screamers made damn sure no one else heard it, the sound systems of the early sixties being primitive. This had an effect on their objects of adoration: it was certainly a factor in The Beatles' decision to scale down their touring schedule in 1965 and give it up completely the following year. If you play music and no one hears, does it even exist?

It was not just a British disease, it was a pandemic. But the sufferers were overwhelmingly female: 'They became emotionally, mentally, or sexually excited. They foamed at the mouth, burst into tears, hurled themselves like lemmings in the direction of The Beatles, or just simply fainted,' wrote Hunter Davies, The Beatles'

* Later chairman of Liverpool Football Club.

biographer. The sexual element was never in doubt: 'Not a dry seat in the house', as the saying went.

'Why?' someone asked the Australian writer Anwen Crawford. 'They don't have anywhere else to scream,' she responded. 'Where can girls give voice to their too-often thwarted desire to become creators, if not in the midst of these concerts where their role is to be fans?' American activist Barbara Ehrenreich saw it as a subconscious protest against girls' roles in an increasingly sexualized society. 'To abandon control – to scream, faint, dash about in mobs – was, in form if not in conscious intent . . . the first and most dramatic uprising of women's sexual revolution.'

But it had all happened before: in Britain with Johnnie Ray ten years earlier* and, in more naturally excitable societies, going back through the response to Sinatra, Valentino, Lindbergh, all the way to Lisztomania and all kinds of medieval madnesses. There were, however, less innocent manifestations. When the mania was still confined to Liverpool and every girl in town *almost* knew a Beatle, hairdresser Maureen Cox, Ringo's girlfriend and later wife, felt herself in serious danger from rivals who filled that role in their fantasies. They would come into the shop and threaten her; once she had her face badly scratched through her car window. 'I just got the window up in time,' said Cox. 'If I hadn't, she would have opened the door and killed me.'

Not all the objects of such adulation found it uncomfortable. Chad Stuart and Jeremy Clyde were a rather upmarket, soft-voiced British duo who went to the US in The Beatles' wake and hit the public fancy. Clyde remembered the screams without any regret. 'A wall of sound, a blast, like a jet engine. Never letting up. No pause for breath. It keeps on going,' he said. 'It was a young man's dream come true. "You're a star, and America's at your feet."'

———◆———

The hormonal compulsions of young men received less appreciation. Over the cold Easter of 1964, the British public awoke to the news

---

* See pp. 145–6.

that the country had two warring tribes, of whom they were previously unaware: the Mods and the Rockers. And they really hated each other, something that was evidently news to most of the actual Mods and Rockers themselves.

The Rockers' equivalent of screaming at unattainable pop stars was to ride motorbikes, making their own wall of sound, cocooned in leather (without, in those days, unmanly helmets), and looking fierce. This helped cover up the fact that quite a lot of them were rather shy.

The Mods rode, if anything, dainty Italian scooters like Vespas and Lambrettas, but were mainly interested in one thing: 'clothes', according to the sixties chronicler Jonathon Green. 'Not as some kind of tribal totem, but clothes as clothes. Sartorial art for art's sake.' Their spiritual home was Carnaby Street in London – for a few weeks anyway, until word spread too far and it became the most uncool place on the planet.

The Mods had far more influence on the decade than the Rockers, especially after The Who gave voice to the Mods' inner demons. But the London-based inner core were not prone to violence, being far more taken by a narcissistic interest in their snazzy suits, a taste for the amphetamine variant known as Purple Hearts, and an occasional tinge of homoeroticism.

That Easter Sunday, Clacton was cool as well as cold. The papers told the story: 'war . . . mob violence . . . day of terror . . . orgy of destruction . . .' Or, as the sociologist Stanley Cohen, who spent years studying the Mods and Rockers, put it: 'A few groups started scuffling on the pavements and throwing stones at each other . . . Those on bikes and scooters roared up and down, windows were broken, some beach huts were wrecked and one boy fired a starting pistol in the air.' Two dozen were charged, hardly any of them for violence.

According to Cohen, the rivalry was originally between local kids and the eternal enemy, Londoners. But after the publicity it became institutionalized. And it was all such fun that repeat days of terror were staged over the Whit weekend in May, notably at Margate where there were indeed two knifings, a man dropped on to a flower bed, and fifty deckchairs broken, slightly more than the bank holiday average.

However, Margate had a secret weapon who had had enough of being secret. Dr George Simpson, chairman of the magistrates, was ready for his close-up. As day trippers from Fleet Street took down every word, he declaimed: 'Vermin . . . long-haired, mentally unstable, petty little hoodlums, these sawdust Caesars who can only find courage like rats, in hunting in packs, came to Margate with the avowed intent of interfering with the life and property of its inhabitants.' Later, after handing out sentences and fines that made policemen gasp, he and his wife posed for pictures on the beach. 'The town was full of dirty grubby teenagers. It must not be allowed to happen again,' chimed in Mrs S.

And it never did. There were a couple of August fixtures at different resorts and then the Mods and Rockers generation – troublesome and untroublesome alike – grew up, had children and grandchildren and grew old, spending their holidays in warmer, more welcoming resorts while Margate mouldered away, forgotten.

———◦———

By astonishing coincidence, that Easter weekend of 1964 brought forth another fragment of sixties history, only a few miles from Clacton. Not in Britain itself but out to sea, just beyond territorial jurisdiction but well within medium-wave earshot for much of England. On board a retired Danish passenger ferry, Radio Caroline began broadcasting day-long pop to a still pop-starved nation. Thus began the era of pirate radio.

Whitehall and Westminster spent the next three years trying to invent a crime the pirate stations might be committing. The stations multiplied, feuded in a way that led to a murder case, and generally behaved piratically. But they attracted huge audiences, and the political price of their eventual suppression was the transformation of British radio. And henceforth it would be possible to *really* annoy people with your transistor set.

6

ENOUGH ROPE

E ARLY AUGUST 1963: THE COMBINED FORCES OF JUDICIARY, executive and his fair-weather friends had just hounded Stephen Ward to his grave. And it was just over a week since the Soviet Union had announced that their former star turn in MI6, Kim Philby, had been granted political asylum.

But there had also been a huge breakthrough in global politics: the West and the Soviet Union had signed the Nuclear Test Ban Treaty, which marked the end of the lukewarm war which had so nearly flared into conflagration less than a year earlier. The threat of global annihilation slowly receded from people's minds. Harold Macmillan, so close to defenestration as prime minister at the height of Profumomania, was breathing a little easier now. The polls showed that the 20 per cent Labour lead in June was now a mere 15: merely horrific for the Conservatives rather than catastrophic.

And then came a more local distraction. At 3 a.m. on 8 August, a mail train from Glasgow to London came to an unscheduled halt at a red signal in the Buckinghamshire countryside. This really was the Great Train Robbery. And though sixty years have passed, and crimes of much greater magnitude (inflation or no inflation) have been committed, it remains the Greatest, its hold on the British imagination undiminished. The test ban treaty? Important but not interesting.

Part of that is connected to the enduring British obsession with trains. But it also fed into the mood of the moment: the government was useless, the elite corrupt, complacent and concupiscent. Yet here were a group of men who set an ambitious plan and executed it with precision, panache, audacity and, well, not *much* violence. Good luck to them, was the immediate response. At least someone knew what they were doing.

There was no red signal: it was presumably created by the magicians thought to be involved in those practice runs on the Brighton line. The fireman, David Whitby, came down to phone the signalman and was bundled down the embankment. The driver, Jack Mills, appeared and got coshed. Bleeding, he was forced to drive the diesel engine to its predetermined position so it could be decoupled, the workers in the mail coach tied up (no coshing required) and the high-value bags passed down to the embankment and into the waiting lorry.*

The bags contained about £2.5 million of what was then Britain's highest-value currency: fivers, one-pound and ten-shilling notes (about £50 million at 2022 prices). They were being sent to the Bank of England to be officially destroyed, because that was the way it was done. They were not rendered unusable in any way, nor was a record kept of most of the numbers. You might think this damn stupid.

The gang, however, had thought of almost everything, including specifically hiring the railway experts, and almost everything worked. As they drove back to their hideout, listening to the police radio, the robbers heard a voice saying: 'You won't believe this. But they've just stolen a train.'

The losers from this were notionally the banks, with the losses covered by Lloyd's of London; there were no weeping grannies left bereft of savings. Nothing to stop the public regarding the

---

* To be more accurate, since it was a diesel engine, Whitby was the co-driver rather than the fireman. The exact roles of individual gang members on the night has been the subject of much speculation and obfuscation, most particularly the identity of the man who coshed Mills. Both Mills and Whitby died within a few years of the robbery, Whitby aged only 34. Both families believed they never recovered from the ordeal, a perpetual stain on the robbers' quasi-heroic status.

gang as somewhere between Dick Turpin and Raffles. And Reginald
Bevins, the Postmaster General, was very aware of this when he
flew back to London from his holiday: 'I don't feel any admiration
for these gentlemen at all,' he said tetchily. 'In fact, I would not use
the word gentlemen.'

But the robbers were not infallible. The first mistake came when
they tied up Mills and Whitby and told them not to move for half
an hour. That suggested the hideout was close by. The police knew
London's cleverer criminals – if not the *most* clever – and soon
noted who was and was not around. And the tasty reward on offer
found takers.

Five days later, the police, sweeping the countryside, began to
get close to the hideout, Leatherslade Farm; the gang left hurriedly,
too hurriedly. One member, Roy James, had fed the farm cats and
his prints were on the bowl. (No good turn goes unpunished.) They
had passed the time by playing Monopoly with the real money,
and there were prints on the board. The police knew nearly all the
men they wanted, had the evidence to convict, and soon enough
only three of them remained at large.

The men in custody were tried in January 1964. Almost all
offered some kind of defence but, as old pros, they knew what to
expect: ten years if lucky (less than seven with remission), fifteen or
eighteen if not. They were wrong. 'Let us clear out of the way any
romantic notions of daredevilry,' said Mr Justice Edmund Davies.
'This is nothing less than a sordid crime of violence inspired by
vast greed.' He also mentioned 'the nerve-shattered engine-driver'
and added: 'To deal with this case leniently would be a positively
evil thing.'*

Seven gang members were given thirty years; the peripherals
twenty-plus. This was not a message to the gang members, nor even
to potential imitators. It was a message to the British public, who
had not been sufficiently outraged and needed to be taught a lesson.

---

* The judge was a Welsh grammar school boy, but once on the bench was said to
have become rather pompous: 'the sort of man who refers to fish and chipped
potatoes,' said one barrister.

As the MP Reginald Paget put it, 'a property-owning judiciary has imposed sentences eight times as long as it would impose for the most brutal crime against a child'.

In a sense, the sentencing was repudiated by his colleagues. The three men who were not caught until much later ended up with much lighter sentences. Bruce Reynolds, the acknowledged mastermind of the caper who evaded capture for more than five years, was given less than the others: twenty-five years, out in nine.*

And two of those inside jail made their own way out, with the support of fellow inmates who thought the sentences unjust. Charlie Wilson went AWOL for four years and Ronnie Biggs famously had thirty-six years on the outside, most of them in broad daylight – because he had fathered a child in Brazil and, under Brazilian law, could not be extradited. The curious criminal sense of fair play also extended to the spy George Blake, a sincere ideologue who became popular with his fellow inmates and who was sprung from Wormwood Scrubs five years into his scheduled forty-two. Blake successfully got out of the country but had to spend the rest of his life in Moscow instead. Biggs seemed to have had the better deal.

———————

The question of very long sentences was about to become extremely significant, because the most reliable method of avoiding them was going out of fashion. In an era when many deep-rooted customs were disappearing fast, one last controversial case finally put paid to hanging.

It was a really ghastly murder. A summer's evening in 1961; Michael Gregsten and Valerie Storie, work colleagues and lovers, sitting in a Morris Minor at a Thames-side beauty spot near Windsor, 'chatting' after an evening drink – he, as it happened, married to someone else. A man taps on the window, pointing a

———————

* After many adventures, Reynolds was living in a pleasant book-filled house overlooking Tor Bay when Tommy Butler of the Yard appeared uninvited in his bedroom. 'It's been a long time, Bruce,' said Butler. '*C'est la vie,*' replied Reynolds.

gun. He forces them into a nightmare drive across the country. They get to a lay-by on the A6 in Bedfordshire: the gunman shoots Gregsten, fatally, then rapes Storie before shooting her too, leaving her alive but paralysed.

The motive was never clear. But what made the case uniquely troublesome is that there was not one suspect, but two. One was James Hanratty, last heard of in this book as the young man building a garage for the Frank family in Kingsbury.

Things had not gone well. He had turned into a petty but serially unsuccessful criminal: not a violent one though. The other was Peter Alphon, who behaved erratically after the murder and on some occasions appeared to confess.

The Scotland Yard man in charge, Robert Acott, concluded that Alphon was a fantasist, dismissed him and built a case against Hanratty. He was charged, faced a trial that lasted three full weeks, found guilty and executed. It was certainly not a murder when the Home Secretary could offer a reprieve – it was too wicked for that. And the jury had spoken.

But the evidence was complex and never clear-cut: it hinged on Storie's evidence after picking him out, second time lucky, at an identity parade: his piercing blue eyes and London accent ('fink' not 'think'). The argument became divisive, like the Dreyfus affair that convulsed *fin-de-siècle* France. The Establishment said justice had been done, and the Left thought not; this would not be resolved for nearly forty years, if then. The barrister Louis Blom-Cooper said it showed the flaws in the entire British adversarial system of justice: there was no one like the French *juge d'instruction* whose chief task was to ascertain the truth. 'My father refused to believe he could possibly have done it,' said Laura Frank (now Spira). 'He was certainly a bit what was called backward. But we never saw him as a delinquent. There was another boy down the road like that, but not James.'

One thing was certain: this was yet another argument against the finality of hanging. For the legislative classes, if not the public, that would now be settled.

—·—

After all the tumult and the shouting, it ended almost unnoticed, at
8 a.m. precisely on 13 August 1964. Not an echo of the roars of
Victorian delight when public hangings were like Derby Day; nor
the vigils and occasional flare-ups outside the jails in Mrs van der
Elst's heyday of the early fifties. She was old and ill now and may
not even have noticed the executions of Gwynne Evans and Peter
Allen, one in Manchester, the other in Liverpool. Hardly anyone
else did. There were two paragraphs in the southern edition of the
Daily Mail and one in the *Daily Telegraph*, on page 17.

The case was as vile as the A6 murder, without the controversy.
They barged in on the modest home, just outside Workington, of
John Alan West, a 53-year-old laundry roundsman. They stole two
bank books and a long-service gold watch, bashed him on the head
and stabbed him in the heart. In due course, laundry roundsmen,
bank books and long-service gold watches would all become
obsolete. But hanging became obsolete at once. These two took the
total of twentieth-century hangings in the UK to 753; thereafter it
was zero.

It is strange that no one noticed the significance. The general
election was only two months away, Labour were hot favourites
to win, and the party, including the putative Home Secretary Sir
Frank Soskice, was now overwhelmingly against hanging. When
he took over, Soskice announced that he would reprieve all
murderers pending parliamentary resolution; in 1965 this turned
into a five-year moratorium; before that time ran out, abolition
became permanent.

This certainly did not put an end to agitation for the rope's
return, which would peter out only through generational change. A
similar process attended the end of corporal punishment via the
courts (in the 1940s), in prison (last used 1962), in schools (later)
and, perhaps, in the home (ongoing). Whether the naughty step
constitutes an adequate replacement for the smack is a question for
another time.

7

THE LAST FROM THE PAST

As POLITICS RESUMED IN THE AUTUMN OF 1963, HAROLD Macmillan was feeling calmer. Whole weeks had gone by without further sexual revelations; he could now consider his own position as prime minister calmly.

He was almost 70; he had survived being forced out in the midsummer Profumo frenzy, and he could retire on his own terms. So he considered the candidates for succession, and concluded that the best choice would be Lord Hailsham, the Minister for Science. This was odd, since he had never cared much for the erratic and bombastic Hailsham.

Perhaps that's why, on the Monday before the annual Conservative conference, he made up his mind to stay on himself. The notion of Hailsham was only even remotely possible by fluke, Britain having evolved beyond having unelected peers as prime minister. But the Peerage Act had passed into law that summer after a campaign by the 2nd Viscount Stansgate – who preferred to sit in the House of Commons, which he had been forced to leave when his father died. He fought to change the law, revert to his old name of Anthony Wedgwood Benn* and have the right to return to the Commons. The Act allowed a one-year window for all peers to

---

* Or, as he later preferred, as the times became less formal and his politics further left, Tony Benn.

renounce their titles, which gave Hailsham an opportunity – and the Foreign Secretary, the 14th Earl of Home, although the idea of Home as PM was unthinkable anyway.

Then, in the early hours of Tuesday, Macmillan woke with an agonizing pain caused by a tumour in his prostate, that mysterious part of the male anatomy that lay undiscovered by anyone until the sixteenth century and by most men ever since until they are, like Macmillan, past 60.

It seems clear now that Macmillan was told very quickly that the tumour was not malignant, and that he did not resign in panic. But he told his surgeon it was 'manna from heaven' in forcing him to make the decision to go. On the Wednesday, from hospital, he drafted his resignation message for Home to read out in his capacity as president of the Tory party's national association, a Buggins'-turn job which gave special status at the conference in Blackpool.

On the Thursday, Home read the message, which talked of starting the 'customary processes of consultation', i.e. the primitive system of soundings that allowed the Conservative Party to avoid the vagaries and vulgarities of internal democracy. To an extent it could be controlled by the outgoing leader, but only to an extent. It is not necessary to have democracy to have politics. Any one of the three main contenders could have seized the prize by taking the conference by storm.

Oh, what a week it was, even by the dramatic standards of 1963. It seethed with intrigue and whispers washed down by the rivers of alcohol that lubricate all party conferences. And one by one the contenders imploded. The first was Hailsham, who theatrically announced he would indeed renounce his peerage, reverting to the name of Quintin Hogg. His fan club in the hall went wild; buttons appeared around Blackpool with just the letter Q; and, having just fathered a daughter* at the age of 55, Q proceeded to (bottle) feed her surrounded by photographers in the foyer of the Imperial Hotel. This might have made him president of the United States but it was too much for the Conservative Party.

---

* In wedlock, unfashionably.

The other two made the reverse mistake and underplayed their hand. The youngest (46), freshest option was the Chancellor Reggie Maudling. He was chubby, chummy, cheery, instinctively idle, but also, said the future Cabinet Secretary Robert Armstrong, 'the most formidably intelligent man I ever worked with'.* Not for the last time, his intelligence deserted him. He composed a perfectly decent speech glossing over the indecent state of the economy, but delivered it in a flat monotone and got minimal applause. Exit Maudling.

And then, as ever, there was Rab Butler. 'The finest political nose I've ever known,' said Armstrong. 'But he was a strange enigmatic character, acutely sensitive.' And his nose sometimes let him down. He lacked the killer instinct, but wounded with cutting comments to colleagues. The chairman of the 1922 Committee of backbenchers, John Morrison, had already told him: 'The chaps won't have you.'

Butler was, perforce, the star of the show. In Macmillan's absence, he had the prime-ministerial suite and the prime minister's speaking slot. He had to poke gentle fun at Harold Wilson to make the party chuckle, tell them how the Tories were going to win the election and how Labour would ruin everything, and rouse the troops by hinting at the great things that would be done in the fourth consecutive Tory term – without quite spelling out that he was the man to do it. Too diffident, he blew it.

It was said he was disorientated by having lunch with Home just before the speech. Home had mentioned casually that he had to see his doctor when he got back to London. Why was that? asked Butler. Because he had been approached to become leader, he replied. Home was supposed to be the man taking the soundings; it is always an error to underestimate the ruthlessness of a charming Etonian.

---

* The young Armstrong was sent to accompany him on a Treasury trip to New York. One day, Maudling had to do a broadcast. 'I offered to show him the briefing paper,' Armstrong recalled. 'He said: "No, let's go to the flicks." When we came out I offered again. He said: "Let's go shopping." He never did read the brief. Then he did the broadcast. He was told he had to speak for thirteen and a half minutes. He did it without a note. It made perfect sense. It had a beginning, a middle and an end. And it lasted thirteen and a half minutes.'

The fix was in, but it was not an unjustified fix. Leaving aside the long-standing grudges between him and Butler, it was legitimate for Macmillan to see the minuses for every other candidate and promote the one most likely to cause least upset – the one the chaps would have. And thus, in perhaps the most bizarre of all prime-ministerial audiences, held in a downstairs room at the King Edward VII's Hospital, the invalid Macmillan – in a silk shirt with a rug over his knees – read out to his sovereign the pros and cons of the possibles and then, in D.R. Thorpe's words, 'like Hercule Poirot disentangling a mystery, Macmillan went through the names of all the suspects, before picking out the one least expected'.

The Queen called Lord Home to the Palace and cautiously asked him just to see if he could form a government. He could and did, for the loss of two pro-Butler ministers, Iain Macleod and Enoch Powell. Then he renounced his earldom (though not the attendant 100,000 Scottish acres), found a convenient Commons seat as Sir Alec Douglas-Home,* and all was calm.

————◆————

In a sense, he was a useless prime minister. There were no major foreign crises, which were his forte, since he had no interest in domestic policy or economics. He had, some years before, admitted he needed matchsticks to do sums. This was not self-deprecation: Maudling, his Chancellor, said Douglas-Home never understood a word he was saying. He allowed the energetic Ted Heath to have his way and abolish retail price maintenance, thus allowing retailers to set the price of their stock. This led to the surge of supermarkets and the slow strangulation of small shopkeepers, which was perhaps inevitable.

But Douglas-Home displayed no interest in the modernization that had preoccupied Macmillan, or much else. Indeed, though he was the first prime minister born in the twentieth century, he came

---

* At different stages of his life, he went under five different names (Alec D-H, the Earl of Dunglass, the 14th Earl of Home, Sir Alec D-H and then Baron Home of the Hirsel). Only much-married women can normally match that.

across as a throwback. The young MP Julian Critchley spotted him one day coming out, alone, from the Carlton Club. Writing thirty years later, he recalled: 'As he walked up the street, passers-by solemnly raised their hats and, in return, Alec gravely acknowledged their salutes. Two points come to mind: in the mid-sixties men still wore hats; and "security" . . . was then quite unheard of.'

Not quite. Douglas-Home was *supposed* to have a burly police-man in attendance, but he spent one night staying with friends near Aberdeen who had no room for the bodyguard. And briefly, he was left home alone; the doorbell rang so he answered it. Two left-wing students were at the door and said they were there to kidnap him. 'I suppose you realise if you do, the Conservatives will win the election by two or three hundred,' he replied gently. He stalled for time and gave them a beer; they departed in peace, and maybe voted for him.

This story did not emerge for forty-four years. But it does seem emblematic: Douglas Hurd said Sir Alec ranked with King Hussein and Nelson Mandela as the most courteous men he ever met in politics. But, as David Frost had said on *TW3*, he was Dull Alec in public.*

At Labour's less dramatic conference the week before the Battle of Blackpool, Harold Wilson had found a way of uniting his party behind a vision of the future. 'We are redefining and we are restating our Socialism in terms of the scientific revolution . . . The Britain that is going to be forged in the white heat of this revolution will be no place for restrictive practices or for outdated methods on either side of industry.'

Of course, nothing like that happened in practice. But it sounded *great* and it was not a speech Sir Alec could have attempted. Wilson, as a contemporary of President Kennedy, loved the comparison, even if he had none of JFK's looks, charisma or raging libido. He also had a talent for mockery, did Wilson, if not for being mocked; and he really did seem the man of the moment. Still, something of Douglas-Home's inner calm must have got through to the electorate because the polls started narrowing. In October 1964 the Labour

---

* It's true. I sat through a speech of his.

Party under Wilson won the election, but with a majority of just five.

Sir Alec was not the only one in the fallen Tory government whose grasp of sums was in question. Reggie Maudling left the customary welcome note for his successor at the Treasury, Jim Callaghan. This one read: 'Good luck, old cock . . . Sorry to leave it in such a mess.' It turned out that Labour's campaign attacks on Tory financial policies had been understatements. On the very day he walked into 10 Downing Street, Wilson was told by the Treasury that the projected £500 million annual balance of payments deficit was really £800 million.

The next evening, Wilson, Callaghan and George Brown, who had been given a nebulous and short-lived job as head of the Department of Economic Affairs, met Treasury officials to discuss the situation. There was one obvious solution: an immediate devaluation of the pound. Wilson would not hear of it.

This was a prime minister who would thrive on crises. He feasted on last-ditch talks, face-saving deals and patchwork solutions. His most important aide was his secretary Marcia Williams, who specialized in screaming insults, often at him. This would be the daily routine of British government for the rest of the sixties. Had he jumped the other way on devaluation, much of that might have been avoided. In that first week, all the blame could have been heaped on the Tories and there would have been breathing space for all the social benefits and go-getting technological policies Wilson had promised. Instead, Labour spent their first three years in office defending an indefensible exchange rate of $2.80 to the pound, by which time his reputation for competence had been shredded.

But Wilson was seared by history. Devaluation in the era of fixed currency rates was a major blow to national machismo; he had been part of the Attlee government when it devalued (from $4.03 to $2.80) in 1949 and was acutely aware of how Labour had been flayed for it. He had constantly rejected it in opposition. It would need major austerity measures to make it work. He also felt a touching duty of care for the 'sterling area', the mostly

Commonwealth countries who trustingly kept their reserves in pounds; they would have suffered collateral damage. And the majority was tiny: the next election could not be delayed long.

The eighteen-month-long parliament from 1964 to 1966 was Wilson's halcyon age. 'He was obviously, delightedly, incomparably in control,' wrote his biographer Ben Pimlott. 'Often he seemed like a juggler spinning plates on sticks, moving rapidly from one to the next to keep all in motion, while maintaining a witty patter to the audience.' Douglas-Home resigned as Tory leader, his route to the summit via what Iain Macleod damned as the 'magic circle' now discredited. The choice was taken over by the party MPs, who narrowly voted for Heath over Maudling, perceiving Heath to be more energetic. In 1966 Wilson trounced Heath: the single figure majority became almost triple figures. And then things really went pear-shaped.

8

MICKEY MOUSE AND RATTÍN

IN THE 1960 OLYMPICS, HELD IN ROME IN SWELTERING LATE summer, Britain won the grand total of two gold medals, compared to forty-three for the Soviet Union and thirty-four for the United States. The swimmer Anita Lonsbrough was one, Don Thompson the other.

Thompson's name is not much remembered, but he was the absolute embodiment of the best of British sport in that era: he was small (five-foot-five), determined, inventive, ordinary (a Home Counties insurance clerk), extraordinary, indeed downright eccentric. He competed in the 50-kilometre walk, a thoroughly eccentric event anyway – and a contentious one, since the rules about what constitutes legal walking and illegal running are somewhat abstruse.

Having collapsed when close to a medal in 1956, Thompson devised his own method of preparing for the heat. Several days a week he went up to the little bathroom of his semi, put on a heavy tracksuit, switched the wall heater on full, brought in steaming pots and kettles of water, stuffed towels round the door and windows, and lit a paraffin stove. He then exercised for half an hour, by which time he felt faint. Lucky, really: it was years before he realized the faintness was due to carbon monoxide from the stove.

In Rome he put clip-on shades over his thick specs, wore a *képi* into which his mum had sown a hanky, and he beat the world. The Italians thought it was hilarious and called him *Il Topolino* (Mickey Mouse). The British, vaguely embarrassed, waited ten years before handing Thompson an MBE, then the honours-list going rate for a gold.* He never made money but he was once the guest celebrity on *What's My Line?*

———◆———

The participants in the national sport were only slightly better off. Footballers could read the front pages as well as the back; they knew what factory workers were earning, and they were getting antsy. And they found a dauntless leader: a grammar school boy, a decent player for Fulham, and a nonconformist (he had a beard). Jimmy Hill became chairman of the Professional Footballers' Association in 1957, and by 1961 he was ready to strike – and so were his men.

It was a big step for them, given their £20-a-week maximum wage and the attendant conditions of near-slavery. And there were doubters. The players held regional meetings, and in Manchester one young player (his name unrecorded) bravely got up and put the case for the status quo: 'My dad's a miner, earning £10 a week. I play in the lower divisions and I earn twice as much. I train in the open air and play football on Saturday – he's down the pit for eight hours at a time, five days a week. That can't be right. We earn quite enough as it is.'

This impelled a player of more stature, Tommy Banks of Bolton and England, to reply. He had been a miner himself, and knew how tough it was down the pit. But, he said, there would not be 30,000 paying spectators watching the boy's dad work on a Monday morning.

The players stayed solid, the government and even the right-wing press backed them, the clubs caved. They tried to renege later but

---

* Ken Matthews, an electrician from Sutton Coldfield who had to take his annual holidays to compete, won the 20-kilometre version of the walk in 1964. He was one of four British gold medallists; the others got MBEs at once – he had to wait until 1977.

the end was nigh. Soon enough, Hill's teammate Johnny Haynes was famously earning £100 a week and the others were pulled upwards in his wake. 'When we got onto forty quid a week, we all started to acquire what we thought were fancy cars,' Terry Neill of Arsenal recalled. 'I'm talking about a Sunbeam – second-hand, of course, knockdown price, a bit rusty.' But it was the start of something massive.

Two years later, the case of Eastham v. Newcastle United was heard before Mr Justice Wilberforce, whose great-great-grandfather William Wilberforce had led the movement to abolish the slave trade in the Empire. His descendant was very conscious of his heritage and ruled that the clubs' practice of stopping players going elsewhere, even if their contracts had expired, was illegal.

———◆———

Football remained troubled throughout the early sixties. As the players began to get a little richer, crowds continued to dwindle, for which a report commissioned by the league blamed family life (or, as the *Daily Express* translated it: 'selfish, jealous, resentful women') and the rise of alternative leisure pursuits, but also bad football and bad facilities. In 1964 there was a match-fixing scandal which led to life bans and jail sentences for ten players, including two England internationals, Peter Swan and Tony Kay, who were allegedly shopped to *The People* by the very man, Jimmy Gauld, who had inveigled them into the fraud in the first place. Curiously, this happened just after players' pay began to rise, which is an interesting comment on human nature. Thereafter, all betting on individual English football matches was banned until the players became so wealthy they were effectively incorruptible.

Hooliganism was becoming a serious problem. British Rail stopped all football specials from Merseyside; referees threatened to boycott matches at Millwall; and Tottenham Hotspur banned four youths for life for obscene chanting. Not everyone involved could be described as the usual suspects. Ex-soldier Bill Brown invaded the pitch to join in an on-field punch-up during a non-league match at Lytham in Lancashire. It was his 82nd birthday. 'I never could resist a scrap,' he said. And when scuffles broke out after a West Ham–Stoke match, Essex housewife Sheila West (obviously not one of the selfish, jealous, resentful women) left her two children in the stand while she went down to punch the referee. Mortified, she went to Swansea the next day and knocked on his front door to apologize. 'A real gentleman,' she said.

Other sports were groping towards the future as well, in their very different ways. Before the 1963 season, cricket decided to initiate a one-day knockout tournament and to abolish the ancient class distinction between 'gentlemen' and 'players': the officer-class amateurs and the professionals who were paid, but even less than the footballers. A trial run for one-day cricket had been staged by four Midland teams the previous summer. Northamptonshire won the final and the players were given an ashtray each.

In 1962, a fortnight before the annual Varsity match, the Cambridge rugby team was ordered to go on the wagon. Their opponents were disdainful of this thoroughly untraditional approach: 'We believe in a good old after-the-match thrash at the bar,' said Oxford captain Joe McPartlin. 'My team are very happy and light-hearted.' Ominously for devotees of sport as fun, Cambridge won.

Top-level sport could be as casual as the businessmen's golf. In 1967, the reigning Wimbledon champion Manuel Santana was knocked out by the unknown American Charlie Pasarell, who explained to incredulous reporters: 'For the last few days I have been training in the locker room – skipping and doing press-ups. Getting a real sweat on.' 'I don't believe in training,' said the most talented British not-very-hopeful of the era, Bobby Wilson.

The 1967 Wimbledon tournament marked the debut of colour on British TV, and the most talked-about character of all was a red-haired ballboy, cunningly given shifts on the show courts to attract attention and bump up sales of colour sets. It was also the last all-amateur Wimbledon. The next year there was prize money: £2,000 for the men's champion, £750 for the women, which made it almost worth a few minutes in a gym.

Other sports, not steeped in British values, were already taking winning more seriously. And the week after that last pure honour-and-glory Wimbledon final, Tommy Simpson, desperate to become the first Briton to win the Tour de France, collapsed and died climbing Mont Ventoux. Fleet Street blamed the searing heat; the inquest talked about the amphetamines in his body. Everybody was at it, and had been for years. The Tour had been professional from its inception.

———·———

In 1966, for the first and as yet only time, the football World Cup was held in England. Three years earlier, Alf Ramsey, who had just made Ipswich the most improbable and rustic of all league champions, had taken over as England manager; his predecessor, Walter Winterbottom, having been bedevilled by interfering committees. Ramsey demanded and was given total control.

He was an aloof, inscrutable figure, ill at ease in some ways – so keen to take Dagenham out of his voice that he could sound like Harold Steptoe, the son in the rag-and-bone sitcom *Steptoe & Son*, chatting up a posh bird. But Ramsey was at ease with footballers and had confidence in his strategy, and when it mattered most it worked. England's World Cup win became an epic of the race, becoming ever more potent as the decades flew by without it being repeated.

And it was a very English epic, beginning in terrible humiliation and continuing through adversity, filthy tricks from the enemy, a damn-close-run-thing in the final, and a lucky break to bring victory. There was even a heroic dog. It was a war film without the bloodshed – unless, that is, you take a very long view.

The humiliation was the theft of the trophy from a pre-tournament exhibition in London; the heroic dog was Pickles, a Thames waterman's mongrel, who got very excited when he found something unusual in the garden hedge.

In keeping with tradition, England's opening match was a miserable o-o draw. But they did enough to win the qualifying group and set up the infamous quarter-final against Argentina. In the English version, the Argentinians behaved like 'animals' (Alf

Ramsey); their captain Antonio Rattín was responsible for 'habitual fouling', 'ranting', 'violence of the tongue' and described as a 'fine player totally without self-control' (the respectable British papers), and was sent off in the first half by a notably officious German referee, though it took the Argentinians a full eight minutes to accept the decision and get on with the game. England still struggled to eke out a 1-0 win.

The name Rattín – suitably evil-sounding to Anglophones – persisted in English football for years as a symbol of villainy. But there was another side to the story. Football was much less global then and, according to the soccer historian Jonathan Wilson, South American football was much more about self-expression than the European game, which meant their referees were tougher on physical fouls and more relaxed about the verbals. There were nineteen European referees in the tournament – and four from South America.

And right from the start, the long-distance travellers had been storing up a set of grievances that began to suggest conspiracy rather than just British arrogance and ineptitude. Both Argentina and Brazil were given training grounds with no goalposts. Travel and hotel arrangements were often dire, most especially for the foreign media, which is an infallible way of undoing years of soft diplomacy. England, of course, played all their matches on their home turf at Wembley.

Pelé, the world's best player, was kicked to buggery by Bulgaria and Portugal, and the Brazilians failed to reach the last eight. As Argentina went down to defeat at Wembley, the only other South Americans left in the tournament, Uruguay, had two players sent off against West Germany by an English referee. From the southern hemisphere, it seemed like a massive Anglo-German conspiracy, an original view of twentieth-century European history.

A nice, quiet win over Portugal and then the unforgettable final against the Germans: an early German goal . . . two for England . . . then a last-minute equalizer . . . the England players slumping on the turf as they contemplated a further half-hour, Field Marshal Ramsey yelling: 'Look at them!' indicating the

equally weary Germans. 'They're FINISHED!' . . . Geoff Hurst's
shot that bounced off the underside of the crossbar and ricocheted
downwards . . . the agonizing wait until 'the Russian linesman'*
ruled it was a goal . . . and finally commentator Kenneth Wolsten-
holme's magic moment: *Some people are on the pitch! They think
it's all over!* [Hurst makes it 4–2.] *It is now!'*

That night, English football officialdom showed that its crassness
was not a sign of xenophobia: the England players' wives were
banned from the banquet, though the dignitaries' wives went in.
Jack Charlton, whose wife was absent giving birth to a son, sneaked
out, found a journalist pal, Jim Mossop, and grabbed him. They
escaped to a nightclub, and never had to buy a drink all night. They
woke the next morning in the living room of a house in Walthamstow,
not entirely sure of the sequence of events.

The South Americans forgot nothing. 'Britain,' concluded the
Buenos Aires newspaper *Clarín*, 'is still the pirate that despoiled the
Caribbean and robbed us of the Malvinas' (aka the Falkland Islands,
the British colony 300 miles from the Argentine coast, 7,000 from
London). Two months after the match, Argentinian hijackers
mounted a quarter-hearted invasion attempt by forcing a plane to
land on the Falklands' racecourse, where it sank into a peat bog. As
islanders innocently rushed to help, they were taken hostage. It
ended in fiasco. But the invaders would be back.

Meanwhile, after the head of Brazilian football, João Havelange,
returned home, he alleged that all the indignities were orchestrated
by Sir Stanley Rous, the English president of international football's
ruling body FIFA; the referees, he said, were both biased and bribed.

Eight years later Havelange unseated Rous, then nearly 80, from
FIFA. Rous was one of the last of the British blazer brigade who
gave Victorian sporting values to the world and enforced them.
Corrupt? Never. Insensitive and out of touch? Certainly. In
particular, Rous kept plotting to the end to keep South Africa inside
football, racist rules and all, against the pressure for an international
boycott. Havelange was the epitome of the new breed of global

---

* Tofiq Bahramov was actually from Azerbaijan, then under Soviet control.

sporting politicians. Corrupt? Funny that he should have accused Rous of bribery. No one knows quite how much Havelange earned from kickbacks in his twenty-four-year tenure of the FIFA presidency. But a lot more than £20 a week.

9

UP, UP AND AWAY

'IT'S THE ERA OF THE EXTROVERT,' PROCLAIMED THE *DAILY
Telegraph* as the 1960 autumn couture season approached.
Short skirts were in! Curves were out! according to fashion columnist
Winefride Jackson, who added: 'Mary Quant could vouch for that.
Her Chelsea and Knightsbridge dress shops have attracted a growing
clientele of lively young sophisticates.'

During a brief heatwave two years later, an American correspondent in London insisted the whole city was full of short-skirted
girls, though it seems likely he did not stray far from Chelsea and
Knightsbridge. In 1964, a fashion expert in the US, Jinny Booth,
said she was taking an inch off every skirt she owned – 'It's all due,'
she said, 'to the increased importance of the leg' – even though the
Paris houses were expected to lower hemlines, which was supposed
to matter, like the banks lowering interest rates.

In March 1966, it was reported that customers in one of
'London's sedatest stores' were buying their normal range of dresses,
knee-length or below, and immediately asking them to be shortened.
In April the *Daily Mirror* ran the headline SHORT-SKIRT GIRL HELD
UP TROUSER FACTORY: 'When Kathleen Yorke's hemline went up,
production at the trouser factory went down . . . The forewoman
Mrs Clarice Farrell said: "The men were staring at her, and they
weren't getting on with their work."' Seventeen-year-old Kathleen's
op-art skirt was four inches above the knee so the fashion had

evidently reached Castleford, though the coinage *mini-skirt* had not yet reached the *Mirror*. Even so, male interest rates were definitely going up.

In May the term *mini-skirt* appeared in the *Sunday Times* for the first time, even though it was only to try to impose the death sentence. The fashion editor, Ernestine Carter, applauded the way the young wore cheap clothes with imagination and flair. 'Just as Cubism was necessary to clarify the basis of painting, perhaps this period of far-out fashion will be seen to have been an equally vital force,' she said sweetly before adding: 'But Cubism had its day. And a great many of us think it is about time that the far-out clothes had theirs too.'

But the couture houses and the fashion editors were suddenly like the Russian nobles of 1917. Nobody was taking their orders any more. And the mini-skirt carried on regardless. On and on. Up and up.

———•———

In the 1960s the American magazine *Time* was a publication of enormous wealth and significance. In particular, the cover each week – usually a picture of a person, most often white, male and American – was the focus of enormous attention: since it was on newsstands across the world, it was not necessary to buy it to know who had been chosen that week. It was a benchmark of celebrity and importance (The Beatles did not make it until 1967). Over Easter 1966 the cover simply asked starkly 'Is God Dead?' (No picture that week.) And no doubt God was duly flattered by the attention.*

The following week was the Swinging London issue, heralded by a wild collage on the cover and a story that began: 'In this century, every decade has had its city . . .' After Vienna, Paris, Berlin, New York and Rome, it pronounced, the title now rested with London. And Britain, cringingly grateful for any recognition

———

* The last issue of the sixties asked, perhaps by way of penance, 'Is God Coming Back to Life'?

from the Americans, was definitely flattered. *Time* was impressed
by London's apparent new classlessness and its place in the vanguard
of change in rock music, culture, attitudes and fashion. And the
greatest of these was fashion, said Andrea Adam, one of the
London-based *Time* journalists who wrote some of the words that
were mashed by editors in New York into the magazine's terse,
bland house style. Well, what she actually said was: 'What prompted
the bloody cover story was not a fascination with a socio-cultural
phenomenon, it was the fascination among the senior editors for
mini-skirts.'

The notion of Swinging London did have its moment, but the
very fact that it was being read about in the dentists' waiting rooms
of Nebraska was enough to kill it stone dead at home. There was
another compulsory text for this: *The Young Meteors* by Jonathan
Aitken, published in 1967. Aitken, then 24, interviewed everyone
under 40, preferably under 30, who in his eyes was anyone in the
up-itself London of the mid-sixties. Then he flattered them. One
suspects the research was far more about networking than the
actual writing.

There were the suddenly trendy photographers like David
Bailey ('hypnotic jet black eyes staring sulkily from his mahogany
thatch'), and the aptly named Tom Hustler; the models Jean
Shrimpton, Bailey's muse, and the chirpy teenage Neasden sparrow
Twiggy (born Lesley Hornby) plus her Svengali, Justin de
Villeneuve (born Nigel Davies), who sang her praises to Aitken:
'Because she's working class and not one of those county types
like Shrimpton, ordinary girls feel they can identify themselves
with Twiggy.'

There were the boutique owners like John Stephen, who by this
stage controlled fifteen shops on Carnaby Street alone, and Barbara
Hulanicki, founder of Biba, who said that 'after a month's wear a
new dress is an antique'. There were even politicians – like Leon
Brittan, who at 27, said Aitken, 'has all the trappings of youthful
political success'. And there was also the 'legendary' businessman
Jim Slater. Amid the supposed classlessness, there were, as always
in Britain, Etonians and even real-life earls like the photographer

Patrick Lichfield and the Earl of Lucan, who Aitken found in his natural habitat of John Aspinall's high-end gambling den on Berkeley Square: 'If the points are going against him, he can be seen anxiously tweaking the luxuriant moustache.'

Some of these fell spectacularly to earth later, as meteors sometimes do. Excluding Lucan – who fell to earth who-knows-where – no one would fall further than the author, whose picaresque life would make a novel in its own right: childhood invalid, gilded youth, roué, journalist, shit, Tory MP, Cabinet minister, perjurer, jailbird, priest.

———◆———

Five months before the mini reached Castleford, it was Jean Shrimpton who gave it its single most spectacular moment, when in 1965 she travelled to then very un-swinging Australia and turned up at its annual social highlight, the Melbourne Cup race meeting, wearing 'a plain, white sleeveless shift, its hemline a full four inches above the knee'. As pictures flew across the world, an Australian fashion expert, Raymond Millward, insisted that of course the country was well up with London styles: 'We were astounded, not with Miss Shrimpton's short dress . . . but at the way she flouted convention by not wearing stockings and accessories.'

Deep in the Melbourne suburbs, an 18-year-old librarian, Helen Elliott, was enthralled. 'The photograph was a composition in movement: her hair swung, her legs were bare, she was hatless and gloveless,' she wrote half a century later. 'A few years later I saw Botticelli's *Birth of Venus* in the Uffizi, painted in 1495. Shrimpton at the races . . . hit my eyes with exactly the same visual gasp that Botticelli had been eliciting for five centuries. There was that mirror to the candour of youth, caught for eternity. How many lives has Botticelli's Venus changed? Melbourne's Venus at the Races changed just as many, I'm sure of that. She suggested that we, too, might be able to be just ourselves.'

Not only was the mini-skirt not imposed by Paris, it was not even imposed by men, much as they appreciated it. Young women were pleasing themselves and were pleased with how they looked.

To borrow again the phrase from the chronicler of fifties' childhood, Ysenda Maxtone Graham, this was Beanpole Britain growing up. They were not all tall but they were slender; plumpness in the young was rare, obesity very rare.

There was the customary response from authority. At Oxford, female undergraduates were warned not to wear mini-skirts into exams for fear of distracting the men; at a Catholic secondary school in Kent, the headmaster decreed that mini-skirts 'bordered on immodesty' and that the more extreme variant, micro-skirts, 'bordered on indecency'; at a Dickens festival in Broadstairs, a barmaid appeared in the streets in a 'Dickensian mini-skirt'. 'We think it's excessively bad form, very stupid and not funny,' said the festival secretary.

Other new fashions brought condemnation in their turn. Kinky boots, which made wearing mini-skirts slightly more realistic in the English climate, were banned by the head of a Peterborough all-girls school who had previously banned black underwear.

And trousers for women were a constant source of contention. Actress Geraldine Chaplin, daughter of Charlie, was refused admittance to the Savoy restaurant in 1967 even though: (a) she was who she was; (b) she was staying in the hotel; and (c) her trouser suit had been designed by Pierre Cardin personally. In 1968, still sweet 16, Jayne Harries was denied admission to the Royal Enclosure at Ascot for wearing white bell-bottom trousers. She had prepared for this eventuality and returned rapidly from her father's Rolls, wearing very little at all. This time she was admitted. Technically, she was wearing a white lace-trimmed micro-dress. She looked as though she had just arrived in one of the Savoy's honeymoon suites and was ready for what came next.

This was not far from the truth. Miss Harries – head girl of Cygnets finishing school, talented showjumper, sought-after debutante, daughter of a self-made millionaire TV manufacturer – climbed out of her bedroom window a month later to marry a 24-year-old hairdresser called Gavin Hodge, who was not in her parents' script. The couple flew to Lisbon, closely followed by her doting parents, who were won round and attended the wedding. But Mrs Hodge would turn into perhaps the most tragic of all the meteors.

———·———

It might not have worried Jayne Harries but in Britain there was a practical reason in favour of the mini. Purchase tax was levied on adult clothes but not children's clothes: for dresses, skirts and coats this was determined by length – hence minis were significantly cheaper. In September 1965, the Customs and Excise department woke up to this and changed the rules.

The fashion also had a curious effect on men, prurient interest aside. Once the hemline climbed several inches above the knee, stockings and their attendant suspenders became unfeasible, except perhaps at tarts-and-vicars parties. So women turned to tights, a trend that proved permanent. These required much more nylon; and the makers of men's shirts found they had a shortage. Nylon shirts had become widely worn in the 1950s, mainly because they needed no ironing, making them popular with put-upon mums; never mind them being sweaty and uncomfortable, with an ever-present threat of being blasted by static when dressing and undressing. This phase – it was hardly a fashion – was dealt a further blow by the 1973 oil crisis, since nylon relies on petrochemicals. It is also claimed that nylon's hard-wearing qualities irritated the retailers, who saw sales fall. Polyester blends took over.*

Was it the sweatiness that made men more self-aware of their personal habits? Or the undercurrent of sexuality that began to infiltrate even mundane commuting in the mini-skirt era? 'When I first joined the Middlesex dressing room in 1961,' the cricketer Mike Brearley told me, 'anyone who wore deodorant or after-shave would have been seen as a fancy-dan. Four years later the stuff was everywhere.' On that timing, one suspects that ITV were probably the main culprit. Old Spice were big advertisers and so

———

* There were also nylon sheets, heavily advertised by a firm called Brentford Nylons, and much favoured by the worst boarding houses. My guess is a fakir's bed of nails or a North Korean prison cell might offer a worse night's sleep, but not by much.

were Lifebuoy soap, with its accusatory slogan 'Someone isn't using Lifebuoy' followed by the whisper: 'B.O.'

Male appearance in the early sixties would soon seem almost as dated as the periwig or the codpiece. This can be gleaned from one small observation. The haphazard pattern of televised football began a new era in August 1964, when the first edition of *Match of the Day* was shown on Britain's newly opened and not universally available third channel, BBC2. The TV audience was smaller than the attendance at the match on offer: Liverpool v. Arsenal. The programme was shown again fifty years later. The football was nowhere near as interesting as the crowd in the stands: nearly all male, of course, mostly working-class, one imagines, and most of them *wearing ties*. An extraordinary sight, and among elderly men it lingered a while longer.

Even before this, there was an inversion of habits between the classes: the middle class, working mainly in offices, wore suits and ties all week but dressed down at weekends (except for church); manual workers, who were the majority of males, tended to the reverse – Sunday best. And football on Merseyside was always a quasi-religious experience.

Maxtone Graham noted the phenomenon of people dressing *up* rather than down to go on holiday. The queues at the northern railway stations in Wakes weeks, when entire towns went on holiday, persisted into the sixties. And there they were – the girls 'in their Whitsun dresses, ankle socks and sandals, the boys in shorts, shirts and ties, fathers and grandfathers in smart trousers, ties and hats, mothers and grannies in their Sunday best, all queuing up with their heavy non-pull-along suitcases'. Steve Hancorn and Anna Coda, a couple who have spent much time at Labour Party meetings over the years, can remember three phases: first all the men wore jackets and ties; then only the working-class members did; then no one.

Andreas Whittam Smith, fresh from Oxford, began working at the merchant bank N. M. Rothschild in 1960, which was still full of family members known as Mr Eddy, Mr Lionel and the like. 'There was no such thing as graduates going in on high salaries,' he said. 'I went in as a clerk on £600 a year. Every night Rothschilds would lend money to the old discount houses*; every afternoon the security would come back, a bill for 107 per cent of the amount. My job was to check the name on the bill against a list and check the amount. I would be wearing a suit, a white shirt, a stiff white collar with studs, a tie.'

'A bowler hat?'

'Many of the members did wear bowler hats. But I think I would have been thought as getting above myself.'

£600 a year not covering an even remotely Rothschildian lifestyle, he moonlighted doing menial work in hotels and nightclubs: 'I was reasonably sure that if a Rothschild happened to wander in they would not know who I was.'

In the early 1960s, even a student's idea of dressing down was wearing a sports jacket and tie; by 1970 this was unimaginably formal. By 1968, as well as admitting girls in nighties, Royal Ascot softened the dress rules for men and allowed them to wear lounge suits instead of morning coats. Apparently, the Queen wanted to emulate 'the easy atmosphere of the Buckingham Palace garden parties'. But she had actually got ahead of the times and under-estimated the British male's enduring if well-hidden delight in actual dressing up: hardly anyone took advantage of Her Majesty's relaxation, and the old rules were reinstated the following year. The baby-boom generation was largely immune to the fancy dress fetish and to an extent has remained so. And it became common for young men to claim they did not own a tie.[†]

Long hair also became ubiquitous. Among the new idols, The Beatles' cautious fringes were rapidly superseded by the flowing manes of Mick Jagger and others, and practically everyone beyond the reach of stern institutional discipline at least made a gesture in

---

*   Financial institutions that acted as intermediaries between lenders and borrowers. They disappeared in the 1990s.

†   Trainee newspaper reporters of that era were told by old-school editors they should always wear a tie in case they were suddenly called on to interview the Archbishop of Canterbury. An odd choice, as the smart-arses would grumble, since he would be wearing a dress.

that direction. Authority resisted, of course. Owen Holmes, 14, was put into a girls' class of a Catholic school in Midlothian, and told to get an apron and cap for the Wednesday cookery lesson. 'Are you the sister of the previous defendant?' a young man was asked at Daventry Magistrates' Court. Trainee miners in Nottinghamshire were told to wear hairnets under their pit helmets.

And Richard McNab, 21, had his dole money suspended by officials in Southampton because his hair was too long even after a trim. 'The issue,' said an official, 'was whether Mr McNab was making himself reasonably available for work.' By 1966, many of the young beaus attending Queen Charlotte's Ball, the highlight of the deb season, had shoulder-length hair; they presumably did not have to worry about labour exchanges. Male fashion being less fickle than female, long hair was normal well into the 1970s, fading, coincidentally or otherwise, when the employment market became tougher.

The early skinheads, who were pioneering rebels against long hair in the late sixties, also helped take Doc Marten boots out of the building site, following a lead from Pete Townshend of The Who. But in the sixties it seemed no one could save the hat. The bowler-hatted army who marched across London's bridges from train to office became steadily more bare-headed – until in due course new generations discovered that hats had their uses in both cold and heat. But the bowler became merely a novelty item.

Across Britain and the rich, free world, the young, and sometimes the less young, dug the music; they let their hair down and their hemlines up; they dressed down and they began to play up; it was possible to get laid with fewer preliminaries and caveats and maybe share joints at parties. Beyond that, their lives continued pretty much as before. And many suspected the decade was only happening elsewhere. Sociologists interviewing Tyneside shipbuilders found themselves being asked about the free love apparently available in universities, and how to chat up female students. 'It's all fun down south, isn't it,' said one of the plumbers.

For some in London, that was true. There was an elite who went in for professional sixties-ism, calling themselves 'the counterculture' or 'the underground', which did not mean commuting from Edgware. 'We lay around and got stoned, had sex, listened to music that exalted lying around, getting stoned, having sex,' as Jenny Diski recalled in her memoir, *The Sixties*. Diski's coterie took their drugs seriously and their work, such as it was, lightly. She understood her life was not the norm: 'Not everyone in France was fomenting revolution in 1789; only a tiny proportion of the new generation were Bright Young Things of the 1920s.' Some of her friends had more trouble understanding that.

'The underground was terribly small and very very localised,' said John Peel. 'I could never understand, for example, why it was that the Country Joe and the Fish LP never got into the charts. I said to the record company, "Why isn't this in the charts? Everybody I know has got a copy." But what I didn't realise was that it was the other way round: I knew everybody who'd got a copy. So the 300 that they'd sold were all to people that I knew.' Peel, briefly on the pirate station Radio London and then for thirty-seven years on the BBC, would become the high priest of obscure rock to several generations. As the decade passed high noon, and Beatlemania became less maniacal, music would stop uniting the world and once more split off in different directions.

It was Peel who led the way up the high road. And most of the road signs pointed to California. Swinging London did not have a decade, as *Time* had suggested – it was about a year. By the summer of 1967, if these kinds of judgments mean anything, it was San Francisco, the summer of love and flowers in your hair.

Try as one might, it is not possible to ignore the old line: 'If you can remember the Sixties, you weren't really there.'* The historian Dominic Sandbrook – who has an alibi, having not been born until 1974 – has debunked the whole notion of a sexual revolution, and most especially the role of the pill. Maybe so. But customs had changed dramatically in a decade. A student party, say, in 1969

---

* Most reliably ascribed to the American comedian Charles Fleischer, circa 1982.

would have been very different from one in 1959: the old rules had been relaxed. And even a Tyneside apprentice would have had access to improved condoms and perhaps to that most underrated aid to sexual liberation: a car.

———•———

In the summer of 1965, the American poet Allen Ginsberg came to London and was willing to read free of charge. So, various denizens of the underground announced the 'International Poetry Incarnation' and hired the Royal Albert Hall: about 5,000 people, mostly young, got in; more were turned away. It was hailed as the revival of this most fragile of art forms. Unfortunately, no one had actually organized it.

It went on for four hours; Ginsberg was drunk; a Dutch poet was on an acid trip. 'The main thing that was wrong with it was that forty poor English poets, poor quality that is, got up and read their awful bullshit and made the whole thing so boring,' said the writer Barry Miles. But he also saw it as the catalyst for the real birth of the underground – 'it created a community and a scene, the framework within which everything happened'. Or maybe it was the death of it. The poet and scriptwriter Johnny Byrne called it 'the end of the genuine feeling of an alternative culture. Everything as far as I was concerned went downhill after that.'

The beginning? The end? It was the sixties – maybe it could be both. But soon the scene would start to cause real ends. Just before Christmas 1966, Tara Browne, heir to the Guinness fortune, racing driver, socialite and hellraiser, was among the first casualties. He smashed his Lotus Elan up near Chelsea and was killed instantly. He was 21. There are discrepancies in the accounts of his speed and what he might have ingested, but most people assumed very fast and very stoned. He was later hymned by good poets: his friend Hugo Williams, and (to an extent) Lennon & McCartney in 'A Day in the Life'. One might see him as a victim of the absence of war.

10

IF YOU CAN MEET WITH TRIUMPH AND DISASTER

T HEY KEPT WRITING THEMSELVES OFF, THE DEBONAIR daredevils. The cull on the racetracks actually worsened in the early sixties: eight men, three of them British, died at the wheel of a Formula 1 car between 1960 and 1962 alone.* The most horrendous came at Monza in Italy in 1961, when the German Wolfgang von Trips, on the edge of winning the Championship, was killed along with fifteen spectators.

Later, the Scotsman Jim Clark, widely regarded as the best and the safest of all Formula 1 drivers, died at a minor race in Germany in 1968; his contemporaries thought there must have been a fault in the car since Clark was so unlikely to make a mistake. He was 32.

And they were all Sunday slowcoaches compared to Donald Campbell, who in 1964 had followed his father, Sir Malcolm, by capturing the world land speed record, surpassing 400 mph on an Australian salt flat. Three years later, he went to Coniston in the Lake District to take his own water speed record above 300 mph. Like John Cobb, it was the second leg that did for him, and he was a fraction of a second from achieving his goal when he uttered his last words on the radio. The definitive version seems to be: 'Hello. The bow's up. I have gone . . .' He was 45.

Like Cobb, Campbell was hailed as a great patriot. Like Cobb,

---

* Not necessarily in an actual race.

his death generated huge publicity and a feeling of inevitability. But in a sense his time had gone. The pursuit of speed records for their own sake was somewhat out of fashion. Campbell had insufficient funding from the kind of backers who were delighted to be associated with his father (who died at home). Which is why he had stuffed a new engine into the now-ancient boat in which he had first broken 200 mph. In that too, there was an all-too-recognizable symbol of Britishness.

Theoretically, Campbell could have saved money by breaking the land speed record at home. Britain's first stretch of actual motorway had been the Preston bypass, which opened in 1958 and was later incorporated into the M6. The first significant stretch, from Watford to Rugby, opened in the closing weeks of 1959. This was the M1, though it would take another nine years to reach its northern terminus at Leeds and eighteen to make its final approach to Staples Corner in London

In its early days the M1 had no crash barriers, lighting, or hard shoulder, and very little traffic. One astonishing fact is that the Newport Pagnell and Watford Gap services were considered cool places to hang out, and even eat.

Oh, and there was also no speed limit. At dawn one midsummer morning in 1964, the racing driver Jack Sears decided to test his AC Cobra before the 24-hour race at Le Mans and made a couple of runs up and down the motorway from Watford Gap service station – at up to 185 mph. Two policemen did come over to him in the car park: they wanted to look round the Cobra. 'It was more likely they would ask for an autograph than write a ticket – because no laws were broken,' Sears said later.

Which was true. Furthermore, being a decent sort, he slowed down to about 120 when there was another car – which did not happen often before five in the morning – so as not to give the driver a heart attack. And hardly anyone would have known if someone had not blabbed in a Fleet Street bar, whereupon it hit the papers. 'I thought it was being blown out of all proportion,' said Sears. 'I didn't think I'd done anything out of the ordinary.'

Some blamed him eighteen months later when the Labour

government imposed a 70-mph limit, experimentally at first then permanently. The motoring writer L. J. K. Setright argued, not very plausibly, that this discouraged engineering progress and thus contributed to the decline of the British car industry. It had to happen: the M1 would soon cease to be empty at any hour, and the sixties did see the first hints of a more safety-conscious culture. Soon, all that would be left of those early days of the M1 was the fading paint of the MARPLES MUST GO! sign on a bridge near Luton to commemorate Macmillan's much-unloved transport minister after he had indeed gone.

On bank holidays in those days there would be daily bulletins of death tolls, issued by the government and widely reported.* The figures for the Whitsun weekend in 1964 were notably dreadful. And 1966 would be the peak year – wartime excluded – for road deaths in Great Britain: 7,985, more than four times the 2019 figure.

The then transport minister, Barbara Castle, brought in the breathalyser the following year, which cannot be wholly irrelevant to the decline in fatalities after that. It was fiercely resisted by the road lobby, which claimed that alcohol was overrated as a cause of road accidents; in the House of Lords the Earl of Arran argued that it would make more sense to turn all roads into dual carriageways, a proposal he had not costed. At the same time, MoT† tests were imposed on cars over three years old rather than just ten, and seat belts had to be fitted on all new cars, though not necessarily worn.

The breathalyser came into force as midnight struck to bring in Monday, 9 October 1967. The streets of London were said to have been deserted long before Big Ben chimed. The roads round Redhill, Somerset were not; and at two minutes past, Garth Jones, 21, won a place in history after hitting a telegraph pole. (Despite testing positive, he was acquitted – the accident happened before midnight.) The following month, schoolteacher Michael Hallewell

---

* 'See you in the statistics,' we would say in our house if anyone went out on a holiday weekend. I suppose it was our way of saying 'Be careful'.

† Short for Ministry of Transport. The abbreviation survives even though the name no longer exists otherwise. It is now the Department for Transport (known unofficially as DafT).

came back from a fancy-dress party, had a small collision with a
wall and was duly asked to blow into the bag. He was wearing bath
towels, an outsize polythene bag and a tall green hat. He had gone
as a very topical object. 'I'm trying very hard to see the humorous
side,' he said.

And for many years, being caught over the limit was widely
seen as one of life's little hazards, like sneaky speed traps. There
was even an organization called the St Christopher Motorist
Association, which insured drivers against bans and offered a free
chauffeur for the duration. Such policies were only outlawed in the
late 1980s.

Planes landed safely more regularly in the sixties than in the
fifties, but there were still terrible exceptions: in June 1967 there
were two major British plane crashes within twelve hours. First a
DC4 from Manston in Kent crashed into a Pyrenean mountain,
killing all eighty-eight passengers and crew. Faulty heating on the
flight deck had leaked carbon monoxide, making the pilot irrational
before he became unconscious. Then a British Midland Argonaut
from Majorca to Manchester lost power and came down in
Stockport; the pilot saved lives on the ground by finding an open
space but seventy-two out of eighty-four on board died.

The most infallible signal of a plane crash was still an outbreak
of exuberance in the patriotic press about how wonderful our planes
were. 'Twenty-six minutes,' trilled the *Daily Express* in August
1963. 'That is the time it took last night to put Britain smack into
the world aircraft big league. As test pilot Jock Bryce took his BAC
One-Eleven down at Hurn Airport after its first flight, he passed a
rainbow. And this bus-stop jet could win for Britain the pot of gold
at the end of the rainbow.'

Come October: 'A boxful of secrets was salvaged last night from
the wreckage of Britain's proud jet hope, the One-Eleven. The box,
a black flight recorder known as Midas, may today give vital clues
to yesterday's major test crash.' Seven died.

Already, Britain had captured the lead in developing the
hovercraft: 'Britain's hovercraft pioneers are skimming even further
and further ahead of their rivals.' Indeed, if they looked behind

there was no one trailing in their wake. The hovercraft was a British invention, conceived Blue Peterishly by Christopher Cockerell using cans of cat food and coffee and vacuum cleaner tubes. There would be only one small disaster (five died in a gale in the Solent in 1972) but the combination of its small size, its preference for calm water and the infernal noise did for it commercially.* For some newspapers, all the pigeons were swifts.

The growth of urban traffic began to drive children's play off the streets, as did the general notion, which reached its peak in the sixties, that the car was king. Panda crossings, which offered part-time lights, were brought in to supersede some of the zebra crossings in 1962, only to be junked themselves seven years later and replaced by the pelicans, which meant asking permission to cross.

How sweet those kiddie-friendly animal names sounded, disguising the underlying reality. Roads belonged to vehicles unless pedestrians begged indulgence and asked nicely. In narrow residential streets, as house after house acquired their Escort or Cortina and needed somewhere to park, cars also took possession of the pavement. Nothing could impede the flow of the traffic, certainly not the urban 30-mph speed limit, which was neither observed nor enforced.

The dictatorship of the motorist was mitigated by the remnants of old-fashioned British anarchism. Unlike Americans, Australians and Germans, those aged between about 8 and 80 continued to use their own judgment. Old-style buses like the London Routemaster offered the chance of getting on or off wherever it stopped or crawled. There was an attempt to ban jaywalking – starting in, of all places, Fleet Street, where no self-respecting journalist was going to allow some piddling law to slow down the rush from office to pub. It never caught on.

And the pattern of childhood had not yet changed. Homes were

---

* It still travels between Southsea and Ryde; it outpaces the ferries and is fun for visitors.

not yet child-centred and kids were still semi-feral. Some of their adventures continued to end badly, with bodies in canals or, mutilated, in deep woods. The vast majority did not, and some of the escapades were still improbably spectacular, especially in the summer holidays. In 1961, a Glaswegian boy and a girl from London separately made it across the Atlantic by just slipping on to planes. Their visits were very brief but the retribution was nugatory – and what an advert for the ingenuity of British youth.

First Harry McIlwraith, a 14-year-old Glaswegian anxious to escape the infamously rough Gorbals, managed to stow away on a plane from Prestwick to Montreal. He was caught because a stewardess noticed the toilet was continuously occupied although all the passengers were in their seats. A note was put under the door saying 'The game's up. Why not come out and be comfortable?' He did come home to face the magistrate, having stolen £15 from his mother's purse. But the boy had spirit: the previous week he had rowed for five hours to the Isle of Arran.

A few weeks later, Angela Reilly, a 12-year-old Londoner, inveigled herself, ticketless and passportless, on to a Pan Am flight to Boston. Before being sent home, she was billeted for the night with an airline executive, whose wife reported: 'We'd love to have her for keeps . . . She's the loveliest, sweetest child I've ever seen.' Back home, Angela wrote a letter to 'Dear Mr Pan American' asking him not to blame the stewardess who inadvertently let her board.* She also put 'xxx' at the end. Even Mr Pan American melted at that.

Two London brothers packed some clothes, raided their piggy banks, slipped away from home and took a tube to catch a train and see their father, who had separated from their mother, in Merthyr Tydfil. They failed, having gone to the wrong station: Euston not Paddington. A foolish error but, in mitigation, they were five and four. The most bizarre was the story of two boys, aged 12 and 10, in Addiewell, Midlothian, who began playing on some new electricity wire laid on the ground to be winched into place. Suddenly the cable erectors, several miles away, began to do

---

* She had pretended her dad was further back in the queue.

just that, lifting the boys seventy-five feet in the air. It could have ended terribly. It didn't.

———•———

In May 1965, at Tonypandy in the Rhondda Valley, thirty-one men were killed 800 feet underground by an explosion caused by a build-up of the coal miners' ancient enemy, firedamp – flammable gas. A familiar and terrible scene was enacted: a tremble felt in the houses, the sound of the emergency hooters, the housewives rushing through the streets in the rain, desperate for news. 'They are stunned and saddened,' said a local church minister. 'But they know the risk is with them always. All they can do is carry on. There is nothing else they can do, because mining is their life.' 'This is the real price of coal,' said Lord Robens, the chairman of the National Coal Board. This was to be the last of many disasters on such a scale in a Welsh colliery. If you exclude the most terrible disaster of all.

In these narrow valleys, generations of housewives would see their miner husbands off for their shifts with the same unspoken thought: that they really might never see them again. The same did not apply when they said goodbye to their children, walking through quiet streets to the safety of school. Seven miles north-east of Tonypandy lay Aberfan, hard by the Merthyr Vale colliery and its attendant slagheaps.

There had been signals of concern about the slagheaps from local officials and councillors, even a petition; but never quite at the volume needed to galvanize an inert coal-board bureaucracy. There was an unspoken fear, a much more obvious risk: collieries were already closing – in Robens's ten-year stint, 1961 to 1971, the number of pits went down from 698 to 292. Moan too much and yours gets it.

In 1963, the borough engineer expressed 'extremely serious concerns' about the 111-foot high No. 7 tip, which had springs underneath, noting: 'The slurry is so fluid and the gradient so steep that it could not possibly stay in position in the winter time or during periods of heavy rain.' The slurry did stay through the next three winters and a great deal of Welsh rain. But in October 1966 it had been raining for days.

It was just after 9 a.m. on a foggy Friday when much of the mountain began to move, fast, and ten minutes later an unimaginable force smashed into Pantglas Junior School. The children of Aberfan would have spent less than one-fifth of their lives in school. Half an hour earlier, they would not have arrived; a few hours later they would have gone – half-term was starting and they were to be let out early. People would have died in nearby houses, but not in such numbers and it would not have singled out the young: 144 died, 116 of them children, nearly all between seven and ten.

'It looked like a plane crash, or a bomb,' recalled a BBC Wales reporter fifty years later. 'A thirty-foot-high tidal wave of mud and bricks and stone. Then I saw the morning shift from Merthyr Vale colliery, some of them still stripped off to the waist . . . They took it over and proceeded to give a masterclass in professional efficiency. The miners worked so gently. A whistle would blow and there would be total silence. There might have been a little cry or they might have seen something.' Ten children were pulled out alive, all within the first hour or so.

But for them and everyone else in Aberfan the agony was just beginning. Nowhere in modern Britain has ever known such a concentration of grief, and it has never gone away.

————◦————

There was at least one more dangerous job than coal mining. And there were places almost as particular as mining villages. Hull, loneliest and least known of the English cities, was still pervaded by the smell of fish.

The real price of fish was pervasive too. 'Mortality rates were seventeen times higher than coal mining,' said Alan Johnson, who became one of Hull's MPs. 'There were nine hundred ships lost out of Hull in 150 years of distance-water trawling. The carnage, the lives, the eight thousand people killed in that period with terrible conditions, fishing in thirty degrees below freezing.'

Ken Knox, who was peeling potatoes at the start of the 1950s, was a skipper in the 1960s. Life never did become that easy. 'When you got to be a deckhand you might have one trip a year off. But many didn't have that. There might be three times as many crew waiting for one. And you might be replaced and you might not get your job back.' One trip normally lasted three weeks; home leave was three days. The shortest trip was Iceland; the longest were Greenland, Labrador and Newfoundland. There was, one way and another, not a lot of sunbathing.

Whatever they were doing it was full on, especially when they reached the fishing grounds. Eighteen hours' work, six hours' sleep. The three days ashore were never wasted either. Christmas? Knox was at sea for seventeen in a row, but some skippers allowed an hour for lunch just the once instead of the normal half-hour. The owners outsourced risk to the skippers, hence the hard driving; if the catch was fit only for fishmeal, everyone lost right down to the deckies. But the rewards were there: out of their oilskins, trawlermen were known for snappy dressing, and the single men had no trouble reaping the traditional shore-leave rewards. When they married, wise wives squirrelled the money away for the bad times.

In the early days of 1968 the worst times came. And, for once, Britain took notice. Within three weeks, three ships – the *St Romanus*, the *Kingston Peridot* and the *Ross Cleveland* were lost. Fifty-eight men died. Harry Eddom, mate of the *Ross Cleveland*, swam ashore and lived. On the day his survival became known, two other things happened. Several members of the crew of the *St Andronicus* forced the captain to turn back as he headed for the storm-tossed north, when they heard the fate of her sister ship the *Romanus*. 'I am disgusted and appalled at some of these modern sailors,' said the owners' general manager, Albert Robinson. 'These men are now banned from our ships.' Meanwhile, a deputation of Hull housewives, led by Lillian Bilocca ('Big Lil') – a no-prisoners matriarch from the Ena Sharples school of femininity – arrived grim-faced in London to meet ministers with a list of safety demands. The government knew when it was licked.

11

SMASHING THE CROCKERY

I F HAROLD WILSON HAD BEEN SPINNING PLATES LIKE A MASTER juggler before the 1966 election, they started crashing to earth almost as soon as he strode triumphantly back into Downing Street. Within weeks the economic situation was laid bare, and by July sterling was back in crisis. 'The most dramatic decline any modern PM has suffered,' wrote the Cabinet diarist Richard Crossman.

It was another moment to consider devaluation; Wilson refused. Instead he announced a package of cuts and charges and taxes and freezes and standstills and restraints. This included a £50 limit on spending money for foreign holidays, which made the champagne socialist wing of the Cabinet gulp.

The crisis was ignited by a six-week national seamen's strike which affected both imports and exports. Wilson was trying to keep inflation under 4 per cent via a prices and incomes policy. The seamen wanted 17 per cent, and in the midst of this an inquiry into medical salaries recommended that GPs should get 30 per cent. Wilson thought both groups had a good case. But he was tied up in nautical knots.

And thus the pattern was set. Notionally, trade unionists supported the Labour government. But Labour could not control the Trades Union Congress; and the TUC could not control the individual unions, who in turn could not control their branches who could not control their shop stewards who could not control their workers.

Shortly after the emergency measures, Crossman thought Wilson might be on the up again, which he ascribed to England winning the World Cup.* But the nation's mood was less febrile than Crossman's. Ted Heath's Conservatives did not take a clear lead in the Gallup poll until April 1967. They then held it unflinchingly and sometimes overwhelmingly for the next three years. Wilson, said Bernard Levin in his history of the sixties, 'had given, for a time, a tremendously effective impression of action, which turned out on inspection to be only activity'.

———·———

In many ways, Harold Wilson came across as a very likeable man. 'He was a good man to work for. He liked a chat,' recalled Lord Armstrong. According to his press secretary Joe Haines: 'He had no side to him at all. He never pulled rank on you as Jim Callaghan did.' His trademark pipe was a prop; in private he preferred cigars, but in his era nothing suggested trustworthiness more than a pipe-smoking Englishman – also, he could pretend to relight it in an interview to cover a little thinking time. But he seems to have been genuinely unpretentious (the holiday bungalow in the Scillies was real), and uninterested in using politics for personal enrichment.

'But you never knew what he was going to do,' added Armstrong, with a hint of exasperation. This was something more than Harold Macmillan's technique of using words as cover for contrary actions; fearful that colleagues would blab and brief self-servingly, Wilson kept his counsel to an extent that made him seem permanently shifty. This may help explain his unusually good relationship with the Queen. She relished, said Douglas Hurd, 'his willingness to talk through with her his problems and possible ways of handling them'. Wilson had a strong marriage – to a woman who hated talking

---

* There is an enduring myth that Wilson won the 1966 election because of the World Cup triumph, which would have been difficult since the election took place three months before the football. This may be due to confusion with the England/Wilson double failure in 1970, when there might have been a connection.

politics; perhaps he saw his Palace audiences as psychotherapy sessions with the one person who would listen but never blab. The Queen Mother, notoriously right-wing, put it another way: 'You've tamed him,' she told her daughter.

Wilson had had a rather sheltered career: precocious Oxford don, civil servant, politician. And he did have a strange streak of naivety in his dealings with the recalcitrant white-ruled remnant of empire: Rhodesia (formerly southern Rhodesia), where the whites, less than 5 per cent of the population, held sway over a fast-growing black majority.

South Africa, wedded to apartheid, its brutal system of black suppression, was beyond anyone else's control. The Rhodesians had no apartheid as such, no 'Whites Only' signs as in South Africa. Unlike the crude Afrikaners, Rhodesia's masters were of British stock and did not behave like that. Their signs said 'Right of Admission Reserved': no need to spell it out – everyone knew what that meant. Like white settlers elsewhere, they accepted there had to be a target date for majority rule: the target date the Rhodesians had in mind was the Twelfth of Never.

Rhodesia occupied a charming chunk of Africa, with a climate so kindly it was said it rained only at night. However, the whites there were rougher-edged than the upmarket exiles of Kenya; newcomers from Britain usually found the prevailing attitudes as well as the weather congenial and saw off the moderate politicians willing to contemplate change. In 1964 Ian Smith, a wartime fighter pilot – polite, puritanical, quietly ruthless – took over, and began to steer the country to its own version of independence: a unilateral declaration of independence (UDI) on the whites' terms.

The United Nations? The British government? Pah! Rhodesia was already effectively self-governing, and what Smith feared most was being ousted by the even harder right. This included the real live duke who sat in his Cabinet, the 7th Duke of Montrose, who once told a visiting UN official: 'The only thing an African understands is a hit over the head with a stout stick.' Rhodesia was, in a delicious phrase of the time, 'Surrey with the lunatic fringe on top'.

Wilson was curiously obtuse about Rhodesia: he kept thinking he could negotiate the problem away. He and Smith talked in London, they talked in the Rhodesian capital, Salisbury,* they talked on a cruiser, they talked on an assault ship, they talked on the phone. But Wilson had already ruled out military force. This was very sensible in itself – the logistics of invading a far-away landlocked country were horrendous, and there was a lot of pro-Smith sentiment at home from the Queen Mother downwards – and, most worryingly, in dozens of sergeants' messes. But the knowledge that it would never happen helped bolster Smith's intransigence.

The UN imposed sanctions. Since Rhodesia had their allies South Africa to the south, and oil came in handily via Mozambique, ruled by fascist Portugal, to the east, the sanctions were challenging but not crippling. Plenty of other countries (including France, West Germany, the Shah's Iran, and Japan) and countless dodgy businessmen surreptitiously helped the rebels. And as Britain's economic plight worsened, the white Rhodesians just laughed, the more so as many of the new African regimes turned into kleptocracies.

In November 1967, sixteen months after the July crisis, another storm surge finally engulfed the pound and forced Wilson and his Chancellor, Jim Callaghan, to devalue sterling, from $2.80 to $2.40. They had wasted three years defending the indefensible. Wilson then made a disastrous broadcast where he told the nation that the pound abroad would be worth less before adding: 'This doesn't mean, of course, that the pound here in Britain in your pocket or purse or in your bank has been devalued.' This was a necessary explanation: many did fear everything would cost more at once. Still, import prices would indeed rise with time, and the tone seemed too smug, as though this were all part of the Wilsonian masterplan, particularly when he added towards the end: 'This is a proud moment.' 'Too complacent by half', noted his colleague Barbara Castle. The damage stuck.

---

* Later Harare.

What then did Labour, with its large majority, actually achieve? In spite of everything, the Attlee settlement was nurtured as well as the situation permitted; the poor and sick were not neglected; beggars did not crowd the streets; the new National Giro, run by the Post Office, helped the working class open bank accounts; comprehensive education advanced, though this was and remains a thoroughly contentious development; the Open University, a second chance for the millions who coulda-woulda-shoulda earned degrees before the 1960s but never had the chance, was a triumph from the start. The Trade Descriptions Act, which banned sellers from making false claims, was so popular it became part of the language for many years, in all kinds of contexts. 'Arsenal do not belong to the First Division,' said a football report in 1976. 'They could easily be accused under the Trade Descriptions Act.'

Two achievements stood out, one grossly underrated at the time. As the US involvement in Vietnam became ever more intractable and unpopular, Wilson was under huge pressure from the Left to denounce it. Three major protests were held in London in 1967–68 which were built up by both participants and opponents as attempted insurrections. British good humour prevailed, narrowly. The real pressure on Wilson was the other way.

A hard-up, diminishing country could not possibly be seen to alienate its rich ally and protector. In fact, on a personal level, Wilson did just that, annoying Lyndon B. Johnson partly by trying to stage his own hopeless peace initiatives but also by cocking a deaf ear to the president's insistent blandishments to send even a token force, perhaps just to Thailand – not the worst posting – to release US troops for combat in Vietnam. Wilson would not budge. Indeed, after devaluation, Britain announced its withdrawal from all its post-imperial bases in Asia.

'All we needed was one regiment,' Johnson's Secretary of State, Dean Rusk, told the *Times* correspondent Louis Heren off the record. 'The Black Watch would have done. Just one regiment, but you wouldn't. Well, don't expect us to save you again. They can invade Sussex and we wouldn't do a damn thing about it.'

Bognor Regis has survived; the reputations of Johnson and Rusk have not.

Wilson also had a particularly good crisis when the *Torrey Canyon* went aground off the Scillies in 1967 and began spilling oil that threatened to pollute beaches along the south coast. He was at his bungalow at the time, sensed the problem quickly and went into dynamic mode. Among the weaponry used was 2,000 gallons of napalm to encourage the flames on the burning ship and mitigate the damage. It might be a source of pride to reflect that while the US was using napalm to kill Vietnamese civilians, Britain was using it to save holiday beaches.

———•———

The main almost-undisputed Labour success was the series of social reforms mostly associated with Roy Jenkins's tenure of the Home Office. His stay lasted less than two years. Before he arrived, the department had a matchless reputation for illiberalism and incompetence. After he left, it resumed as before. It was not that he was an exceptionally advanced thinker; nearly all the changes had been screamingly obvious for decades. But he understood how to manage both his sprawling empire and the politics, and he did so with determination, skill and panache.

And it was Jenkins who had written the book. Before the 1959 election, aged 38, he wrote a slim paperback called *The Labour Case*, the final chapter of which set out a list of essential changes, hardly any of which made their way into Labour's flaccid and failed manifesto that year: an end to capital punishment, the legalization of male homosexuality, the abolition of theatre censorship, and reform of the laws affecting Sunday observance, betting, suicide, licensing, abortion, divorce and immigration.

Rab Butler, who served five years in this Whitehall penal colony under Macmillan, did talk about loosening the 'Victorian corsetry' that restrained the nation's life. Suicide or, more relevantly, attempted suicide ceased to be a crime; and cash betting was allowed away from the racecourse (not that either law had ever stopped anyone). Under Labour, capital punishment was abandoned before Jenkins reached the Home Office and finally abolished after he left.*

Indeed, only two big reforms actually came during Jenkins's stint: abortion and homosexuality. In both cases he obeyed the Westminster custom of advancing social legislation at arm's length, leaving the heavy lifting to a backbencher while providing enough parliamentary time for it to go through. This allows matters of conscience to be decided without involving the whips and gives the government plausible deniability if the voters don't like it. Wilson was afraid both issues were vote-losers.

The abortion law – allowing termination of pregnancy under medical supervision up to 28 weeks – was pushed through deftly by a new Liberal MP called David Steel, not yet 30, who struck the right tone. But every worldly adult knew what went on. The feminist movement hardly existed then and the religious opposition had no numbers, so there was little American-style stridency on this. Legal abortion was accepted on the basis that, if it was evil, it was a necessary one.

And ten years on from parliament's refusal even to contemplate the Wolfenden committee's recommendation to legalize male homosexuality, parliamentary opinion had shifted, partly because Labour now had a big majority, not the Tories, and partly because a new generation of MPs were more relaxed. The old implacables were still there: 'I am rather tired of democracy being made safe for the pimps, the prostitutes, the spivs, the pansies and now the queers,' said Sir Cyril Osborne (Conservative). 'It is high time that we ordinary squares had some public attention and our point of view listened to.' But the squares were a minority now.

Nonetheless, it applied only to 'consenting adults in private', which meant over-21s. The laws affecting under-21s were actually strengthened. Nor did it change the general sense of shame attached. None of the significant number of gay men on the pop scene were

---

* Notionally, capital punishment remained for treason, piracy and arson in the royal dockyards until the 1990s. The last gallows stood ready and waiting in Wandsworth jail, just in case. It is now in the National Museum of Justice in Nottingham.

ready to proclaim themselves to the fans; no one rushed home to come out to their mum. This would take longer. But it was a start.

Jenkins's next target was theatre censorship, a farce which had the virtue of being funnier than almost anything actually performed. Since 1737 this had been in the hands of the Lord Chamberlain, a royal flunkey whose duties originally included the royal bedchamber but were now more to do with state visits and garden parties. The incumbent was Lord Cobbold, a former governor of the Bank of England, whose qualifications for the censor's role were not obvious.

Theatre managers had not been wholly averse to the system, because it offered some protection against the whims of councillors, police and magistrates. But as theatre became more vibrant after the mid-fifties, censorship became increasingly absurd: John Osborne's agent had to conduct fruitless negotiations with a random aristocrat's office about the use of *pouf*, *rogered* and *balls* in *The Entertainer*. In the sixties, halfway through the run of the musical *Fings Ain't What They Used T'Be*, the censor intervened to stop a plank being carried at a phallic angle.

Worse, the censorship was not just about alleged obscenity: plays could be stopped from upsetting the royal family, foreign powers and indeed all living persons. In 1965 a revue at the Lyric, Hammersmith, was ordered to remove two songs three hours before opening night. The *Daily Mail* decided to print the text of one of the songs, about Britannia. It thus reached 6 million readers. To achieve that onstage, as Michael Frayn pointed out in his *Observer* column, it would have had to run at the Lyric for the next thirty years. With more notice, this nonsense was easy to evade: theatres could turn themselves into private clubs for the duration. But there was still a risk of prosecution, which happened to Edward Bond's play, *Saved*, which had a harrowing baby-stoning scene (no real babies were harmed). The final straw came when satire burst back on to the stage and the *Private Eye* team put on a jolly spoof called *Mrs Wilson's Diary* gently mocking the government. Cobbold not only wrote his own review – 'cheap and gratuitously nasty . . . worthless' – but sent the script to Wilson to let him censor it himself, which, with the help of George Brown and Jim Callaghan, he did. Eight scenes were cut before it was finally staged. This was outrageous: the BBC did not seek prime-ministerial approval for comedy sketches. Stupid too: if Wilson still had the Supermac touch, he would have been in the audience, laughing.

In discussion, Wilson began to muse disingenuously that maybe representations of living people should remain subject to censorship. Jenkins mused about resignation. However, a Labour MP, George Strauss, had won a high place in the private members' ballot for time to introduce their own legislation and was delighted to put it forward. Theatres were finally freed in July 1968. For a while there were bacchanalian excesses, as with the brief nudity in *Hair* and the more pervasively sexual show-offery of *Oh! Calcutta!* Eventually, Britain became more grown-up.

By then Jenkins had a more grown-up job. After an exchange of hostages with the Treasury after devaluation, he became a confident Chancellor of the Exchequer and Callaghan a much more conventional Home Secretary. Lord Gardiner, the progressive Lord Chancellor, saw through divorce reform, ending another mad situation whereby one half of a marriage had to blame the other to escape them. This often involved staging bogus dirty weekends (traditionally in Brighton) so that a private detective could barge in, take a photo and show one of them in bed with someone else. In 1964 a judge had refused a Hornsey couple permission to divorce because they did not argue enough. The new law made that somewhat simpler.*

But Labour left office with the drinking laws and Sunday observance untouched. Nor did Callaghan have any truck with the idea of making cannabis legal, which Jenkins had been considering. Nor would any other of the eighteen men (including Jenkins himself when he returned in 1974) and four women who would hold and often further disfigure the role of Home Secretary over the next half-century. It is, though, fair to say that most of them were too hard-pressed just surviving each day in that grim posting to worry about improving people's lives.

---

* Although full no-fault divorce did not arrive in England and Wales until 2022.

Crime rose throughout the sixties, and there were two cases around the Jenkins era that sent a collective shudder through Britain. First came the Moors murders, in which Ian Brady, aided by his girlfriend Myra Hindley, killed five blameless young people: three boys, two girls, aged between 10 and 17. No case has ever left such a lasting scar on the nation's psyche; the public were transfixed by the mixture of sadistic cruelty, sexual depravity, the involvement of the bewitched Hindley, and the cold, bleak moors north of Manchester where the bodies were buried. Had they been caught earlier, with hanging still available, reprieve would have been unthinkable (unless Brady had successfully played the insanity card). As it was, the horrors not surprisingly stirred the nation's vengeful instincts.

Then, in August 1966, three men in a car parked outside Wormwood Scrubs prison in West London were approached by three plain-clothes policemen who briefly questioned them. One of the suspects, Harry Roberts, then drew a gun. All three policemen were shot dead. By nightfall, the Police Federation had called for the return of the death penalty to protect its members.

The other two fugitives were found quickly enough, but Roberts stayed at large for three months, mainly in Hertfordshire woodland – he had been a soldier in the Malayan jungle and hunkered down well while police hunted everywhere else. Six thousand people rang up with presumably bogus sightings. Mrs Joy Lewin, who served him regularly for six weeks in the village shop in Thorley, was not among the 6,000. 'I didn't want to look a fool,' she said. 'I knew the first time he walked in it was Roberts. But people laughed when I told them so I did nothing.' That was one type of Britishness: fear of embarrassment.

That autumn, football crowds taunted the attendant coppers:

> *Harry Roberts, he's our man.*
> *He shoots policemen, bang, bang, bang.*

That was a newer type of Britishness.

These three would also have hanged – Roberts, the instigator, ringleader and firer of two fatal shots, most certainly of all. Instead, aged 30, he got an indeterminate life sentence and was left to rot. He deserves no sympathy; he had minimal remorse. Twenty-six years into what turned into a forty-eight-year stretch, he told *The Guardian*: 'The police aren't like real people to us. They're strangers, they're the enemy . . . it's like people I killed in Malaya.' He was paroled in 2014, aged 78.

Hanging had at least been quick and cheap; long-term prisoners posed serious management problems. Gangsters were now generally far nastier than the Ealing Comedy figures of the fifties. South London was ruled by the Richardson gang, who specialized in 'long-firm fraud'. This involved setting up companies which bought and sold modest amounts of goods from a load of wholesalers for a while, building up reputation and credit. They then placed a batch of much larger orders, sold them and vanished.

Those who affronted the Richardsons were invited to their HQ for 'a discussion' at which there would be impromptu dentistry. Nailing feet to the floor and electric shock treatment would also be part of the conversation. Eventually, some victims thought this worth mentioning to police. Nine men were convicted. The gang leader, Charlie Richardson, got twenty-five years, which was considered high for what was merely grievous bodily harm. At the lengthy trial, the defence denied the existence of the black box said to cause the electric shocks; Eddie, Charlie's brother and henchman, said years later it did exist but the shock was no stronger than that of a farmer's electric fence: 'That's not to say it wasn't unpleasant, especially as Charlie liked to wire it up to blokes' bollocks.'

This was merely the hors d'oeuvre for the trial of the self-appointed monarchs of the East End. The twins Ronnie and Reggie Kray were both ex-boxers who first came to public attention in the early sixties when they popped up in celebrity photos in the papers for no obvious reason. They did a bit of long-firm fraud themselves, but mainly they owned their own nightclubs and took protection money from many others. Above all, they seemed to enjoy being famous gangsters – especially Ronnie, who was not just a psychopath

but, more unusually, obviously homosexual. Still a crime – though in his case, the least of them. They employed about thirty people in what they privately called 'the Firm'* and raised a lot for charity.†
It was widely understood that those approached for donations did not apologize and say they had already given to Oxfam.

In 1965, both were arrested for 'demanding money with menaces'. After a little light witness-tampering, they got off and were greeted on their return to the family home in Bethnal Green like conquering heroes. 'A couple of real nice boys, Ron and Reg,' one caller told the press. After that, they felt invulnerable. Ronnie shot George Cornell, a Richardson man who, aside from other misdemeanours, had called him 'a fat pouf' in the bar of the Blind Beggar pub; Reggie later stabbed another gangster, Jack 'The Hat' McVitie, to death, evidently for being a nuisance. There were witnesses; and this time the police got them to sing by offering immunity. Chief Superintendent 'Nipper' Read, a boxer himself, planned his campaign meticulously. And he nabbed them.

The Krays came up against a judge who also cherished his reputation: Mr Justice Melford Stevenson, who lived in a house called Truncheons. Like the Krays, he exuded menace and sternness. He accompanied the life sentences with a recommendation of a thirty-year minimum. It was obvious there were many crimes, including murder, for which evidence was lacking. It was still not, however, obvious to elements in the East End and the residents of Bildeston in Suffolk – where the Krays had bought a 'retirement home' and gave the children donkey rides. Even one of their old teachers, who had himself gone to Bildeston to retire, said he 'thought the world of them . . . They brought honour and glory to the school.'

Stevenson said later there were only two correct statements made by the twins throughout the trial: that he was hopelessly prejudiced against them, and that the prosecuting counsel was a 'fat slob'.

---

* As the Royal Family call their business.
† As even the most rapacious public companies would do in the future.

There was another gang operating in London at the time. Its activities were extensive in the most profitable areas of business: bank robberies, drugs, porn, nightlife, sex. Many of those involved were never brought to justice. Even Charlie Richardson was shocked: 'The most lucrative, powerful and extensive protection racket ever to exist was administered by the Metropolitan Police . . . I made regular payments to the police. It was a sort of taxation on crime.'

By the mid-sixties, there were no doubt innocents who thought the police force was still that of Dock Green. But the London football fans chanting for Harry Roberts were on to something. And it was especially a London phenomenon: the pickings were richer, and the Metropolitan Police totally inward-looking and contemptuous of outsiders – particularly of Robert Mark, the former chief constable of Leicester brought in at a senior level by Jenkins to do a clean-up job. Mark reckoned that 90 per cent of all London policemen welcomed what he was doing. This still left a large number, mainly in the CID, who had reason to be very nervous.

Some, though not many, would go to prison in time. But in the sixties it often seemed easier to get out of jail free than to escape an old-fashioned boarding school or a Butlin's holiday camp. The end of hanging meant that even the worst murderers were eternal escape risks, and the new extreme sentences meant that for some there was nothing to lose. Harry Roberts told *The Guardian* he made twenty-two escape attempts in his early years, but he must have lost his jungle skills. Hindley was involved in a plot with a warder which was foiled. Charlie Richardson, having completed an Open University degree in sociology, was put in an open prison and wandered off for almost a year.

And after George Blake fled in October 1966, it started a fashion. Jenkins, as Home Secretary, asked the eternal panjandrum Lord Mountbatten to investigate. Mountbatten reported just before Christmas and said no British jail was really secure, whereupon thirty-nine more inmates decided there might be more festive cheer elsewhere. The world laughed, especially when bookmakers began offering odds on each day's score.

Most notorious of the Christmas escapees was Frank Mitchell, the Mad Axeman. Four years earlier, Mitchell had become, it seems, the last prisoner to receive a judicial birching (fifteen strokes) for attacking prison officers in Hull. By 1966 he was in Dartmoor, regarded by the public as the British Alcatraz but actually very come-day, go-day because working parties went out on the wide-open moor. Mitchell was out there when he asked to be allowed to feed some nearby ponies. Just of sight was a car containing Kray associates; Mitchell was in London before anyone realized he had gone.

However, his incarceration there was much sterner than on Dartmoor: the boys soon realized he was a liability – he was being hunted and was recognizable, big and psychotic. So the Krays resorted to their own version of capital punishment, which had not been abolished. Mitchell's body was never found.

And somehow, around this time, without the catharsis of the hanging rituals – from the black cap to the scenes outside the prison gates – murder lost some of its dangerous allure. The teasingly thrilling popular press headlines – THE CARBON COPY MURDER IN CLOD HALL LANE . . . THE BLUE GARDENIA KILLER . . . THE KILLING OF LITTLE MISS CHATTERBOX . . . THE GREEN TIGHTS MURDER . . . THE FIEND OF BEENHAM – began to fade away, and readers began to get such kicks from detective fiction instead.

12

YE BLOCKS, YE STONES

IN JUNE 1965, THE QUEEN – OR TO BE MORE EXACT HAROLD
Wilson – was graciously pleased to give all four Beatles the MBE
for 'services to export'. It was in part a Wilsonian publicity stunt
but also a genuine attempt to make the honours more inclusive.* At
least five men from previous honours lists pompously sent back
their own medals in protest and, from America, the award was
criticized by the head of the Ku Klux Klan. 'The whole matter is
becoming a drag,' said Ringo.

Four months later, when The Beatles went to the Palace, it was
besieged by young females in a manner that, for them, was becoming
almost as ritualized as the honours system itself. The Fab Four were
starting to find this a drag too. In 1966, there were fraught visits to
the Philippines – where they were alleged to have been insufficiently
respectful to the Marcos dictatorship – and to the US where, in
Memphis, John Lennon's humour, always a tightrope act, stumbled
when he said they were more popular than Jesus. They stopped
touring. Forever, as it turned out.

Instead, they spent more time dropping acid and imbibing the
wisdom of the Maharishi Mahesh Yogi. At Christmas 1967, their
long-awaited BBC special, *Magical Mystery Tour*, flopped

---

* Simultaneously, Violet Carson, who played the battle-axe Ena Sharples in
Coronation Street, was awarded the OBE.

spectacularly ('O Beatles, O grief' – *Daily Mirror*; 'blatant rubbish' – *Daily Express*). This was the moment a great many people had been predicting ever since the Dave Clark Five knocked them off No. 1 in the charts in January 1964, if not before: gone, finished, has-beens.

The calm presence of Brian Epstein was absent: he had died of a drug overdose in August 1967, aged 32. Maybe he would have prevented the TV disaster, a mess born of overconfidence but not without musical merit. Without him, the business suffered but not their skills.

They had reached their pinnacle the previous summer with the *Sgt. Pepper* LP. The later output was partly a tribute to the effects of both LSD and gurus. But, above all, it was a huge tribute to John and Paul's work ethic. 'They were always being told they were not going to last,' said Philip Norman, one of their biographers. 'Lennon and McCartney believed this so they kept writing songs. That's why they moved in such huge leaps.'

'What perfectionists they were. Particularly Paul,' said another, Hunter Davies, who had special access. 'They would endlessly work on the same bit till I was screaming with boredom. It seemed fine to me the first time, so why do it a hundred times?' The Beatles' pre-eminence was never lost in the group's lifetime, or ever after. However, they were no longer ubiquitous, and others filled the gaps.

Culturally the whole decade moved in huge leaps. The Beatles had pushed the envelope of acceptable dress and demeanour a little; the Rolling Stones then ripped it to shreds. This strategy is generally credited to their first manager, Andrew Loog Oldham, a teenage Svengali – younger than any of the group – who occupied a totally different role from the dodgy-uncle type like Larry Parnes or the steady older-brother figure of Epstein. He functioned more as an agent provocateur.

'What Oldham did was to take everything implicit in the Stones and blow it up one hundred times,' wrote Nik Cohn. 'Long-haired and ugly and anarchic as they were, Oldham made them more so and he turned them into everything that parents would most hate, be most frightened by.' By 1964 their hair was collar-length. A year later, Mick Jagger, Bill Wyman and Brian Jones were fined £5 each for urinating against a garage wall in East London after a concert. Just what Oldham wanted.

An arms race of outrage developed between competing groups: partly calculated attention-seeking, partly the drugs. The Pretty Things – neighbours of the Stones in South East London, who played 'anarchic R&B' with large dollops of LSD – never got above No. 10 in the charts, but they did get banned for life from New Zealand. It was either there or somewhere else that Viv Prince was said to be 'drinking a bottle of whisky a day and there were a number of incidents with a tear-gas gun he'd got hold of in Germany'.

There was the Texan P. J. Proby, much more famous in Britain than back home, who was touring with Cilla Black when his trousers astonishingly managed to split three nights running, in Croydon, Walthamstow and Luton. He was barred from the next night in Northampton but turned up anyway for the mobbing outside.

The truly gifted were not immune. Syd Barrett, the guiding genius behind Pink Floyd's early success, became so acid-addled that he had to be replaced, to everyone's disadvantage. For him, there was no cathartic early death; he went home and lived reclusively with his mum. And there was Jimi Hendrix, who struggled to make a living as a blues guitarist in New York, but came to London in 1966 and astounded everyone with his talent, his virtuosity, the blatant sexuality of his act, and the extra bit of outrage when the top of his guitar caught fire. 'He became a symbol for the entire decadent London rock scene,' wrote Anthony Scaduto, 'the epito-misation of raw sensual power, of drugs and drink and dissolution. He was delivering what Jagger had only been hinting at.' Even teenagers found it hard to keep up; authority decided retribution was required.

———·———

The future Metropolitan Police commissioner Robert Mark identified three different types of police corruption: the small-scale bribe of the African border post variety; the large-scale nexus within the Met linking coppers and gangsters, which he would tackle later; and 'corruption for the job', bending the rules to get convictions. The drugs bust at Keith Richards's rather grand Sussex thatched cottage was partly in that third category – the unofficial 'filthy fellow' prosecution that caused the death of Stephen Ward. It also involved a conspiracy between the disreputable drugs squad and Britain's most disreputable newspaper, the *News of the World* aka the Screws.

What happened was that the Screws had run a series of articles highlighting drug-taking rock stars, based partly on overhearing Jagger talking in a nightclub. But it was not Jagger, it was Brian Jones, the *News of the World* having sent a most unworldly reporter. Jagger issued a libel writ. To stave this off, the paper began spying on him, got wind of the Sussex party and tipped off the police, who raided it and seized 'some Ambre Solaire, a few bars of hotel soap, Earl Grey tea and other suspect substances for analysis, and even a few traces of pot'.

Richards was charged for allowing the pot on the premises, Jagger for possession of four amphetamine tablets found in a jacket pocket, bought legally in Italy and which his doctor at home would have prescribed had he asked. No charges were pressed on the best-remembered rumour of the night: that Marianne Faithfull had a Mars bar in an orifice not normally used for the purpose. She was indeed wrapped only in a towel during the appearance of the uninvited guests, and maybe they could have invented a law against that. And the raid, by chance or design, was timed to come after the departure of one George Harrison MBE, whose honoured presence might have been a complication.

The judge, an old naval man called Block, told the jury Jagger's defence was worthless and sent him to prison for three months. Richards got a year. The normal going rate for their crimes, even then, was probation. Jagger was very publicly handcuffed as he was led to jail.

The leader columns of newspapers are normally very much less influential than their authors like to think – *The Times* helping convince Princess Margaret to give up Peter Townsend a possible exception. But they can make a difference when they escape their normal philosophical shackles. And the newish editor of *The Times*, William Rees-Mogg,* wrote a devastating leader attacking the convictions. It was headed with a quote from Alexander Pope: 'Who breaks a butterfly upon a wheel?' and went on: 'Mr Jagger's is about as mild a drug case as can ever have been brought before the Courts . . . It should be the particular quality of British justice to ensure that Mr Jagger is treated exactly the same as anyone else, no better and no worse.'

The two were already out on bail pending the appeal; Jagger, who had had three nights in jail, said he had some 'interesting experiences' and that the cells were 'not much different to a hotel room in Minnesota'. Lord Parker, the Lord Chief Justice, then brought their appeals forward, sat on the bench himself and set them free. Judge Block later made it very clear that Rees-Mogg had rumbled him. Addressing the mighty legal brains of the Horsham Ploughing and Agricultural Society shortly afterwards, he said: 'We did our best, your fellow countrymen, I and my fellow magistrates, to cut these Stones down to size, but alas, it was not to be because the Court of Criminal Appeal let them roll free.'

Later in the year there was a similar charade with Brian Jones, who by now really did have a drugs problem: a raid on his flat, a piffling amount of cannabis found, pomp and piety from the bench, nine months in prison, out on bail, quashed on appeal. By now the legalization of cannabis was becoming an issue; in 1969 a government committee under Baroness Wootton did not go that far but recommended liberalization and an end to the kind of nonsense the Stones suffered. Jim Callaghan, as Home Secretary, brushed it aside. No votes in it.

In practice, the Wootton compromise on pot would more or less become the norm that persists to this day. It was a bit like the homosexuality law before 1967. If you had your own home and were discreet about it, no one would bash the door down to see

---

* Father of the much less liberal future government minister Jacob.

SIXTIES PEOPLE: (*top left*) Twiggy, the model whose common touch helped define the decade, poses in King's Road, Chelsea, holding a maple twig for reasons unclear, 1966; (*top right*) John Stephen, 'the King of Carnaby Street', strides out discreetly, 1967; (*below*) photographer and activist John 'Hoppy' Hopkins, once described as the nearest thing to a leader the counterculture ever had, returns to his girlfriend Suzy Creamcheese after nine months in jail for possessing a small amount of cannabis, 1967.

NOVELTIES

(*Top left*) Twisting the night away in the baronial-style Saddle Room, London's first discotheque, 1962.

(*Top right*) Daytime in the sixties: mini-dress, boots, transistor and probably a pirate station, London, 1966.

(*Left*) Saturday night fever: the cast of *That Was the Week That Was*, the BBC's smash hit satirical show, at the height of its glory, January 1963.

THE MOPTOPS WHO TRANSFORMED POP: The Beatles, John, Paul and George and Ringo, pose before their performance at the Royal Variety Show, November 1963 . . . And again, almost four years, many triumphs and costume changes later, as they launch perhaps their greatest album, *Sergeant Pepper's Lonely Hearts Club Band*, June 1967.

THE AFFAIR THAT TRANSFIXED THE WORLD: (*top left*) John Profumo, the war minister who strayed and fibbed; (*top right*) Christine Keeler, with whom he slept a few times; (*bottom left*) Stephen Ward, her friend and mentor who became the scapegoat; (*bottom right*) Mervyn Griffith-Jones, the barrister who helped drive Ward to suicide.

THE OPEN ROAD

No crash barrier, no hard shoulder . . . hardly any traffic. The newly opened M1 near Little Linford, Buckinghamshire, 1960.

THE DOOMED ARCH

The much-loved Euston Arch in 1960. Built in 1837, it was demolished in 1962 to make way for the modernization of the station. The government refused funding to allow it to be relocated.

GOING . . .: (*above*) children make use of the temporary playground created by cleared terraced houses in Hulme, Mamchester. The surrounding homes await their fate, 1962; (*below*) the last British Rail steam train, 'The Fifteen Guinea Special', leaves Liverpool Lime Street heading for Manchester, August 1968.

(*Top left*) BANNED: sixteen-year-old heiress Jayne Harries was refused admission to the Royal Enclosure at Ascot for wearing a trouser suit, June 1968. (*Top right*) UNBANNED: a few minutes later, after a quick change into a less demure micro-dress, she is allowed in. (*Below*) UNCONSTRAINED: Yorkshire miner Keith Nicholson and his wife Vivian, who promised to 'spend, spend, spend', receive their winnings from Bruce Forsyth on behalf of Littlewoods Pools, 1961. Subsequently, things turned out badly for both Jayne Harries and the Nicholsons.

IMPROBABLE FAME, CERTAIN INFAMY: (*top left*) Don Thompson, who the Italians christened Mickey Mouse, wins the 50 km race walk at the Rome Olympics, having trained for the heat in his bathroom in Middlesex. He was one of Britain's two gold medallists at the 1960 Games; (*top right*) Pickles, the collie who found the stolen World Cup in a south London hedge, became an unexpected star in 1966; (*bottom left*) PC Norwell Roberts (who changed his name from Gumbs) became London's first black policemen in modern times, 1967; (*bottom right*) his namesake, Harry Roberts, was involved in the fatal shooting of three policemen outside Wormwood Scrubs prison and served 48 years in jail.

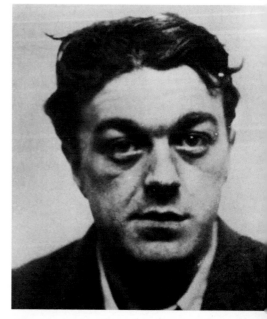

what you were doing. On the streets, in pubs, parks and public toilets, you had to be more careful. The hounding of pop stars eased off long before the biggest names were routinely given not MBEs but knighthoods.

13

CLOSING TIME

IN 1961, DAVID BRADSHAW AND HIS BROTHER JOHN, EIGHT AND seven, from the Caribbean island of Montserrat, docked in Southampton on their way to join their parents in Swindon. The on-board minder assumed they would be met, which they would have been had not the ship docked two days early.

With the adventurous spirit of sixties children, they made their way to Swindon. All they knew was that the house was No. 64 in a street beginning with G. By now it was after midnight. A policeman helped and they were third time lucky. There was hot water, a bathroom, flushing toilet, a TV, cornflakes – and a younger brother they had never met.

That year, the Commonwealth Immigration Bill began its passage towards the statute book to curb the flow of migrants. It was, of course, discriminatory in intent without being specific. In keeping with British legislative tradition, its effects were largely the reverse of those intended.

It was opposed passionately by the Labour leader, Hugh Gaitskell, who denounced 'this miserable, shameful, shabby bill' and insisted atavistically 'we are the mother country and we ought not to forget it'. When the Labour party came to power, however, it made no attempt at repeal. True, the high-minded Gaitskell had died, to be replaced by the wily Wilson. But politics is always the art of the possible; Labour's 1964 manifesto accepted there had to be limits and Gaitskell would have had to do the same.

The new law ended walk-in rights for ex-imperial all-comers; classified potential workers under three categories (those offered jobs, those with special skills, and those with neither); and allowed the government to decide on numbers. It also gave authority to bar the sick, the criminal and the politically undesirable – the three fences the US had traditionally made the huddled masses jump when they arrived at Ellis Island. The first consequence, inevitably, was to create a huge rush to get in before the law was enacted. The second was to bind those already in Britain without documents much closer, because they feared if they went abroad at all they might not be able to prove their right to return.*

The third was that it allowed workers to bring their dependents, which ended any notion that the newcomers were temporary remittance men. The new law increased the flow of wives and children like the Bradshaws, and guaranteed Britain's future as a multiracial country to an extent the Macmillan government had never envisaged or could have accepted if they had. Net immigration was higher in the fourteen years after the Act than the fourteen before, dating back to the arrival of the *Windrush*.

'The clumsiness of the 1962 Act was consistent with characteristic British traits: a distaste for absolutist solutions, a preference for muddle over clarity, a refusal to be entirely guided by the promptings of either conscience or prejudice,' wrote the immigration historian Robert Winder. 'Britain pursued a policy which reflected both its generous and its mean streak, often simultaneously.'

This was true. A successful and humane immigration policy depends on a country (a) admitting the migrants it wants and needs for its own purposes, while (b) amending that to cope with overriding humanitarian crises. Britain's failure to fulfil the first criterion directly reduced its willingness to fulfil the second. There was still minimal consideration of the impact on education, health, welfare

---

* The failure to insist on retrospective documentation was the prime cause of the Windrush scandal that exploded nearly sixty years later.

or housing. As late as 1965 the Home Office said they had no idea
how many migrants were in the country.

————⋅————

The main source of migration was now Asia, not the Caribbean. In
particular the newcomers came from the rural Mirpur region of
Pakistan, where more than 100,000 people were being displaced by
the huge Mangla Dam project. Britain's textile mills, backed by
public money, were still investing in a futile attempt to compete
with cheaper Asian rivals, not least the subcontinent itself. Pakistan's
new homeless had enough compensation to travel, and the pay for
doing night and weekend shifts in British factories was far more
attractive to them than to the British indigenes, so they could be
recruited even after 1962. And the dam meant that the Pakistani
government, which had previously made emigration difficult
(though a little bribe always went a long way) was now more
supportive. Again, this brought permanent migration to fulfil a
short-term need.

   This was to prove the most problematic of all the waves of
migration. The different social habits of young Jamaicans and
elderly Londoners had caused friction enough, but the Mirpuris
might have dropped in from a distant planet. These were country
boys, without English or any other point of connection. In the
absence of women, they only had each other. Seventeen men from
the same village lived in a two-bedroom house in Oxford, sharing
beds, sleeping on the stairs or in the garden. No one had given them
any advice or support. 'I was all right because I had been in the
army and had learnt some of the English ways,' recalled one of
them, 'but the others did not even know how to use English
bathrooms or toilets. No wonder our neighbours disliked us.'

   The Indian newcomers were usually better prepared but equally
crowded. One migrant, Avtar Singh Jouhl, found himself one of
'fifteen or sixteen' in his brother's house in Smethwick. Tin bath; no
hot water; outside toilet. Local teenage boys were inclined to
conclude that 'all Pakis are homos', as the writer Jeremy Seabrook
heard one say in Blackburn.

It was not about sex but saving. This was not difficult, because terraced houses in northern industrial towns were available for around £750 and the Asian migrants were quick to sense the pluses of owning property. Their lives would become much more domesticated with time, but not necessarily more integrated.

Many of the British were convinced, as they were with earlier waves of migrants, that the newcomers were up to no good. The most common suspicion, benefit fraud, was rarely well founded. However, post-1962 it was easy to bring in a nephew or two and call them sons – and the subcontinental marital market was a nightmare for officials to comprehend. But mostly the migrants themselves were the victims, having to pay off corrupt officials at home before they could leave. Later in the decade, in a pattern that would recur, gangsters would ferry illegals across the Channel and dump them on the south coast with even less aftercare than the legals received.

On a foggy November morning in 1967, three men were put ashore in Kent, found the nearest railway station and waited for a train. They waited and waited then finally asked a man on the street: 'Next train, please?' 'Easter,' he replied. It was the miniature Romney, Hythe and Dymchurch Railway. They were arrested. Others must have melted into the mist.

There were also suspicions of African 'cuckoo babies' being fostered on the south coast, which broke cover when a five-year-old Nigerian boy was found starving in a cellar in Sussex. 'For all we know scores of babies may have been taken by foster parents,' said an NSPCC official. Adoption and fostering in those days was largely unregulated.

As soon as Harold Wilson took power, he insisted he would not tolerate racial discrimination. One of the few seats Labour lost in the 1964 election was the West Midlands town of Smethwick, which already had a large immigrant population; the successful Tory, Peter Griffiths, fought an overtly racist campaign and Wilson demanded that he be treated as 'a parliamentary leper'.

Unfortunately, his own local party in the constituency had not noticed that its own HQ, the Smethwick Labour Club, operated a colour bar and would not even allow the defeated member to invite black supporters to his own rather sombre post-election booze-up.* Shamefacedly, the politicians severed the connection.†

These attitudes were endemic. Across the planet, people were intrinsically suspicious of strangers who did not look, talk or necessarily think like them; they still are and probably always will be. This could be modified by close acquaintance or celebrity. In the early sixties the greatest cricketer of his era, the Barbadian Garry Sobers, was playing in the Lancashire League, where the clubs had enough money to make it worth his while. The opposition had several local West Indians in their team and Sobers took them to his local pub. 'You are OK, Mr Sobers,' he was told. 'But these boys can't come in.' He took them elsewhere.

To stop such incidents, the Wilson government pushed through the first Race Relations Act in 1965 but, with its small majority, it wanted Conservative support. To get that it had to opt for tepid minimalism, which put a stop to racial bans in 'places of public resort' like Sobers's local pub and the Goring Hotel but not much else. And the first step after a complaint was 'conciliation'. But it was a start. A tougher act would follow three years later.

In the meantime there were continuing outrages. That same year Balwant Singh, a Wolverhampton bus conductor, was told he could not buy a home on the new Lyndale Park estate at Wednesfield (between £2,850 and £4,250) by order of the developers. 'Our clients reserve the right to sell to whoever they please,' said a spokesman for the agents. In 1966 a Wimbledon car hire firm refused to carry the secretary of the Ugandan Trades Union Congress, D. G. Nkuuti, who was in Britain on a fraternal union

---

* The defeated candidate was Patrick Gordon-Walker, who was appointed to his intended position as Foreign Secretary, but had to resign early in 1965 after also losing the supposedly safe seat at Leyton at a by-election.

† It was and is quite normal for supposedly political clubs to exist with minimal regard for ideology – many Conservative clubs thrived in mining villages which had hardly any Tory voters. They are sometimes lightly camouflaged as 'Constitutional Clubs'.

visit. 'We do not carry blacks, not for Harold Wilson nor for anyone,' his hosts were told. 'The country has gone to the dogs.'

Employment remained contentious. In 1963 came the Bristol bus boycott. It coincided with and received inspiration from somewhat more dramatic events in Birmingham, Alabama, where Martin Luther King was thrown in jail for protesting against segregation. Just about everyone in Britain knew about racism in the American South. In Bristol, only regular bus users (and maybe not all of them) would have noticed that all the crew were white. Finally, the company admitted that was not a coincidence, and blamed their employees.

Local West Indians, backed by students, began a protest. The affair was brief, bloodless, and was ended by an announcement from the nationalized body that owned the Bristol Omnibus Company that the colour bar would end. Retrospectively, the dispute has been sanctified into a major landmark in Britain's racial history, though it received limited publicity outside Bristol at the time. Nor did it unite white progressive opinion with the vehemence attached to their view of Alabama. The columnist Claud Cockburn thought he detected a certain unease among this group. Of course they opposed the colour bar, but would have preferred that it had been dealt with differently: 'Quietly. Tactfully. Without undue publicity.' The British way.

And the British way was certainly better than the Alabama way. In 1962, Jamaican-born Wilston Jackson, after ten years on the railways, was promoted from fireman to become Britain's first black train driver. The firemen threatened to refuse to work with him, but a strong-minded foreman saw that off. Jackson now has a plaque in his honour at King's Cross.

Three years later, Asquith Xavier, a guard born in Dominica, requested a transfer from Marylebone station – hard hit by the Beeching cuts – to Euston, where there were vacancies. This was refused because of 'staff resistance' to black workers – something that had existed at Euston for years and been accepted by management for the sake of a quiet life. However, publication of the reason for the rejection put a stop to the quietude. The transport minister, Barbara Castle, intervened, and within a week the decision was reversed. This was uncomfortable for everyone, most especially Leslie Leppington, the divisional manager obliged to face the press. 'The staff representatives at Euston were not so much anti-colour as pro-white, pro-fellow railwaymen,' he said, to derisive laughter from the hacks. He added the men were afraid of losing their jobs. Xavier now has a plaque at Chatham, where he lived.

The fear of losing jobs was real enough. Unemployment was rising generally and the railways were retrenching as the Beeching cuts bit. It was also true that the Euston and Bristol situations (which were nowhere near unique) were obviously untenable. But white unease was growing, and sometimes it could not be handled quietly.

Gladstone Buchanan, his wife and four children, who had been living in one room, finally got their wish and were allocated a three-bedroom council flat in a small block at Bradley, on the edge of Wolverhampton. The new neighbours were not welcoming. 'The coloured family's door will be eighteen inches from my door' . . . 'I'd have to share my washing line with them' . . . 'It's the smell of their cooking we object to'. 'Tenants should give it a try,' said Wolverhampton's housing chairman, Alderman Herbert Lane. 'They're being unfair.'

Of course they were. But to understand history one has to see the views of those who ended on the wrong side of it. Most British people led sheltered lives before the 1960s. If they had been abroad at all it was probably in uniform; they would have dealt with non-whites only as inferiors or enemies. The narrative of empire did not suggest to them that whites and non-whites were equally competent (and nor did the performance of the newly independent African states). The working classes ate traditional English food and enjoyed traditional English pastimes. They sensed their already scarce housing was getting scarcer; that their jobs were under threat and also their communities – by urban clearances, the building of high-rises and the scattering of friends and family. And no one seemed able to articulate their feelings. Soon one man would do so.

———◊———

Enoch Powell was a most unusual person and an extremely unusual politician. He was certainly, as we say now, on the spectrum: the clarity of his own mind being muddied by its inability to discern the working of other minds, or the customary process of politics as half-measures.

His most effective Commons speech was his denunciation of imperial brutality in Kenya in 1959; his most effective ministerial speech came when he was health minister in 1961. It is still remembered reverently by erudite health professionals as the 'Water Tower speech'; it presaged the closure of the old lunatic asylums and their replacement by 'care in the community'. 'There they stand,' he said, 'isolated, majestic, imperious, brooded over by the gigantic water-tower and chimney combined, rising unmistakable and daunting out of the countryside – the asylums which our forefathers built with such immense solidity . . .'* He then talked of lighting 'the funeral pyre' of the mental hospitals. On the political spectrum, Powell was not someone who could be easily classified.

His most famous speech of all – *the* most famous or infamous of all post-war British political speeches – was made in Birmingham, near his Wolverhampton constituency, in April 1968. There he stood – isolated, majestic, imperious – at a small gathering of Conservatives, and attempted to light the funeral pyre of multi-racial Britain. This was the speech known much more widely as 'Rivers of Blood'.

April 1968 was when the global political frenzies of the decade were reaching their dissonant crescendos. It was the height of the Prague Spring, when it seemed briefly possible that Communism could be made decent; it was weeks before France erupted and the de Gaulle government tottered; Lyndon Johnson had just announced he would not seek another term as president; days after that, Martin Luther King was murdered in Tennessee. More relevantly, in banal

---

* He also instituted a huge programme of general hospital-building which Kenneth Robinson, a Labour successor, said could only have been done by a minister with Powell's reputation for financial frugality.

British terms, it was two months after the Labour government had rushed through an act in a single day to control the admission of Asians from Kenya.

Asians, mainly Hindu Gujaratis, were the mercantile classes of East Africa, sometimes very wealthy. As such they were held in contempt by both the native Africans and the British colonialists. The British confined their disdain for these upstarts to social snobbery and snubbery but, with Kenya now independent, African grudges had freer rein. And the Kenyan government was starting to make Asian life uncomfortable. Many got out and, in keeping with a promise made by the Tories at independence, turned up in Britain.

The refusal to admit them was a shameful betrayal by Labour, as the Cabinet well knew. But perfidy of this kind was a natural outcome of the general immigration shambles. There were issues on the Tory side too: they were struggling to come to terms with the government's second, more potent, Race Relations Bill. Into this delicate situation strode Powell, boots and all.

Powell had for some time been concerned that the 1962 Act was failing to curb the influx, and had made a speech at Walsall in February calling for further controls. The Walsall speech had made little impact; he wanted to make himself clearer. The Birmingham speech, he told the editor of the Wolverhampton *Express & Star*, 'will go up *fizz* like a rocket'.

Aside from the small number present, hardly anyone heard the speech in full until the fiftieth anniversary when the BBC broadcast it read by an actor (to much fury from Powell-haters). Reading the text now, it feels very strange indeed.

He allowed himself to be sidetracked by the Race Relations Bill and his support for the ridiculous local bans on Sikh bus conductors wearing turbans. The central anecdote was about a woman who had excreta pushed through her letterbox. It was almost certainly false, a conflation of different items of local gossip. The woman existed all right but was well known locally to be sad, drunk, unreliable and, if anything, dependent on her kindly West Indian neighbours.

According to Powell, if she went out, she was followed by

children: 'charming, wide-grinning piccaninnies. They cannot speak English, but one word they know. "Racialist," they chant.' Can't speak English? What language did he think the West Indian immigrants spoke? The *one* word they knew? Although I do doubt if anyone in Wolverhampton had been rude enough to call them 'piccaninnies' before.

And then the peroration: 'As I look ahead, I am filled with foreboding; like the Roman, I seem to see "the River Tiber foaming with much blood".' Powell's one regret, according to his biographer Simon Heffer, is that he did not leave that in Latin in the press release.

The following day, Ted Heath sacked him from the Shadow Cabinet. Powell, aged only 56, would never again play a central role in forming policy, though he hung around Westminster for the next two decades causing intermittent mayhem on many issues. One long-term effect of the speech was that it became to some extent a self-denying prophecy – not least in Wolverhampton, where community leaders got together afterwards to maintain calm and prove Powell wrong. Mass intercommunal violence in Britain did not happen. Race-motivated murders, occasional riots, bitter hatred between black communities and the police, these did happen. But Britain's rivers did not foam with blood.

The speech's other effect was that it closed down discussion of the very subject Powell was trying to raise. For the rest of the twentieth century, immigration policy was hardly discussed in public: the political elite was terrified of mentioning it. Even Margaret Thatcher, who was not unsympathetic to the Powell thesis, was very cautious in government, and the liberal nothing-to-see-here thesis held solid.

Yet had Powell concentrated on the facts and foregone the fizz, it might have been different. He predicted the million non-whites of 1968 would become 5–7 million by 2000, a figure that seemed absurd; the 2001 census suggested almost 4 million, so he was exaggerating but not that much. And he was right to believe he spoke for the country.

Dockers along the Thames went on strike in his support and

3,000 marched on parliament; Smithfield meat porters delivered a ninety-two-page petition. Most chillingly for other politicians, a Gallup poll showed 74 per cent of those questioned supported Powell, with only 15 per cent against. He claimed to have received 30,000 letters in the first three days' post, only thirty against him. This would be skewed because most who opposed him would not have written to him, but it is not implausible.

The fuss died down, dockers found other things to strike about, a flurry of racial incidents and neo-Nazi activities came and went. The British working class settled into a state of general pissed-offness. But this subject would never quite go away, and that was not Powell's doing. The secret people of England, G. K. Chesterton called them; they would have their say, but it would take them nearly half a century to clear their throats.

———◦———

Slowly, pioneer migrants did climb through ceilings that appeared from below not to be made of glass, but more like reinforced concrete. In May 1962, Eric Irons from Jamaica was appointed a magistrate in Nottingham. That very month, John Charles, a mixed-race East London boy, played football for England Under-18s* and built a decent if too brief career for West Ham. In 1965, Dwight Whylie, already an accomplished broadcaster in Jamaica, became an announcer on BBC radio.

For at least some of these early achievers, it was much harder than it looked. Norwell Roberts from Anguilla became a poster boy for integration when he became London's only black policeman in 1967.[†] He actually joined as Norwell Gumbs but changed his surname, tired of it being misspelled. His colour was harder to eradicate. Roberts was wheeled out regularly for public relations purposes during protests, especially left-wing ones. The public took to him, as a novelty; so did the police hierarchy. Among his

---

* Charles's achievement was hardly noticed at the time. He is not to be confused with John Charles, the Welsh international.

† Later researchers discovered there had been a black superintendent in the nineteenth century, so he was not the first.

colleagues it was different. Posted to Bow Street police station, he was bullied viciously, even to the point of being ignored if he requested backup. His black friends thought he was a traitor. He took it all, stayed the course and retired as a detective sergeant.

Jocelyn Barrow from Trinidad was a schoolteacher and founding member of the Campaign Against Racial Discrimination who persuaded Lord Sieff, the chairman of Marks & Spencer, to change their policy of employing black people only in the stockroom. One day she wandered into the Brixton branch, full of black customers but with all visible staff white. So she went home, rang to enquire about a job and was invited for interview, where she was quickly told all the posts had been filled. She pulled out her letter from Lord Sieff; the manager 'turned puce'.

The government set a limit of 3 per cent non-whites in most army units, which may well have been illegal under its own newly enacted law. MI5 rejected them, saying 'they could not be trusted'. And so on, and on. The worst of all worlds: Britain neither imposed workable controls nor wholeheartedly accepted the migrants who were already entrenched. After The Speech, Powell would focus on the need to encourage them to Go Home. This was, short of deportation, a fantasy.

The dominant fact of this era, wrote the immigration historian David Goodhart, was the newcomers putting down solid roots: 'Families arrived, children were born, or started going to school – there was no turning back. And however hard life in Britain sometimes was for the pioneers, there was now a good reason to stay and make whatever sacrifices were necessary: for a better life for the children.'

14

A WOMAN'S WORK

THERE WAS ANOTHER GROUP THAT MIGHT HAVE REGARDED itself as downtrodden. Towards the end of the 1960s, the Bishop of St Andrews told the boys of Trinity College, Glenalmond,* the Scottish public school: 'You are being educated to become the leaders of men.'

In the same decade, the headmistress of King Edward VI High School for Girls, Birmingham, an institution of roughly comparable academic distinction, told her pupils: 'You are being educated to become the mothers of leaders of men.'

Women certainly benefited from sexual liberation as well as men, and the contemporary arbiters of public morals – the agony aunts – were telling them to embrace it. In the midst of the Profumo affair, even the *Mirror*'s normally balanced Marjorie Proops was getting carried away: 'Take the myth, so often propounded by those who have very little of it, that sex isn't everything. Let us not kid ourselves. It is.' *Everything?* It is impossible to imagine those sentences appearing in a popular paper a few years before.

But for all the pretensions of the decade, the distinction between male and female roles hardly altered. In 1961, a successful British actress called Maureen Swanson – billed as 'the next Vivien Leigh'

---

* Now co-educational and known as Glenalmond College.

– married Viscount Ednam, later the 4th Earl of Dudley. Just like Valerie Hobson in the fifties she immediately gave up acting, aged 28. She became a mother of six and otherwise devoted herself to interior design.*

Throughout the sixties, women alone, or even together, were made unwelcome in bars and restaurants any time after early evening. It was assumed they were prostitutes. In offices, adulterous affairs were presumed to be the woman's fault. But their issues extended far beyond Marge Proops's 'everything'. No woman was too high to avoid being patronized at work. The Wilson government had more female ministers than its predecessors but they were still regarded as a novelty act. When Judith Hart, the No. 2 minister at the Commonwealth Office, had to go to Zambia to deal with one of the many subplots involving Rhodesia, the *Telegraph* front-page headline was WOMAN MINISTER FLIES TO CRISIS, as if in shock that such a fragile creature could get on a plane.

Notionally, the Civil Service was quite advanced in the matter of equality. But when Wilson made Shirley Williams parliamentary under-secretary at the Ministry of Labour, the senior civil servant, Sir James Dunnett, simply refused to communicate with her. It was nothing personal: Dunnett would not promote women civil servants above the middling rank of principal. The Foreign Office, meanwhile, maintained until 1973 a total bar on married women as diplomats. It was quite brutal. One victim, Sheila Skinner, recalled her wedding day: 'In the morning we got married. By the evening I was without a job. I think technically I resigned. In practice of course I was thrown out.' She did ask a senior official if, with her language skills, there was *anything* she could do. 'Wives do not work,' was the firm reply.

This policy may have been cruel and wasteful – and would soon become unacceptable. But it was not irrational. The Foreign Office wanted its senior representatives to go where needed, and wives

---

* In contrast to Hobson's glittering wedding to John Profumo, even the recently divorced Ednam's own father, the 3rd Earl, declined to attend, preferring to play bridge. She had better luck than Hobson thereafter. There was a curious connection: Swanson had had a fling with Stephen Ward before either became famous.

were a useful adjunct because entertaining was one aspect of the job. But wives with their own careers complicated the great chess game of getting the right chaps (or just occasionally unmarried chapesses) in the right places. Plus there was the question of maternity to consider.

Other organizations had less excuse. Renée Gerson's fraught academic progress had taken her to be dean of history and politics at the City of London Polytechnic. Even then, she felt a lack of respect. 'In meetings men didn't always take you up on what you said but pinched the idea later in the discussion. It was quite subtle but the men around had to take the credit for everything.'

The popular press had its own way of dealing with female achievement. In 1965, when the Nobel Prize-winning chemist Dorothy Hodgkin became the second woman, after Florence Nightingale, to be awarded the Order of Merit, it was reported that she 'likes to be mistaken for an ordinary housewife'. Dame Elizabeth Lane, the first woman High Court judge, loved 'cooking, tennis and needlework'. Two years later, both the Oxbridge unions elected their first female presidents. 'Blonde' Ann Mallalieu of Cambridge had to invent a new dress code to match male presidents' tails: 'True to the Emily Pankhurst tradition, her tangerine chiffon dress was full-length. It was also low cut, fetching and enchantingly feminine.' At Oxford, Geraldine Jones wanted to take her mind off the voting so 'she prepared a chicken casserole and trifle'.

This was not wholly drivel. It sent a message that success in hitherto masculine worlds did not necessarily involve any loss of femininity. Women, as well as men, wanted to know that. Sometimes even the government needed to say it. In 1969, June Spens became the first engineer employed by the construction firm George Wimpey, and she was feted at a lunch to inaugurate Women in Engineering Year with Shirley Williams – by now an education minister. Williams pointed out that in Britain only one engineer in five hundred was female, compared to one in twenty-eight in France and one in three in the Soviet Union. Communist engineers did not have a sexy image but Williams said there was no reason why a girl in engineering should be less feminine than one in home economics.

Reinforcing the point, Spens arrived in a mini-skirt, not her donkey jacket and boots.

And bright women who had taken the traditional route of domesticity often found themselves bored and lonely, especially if they moved to impersonal suburbs. A newer breed of women's magazines did not gloss over this. A former journalist, 'Louise', confessed to spending her days planning menus for her husband's return, whereupon he would fall asleep exhausted in front of the TV. She turned to cocktails; others needed antidepressants and tranquillizers – mother's little helper, in the Rolling Stones' enduring phrase.

And yet those on the cutting edge of social change can be seen in hindsight as having been as conservative as the crustiest Whitehall mandarin when it came to gender relations. 'A lot of girls just rolled joints,' recalled Nicola Lane, an American who gravitated to the underground scene in London. 'It was what you did while you sat quietly in the corner, nodding your head . . . You were not really encouraged to be a thinker. You were there really for fucks and domesticity. The old lady syndrome. "My lady": so Guinevere-y . . . It was quite a difficult time for a girl.'

The BBC, the embodiment of the nation, had begun the decade by appointing a woman newsreader, Nan Winton. She was not the first on British TV: Barbara Mandell had read lunchtime and Sunday-evening bulletins in ITV's daring early days, but it was thought too gimmicky to make her a star turn.

But in June 1960 Winton was elevated to the elite on the evening rota. 'We feel women should have equal opportunity with men,' said a BBC spokesman. Nine months later they no longer felt that and she was sacked. It appears to have been discriminatory rather than personal: 'If any woman could read the news, Nan could,' her colleague Richard Baker wrote later, tantalizingly. There seemed to be a sense that women could not convey objectivity. Winton herself could never shed any light on her dismissal, since no one ever gave her a reason.

On radio, things worked less brutally but no less oddly. For more than thirty years what was the BBC Home Service, and in 1967 became Radio 4, was adorned by a programme called *My Word!* It was a light-hearted panel game which was notionally a literary contest involving two men – Frank Muir and Denis Norden – and two women – for most of the run, Dilys Powell and Anne Scott-James, two combative top-flight journalists.

But, as time went on, the women would contribute less and less, because the whole second half of the show was taken over by comic monologues from Frank and Denis ending with a pun on a preordained quotation. In terms of entertainment, this was wholly justifiable because these were masterpieces of humorous writing.* But since the two women had no further role in proceedings, the format did seem rather unbalanced, even for those days. Had they all been a generation younger, the women could have spent the time rolling the joints for everyone to share later.

Some women, even those with careers, were content to devote at least some years to motherhood and housewifery. The teacher Ruth Patrick, now Mrs Borrill, began the 1960s in a three-bed semi on the outskirts of Penrith. She had a new baby and a new washing machine but no fridge, TV or telephone. Nor did she drive.

'I used to push the pram into Penrith and go to Wilsons the grocers, order the groceries and pay the bill for last week. Then I'd go to the greengrocers and the butchers. Mostly they would deliver by bike. If I went to the fishmongers I'd take it home and we'd have it that night.' It was a pattern of shopping – relaxed and sometimes sociable but limited – that would have been familiar to her mother's generation.

Supermarkets were coming. Northampton's first was a plate-glass cube, Fine Fare, on the site of the demolished New Theatre. But in the early sixties their impact was limited. Most of the early ones were in town centres with no dedicated parking. And driving in Penrith was a nightmare since, until the M6, the Anglo-Scottish traffic was funnelled through the centre. In any case, Mrs Borrill

---

*   My copy of *The My Word! Stories* sits, much-thumbed, by the loo.

was in the majority: only at the very end of the sixties did even half Britain's households have a car, and only a tiny fraction had two.

So, in Herefordshire, Michael and Maisie Griffith's shop was still expanding. 'The sixties and seventies were the best years,' said Michael. 'The existing village shop only did food and, until electricity came, oil for the lamps. So we expanded to do anything they didn't: china, glass, hardware, garden tools. We had six wallpaper books and they were out all the time. And we employed a full-time assistant, Miss Tovey.'

Most crucially, the abolition of resale price maintenance – that rare achievement of the short-lived Douglas-Home administration – kicked in only gradually from 1964. Only then could the chains fully compete on price and turn Britain from a nation of shopkeepers to one of checkout operators and shelf-stackers.

In the meantime, the competitive weapon of choice was stamps, Queen's head-less and mostly green. Richard Tompkins, who ran a print business, had spotted them in the US – where garages and supermarkets gave them away for every dollar spent, to be stuck into books and redeemed for 'gifts'. There was a lot of licking involved to get a benefit estimated at 2.5 per cent. Tesco linked up with Tompkins's company, Green Shield; Fine Fare, owned by the Anglo-Canadian magnate, Garfield Weston, offered the American-owned rival pink stamps; Weston also owned Allied Bakeries, and Sainsbury's – appalled by the whole thing – stopped selling his bread. Tompkins won the early battles and dominated the British market.

'The consumer is not a moron,' said the great advertising guru of the era, David Ogilvy, 'she's your wife'. The Green Shield craze did not say a great deal for the sagacity of the consumer, whoever it was. Advertising and marketing were becoming more pervasive and more professional but also more aspirational. The classic case was After Eight mints, launched by Rowntree in 1962. They competed on price – by being made deliberately expensive: about nine times the price of a normal bar of chocolate. The name, the box, the design, the individual wrapping, the thinness of the actual mint: it all oozed class.

And so did the adverts. 'There was a crude view of advertising that said your target group had to be represented in the ads,' said Jeremy Bullmore, later chairman of the agency involved, J. Walter Thompson. 'What JWT did was show people in dinner jackets and party frocks. We weren't selling to them.' After Eight sales went whoosh from the start, a huge percentage being sold as presents – especially to dinner guests.

Nervously, falteringly, abetted by the supermarkets offering a wider range of produce, the British became a little more adventurous in their eating habits. Package Mediterranean holidays, which were still possible even during the Wilson-era clampdown on foreign travel, were one factor.

In 1967, a new factory in St Albans began turning out a hundred forms of British pasta, though the *Times* reporter sent to cover the opening was somewhat bewildered by the 'long muscular tubes, short plump barrels, letters of the alphabet, coils, and stars, silver bells and cockle-shells, and things with scalloped edges'. The paper thought it safest to revert to the fifties nursery menu and call it a 'macaroni factory'.

Glamorous Italian eating is said to have come to London in 1961, when the Terrazza restaurant in Soho did away with the traditional décor of fake vines, hanging garlic and candles, went in for 'white walls, ceramic tiles, curved archways', and all the stars flocked in. The sophisticates took ownership of such places by casually referring to them not as 'trattorias' but 'trats'. To less-favoured parts of the country, two Italian brothers brought the Berni Inns, offering fake half-timbering on the walls and the classic sixties meal of prawn cocktail, steak and Black Forest gateau on the tables, and not much choice.

Chinese and Indian restaurants began to spread, and eventually the customers became adventurous enough to look above the English food options and attempt the unfamiliar. This may have been because the Chinese way with egg and chips was invariably disgusting while the sweet and sour might not be. The concessions made to British tastes by Indian restaurants (staffed mainly by Sylhetis, from what would become Bangladesh) were scorned by discerning migrants. But, if the spices were not up to scratch, the meat was better than at home. Britain's six Indian restaurants in 1960 became 1,200 in 1970, and it was no longer necessary to ring a colonel in Devon to get a curry.

The British version of a hamburger joint, the Wimpy bar, was soon everywhere, each franchise serving variations on the familiar theme – something that would never be allowed when the American chains muscled in like GIs on a wartime dance floor and thrust their local rivals aside.

Wine consumption increased steadily in the sixties, though the big leap was still to come. And with it a new form of class distinction gradually developed: those who drank wine felt superior to those who did not. Those who bought drier, dearer wine, and sniffed it knowingly, looked down smugly on those who drank cheap and nasty Blue Nun and Asti Spumante. Smuggest of all were those who thought they knew what they were doing and drank cheap but classy wines no one else had heard of.

Some eating habits were getting worse. Pre-sliced bread was invented in 1912 and was indeed a great thing. Modern factory-made sliced white bread derived from the Chorleywood process, a British invention, though not necessarily a proud one. It made bread more profitable to the manufacturers and cheaper to the consumer, but significantly less nutritious and with the taste of 'boiled flannel', as the food writer Felicity Lawrence put it. Special rules protected wholemeal bread until the 1980s, by which time traditional bakeries had largely vanished.

Later in the decade, big brewers gobbled up small brewers and moved to ensure that beer went in the same direction. The old pub hand-pumps were replaced by new easy-to-use taps dispensing mass-produced keg bitter rather than English ale. Nescafé came to Britain, providing quick but dull coffee, and the sales of teabags overtook loose tea.

But in the home, the new generation of housewives – middle-class ones, anyway – were far more willing to experiment than their parents had been. It was chic to have prawn cocktail, sole véronique, fondue, spag bol, paella (but not yet pizza), plus infinite ways of having the former special-occasion dish, chicken. There was chicken Maryland, chicken-in-a-basket, chicken chasseur and coq au vin (sometimes translated as 'sex in the back of a lorry'). And if that was not followed by Black Forest gateau, it might just be profiteroles.

For the really modish dinner party, garlic, sold in a single shop in London just after the war, became respectable instead of foreign and smelly. And olive oil became available other than through chemists selling it as a remedy for earache. Progress indeed.

15

DOWN WITH SKOOLS

I N 1957, JOHN CLARKE, THE SON OF A RAILWAY CLERK, SAT AN exam at Brackley Junior School in Northamptonshire. This was the 11-plus, the test that set the lifetime trajectory of millions of British children even before they reached puberty. If they passed, they were eligible for a grammar school – often ancient institutions, devoted to academic excellence. If not, they would go to one of the new secondary moderns and while away the time before being released into the real world four years later.

Clarke failed. In his case, though, he had taken the exam before his eleventh birthday and was, unusually, eligible for a second attempt. This time, his father – a keen reader whose own father had discouraged his schooling – was galvanized, and so was the boy, and he passed. In 1967 John Clarke was elected a fellow of All Souls, Oxford, the youngest of the century. He later became professor of history at the University of Buckingham.

We will never know how many John Clarkes lie unknown and forgotten in country churchyards or municipal cemeteries without ever having had the chance to prove their potential. It was this evil that the Wilson government set out to eradicate by trying to abolish selection in the school system; the aim was to make all schools comprehensive. The word of the moment was *meritocracy*, popularized by Michael Young in his 1958 satire

*The Rise of the Meritocracy.** And everyone thought meritocracy must be A Good Thing.

Unfortunately, Young was too subtle. Yes, he was against the 11-plus; he was against the whole idea of intelligence as the benchmark of merit. He wanted schools to encourage all skills – including manual ones – and saw a meritocracy as creating yet another self-perpetuating elite as pernicious as heredity and aristocracy. Instead, the notion of IQ, systematized by the American psychologist David Wechsler in 1939, became immensely popular.

Labour's policy was pushed through by the Education Secretary, Anthony Crosland. A public school boy himself, he knew what he didn't like about the state system. 'If it's the last thing I do,' he told his wife, 'I'm going to destroy every fucking grammar school.' He did not have the power to compel their abolition but, if local councils did not submit plans to go comprehensive, there would be no money for new schools; and in 1967 even true-blue Surrey sulkily surrendered.

But public attitudes were not straightforwardly left v. right. The movement towards comprehensives was already happening when the Tories were in power, often under the aegis of Tory councils. According to the long-time education correspondent Peter Wilby: 'The impetus for comprehensives really came from the middle class because they couldn't cope with their children failing the 11-plus. It was regarded as a disaster. They didn't want their children going to school with the oiks from the council estate. There were many minor private schools who catered mainly to 11-plus failures.'

The secondary moderns had only been invented in 1944, when Rab Butler set up what was supposed to be a tripartite system: grammars, sec mods and technical schools. Before that, scholarship children were spirited away to grammar school and the vast majority just stayed in the elementary schools, mouldering. The Act also raised the leaving age to 15, so that could hardly continue.

---

* Young was the author of *Family and Kinship in East London*, discussed earlier. He was also a major figure in the creation of the Labour manifesto for its 1945 election win, the Consumers Association and its magazine *Which?*, and the Open University.

Alas: hardly any techs were built (with terrible effects on Britain's industrial skills) and the sec mods were underfunded and useless. The selection system was not just brutal but unjust – pass rates depended not on a national standard but on how many grammar places were available locally, which could vary hugely. There was also evidence that working-class children who did pass – and were separated from their friends – tended not to thrive in the grammars.

Yet some of them certainly did, like Professor John Clarke. 'I'm still fundamentally torn about the whole selection process,' he told me. 'I can see how bad it was. The idea of levelling up was very powerful in the sixties and seventies. But my impression is that isn't what happened. The grammars joined the secondary modern schools rather than the other way round. And the ethos of the grammar school was lost.'

———•———

Magdalen College School, Brackley, Clarke's grammar, was very strong on ethos: a cadet force, an ancient chapel, house colours, prefects, the whole public school bit except the fees. That was quite normal. And in many ways such places were more successful in the sixties than they had ever been.

The fee-paying schools were just starting their journey of becoming less like eccentric quasi-penal institutions and more like five-star hotels. They even had to work harder at education, because Oxbridge was coming under pressure not to admit their products just because they talked posh, were good at cricket or the dons remembered their dear old dad.

The eight brand-new universities of the sixties – York, Lancaster, Sussex, Essex, Kent, East Anglia, Warwick and Stirling – offered more chances to state school pupils, and indeed started to threaten the Oxbridge monopoly by offering innovative courses, more places for women and a certain modish cachet. Sussex became especially hot in the mid-sixties when the trendy twin daughters of the Cabinet minister Douglas Jay got the gossip columns enchanted the moment they arrived for freshers' week. This was way cooler than dreaming spires.

But the new universities' ambience – brutalist architecture on greenfield sites – did not weather well. As one student put it, only cemeteries were sited further out of town than a new university. Meantime, the ancient institutions woke up, scratched themselves, obsessed less with Latin, accepted the existence of sociology and the like, got ever richer, and retained – even enhanced – their right to have the pick of the students.

The non-Oxbridge universities, both new and older, had something in common with the comprehensives. They were big and impersonal, developed few traditions, inspired little loyalty. Even bog-standard American high schools and colleges have sports teams that suck in the alumni for life. The Boat Race and the varsity rugby match still have a minor-key role for Oxford and Cambridge. The failure to build anything similar elsewhere would prove a serious disadvantage to British higher education after the warm financial breezes that blew through the sector in the mid-twentieth century turned chillier. Because some graduates get rich, and some of those feel philanthropic. They give money to a cause to which they feel connected. But the new seats of learning were born at a time when continuity, conservative values and the significance of symbolism were out of style.

———•———

If getting rich was in the forefront of the thoughts of a late-sixties undergraduate, it was unfashionable to admit it. Scientists were expected to turn up early in laboratories to fan the flickering embers of Harold Wilson's once white-hot technological revolution; less focused students were also interested in a revolution, far more nebulous even than Wilson's. Indeed, it was hard to comprehend anything about it, except that it was considered essential.

After the summer of love came 1968, the summer of hate, when the Chicago convention riots followed hard on the murders of Martin Luther King and Bobby Kennedy. American male students were at risk of being despatched to fight an unpopular and futile war in Vietnam. Elsewhere, the Czechs and Slovaks craved freedom; French grievances were less obvious but the protests were characteristically theatrical. The causes of the widespread unrest in Britain were more obscure still.

Its first manifestation did have a clear *casus belli*. In late 1966, the London School of Economics named its next director: Walter Adams, a historian who had spent the previous twelve years running the university in Rhodesia. His compromises with the rebel Rhodesian regime appeared less than heroic, certainly from afar. It was a risky choice, especially for the LSE, which of its nature had a highly politicized student body. And when the students did raise objections to Adams, the governing body's response was pedantic and ill-judged, which moved the argument on to other subjects.

In the new year, a planned protest meeting was banned by the outgoing director, Sir Sydney Caine. Six hundred students decided to go ahead anyway, and in the ensuing ruckus British student protest immediately delivered a fatality: an elderly hall porter had a heart attack. But even at LSE, where no one slogged away in the labs, student apathy exceeded student anger. 'Even at the height of it, probably two-thirds of the students were quite uninvolved,' said Alex Finer, who was a student union official. 'It was a minority that felt like a majority. Partly because it was London and lots of people from other colleges turned up.'

Over the next few years, the epidemic apparently reached all but one of Britain's forty-five universities in some form, mild or chronic.* The issues at LSE moved away from Adams, mutated and spread elsewhere: attacks on the bourgeois and/or capitalist nature of the education on offer, whatever that meant – and the lack of student participation in decision-making. This did get addressed, rightly.

The infant University of Essex became notorious after demonstrators blocked and damaged a car carrying Enoch Powell (this was a month before The Speech) and then barricaded the vice-chancellor, Dr Albert Sloman, in his office. A few weeks later, Sloman had to wait outside a meeting of a 'free university' before

---

* The exception was presumably the newest of all, the Open University, which specialized in distance learning, making sit-ins, etc. impractical.

being permitted to explain himself in the gaps when they were not shouting him down.

One irony was that Sloman was famously liberal, but this was no time for liberals. Another irony came in 1969 when the moderate president of the National Union of Students, Trevor Fisk, was unseated by a fiery radical called Jack Straw. Later Straw would become a notably authoritarian Labour Home Secretary – though not as authoritarian as Charles Clarke, who followed him in both jobs.

And this 'free university'? What did that mean? University education in Britain *was* free: no tuition fees for UK-based students from 1962, and means-tested maintenance grants. The state demanded nothing in return, not even National Service. The last conscript was formally discharged in May 1963, a personable lieutenant in the Pay Corps called Richard Vaughan.* And that was the year when the nuclear threat receded – and, for the British, so the whole notion of an existential war started to feel obsolete. 1968, with all its global strife, was the first year since 1945 – and possibly the seventeenth century – when no one in Britain's armed forces was killed in combat.

No one really cared what you did as long as you did not do it in front of visiting dignitaries' cars. The young had unprecedented sexual licence and had seized control of the culture. And still we complained. What an ungracious bunch of shits we must have been.

————◦————

The mood percolated down to the public schools, where things had moved on since 1832 – when the headmaster of Eton flogged eighty boys in a session – but not that much. At Eton the enigmatic reformist head Anthony Chenevix-Trench did away with the birch and banned boy-on-boy whackings but still caned pupils on the bare buttocks himself; the system of fagging, whereby younger boys were enslaved by older boys, persisted. John Dancy, the more

---

* At least, Vaughan was the one chosen for publicity purposes. It is possible a few others were still in army hospitals or glasshouses.

skilfully progressive head of Marlborough, made it the first of the traditional leading schools to go co-educational (a great success) and brought in selected local children as sixth-form boarders (not quite so successful).

At another all-male institution, Aldenham School in Hertfordshire, the headmaster, Paul Griffin, also saw an opportunity. He was approached by the film director Lindsay Anderson, who was working on a project about a boys' public school. Could he film some of it there? Suspiciously, Griffin asked to see the script; he was given *some* of it. 'Everyone thought Anderson was the cat's pyjamas,' he recalled later. 'I was a useful idiot, I suppose.'

Filming took place at the school during the summer holidays of 1968,* while the Chicago cops were whacking protesters and Soviet tanks moved into Prague. Some of the day boys took part as extras in scenes shot in the gym, study hall and corridors of Aldenham. They had no idea what the film was about until they were invited to a press showing in London. It was *If . . .*, which depicted the murderous fantasies harboured by every red-blooded and rebellious sixties boy at a rule-bound and hidebound British boarding school. The effect on every boarding school boy of the era was electric; at Aldenham the shock was multiplied a hundred times. 'It was our school, our story, our fantasy,' said Simon Worrall, who was there at the time. 'And life did begin to imitate art.'

'All through the winter of 1968, the mood of rebellion grew,' he wrote in *The Times* forty years after the filming. 'A group of sixth-formers refused to be prefects and preached subversion. A mass walkout was staged at a debating society event. Drugs and counter-culture publications such as *International Times* flowed in.' There was also a vague attempt to break into the school armoury, with the thought of recreating *If . . .*'s cathartic climax. And the head had a breakdown.

Eventually, the school calmed down a little; so did the universities; and so did the world. As the sixties headed towards their close, that was the last thing anyone expected.

---

* The outdoor scenes were shot at Cheltenham College, Anderson's *alma mater*.

16

THE PAST BLASTERS

ONE PHRASE, COMPLETELY FORGOTTEN NOW, ECHOED constantly through the sixties. Mrs Jane Smyth of Belfast said it when she was forced to move to make way for a ring road: 'I don't mind moving,' she said. 'You cannot stand in the way of progress.' The local councillor for Sampford Peverell said it when confronted with the notion of an overspill town for 40,000 Londoners on his doorstep in Devon: 'You can't stand in the way of progress by saying "anywhere but here".'

Anthony Giles of Reading University was engaged on working out fair compensation for farmers being displaced by the new town of Milton Keynes (which, unlike the Devon plan, did happen). Then he discovered that his house in suburban Reading was in the way of a new link road, the prettily-named A329(M). 'I didn't realize it would suddenly happen to me,' he said. But he still added the mantra: 'One does not want to stand in the way of progress.'

Even those who were doing just that would utter the words, thus showing they were not heretics and still worshipped at the shrine of modernity. Protesters in rural Leicestershire successfully campaigned to put the M1 out of sight in a cutting through the Charnwood Forest. Said farmer John Pettitt: 'Nobody was at all keen to have the motorway through the woodland at all, but we realised that you can't stand in the way of progress.'

One point that Anthony Giles, from his dual perspective, mentioned was the importance of compensation, which he defined as ensuring that no one who lost their homes and businesses lost money. This was wholly the wrong approach, which made no allowance for the uncertainties and trauma of the process. The Whitehall way was grudging, minimalistic and entirely stupid. Had they stuffed the victims' mouths with gold, which is how Aneurin Bevan sold the NHS to the consultants, people would have clamoured to have a motorway, runway or high-speed rail line through their kitchens. It would have saved billions over the years in public inquiries.

———·———

In the history of modern Britain's love affair with old buildings, the Doric arch at Euston station occupies the same role as John Brown's Body played in the abolition of American slavery: the martyrdom that created a rallying cry and made future victories possible.

The arch had stood symbolically at the entrance to Euston since the early days of railways – loved by many, hated by some. In 1960 it was announced that, to allow for the long-overdue electrification of the main line to the north-west, the old station – with its awesome Great Hall – and the arch would have to be demolished. There were many protests, and a deputation of traditionalist architects and conservationists, including the poet John Betjeman, went to see Harold Macmillan. 'He sat without moving with his eyes apparently closed,' said J. M. Richards, who led the group. 'He asked no questions; in fact he said nothing except that he would consider the matter.' There was no sign that he ever did.

It seems there was indeed a binary choice between electrification and the removal of the arch, but also that the government exaggerated the cost and difficulties of re-erecting the arch elsewhere. And the resulting bitterness helped ensure that the inchoate plans for the far more significant demolition of the nearby Gothic Revival gem of St Pancras were stillborn. There was no need in engineering terms, and the proponents of it were flippant.

One headline read RED ELEPHANT ON THE EUSTON ROAD, and Sir Edward Playfair, a civil servant turned businessman, railed about maintaining 'a national junkyard' and hamstringing 'today's architects in favour of the dead'. But as the sixties passed their zenith, living architects were beginning to be held in some contempt.

Londonderry House, a name synonymous with pre-war aristo-cratic decadence, was razed and that end of Park Lane became dominated by the Hilton Hotel and the Playboy Club, a name synonymous with post-war plutocratic decadence. The counter-intuitively ornate Coal Exchange by the Thames was sacrificed in 1962 to road widening. But the new buildings made no concessions to beauty or sometimes even functionality. And there was nothing quite as unpleasant to use or to look at as the new Euston.

———◦———

After the Great Fire of 1666, the heart of London was rebuilt by Christopher Wren; after the war it was rebuilt by a handful of property developers and, to a large extent, a single architect, less affectionately remembered than Wren. The developers picked up promising sites for office space. They were backed by insurance companies and pension funds who sensed a safe haven for their cash reserves and were rewarded, in the Macmillan years, by the first of the many post-war London property booms.

The architect of choice was Richard Seifert, whose greatest skill was understanding the planning regulations far more profoundly than the people who enforced or even drafted them. 'There was a certain unashamed vulgarity about many of these buildings,' wrote the architectural critic Gavin Stamp. The modernism was accent-uated by the space-age names Seifert chose – Orbit House, Telstar House, Planet House – hinting at how high he would have liked to build if he could have slipped the plans past the dozy councillors. He worked closely with Harry Hyams, the most elusive and reclusive of the leading developers, whose company held its AGM at 4.15 p.m. on New Year's Eve to discourage attendance. The pairing's most infamous construction was Centre Point, which still defaces the east end of Oxford Street and notoriously remained empty for more than a decade. It made little difference to Hyams: due to rising values and quirks in the tax and accountancy rules, he was still making money from it.

The rising star of the property business had been Jack Cotton, an expansive Brummie who lived in the Dorchester Hotel and whose filing system was inside his head. He then flew too high by acquiring a chunk of Piccadilly Circus and proposing a scheme so obnoxious that the public, even at the height of can't-stand-in-the-wayism, rebelled and forced the complaisant planners into retreat.* In 1961 Cotton linked up with his more focused rival Charles Clore, was soon shafted and died in the Bahamas.

Clore, last heard of in this account in bed with Christine Keeler, kept on rolling through the seventies. 'Sexually gluttonous . . . crude and impatient . . . his relationships were almost all mutually vigilant and calculating . . . Though luxury and power gratified him, money was his only passion.' Clore gave enough of it away to earn a knighthood but, as that extract shows, not enough to earn a kindly memorial in the *Oxford Dictionary of National Biography*.

Some believed in making money by remaking Britain's cities, but some were true believers. One was Sir Herbert Manzoni, city engineer and surveyor of Birmingham, who bulldozed his ideas through the city council and then through the city itself. He disdained sentiment, thought Birmingham had almost no buildings worth keeping, and did not waste time consulting anyone. At the time he was regarded with awe in planning circles, but his reputation has not weathered well, and nor have his high-rises and inner ring road. Birmingham became the object lesson in how not to do development, and has still not wholly recovered.

Britain's housing problems, however, were real and intractable. At the start of the sixties one in seven homes remained reliant on an outside toilet. And Birmingham still had people living in

---

* All through the sixties and seventies the authorities kept trying to remake the Circus, but people seemed to like it as it was: jams, junkies and junk souvenir shops.

real back-to-backs, i.e. with only one outside wall. The horrors of 'Rachmanism'* appear to have been over-personalized and somewhat exaggerated. One of the many committees to which governments of the era outsourced problems (and then often ignored), Milner Holland on housing, reported in 1965 that only 1 per cent of London tenants had faced intimidation and 80 to 90 per cent were happy with their landlords.

But governments of different colours found it hard to get a balance between exploitation on the one hand and unattractive returns to landlords on the other – and private rentals dwindled against the competition from subsidized council housing and, for those who could afford the outlay, what became the tax-free bonanza of ownership. So the council waiting lists got longer.

Then, in November 1966, the BBC showed its most talked-about single drama of all time: *Cathy Come Home*, a gruesome tale about how a concatenation of minor difficulties with housing leads a young family to disaster. It might have evoked the customary short-lived response from viewers ('How terrible! Somebody must do something!') but for a coincidence more improbable than those depicted onscreen.

A charity precisely designed to help such families was launched – with no prior knowledge of *Cathy* – a few days later. Shelter was run by a sparky young New Zealander, Des Wilson, who shook up the whole genteel business of giving ('dominated by ex-colonels and Lady Bountifuls', as he put it) with shock adverts and quasi-political campaigns.

And it was a huge success. Shelter was not focused on rough sleepers, but getting families living in slums into less crowded, more sanitary conditions. Such homes were becoming available, and it took a while for Des Wilson – like almost everyone else – to see the drawbacks. Because the solution was deemed to be on the umpteenth floor.

---

* Named after Peter Rachman, another of Christine Keeler's sugar daddies. Defined in the *Oxford English Dictionary* as 'the exploitation and intimidation of tenants by unscrupulous landlords'.

Demand was increasing, the subsidies for tower blocks were still in place, and expert opinion was still opposed to distinguishing between the hopeless slums and the many thousands of homes that could and should have been modernized. Manzonis lurked everywhere. Wilfred Burns, who made his name redeveloping Coventry and Newcastle and later became chief planning officer at the Ministry of Housing (and Sir Wilfred into the bargain), admitted that slums broke up communities but insisted: 'This is a good thing when we are dealing with people who have no initiative or civic pride. The task is surely to break up such groupings, even though the people seem to be satisfied with their miserable environment and seem to enjoy an extrovert social life within their own locality.' Then they could sit in their new toileted homes and watch the old-fashioned extroversion of such places on *Coronation Street*.

The ill-conceived concept of high-rises and their shoddy construction quickly earned them a terrible reputation, for families above all. The children confined within them became the first generation to lose the ancient right to unsupervised play. The alternative approach of 'streets in the sky' – which reached its apogee on the massive Park Hill development in Sheffield, completed in 1961 – proved more popular. At first.

The failure of the towers was sealed on a May morning in 1968, when Ivy Hodge went into her eighteenth-floor kitchen and struck a match to light her gas ring to make a cuppa. When she regained consciousness, having suffered only minor burns, the four floors above the kitchen in the East London block known as Ronan Point had collapsed and four people were dead.

The death toll itself was not, in news terms, significant: just a bad car crash. Seven members of a Ukrainian-Greek family in Bedford were killed by gas in 1969 and rated only a few sad paragraphs. But Ronan Point spoke to the whole country's deepest fears about these alien monsters, and most especially the fears of those forced to live in them. The block had been built using a new 'large panel system' design which did away with the need for scaffolding or even much skilled labour. It simply involved putting up one concrete wall and floor on top of the one below, which was

probably fine if everything had been done correctly, with no missing
bolts or that'll-do bodges. But it hadn't.

The BBC reported fifty years later that there were 1,585 blocks
still standing built to the same design. By this time, even if the bolts
are still there, they may well have rusted, causing 'concrete cancer';
gas cookers are banned in these blocks as a precaution. Ronan Point
is not one of them: it was 'scientifically dismantled' – though not
until 1986, when it was found that what were supposed to be load-
bearing wall joints were packed with wadding, cigarette ends, tin
cans and newspapers.

Jeremy Sandford (Eton and Oxford), who wrote *Cathy*, was visiting
London's council-run hostels for the homeless for a series of
Observer articles five years before the programme was broadcast.
These were sometimes old workhouses, but without the work. At
Newington Lodge in Southwark, he found up to three families in a
room and two toilets for sixty-five people; dysentery was endemic.
Husbands were banned and had to pay for separate lodgings.
Starvation rations were available. At Norwood House near Gipsy
Hill, mothers and children lived in a huge hall behind seven-foot-
high partitions and curtains.

No one was meant to stay long in such places; indeed, they were
liable to get kicked out after a few weeks as new supplicants arrived.
But even in the 1960s houses in the south-east were getting beyond
the reach of unskilled workers; the council lists were hopeless,
and the remaining private landlords did not want the nuisance of
children. Eventually there was a rebellion. It came out of Kent, as
rebellions did until Tudor times: a decorator and father of four
called Stan Daniels – turned out of a rented home when it was
sold – barricaded himself into his family's quarters at Kent County
Council's homeless hostel protesting about his own exclusion,
and his wife and children's impending eviction after the maximum
three months. Other families joined in; two men were jailed. It was
a long battle – but after *Cathy*, this kind of Victorianism became
politically unviable.

These were not generally overseas migrants: many of them were arriving from rural England, hoping the streets of London would be paved with gold. The collapse of the countryside had already been going on, wars excepted, for almost a century, but now it took on a new form: many farmers were doing fine, but mechanization did for almost all the remaining farm labourers.

The 300,000 working farm horses in 1950 were nearly all gone by 1960. Now the men followed. In 1969, *Akenfield*, Ronald Blythe's classic study of Suffolk rural life, was published. Blythe noted that only a tenth of boys leaving country schools in 1967 wanted to do agricultural work. Twenty thousand men had left the land in the five years before that, and the process was far from finished. He compared the exodus to the 1870s, when 200,000 rural labourers emigrated.

The first time it was failure – North American cereals, grown on vast prairies in more trustworthy summers, could outcompete Britain once their railroad system was in place. This time it was what Blythe called 'a second agricultural revolution', based on machinery, fertilizer and weedkiller. By 1969, more than half the farmers in England and Wales had no non-family help at all, not even part-time. 'When I wrote *Akenfield*,' he said many years later, 'I had no idea that anything particular was happening, but it was the last days of the old traditional rural life in Britain. And it vanished.'

Rustic railways were nearly all victims of Dr Beeching, and the bus services began to dwindle too. Schools, churches, pubs, shops and post offices began to disappear; blacksmiths and wheelwrights moved into the motor trade or gave up. Country cottages were becoming ever more derelict and unwanted, so much so that a national survey was commissioned to see what could be done about it.

Most of the rural refugees did not go as far as London, save the small percentage wafted there by higher education. Those who did might have found one pleasant surprise. In early December 1962, the smog descended again and the death toll was estimated at more than a hundred. But it was never repeated on that scale: clean air legislation, the decline of industry in the capital, the Barry Bucknell-inspired boarding-up of fireplaces, and, eventually, central heating had their effect.

There was still traffic, more and more of it and some of it ever more intrusive. High above Acklam Road, on the edge of Notting Hill, a new dual carriageway, the Westway, was taking shape. Already, daylight ceased to penetrate the ground floors and most of the first floors, but the twenty-four-hour noise had not started yet. This was scheduled as the first in a series of new roads designed to modernize London. Still, at least the houses in Acklam Road might become more affordable. And you can't stand in the way of . . .

17

NOW WE ARE FORTY

I N THIS HURTLING DECADE, WHEN EVERYTHING THE MONARCHY stood for – protocol, convention, continuity, respect, restraint – was under siege, it was perhaps as well that the royal family maintained a relatively low profile.

In 1968, Prince Philip reflected on this in an astute and mellow TV interview: 'In 1953 we were a great deal younger. Now we are getting into middle age. I dare say when we are a bit more ancient there might be a bit more reverence again. But now we are in the least interesting period of a glamorous existence. People have got accustomed to us.'

He was not always that astute. While visiting Paraguay in 1962 he supposedly told its dictator, Alfredo Stroessner, that it was a pleasure to be 'in a country that isn't ruled by its people'. He was, luckily, a long way from the nearest British pressman. But it was the gaffes that made him a character, a fallible human to set off his wife, who remained dutiful and only a little less beautiful. She had no difficulty negotiating the change to a Labour government, which had taxed her father and grandfather. Perhaps it helped that she had too little adult life before her accession to align natural royal conservatism with political Conservatism. And that Harold Wilson was her first prime minister not old enough to be an ancestor.

She also maintained her courage. In the midst of the Profumo summer she had to endure a state visit from King Paul of Greece,

Prince Philip's first cousin, and his notorious German-born wife, Frederica, whose compulsive right-wing meddling did more than anything to turn Greece into a republic. There were furious demonstrations ('Fascist swine'; 'Nazis out') in London, and as collateral damage Elizabeth herself was booed.

She was booed again in October 1964, and this time it was aimed at her. She was visiting Quebec, where French-speaking separatism was in full cry with a genuine hint of menace. Separatist leader Dr Marcel Chaput had warned in advance, 'I fear that her safety simply cannot be guaranteed while she is in Quebec.' But he added reassuringly: 'If it should come to an assassination then it would be simply the assassination of a symbol, not of a woman.' In fact, the expected flashpoint, her visit to Quebec City, passed off relatively calmly – though the police beat the hell out of the demonstrators after her motorcade passed by. The Queen then had to rush back to London for the election and the apotheosis of Harold Wilson. It must have felt very relaxing.

The cast of adult royal characters was thin in the 1960s, hence a lot of work and attention fell to cousins like Princess Alexandra, whose wedding in 1963 was watched by almost half the nation, many of whom cannot have known precisely who she was. Her second child, Marina Ogilvy, was born on Sunday, 31 July 1966, the day after England won the World Cup final. On the Monday, the front-page splash in Britain's two biggest-selling dailies, the *Express* and the *Mirror*, was the baby and not the football, which beggars belief.*

But the sixties left some mark on royalty. In 1967, another first cousin, the Earl of Harewood, was sued for divorce in a manner that ten years earlier would have been unspeakably scandalous: he was living with his mistress with whom he already had a child. The fuss was brief, though he was sentenced to ten years off the Palace invitation list.† Princess Margaret, like the Queen, was making

---

* By January 2022, Marina Ogilvy was sixty-second in the line of succession to the throne, after such famous figures as Tāne Lewis, Rufus Gilman and both Columbus and Cassius Taylor.
† His first wife later married Jeremy Thorpe. She was not a lucky woman.

babies and presumed happily married, though not by her closest friends. American tabloids reported a rift between her and Lord Snowdon as early as February 1967, less than halfway through their actual marriage. The denial was reported at home, and the matter was laid to rest. Against the tenor of the times, British papers were getting a little less disrespectful and the gossip columns were relatively restrained. It was a short-lived phase.

The quietude, however, produced a chink of light. It coincided with the retirement in 1968 of Commander Richard Colville, the ineffably useless head of the Palace press office who in a twenty-one-year career alienated everyone connected with royal reporting except the person who mattered most. It suited the Queen for his operation to be run like MI5 without the transparency.

His successor was very different. Bill Heseltine was a high-flying Australian civil servant who understood the niceties but brought in a breath of eucalyptus-scented fresh air at a time when the Queen was willing to try opening the windows. Thus began the process that led to the documentary *Royal Family*, first broadcast on the BBC in June 1969 – just before the investiture of Charles as Prince of Wales. As it spread across the planet it probably became the most widely watched TV programme up to then.

It was perhaps the most charming ninety minutes of propaganda ever shown, put together with great skill by the filmmaker Richard Cawston – and everyone was delighted, including the Queen, who could have censored any of it but did nothing. The most remembered scene was a barbecue by a Highland loch; the most touching, to my eyes, was a snowball fight between Andrew and Edward at Sandringham, acting like any pair of under-ten brothers in the kingdom.

In myth, now perpetuated by the Netflix series *The Crown*, *Royal Family* was a disaster, suppressed almost at once. In fact it was a rip-roaring success, shown eleven times in Britain over the next five years and watched in total by an estimated 400 million worldwide. The reviews were 'ecstatic', said the royal biographer Ben Pimlott. And the Queen seemed contented: Heseltine advanced up the hierarchy and eventually became her private secretary.

It was the consequences that the Queen disliked. 'The Palace expected the press to feel grateful,' said Pimlott. 'This was naive. Appetites were whetted, that was all.' Later the film was indeed suppressed, to be discovered in little-known archives and occasionally passed around like samizdat. Experts shook their heads and quoted the Victorian constitutionalist Walter Bagehot about the perils of letting daylight in on magic. In the context of the time it was worth doing, though perhaps once a reign is enough.

One family member seemed notably ill at ease on screen: the heir. He was 20 now and facing the kingly rite of passage by being invested as Prince of Wales. After almost half a century's quiescence, the non-English constituents of the kingdom were stirring and the Welsh had made the first move. In 1965 the Tryweryn valley in North Wales was flooded to pipe water into Liverpool; the Welsh had no say at all. Fired up by this, a couple of paramilitary groups strutted around and went in for minor bombings. Meanwhile, at the respectable end of the spectrum, Plaid Cymru, the Welsh nationalists, won their first-ever by-election and the Welsh language began to recover from attempted eradication.

It was not the easiest time to impose a gauche young Englishman as an absentee prince. And when he went on a preparatory tour in 1968, Charles was met by go home banners, smoke bombs and eggs. But he went over and gamely talked to the protesters. The situation remained tense. The night before the ceremony in Caernarvon, two activists were killed by their own bomb near the route of the royal train. The occasion itself went well.

In one way, the royal family had something in common with everyone else in 1969: they wanted a pay rise. This was brought to public attention, in one of his less well-judged interventions, by Prince Philip in an interview on American TV. He talked of moving into smaller premises, having to sell a small yacht and maybe giving up polo. He had a point, since the Queen's allowance had remained static since 1952, and the government dealt with it. But the comments did fuel the view that the visibility project had been a tactic leading up to this.

That same month, November, perhaps the very first story

emerged of a Prince Charles romance: he was linked with Lady Leonora Grosvenor, daughter of the mind-bogglingly rich Duke of Westminster. She called the rumours 'silly'. Obviously, why on earth should she dally with a gold-digging pauper?

18

THE FAINT ECHOES
OF EMPIRE

WALES WAS NOT THE ONLY PLACE STIRRING. IN 1967 THE Scottish nationalists followed their Welsh counterparts with a shock win in a by-election at Hamilton, though it was just a fling, a sign of disillusion with the Wilson government, rather than any coherent commitment to independence. It was, thus far, just a wavelet. There was, however, a fourth component of the United Kingdom, a place everyone else had spent years trying to forget – and doing that rather well.

Northern Ireland was a disgrace – JOHN BULL'S POLITICAL SLUM, as a rare headline put it: an effective dictatorship by the Protestant majority using gerrymandering and blatant discrimination to deny the Catholic minority jobs, houses and rights. Alabama sans sunshine. Westminster politicians knew about this on some level but were deterred by an absurd convention of non-interference agreed after Ireland was partitioned in 1921 – even though the province was wholly dependent on subsidy from London. Conservative governments enjoyed reliable support from their cohort of Ulster Unionist MPs, and Labour had no wish to poke a hornets' nest. The Irish Republican Army slumbered, fantasizing about a united Ireland the way the priests did about heaven. Let it be.

It was the hint of reform that stirred the hornets. Captain Terence O'Neill, who had succeeded the sempiternal Lord Brookeborough as prime minister, was open to reform and had meetings with the leaders of the Irish Republic. This awakened dark and implacable forces among the Protestants, headed by a vile-tongued preacher called Ian Paisley, and countervailing Catholic spirits, mainly – it being the sixties – among the youth.

The first major flashpoint came in October 1968 when a banned civil rights demonstration in Londonderry* took place anyway and was attacked by the Royal Ulster Constabulary, the armed enforcers of Protestant power, who administered their own rough justice. The following August there was rioting across the province. This time there was bloodshed – eight dead – and the Dublin government set up field hospitals on their side of the border.

By now the agents of traditional Ulster authority, official and unofficial, appeared to be merging together to maintain the status quo by whatever means necessary. And so, in August 1969, the British government sent in the Army, who were welcomed in Catholic areas with smiles and cups of tea. Jim Callaghan, as Home Secretary, was in charge and acting decisively.

O'Neill had already been forced from office by his own back-benchers. But on the other side, the moderates and republicans put aside their own differences to win a by-election and send a charismatic 21-year-old Catholic, Bernadette Devlin, to Westminster, where she instantly entranced the House with a devastating maiden speech. Never before had British opinion been so committed to enacting sensible democratic reforms and sorting things out.

But the decade of high hopes was ending. And the British could make a mess of even the simplest problems among its imperial remnants.

———◆———

A few months earlier, the Wilson government had sent troops to the tiny Caribbean island of Anguilla, the size of the Isle of Sheppey with the population of a mid-Wales market town but none of its pulsating energy. There was not even a telephone. A junior foreign minister, William Whitlock, had been sent out by the Wilson

---

* Known as Derry by its Catholic majority, who were always in the minority on the city council.

government to investigate reports of an armed rebellion and Rhodesian-style unilateral declaration of independence. During his visit he heard a few gunshots some distance away and hurried home, to be replaced by a consignment of paratroops, Metropolitan policemen and Fleet Street's finest on one of their jauntiest adventures. In Bernard Levin's words, 'they were greeted by a withering fire of curious stares'. The Army had called it Operation Sheepskin. Levin christened it the War of Whitlock's Nerves.

Anguilla's grievance was that Whitehall had lumped the island together with nearby Saint Kitts and Nevis to prepare for independence, working on the usual Whitehall principle of drawing lines on a map. The Anguillans resented being bossed around by their more numerous neighbours, a matter that was easily resolved by extracting it from the proposed federation. The main damage was to Whitlock's ministerial career; there was also a certain amount of sniggering at the expense of the prime minister who, it was said, had finally picked on someone his own size.

———•———

In thousands of classrooms round Britain and perhaps beyond, old-fashioned maps of the world hung close to the old-fashioned blackboard. Much of the world was traditionally coloured red to denote the British Empire – or more usually pink, making it easier to read the names of the countries. If the map had been there from the start to finish of the 1960s, many of the names would already be out of date – Northern Rhodesia, Nyasaland, Bechuanaland and British Guiana had become independent Zambia, Malawi, Botswana and Guyana. At the start of the decade there were still swathes of the map under British control. By 1970 there were only blotches, and there was very little left much larger than Anguilla that was now accurately in the pink.

However, the Empire had managed to morph into the Commonwealth, something that is easy to deride and overlook. Its existence says one thing: that the former colonies' sense of their history is complex and nuanced, and a lingering affection is somewhere in the mixture.

Meanwhile, Britain still had unfinished business. There was Rhodesia, of course. But Britain was still fighting post-imperial wars that were fairly obscure at the time and completely baffling now. Between 1962 and 1966 British forces were involved in what was discreetly known as 'the confrontation' with Indonesia in the jungles (or, as we would now say, rainforests) of Borneo. It was a confrontation that saw 126 British soldiers killed in combat in the cause of defeating Indonesia's aim of destabilizing the new federation of Malaysia, a potential regional rival.

It could have been Britain's Vietnam. But it resulted in a clear-cut victory, one that was hardly noticed at home. The anonymity was partly because of the abolition of conscription, which severed most of the public from the reality of distant wars; partly because the whole business of empire was being consigned to a mental oubliette; partly because the cause itself was complex; and partly because what goes on in the jungle tends to stay in the jungle.

Humiliation was readily available elsewhere. After nearly 130 years of ruling Aden, the strategic but hot-as-hell port on the heel of the Arabian Peninsula, Britain was trying to withdraw, but they were beset by two rebel groups, who were also fighting each other, with the Egyptians stirring the pot.

The business is best remembered, if at all, for the theatrical re-capture of the Crater district of Aden in 1967, led by Colin Mitchell ('Mad Mitch') – a small, charismatic, completely disobedient lieutenant-colonel from the Argyll and Sutherland Highlanders whose men marched in accompanied by a pipe band playing 'Scotland the Brave'. The occupation was partly a revenge mission for a massacre of British forces in a mutiny by local police. Revenge was assuredly taken before Britain's brave boys said a very unfond farewell four months later. Britain left what is currently the de facto capital of Yemen, and the folks at home thought nothing more about it unless reminded by televised pleas for famine relief.*

Through those closing years of occupation, Britain had lumped

---

* Lauded by the popular press, but not by the Army's hierarchy, Mitchell served a single term as a Conservative MP but chafed at the discipline required.

Aden in with its hinterland to form something called the Federation of South Arabia to prepare this benighted place for independence. And here, in the dying months of the Tory government, was fought the least-known and perhaps most ill-advised of all Britain's late imperial wars.

Deep in the mountains lay the province of Radfan, on what had been the Aden to Mecca caravan route – where the Qutaibi tribesmen made an unofficial living collecting tolls from passing travellers. It was a protection racket, but they did not have much else. The route was now being used as a conduit for arms from Yemen for feuding rebel groups, and Britain, convinced the tribesmen were in league with rebels, decided to put a stop to this. As one army officer explained: 'The locals were a xenophobic lot, equipped from boyhood with rifles, who regarded the British arrival in their mountains as an opportunity for target practice.' As well they might.

So they decided to thwart the rebels by building a bypass, very fashionable at home, which they could control from the high ground, cutting out the Radfanis. But they had no idea about Radfan. An old tradesman told a correspondent from *The Times* that he was the first Englishman he had met since 'a man called Jacobs'. The *Times* man made enquiries back in Aden and concluded Jacobs must have been there in 1904.

The target practice included the killing of two SAS men, who were beheaded and (so it was rumoured) had their heads displayed on poles in Yemen. The British had promised 'minimum force and minimum bloodshed'. What this meant was reinforcements from home and thousand-pound bombs.

Then the Radfanis were driven from their villages. 'Patrols are systematically burning food stocks and farm stockades, and destroying livestock left behind,' said the *Sunday Telegraph*. 'They are also preventing the inhabitants returning to their villages to sow their crops now that the rainy season has arrived.' There was no attempt to resettle them; they were just forced into the mountains. British officials were keen to avoid visits by aid agencies because they might 'misunderstand', i.e. discover the truth.

Thirteen British troops were killed in this sideshow and an unknown number of tribesmen. If they remembered Mr Jacobs's pacific visit from 1904, then the survivors would certainly remember the British Army's last fling of imperial arrogance another sixty years later. They would not remember what Britain achieved by this business, because the answer seems to be: nothing.

———•———

Maybe one time in a million, old warriors get heart-warming news. By the 1960s, Brian Hough, the Korean War veteran, was a bus driver in Manchester. An acquaintance caught sight of him at Piccadilly bus station in the city centre. 'I've seen your mate, Huffy,' he said. 'Who do you mean?' asked Hough. 'Jack Goulding.' That was the soldier married the night before he left for Korea and airlifted from the battlefield, presumed dead or dying.

'I blew my top a bit,' said Huffy. 'But it was true. He had spent eighteen months in a military hospital in Chester. He could walk with a stick and eventually he went back to work. They had three kids and it was marvellous. Jack always looked poorly but we got back in touch and we had some good times together. He died in 2002. And for fifty years Veronica had to dress his wounds every day. They never healed. What that girl did for him, it's unbelievable.'

19

THE MOON, MONEY AND MURDOCH

IN JULY 1969, HUMANKIND WALKED ON THE MOON FOR THE FIRST time. The two men were of course American. That was an important victory for capitalism and liberal democracy but hardly a British victory. Britain had come closer than any other country to conquering planet Earth; it fell to other nations to blaze a trail to other worlds.

The British Empire was perceived to have been laid to rest more than four years before when the long-planned Operation Hope Not had to be activated: Sir Winston's Churchill's funeral. In November 1964, the world celebrated his 90th birthday: thousands of cards arrived at his home – some with addresses like 'The Greatest Man Alive, London' – plus 120 cakes. A crowd stood outside and serenaded him and, leaning on two servants, he came to the window to wave. His doctor, Lord Moran, said he was 'very well', which he clearly was not.

Six weeks later Churchill had a stroke and, over the next nine days, slipped inexorably away, and before a cold January ended, the world's great and (mostly) good made their way to a frigid London for the state funeral. He asked for 'lively' hymns and got 'Fight the Good Fight' and 'The Battle Hymn of the Republic'. Clement Attlee, frail now himself, had promised to be a pall-bearer and kept his word, though he had to be helped by a guardsman. Most famously and picturesquely, the dockside cranes lowered the jibs in Churchill's honour, like sad giraffes, as the barge carrying the coffin passed by. It was seen as a spontaneous gesture, which was improbable since it was Saturday afternoon, and later speculation suggested they had to be bribed, or at least paid, to do it. The coffin then left from Waterloo station, although Paddington would be the normal station to reach Bladon; the choice may have been dictated by proximity to the river but the version that Churchill insisted on Waterloo so the station name would annoy General de Gaulle, the president of France, is too delicious to ignore.

Still, de Gaulle had the last word. 'Now Britain is no longer a great power,' he said. The British, said the historian Piers Brendon, were 'grieving a potent symbol of their lost greatness and their finest hour.' American author William Manchester added: 'They mourned, not only him and all he meant, but all that they had been, and no longer were, and would never be again.'

This is all very pretty but was it not possible they were simply mourning a great man? The nation was growing out of imperial grandeur.

Richard Dimbleby commentated on that occasion for the BBC, as he always had done and, it seemed, always would. But he died before the year was out, of cancer, which he insisted should be made public, breaking the taboo. He was only 52 but seemed, not so much older but more mature than that. He was an almost grandfatherly figure even on Coronation Day, when he'd just turned 40. Revel Guest, who worked with him as a producer on *Panorama*, thought the world of him: 'he had clarity, humility, a listening ability, bonhomie and a desire for accuracy'.

The triumphs Britain could offer were individual ones. The upmarket adventurer Francis Chichester circumnavigated the globe single-handed in nine months in 1966–67, and was knighted by the Queen at Greenwich with Francis Drake's sword. He was 66 at the time. He was followed quickly by Alec Rose, a green-grocer from Southsea who was still short of turning 60. An estimated quarter-million people saw Rose return to Portsmouth Harbour. Perhaps even more than Churchill's funeral, these feats brought the lost spirit of empire to the surface.*

One Englishman was able to share in the lunar success. A 25-year-old bachelor from Preston, David Threlfall – for reasons he could not actually explain – had placed a £10 bet on man landing on the moon before 1971 with bookmakers William Hill at 1,000-to-1, five years earlier. He was presented with his £10,000 cheque in the ITV studio as soon as the *Eagle* landed. It was a huge win for him – worth at least sixteen times that fifty years on – and in the long run for Hills too: the publicity value was immeasurable. Sadly, Threlfall died in a car crash only a year later.

There was an understanding in Britain (less so in America) that money did not necessarily bring lasting happiness. The cautionary tale throughout the sixties was Mrs Vivian Nicholson, a Yorkshire miner's wife who first came to attention when her second husband Keith won £152,000 on the football pools and she brought forth the phrase that stuck to her: 'I'm going to spend and spend and spend.' She kept her word, and her adventures filled the papers in the manner of Lady Docker in the fifties. She was lonely even before Keith suffered David Threlfall's fate and was killed in his Jaguar in 1965. Her descent, involving three more short-lived marriages, was long, pitiful and increasingly penurious.

The pools coupon was just a licence to dream. But the idea of a personal moon shot – having an idea, building a business, taking risks and getting filthy rich – was deeply unfashionable in Britain. The tax system discouraged it. The upper classes still looked down on 'trade' and people who had bought their own furniture. And the incessant troubles of British industry continued to focus on the differentials, making sure that, however much or little one earned, others must not have more. The word 'breadhead', implying someone obsessed with money-making, was first noted in the US in 1969, but its implicit contempt was already endemic in Britain. There were exceptions: in 1968 a precocious 17-year-old ex-public schoolboy achieved significant publicity in *The Guardian* for a

---

* More importantly, they signalled to their contemporaries that 60 was not extreme old age and that life was for living not telly-watching.

new national magazine called *Student*. Little was heard about *Student* thereafter, and the press turned out to be one of the few fields of endeavour in which Richard Branson did not at least dabble in his adult life – sometimes successfully but always with much publicity.

The existing business community wanted to make a profit, and would often moan about the impediments to that while playing their afternoon round of golf on early closing day. But they did not necessarily fixate on the notion of making *more* profit for its own sake. They would certainly grumble about the trade unions, who were seen as greedy, and that grumbling trickled down the social scale, especially among women. In 1961 a Penguin paperback by the journalist Michael Shanks with the doom-and-gloom title *The Stagnant Society* sold 60,000 copies. Shanks was particularly obsessed with the tea break but posed a general question that went with the grain of opinion: 'Why *won't* our workers work harder?'

Just before New Year 1968, a short-lived patriotic campaign was started by five secretaries in Surbiton, who offered to work half an hour longer each day without pay. The unions were appalled, as was fashionable opinion. 'I'm Backing Britain' had a shelf life of several weeks; the revelation that its T-shirts were made in Portugal was unhelpful. But it was notably supported by the Labour Party's most reliable press ally: the *Daily Mirror* said the unions were being 'pathetic' and 'sourpusses'. The whole campaign left such a lasting legacy that when it came to the next New Year . . . there was a massive stay-away from work, especially in the heavy industries of the North. 'We are a nation without a conscience,' said one employer. This followed widespread absenteeism a week earlier, on 27 December. New Year was also not then a bank holiday.

Early in 1969 the government made its own move. The hyperactive Barbara Castle, now at the Department of Employment, published a White Paper called *In Place of Strife*, to reform industrial relations and make strikes more difficult. It was quite cleverly crafted, including many features to please the unions, such as protection against dismissal, but not quite clever enough. As well as industrial strife, it brought internal party strife.

Harold Wilson saw it as a way of finessing the Tories; Jim Callaghan, who led the Cabinet rebellion, calculated union and backbench feeling more accurately and sensed personal opportunity. His star was rising again – he seemed to be getting a firm hand on Ulster – and with the volatile George Brown having offered his resignation once too often and had it accepted (the best guesstimate is that it was his seventeenth resignation threat), Callaghan was now the obvious leader of the horny-handed wing of the party. For a while Wilson's leadership tottered. In June he patched up a face-saving deal with the unions.

In return for him dropping the bill, the leaders made a promise to do something about union reform themselves. It was 'solemn and binding'. This was characterized by the press as 'Solomon Binding', a fictional character who might have been one of the Tolpuddle Martyrs and took on a life of his own, but a rather elusive one. The union leaders definitely said they would do something. 'What it was that they were to do was never specified,' wrote Bernard Levin. 'Nor, in the event, did they do it, whatever it was.'

In 1964, inflation ensured the return of the £10 note, abolished in wartime. In 1965, the price of posting a letter supposed to arrive the next day went up from three old pence to four, and then five pence (just over two pence in today's money) three years later when the two-tier post came into operation. Also in 1965, following a devastating report by the Royal College of Physicians three years earlier, cigarette adverts . . .

'Take a tip, take a Bristol, take a real cigarette, that's a Bristol'
'You're never alone with a Strand'
'Consulate: Cool as a mountain stream . . .'

were banned on TV, although pipes and cigars were exempt . . .

'Happiness is a cigar called Hamlet'

And Kenneth Tynan uttered the first nationally audible *fuck* on TV.*

The first credit card, Barclaycard, arrived in 1966, introducing once-cautious Britons to the joy of debt. The same year came the now obsolete cheque cards, which helped reduce the possibility of fraud through stolen cheques.

In 1967 the government sank the pirate radio stations bar a few posthumous gurgles, and in return the BBC made its peace offering to the nation's youth. It abandoned its time-honoured wireless offering of Light Programme, Home Service and Third Programme (Slight, Drone and Weird, as someone once put it) and created Radios 1, 2, 3 and 4. But the pop station Radio 1 was far from full-time at first and it was often subsumed by Radio 2 – which at that time, in the mind's ear, mainly played Mantovani and his cascading strings. Audio cassettes went on sale hereabouts, though the quality was not yet up to much.

The picturesque London telephone exchanges, from ABBey to WORdsworth, were replaced by numbers in 1968. These were never future-proofed, which led to incessant further changes. That same year, the much-loved K6 red telephone kiosk, designed by Sir Giles Gilbert Scott in the 1930s, was superseded – though not necessarily replaced – by the joyless, heavily glazed K8.† The Trimphone went on sale: a lightweight home phone with a trendy look (though still with a dial), it had a trilly ringtone which unfailingly conjures up the late sixties.

The last British Rail steam train on the slimmed-down post-Beeching network ran in 1968; nostalgia was limited and to some extent forbidden – for several years thereafter the old locomotives were completely banned from the system. The previous year, the last of British Rail's shunting horses, Charlie, was retired, aged 24,

---

* The historian Joe Moran says that the Irish playwright Brendan Behan used the dread word several times during an interview on *Panorama* in 1956, but he was so drunk no one heard it properly. And in a teatime interview on Ulster TV in 1959 the man whose job was to paint continuously the railings by the River Lagan in Belfast was asked if it was boring. 'Of course it's fucking boring,' he replied. No one complained on either occasion.

† The K7 (1959) existed, but only on the drawing board.

having spent his final six years in the appropriately horsey environs of Newmarket station.

In 1969, Simon Dee, the biggest star to emerge from the pirate stations, lost his BBC chat show, and thereafter fell like Lucifer. And John Lennon returned his MBE in protest at Britain's involvement in the Nigerian civil war, support for the US and the fact that his record 'Cold Turkey' had fallen from No. 15 to 18 in the charts. 'Jolly good,' said a schoolmaster who had returned his own award when The Beatles received theirs. 'I'll apply for mine back.'

And late in 1968 a bizarre-sounding lunch took place between two of the decade's quintessential figures: Lennon and the railway axeman Dr Beeching. Lennon hoped Beeching might sort out the chaos of The Beatles' short-lived Apple empire, the Fab Four's shambolic final endeavour as a foursome. Nothing came of this mind-boggling meeting, though Apple did close down quickly enough, which was presumably Beeching's solution. In January 1969 came the group's impromptu final concert, on a rooftop in Savile Row, brought to a conclusion by the appearance of an earnest young constable.

Life was changing in the home too. In 1969 *The Guardian* mentioned tentatively the growing popularity of 'Scandinavian dynes or duvets' instead of a top sheet and blankets, although Habitat had been selling them since 1964. As increasing numbers of Britons acquired their first bathrooms, the bourgeoisie began to install time-and-space-saving showers, rather than a second bath. And holidays increasingly involved towing caravans, an uncool fact about the decade of cool.

———·———

In 1967, John Simpson, later the BBC World Affairs editor, then fresh out of Cambridge, was working as a junior sub-editor in the newsroom when he was handed a story about a well-known children's broadcaster who had just died. It was suggested that he ring the woman he worked with on *Children's Hour* for many years and ask for a tribute.

At first Simpson could not make out the sound coming from the other end. Slowly he realized it was laughter. Then came her tribute: 'That evil old bastard,' she said at last. 'I hope he died in agony.' The woman told him that children would win competitions to meet the great man at Broadcasting House. He would show them round, give them lunch, take them to the gents and interfere with them.

If they complained, the director-general's office would write and say 'the nation wouldn't understand such an accusation against a much-loved figure'. The evidence suggests that the allegation was basically correct; that the man in question was Derek McCulloch, 'Uncle Mac' from *Children's Favourites*, and that his accuser was his *Children's Hour* colleague Kathleen Garscadden, 'Auntie Kathleen'. Her words were somewhat amended for broadcast purposes, said Simpson. According to the BBC she said, 'He had a wonderful way with children.'

On my shelves I still have a copy of a 1955 Ladybird book by Derek McCulloch: *In the Train with Uncle Mac* about Bob and Betty, two classically smartly dressed and well-behaved Ladybird children travelling alone to see their uncle in what appears to be an old-fashioned non-corridor train. I have become rather worried about Bob and Betty.

Even if McCulloch had been caught and exposed, the consequences might not have been that serious. In 1962, Sir Ian Horobin, a former Conservative MP and junior minister, admitted offences against five boys at a youth centre in the East End, where he had been warden for thirty-eight years. The five were a fraction of the total. He boasted of 'a succession of sweethearts' and that he had lately had sex with the sons and even grandsons of the boys he'd had in the early days. He got four years and then retired to Tangiers. Just before his arrest, he had been gazetted as a life peer but tactfully withdrew. He was said to have been very brave when tortured by the Japanese as a POW.

———•———

New names were starting to rise. That autumn the eternal dirty old uncle of every British sabbath, the *News of the World*, came up for sale. A rich and, it was already clear, repulsive Labour MP, Robert Maxwell, wanted to buy it – which sent its owners, the shambolic Carr family, into an improbable fit of fastidiousness. Enter a clean skin: a 37-year-old Australian with an air of colonial innocence. His name was Rupert Murdoch. He prevailed.

Murdoch also defeated Maxwell to acquire a failing newspaper then owned by the International Publishing Corporation. Until 1964, it was the *Daily Herald*, the organ of the trade union movement. It was sustained by the profits of the mighty *Daily Mirror* and a vast array of successful magazines. Unable to close it for fear of antagonizing the even mightier print unions, the *Mirror*'s presiding genius, Hugh Cudlipp, turned it into a self-consciously modern paper called *The Sun*. It was aimed, according to Cudlipp, at 'a middle-class couple, aged 28 with two children and living in Reading'.

The Sun's original version was a decent if underfunded newspaper. However, Cudlipp's genius failed him this time, there being insufficient couples fitting that description to make it profitable. Still, it could not safely be closed. But luckily Maxwell and Murdoch were interested in this paper too. And Murdoch, to IPC's delight, handed over £1 million for it. It was as if he thought he knew something about the British public – supposedly better fed, better educated, less bellicose, more serious, more intelligent, more aspirational than ever before – than anyone else. And maybe he did.

NEAR MISS

In Hammersmith, an
unperturbed Harold
Wilson sees an egg fly in
his direction, one of many
thrown at him in the 1970
election campaign. But he
was days away from losing
his job as prime minister.

DIRECT HIT

. . Five days later a
woman carrying a four-
year-old throws a pot of
red paint at Ted Heath as
he enters 10 Downing
Street, having defeated
Wilson. 'That was a stupid
thing to do, wasn't it?' he
said.

THE DISROBING DECADE: (*above*) the London cast of *Oh! Calcutta!* prepare to reveal their all, August 1970; (*below*) after a lot of lager and a £10 bet, Australian Michael O'Brien revealed his all to the crowd at Twickenham for the England-Wales rugby international in March 1974, and was blamed for starting the craze for streaking at major sports events. PC Bruce Perry was responsible for the inventive cover-up.

LAW AND DISORDER: (*top left*) Sir Robert Mark, the stern Commissioner of the Metropolitan Police, pictured in 1973, was responsible for weeding out dozens of his force members on suspicion of being 'bad apples'; (*top right*) looking surprisingly jaunty, former Commander Ken Drury, a prominent victim of the purge, makes his way to court and jail on corruption charges, 1976; (*below*) always game for a stunt, the Sex Pistols sign their new recording contract outside Buckingham Palace, 1977.

TROUBLE LOOMS: (*above*) peace descends on the decibel-heavy weaving shed at Bancroft Mill, Barnoldswick, as the end draws near for Britain's cotton mills, 1978; (*bottom left*) diminutive Michael Edwardes, the boss of British Leyland; (*bottom right*) Edwardes would eventually see off the burly Communist union convenor Derek Robinson ('Red Robbo'), held responsible for 523 disputes at the company's Longbridge plant in 1978–79.

ODD COUPLES: (*top left*) Xaviera Hollander, call girl, madam, and author of *The Happy Hooker*, stands tall above the anti-permissiveness campaigner Mary Whitehouse at the press conference to launch Lord Longford's report on pornography, 1972; (*top right*) topless together: a couple at the Isle of Wight pop festival, 1970; (*below*) the new Conservative leader Margaret Thatcher and her embittered predecessor Edward Heath while campaigning to keep Britain in the Common Market, 1975.

IN DARKNESS AND IN LIGHT: (*above*) at the height of the Troubles, IRA men check a weapon, Derry, 1972; (*below*) more pacific activists gather in Trafalgar Square to campaign for Christian values and against moral pollution at the Festival of Light, 1971.

WHEN YOU'RE SMILING: (*top left*) Freddie Laker, the pioneer of cheap transatlantic travel, takes delight in one of his DC-10 planes, 1976; (*top right*) John Tyme, the anti-motorway campaigner, smiles wryly as he passes his supporters; (*bottom left*) Joyce McKinney, who added a new dimension to the idea of transatlantic relations, in a police van en route to Epsom Magistrates' Court for a hearing in the strange but entertaining Case of the Manacled Mormon, 1977; (*bottom right*) Morecambe and Wise, the comedians whose TV ratings reached Miss World and World Cup levels, perform on stage at Croydon, 1973.

GOOD TIMES, BAD TIMES: (*above*) Jim Callaghan (*second left*) forgets his troubles back home, flanked by Chancellor Helmut Schmidt, President Jimmy Carter and President Valéry Giscard D'Estaing, at the four-nation summit in sunny Guadeloupe, January 1979; (*below*) in chilly Leicester Square, rubbish piles high, along with Callaghan's troubles, in the Winter of Discontent, February 1979.

THE 1970s

1

IS THE SHOW
REALLY OVER?

C AN WE IDENTIFY THE APOGEE OF SIXTIES-ISM, THE SET OF
attitudes associated, fairly if sometimes misleadingly, with the
reign's most ostentatious decade? Anyone, present at the time or
not, is entitled to an opinion.

So how about this one? It actually happened in the 1970s;
decade-ism is not an exact science, and the distinction between the
sixties and the seventies is a particularly complex one. It was
something that emphatically could not have happened ten years
earlier, and would not have happened ten years later. It was a nude
picture. In *The Times*.

On 17 March 1971, when the paper's lead story assured readers
that firm action would be taken to end the violence in Northern
Ireland,* all the display advertising space had been bought by a
single company, Fisons, to promote its various wares. Almost
the whole of page 7 comprised a picture of a 23-year-old model,
Vivien Neves.

She was kneeling, so the shot was not quite full-frontal. Her
arms were held aloft, tugging her long, blonde hair. Her breasts and
nipples were very visible. At the foot of the page was a small amount
of text making a tenuous connection between the photo and one of
Fisons' products, Bisks slimming biscuits. The picture then and now

---

* A kind of scoop, since the prediction was twenty-seven years ahead of reality.

seemed to me somehow beyond erotic. My response was more like that of the Melbourne librarian seeing Jean Shrimpton's mini-skirt at the races. Here was a goddess.

The Times in that era still held an unchallenged place in reputation, its own self-esteem and in its influence on the Establishment, though certainly not in circulation. Its status was epitomized by its slogan, 'Top people take The Times'. The long-serving editor, William Rees-Mogg, was an impeccably elitist figure but, as with his leader column on the Jagger drug bust, was not above occasional acts of mischief. He had declined to veto the Fisons advert.

Two days later, the letters column printed some of the predictable harrumphs from the readers. But the opposition was far from unanimous. 'I hope this delightful picture has the same effect on The Times' circulation as it does on mine,' wrote James Marchant of Bletchley. And F. S. Macdonald, a schoolmaster from Leatherhead, wrote simply: 'Topless people take The Times?'

Three decades later, after Neves had died of multiple sclerosis aged only 55, Rees-Mogg himself reflected that he wished he had met her to say thank you. 'She was good for Fisons and good for The Times. I knew running the advert would please a large number of our readers. In fact, I happened to be having lunch with the judges at the Old Bailey the next day and they were all entirely in favour.' Indeed, Fisons bought up the whole paper again later in the year. This time, Page 7 featured an unidentified feminine fundament, semi-prone on an armchair, vaguely promoting Genitron – which was said to make vinyl upholstery softer. Her bottom was clothed, though only lightly.

———•———

All this would have been unthinkable in 1961, and indeed in 1981. Above all, that was the year Rupert Murdoch, already owner of The Sun and the News of the World, added The Times and Sunday Times to his portfolio: the deal was controversial enough without encouraging the accusation that he was turning the top people's paper into a tit-sheet.

The Sun had taken that step definitively late in 1970, on page 3 not 7, and for the next forty-five years the Page 3 pin-up was the most famous, most talked-about and, especially towards the end, most controversial feature in British journalism. Rivals emerged over the years and at times there were suggestions that Murdoch might respond to the competition by 'playing the pubic ace', as one commentator put it. In fact, the dress code – bra off, knickers on – became as formulaic as the crossword.

The paper was exactly a year old when the tradition began with the appearance of most of Stephanie Rahn from Munich, maintaining the German tradition of being forward in stripping off. Thereafter, hundreds of young women appeared in varied though repetitive poses over a period of more than 13,000 days. But even before this, *The Sun* had stamped itself on the nation's consciousness with cheeky headlines, sex-related stories and breathless TV ads promoting the theme of the week: Pony Week, Laugh Week. Doggy Week, Down Under Week and Ooh-la-la Week – free weekends in Paris and half-price French knickers. This worried the Independent Television Authority, though not as much as Pussy Week.

From the start, the paper's news stories had an emphasis that had never been seen in a British daily paper and were far removed from the traditional faux-prudery of its Sunday sister:

GIRLS, DON'T BE CAUGHT BENDING

SEX IS A PLEASURE – EVEN FOR CHELSEA PENSIONERS

LADIES OF THE W.I. STRIP FOR PANTIE PANTO

It was rough, raggedy-arse, iconoclastic. Yet it proceeded with a certain caution: politically it did not yet deviate too far from the *Daily Mirror*'s support for the Labour Party – it perceived its readers as little interested in politics. And it was nowhere near as cruel and reckless as it later became. The sales rocketed and, from a standing start, it headed to 4 million a day, overtaking the *Mirror*, which had sold *The Sun* to Murdoch, within eight years.

The old *Mirror* had been devoted, consciously or not, to the theory of embourgeoisement: that working-class people were becoming more enlightened and sophisticated. Murdoch demolished this. By the mid-1970s the *Mirror* had started to compete on *The Sun*'s terms, losing its soul in the process without much gain in sales. In 1978, the *Daily Express*, its own circulation falling rapidly, started the *Daily Star*, which made *The Sun* look staid. The upshot was that 'permissiveness', that very sixties word, became far more embedded in Fleet Street than it had been in the actual 1960s.

This was not wholly typical, and attitudes in the new decade would prove far more complicated. One can see the tide of change in the sixties as a mighty river roaring onwards. In the seventies it found its delta. Some of the changes in culture and attitude kept their course. Others moved on and mutated. Some things stagnated, even went into reverse. Popular music, for instance, after an era when even great-grandmas might know the hit tunes, became much more fragmented. The seventies was not, as is sometimes claimed, a drab decade. It was an intricate and idiosyncratic one.

———·———

At first there was a sense that everyone was still testing the boundaries, especially over nudity. It was even demanded in a Radio 3 play in which the actress Rosalind Shanks was being massaged by another woman. Clothes would spoil the sound effects, she was told. A reluctant Shanks won a compromise and wore a body stocking.

The summit of this particular craze was reached in July 1970 when *Oh! Calcutta!* came to the now-uncensored London stage. The title was an obscure pun on the French for 'what an arse you have!' and there were allegedly sightings of occasional homesick and bewildered Bengalis entering and rapidly departing the Roundhouse when it opened. There were also thousands of thrill-seekers well aware it was a revue about sex – or, as its creator Kenneth Tynan put it, an 'experiment in elegant erotica'.

The London critics were kinder than the Americans had been, perhaps because Tynan was a colleague. They mostly considered the sketches only patchily funny and that the actors, who went starkers three times, were well chosen for their physical attributes.

No, they did not feel corrupted. 'As erotically steamy as a Darby & Joan outing,' said the *Mirror*. 'As depraved as a Welsh Sunday.'

The Lord Chamberlain could no longer demand that scripts be changed in advance, but that was no protection from an obscenity charge – indeed it heightened the risk. During the previews, police officers arrived, had a little ogle, then came back for more ogles, and Inspector Fred Luff of the Obscene Publications Squad, a group that later turned out to be depraved themselves, decided it was obscene. They were foiled by the Director of Public Prosecutions' crack troop of porn experts: a law professor, a vicar and two headmistresses. More robust and worldly than the boys in blue, they agreed with the critics. The show ran for almost ten years.

Even so, it was all too much for some of those who had fought hardest for this very freedom. The humorous writer and sometime MP Sir Alan (A. P.) Herbert had chaired the committee of literary types who began the successful campaign to reshape the Obscene Publications Act in the fifties. He had not seen *Oh! Calcutta!* but he knew what he didn't like. Now aged 80, he concluded: 'I am sorry to think that our efforts seem to have ended in a right to represent copulation, veraciously, on the public stage.' Public copulation did not take place often but there was a craze for *streaking* (word first recorded 1973), mainly at major sporting events.

———•———

For Fred Luff there were plenty of other fish in the sea of iniquity. In January, Luff had led a raid on a London art gallery, seizing eight lithographs depicting the artist, one John Lennon, and his new wife, Yoko Ono, 'in various stages of their love life'. It was hard to know who was the most crazed publicity-seeker: Lennon, Ono, the gallery owner or Luff. The art, it was agreed, had little merit: one was a sketch of Yoko being penetrated by either a very large penis, a champion banana or the crescent moon.

Luff's men took names and addresses of everyone present, and three of them gave evidence when the case came to court: 'I deny that John Lennon or the organiser, have or had the right to shock me,' said a housewife and magistrate from shockable Egham. But

the court was sitting in the West End, and the magistrate, St John
Harmsworth, had seen just about everything except a banana
almost as big as Yoko. He threw the case out.

In many ways, the cultural revolution was rolling onwards.
Three years after *Hair*'s nudity had first shocked the shockable
classes, the Dean of St Paul's held a special evensong featuring
numbers from the show to mark the anniversary. The cathedral was
packed; a man who shouted at one of the actors, 'You're a disgrace
to the name of Jesus Christ,' was chucked out to join other
conservative protesters outside.

But Luff was far from done. The underground magazines – which
flourished in Britain only fleetingly – were regularly harassed. And
because distributors and retailers could also be prosecuted for libel,
the scene was fragile and enfeebled. Even *Private Eye* (continuously,
for many years) and *Time Out* (sometimes) were banned by
W. H. Smith shops. Magazines that pushed the boundaries further
were constantly at risk from the police. *International Times*, which
was said to be selling 40,000 copies, was regularly raided and finally
got closed down because it ran gay contact adverts. And then there
was *Oz*, whose fame far outlasted its brief but merry life, because
authority went berserk.

Oz was originally started in 1963 in Australia, then a country as
worldly and sophisticated as other remote Pacific islands. The
magazine's presiding eccentric, Richard Neville, after a couple of
brushes with prudish Aussie laws, eventually took the hippie trail
north, fetched up in Swinging London and began a British version
in 1967. In February 1970 *Oz* published the Pussy Power issue
(that's another story), which included an advert inviting under-18s
to edit the April issue: 'no money, except expenses, and offering
almost complete editorial freedom'.

About twenty teenagers, almost all male, turned up. Thrilled by
editing a real national magazine, some did what adolescent boys do
when excited and became adventurously lewd. A lot was censored
by the adults. But alongside a long moan about the exam system, a
cartoon strip appeared in which a schoolboy called Viv Berger put
the head of Rupert Bear, whose innocently dull adventures had

appeared in the *Daily Express* since the Neolithic age, on to the work of the famously scabrous American cartoonist Robert Crumb. It was revolting, but the text was actually quite clever: cleverer than most of *Oz*'s normal mix of sex, drugs, rock, and Day-Glo colours. The Schoolkids issue, it was said, did not sell that well, which might explain why the police found so many copies when they raided the *Oz* office.

Rupert's erect penis would then become the centre of perhaps, despite much competition, the most crackpot trial ever seen at the Old Bailey. Neville and his two cohorts, Jim Anderson and Felix Dennis, were charged with 'conspiring to produce a magazine containing divers obscene lewd, indecent and sexually perverted articles, cartoons, drawings and illustrations with intent thereby to debauch and corrupt the morals of children and young persons within the Realm and to arouse and implant in their minds lustful and perverted desires'. Fifty years on, the concern would have been for the morals of the young persons who wrote it – but, no, this was about everybody else.

It was eight months from the arrests to the trial, all of which – had the police got their way – the three would have spent in jail. By this time the Conservatives were back in power, but this was not relevant because the Obscene Publications Squad was now beyond anyone's control. The chosen judge was Michael Argyle, Recorder of Birmingham, famously stern if unpredictable, and very keen on self-publicity. He revelled in his starring role, and so – at least at first – did the defendants. The case was strung out over six weeks before the jury rejected the conspiracy charge and convicted them on four minor counts.* Argyle then remanded them in custody for 'medical and social reports', at which point their fashionably luxuriant locks became subject to the untender attention of the prison barber. This offended the British sense of fair play, and the Home Secretary, Reginald Maudling, promptly changed the rules – deferring the shears until after sentence.

---

* The *Oz* trial was one of the last to be tried under the old rules which restricted jury service to property owners – which made juries older, richer and more masculine.

A week later, Neville, Anderson and Dennis were sentenced to
fifteen, twelve and nine months respectively, Dennis being considered
'very much less intelligent than the others'. The usual liberal suspects
were duly outraged by the sentences and, outside the court,
protesters burned an effigy of Argyle. But there was also a sense of
general opinion turning in the Oz Three's favour, especially in legal
circles. They were quickly released from jail pending appeal by a
more senior judge, and in November the Lord Chief Justice, Lord
Widgery, quashed the sentences, saying Argyle had seriously
misdirected the jury.

The circulation of Oz spiked briefly then fell back; in 1973, it
went bust and ceased to exist. Neville and Anderson returned to
Australia and aged quietly. Dennis, the allegedly stupid one, founded
a more successful and respectable publishing company, and by
1995 was listed as the fifty-sixth richest person in Britain.

As times grew darker, many of the fashions of the recent past
faded away: student rebellions, long hair, mini-skirts. But there
were still dirty magazines. Maudling was a little puzzled. Why
did Rupert Bear get prosecuted when there was hardcore porn all
over Soho? There was an answer to that question, but it took a
while to emerge.

————◆————

Yet in 1971 the battle between the counterculture and the counter-
counterculture was being fought much more evenly than in the
sixties. And the moralists, under the banner of the Festival of Light,
began to ape the tactics of the Left by taking to the streets. In
September they held a rally in Trafalgar Square: with the innocence
of evangelists, they talked of 100,000 turning up, so when they got
about half that it seemed like a failure. They were addressed by the
controversialist Malcolm Muggeridge, a Soviet sympathizer who
had found God, the 'clean up TV' campaigner Mary Whitehouse,
and Lord Longford, a former Labour minister who held a strange
honorary position as the nation's favourite batty uncle. None of
them traffic-stopping spellbinders in the Billy Graham manner.

But the crowd would have cheered anyone who told them they

were not alone in believing in Jesus in a world full of ungodliness. When they marched to Hyde Park they met some opposition from *Oz*-type libertines who lobbed a few smoke bombs. What was notable, said the *Sunday Telegraph* reporter, was that – excepting the wording on their banners – both sides were indistinguishable: nearly all young, casually dressed and having their own version of fun. This appeared under the headline SILENT MAJORITY* FINDS A VOICE FOR MORALITY.

A month later, just before their appeal was heard, Neville and the *Oz* team's barrister John Mortimer debated the legitimacy of pornography with Longford and Whitehouse at the Cambridge Union. The old guard were defeated but only by 442 to 271, far from a landslide. And if supposedly outdated attitudes had such support even there, what did that say about Middle England? Even the car manufacturers, always aware of the sexual implications of their sales pitch, had their limits. At the 1970 and 1971 motor shows, the TVR sports car company drew far more attention than their rivals when they hired nude models to sprawl across their new models. The second time, the firm was threatened with expulsion from the hall.

Whitehouse, a retired schoolmistress from Shropshire, had an annoying habit of disarming interviewers by being charming and mumsy. Though she was *persona non grata* at the BBC when run by the quintessentially sixties figure Sir Hugh Carleton Greene, she was taken seriously by his more cautious successor Charles Curran.† Longford was a different case. His other preoccupation at the time was preparing a report on pornography.

He researched partly by visiting strip clubs with the press in tow. Sir Hugh might have commissioned this as a sitcom. His Lordship was not shocked by his visits to Soho, but the fleshpots of Copenhagen proved too much for him and he walked out of two clubs very rapidly. At one the manager hurried after him:

---

* A phrase coined in the US by President Nixon.
† Not to be confused with a Conservative MP of the same name, quoted elsewhere in this book.

'But sir, you have not seen the intercourse! We have intercourse later in the programme!'

The report appeared in 1972, backed by a committee of fifty-three including Kingsley Amis – turning from angry young man to grumpy old one – and Cliff Richard, who had by now completely thrown off the mantle of raunchy teenage idol to become very Christian and a bit weird. Its headline proposal was a new definition of obscenity as anything that 'outraged contemporary standards of decency or humanity which were accepted by the public at large' rather than tending to 'deprave and corrupt'. But who would decide that? Judge Argyle? Kenneth Tynan? A Gallup poll? Longford moved on to a new cause: campaigning for the release of the Moors murderer Myra Hindley. On his own definition of obscenity, any jury in the country would have convicted him for that.

———·———

But the loud minority had not gone away. Another endpoint of sixties-ism might have been the third and last of the original annual Isle of Wight rock festivals, over the 1970 August bank holiday. It was in many ways an object lesson in what not to do on these occasions. The locals forced the event into a giant bowl on a relatively remote bit of coast (though most residents would have preferred it on a sandbank in the Solent). This made it easy to watch from beyond the fences, but French anarchists and Hells Angels forced their way in anyway. It is said the toilets at the top continually spewed sewage in a waterfall down the hill.

Dave Brock of Hawkwind compared the site, full of corrugated iron, to a prison camp (and the disc jockey John Peel said all rock festivals brought back memories of National Service). By the weekend there were an estimated 600,000 people – yet somehow the organizers went broke. The climax came from Jimi Hendrix, somewhat off his game like most of the performers – because even if they stuck to orange juice it was usually spiked. My university flatmate Mike Lazar was there. 'Did you see Hendrix?' I asked him excitedly. 'I saw a dot on the horizon. We were all stoned anyway.'

Still, the chief constable of Hampshire was relaxed, saying the vast majority were less violent than a football crowd, which was testament to the soothing power of marijuana.*

Eighteen days later, Hendrix was found dead in a basement flat in Notting Hill. The cause of death – suicide, accident or even murder – was unknown, though the coroner was able to rule out an absence of drugs, drink and general excess. Hendrix was the guitarist's guitarist and a sensational showman. He was also one of four world-famous rock stars who died within a two-year span – after Brian Jones and before Janis Joplin and Jim Morrison, who had told the island throng: 'We want the world . . . and we want it now!' All four were 27, giving rise to the notion that it was a uniquely dangerous age for the famous and hedonistic.†

The day after Hendrix died, a smaller-scale festival was staged for the first time at a farm in Somerset. The poster, in fashionably psychedelic lettering, was headed 'Pop, Folk & Blues'. The attendance: about 1,500. Price: £1, free milk from the farm included. The event later became known as Glastonbury. Among those appearing was the then little-known figure of Marc Bolan, who would himself be killed in a car crash in 1977, aged 29.

In the years ahead, the 'live fast, die young' ethos did not disappear from the rock scene but it became less compulsory. And converts to wholesomeness could be found in the most improbable places. Keith Curtis, a projectionist working for a cinema club in Newport, South Wales, switched off a film called *Danish Blue* during a nude scene and announced 'No more'. He rejected appeals to keep running the film while looking the other way, and went home to find another job. 'In my opinion the scenes went too far,' he said.

In 1973, one of the BBC's comedy classics began: *Whatever Happened to the Likely Lads?*, which was a follow-up to an earlier series, *The Likely Lads*. Two randy and pint-supping young Geordie mates – Terry (James Bolam) and Bob (Rodney Bewes) – met again

---

* The event was revived, more decorously, in 2002.
† Much later, Kurt Cobain and Amy Winehouse joined what became known as the 27 Club.

by chance years later: Terry had joined the Army, serving in Germany, and was (characteristically) bemoaning his fate: 'When this country goes through a social transformation I'm not here to see it . . . Death of censorship, the new morality, *Oh! Calcutta!*, topless waitresses . . . Permissive society, I missed it all.'

Well, he had and he hadn't.

———•———

One old-fashioned piece of licence, hallowed since 1692, ended in 1970. At the end of July, the ancient naval custom of the midday rum ration was abolished. The chaps were not happy: some even chanted 'Save our tot' to Prince Philip, as Admiral of the Fleet, when he opened the Commonwealth Games in Edinburgh. A naval spokesman shrugged it off: 'Just high spirits.' Nuclear submarines on patrol had already amended the regime by serving the rum off duty, which was reassuring.

There is a quote, hard to pin down but attributed to Winston Churchill, dismissing naval traditions as 'rum, sodomy and the lash'. Two of them had now gone. Difficult to be sure about the middle item.

2

LISTEN TO REASON

S PORTING CONTESTS EXCLUDED, THERE WERE THREE EVENTS, televised by the BBC, that brought Britain together in the 1970s to an extent unthinkable when the three TV channels began to multiply towards infinity. As a rite of spring there is and was the Eurovision Song Contest, which was still taken seriously by the British music industry, the public and whoever was assigned to commentate on it (in 1970 it was the disc jockey David Gell).

There was the *Morecambe and Wise Christmas Show*, in which performers of the utmost distinction, from Sir Laurence Olivier down, came along to be cheerfully insulted by Eric and Ernie, the most popular double act in the land. It regularly outdrew the Queen's Christmas message earlier in the day.

And there was one other annual event that united the British round their TV sets. On a Friday night in November 1970, the *Radio Times* felt able to predict that 'nearly 28 million people', half the UK population, would watch BBC1's offering against the only two other channels' efforts – deliberately feeble for its companion BBC2, despairingly so for its rival ITV.

The show involved the presentation of fifty-eight attractive young ladies from most of the world, parading in one-piece swimsuits before one of them would be singled out to be Miss World 1970. Watching this was something like viewing the already defunct presentation of debutantes at Buckingham Palace, or being the quality control inspector at a Barbie doll factory. One contestant, Miss Sweden, had described it the previous day as 'a cattle market'.

This edition did not quite run to time. Just as the host, the ageing comedian Bob Hope, was making his peroration before the finalists were announced, the sound of a football rattle* was heard. Then came chanting from a few sections of the vast Royal Albert Hall, a light shower of debris on to the stage, including bags of flour and rotten tomatoes, the odd smoke and stink bomb in the auditorium, showers of leaflets from the upper decks, and the enforced departure of a number of what the newspapers later described as 'girls', who had been planning the protest for some time. 'We had no quarrel with the contestants,' Sally Alexander, one of the 'girls', summed up years later. 'Our argument was "Why do you have to be beautiful and looked at like this to be noticed as a woman?"'

At the time, the effect of the protest was muted by an argument about the winner, Miss Grenada, given that Grenada's premier, Eric Gairy,† was on the judging panel. It was said that Miss Sweden had the most first places, but that only the chief organizer, Eric Morley, understood the voting system. And one can see that freethinking Miss Sweden would not have been his idea of a Miss World. But retrospectively the night has been sanctified as the birth of Britain's feminist movement.

However, the contest took place four days after *The Sun*'s invention of the regular Page 3 girl, which most feminists saw as a perpetual insult. And yet millions of women read or skimmed *The Sun*. And the half of the UK that watched Miss World was certainly not all male either. Indeed, one has a sense that most men watched it in the way one might expect; it was the women who were most judgmental, looking out for any flaw or blemish. Which is exactly what farmers do at cattle markets.

---

* A noisy, whirling solid-wood device popular with soccer crowds – used to express support for their team and occasionally maim the person next to them.
† One of the Caribbean's nastiest tyrants after the island became independent in 1974.

In 1968, in Atlantic City, New Jersey, a group of demonstrators picketed the Miss America pageant and hurled bras, girdles, hair curlers, false eyelashes, high-heeled shoes and detergent into a giant rubbish bin. There had been talk of burning bras, but the mayor asked them not to, because the wooden boardwalk had already caught fire once that year. This was the first significant sighting of the Women's Liberation Movement.

The intellectual underpinnings had started much earlier, when the American Betty Friedan discovered that her contemporaries at the elite all-female Smith College in Massachusetts had reached their early forties feeling as under-fulfilled as she did. Thus emerged her 1963 book *The Feminine Mystique*. The British equivalent, *The Female Eunuch*, by the trenchant and witty Germaine Greer, did not appear until just before the Miss World demo.

Then early in 1971, *The Observer* ran a series of long articles on what it called 'women's lib', heralding its arrival into the mainstream. One was written by a 23-year-old, Anna Coote. It did not reveal anything that was not known – or at any rate, was not knowable. But it set out the facts of the disabilities and discrimination imposed on British women with a cool clarity that must have been revelatory to the vast majority of men and a great many women. Starting with children's books:

> Elizabeth is taking off the doll's clothes. She is going to wash them and put them out on the grass to dry in the sun . . .
> . . . Simon is making a boat. He is making it of bits of wood. This is like my daddy's boat, he says.

Coote worked through the issues of A levels, university entrance, the jobs market, dating rules, equal pay, matrimonial law and, above all, the conditioning that women receive for their subsidiary role in society: 'The prime minister is a man, the doctor is a man, the television news is read by a man, the vicar is a man and God is a man: it is not surprising that children develop the idea that authority is naturally invested in the male of the species . . .' It was a devastating case for the prosecution.

Fifty years on, Coote herself believes the awakening of British womanhood was a direct result of the expansion of higher education in the mid-sixties, which made much more difference to teenage girls than boys because expectations were so low: 'My sister is only eighteen months older than me and much cleverer, but she went to secretarial college because that's what you did. I went to university. Attitudes changed that quickly. And though in the counterculture women were meant to be just dolly birds, it brought us the capacity to revolt against it.'

From the mid-sixties to the mid-seventies, there was a radio programme called *Petticoat Line* in which an all-woman panel answered listeners' questions, mostly light-hearted. Some of the panellists were serious figures and some were young, though both the chair, Anona Winn, and the most regular panellist, Renée Houston, were old troupers who had been in showbiz since the 1920s. It was not exactly on the feminist cutting edge.

For a while there was a male counterpart called *Be Reasonable!*, a phrase probably used by the husband in every marital sitcom since the early days of wireless. Both were rather jolly but loathed by many BBC executives, and would have been axed much quicker except that Tony Whitby, the controller of Radio 4, knew he would be 'hanged from the lampposts of Bond Street' if he laid a finger on Anona and Renée.

But their presence, as feminism grew more serious, did encourage an urgency in gradually tilting the much longer-running radio staple, *Woman's Hour*, away from domesticity and towards the outside world. It also sped up the hunt for female continuity announcers (Hylda Bamber and Barbara Edwards were appointed in 1972) and, more sluggishly, newsreaders: Sheila Tracy made her Radio 4 debut in 1975. 'It was the midnight bulletin,' she recalled, 'so it didn't cause too much fuss.'

And slowly, one by one, women did begin to kick open the barred gates into traditional male enclaves. Sometimes the process was inadvertently helped by its opponents. In the City, the Stock

Exchange had rejected the notion of women members for the third time in four years, and its maritime equivalent, the Baltic Exchange, was just as recalcitrant. Graham Greenwell, a Stock Exchange member for fifty years, wrote to *The Times*: 'In essence, both the Stock Exchange and the Baltic are private men's clubs and not business institutions, and wish to remain so.' This was probably at least half true and he was probably also half joking. But it was not a wise intervention. The following day there were rebukes for Greenwell from both the Exchange chairman and another, younger, member:

> Sir,
> It is more usual for sons to be put right by their fathers.
> However, on other less frequent occasions the reverse
> applies . . . In my opinion it is purely a question of time
> before the Stock Exchange admits women and the present
> reluctance is just another example of resistance to change of
> any kind which is only too prevalent in this country today.
> Incidentally, if the Stock Exchange is a private men's club I
> have yet to find either the dining room or the card room.
>   Yours faithfully, Philip Greenwell.

The Stock Exchange gave way in 1973, the Baltic a year later.

Prince Charles's spartan alma mater, Gordonstoun, admitted girls in 1972. 'It is really a very civilised place,' said the headmaster, John Kempe. Their presence may have brightened Prince Andrew's years there. In 1971, Professor Margaret Burbidge was made director of the Royal Greenwich Observatory and the Jockey Club announced that women could ride in a handful of special races but not compete against men.

That summer, a wholly unofficial England football team arrived in Mexico to play in a wholly unofficial World Cup. It comprised women. 'It was utterly surreal, like going to Narnia,' said Chris Lockwood, who played as a 15-year-old. 'We'd gone from playing on park pitches and suddenly we were running out in front of 80,000 people.' They lost both their games, but when they came home the Football Association rescinded a fifty-year-long ban on women playing on any of their affiliated grounds. The welcome was a bit grudging but the 80,000-strong crowd in Mexico must have made an impression on the FA.

In 1972, Rose Heilbron QC became the first woman judge at the Old Bailey, and three of the previously all-male Cambridge colleges began to admit women. Oxford followed two years later, having just made amends to the physiologist Mabel Purefoy FitzGerald, aged 100, who was given an apology and an honorary MA, having not been eligible to receive a degree when she finished her studies there in 1899.

The Church of England began informally debating the possible ordination of women in 1972 with most speakers in favour. However, in 1973, the Bishop of Exeter, Robert Mortimer, said the old pagan religions had priestesses 'and we all know the kind of religions they were'. That was the start of a long battle. In 1974, after a very short battle, liberationists persuaded the Passport Office to allow them to call themselves 'Ms': they kept turning up to enquire annoyingly. And Jill Viner, 22, became London's first woman bus driver. In 1975, to mark International Women's Year, six dames were in the Birthday Honours list instead of the usual one (compared to a score or more knights).

In 1976, women tennis players, led by the champion Chris Evert, threatened to strike if their prize money at Wimbledon was not raised to the same level as the men, even though they did not do equal work: a maximum three sets to the men's five. Though the differentials were narrowed, it took until 2007 to close the gap completely – by which time, more significantly, the winner, Venus Williams, pocketed £700,000. Evert had won £10,000.

In 1977, three women were actually invited to join the Jockey Club, rulers of horse racing and seemingly the most unbiddable of all the patriarchies. They included Helen Johnson Houghton, who in 1956 did and did not train the 2,000 Guineas winner.* A year later, on another part of the battlefield, there re-emerged the force

---

* See pp. 67–8.

of nature who had earlier vanquished the Jockey Club: Johnson Houghton's fellow trainer Florence Nagle, now 83 and still up for a fight. This time, as a long-standing breeder of setters and Irish wolfhounds, she took on the Kennel Club, the masters of British dogdom, whose all-male committee took the decisions and ate jolly good lunches at their Mayfair HQ on the fees paid mainly by women, who bred most of the dogs. Nagle lost the first round on a technicality but the enemy raised the white flag before making further fools of themselves. 'Women always have to fight for things,' she said, 'and someone has to stick their neck out.'

In 1978, Hannah Dadds became the first woman driver on the London Underground. And in 1979 Scotswoman Agnes Curran became the first to be made governor of a men's prison: Dungavel in Lanarkshire. She was quite undaunted: 'Women handle wee boys until they grow up and the average woman does not consider that a problem.'

In time, shame and legislation put paid to the most egregious anomalies. The Equal Pay Act and the Sex Discrimination Act both became law in 1975, but the concept of equal pay for equal work in particular proved devilish to enforce because it was so hard to define equal work. Those in the forefront of the process were not ordinary women and did not necessarily lead ordinary lives; as Margaret Thatcher had ill-advisedly told the Maidstone Tories when she wanted to be their candidate all those years before, good nannies made a difference.

———•———

In the case of small businesses, there was a genuine cause to be wary of employing younger women. It might no longer be lawful to advertise for a butcher's boy or a baker's roundsman but there was good reason for Mr Bones or Mr Bun to prefer one to the alternative.* Especially as communities were being broken up and the supply of real or honorary grans and aunties to help with childcare was less plentiful.

---

* The 1975 Act exempted businesses with fewer than six employees.

Even big companies made the same calculation. And some of the most blatant were nationalized. Delphine Gray-Fisk went in a glider as an 11-year-old in 1965 and was completely smitten. At 20, she qualified as a pilot and worked as an instructor. Then she fancied the idea of flying one of those fancy long-distance VC10s.

Those were still the days of two major nationalized airlines: long-haul BOAC and short-haul BEA, which merged as British Airways in 1974. So Gray-Fisk applied to BOAC, had an interview and was given the traditional 'no longer any vacancies' code. 'I think half the board wanted me and half didn't,' she reflected later. Then she applied to BEA as second-best. They were much blunter: 'We do not employ women pilots.'

That was rather a relief: 'I didn't want to join them, flying rotten Viscounts and things.' But it happened that a former pilot, by now a Conservative MP, lived next door to her boyfriend's parents. And one day they were all having lunch and she told the story. 'That's very interesting,' said Norman Tebbit. 'Can I borrow it?'

Thus the matter came to parliament. 'If she was a coloured woman they would have had to interview her, otherwise they would have been accused of colour prejudice. This is a blatant sexual bar, which ought to be stopped,' Tebbit said. As it happened, Gray-Fisk was more relaxed than he was. She had no truck with the liberation movement and quite saw the other side of the argument: 'It is a problem if you employ women of childbearing age. They might just decide to pop off and have a baby.' She went off to the medium-sized airline Dan-Air, who did not think it a problem, and had twenty good years before it folded.

Sometimes old ways and new met uneasily. Princess Anne, about to marry army officer Mark Phillips in Westminster Abbey, went along with normal Abbey ritual – based on the 1662 Book of Common Prayer – and agreed to love, cherish and *obey* her husband. Even though, through accident of birth, she held the rank of colonel and he was a mere captain. The Labour peer Lady Summerskill thought this was an anachronism. 'The groom would say "With my body I thee worship"', the Dean of Westminster, Dr Eric Abbott, pointed out. He thought that made it 'fair do's'. Prebendary Frank

Rodgers, ordained in 1971, began his clerical career as a curate in the Midlands where brides still routinely promised to obey. 'I don't remember anyone raising it as an issue. Maybe they did in more sophisticated areas. But as the newer prayer books came in it just faded away.'

Clearly modern women were not interested in automatic obedience. But the drive towards equality threw up many complications, some of which reached the courts. What would be the correct feminist position on the case in Brighton where a man on a date left the table halfway through the meal, said he was going to the toilet and never returned? She was unable to pay the £2.09 bill and charged with obtaining food and wine by deception – but was cleared. 'A woman who goes to a restaurant with a man can reasonably expect her escort to pay – even in 1971,' said deputy recorder Basil Webb.

What about the couple, divorced after less than a year, no children, both working at not dissimilar rates of pay? Stafford magistrates ordered the husband to pay the wife £8 a week, a quarter of his gross pay. The High Court made it a nominal 5p a year (just in case the circumstances changed). The message was that marriage was not an automatic meal ticket for life.

And if there was going to be equality, what about male midwives? They were officially banned from 1951 to 1977 and by the 2020s constituted about 1 per cent of the workforce. Women had long been used to seeing male gynaecologists. Was there such a difference?* Meanwhile, the head of a comprehensive school in Newcastle, beset by unruly girls, brought in equality by extending corporal punishment to them as well as boys. This was not quite what the early feminists had in mind.

And some organizations stood aloof from the gallop towards inclusivity. As *The Times* solemnly reported on the last day of 1971: 'The North Wales branch of the Contractors Mechanical Plant

---

* In 2022, the Royal College of Midwifery website did not mention males in its 'How to Become a Midwife' section, which suggests that this diversity is tolerated rather than encouraged.

Engineers association has been instructed by its national executive
to expel its only woman member.' Mrs Joan Bulman, of Ellesmere
Port, was in charge of thirty men.

Perhaps genuine equality could only be achieved when women
could act every bit as ridiculously as men. Jenny Diski watched as
the women-only Sisterwrite feminist bookshop in Islington refused
admission to the male companion of a woman who had just arrived
in London and wanted to look at the noticeboard. The male was
her two-year-old son. Oh, *be reasonable*!

------·------

There was another front in the cultural war – the verbiage, much
mocked by opponents: 'Madam Chair' . . . 'the sisterhood' . . .
'wimmin' (a feminist coinage used scornfully by opponents) . . .
along with 'do we have to call it Personchester?' . . . 'they're all
lezzies aren't they?' . . . and the most terrible accusation of all
leftish British discourse, 'middle-class'.

So it was with great delight that the sisterhood found a proper
working-class cause: the night cleaners, employed at pitiful rates in
pitiful conditions in London's new skyscraper offices. And they
found a voice, belonging to a feisty old-school East Ender and
mother of four, May Hobbs, who founded an action group after
being blacklisted by employers.

It turned out that one of the worst offenders was the government,
who had contracted out the cleaning of ministerial buildings. The
2,300 cleaning contracts all went to the lowest bidder, which meant
the lowest payer. The Civil Service had a minimum rate for cleaners
of £18, whereas the contractor was paying £12.50.* MPs began to
ask questions. It was reported that one Ministry of Defence
establishment, the Empress State Building in Fulham, had twenty-
six storeys, 1,200 rooms, ten women to clean it, three vacuum
cleaners (all broken) and no dusters (they brought their own).

So in 1972 the cleaners went on strike, backed by the Civil
Service Union, and won after two weeks on what sounds like a

---

* Not hourly, weekly.

notably sociable picket line that touched a great many guilt nerves, including the government's. There was a general rise of £2.50, and Empress State workers pushed their pay up to £21 a week.

Then in 1975 there came a documentary, *Nightcleaners*, made by an avant-garde collective. It was watched and approved by the people who watch films made by avant-garde collectives. In time the cleaners returned to nocturnal obscurity and their pay rates stagnated again, and they resumed both their Dickensian routine and their perpetually fragile family life.

And the trade unions rapidly lost interest. The members and leaders being overwhelmingly male, they were unsure whether women in the workforce were a source of new strength or a threat. There was a more specific problem, Sally Alexander thought: 'Trade unions understand one thing and that's wage demands. But the night cleaners wanted to change their conditions more than their pay.' They were also a nightmare to organize: May Hobbs emigrated to Australia, and no wonder.

———•———

Whatever became of the Miss World contest? In the short run it remained as popular as ever with the British TV audience and the press. In 1973, Eric Morley, who ran the contest with his wife, Julia, achieved a long-term aim in getting an American winner to broaden the contest's appeal. The new Miss World was Marjorie Wallace from Indianapolis, 19 and 35-24-35; she got him publicity all right.

Wallace's boyfriend was the playboy racing driver Peter Revson. Then came alleged flings with George Best and Tom Jones. Never one to miss out, Warren Beatty was linked with her by the *Daily Mail*. After 104 days, Morley had had enough and fired her, saying all contestants were warned about their private lives bringing adverse publicity. But the show was not over. Two weeks later Revson was killed in practice for the South African Grand Prix. Marjorie was in the front row at the funeral, weeping. Two months later she took an overdose but survived. Later she bagged, briefly, another famous scalp in Jimmy Connors, actually married twice and appeared a lot on television, carrying with her always the tagline 'former Miss World' – they can't take that away from her.

In 1974, the judges went for Miss UK. Helen Morgan, also 35-24-35, from Wales, was an unlikely candidate for immediate hanky-panky since she had a two-month-old baby. This was no secret and not against the rules, though husbands were.

But the Morleys did not share Britain's patriotic enthusiasm. Apart from anything else, the baby would affect the new queen's ability to perform her regal duties. Immediately after the event it was announced that mothers would in future be banned as well as wives, following the discovery they were not necessarily the same thing. Or, at least, the Morleys and Helen Morgan discovered that many viewers still thought they should be the same thing.

Flushed with pride, Morgan walked into a hotel bar two days after winning to be confronted by a stranger who said: 'You have certainly not won any competitions for Victorian morality.' She resigned the next day.

'How can you set down a moral standard for a contest anyway?' Morgan said despairingly later. 'No one would expect the girls to prove they were virgins.' In a sense, she now stood shoulder to shoulder with the sisterhood who had tried to sabotage this very event four years earlier: in shared recognition that humanity does not deal in perfection.

3

THE ICEMAN COMETH

O N NEW YEAR'S DAY 1970, THE CHANCELLOR OF THE Exchequer, Roy Jenkins, pleased himself and his metropolitan friends by abolishing the £50 travel limit which had hampered all but the most rudimentary Continental holidays for the previous three and a half years.

That might have been taken as the first harbinger of an early election, with the expectation of whole flocks of springtime swallows emerging from the Chancellor's red box in April. But Jenkins refused to play the customary game of bribing the voters with tax cuts: 'a vulgar piece of economic management below the level of political sophistication of the British electorate,' as he put it later. It also pleased the Treasury mandarins, seared by their complicity in the disastrous Tory giveaway of 1964.

It even pleased the *Daily Telegraph*, no friend of Labour, which admired the dullness of his measures and praised his 'extraordinary self-restraint'. And to an astonishing extent it appeared to please the electorate. The Conservatives, who had led every Gallup poll for three solid years, suddenly found themselves staring at a 7 per cent deficit. This was ratified by the local elections, which went brilliantly for Labour. With hindsight, one might fancy the voters were so sophisticated they lied to the pollsters to con Harold Wilson into calling an election nine months early. He certainly took the bait.

Wilson did not treat the voters as adults. Everything possible was done to stack the odds in his favour. Those troublesome long-haired lefty layabouts, the 18- to 20-year-olds, had the vote for the first time; the government refused to implement recent boundary changes which were thought to favour the opposition; the planned South African cricket tour of the UK, due to take place behind barbed wire to deter anti-apartheid protesters, was cancelled because Wilson was not going to have his election wrecked by mayhem.*

Meanwhile, Wilson ingratiated himself with the rapidly growing readership of *The Sun* by presenting the paper's TV awards, and sang 'Cockles and Mussels' with Violet Carson (aka Ena Sharples). This would have been unimaginable for starchy Ted Heath. Starchy old Heath was talking about the boring old issues.

Every general election subtly changes the nature of electioneering as new techniques and new media replace old. But in 1970 politics still had an old-fashioned flavour. The Conservative Julian Critchley, who had been evicted from a marginal seat in 1964, now found a safe haven in military-minded Aldershot. He researched local issues before the selection meeting and talked about those, not Wilson. Later, an old colonel told him why he had really won: 'It was your wife . . . Damned fine woman. And she was the only one of them to stand up when we asked her a question.'

Candidates still addressed quite well-attended meetings in parish halls hoping to be elected to what was still quite an old-fashioned parliament. Ken Clarke made it in 1970 to join a Conservative Party where just about every backbencher did other work and then strolled to the Commons afterwards. 'And it was a much more powerful House of Commons,' he recalled before he left 49 years later, 'a much more effective political system.'

Bryan Magee, already well known as a philosopher and TV presenter, was less enamoured when he was elected for Labour in 1974. The Palace of Westminster being exempt from the licensing laws it inflicted on the nation, there was always one bar open whatever the hour. And there being little else to do before the

---

* South Africa would not tour England again for another twenty-four years.

10 p.m. vote (except, God forbid, listen to the debate), most of the members drank. Magee was conscientious about constituency work, which took two to three hours in the morning. He filled his time until 10 p.m. writing a book about Schopenhauer.

Critchley, on his return to the Commons, was pleased to note that the salary had doubled and there was now an allowance for a secretary and stamps. He was less pleased to find that the Commons' once-famous wine cellar had been sold off, though the records of the transaction had disappeared. The chairman of the kitchen committee in his absence had been one Robert Maxwell.

———•———

What was new in 1970, some felt, was the complete hegemony of the opinion polls. Ever since 1945, when these new-fangled fortune tellers correctly predicted a Labour landslide and were ignored, the pollsters had acquired a reputation close to infallibility. Six days before this election, Ted Heath finished a speech in Manchester and was confronted by the news that the latest poll, in the *Mail*, showed a 12.4 per cent lead. '*Against* us?' he asked, piteously. It was indeed against them, just like every other poll bar one (and that by only 1 per cent) all the way to election day. And yet his team kept telling him that the canvass returns were very encouraging, especially in the Labour-held marginals.

There were doubters on the other side too. 'I have a haunting feeling that there is a silent majority sitting behind its lace curtains, waiting to come out and vote Tory,' wrote Barbara Castle in her diary on the final weekend. And Labour's campaign was cynical, evasive and *ad hominem*, centred on a series of posters showing pastiche puppets of leading Tories captioned 'Yesterday's Men'.

Wilson puffed his pipe, avoided mass meetings and kept his itinerary largely secret, in a manner not then the norm. Nonetheless, fourteen eggs were thrown at him in the fortnight leading up to the election, which brought forth the best joke of Heath's life. It was a very serious matter, he said: 'This was a secret meeting on a secret tour which nobody was meant to know about, and what it shows is that there are men walking the streets today, also women, with eggs in their pockets, just on the offchance that they'll meet the leader of the Labour party.'

Eggs or not, Wilson exuded bonhomie and complacency. The sun was shining that June, literally and metaphorically. If the voters were indeed sophisticated, they would have sensed downpours could not be long delayed. One theory is that, after Labour gave up on trade union reform and pay policy, people began to feel more prosperous, but by June price rises were eroding that; Jim Callaghan even accused business of helping the Tories by upping prices during the campaign.

And they would also have noticed the balance of payments, a monthly statistic weaponized and fetishized by Wilson to pinpoint Tory profligacy before 1964, and now awaited with as much excitement as the football results. Just before the poll, the May figures revealed a gaping deficit of £31 million. It was a freak, said Labour; that month included two new jumbo jets. But those who live by the trade figures can also die by the trade figures.

Or maybe Labour were killed by a football result. Far away in Mexico, England were trying to defend the World Cup won at home in 1966, and duly received a certain amount of payback for the indignities felt by the Latin Americans in that tournament. If they had forgotten at all, the Mexican press and public were reminded when the now-knighted manager Sir Alf Ramsey, whose tactics were superior to his tact, led his squad on a badwill tour in 1969.

The major vengeance came before the World Cup itself, when England played warm-up matches in Ecuador and Colombia and the captain Bobby Moore was arrested, almost certainly unjustly, for the theft of a bracelet in Bogotá. Despite that, despite their distrust of the Mexican food, despite the heat and the altitude and the fact that, as Bobby Charlton later recalled, 'we were unpopular throughout the country. Nobody wanted us to win,' England played well to reach the quarter-final in León. There they were 2–0 up against West Germany with twenty minutes to go and coasting towards the last four.

And then. Popular memory blames Peter Bonetti, the stand-in goalkeeper, deputizing for the sick Gordon Banks. Journalists present noted Ramsey's decision to sit on the lead and cede the mid-field to the Germans; the knackering effect of Ramsey's 4-4-2 system in extreme conditions; the pro-German (or anti-English) roars from the Mexican crowd. Whatever, the defeat in extra time was the anti-dote to 1966, a more typical English experience – one more suited to the nation's phlegm, fatalism and dark humour. Part of the backstory of *Whatever Happened to the Likely Lads?* was that Terry had married a German girl and was watching the 1970 game with her family. After the whistle, he walked out forever. 'Did they laugh?' asked Bob. 'Laugh?' said Terry. 'They nearly invaded Poland.'

The British TV audience for the Mexican fiasco was around 28 million, closely matching the number who voted four days later in the election.* On the Thursday morning, a letter appeared in *The Times* from the journalist Peter Grosvenor: 'Could it be that Harold Wilson is two-nil up with twenty minutes to play?' The question of a connection with losing the football had been quietly troubling Labour minds all week, and would do so long afterwards.

It is true that the swing to the Tories was smaller in Scotland and Wales, where voters were less moved, and perhaps even delighted, by events in Mexico. Four more times in the next fifty years we would see the polls confounded by a late swing – twice to and from each main party – and in each case it involved some combination of flawed leadership and a vacuous or overconfident campaign. I suspect that in 1970 the voters remembered in time just how chaotic Labour's term had been and wanted a change.

The Conservatives gained seventy-seven seats for a majority of thirty. There were notably large pro-Tory swings in Wolverhampton, Enoch Powell's fiefdom, and an even bigger one in Clapham where the defeated Labour candidate was a much-respected doctor of high calibre and principle, Dr David Pitt. Had he won the seat, he would have been modern Britain's first black MP, and a superb, passionate one.† But the man on the Clapham omnibus was not ready for him.

---

* And that year's eventful Miss World.
† Pitt later became chair of the Greater London Council and Lord Pitt of Hampstead (he grew up round Hampstead, Grenada, and lived in its London namesake).

As one said, 'I fought for England and I think it should be a white man that does this job.'

Election data was not as sophisticated as it later became, and there is no clear evidence of the effect of giving the nearly 2 million 18- to 20-year-olds the vote, which Labour expected would benefit them. But in January, when the Tories were still ahead in the polls, a Gallup survey showed the Tories actually had a much *bigger* lead among the newly eligible. Perhaps this was indeed the new silent majority. But campaigners just sensed total apathy among the young. Many were not even registered, never mind willing to get out of bed and vote.

———•———

Edward Heath was perhaps the most enigmatic of British prime ministers. He was almost 54 when he entered Downing Street, an imposing figure with a slight hint of faded matinee idol. And he was not without charm, though it was rarely deployed when more adept politicians would use it most: with women and his own backbenchers. He also had a strange sense of dark humour which was inclined to leave people either baffled or affronted, and a unique, much-parodied, shoulder-shaking laugh.

There was never a silver spoon: his father was a carpenter, his mother a maid. But he moved inexorably upwards: grammar school, a stickler of a prefect, scholarship to Balliol, Oxford, president of the union, a good war (an artillery major), into parliament, Conservative chief whip, Cabinet minister, party leader, successful yachtsman, PM . . . though he never quite shook off the values of a school prefect. And his upward mobility left him with a strange set of strangulated vowels which was another source of mockery.

His politics did have a foundation of underlying decency. He did not hate the trade unions or wish to crush them, even if he felt, in that prefectorial way, constantly disappointed by their misbehaviour. He did not want to destroy the welfare state. He had principles and beliefs: he really did believe that Britain's future lay in Europe, and he successfully placed it there, for his lifetime at least; he also believed in modernizing Britain, which Wilson had articulated better but less sincerely. Heath's assistant Douglas Hurd said that his instinct was always to find the right answer, not the politically convenient one. Only then would he worry about tactics and communication. Indeed, the last one was often badly neglected.

Poor old Ted – even his great moments seemed to be ruined, as though he wore a kick me sticker on his back. On his great election night, a Labour supporter stubbed out a fag end on his neck; in Downing Street on the Saturday, a young woman carrying a four-year-old threw red paint on him; eighteen months later, the signing ceremony in Brussels for Britain's agreement to join the Common Market was postponed because a German woman threw ink over him. The ink made the headlines, not the historic moment. Wilson's eggings never defined him in the same way.

Perhaps the public urge to inflict light damage on Heath was down to his awkward demeanour. He could come across as awfully obtuse, even in his principles. He detested the ritual handout of knighthoods to deadbeat MPs, as did everyone else except a couple of hundred Tory backbenchers – the people he most needed to keep sweet. He was the Mr Spock of politics, thoroughly logical but stunted in his emotions. This encompassed the most powerful emotion of all. So far as is known, he never had a sexual relationship.

Whether Heath was a repressed homosexual or asexual (whatever that means), or simply too shy to make a rash move, remains a matter of conjecture. The late Ronald Higgins, who worked in his private office in the 1960s, once told me he had never known an adult so ignorant of sexual matters, and that Heath had needed an explanation of what it was John Profumo and Christine Keeler actually did. This makes one wonder how he ever survived four years as chief whip – who is meant to know what every MP is up to.

———•———

Heath was always energetic and competent: Downing Street was a more efficient place during his regime, with the calm Hurd as chief aide rather than manic Marcia Williams. And once they had learned his ways, it seems his crew both on land and on his yacht could grow quite fond of him. The major difference between him and the infinitely flexible Wilson was that Heath liked to have a clear plan. But then, as the boxer Mike Tyson later put it, 'everyone has a plan till they get punched in the mouth'. And the first punch for this government was brutal. A month after the election, Iain Macleod, the Chancellor of the Exchequer, died suddenly, aged 56. This was no ordinary loss. He was the government's most combative debater and its sharpest and most original mind; a man who had made a fortune in his youth from his skill at bridge and poker. His successor, Anthony Barber, was regarded as a poor substitute.

The Tories had done some right-wing posturing before coming into government, notably at a pre-election get-together at the Selsdon Park Hotel in Croydon – from which Labour created an imaginary neolith called 'Selsdon Man' in an attempt to define their opponents as reactionary. But Heath did not want to dismantle Clement Attlee's legacy, and the ministers who would later embark on that project – Margaret Thatcher (then at Education) and Sir Keith Joseph (Health and Social Security) – were at this time both very anxious to spend money.

At first the government quietly did what Tory governments do: lower taxes and raise prescription charges. Of course, it was looking for cuts – as any new government must do – and Terence Higgins, a junior Treasury minister, gave Thatcher a choice: a huge list of cheeseparing savings, or axe the Open University, Labour's new pride and joy. 'To my surprise,' Higgins recalled, 'she chose to save the Open University.' Free milk for older primary school children was an early casualty, hence she had her first brush with infamy – as Thatcher the milk snatcher.

More generally, the Heath regime had two problems it never overcame. One was the urgent desire to follow the plan without Wilsonian ducking and weaving, which left him ill prepared for each further punch in the mouth. And then there was the sheer pettiness of some of his principles. He was adamant that people who went to art galleries and museums should pay for their pleasure, even if the nation owned the treasures. This exercise cost a vast amount of time and political capital for a trifling amount of income.

In the event, after many delays and compromises, charges were not imposed until January 1974, whereupon the nation's great cultural cathedrals emptied. Two months later Heath was out of office and the charges were abolished. The money collected barely covered the cost of installing the turnstiles.

Swirling around Westminster were the great issues of joining Europe and trying to resolve the issue of Ulster. The vast majority of the British public were bored rigid by both these subjects, except when the horrors of Ireland escaped across the stormy sea. But the defining political issue was what went on – or did not go on – in the nation's workplaces.

4

EVERYBODY OUT

ALONG WITH JENKINS'S RESTORATION OF RIGHTS TO holidaymakers, New Year's Day 1970 was when it ceased to be compulsory for the English to attend church on Sunday. The 1552 law had not been enforced since 1846 and even the archbishops registered no objection to the repeal. The only possible earthly retribution had long since been the chance of a Monday scowl from the vicar if you passed in the street.

Some people were ignoring more pressing obligations. Many thousands of workers stayed away from work that New Year's Day, even though it was not then a bank holiday. Dockers and car workers were prominent absentees. The Confederation of British Industry called on its members to get tough on malingerers. A year later, at least 125,000 stayed away, including all but 300 of Merseyside's 10,000 dockers. By now the CBI was getting so tough it floated the idea of making 1 January a bank holiday in England and Wales, as in Scotland and the rest of Europe, and in 1974 it came to pass. The effect was that many offices and factories decided not to open during the gap between Christmas and New Year, creating a nine- or ten-day holiday and diminishing British productivity yet further.

There were statistics around in the 1970s showing that Britain was not necessarily more strike-prone than other countries. This is quite possibly true. In other countries, strikes happened on a

grand scale: 1.7 million Indian Railways employees walked out
in 1974.

What was unusual was the extent to which British strikes and
their annoying variants, the go-slow or work-to-rule, became a
national pastime. And for every action like the night cleaners' strike
that drew attention to serious grievances, there were many more
that were irresponsible and nit-picking; adult versions of playground
spats. Small groups of workers – this was a motor industry speciality
– could hold up a huge operation to improve their own differentials:
the fetish that it was not so much about earning more, but about
ensuring others earned less. Often workers were at odds with their
own union leaders, sometimes even their own shop stewards. But
there was a general sense, which was not unjustified, that if you did
not fight your corner you would be trodden on. Management could
be equally self-serving.

The old favourites were all in the mix: the car workers, the
dockers, the three competing rail unions and so on. But as
the decade wore on practically everyone had a go: the postmen
(nationally, for the first time ever), hospital consultants, university
lecturers, Newmarket stable lads, West End actors, stagehands at
the new National Theatre (several times), staff at ITV, Claridge's
hotel, the Tate Gallery and the Royal Ballet, pit rescue men, the
civil servants running Ernie the premium bonds computer, AA
patrolmen and Playboy Club bunnies.

Some strikers started young. A thousand London schoolchildren
played truant in 1972 to march to Trafalgar Square – under the
aegis of the 'Marxist-Maoist' Schools Action Union – to protest
against uniforms and caning. Choirboys in Nottinghamshire
demanded 'unsocial hours' money for weddings because they were
forced to miss football. They won an extra 2p each. In Bedfordshire,
another set of choirboys threatened action unless the monthly
matins service was abolished. 'It is such a boring service,' said Keith
Fountain, 11. 'We all like Holy Communion best.'

And on a single day towards the end of the short, cold summer
of 1972, about 4,000 prisoners in thirty or so British jails staged
sit-down strikes to protest against bad conditions. It was a

tremendous tribute to the power of the bush telegraph in those pre-internet days, and to the organization behind it: PROP, Preservation of the Rights of Prisoners. And it might have led to an intelligent public debate about the purpose of imprisonment. But it all got messy and faded away.

Still, that might have been the *reductio ad absurdum* of strike fever but for the exchange created by Douglas Adams for that other 1970s phenomenon, *The Hitchhiker's Guide to the Galaxy*:

> 'You'll have a national philosopher's strike on your hands.'
> 'Who will that inconvenience?'
> 'Never you mind who it'll inconvenience . . . It'll hurt, buster!
> It'll hurt!'

———·———

There was another confrontation with symbolic significance. It happened at the prime minister's old school, Chatham House Grammar in Ramsgate. At the start of term in September 1970, the head, Kenneth Potten, attempted a clampdown on long hair. Fifty sixth-formers shut themselves in their common room smoking and listening to records; Potten backed off. 'It is damnable. I loathe this longhaired business,' said a retired teacher, Cecil Curzon. 'When Mr Heath was a prefect he would not have tolerated it.' But Potten bided his time. Nine months later, just before the cooling-off period of the summer holidays, he announced that from the following term boys' hair would have to be above the collar on pain of expulsion.

A few weeks of parental pressure seems to have done the trick. And the ex-prefect's industrial strategy was along the same lines. Heath had been handed a hospital pass by Wilson, who had abandoned both an incomes policy and union reform. In the short term Heath would ignore the affronts until his master plan of an overarching Industrial Relations Act reached the statute book in the summer of 1971. And there were plenty of affronts.

Even before Macleod's death, the Queen came back home from Canada and within ten minutes – barely time to pat the corgis – had to sign a state of emergency to deal with a dockers' strike. She had done that twice before, in 1955 (rail strike) and 1966 (seamen); Heath forced her to do it five times in less than four years. This allowed him to use troops if required and ban profiteering, though it was hardly needed on this occasion: Lord Pearson, a judge wise in the Wilsonian wiles of finding just enough money, was appointed to end the dispute and it was over inside a fortnight. The worst casualties were several million rotted bananas.*

In the autumn came a strike by council workers. Eventually this led to untreated sewage pouring into the rivers. The main casualties were thousands of fish; winners included millions of rats and billions of flies – and, in the end, the strikers. They got 90 per cent of their demand from another experienced and kindly conciliator, Sir Jack Scamp, and a good deal of sympathy. 'We wash and we wash but the kids turn away from us and shout "Pooh, dad,"' said a picket at the Luton sewage works, where most of the strikers were former farm workers, driven from the land by automation.

In December, electrical workers staged a work-to-rule, causing power cuts. The Queen was obliged to declare that an emergency too, and the Commons had to sit and discuss the matter lit by lanterns and candles. That winter the government swerved a miners' strike – a majority was in favour but not the two-thirds required by the National Union of Mineworkers' rules. They also saw off the postal workers, who did strike but overestimated their indispensability. By the summer of 1971 there were rays of sunshine: there was an optimistic tax-cutting budget and Heath began to think they might hold on with 'guidelines' for pay rather than actual curbs until his new bill came into force the following year and tamed the unions.

But when the next pay round came, out went the miners. It was never meant to happen. The government was aware that the working-class heroes had fallen behind in the rush for pay rises and still only had two weeks' holiday, while elsewhere three was the norm and four the new objective. The new head of the coal

* Pearson's pupil master when he was a young barrister was Walter Monckton, who later became Churchill's fixer in these matters.

board, Derek Ezra, was sympathetic; the miners themselves were wary. Their fathers and grandfathers had been the great losers of the 1926 General Strike and memories were long in the inward-looking pit villages.

The demand was for 25 per cent against a guideline of 8 per cent. If they achieved anything like that it would set off a tsunami across every industry. And wage inflation would increase unemployment; the government's position was not unreasonable. But the miners were becoming less pliant: outright Communists now had a foothold on the miners' executive, and in Yorkshire, the most agitated coalfield, a young firebrand called Arthur Scargill was making noises. In 1971 oil had overtaken coal as Britain's staple fuel, and pit closures were continuing at pace. If not now, when?

Even so, the majority for striking was only slightly higher than the previous winter. However, the union's rules had been changed: a strike no longer needed two-thirds in favour, just 55 per cent; they got almost 59. And miners' ballots were done fairly and secretly: the government could not try to overturn the decision. Anyway, coal stocks seemed adequate, the union's strike fund low, the miners very much the underdogs. The government remained sanguine; instead of reaching for an emergency proclamation under stress the way other men of his era reached for cigarettes, Heath held off for a month.

The strike began in early January 1972. Before the month was out, unemployment reached a million for the first time since the early days of the war* and, though it was foreseeable, the government was dismayed – as was *The Times*, which in advance had declared such a number as 'morally, economically, socially and politically intolerable'. The flame of liberal Conservatism still burned. January turned to February and the miners were rock-solid. With no strike-breakers there was no need to picket the pits and they turned instead to stopping coal movements. On 10 February, rolling electricity blackouts began, even during *Coronation Street*. The next day came the climax.

---

* Excluding a brief spike in the frigid winter of 1947.

The West Midlands Gas Board's coke depot at Saltley in Birmingham was now said to be Britain's last remaining major stockpile of coke – nuggets of coal with few impurities – which was essential to industry. Pickets had been gathering all week to prevent lorries getting through with mixed success, and on that Thursday they were joined by busloads of local union members who had walked out for the day in sympathy. Seven hundred policemen met 7,000 protesters. The most sober accounts suggest the mood was non-violent and even good-humoured. But the possibility of a new Peterloo was not unthinkable. The chief constable of Birmingham, Sir Derrick Capper, ordered the gates to be closed for safety's sake.

There were a number of consequences. First, Scargill, who had seized control of the situation from more senior union officials, climbed on to a toilet block to declare victory. Second, the government were very cheesed off with Capper. Third, the tribune of the bourgeoisie saw it as the end of civilization: 'Vast mob of militant and potentially violent strikers . . . a clear victory for intimidation . . . utterly deplorable,' said the *Telegraph*.*

Fourth, Heath announced new measures to save electricity – including a possible three-day week – while simultaneously readying himself for defeat. His aide Douglas Hurd wrote in his diary: 'The government now wandering vainly over the battlefield looking for someone to surrender to – and being massacred all the time.' Fifth, the *Telegraph* published a Gallup poll showing that the public were on the miners' side by a 3–1 margin, having obviously failed to read the paper's leader columns. And last, Scargill's ego swelled to the size of a middle-sized planet.

Meanwhile, the government found another kindly arbiter, Lord Wilberforce, the judge who had ended football slavery. Heath promised Wilberforce's words would be holy writ. The offer was 20 per cent, which was a phenomenal outcome for the miners, but their negotiators kept niggling away at the small print. 'We have gained more in the last twenty-four hours than we did in the last

---

* However, bizarrely and quite coincidentally, the stock market reached a three-year peak that very day.

twenty-four years,' said the union general secretary Lawrence Daly.

'We were in a class war,' wrote Scargill later. 'We were not playing cricket on the village green.' Few miners really shared his venom, and the team captains – Heath and the miners' president, Joe Gormley – did indeed utter half-sincere pleasantries as if it were the end of a one-sided Ashes series.

Afterwards, Heath addressed the nation and talked about 'the invisible danger of violence' and that it would not be tolerated. The very next day, 28 February 1972, the main body of his Industrial Relations Act came into force. This was supposed to be the *coup de grâce*, taming unruly trade unions just as his old school head tamed unruly hair.

———•———

The new Act was even-handed, in a very Heathian way, and it did offer workers advantages. Unions could register under the Act, or not. If they did, they have would have rights, immunities and tax concessions. Workers had an unfettered right to join a union, but also (with a few exemptions) not to join one, putting paid to the 'closed shop' which meant workers who refused to join in some workplaces could be sacked. Agreements would be legally binding, and the new court being set up could order secret ballots and cooling-off periods before planned strikes on pain of heavy fines.

But employers would lose the absolute right of dismissal. The Act may or may not have banned the kind of secondary picketing seen at Saltley; no one seemed quite sure. All this was to be left in the hands of a National Industrial Relations Court, so the government could stay out of it. It was headed by Sir John Donaldson, who was not a cuddly judge.

It was obviously going to be great for the lawyers: the whole bill was so complex even one of its fathers, the employment minister Robert Carr, said he could not understand the final wording. Nor, evidently, did some of the judges. The very first test case, in July 1972, produced a disagreement between Donaldson's court and the idiosyncratic Lord Denning in the appeal court: five dockers blockaded a cold store to protest against containerization threatening their jobs. This was definitely against the new law but it was not clear who was to be punished: their union, the mighty Transport & General, or the men themselves. The men, said Denning.

The farcical upshot was the appearance of two Dickensian characters from the dusty heart of government: the tipstaff to arrest them and someone called the official solicitor – whose normal duties involved representing infants, the infirm and the insane – to get them out. But the men were all for a little light martyrdom for contempt of court, and happily went off to jail.

That set off a national dock strike, a Fleet Street printers' strike and the threat of a one-day general strike. Heath told Vic Feather, the general secretary of the TUC, that the matter was out of his hands while frantic backstairs deals were done. Wilson called Heath 'the face that stopped a thousand ships', but there being no printers, there were no national newspapers to record the phrase.

Deals were clearly done: the House of Lords rapidly reversed Denning and put the onus back on the union; Donaldson immediately released the prisoners and they were chaired shoulder-high by one of the largest crowds outside any prison since the abolition of public hanging.* The union hierarchy thought these heroes a damn nuisance.

There was still a dock strike to be settled (national emergency No. 4) but the government stitched up a long-term featherbedding scheme, which in time ensured that little Felixstowe, too insignificant to be part of the deal, would end up as Britain's No. 1 port in the containerized era to come. Donaldson's court limped on, but everyone understood that the roulette table of the law was no place to conduct industrial relations. Employers and unions routinely added a rider that agreements were not legally binding.

---

* The Pentonville Five would later take their place in the numerical list of 1970s judicial martyrs: the Shrewsbury Two, the Oz Three, the Guildford Four, the Birmingham Six and the Maguire Seven. The Shrewsbury Two were building workers – one of whom, Ricky Tomlinson, had a second bout of fame when he starred in the 1990s BBC sitcom *The Royle Family*. The last three cases, all Ulster-related, were very unfunny indeed.

Two years on from the election, this was now a very different government to the one that had taken office. It had promised not to emulate Labour and pump money into 'lame duck' businesses. That became untenable barely six months into Heath's rule, when Rolls-Royce nearly went bust after it signed a bad deal for a good product: its RB-211 jet engine. The most resonant name in British manufacturing had to be part-nationalized to avoid humiliation (and spare 80,000 jobs). The government then became almost as enamoured of wiping the bottoms of incontinent businesses as Labour had been. 'We have bent our own rules under the pressure of other considerations, notably unemployment,' the Trade and Industry Secretary John Davies explained.

Barber's 1972 budget pumped £1,300 million into the economy – an unprecedented amount.* He cut taxes and increased pensions to create a growth spurt – 5 per cent a year was mentioned – in an attempt to make Britain fit to join the European Common Market the following year.

By now the fixed exchange rates negotiated at the end of the war, which made devaluation such a big deal, had started to break down. And with the dollar for once under pressure, the pound had risen from 2.40 to the dollar to 2.60, making exports less competitive, heading back to the 2.80 that had proved unstainable for the Wilson government. For a man who disdained trickery, Heath then did something unusually cunning: he allowed sterling to float 'temporarily'. Floating in this situation meant standing aside while sterling plummeted. The clever part was not calling it a devaluation, so the public did not notice until prices went up. As for temporary, the pound never glimpsed 2.60 again at any point in the next fifty years and has only rarely gone above two dollars. It was a government whose fixed policies turned out to be very temporary and its temporary ones eternal. As for 5 per cent growth, it was a nice thought.

---

* At the time the word *billion* was not used in Britain for a thousand million, a sum beyond anyone's avarice. It denoted a million million, which meant it was hardly ever mentioned except among astronomers observing distant galaxies. The inflation of the 1970s made the alternative American usage more useful.

Heath genuinely believed in the necessity of economic growth for its own sake. It was a lasting passion for him, to rank with music and above sailing. And in perhaps the most lyrical passage of his oratorical career, he pressed the case: 'The alternative to expansion is not, as some occasionally seem to suppose, an England of quiet market towns linked only by steam trains puffing slowly and peacefully through green meadows. The alternative is slums, dangerous roads, old factories, cramped schools, stunted lives.' It was perhaps the most lyrical passage of his entire political life.

British Rail's steam trains had stopped puffing in 1968 and many of the lines had fallen silent, to relatively little fuss at the time. But, having elected an arch-modernizer to lead them, the British suddenly fell prey to a fit of nostalgia. And not just about trains.

5

DOWN AMONG THE DEAD ELMS

B Y 1970, BRITAIN'S MOST FAMOUS VILLAGE WAS IN TROUBLE. The distant Lord of the Manor and his henchmen were unhappy; the land agent who had managed the place with great success for twenty years was now behind the times and losing his touch. The previous year, faced with similar problems in an urban property, the lord had simply obliterated the place. The villagers had reason to be uneasy.

In other words, the BBC hierarchy were worried about the state of things in Ambridge, fictional home of *The Archers*, and word was sent down that if the scripts did not improve in six months, the series would be axed – the fate that had met radio's other daily drama, *The Dales* (previously *Mrs Dale's Diary*) the previous year.

Ambridge had made some concessions to the 1960s: Jennifer, Dan and Doris Archer's wayward teenage niece, had an illegitimate son. Both the event and the initially horrified yet ultimately loving reaction were true to the spirit of the times: 'A baby is a baby and that's all that matters,' declared Doris finally.

But the man who created the programme twenty years earlier, Godfrey Baseley, was still the editor. Baseley – known as 'God', and not just because of his name – was reluctant to change the old format, which included a traditional ration of lightly dramatized Ministry of Agriculture instructional circulars which real farmers would rapidly bin. He had also wangled himself a role on-air as a whip-cracking master of foxhounds called Brigadier Winstanley, art imitating life.

Perhaps feeling the pressure, Baseley came up with a new dramatic storyline to begin the new decade: Jennifer's son Adam, now two, was kidnapped. This was not well executed: Adam would survive, Baseley would not. The appointment of a new head of BBC radio in Birmingham, where the programme was based, was decisive. 'When the stories weren't insipid, they were incredible,' reflected the new man, Jock Gallagher. 'One minute the cast was drooping over the teacups, the next Jennifer's son was being kidnapped. People were switching off in droves.' One could have made a soap opera about the soap opera.

Eventually Baseley was forced out; he would occasionally direct sniper fire at his old redoubt from a distant turret over the next two decades. Brigadier Winstanley, though, would crack his whip no more. Headstrong horse riders are always at risk in the countryside, and Winstanley met a predictable end. But it got worse before it got better: a *Coronation Street* writer called Malcolm Lynch was brought in as script editor. It is said that in 1971 Lynch managed to confect *in a single week* 'a plane crash, a train crash, a quasi-rape and a beam in the church falling on Dan Archer's head'. As with the kidnap, the normally meticulous collective memory of the village gets a little hazy here. The actors were terrified they would all be Grace Archered, but it was Lynch who disappeared.

From around this time the BBC came to terms with its creation: *The Archers* was a rural programme for urban listeners. They did not need to know the details of dealing with the multifarious diseases of sheep, nor did they want multiple catastrophes. They wanted a sense of the countryside that was simultaneously a bit idealized and a bit over-dramatized. The programme had to speak to a specifically English dream: the eternal fantasy of a cottage in an eternal springtime with cheery, caring neighbours. For most of the population living in their cramped reality, 'their relationship with this arcadia is that of some emotional remittance man', as Jeremy Paxman later put it in *The English*.

But now an increasing number of people were starting to make the fantasy come true.

———·———

Suddenly people wanted to live in Ambridge or somewhere very like it. City life was losing its allure, as house prices, traffic and the crime rate all went up. A generation with little or no memory of the war and privation were now meeting, marrying, mating and making a home (though no longer necessarily in that order). Most were now able to take for granted the luxuries for which their parents had saved and strived.

So just at the very moment that the Heath government was prioritizing economic growth, the whole concept was being questioned from below. This counter-revolution took many forms: the long-haired undergraduate who protested about the evils of capitalism a few years earlier might now be a long-haired hippie weaving baskets in an off-grid commune in mid-Wales – or a smart young executive commuting long distances on the still relatively uncluttered motorways, or heading off on Fridays to a weekend cottage.

The nostalgia for Paxman's arcadia was an early manifestation of the change. The cottages that survived the habit of demolishing them, which had been going on for centuries, now became highly desirable, partly because London prices were already off the launch pad and heading for outer space, and partly because the baby boom generation had acquired a taste for the old and quaint.

In December 1970, *Country Life* said demand was now exceeding supply. By 1971 ('a year of never-ending demand') it was shocked to report that three-bedroom thatched cottages in Sussex with a quarter of an acre were now going for almost £14,000. A cottage in the Mendips was on sale in 1972 for £7,950, very steep that far from London. By November 1973 it was 'increasingly difficult to find an unmodernised cottage for sale in England . . . hardly any left in Suffolk'.

This had effects that have never gone away. Cornish coastal villages were already deserted in winter. In 1972, the vicar of

Birchover, Derbyshire, said that he himself had given space in his home to a local boy and his bride for the past year. 'A cottage on the edge of the village was recently sold for £10,000,' he said. 'What chance do young people have of finding a home?' Even the magazine *Industrial Management* was a little shame-faced about the trend: 'The villages are no longer the sort of place where a country person can feel at home. The talk in the bar tends to be about production figures instead of harvest yields.' However, the message that came through was buy now, don't dither.* Harrods estate agency commented: 'Everyone now wants honeysuckle over the door, oak beams, Elizabethan bricks and a modernized kitchen.' Well, there were limits to the nostalgia: the incomers were not seeking a return to frozen pipes and the mangle.

Another aspect of the new mood was a sudden upsurge of grief for the loss of houses once again beyond the reach of all but the topmost industrial managers, though they could have been bought for a song in the fifties. This was precipitated by an exhibition at the Victoria and Albert Museum in late 1974, *The Destruction of the Country House*, recording the loss of the stately and semi-stately homes of England in the previous hundred years. There were at least a thousand of them – perhaps two thousand – that had been demolished, gutted, left to decay or accidentally, you know, burned down. Not much disappeared before 1914, much went in the upheaval after the First World War, but more than half the destruction came after the Second – when the process of listing and protecting historic buildings was already under way. One lost house every five days in 1955, it was estimated.

It was actually a Labour government – some way beyond its traditional sphere of interests – that finally halted the carnage in 1968 by stiffening the law and forcing owners to ask permission to demolish listed buildings rather than merely telling the council.

---

* Circa 1974 I was living in the Northamptonshire village of Badby. I would stare lovingly and hopelessly at an eccentric cottage in the village, on the market at £14,000, and mentioned this to a fellow drinker in the Maltsters Arms. 'That place?' he said. 'I saw it sold in this very bar just after the war. Twenty-five quid on a handshake.'

It had tapered off before then, because land and property were already starting to look a good investment after many years of decline. But still, multiple environmental disputes were now taking a shape that transcended party lines. Sentimentalists v. pragmatists, if you like.

'Many was the time I stood in that exhibition watching the tears stream down the visitors' faces,' said Roy Strong, the young director of the V&A. The demolitions were 'a social cataclysm . . . an architectural and cultural tragedy', wrote the architectural critic Giles Worsley. That all may seem a touch over the top, but the British formed a firm view around this time that old buildings will generally be replaced by something uglier, less lasting and often less practical.

———•———

It was hard to know whether the retreat into the past was primarily a refuge from the pessimism that would slowly engulf Britain in the 1970s or a reaction to the excess of modernity that preceded it. But it was very real. Old oak furniture started fetching surprisingly high prices at London auction houses. The wistfulness extended to the recently closed railways – and above all the steam trains that had puffed slowly through the green meadows. Three enthusiasts were fined £25 for trying to take a TRESPASSERS WILL BE PROSECUTED sign from the closed-down station at Abingdon, which, like much else, was being left to decay. If the railway managers had had any imagination, they would have collected such objects and sent them to Sotheby's.

Hundreds of folk song clubs operated in pubs, bridging the gap between rock and the nation's rustic roots. Village cricket took on a new lease of life as the industrial managers linseed-oiled their bats; and in 1972 a national tournament began and 795 villages entered, each with a population of under 2,500, culminating in a final at Lord's. The Test-cricketer-turned-writer Ian Peebles was there, and bemoaned the absence of 'sheep, braces, cow pats, long grass and the vicar'. He was also troubled by the immaculate kit and the high standard, but then he hadn't seen the other 793 teams.

And this same mood brought forth perhaps the most effective of all British consumer campaigns, conducted against overwhelming odds. Historically, Britain had many hundreds of local breweries producing beer that varied from the delectable to the disgusting. And there were strong regional preferences among drinkers: in Yorkshire they liked a good head of froth; Birmingham remained loyal to mild ale rather than bitter.

By the end of the 1960s, the breweries had been whittled down to around a hundred, dominated by seven huge combines that were rapidly eating the survivors.* As they did so, they modernized the product and introduced keg bitter, which had many advantages: it was easy to transport, could be advertised nationally, did not go off, required minimal skill from the landlord, and the bar staff did not have to pull heavy hand pumps. It had just one disadvantage: it was gassy and tasteless.

The best known was Watney's Red Barrel. Now only the earworm remains:

> Drink Red Barrel, near or far
> In pub or club or any bar
> It's always good wherever you are
> Watney's Keg Red Barrel.

It had been developed in 1931 to be shipped to the expats running the empire and was ideal for that purpose. But it was a poor imitation of the ale of Olde England. Even so, Watney's were now imposing it on the thousands of pubs at home who were contractually obliged to sell its products.

In early 1971, four blokes in a bar were moaning about the quality of the beer, as well one might. This turned into the Campaign for Real Ale (CAMRA). During an early argument with Bass Charrington, who controlled even more pubs than Watney's,

---

* Manchester (especially) and Nottingham still had strong competing local breweries, and pints there were cheaper than anywhere except Carlisle, where the brewery was nationalized – a charming historic quirk until it offended Ted Heath's tidy mind and he insisted on selling it off.

the company accused them of talking 'romantic hogwash'. Slowly, CAMRA's membership grew, and traditional ale began to return to the nation's pubs. Bass Charrington and Watney's no longer exist.

———·———

Another much-loved staple of Arcadia was less fortunate. There is evidence of the elm tree in Britain from the Pleistocene era; there is precious little evidence left from the 1970s. It was, and all too rarely still is, a lovely tree that graced the hedgerows of southern England in particular: a kind of feminine counterpart to the sturdy, masculine oak. The elm was varied; even experts might struggle to distinguish one type from another because they interbred. It was moody and inclined – according to folklore – to drop a branch at whim as soon as anyone walked underneath ('elm hateth man, and waiteth'). The wood was versatile though regarded as a bugger by craftsmen because it was tough to work. But underneath the façade of temperamental beauty, the elm turned out to be pathetically vulnerable.

Dutch elm disease had been identified in the Netherlands in 1919 and noticed in Britain in 1927. It was caused by a fungus spread by a beetle that burrowed into the bark, set up home and trashed it. At first, the damage was limited: it was possible to lop off an infected branch and save the tree. But a more virulent strain spread across North America in the 1960s. And Britain, in keeping with its erratic attitude to immigration, never noticed the imports of Canadian rock elm that were blamed: research suggested it spread from the south coast ports around 1970. By the time anyone spotted the first indicator – leaves turning brown in midsummer – each tree was doomed.

The figures are erratic too. But an informed guesstimate was that Britain had 22 million mature elms and that two-thirds had gone by 1980. Most of the survivors went later and there has still been no ceasefire: healthy saplings get picked off as soon as they reach adolescence – the beetles must have an intelligence network far more effective than MI5.

Round about 1975, by which time they had ravaged all the elms in sight but before most of the dead trees were felled, a sense of desolation settled over the landscape which fitted the melancholia that was starting to blight the country. People who had never noticed the elms in their lifetime now mourned their loss. The one plus was that there was a little more realization about what else was at risk.*

———⸱———

In February 1970, BBC1 introduced a new drama series, *Doomwatch*, about a secret government department which had to save the nation from destruction every Monday for the next three months. It was written by Dr Kit Pedler and Gerry Davis, who had been involved with *Doctor Who* and were credited with creating the Cybermen. This was not, however, science fantasy; it was science fiction which at times touched on the wilder shores of science fact. And this spoke to the growing doubts about the Heathian worship of unmitigated progress for its own sake.

The first episode concerned a plastic-eating microorganism that was causing planes to fall out of the sky. The *Daily Mirror* thought it 'incredible', and not in a good way; 'veered towards the ridiculous,' said the *Express*. But *Doomwatch* became a big hit, the word itself successful enough to enter popular-press language (and the *Oxford English Dictionary*). Those heroes of the last two decades, the boffins, were now the potential enemy. The multiple fears this roused replaced the fading worry about being nuked.

Indeed, the *Mirror* started to use *doomwatch* as a decorative device on relevant stories: a black border with white lettering intoning the mantra

DOOMWATCH . . . DOOMWATCH . . . DOOMWATCH . . .

---

* Through a rare example of energetic and effective local government, with some assistance from the topography, East Sussex retained more elms than anywhere else. A mature wych elm close to my own home somehow survived until 2021. I miss it terribly.

Two years later, this surrounded the *Mirror* report on a long and portentous article called 'Blueprint for Survival', which had been published to great fanfare in *The Ecologist* magazine. Some of its prescriptions seem quaint: e.g. a two-child maximum. Others, like the threat posed by man-made chemicals, were very perceptive. The edition sold out, and some buyers may have read it all. The article did mark a starting point for the embryonic political wing of the environmental movement, but its progress was as slow as that of the earthworms its activists so valued.

Prophecies of doom came thick and fast in the 1970s: the possible extinction of the blue whale and the tiger; plastic beads in the Bristol Channel, believed to come from polystyrene manufacture; the dangers of lead in petrol; the threat of aerosol sprays to the ozone layer; and an alarming report in 1977 that enough material to make fifteen nuclear bombs had gone missing in British nuclear establishments in the past seven years. Officials would not reveal what safeguards were in place: security reasons, they said, or maybe embarrassment.

Britain was notably sluggish in taking environmental measures that would actually cost money. But in 1977 bottle banks made their British debut, in the contrasting settings of Oxford and Barnsley. And amid the post-imperial torpor, perhaps it was wise for the British to conclude that environmentalism begins at home.

Now people did stand in the way of progress, literally if necessary. Capitalism was of course on the other side. 'What we want are fifty-ton juggernauts,' said Sir Joseph Bamford, boss of JCB and patron saint of the backhoe. But the old sentiments had Labour adherents too. The party's leading intellectual, Tony Crosland, called conservationists 'a rich, upper-middle-class coterie bent on frustrating national growth to the detriment of the working class'. But that was not a unanimous view, and in the Tory party there was a clear distinction between conservative Conservatives and acquisitive Conservatives. Though they could be the same person: the developer Harry Hyams lived on a 600-acre estate in Wiltshire and guarded it ferociously against the slightest annoyance.

New estates, new factories and new roads in pristine places all led to regular fallouts about the value of aesthetics against homes and jobs. In the countryside the battle lines were often drawn between the leave-things-alone incomers and those whose grandparents lay in the churchyard.

In urban areas it worked a little differently, and the greatest battleground involved roads. In the late sixties, when Harold Wilson's ratings hit the floor, the Tories had swept the board in local elections. This included gaining control of the Greater London Council. London's new leader, Desmond Plummer, was a consensual kind of politician, but he loved his gold-coloured Mini Cooper and he did love his roads, seeing them as London's salvation.

Weeks after Plummer won a second term in 1970 and Heath entered Downing Street, that certainty collapsed. The new transport minister, John Peyton, and his young junior, Michael Heseltine, attended the official opening of the elevated Westway, the planned first stage of a network of urban motorways circling inner London. The neighbours turned up in force, and they were not after champagne and canapés. As Heseltine tried to cut the ribbon, they blocked the road within sight of a huge banner below the roofline of ill-fated Acklam Road: GET US OUT OF THIS HELL – REHOUSE US NOW.

Both ministers were shaken. 'What a mighty human problem roads like this pose,' said Heseltine. 'You cannot but have sympathy for these people.' Later that week, the noise in the nearest homes was recorded at twice the officially recommended maximum. Further information was hard to come by. As Liz Reeves, a 79-year-old widow whose house held the recording device, reported: 'It ticked like a giant alarm clock and went bang every hour. So I turned the damn thing off.'

One estimate was that by this time there were already a hundred local anti-motorway groups in the London neighbourhoods where people had seen the maps with dotted lines of projected motorways superimposed, and reacted in horror. And the lesson was that moderation did not pay. Residents of a block of flats in Hendon who just wrote polite letters when the M1 extension came past found their lives made misery and their home's value more than halved (from a notional £8,000 to about £3,500, if they could find someone desperate enough to buy it).

The government and council now began the familiar British process of dealing with failing policies: they set up committees, awaited reports, sidestepped, backtracked, made grudging concessions . . . In the end, the Labour opposition on the council withdrew support for the spider's web of ringways, fought the next London election on that basis, won – helped by Heath's unpopularity – and scrapped almost all of them. Which did not solve London's problems but did avoid a terrible answer: it was never clear where these cars would all end up – there was no room in the middle.

Rebellion spread. There was Bath, which in the early 1950s was still an almost complete Georgian city. Twenty years on, the artisan houses that made up much of the town, instead of subtly being given mod cons, were demolished and replaced by the standard mid-century cack: the set pieces like the Royal Crescent and the Pump Room were preserved of course, but, wrote Adam Fergusson in *The Sack of Bath*, 'they were like mountains without foothills, like Old Masters without frames'.

Conservation groups belatedly fought back. When a Birmingham-style tunnel was proposed to take traffic under Bath in 1972, it was howled down. The proposal came from a committee headed by Sir Colin Buchanan, who ten years earlier had been Ernest Marples's go-to man for separation schemes then much lauded as the solution to accommodate both urban traffic and pedestrians. But people hated them. When this plan was torn to pieces by public opinion, Buchanan reacted like a man from a lost world: 'Have attitudes to comprehensive redevelopment changed?' he asked pleadingly in *The Times*. 'Now there seems to be a hullabaloo if so much as a single house is threatened. What has happened?'

What had happened was a rebellion against top-down ideas. Oxford and York, two other urban gems, fought off inner ring roads. It could work the other way too: an ambitious park-and-ride scheme in Nottingham was junked when the motorists fought back. But pretty much every major road project was now under threat. And one man was largely responsible.

The very name John Tyme seemed to have come from the deepest mists of ancient England; he might have ridden with Wat Tyler or Hereward the Wake. He was in fact a slender and inoffensive-looking polytechnic lecturer who spent the 1970s terrorizing planning inspectors charged with assessing or, the government hoped, rubber-stamping plans for new motorways. Tyme first sprung to life fully armed when he arrived at an inquiry into the M16 north of London, which was due to batter its way through Epping Forest, and declared it illegal under Section 11 of the Highways Act 1959, and possibly an offence to Magna Carta and various pronouncements of the Witenagemot. When he was brushed aside, the inquiry was 'abandoned in uproar' and local protesters staged a sit-in.

Tyme would then reappear regularly at such inquiries, the reports being regularly sprinkled with the word *uproar*. With a grant from the Rowntree Trust he was able to take leave from his job to become a full-time anti-road protester. When argument failed, he and the local groups he was supporting attempted various forms of disruption. In the inquiry into the M3 at Winchester, he was joined by the headmaster of Winchester College – who got thrown out – and a man dressed as King Alfred. The inspector was greeted with Nazi salutes. In Ipswich (new bypass), Tyme himself refused to leave and padlocked himself to a table; he was carried out, table and all. At Accrington (M65), activists brought their children, who started playing with model cars on the inspector's desk and plonked a train set on the floor. In North London (Archway Road widening), the inspector retreated into what protesters called 'the bunker' and held hearings in private which were meant to be broadcast to the multitude – except that the equipment didn't work.

Tyme did work some miracles. The M16 never did happen as such: it was incorporated into the M25 and almost tiptoed round the forest in a tunnel under some heathland. Archway Road was not widened. The M3 round Winchester was delayed for twenty years and the line was moved, though it remained, to say the least, controversial. Peter Simple, the *Telegraph*'s romantic Tory columnist, suggested Tyme would be seen as 'a prophet and hero'. In fact, he has been largely forgotten but, twenty years after a brief *Times* obituary, his soul goes marching on.

———·———

There was one clash between the go-ahead nation the politicians wanted and the peaceful, unchanging land their voters wanted (certainly in their earshot and eyeline) which exceeded all the disputes over motorways laid end to end.

When traffic at Heathrow, then known simply as London Airport, expanded in the 1950s, thoughts turned to alternatives. After the usual prevarication, one wartime airfield, Gatwick, was preferred to another, Stansted. And when the working classes discovered that mysterious exurb of Britain known as 'Abroad' in the 1960s and a third airport loomed, Stansted seemed the obvious choice, though not to the residents of west Essex and east Hertfordshire.

An inquiry opened in 1965 and heard 260 objections, none of them from John Tyme. The inspector did not think Stansted a good site but his decision was not binding. Ditto John Betjeman: 'a place of elmy hills,' he called the district, 'willow-bordered streams, plaster and timber and old brick farms and cottages, water mills. flint churches and winding lanes and villages with greens and inns'. Misgivings spread, especially in parliament, but it was rammed through by the government – a decision that lasted until Harold Wilson's next reshuffle, which put Anthony Crosland at the relevant ministry, the Board of Trade.

Crosland did not care for elmy hills but he studied the cost-benefit analysis and concluded Stansted was wrong, took the matter back to Cabinet and prevailed. So in 1968 a full-scale commission was set up under the judge Sir John Roskill to make a judgment. There were seventy-eight (!)* possibles on Roskill's original long list, stretching across the south-eastern third of the British mainland

---

* All these sites – and a few more considered at other times – are mapped in David McKie's book *A Sadly Mismanaged Affair* (a title that could be used for hundreds of other books on British political fiascos).

from Ferrybridge in Yorkshire, a mere 180 miles from London, to the south coast and west Wiltshire.

This was whittled down to twenty-nine and then a final four: Cublington (Bucks), Nuthampstead (Herts), Thurleigh (Beds) and Foulness (Essex). Stansted was considered but did not make the short list. The judges eyed them up as if it were a Miss World contest, vital statistics and all. Cublington had the most vociferous objectors, and Betjeman said it was the worst choice. But it was relatively cheap and the airlines liked it, as did all but one of the six-strong panel. The exception was Colin Buchanan, proponent of the Bath tunnel.

By 1971 the Tories were back, under Heath, and he was very interested in Buchanan's thoughts. While the commission announced their choice of Cublington, Buchanan went for Foulness, the near-empty, numinous marshland on the tip of Essex. It was far more expensive than the others but he contended that the inland sites were all unacceptable on environmental grounds and the government agreed, not so much because the environment bothered them as such but because solid Tory Buckinghamshire was mutinous.

And for a while Foulness was all the go: its name was duly sanitized to Maplin, after the nearby mudflats not the island. Work would begin in two years, the government said; an eight-lane 'superway' would speed travellers to London; a new city would be built housing 300,000, and so on. But opinion was turning. Airlines thought Maplin a dreadful choice. And when the 1973 oil crisis struck, choosing the dearest option did not seem so attractive.

And Buchanan's notion of 'environment' was a limited one: he did not consider the thousands of Brent geese who spent their mating seasons in the Arctic and their winters feasting on eelgrass in Maplin Sands. Ornithologists were divided on the likelihood of bird strikes at the airport. But if a goose or their attendant mallard or wigeon staged an attack on a jet engine over Maplin it could wreak vengeful havoc in a manner far beyond anything the cricket-playing, cottage-dwelling, real-ale-drinking industrial managers of Buckinghamshire could ever manage.

Anyway, Labour came back to power in 1974 and scrapped the project. Thereafter it seems to have become generally understood that the whole business of commissions was absurd; siting an airport was a political decision, though it needed to be better thought-out than Maplin. So Stansted, which was already a functioning airport, began to experience 'limited growth'. No one said it had been chosen as the third London airport; it just happened. In the end, from a brutally political point of view, it was quite a well-managed affair.

6

AND THE BANDS
PLAYED ON

I F THE 1970S WAS A DECADE OF BLIGHTED HOPES, NOTHING
epitomized that more than Northern Ireland: a little local
difficulty that turned into a near-thirty years' war. And for what?
The situation was perfectly simple: a part of the United Kingdom
was being run in a manner not that dissimilar to Rhodesia, but with
discrimination based on religion rather than race.

For this outrage, the eternal Ulster Unionist regime and their
Protestant support base were responsible, abetted by the indifference
of successive British governments. Forced to act in 1969, the Wilson
government had insisted on 'reforms being carried out . . . based on
the practice and principle of non-discrimination', as the 1970
Labour manifesto put it. And the Northern Ireland prime minister,
by then James Chichester-Clark (Eton and Sandhurst), had publicly
agreed to that.

How on earth did this lead to the loss of 3,500 lives? Civilians,
soldiers, police and paramilitaries; in Ulster, the Irish Republic,
England, even the Netherlands and Gibraltar; killed in action, in
pubs, in their own homes, on buses, at remote border crossings;
targeted killings, random killings, cock-up killings; by guns, bombs,
landmines; the Dowager Baroness Brabourne, aged 83, by the bomb
targeting Earl Mountbatten; Colin Nicholl, 17 months, in his pram.

For all these outrages, the responsibility must be shared more
evenly. In 1963, the segregationist governor of Alabama, George

Wallace, 'stood in the schoolhouse door' to prevent two black students being registered at the state university. Wallace gave over after making his point. For decades the malevolent preacher Rev. Ian Paisley metaphorically blocked the door by firing up Protestant opinion against any glimmer of compromise in his benighted province.

The worst excesses of official sectarianism were softened in the early years. But there was still a nexus of unionist control – the quasi-masonic Orange Order; the police and the locally recruited Ulster Defence Regiment linked on the one hand to the Protestant paramilitaries and on the other to the British Army. And once the Army had alienated the Catholic minority and the Irish Republican Army effectively declared war on the British, the military had no idea at all what was really happening in Catholic areas. They had very weak intelligence, often in both senses of the word.

Then there was the Provisional IRA itself, once it had vigorously thrust aside the old-style Official IRA. Operationally, its guerrilla activities had mixed success: sometimes brilliantly executed (in their own terms), but often botched; bombers regularly blew themselves up. Tactically, they were sometimes brilliant, switching tack and finding new targets no one else had foreseen. But the whole IRA strategy had a fundamental flaw. They thought they would drive the British out of Ireland. Yet each new horror made that less and less thinkable. And had they persisted with bombing London tubes and trains in rush hour (which they toyed with briefly), the retribution might have been fearful.

In due course, the British police and legal system disgraced themselves when a succession of suspects were arrested, beaten up in some cases, charged, convicted and imprisoned for several of the worst atrocities committed on the mainland – only for their convictions to be reversed after they had languished in jail for years.

And then there was the British government. Even before the 1970 election there were signs that Jim Callaghan's mercy mission from 1969 had turned into something different, as the Provisionals became increasingly daring. Asked what he felt when Sir Ian Freeland, head of the Army, warned that troops would shoot-to-kill petrol bombers if they defied warnings, Callaghan replied:

'How is the Army supposed to behave when petrol bombs are thrown at them?'

A few weeks later, Labour was out and Callaghan was replaced as Home Secretary by Reggie Maudling, less engaged with politics since Heath had beaten him to the leadership and with little appetite for, or empathy with, the increasing horrors of Ulster. His most famous quote may well be his remark as he flew back home after his first visit, which went something like: 'What a bloody awful place. Get me a large Scotch.' The brief passage on the province in the Tories' 1970 manifesto looked as though it had been drafted by the Ulster Unionists – as, at first, did many of their policies.

Two weeks after the election, the Army moved into the Catholic stronghold of the Lower Falls in Belfast, which had been allowed to stand as a no-go area. Looking for weaponry, they found themselves in a gun battle and used CS gas to quell rioters. Then General Freeland imposed a 36-hour curfew, which was probably an abuse of his authority. The soldiers did not behave kindly and there were accusations of looting. Four civilians died. In 2019, a bright and thoughtful Belfast woman was interviewed by the BBC on the fiftieth anniversary of the first major riots.

'I think the curfew was the turning point in terms of how the Catholic population saw the soldiers,' she said.

'To this day you believe the IRA's cause was justified?'

'Yes.'

It was also a time when Northern Ireland hinted at one of its best-kept secrets. At one point of the curfew, journalists were allowed in under armed escort. The idea of Belfast as a war zone was still novel: 'We roared around the debris-strewn backstreets, with the householders' faces peering – frightened, angry, contemptuous or blank – from behind the lace and aspidistra,' wrote Harold Jackson of *The Guardian*, who had been in many war zones before and was not shocked. But . . . 'This was Belfast on a Saturday afternoon. It was grotesque.'

Jackson had also been there on the Friday night when the gas was flying. He had only a handkerchief to protect him, which was not enough. But women put out buckets of water and a dash of vinegar. '"Here, love," one shouted to me, "dab it with this," and she ripped a length from the bottom of her apron to dip it in the bucket. Another took me into her house to soothe my burning throat with water. No one asked who I was.'

And this was the secret. To their close-to-hand enemies, the otherwise ordinary people of the province could be callous and implacable; to the neutral stranger it was 'come into the parlour.' On mainland Britain, news bulletins were full of the terrors, which were real enough, but none of the context. In the 1970s your mum might just about accept it if you said you were gay; tell her you were heading to Ulster and she would recoil in horror. The very accent became inextricably associated with the stern threats of Paisley and Gerry Adams.

Yet those who were posted there had a habit of falling deeply in love with the place. For the squaddies, it was not a drill but real soldiering, which is what most wanted. The attendant civil servants flown over when London's involvement got ever deeper loved it too. 'It was like stepping back into a warm cocoon,' recalled one. 'Clean air, empty roads, friendly shops. If I could ever persuade anyone to come over and stay with me, they felt just the same. I know people who decided to retire there.'*

Of course there was danger. Anyone associated with the government had to steer clear of the Catholic areas. Only journalists had the run of the place, more or less safely. 'Everyone was terribly nice,' said Bob Chesshyre of *The Observer*, a frequent visitor in the early seventies. 'They might be killing each other at night but in the daytime they were absolutely charming.'

As so often, it looked far worse on TV. The average annual death toll attributed to the Troubles was very similar to the number killed on Northern Ireland's roads in the years beforehand. Admittedly, the first five years of the Troubles were particularly bloody.

---

* Derry/Londonderry is the only city I have ever visited, rather than a small town or village, where people habitually said 'Good morning' to strangers in the street.

But even in the worst places, at the worst times, normal life went on.*

The partially immunized press needed a sixth sense for possible danger. Chesshyre, like almost everyone, had the odd near miss. But these situations can be invigorating. As in wartime London, the heightened possibility of sudden death encouraged and enhanced both sexual coupling and laughter. There was also a particular, well, Irish dimension: whatever ghastliness was being perpetrated a certain madcap quality would often emerge. As G. K. Chesterton put it:

> *The great Gaels of Ireland*
> *Are the men that God made mad,*
> *For all their wars are merry*
> *And all their songs are sad.*

———•———

It was, surprisingly, February 1971 before the first British soldier was killed: Gunner Robert Curtis, who had just received a letter from his wife saying he was about to be a father. The Provisional IRA had now seized the initiative from the outmoded Official IRA. They brought a new casual brutality to Irish violence, typified by the five men killed by a landmine in County Tyrone on their way to inspect a BBC transmitter. The mine was intended for an army patrol but, well, these things happen. It was nothing personal. It was for the great cause of a united Ireland. No matter that the Irish Republic had very little interest in taking over their batty neighbours; and that the Republic itself – poor, behind-the-times and priest-ridden – was a thoroughly unattractive proposition in the 1970s.

That March, Maudling told the Stormont parliament that violence could not be tolerated. By December he was talking about 'an acceptable level of violence'. In between, Ulster had acquired its

---

* I met a woman who lived near the border in South Armagh, 'bandit country'. She was telling me how they had to search under the car every morning in case there was a car bomb. I must have grimaced. 'I don't know how you live in London,' she said. 'All that crime.'

sixth, last, most professional and, as it turned out, shortest-serving prime minister. Brian Faulkner replaced Chichester-Clark, who had failed to persuade Heath to improve security and given up. Faulkner was a Harold Wilson figure, admired but distrusted. His big idea was internment – rounding up all the suspects. He got it past a despairing Heath and Maudling, who had no other ideas.

So, before dawn on 9 August 1971, 342 men, all from Catholic areas, were taken from their homes. There followed a series of self-satisfied announcements from the Army and officials: 'successful because of the complete secrecy'; 'by no means dissatisfied', culminating in 'the hard core of the IRA has been virtually defeated' from the Army's chief of staff. These remarks came from the school of self-delusion that simultaneously characterized American statements about the war in Vietnam. More objective observers quickly concluded it was a blunder, and more slowly realized it was a blunder that covered up British crimes comparable with the worst excesses of empire. Not in the rice paddies or the Highveld or the South Arabian badlands, but inside the United Kingdom.

First, the fiasco. Complete secrecy included not alerting and squaring Jim Callaghan, now Maudling's shadow, but the IRA knew all right and many of their men had slipped away. Often, their fathers and brothers were arrested instead. More than a hundred were so obviously innocent they had to be released within forty-eight hours. Thousands of homes were raided, much property being destroyed in the process. The prisoners were held in terrible conditions. There would in time be much semantic discussion about whether the internees were greeted with 'ill-treatment', 'brutality' or 'torture'. There can be little doubt the techniques veered towards the upper end of the scale, and it was mindless brutality at that.

Many more suspects were picked up in the months ahead, some of them actually Protestants. It all constituted the most successful recruitment campaign since Lord Kitchener's pointing finger in 1914; the IRA could never have been so successful without governmental help. The violence increased exponentially, which in turn electrified the inchoate Protestant paramilitaries and led to the tit-for-tat killings that would characterize the years ahead.

One microcosm of the first seizures occurred on the Ballymurphy estate, where ten civilians, including a priest, were shot dead during and after the initial raids. Ballymurphy was a sullen and impoverished post-war Catholic sink estate, reputedly without the vibrant laughing spirit of the hugger-mugger terraced streets. No one saw anything except local people and members of the first battalion of the Parachute Regiment, neither group impartial; investigation at the time was perfunctory at best. The initial inquest was inconclusive; forty-nine years and nine months later, a second inquest was very conclusive. Dame Siobhan Keegan, shortly to be Northern Ireland's chief justice, concluded that the residents were more reliable witnesses than the soldiers; that at least nine of the ten had been shot by the British Army; that all the dead were unarmed and posing no threat; and that several had been shot in the back, including the priest, Father Hugh Mullan, who was tending a wounding man.

The regiment learned nothing from this, and just under six months later they were involved in, and much later held responsible for, a mass killing that was far more public, would have far more resonance and had a catastrophic effect on Britain's reputation. This was Bloody Sunday.

The occasion was a civil rights march through the streets of Derry to protest against internment. It had been banned by the Faulkner government but this was a regime whose legitimacy was now questioned from every quarter. There was clearly the potential for a riot, and indeed one broke out when the marchers hit army barricades – though not in the Rossville Street square where the men of 1 Para, who already had Ballymurphy on their record, opened fire.

The scene there, as reported by Simon Winchester of *The Guardian*, was of thousands of people drifting towards a protest meeting until a group of armoured cars careered in, paratroopers got out and began firing into the crowd. The Army said this was because 'a number of snipers' had opened fire on them. But Winchester said that he and others present had only heard one shot. 'One came away with the firm impression, reinforced by dozens of eyewitnesses, that the soldiers may have fired needlessly.'

This instant judgment, dictated under pressure down the telephone, took more than thirty-eight years to be verified, by the ineffably painstaking inquiry set up under Lord Justice Saville in 1998 which reported in 2010. Thirteen unarmed civilians died on the day; a fourteenth death later has been attributed to the shooting. Eleven thick volumes of evidence and an estimated £191 million later, Savile rejected the verdict of Lord Widgery at the initial inquiry that the Army was not to blame. Instead he singled out the battalion commander, Lieutenant-Colonel Derek Wilford, for disobeying orders and sending his men into a situation where just this outcome was likely to happen.

———·———

After Bloody Sunday, madness became endemic. 1972 would be the most deadly year of all: 476 deaths, more than half of them non-combatants, unfortunates who happened to be in the wrong place at the wrong time; 2,000 explosions, 2,000 armed robberies, 10,000 shooting incidents. It was the year the IRA discovered the car bomb. Even before this, stupidity lurked on every side. Just before Christmas 1971, a bomb killed fifteen in a Belfast Catholic bar, McGurk's, and the Royal Ulster Constabulary, deeply rooted in the loyalist community, assumed it was the IRA blowing themselves up.*

The Army was even more hopeless. 'Because we could talk to both sides, you learned more as a journalist in a week about what was happening there than the authorities ever did,' recalled Bob Chesshyre. 'They didn't know who the enemy was. The army

---

* 'Loyalist' and 'unionist' in Northern Ireland refer to those Protestants who are loyal to the Union, the Crown and Britain, though their loyalty tends to be greatest when they get their own way. The constitutional Catholics became the Social Democratic and Labour Party (SDLP) and were considered 'nationalists'. The more extreme wing voted for Sinn Féin – considered 'republican' when they deigned to stand for election. By 1973 a new middle-of-the-road party, Alliance, had been formed for the very small minority who thought religion did not matter. If you half understand that you are better informed than at least one recent Northern Ireland Secretary of State. Technically, Northern Ireland is not historic Ulster, which has nine counties not six, but they have long been used as synonyms in Great Britain.

officers and men were rotated in and out too regularly ever to get an understanding of the place. And they couldn't get beyond blaming the Catholics for everything.' At times it was like *Lord of the Flies*. Another writer, Kevin Myers, told of a group of teenagers splattering ammo everywhere with huge sub-machine guns and semi-automatic rifles from the infamous Belfast sniper base called the Divis Flats. By pure chance, one bullet penetrated the observation slit of an armoured car and killed a newly arrived lieutenant. The Army thought a new super-sniper was at large.

The gang was led, said Myers, by an 'infant-Rommel'. This was Gerard Steenson, whose short life was an extreme case of growing up in the wild West Belfast of the 1970s, much like Billy the Kid in the wild West of the 1870s. In time Steenson would become involved in multiple assassinations, acquire the nickname Dr Death, and be described by a judge as the most dangerous man he had ever dealt with. He died in a flurry of bullets, aged 29, during a feud between rival republican factions. His mum said he was a keep-fit addict who 'lived for athletics and gymnastics'.

It is fair to say that those drawn to the paramilitaries shared a mixture of some or all of these characteristics: idealism, initiative, thrill-seeking, bravery, an urge to emulate their forebears, ruthlessness, Caponesque gangsterism, vindictiveness and psychopathy. And some were more psychopathic than others.

There was, however, a different quality to the violence from each side and the general attitude to the other community. 'The Protestants really despised the Catholics,' according to Chesshyre. 'They were seen as feckless, living off the state with millions of children. There wasn't the same feeling in reverse. The Catholics didn't hate the Protestants, they just hated the way they had treated them.' There did seem to be more venom when the Protestants were doing the killing. With the Republican paramilitaries, murder was business, not personal – unless they were killing one of their own for some reason, in which case it was very personal.

Loyalist murders could also have strange connections. In 1975, three members of the Miami Showband, a group whose popularity spanned all sections of the island, were murdered in an act that stood out for its vileness even in this vast catalogue of horrors. It was carried out by the paramilitary Ulster Volunteer Force, who pretended to be soldiers, set up a fake checkpoint and stopped the band's minibus.

They planted a bomb on the bus, which exploded prematurely and killed two of the gang. The surviving gang members then shot three of the bandsmen instead. The weird part is that at least four of the killers were also real soldiers – past or present part-time members of the locally raised Ulster Defence Regiment, and thus attached to the British Army. There were also suspicions that British intelligence was involved. No wonder the Catholics were bitter and distrustful.

Amid their own bloodthirstiness, the IRA were capable of a certain whimsical showmanship. To the outside world, the Europa Hotel in Belfast sounded like the hotel from hell. Between 1970 (before it even opened) and 1994, it was bombed thirty-three times, twenty in the first three crazy years. But actually this was the safe haven: every journalist would check in because it was the base for all the news and gossip – and for all those, even some paramilitaries, who wished to impart it. And it was run with an imperturbable efficiency – even, or perhaps especially, when it was bombed or a nearby bomb blew the windows in.

And the band played on – or at least the Penthouse Poppets, Belfast's answer to the Bunny Girls, kept serving the drinks. Once a customer in one of the bars found himself getting drenched because a bomb had gone off in a rooftop water tank and it was dripping down through the floors. He unfurled his umbrella and held it aloft with one hand, his glass in the other. Only in Ireland. This was terrorism as statement, to make sure the hacks got the message about what the IRA could do if it wanted. The total death toll at the Europa was zero, and very few were even slightly hurt.

———·———

The day after Bloody Sunday, the fiery Irish MP Bernadette Devlin marched across the floor of the House of Commons and started thumping the fleshy Home Secretary; no punishment ensued. ('She almost woke him up,' someone remarked.) The next day, Heath set up the Widgery inquiry, the Lord Chief Justice sitting alone to avoid dissent muddying the intended result. The following day, a huge crowd in Dublin burned down the British Embassy.

Nine weeks later, Widgery did what he was meant to do: heaped the blame on the marchers and putrefied his immortal soul. But Heath was truly engaging with the issues now and he'd had enough of Faulkner, who had bounced him into internment. He demanded that London take charge of security and move towards the end of internment and the start of power-sharing. Faulkner, under severe pressure from his potentially violent right-wingers, resigned with all his Cabinet. The Stormont parliament was suspended (in practice abandoned after fifty years of dismal one-party rule) and direct rule imposed from London. In a sense it unified the two extremes: Protestant opinion was rancid, and the last thing the IRA wanted was being bound closer to Britain. But Heath, in many ways the least political of prime ministers, had outsmarted the supposedly serpentine Faulkner, just as he had outsmarted Wilson in 1970.

William Whitelaw was appointed Secretary of State, in practice governor, of Northern Ireland. It was a well-crafted appointment. He was an emollient man with much charm (and very occasional volcanic eruptions) and the great gift of appearing more stupid than he actually was. And Maudling no longer had to deal with the 'bloody awful place'.*

Whitelaw reached out to everyone he could and, during a brief ceasefire by the IRA, one of his conciliatory gestures was to give paramilitary prisoners 'special category' status – in effect accepting they were political prisoners, not the criminals the British had always maintained. He later admitted this was a huge mistake.

It did give cover to an extraordinary event in which six Provisional IRA leaders were flown under safe passage to a secret meeting with Whitelaw in London. They included the rising stars of the

---

* Maudling's intake of scotch that night must have been celebratory rather than consolatory; but in time, his reputation shredded by his association with the crooked architect John Poulson, alcohol became the death of him.

organization, Gerry Adams and Martin McGuinness, aged 24 and 22; McGuinness was very impressed by the fancy cars involved; Whitelaw was not impressed by their skills. All they demanded was for the British to signal their intent to withdraw from Northern Ireland. Nothing would have given the vast majority of Britain greater pleasure than seeing the whole place sink into the sea, but it was obviously impossible for the government.

The IRA leaders went home, and in July – the month when Satan reigned supreme – made two massive mistakes of their own. On a rare balmy Friday afternoon, the streets of Belfast crowded with shoppers from both communities, nineteen bombs went off in sixty-five minutes, the most deadly in the Oxford Street bus station. The IRA claimed they gave warnings, but many were said to be hoaxes and the sheer scale of the operation meant that anyone who escaped one bomb might find only false sanctuary somewhere else. Nine people were killed, and many of the 130 injured people were maimed terribly. Outside the bus station, said a report in *The Observer*, 'there were large, mainly unrecognisable pieces of flesh scattered all over the road as if somebody had looted a butcher's shop'. Some vertebrae and a rib cage were found on a nearby roof a few days later, but only because seagulls were pecking at them.

Can any good redeem such evil? In the South, the infatuation with the IRA that had taken hold after Bloody Sunday plummeted after what became known as Bloody Friday. 'There is a black sin on the face of Irish Republicanism today that will never be erased. Murder now lies at the feet of the Irish nation,' said the Dublin *Sunday Independent*.

In the short term it gave Whitelaw political cover to authorize the Army to undertake Operation Motorman, regaining control of the no-go areas in Belfast and Londonderry, including the long-standing stronghold of Free Derry.

And in the long term Belfast's Royal Victoria Hospital acquired remarkable expertise in dealing with such disasters. It is said that the technique of 'triage' for instant assessment of patients' needs was developed here. And, more definitively, the 'intraluminal shunt', a means of preventing the build-up of fluid. This was mainly relevant to the gruesome but non-fatal injuries caused by punishment shootings, particularly the phenomenon known as kneecapping, what medics called Belfast Limb Arterial and Skeletal Trauma (BLAST). Decisions on whether to amputate or not were taken on the basis of the Mangled Extremity Scoring System (MESS). Doctors have always had a taste for *noir* humour and never was it more needed than in Belfast in 1972.

But there was another outrage even as the troops swept on with Motorman, untroubled by any direct republican retaliation. Three car bombs went off in the tiny village of Claudy, County Londonderry, 'a lazy, happy-go-lucky little place' as the local MP put it, and previously untouched by the insanity. Nine people were killed, shared between Catholic and Protestant as on Bloody Friday. Someone did apparently try to phone a warning but could not find a working telephone box due to previous bombings. No one has ever claimed responsibility, but suspicion has centred on a now long-dead Catholic priest who was swiftly translated to a parish across the border. Cry, the beloved island.

———◦———

When it opened in 1964, the Post Office Tower was the tallest building in London. It was a source of great excitement and fascination: it was full of gadgetry to make London part of the dawning age of telecommunications; you could take a lift to the top and see the view; and what's more you could eat in the thirty-fourth-floor revolving restaurant, run by the holiday camp king Billy Butlin. The restaurant, just like the Hilton Hotel and Bunny Girls, was an alluringly American concept. On 31 October 1971 a bomb was left close to the restaurant. It exploded at 4.30 a.m., no one was hurt and the IRA claimed responsibility. But something was damaged beyond repair: the nation's sense of safety.

The British mainland, with the odd small lapse in Wales, had effectively been a terror-free zone since the last V-2 bomb in 1945. Terrorism was what happened abroad; the very word came from the French Revolution. In 1968, *The Guardian* used the word just four times in a UK context: three of them about the handful of Welsh bombings, the other about a racist attack on a bus conductor in Oxford. In 1969 it came up twice, obliquely, in the context of Ulster.

Even when hijacking became a trend in the late sixties, the early cases tended to have elements of lunacy, humour or heroism, e.g. attempted escapes from Communism. Even when it got more serious, this brushed Britain lightly. In September 1970, during a series of hijackings by Palestinians and their supporters, a man and a woman took over an El Al flight to New York over the North Sea. Sky marshals shot the man dead and the pilot landed in London, leaving the charismatic Palestinian refugee Leila Khaled in the care of the British government.

Ministers had to decide whether or not the hijack took place more than twelve miles from Clacton and thus whether or not Khaled had done anything wrong under British jurisdiction apart from landing without a visa. Having concluded the answer was 'no', they exchanged her for hostages. And when the *Queen Elizabeth 2*, the pride of the Cunard fleet, was threatened with being blown up in mid-Atlantic, it turned out to be not just a hoax but one perpetrated by the desperate owner of a failing shoe shop (Joseph's Bootery) in the New York commuter belt.

The first bombings in London came in 1970 and 1971 from the Angry Brigade, an organization that operated somewhere between old-fashioned anarchist bomb-making and a varsity rag week. They spread alarm but hurt only a single soul. The first confirmed IRA attack on the mainland since the 1930s came just three weeks after Bloody Sunday, in Aldershot, outside the Parachute Regiment's officers' mess. It killed seven people: five women who worked as waitresses and kitchen staff, a gardener and a single army officer – a Catholic chaplain. Genius. This was an Official IRA operation, and they more or less gave up after this wicked imbecility.

But every bombing chipped away at Britain's self-assurance and invulnerability. No more would prime ministers walk home alone from the Carlton Club, as Sir Alec used to do. It was not until 1989 that Margaret Thatcher put security gates across the time-honoured pedestrian shortcut from Whitehall to St James's Park known as

Downing Street, but by then it was a natural next step. Left luggage lockers disappeared from railway stations, as did wastepaper bins. No more would passengers see an unattended piece of luggage on the tube and think, 'Oh, poor chap's left his bag behind.' After the QE2 bomb threat, passengers could no longer invite their friends to tour the ship before sailing. In time the restaurant at the Post Office Tower closed for ever, as did the viewing platform. And the whole country became more uptight, nervous and mean.

————∘————

The Provisional IRA, having concluded that subjecting their own supporters to random massacres was not the best strategy, were quieter for a while – though there was still plenty of violence. Meanwhile, Whitelaw worked tirelessly to put together a constitutional package which reasonable people on both sides might accept: a new assembly elected by proportional representation, essential given Ulster's demography; a coalition executive; a much tighter rein from London; and some kind of cross-border co-operation.

The trouble was that reason was in retreat. The assembly was duly elected, and did meet for a while even though there was no executive. And although Faulkner still led the Ulster Unionists they were outnumbered by the Protestant extremists. The same might have happened on the Catholic side except that the IRA's allies, Sinn Féin, boycotted the whole thing.

The assembly was not a meeting of minds: the day before the more moderate party leaders were due to meet the leaders of Britain and Ireland, the immoderate loyalist assembly members started thumping their less bellicose co-religionists. Among other excitements, a representative of Paisley's Democratic Unionists raced along the backbenches punching heads in turn with a moderate voice calling out, 'Vile beasts! Vile beasts!'

The next day, the men of reason met amid the calm neo-Georgian surroundings of Sunningdale Civil Service College in Berkshire. It was a little ill-starred from the off: Whitelaw had just been yanked out of Belfast to try his special balm on the mutinous miners and was replaced by Francis Pym, another conciliator. Both were ill-prepared for the challenges they now urgently faced.

But the Sunningdale deal was hailed as a triumph, with all the conditions for a new cross-party executive being met. When Heath returned to the Commons the following week he was cheered even by the Labour benches and indeed one Ulster Unionist MP, Stanley McMaster, who called it 'far-sighted'. Too far-sighted, it turned out. When all parties to the conflict finally signed a remarkably similar agreement, the SDLP politician Seamus Mallon called it 'Sunningdale for slow learners'. This was twenty-five years and thousands of violent deaths later.

The executive did exist briefly, limping on until after Heath lost power to Wilson in February 1974. But in the Northern Ireland seats the Protestant moderates were crushed by the extremists – and though Faulkner was notionally in charge of the executive he kept being jostled and spat on inside the chamber. Finally one loyalist group called a general strike to bring an end to the whole notion of power-sharing.

It was hardly taken seriously at first; most Protestants went to work as usual. But it grew, partly because of the use of 'persuasion', a word that can mean something different in the Shankill compared to Sunningdale or even Saltley. Barricades blocked the roads and oil depots, guarded by fierce young men uninterested in intellectual discussion. The Army and police shrugged.

Another factor was the province's largely segregated workforce, and the Ballylumford power station, which served most of the province including Belfast, was overwhelmingly loyalist and pro-strike. The Army did not have the expertise to run Ballylumford even if ordered, which they weren't. And that was the end of Sunningdale; direct rule would go on and on; and the remedial learning was a long way from even starting.

———·———

By now the Provisional IRA had moved on. Like a provincial repertory company wanting to hit the big time, they had taken their show to the West End – including high-profile targets in London and the big provincial cities. The British public now took little notice of murders in Northern Ireland. Bombings in or near places they knew – the Post Office Tower, the Tower of London, main-line stations – got through to them. Attacks on the bastions of the Establishment – Parliament, Scotland Yard, the Old Bailey, the Home Office, Brooks's Club – cut to the heart of the British state. Attacks on pubs frequented by soldiers – in Woolwich, Caterham, Guildford – directly weakened the morale of the Army.

Forty-one innocent people in 1973 and 1974 were killed in bombings in England and more than 400 were injured, plenty of them terribly. As usual, the wounded tended to be forgotten by all but their families. All but three of the dead were casualties of just three mass murders: the bomb on a coach carrying military personnel on the M62 early in 1974, and the Guildford and Birmingham pub bombings that autumn. The two Birmingham attacks, which killed twenty-one and injured 182, were the deadliest ever committed by the Provisional IRA.*

All these cases had something else in common. The convictions were reversed and the prisoners had to be released and compensated, but only – in each case – after they had spent more than fifteen years in jail. A year later, four IRA men (the Balcombe Street Four) were cornered in Central London and surrendered after a six-day siege that ended peacefully. It was clear they were the lynchpins of the entire London operation. At their trial they were charged with seven murders but also told the court they committed the Guildford bombing, for which four people were already in jail. But better for them to suffer than for the state to contemplate an error.

So no one listened.

---

* Twenty-five were killed by loyalist bombs in Dublin and Monaghan earlier in 1974, and twenty-two, including Lord Mountbatten, in separate IRA attacks on the same day in 1979. The Omagh bombing, after the Good Friday agreement in 1998, which killed twenty-nine, was the work of the Real IRA, a splinter group opposed to the peace process.

7

WE'RE IN

IN ONE RESPECT, EDWARD HEATH CAN COUNT AS ONE OF THE
most successful prime ministers Britain has ever had. He had one
overriding mission that he wished to undertake for his country, and
he achieved it: on 1 January 1973, Britain joined the Common
Market. It was a blessing that he died before his achievement could
be dismantled. His (rather clunky) maiden speech in 1950 was
about co-operation with and magnanimity towards Europe. In the
1960s, when he was in charge of the abortive negotiations with
Europe, he never faltered. In 1970 he got his chance.

De Gaulle had resigned as president of France the previous year
and died just after Heath came to power, which stopped him
sniping. His successor, Georges Pompidou, was well disposed. The
result was what the columnist Hugo Young called 'a textbook
exercise in the art of government'. There were two flaws. Although
Labour had been pursuing the same policy in government, Heath's
very zeal made it possible for Harold Wilson to claim later that he
had not negotiated hard enough. And if Heath looked behind him,
the British were hardly marching in step: they were wandering all
over the road. A Gallup poll in April 1970 had shown only 19 per
cent in favour of joining and more than half opposed even to
negotiating; the Conservative manifesto a month later was thus
very cautious.

The truth was that hardly anyone else was consistent in their views. Even those who were now most vehemently opposed had left behind them regrettable droppings in the other direction. Enoch Powell had been associated with a pamphlet that Young called practically 'a federalist tract', and Tony Benn had said that 'we had to cut Queen Victoria's umbilical cord'.

The two main political parties were always split; although eventually Labour became quite rational on the subject and the Tories hysterical, the Labour grassroots turned sharp left and anti-Europe in opposition in the early 1970s. Roy Jenkins, Labour's most Heathian Euro-believer, resigned as the deputy leader and began a slow shuffle away from the party. Only the Liberals, as they were then known, remained almost unanimously pro-Europe, but there was much anecdotal evidence suggesting they attracted protest votes from confused Europhobes.

Then again, the *Daily Mail*, later to become perhaps the most influential voice for withdrawal, was wildly enthusiastic. EUROPE, HERE WE COME it proclaimed on the day Britain joined: 'The *Daily Mail* has not wavered from its conviction that Britain's best and brightest future is in Europe.' Even the *Daily Express*, which had fought ferociously against anything that weakened Britain's relationship with the White Commonwealth, was gracious in defeat: 'Now that we are in . . . it would be fatal for this country to hang back . . . there can be no purpose in pining for the past.'

The Scottish and Welsh nationalists were vehemently anti, but they changed their mind once they saw how the Republic of Ireland (which joined the same day, along with Denmark) milked the European dimension both financially and emotionally and was able to detach itself increasingly from its dysfunctional relationship with Wicked Stepmother England. Meanwhile, the average Briton's viewpoint, as Young tartly put it, was 'changeable, ignorant and half-hearted'.

And overall it was a pretty half-hearted transformation. There was a 'Fanfare for Europe' of 300 events, with a gala launch at Covent Garden featuring the Queen, Prince Philip and a very proud prime minister. Their arrival was greeted by 200 booing protesters and the odd stink bomb. But it was all rather muted: a football team drawn from the three new Common Market countries beat the original six at Wembley – but the ground was only one-third full. In Brussels, the Union Jack was flown upside down.

The one immediate benefit was that travellers' allowances increased, and British tourists could cart home 300 much cheaper cigarettes from the other member states. British workers could be employed in the other eight countries, and vice versa. There was a promise of a regional fund to distribute aid to poorer areas, which indeed happened. But since the UK paid more money to Brussels than it got in, that merely represented both a tax and a loss of democratic accountability.

Three months later, Continental-style value-added tax came in to replace purchase tax, initially at 10 per cent. VAT was designed to be less flexible than purchase tax, which was highest on luxury items. In late March there was a big rush on pianos, cookers and lawnmowers, which were due for a price rise. Customers got understandably muddled and they also had a spree on colour TVs and cameras, which were due to go down. On restaurant menus in particular, it was often unclear whether VAT had been included or not.

Generally, it was not easy for voters to see what benefits they were getting from Europe. VAT was classic: the British were just told they had to have it. And, looking ahead, one could sense a slight chill about the future of British independence. In 1974, in the case known as Bulmer v. Bollinger, Lord Denning – the apple-cheeked exemplar of British judicial tradition – upheld the rights of two British drinks companies, Bulmer and Showerings, to market champagne cider and champagne perry, even though the word *champagne* was protected under European law.*

Denning insisted this protection only applied to wine and that English law prevailed, then added: 'But when we come to matters

---

* Champagne perry was known to every TV advert-watcher as Babycham, and was aimed, wholly and successfully, at women. It appeared to be a triumph of marketing ('I'd love a Babycham') rather than taste. This case kept coming back to court and, though Showerings were not banned from using the word *champagne*, they surrendered for the sake of a quiet life.

with a European element, the Treaty is like an incoming tide. It flows into the estuaries and up the rivers. It cannot be held back . . . In future, in transactions which cross the frontiers, we must no longer speak or think of English law as something on its own. We must speak and think of Community law, of Community rights and obligations, and we must give effect to them.'

The public, like the judges, sank into a resigned acceptance. But the Common Market became the European Economic Community and then the European Community and then the European Union, and the family grew and its tentacles became ever more pervasive. And there was Britain, always saying 'No' or 'But . . .' or sitting on the sidelines, scowling.

———◦———

Even without the Common Market this was a disorientating time for the British. Everything seemed to be changing, often for reasons that made sense in Whitehall but not outside. Much of the groundwork had been done in the unsentimental sixties, and when the seventies brought forth a prime minister who had little time for sentiment or symbolism, these came to fruition in ways that – piled on top of each other – just added to the general tenor of the nation's low-level pissed-offness.

The most significant change was decimal currency, which had been on the parliamentary agenda on and off since 1824. In the 1960s, South Africa, Australia and New Zealand all junked twelve pence in a shilling, twenty shillings to the pound, and indeed the pound itself. The last two unimaginatively and rather disloyally chose to have dollars and cents instead.

There was no serious discussion of Britain not going decimal. Brian Parkyn, an industrial chemist, Labour MP and 'confirmed duodecimalist', protested in the Commons but the Speaker got cross with him: it was already too late. It was proclaimed that the change would save 10 per cent of maths teaching time in primary schools. I have no memory of a problem, and I hated maths. Kids learned £sd instinctively, just as Chinese kids learn their fearsomely difficult language. The old currency was also a history lesson. Right through the sixties, children's pockets had pennies featuring five different monarchs dating back to Victoria. And it was rumoured (falsely) that there were eight pennies in circulation minted in Edward VIII's ten-month reign, so one always looked in case of a jackpot.*

But the principle was decreed unarguable, so discussion centred on two questions. The first was whether the new currency would remain the pound as previously understood, or split into two making it equivalent to the old ten-shilling note. This was a serious argument at a time when most everyday purchases were for well under £1.

It fell to Jim Callaghan, as Chancellor, to make the decision, and he gave five years' notice of the change in 1966, saying that he would keep the pound intact – making a new penny worth 2.4 old pennies rather than 1.2. (Do keep up.) A possible devaluation was a constant shadow for Callaghan at the time; he did not need an unnecessary one. Inflation would prove him right.

The second question was whether the secondary unit would be a penny or a cent. He opted for penny – or new penny at first – which should have been obvious. As R. E. Plummer of Kent had written to *The Times* three years earlier: 'The Americans tend to call their cents pennies. Must we call our pennies cents?' Anyway, Callaghan said, the British would find their own pet names for the new coins; they always do.

So the great day came, on 15 February 1971. There were a few predictable incidents: an 80-year-old woman in Coventry was turned off a bus because she only had old pennies; a man who went into Woolworths in the Strand was given the wrong change – he just happened to be Lord Fiske, chairman of the Decimal Currency Board. Then everyone learned to live with it. Soon enough, there would be far more inflation than could be attributed to decimalization.

But Callaghan was wrong about one thing: the British never did give the new coins nicknames. Before, there had been ha'pennies,

---

* There were, genuinely, only a handful of 1933 pennies, because there was a surfeit at the time and the mint stopped making new ones.

coppers, thruppenny bits, tanners, a bob (always singular however many were involved), ten-bob notes.* But the public treated the newcomers as strangers, not old friends. 'Have you got a one pee?' they would say in the only country in the world to share its basic coin with its most popular word for urination. Or sometimes 'Have you got a one pence?' Half a century on, in a world that has become increasingly informal, we are still not chummy. Pocket calculators arrived the very same year, and could easily have been adapted to duodecimal.

If the currency constituted a lightning victory for the tanks of change, metrication was more like the Irish Troubles, though not as short. Throughout the 1970s there was a body called the Metrication Board, to encourage and advise on changing from imperial measures. In 1974 it took an advert in the *Daily Telegraph* to explain, as if to infants, what it all meant: 'The metre is used to measure length. Pronounced "meeter", it is increasingly being used for measuring things like floor tiles, timber, furniture, bedding, dress patterns, sewing thread and adhesive tapes.'

It was fine and dandy to mess about with the length of adhesive tape, which only professionals were likely to notice, but as soon as this project touched ordinary life, politicians ran for cover. As early as 1972, the Heath government kicked any change to pints of milk and beer, pounds of butter and sugar, and ounces of sweets into a very distant future. In 1978, under Labour, compulsion was on the agenda for the early 1980s. The Department for Prices and Consumer Protection claimed 'universal support for metrication'. Then they took another look. It is 'clearly impossible to proceed against a background of hostility', a minister said, walking rapidly backwards.

At one point the British were told that only Burma, Brunei, Liberia, and both North and South Yemen were not already metric or in the process of changing. 'Is that the company we wish to

---

* Half an old penny, pennies, three pennies, sixpences, shillings, ten shillings.

keep?' was the unspoken message. There was in fact another country which, though going through the motions, was even more attached to its own (adulterated) form of imperial measurement than Britain: the United States.

Margaret Thatcher abolished the Metrication Board soon after taking office, and her soulmate Ronald Reagan would do the same to the US equivalent. The British board's final report, in 1980, admitted that public opinion was against their project (46 per cent to 31). Its final act was the metrication of shredded suet. But in Britain, this issue would not go away.

Close by on the battlefront was the question of weather. The BBC and Meteorological Office spent many years trying to wean the British off the Fahrenheit scale of temperature and on to Centigrade. But it kept creeping back, because people understood what they had learned as children and not the foreign muck. By the twenty-first century, authority gained the upper hand because it used the schools to indoctrinate the children. But for a whole generation, the young thought thirty degrees meant blazing mid-summer and their elders thought it was time to dig out the long johns. *Cui bono?*

———·———

And then there was the map of Britain. In a botched attempt to reform local councils, in 1974 (1975 in Scotland) millions of people found themselves living somewhere different. Lines were drawn on maps in Whitehall, using the precedent of the division of Africa. Counties that had existed since medieval times were sliced, diced, merged, abolished. New ones were created with names too boring even to mention. The maps of Yorkshire and Lancashire were attacked by an axe murderer and left for dead.

There were bland assurances that this was purely an administrative change for greater efficiency, and would not affect longstanding loyalties. But it did, partly because the Post Office initially demanded that the new addresses – affecting a fifth of the country – be used or else, and partly because the media fell into line. The rotting hulk of British local government became more remote and opaque. Apathy and anomie grew. On the plus side, thousands of petty officials used the change to grab pay rises.

There is something else to add to this list: bank holidays. In addition to making New Year's Day an official holiday for the whole UK rather than a day for French leave,* successive governments tinkered with the entire holiday calendar. Heath had begun the process as Minister for Industry in 1964 by moving August Bank Holiday – the traditional commencement of school holidays, fun and maybe sun – from the start to the end of the month, with autumn and school beckoning.† The main aim was to help the tourist trade by encouraging people to have a holiday when the landladies and hotels wanted them, not when people wanted to go.

In the seventies, Labour made the first Monday in May a holiday, for reasons more connected with a gesture towards international socialism than Merrie England and maypoles. Ever since, it has been almost invariably wet, associated only with snooker on TV. Already, the movable feast of Whitsun was abolished to be replaced by the last Monday in May, a date with no resonance or meaning. Thus most of Britain was left with a single day off in the three months of high summer, and nothing else until Christmas.

Whitsun! What a lovely word that is, full of summer and the hum of honeybees. The holiday was deeply rooted in religion and English custom and folklore: Whitsun weddings, Whit walks, Whitsun ales, Whit weeks, the Whitsun boss (aka the snowball tree), 'the ladies go dancing at Whitsun', white dresses in church, Roses cricket matches between Yorkshire and Lancashire – in so far as such places still existed . . .

In a country that in some ways was regaining touch with its mystical roots, this was another pointless loss of soul.

---

* In church calendars, New Year's Day is marked as Circumcision (it being eight days after Jesus's birth). Not something one cares to think about with a hangover.
† This did not apply in Scotland, where children are already back in school.

8

HE'S OUT

IN JANUARY 1970, THE INTERNATIONAL PRICE OF OIL, AS MEASURED by the traditional benchmark of West Texas Intermediate Crude, was $3.35 a barrel, making it slightly under an (old) English penny a pint.* A gallon of petrol at a British petrol pump was six shillings and ninepence, or just over 33p. That, note, was a gallon – so about 8p a litre. As the adverts said: 'The Esso sign means Happy Motoring'.

When Lord Rothschild, a former Shell executive, came to Downing Street to head the policy unit under Heath, he warned that oil prices were likely to rise during the decade. Well below the public radar, a suave lawyer called Sheikh Ahmed Zaki Yamani, Saudi Arabia's oil minister since 1962, was negotiating with the oil companies for greater control of the country's oil resources. The West did not take Arabs very seriously in the early 1970s.

By 1973, the government was in relatively calm water. There was indeed a boom – though, in the British manner, it mostly involved property speculation rather than business investment. Relations with the unions were less chilly. Heath's latest U-turn was imposing statutory wage control, but it had not yet fallen apart. The miners had voted strongly against a repeat strike the previous winter and, after a cordial meeting with the NUM president in the

---

* And not much less palatable than Watney's Red Barrel.

Downing Street garden in July, Heath was confident another deal was possible. In September, *The Economist* claimed that 'Britain was two-thirds of the way to an economic miracle'.

Then came October. On Yom Kippur, the holiest day of the Jewish year, Egypt and Syria launched a co-ordinated attack on Israeli forces to get back the land they had lost in the Six-Day War, six years earlier. Israel was not properly prepared and was rocked backwards. When the guns fell silent nineteen days later, it was not another rout, more a draw.

But the Arabs had found a new weapon – non-lethal but very effective. And before the war was over, their oil-producing nations started squeezing supplies to Israel's allies. Britain actually had a relatively easy ride: Heath did not share Harold Wilson's attachment to Israel, and during the Yom Kippur War the government refused to allow US spy planes to support Israel by using handy British bases in Cyprus. The 'special relationship' wobbled but the Arabs treated Britain lightly. But by January the price of oil had tripled. And the contingency plan for another miners' strike was to rely more on oil. Now the miners had the chance of a lifetime. They demanded a 35 per cent rise.

All along Heath had done his utmost to court them. In many ways, this was now like a Wilson government – lame ducks coddled, nationalization available on request, statutory pay policy, pump up the money – but with an air of rather comic rectitude, as though the prime minister was hoping no one would notice the absence of his trousers. He twiddled the rules of his incomes policy, now in stage three, to keep the miners sweet by offering funny money to evade his own rules.* But the coal board maxed out too early, offering 17 per cent at the first meeting, which was no way to play pay-rise poker for these high stakes. Joe Gormley, the miners' president, was under pressure from militants like the Communist vice-president Mick McGahey and Arthur Scargill; he had to be tough.

And so another winter of crisis unfolded. In November, Britain's

---

* During the incomes policy years, some staff, mainly managers, would be rewarded with company cars even if they never left the office.

260,000 miners began an overtime ban, as did the power station workers – who had a much more immediate effect on the economy. Heath retaliated by asking the Queen for his fifth state of emergency. The next day Princess Anne was marrying Captain Mark Phillips in her obedience-and-all ceremony at Westminster Abbey. *The Times*' front page was full of it: 'solemnity and splendour . . . magnificent pageantry . . . November sunshine . . . fluffy white clouds . . . glittering procession . . . crowds waving flags and cheering exuberantly . . . The bride smiled so gaily . . . radiant . . .'

Two days later, the paper was back to normal: 'Esso rations petrol . . . long queues at filling stations . . . tourists face winter surcharges . . . food price rises sharpest in 20 years . . . commuters face rail crisis . . . 300,000 take industrial action . . . Weather: trough of low pressure . . . wintry showers . . . North Sea rough.'

Ah, the North Sea: the drumbeat from the oil companies that there were plentiful quantities of oil and gas deep under those stormy waters had been getting steadily louder. Everyone just needed to be patient. But, dammit, Britain needed the oil now.

Interest rates were rising fast. Inflation was rocketing. The balance of payments figures were horrendous. Then the Southern Region train drivers joined in with a work-to-rule. This involved refusing to take out a train if, say, the cab was draughty or the ashtrays were full. In December, a 50-mph speed limit was imposed on all roads; TV channels were ordered to close at 10.30 p.m.; open-air Christmas trees could be lit on only three days; and the nation was warned of an impending three-day week. Then the blackouts began. And the IRA decided it was time for London to have a few bombs. The Book of Job had nothing on this.

And then . . . the polls started to turn in the government's favour, after three solid years of buyers' remorse about choosing Heath. In a sense it was not so surprising: during the strike two years earlier, it was easier to see the miners as put-upon underdogs doing the job from hell for an ungrateful nation. Now the raw opportunism of turning the oil crisis to their own advantage made them a little less lovable. But the miners still had sympathizers, even in Downing

Street; Heath could not bring himself to hate them. He was damned whatever he did.

Just before New Year, the power engineers extracted a backdated pay increase which was deemed within the rules. There were also hopes that 'waiting time payments' might be the answer to square the miners. But this was ruled out by the Pay Board, the very seventies body that would attempt to interpret whatever arcane rules were in force, in the manner of a rugby referee peering at the dark goings-on inside a scrum.

Armageddon was slow in coming. Neither oil nor coal was yet running out. Once the electricians had gone back there were none of the 'oh not again' power cuts that characterized the 1972 strike. The three-day week, never imposed in the earlier strike, took the strain; and, with firms operating longer hours, it worked so well that before it was over, industrial output was almost back to normal – which, as Heath's biographer John Campbell noted, 'cast a revealing light on "normal" productivity in British industry'. Histories even record it as a mild winter,* though the British had lower expectations of mildness then.

The three-day week also produced an innovation that would transform the British weekend. Because many towns now had Saturday as a working day, football matches began to be played on Sundays. It was technically unlawful under Sunday observance laws, but the notional way round this was to sell the programme at the turnstiles for the normal admission price – cricket was already using this trick. There was some resistance from the perpetually embattled sabbatarian lobby ('the thin end of a pernicious wedge') and some conservatives within the game (Arsenal). But the crowds at the four FA Cup ties that began the experiment were all above average, and that was the end of that argument.

The government continued to try to save electricity where it could. In the middle of January 1974, the energy minister, Patrick Jenkin, made the only memorable remark of his career by telling

---

* This is certainly not my recollection: I was lodging weeknights in a frigid bedroom at a pub in Essex.

people to brush their teeth in the dark. By now the *Daily Mirror* was bordering such stories with

CRISIS BRITAIN . . . CRISIS BRITAIN . . . CRISIS BRITAIN . . .

Within government, the greatest crisis was a darkly guarded secret: the only public intimation was a well-hidden paragraph in *The Times*, two weeks after the event, saying that Sir William Armstrong, the head of the Civil Service, was ill. Armstrong was no ordinary civil servant. With a prime minister who liked formal channels and had no cronies, Armstrong wielded exceptional influence. And this was no routine illness: it was a breakdown.

Precise accounts vary, but he had certainly been found, naked and babbling, at a weekend conference for *prominenti* at a stately home in Oxfordshire. He was also said to have told all his permanent secretaries to go home 'and prepare for Armageddon', before being led away, like Anthony Eden, to recuperate in the Caribbean.* The middle classes might have agreed about Armageddon: the following day the NUM's McGahey was reported to be inciting troops to mutiny if they were called in to assist in strike-breaking duties.

Armstrong's absence can only have added to the pressures on Heath, beset by the greatest crisis of his own life. The government was sending out mixed messages, which prompted the miners to raise the stakes: they turned the overtime ban into an all-out stoppage. The executive vote was only 16 to 10, but the pithead ballots were 81 per cent in favour – and on 10 February there was a total walkout.

Ever since the new year, the election drums had been getting louder. Heath wanted to renew his mandate and make the miners understand he just wanted to be *fair*. But he had dithered about the timing. Fastidious as ever, he did not want to have an election before the up-to-date register was published on 15 February, a trick Labour was already pre-emptively denouncing. By the time he blew the whistle, for 28 February, Armageddon was receding. There

---

* Happily he recovered well enough to become chairman of the Midland Bank.

were hints of spring. This was the third Heath v. Wilson match-up, the score 1–1, and no one had many positive feelings about either.

Two things happened in the final week of the campaign that may have had some solid effect amid the usual froth and bubble. One was the discovery that the coal industry had calculated its employees' earnings to include holiday pay, whereas manufacturing industries did not. If known, that could have allowed the miners enough money under the Heath rules to avoid the strike. The next was the re-emergence of the Ghost of Elections Past. Enoch Powell had refused to stand this time, surrendering his Wolverhampton citadel after twenty-four years and calling the election 'essentially fraudulent'.

On the final Saturday he spoke in Birmingham: 1,500 people queued to get in. They were all searched by stewards, a foretaste of the untrusting Britain that lay ahead. He told them to vote Labour as the best hope of getting the country out of the Common Market. He had burned any bridge back into the Tory party without any hope of being elevated to a Labour Cabinet as Lord Powell of Erewhon. But he helped achieve what was probably his main objective: inflicting the killer blow on his enemy Heath.

In contrast, the anti-Labour nuclear option never left the launch pad. The *Daily Mail* had a story linking Wilson to a dodgy land deal due to run on pre-election Monday. In a magnificent exercise of witchcraft, his aide Albert Murray rang his mates in the print unions, asking them to threaten a walkout and stop the paper.*

The question Heath asked was 'Who rules the country? The government or the unions?' He thought it was a simple question, and the polls consistently showed the Tories with a narrow lead over Labour while the Liberals staged a late surge. The notion of *fair* – and the sense that's what the miners were not being – pervaded the Tory manifesto. Labour's main proposal was a 'Social Contract', no statutory pay norms, and government favours in return for wage

---

* The story appeared later, when it mattered less, with only a muffled explosion. Wilson's signature was involved but it was a forgery; the fraudster, Ronald Milhench, got three years.

restraint. It sounded suspiciously like a sequel to the last Wilson government: Solomon Binding Rides Again. Mathematically, the soothsayers had it right: the Tories won 300,000 more votes than Labour. But the prophecy was oracular: Heath lost because he won four fewer seats. The main reason was that 'bloody awful place': the old Ulster Unionists, who had long functioned as a Tory subsidiary, were wiped out by the hard-line naysaying Protestants. There was also a big swing to Labour in the West Midlands – Powell country.

The people had spoken but they babbled; nobody was close to having an overall majority or even having a dance partner who could help out. Neither the Liberals (6 million votes, fourteen seats) nor the new phalanx of nine Scottish and Welsh nationalists could offer a pact that would give anyone a workable majority. It was a shambles. The Conservatives later concluded that they had actually gained votes from Labour but lost more to the Liberals; there were also very early hints of what became known as tactical voting, which would come to mean mainly backing the party most likely to beat the Tories.

Heath clung on through a strange weekend, overshadowed by a Turkish plane crash in Paris killing 346 people, most of them British, many of them rugby fans returning from an international. He talked to the Liberal leader Jeremy Thorpe, but it was useless both mathematically and politically – the Liberal grassroots would not have it, even when Heath talked of their holy grail, proportional representation. On the Monday, the Queen sent for Harold Wilson again.

9

IT'S THAT MAN AGAIN

HAROLD WILSON WAS STILL ONLY 57, THEORETICALLY AN IDEAL age to be prime minister. But he had aged rapidly. In opposition to Heath, he had been only intermittently engaged and effective. He was the second post-war prime minister, after Churchill, to have a second coming. And in many ways, their reincarnations had much in common.

Both were by this time heavily dependent on brandy, starting early – well diluted so as not to make them drunk, but enough of it never to be entirely sober. Both could still rise to the occasion when they had to. For both, the vindication was wonderful; it was just the governing that was rather a bore. And Wilson now faced crises more urgent than Churchill had done in 1951 (though not more urgent than those of 1940). The first job was getting the miners back to work.

Ageing fighters can use ringcraft to compensate for their slowing reactions, and Wilson could do something similar. He said before the election that he no longer intended to play every position on the field, and he allowed the campaign to dwell more on his colleagues. This may have been because of his sense of failing powers, but he did have a Cabinet that was experienced and recognizable but also refreshed by a three-and-a-half-year break in the wilderness.

The most important player of all, in that immediate aftermath, had never held office before: the universally beloved Employment

Secretary, Michael Foot, Labour's shaggy white-haired prophet. And the Industry Secretary was the less beloved Tony Benn. This meant Wilson outsourced handling of the crisis that had brought him back to office to the two men who embodied the party's Left.

As they woke to the news of a Labour government, the stock market and sterling counter-intuitively went up. The City wanted an end to a miners' strike. And they got that promptly – a new £45 minimum for workers at the coal face. Even then there was twelve hours of negotiation over bits and bobs before the miners' executive was finally sated. And the next day, Scargill's Yorkshire area announced they wanted a £65 minimum in the next round. The markets' enthusiasm evaporated soon enough.

During its previous term in office, Labour had become a shadow of a mass movement. Wilson's manoeuvrings turned off the idealists; the biddable members happy to lick envelopes were dying off, to be replaced by a group characterized as polytechnic lecturers* (which many of them were), often addicted to Marxist dogma. Thus some constituency parties became a dictatorship of the polytariat, and this helped empower the parliamentary Left.

Most major Cabinet jobs belonged to the safe centrists. The new Chancellor was Denis Healey, given the job in preference to an increasingly disillusioned Roy Jenkins, who was sent back to the Home Office. Income tax went up, back to 83 per cent for the highest earners; pensions and benefits were increased. Healey said later he would have been meaner had the Treasury not given him duff figures.

In the meantime, Foot had quietly met TUC leaders to ask them for their Christmas wish list. The No. 1 priority was the repeal of Heath's Industrial Relations Act – well ahead of the ending of statutory pay curbs, which could wait. 'The unions have tailored their demands to the realities of the political situation,' said *The Times*. No one believed this impossible parliament could last beyond autumn, and everyone was trying to avoid trouble before the

---

* Polytechnics were tertiary colleges that did not have university status. They were promoted to become universities en masse in the 1990s.

inevitable rematch. Even the defeated Tories put aside their doubts about their own leader. For the moment.

That certainly ruled out any difficult decisions for government. The social contract was, in the historian Paul Addison's phrase, 'the semblance of a strategy'. Healey and Foot were starting to fulfil their side of the deal; their unruly partners responded more patchily. The government were stuck for the moment with a persistent hangover from the Heath era – 'threshold agreements', which meant new wage rises were triggered if the cost of living rose above a certain level. Eight million qualified in June alone. This meant that inflation begat more inflation and the thresholds must surely be a contender for the title 'Stupidest Policy Ever'. In 1974, the word *Weimar*, the shorthand for the German hyperinflation that helped bring Hitler to power, was mentioned more often in *The Guardian* than it had been in the other twenty-nine years since the war. In mid-May, Wilson's policy adviser Andrew Graham warned of just this; no one was listening.

The next week the FT index hit 246, its lowest in fifteen years. Come September it was below 200. By then the nurses had also got 30 per cent, although the building unions backed away from their original bid for rises of up to 107 per cent, which was sporting of them and a win for the social contract. Now the election was under way, set for 10 October, and the car workers were on strike again. This time it was Ford's turn, only seven months after the last settlement. The company offered 37 per cent spread over two years. Although even this was rejected, it was enough for the workers to drift back pending further talks. The government were miffed by Ford, whose management pointed out that the company was not party to the social contract.

These were halcyon days for one group of workers: the labour correspondents of the national press, who constituted a significant sub-department in every newspaper. Their routine was extreme even by the standards of 1970s Fleet Street: it involved a huge amount of compulsory hanging about in pubs, waiting for the negotiators to emerge from their discussions, often very late at night.

Ford had one great advantage over their rivals British Leyland in that they had company-wide bargaining, which did not save them from large set-piece strikes but cut out a huge amount of petty disruption and bickering between each walkout. Ford negotiations took place near Paddington, and the press would strike camp in, of all places, the Moscow Arms.* Much of the news from the talks was filtered through a character called Reg Birch, a member of the TUC General Council and a creature rarer than a yeti: a disarmingly genial and funny Maoist. 'Actually there were a lot of personal contacts and bantering relationships between unions and management,' said Don Macintyre, who was on the labour staff of *The Times* in the mid-seventies.

———·———

The election weather was dreary; the arguments dreary; the leaders, both battered, heading for their fourth battle – more even than Gladstone v. Disraeli.† Heath talked of forming a government of national unity and being willing to stand down if he were the obstacle. Two days before the vote, he said that if he won, even with a majority, he would invite the other party leaders on Saturday to explore the possibilities. Wilson said he would not answer such a hypothetical question and anyway was planning to spend Saturday at Chequers.

So Labour got safely to the big day with hopes of repeating 1966, when they turned a small majority into a large one; this time, starting with a minority, they won a small majority. They won fair and square, with a million more votes than the Tories and three more seats than everyone else put together. In the short term they were pretty secure, since their lead over the Tories was forty-two and it would be a rare issue that would bring all the opposition parties together. But, chillingly for Labour, the nationalists got almost a third of the vote in Scotland, and eleven seats. Fire burn and cauldron bubble.

And, chillingly for everyone, Enoch Powell was back after his

———

* On Moscow Road.
† Since 1974, no pair of main-party leaders have faced each other more than once.

brief absence, as one of the reinvented Ulster unionists who had no allegiance to the Conservatives and brought a problem to every solution in the province. Powell forsook his traditional three-piece suit and homburg for tweeds and a cloth cap to greet the Protestant farmers of South Down, while avoiding the urban Catholics. Not everyone understood what he was talking about, but his air of total certainty about everything fitted the loyalist view of the world.

The new maths enabled Labour to complete the accommodation with/capitulation to (delete to taste) the unions. The Industrial Relations Act had already been transformed into the less emotively initialled Trade Unions and Labour Relations Act and was now quickly amended by Michael Foot to restore 'closed shop' rights. Then came the Employment Protection Act, strengthening the worker-friendly parts of Heath's original act – which had, characteristically, been both even-handed and cack-handed – and making it very difficult to fire people. This was a lasting change which largely survived even the bombardment of union rights that came in the next decade.

Right from the start, the watchword was *process* – the boxes that had to be ticked before even the most incompetent employee could be dismissed. On top of that, decades of case law built up. By 1975 it was already established that a factory fitter could not be fairly sacked for having a beard or being a minute late, though a teacher showing porn to his pupils could. There was much more to come.

'Of course, the lawyers were the winners,' mused one solicitor in 2022. 'The first edition of the textbook on the subject, *Harvey's Employment Law*, ran to 150 pages. By now if you had the print version you would need to take a very large wheelie suitcase into court. But there is a short cut. I lost my first case before a tribunal even though I knew all the law, so I asked the opposing lawyer, an old hand, what I'd done wrong. The rule, he explained, is: "The one who says the word *reasonable* most often always wins." That's still true.'

The early months of what was officially Wilson's fourth administration constituted the apogee of trade union power. They now
had 'a degree of legal privilege nobody had enjoyed in Britain since
the medieval Church', as the anarcho-conservative historian
Christopher Booker put it. Sir Leo Pliatzky, a senior official at the
Treasury, dated the period of what he called – from the safety of
retirement – 'collective madness' as eighteen months.

In November 1974, Wilson wrote a memo saying: 'I regard any
attempt to regulate incomes by statutory means to be out.' By
January 1975 prices were going up at an annual rate of 20 per cent,
wages 28. On Twelfth Night, the FT index – which then included
only thirty companies – touched 146.6; one might have wondered
whether it was being calculated in centigrade and could soon go
below zero. In February, miners' leaders rejected a 22 per cent offer
a year after their second victory. Arthur Scargill called the offer 'a
bag of crisps'. By March the stock market was above 300. The
Telegraph's explanation was that, with hyperinflation imminent,
shares were the safest haven.

By this time Cabinet ministers were indulging in line-by-line
battles with the Treasury to save their department's budgets. In
May, wage inflation reached 33 per cent. On the last day of June,
the governor of the Bank of England came to Downing Street to tell
the prime minister sterling was collapsing. For a few hours Wilson
was about to ordain a Heathian statutory policy, which he had so
vigorously denounced. Since what emerged instead was something
of a success, even in the medium term, its fatherhood is in dispute.

The plan was a £6 flat-rate maximum wage increase (and nothing
except 'increments' for those above £8,500), agreed between the
government and the big three of the TUC: Jack Jones and Hugh
Scanlon, leaders of the two biggest unions, and the TUC general
secretary, Len Murray. For once they meant it, and though it was
voluntary the support of the most baronial union leaders carried
much clout. It was obvious the dread word *differentials* would
return in due course. In the meantime, with painful slowness, the
ghost of Weimar now receded.

Labour could still do worthwhile things, even in these straitened times. Reluctantly back at the Home Office, Roy Jenkins was no longer the rising star of his party, and his in-tray was dominated not by exciting and overdue liberal reforms but by the day-to-day crisis management that Home Secretaries usually face. And although there was now a separate Northern Ireland department, bombs in Britain were his problem. But he was responsible for two important and not dissimilar bills along similar lines, the Sex* Discrimination Act and a new and more encompassing Race Relations Act.

In those years, no one was revered more in the Labour Party's iconography than the poor pensioner, always presumed to be eking out their widow's mite on the last shovel of nutty slack – which was diminishingly true. Which was why Healey had had to raise pensions in his first budget, before he worked out that he could not afford it. But Barbara Castle, now in charge of the sprawling Department of Health and Social Security, did what both parties had tried and failed to achieve before, seeing through a complex and non-partisan bill that made pensions potentially less basic and more flexible for the post-war generation, who could not yet imagine growing old. This was SERPS, the State Earnings Related Pension Scheme. 'The country as a whole had begun to demand the privilege of the prosperous. A nation which felt middle-class expected the advantages of that status,' Roy Hattersley, by now a junior minister, reflected much later. But the Labour Party did not fully understand what that entailed. It still had that slightly Soviet streak which had prolonged the post-war ration queue and did for the Attlee government.

Castle herself was responsible for one egregious example of that. The Labour Party had promised to phase out private beds in the National Health Service and somehow this became an ideological red line. There were genuine issues about priorities and distribution of income (the consultants cleaned up), but this option kept the top doctors in the system and on site for emergencies; the rooms made a significant profit and the choice was legitimate in a free society, like travelling first-class on the railways. Some patients might think it was bad enough to be ill without being compelled to endure huge

---

* The word *gender* was not widely used except in foreign language classes.

dormitories, wretched food, and visiting hours which were then
only slightly more generous than those in prison.

The ancillary staff unions were very militant on the subject, and
so was Castle. At the Christie Hospital in South Manchester an
operating-theatre-assistant-cum-union-official called Victor Chester
had the right to decide which patients were allowed to have these
rooms. 'It's like working under a revolutionary council,' said one
consultant. The consultants removed the Chester veto but Castle
got rid of the private beds. And private health care, which had
almost withered away because of the success of the NHS, returned
with a vengeance.

Just up the road from the Christie lies Manchester Grammar
School, founded in 1515. After the education reforms of 1944 it
became a 'direct grant' school, a very British sort of anomaly –
quasi-independent, selective, but largely funded by the state in
return for having about half the places free. Not merely did it
work, it was one of the most admired schools in the country. It still
is. But in 1975, after an hour-long Commons debate starting at
10.30 p.m., MGS and the other 153 direct grants faced a choice:
go all-in with the state system or go independent. Two-thirds
sailed off to join Eton, Harrow and the rest of the traditional public
schools, out of the government's grasp. The less successful ones,
mostly Catholic-run, became comprehensives. Instead of further-
ing Labour's supposed long-term aim of making the state system
so strong and brilliant, all its fee-paying rivals would go out of
business; once again their dogmatism had given the independent
sector new vigour.

———◆———

After the February 1974 election, the Conservative Party had
observed an uneasy internal truce. The whispering against Ted
Heath had begun all right, but the rerun could come at any moment:
changing the leader was impossible. In October it was different.
Three days after Ted Heath's defeat, the Sunday papers were touting
the name of Willie Whitelaw. But the party's right wing was already
at work; earlier in the year Sir Keith Joseph had founded a new

partisan think tank, the Centre for Policy Studies (CPS), to convert the party to 'economic liberalism' – including the newly fashionable doctrine of monetarism* as the answer to inflation. His deputy was Margaret Thatcher.

Joseph began making a series of speeches setting out his thoughts, with a view to a challenge of his own. The very next Saturday he went to Birmingham, that city of provocative oratory, in what was said to be 'a calculated step' towards the Tory leadership. Not very well calculated, it transpired. He said that 'a high and rising proportion of babies are being born to mothers least fitted to bring children into the world and bring them up . . . these mothers, the under-twenties in many cases, single parents, from classes 4 and 5,† are now producing a third of all births. If we do nothing . . . the nation moves towards degeneration'.

In other words, it seemed he was nudging towards eugenics: compulsory birth control, abortions and sterilization for riff-raff. All hell broke loose. Sir Keith was a well-meaning man with a perpetually tortured expression, as though he had just come from a session flagellating himself. On this occasion, despite being a Fellow of All Souls, he seems not to have quite understood what he was himself saying. Eventually he realized self-flagellation was no longer enough: it was time for the pearl-handled revolver. Shortly afterwards, John O'Sullivan, who was attached to the CPS, went to the office to see Joseph and Margaret Thatcher, who had been functioning as his aide for the inchoate leadership contest. 'Look,' Joseph told O'Sullivan, 'I just don't have the kind of temperament that can take this kind of assault. She's a much tougher person than I am.' And as a politician, he was, as Denis Healey put it, 'a mixture of Hamlet, Rasputin and Tommy Cooper'. There would be a challenge to Heath, but it was Thatcher, not Joseph, who would be in the mix.

Meanwhile, Heath was refusing to go quietly, even after three election defeats, but he was also refusing to do anything to make

---

* The theory that economic goals can be achieved by regulating the supply of money into the economy as a whole.

† i.e. the lower classes.

people feel warm towards him. Julian Critchley was dining in the Commons one night with Heath's old ally Jim Prior and two other Tory MPs. Heath came by, greeted Prior warmly and just ignored the other three. 'What can I do with him?' asked Prior despairingly. 'He seemed to disregard the small change of politics,' wrote Critchley later, 'gossip, humbug and knowing the name of one's wife.'

Heath did hold occasional gatherings for backbenchers but they were always stiff occasions. 'I'm a home-loving man,' one MP said. 'Well, why don't you go home then?' grumped the leader. Whitelaw was never going to stand against Heath, which left only one serious contender, who he did not take seriously. But Thatcher had an ad hoc coalition on her side: the right-wingers, the anti-Europeans, the pro-Rhodesians (often the same people), but also the MPs he had affronted, the ones embittered by his meanness with knighthoods ('Not for me, you understand, but Marjorie would have so loved being Lady M'), plus many more who just wanted a change, any change, and were lending Thatcher their vote just to get rid of Heath and hoping someone better might appear on the second ballot. They included liberals like Critchley.

Thatcher's campaign was rousing but non-specific. Her manager, Airey Neave, had successfully escaped from Colditz in the war so he knew about using low cunning to beat the odds: 'Margaret was wondering why Ted never gave you a job,' he might say to a wavering MP. 'Did you refuse?' He would also tell them dolefully that, while Margaret was doing well, Ted might still win without a second ballot . . .

She beat Heath 130–119, with sixteen for the makeweight Hugh Fraser. Heath resigned with more dignity than he sometimes mustered in the years ahead. More candidates came in for the second ballot, including Whitelaw. But the ship had sailed; there was no catching her now. 'She had the courage to declare herself in time. I think people respected that,' said the frontbencher Geoffrey Rippon.

As Brutus said: 'There is a tide in the affairs of men. Which taken at the flood, leads on to fortune . . .'

Women too.

———— ❧ ————

Harold Wilson had one last hurrah to come. In June 1975, with Britain up to its armpits in the quicksand of the inflation crisis, he conjured up a victory that would define British politics for the next forty years. Wilson held and handsomely won a referendum to keep Britain in the European Community. There was no constitutional necessity for this vote: the UK had never had a nationwide referendum before, though the Welsh used to vote regularly about whether they wanted pubs to open on Sundays.

Wilson had never previously agreed with referendums. 'It is contrary to our traditions in this country,' he told the Commons in 1969. Margaret Thatcher, in her first speech as Conservative leader in March 1975, approvingly quoted Clement Attlee saying it was 'a device of demagogues and dictators'. But perhaps a referendum, like joining Europe itself, is a subject where almost no one is consistent.

Back in office, Wilson had to find a way of finessing the insularity he had allowed to fester in opposition. The anti-Europe Tony Benn was calling for a referendum, and Wilson, having dismissed it – partly because of its source – finally seized on that as a good wheeze. Jim Callaghan, who went a bit Bennish on the subject in opposition, added the idea of renegotiating beforehand to create a veneer of consistency: Europe was a good idea, ran the narrative, but Heath had failed to get a good deal.

And it was now Callaghan, as Foreign Secretary, who was in charge of getting a better one. People took a contemptuous view of the renegotiations, seeing them as a machination cooked up by two cynics as a piece of party management. But Callaghan's biographer, Kenneth Morgan, insisted that serious problems were resolved, especially over Commonwealth matters – never a priority for Heath. There were better deals for Caribbean cane and for beef from Botswana, where Callaghan was thereafter much admired. The Brussels negotiators, not yet fed up with British whingeing, thought London was worth a few steaks and sugar lumps.

Nonetheless, Wilson's eternal aim of keeping his party together

may safely be ranked ahead of keeping Britain in Europe on his list
of priorities. And it was all just credible enough to present to the
public, even though it was, in the words of one of his biographers,
an 'unprecedented spectacle . . . a government asking, and getting,
the support of its own voters for the policy of the Opposition against
the declared wishes of its own party, both inside and outside
Parliament, and then carrying on almost as if nothing had happened'.
The conjuror's last great trick.

The previous autumn, polling had shown the British in favour of
withdrawing from Europe, 2–1. With five weeks to go, the Labour
Party held a special conference which voted 2–1 to come out. But
well before the big day, all doubt had been blown away: Middle
England went all docile and stood in line behind the middle ground
of politics.

Neither the prime minister nor the Foreign Secretary nor the new
opposition leader campaigned over-zealously. Margaret Thatcher
was photographed wearing a Christmas-style sweater featuring the
nine members' flags, though the Union Jack was very much front
and centre. And she shared a platform with the vanquished Ted
Heath – he uncomfortable, she fawning with unctuous insincerity:
'It is naturally with some temerity that the pupil speaks before the
master, because you know more about it than the rest of us.'

The electorate's resolve was fixed; perhaps the times seemed so
bad they had no wish to stir up more trouble. Had Britain been out,
they might not have gone in; once in, they voted for the status quo,
a common though not inevitable reaction in existential referendums. Christopher Soames, Britain's senior commissioner in
Brussels, said: 'This is no time for Britain to be considering leaving
a Christmas club, let alone the Common Market.' Farmers were in
favour. God and Mammon marched in lockstep: 415 out of 419
company chairmen in a survey, every Anglican bishop. Not
surprisingly, given such overwhelming support from business, the
pro-European camp had an overwhelming financial advantage.
Every national daily except the Communist *Morning Star* was
onside, even the *Daily Express*, which appeared to be the victim of
some strange enchantment – it hated Brussels and all its ways for

decades before and afterwards. The best-known opponents were Foot, Benn, Powell and Paisley, hardly a meeting of minds. The neo-Nazis and the Trotskyites joined hands, if only metaphorically.

The pro-Europeans did not talk about national sovereignty, nor were the public interested. Polling showed that the cost of living was the main issue. On the day the result was indeed 2-1, but now it was to 'Yes', i.e. staying in. Even Northern Ireland failed to say 'No' to something: only Shetland and the Western Isles did that. Rural England was most enthusiastic, with North Yorkshire top at 76.3 per cent; in England the closest margins were all in the big conurbations. The *Guardian* political columnist Peter Jenkins speculated the result was a vote against Benn.

Harold Wilson must have thought so too: he briskly went back to Downing Street to start finding a way to manoeuvre Benn out of his post as Industry Secretary, where he was plotting mass nationalization. Four days later he was switched to Energy, a post where he could expend his own energy with less political risk.

————•————

On his first day back in office after the February 1974 election, Wilson was sitting in the Downing Street study he had just recaptured from Ted Heath, talking to his friend, the businessman Harry Kissin. 'There are only three people listening,' Wilson said, 'you, me and MI5.' In his official history of MI5, Christopher Andrew insisted that 'MI5 was not, of course, listening in to the Prime Minister'.

There was always a side to Wilson that loved both intrigue (the fun he had ramping up the Profumo affair) and fantasy (the notion that he was Britain's President Kennedy). And as time went on he certainly became more paranoid. But that is not the worst trait in a prime minister: it was arrogance and complacency that made Heath underestimate Margaret Thatcher.

And Wilson was not alone in finding MI5 a worry. 'I never entirely dismissed the suggestion . . . that my own room was bugged,' said his level-headed policy chief Bernard Donoughue. 'One day I passed the Head of MI5 in the corridor. I had never met him before, yet he said to me, "Enjoy your football on Sunday?"'

Certainly, there were people in MI5 – and across the British upper classes – who felt, subconsciously at least, that Labour was not really a legitimate government. MI5 had kept a file on Wilson, under the codename 'Henry Worthington', going back to his regular trips to Moscow in the fifties. But with Wilson now the boss again, MI5's director general, Sir Michael Hanley, had the card affirming its existence removed from the agency's internal index – though not the file itself.

But Wilson knew something that perhaps even Hanley did not: he was preparing his exit strategy. He had promised his wife after his unexpected comeback he would retire when he was 60, in March 1976. This was increasingly urgent: he knew he was no longer up to the job. Somehow he got through the next nine months but he was a spectral presence. He chaired the Cabinet and handled question time in the Commons, which was difficult, partly because he was facing Margaret Thatcher and men of his generation found it difficult to be rude to women. He was still the most powerful person in Britain but perhaps no longer the most influential: that was assumed to be Jack Jones, leader of the Transport and General Workers' Union and enforcer of the new £6 limit on pay rises.

The PM's close associates saw his decline at first-hand. Speaking in public, he needed a script. The brandy intake increased further. Donoughue recalled that, towards the end, he had to write him out a single sentence before a lunch saying welcome and that he hoped the guests would enjoy their meal. He no longer whizzed through the red boxes of government papers that came to him; long papers sometimes lay unread for weeks. He consulted his doctor regularly, often about 'psychosomatic stomach pains before difficult meetings'. Occasionally he would air his grievances. He told the Commons there had been eight burglaries of different offices, all attempts to steal his own private papers. He also accused the South African security service BOSS, ever active against enemies of the white regime, of being behind rumours about the goings-on then starting to engulf the Liberal leader Jeremy Thorpe.

The country was hardly in clover. In 1975 unemployment rose to 1.25 million; bankruptcies and company liquidations reached a fifteen-year high. And on 5 March 1976, for the first time since the upstart ex-colonists established the US dollar in 1792, the pound was officially worth less than two dollars. But there was one even more startling statistic: the PM might be borderline gaga, but Labour and the Tories were still closely matched in the polls.

Eleven days later, Wilson's Cabinet met. Only one other member suspected anything: Jim Callaghan had been tipped off. Wilson read out a long statement, milking his moment and the *coup de théâtre*. There was a theory that Wilson had chosen the day to help the Queen out by overshadowing the announcement of Princess Margaret and Lord Snowdon's imminent break-up. It worked well enough for the posh papers, but the others were far more interested in the Snowdons' split.

Wilson had decided he wanted Callaghan, four years older but more vigorous, as his successor. It was, in any case, his time. As with the Tories, the electorate was just the party's MPs. Six stood: Foot topped the first ballot and was a very respectable runner-up in the end; Jenkins's aloofness and pro-Europe staunchness cost him dearly – he was a poor third, and was treated roughly. Callaghan won cosily: the victory was not overwhelming but never in doubt. Jenkins would have taken the Foreign Office but it went, gallingly, to Tony Crosland – his long-time friend, rival and, it was said, (on a single drunken Oxford evening) lover. Soon afterwards, Jenkins did win the glittering consolation prize of becoming Britain's first and only president of the European Commission – where he was known as *Le Roi Jean Quinze*, which was something more than a pun.

Barbara Castle, whose relationship with Callaghan contained minimal affection, was sacked. She had known what was coming. Callaghan told her that Harold had said the worst part of the job was Prime Minister's Questions, then added, 'It isn't that, it's *this*.' She said she wouldn't pretend she was going willingly: 'But, don't worry Jim, I won't attack you personally, I shall just tell the truth.' He then asked, 'Will you let me do this?' and kissed her on the cheek. It sounds like a scene from *The Godfather*.

It was widely noted that, in Callaghan, Labour was getting a prime minister in the same mould as Wilson: long on political skill, short on principle. In the *New Statesman*, James Fenton wrote: 'I wish someone would take the mould, and break it, before any further casts are made.'

The last prime minister to retire gracefully of his own volition was Stanley Baldwin in 1937, and his popularity did not survive the war when he was blamed for Britain's lack of preparation. Every subsequent exit over the next eighty-five years was forced either by outright defeat or extreme pressure from the party. Except Wilson's.

The wave of good feelings towards him lasted about two months. Then came his Resignation Honours – what became known as the Lavender List. This is the perk given to departing prime ministers, allowing them to hand out the strange baubles that bedevil British life to almost anyone they fancy.

Folklore has overstated the extent that criminality and cronyism permeated Wilson's list. Only a couple of the twenty-one handed major honours appear to have been actual rogues; the others would have passed without comment at any New Year or Queen's Birthday. The strangeness was the surfeit of buccaneering capitalists, most of whom Wilson hardly knew and were not known for even theoretical support of his party. Had he outsourced it all to Margaret Thatcher? Even his intimates could never explain it. The least implausible explanation is that he was already too far gone to concentrate, and outsourced it to Marcia Williams – or, as she had been formally known since 1974, Baroness Falkender.

10

CHANGE AND DECAY

SOMETIME IN THE MID-1970S, A STARK POSTER APPEARED ON advertising hoardings across Britain. The background was black; the lettering was white; there was no illustration or explanation. It said simply: Now for Britain itself.

What did it portend? Was it a hidden message from one of the strange organizations founded by retired military men to save Britain from anarchy? General Sir Walter Walker was openly talking of recruiting 3 million people to his organization, Civil Assistance, to defy the wreckers. Meanwhile, Colonel David Stirling, founder of the SAS, was secretly recruiting 'patriotic' volunteers for his rival outfit, GB '75. However, his new project did not quite match the SAS tradition of discretion. 'We have been rumbled before we were ready,' he groaned.

But this new one, with its chillingly terse message and the budget for a national poster campaign, seemed really serious. These could really be people ready to march into Downing Street and arrest the Wilson gang for treason. A couple of weeks after it appeared, all was revealed. The new version suggested the top half had been torn away to reveal something new and gaudy: **Now for Britain it's Elf!**

In other words, Elf Aquitaine, the giant French oil company, was rebranding a lot of petrol stations and wished us to know about it.

Nothing was unthinkable. Six months before Wilson scraped back into office in February 1974, Chile, which had the strongest democratic tradition in Latin America, experienced a right-wing military coup turfing out a left-wing minority government with extreme brutality. When Sir Douglas Allen, the permanent secretary of the Treasury, talked about finding tanks drawn up on Horse Guards Parade, his colleagues were not quite sure whether it was a joke or not.

A left-wing coup in the UK was obvious fantasy. But no one knew how savage the IRA bombings might get. And the armed forces and security services were already getting deeply entwined with right-wing paramilitaries in Northern Ireland. Who knew how far these tentacles stretched? Certainly not Wilson. Because it didn't happen, that didn't mean it was impossible.

The idea that the country was going to pot, the dogs or hell in a handcart was by no means new. The people of Glastonbury probably greeted Joseph of Arimathea with the same grumble. But it can never have had the intellectual dominance that it did in the 1970s. Since both sides had two spells of government of not-far-off equal duration, it was not even a partisan issue. Denis Healey said in January 1974: 'No amount of dithering and double talk . . . can disguise the fact that the British economy was going to hell in a handcart.' He only stopped saying it because six weeks later he became Chancellor and was put in charge of the handcart. This changed the route but not the direction of travel.

In 1973, with the Tories still in power, the bosses' spokesman, Michael Clapham of the Confederation of British Industry, had said the British risked becoming 'the peasants of the Western world' due to low productivity. Six months later, Lord Rothschild, the head of the Downing Street policy unit, warned that Britain could be Europe's poorest country by 1985. Heath was livid (LORD THINK GETS A ROCKET, said the *Express*); Enver Hoxha, the dictator of dirt-poor Albania, was probably flattered.

The economic sages Samuel Brittan in the *Financial Times* and Peter Jay in *The Times* were if not outright declinists then certainly pessimists; Peter Jenkins, *The Guardian*'s political columnist, made national decline – as his colleague Alan Watkins put it – 'his preoccupation, some might say obsession'.

The theorists of Britain's decline certainly reached well back for its starting point. In *God is an Englishman* (1970) the Australian Donald Horne, perhaps the most damning of all the critics, goes back to the Great Exhibition in Hyde Park in 1851, when Britain won eighty out of the ninety gold medals – whereas at the Paris Exhibition in 1867 it won only twelve. Home advantage usually plays some role when gold medals are at stake, and though the official title was the 'Great Exhibition of the Works of Industry of All Nations', the whole point was to show who was top dog.

Clearly, the new world (and to an extent Germany) began to outcompete Britain in the late nineteenth century and excelled in the hi-tech of the day: electricity, telephones, petroleum. Was this when decay set in? It was followed over the next century, according to Horne, by a 'strong element of frivolity in British business' . . . 'notorious slowness of British management' . . . 'One self-delusion following another' . . . 'aristocratic autocracy, corruption, and muddle'. And so on. Other writers followed a similar line of attack – most relentlessly the Englishman Correlli Barnett in his four-volume *Pride and Fall* sequence, published between 1972 and 2001, chronicling 'a fateful pattern of national over-ambition combined with industrial underperformance'.

The American Martin J. Wiener, writing at the start of the Thatcher era, disapprovingly noted a survey of Britain commissioned by the magazine *New Society* which showed a nation 'remarkably unambitious in a material sense . . . Very few sincerely want to be rich. Most people in Britain neither want nor expect a great deal of money. Even if they could get it, the vast majority do not seem prepared to work harder for it: most of our respondents thought we should work only as much as we need to live a pleasant life . . . It seems clear that the British today prefer economic stability to rapid economic growth.' Wiener made it sound like damnation.

But there is another school of thought that denies the whole declinism thesis. It has been expressed most vigorously by Professor David Edgerton of King's College London. He agrees that Britain's position in the world was in relative decline – economically, militarily and diplomatically – in the second half of the twentieth century and before. But he rejects the blame culture that attends it.

'Mostly it wasn't anybody's fault, it was just inevitable,' he told me. 'The declinist explanation was doubly false – it assumed that it was all the nation's fault, and found the wrong explanation – about what happened before 1914, not what happened after 1945. It refuses to recognize the obvious fact that Britain was more modern in crucial respects before the first war than Germany or the US.

'After the second war other countries were growing faster because they had scope to do so: most British workers had left the land long before so there were fewer workers available to go into factories. Yet Britain had become self-sufficient in agriculture, which it never was at the height of empire. And Britain was still growing steadily at 2.5 per cent a year. In the fifties and sixties most British people could see their lives getting better faster than ever before.'

But the overall sense of decline in the seventies, Edgerton says, was experienced from the upper-middle class – which was expanding numerically but losing ground relatively to the working class. He certainly accepts there certainly were failures – like the car industry. British motor manufacturers' sales peaked in 1972. From then on, buyers began to get the message.

———◦———

'Quite a lot of makes have significantly good reliability and, sadly, nearly all of them are foreign,' said a *Which?* report in 1974. 'Foreign cars had on average only half as many faults as the four main British makes,' said a survey in the AA magazine *Drive*, which proposed a Square Wheel award for the owner with the most troublesome car. Interesting name that: it was also the symbol that defined the Austin Allegro (the 'All-aggro', as it soon became known), which appeared in 1973 with what everyone called a square steering wheel.

It was not exactly square, but it was not exactly round either. The intention was to give a clear view of the instrument panel, not

that there was much to see. It was all well intentioned and it was
not that dreadful a car: it just had too many compromises and not
enough virtues to transform the future of failing British Leyland.
Within five years, foreign cars – mainly Japanese or German – were
taking half the British market even though there were still millions
of people whose wartime memories were raw enough to make them
insist they would never buy such a thing. Until they bought another
British clunker. In the seventies, the journalist Neal Ascherson
drove back regularly from Germany, and when he joined the British
motorway network kept noting the broken fan-belts strewn across
the hard shoulder. 'British cars hadn't been designed for motorway
speeds,' he reflected.

One sure sign of national decline is caring what other people
think. In May 1975, Eric Sevareid, a big-shot newsman from the
American CBS network, proclaimed that 'Wilson's government is at
the stage of Allende's Chilean government when a minority tried to
force a profound transformation of society upon the majority'. It
was a fatuous analogy given that Wilson's sole aim each day was to
get through it. But it made big news in Britain.

Anyway, some Americans thought that, if this was decline, they
liked it. Bernard Nossiter, London correspondent for the *Washington
Post* during the 1970s, found it appealing. The British, he wrote,
appear to be 'the first citizens of the post-industrial age who are
choosing leisure over goods on a large scale'. Anthony Lewis of *The
New York Times*, going home after a stint as London correspondent
in 1973, hymned just this: 'There is a larger reality than the pound
and inflation and the Gross National Product. It is life, and the
British are good at that. They know how to live.' *Live?* Isn't that
what foreigners do?

Was national life really some perpetual Olympics competing
against everyone else? Did we have to live to work rather than work
to live? Seen from fifty years on, and what we now know about the
planet, maybe Britain was ahead of its time, not behind it.

But change and decay was visible. As a Tory back-room boy, the
young Ferdinand Mount was sent on a tour of the northern
constituencies in the early sixties. He saw a Britain that still hummed

with industry but with profit margins 'melting like butter in the sun under competition from the Continent and the Far East'. Ten years later he passed that way again: 'Through industrial wastelands with roofless workshops, scenes of desolation as grim as any I have seen.'*

Scenes like these were visible across ex-industrial Britain. In 1972, as the mills were fading away in the Pennine cotton town of Barnoldswick, Slaters Mill closed down and Mary Wilkin, much admired by her colleagues as a top-notch loom weaver, had to move to Bancroft Mill, originally owned by the Nutter family. She didn't think much of it: 'Slaters were modern, Bancroft were ramshackle, run-down and nobody bothered . . . it were gradually going downhill weren't it?'

On 22 September 1978 – on old-fashioned notepaper with an ornately old-fashioned letterhead (James Nutter & Sons Ltd: Shirtings, Twills, Jeanettes, Drills &c.), with an old-fashioned telegraphic address (NUTTERS, BARNOLDSWICK) and an old-fashioned telephone number (2191), on an old-fashioned typewriter, using old-fashioned punctuation – Nutters announced that production would cease, citing the effects of running at half-capacity, persistent 'adverse trading conditions', and the cost of complying with clean air regulations. It was the last mill to be built in the town, and the last to be closed.

———◆———

Perhaps nothing embodied the perception of decline quite so much as the Cod Wars, in which the might of whatever was left of the British Empire was defeated not once but three times by a country with a population slightly larger than a middle-sized English city – Hull, for example.

The opposition was Iceland, which, under international law, was wholly in the wrong and morally wrong too – in that it was quite

---

* The rooflessness, said Mount, was due to a crazy regulation that levied business rates on any disused workshop with a roof on it. In the early 1970s I travelled regularly by train through the West Midlands. In Smethwick there was a scene very like the one he describes, plus a huge sign: WHERE WILL YOU SPEND ETERNITY?

happy to stoop to recklessness, mild piracy and blackmail. But it was an illustration of how a small country that feels itself existentially threatened can defeat any power on earth. And the final war was contested through the winter and spring of 1975–76, shortly after the United States was chased out of Vietnam. The three Cod Wars caused just one death (accidental), possibly making the conflicts less dangerous than normal fishing in those latitudes.

The last one began in November 1975, when Iceland declared a 200-mile exclusion zone to protect its fish stocks. A month later, British trawlers sheltering off Iceland in a gale were harassed and an Icelandic patrol boat was rammed. The Royal Navy was sent north and there were some nasty moments – reportedly twenty-two incidents of ramming – even if it was never quite all-out war. Veering towards the frigate HMS *Leander* one day, Captain Helgi Hallvardsson of the patrol ship *Thor* was roaring with laughter: 'Anybody want to come aboard for tea?' Captain John Tait of the *Leander* shouted back: 'No thank you. I prefer coffee.' They still collided, with minor damage.

It was the blackmail that settled it. Iceland said that if Britain did not give in, they would leave the Atlantic Alliance and NATO would be expelled from the Keflavik air base. At this point the Pentagon blew the whistle and effectively declared Iceland the winners. The Cold War trumped the Cod War.

'In the late sixties, Hull was the biggest white fish port in the world,' said local boy Barrie Rutter. 'Then it was just gone. It was the devastation of this city. It took decades to recover.' Skipper Ken Knox saw which way it might go and took a dry-land job as a marine cartographer: 'But we didn't think it could be as drastic as it was. Two to three hundred ships down to nothing. The fish stocks off Greenland all failed. Nobody could figure it out.' It was the next century before the actual trawlermen got any compensation. Those who had lived to collect it.

———•———

In London, the new oil-rich masters were moving in. In 1974 Kuwait bought St Martins, one of London's leading property groups, for

£107 million. More cheaply but more flashily, a Middle East consortium bought the Dorchester Hotel two years later. Thereafter it passed to Lebanese and then Hong Kong interests, before settling in the safe arms of the Sultan of Brunei (and home, it was alleged, to his brother Jefri's forty-strong harem). By 1976 it was reported that some Arabs were losing up to half a million a night in London's casinos.

That was the year Sheikh Mohammed Al Maktoum, the future ruler of Dubai, started to send over his private jet on a monthly basis to collect eight tons of feed from Norfolk to be flown back home for his horses and game birds. The next year, his racehorse Hatta won at Brighton to start the sheikh's progress towards pushing aside the petty local aristocrats who once ruled the turf. Winners of big races – owners and their horses – henceforth would increasingly have Arabic names. Soon Witanhurst, London's biggest private house, complete with thirteen acres on Highgate Hill, was marketed for £7 million. Various potential buyers had inspected it, all reportedly from the Middle East.

All this marked the start of a major change. London had once been the epitome of England and Britain. Now, while some were still feeling discomfited by the presence of non-white neighbours, the upper classes were being outcompeted by overseas buyers – a process that was only just beginning. And London was on its way to becoming an increasingly cosmopolitan city, and much less a collection of villages. Its Britishness became a veneer for the tourists. Behind closed doors, even West End gentlemen's clubs were in trouble: closing, merging, letting in women.

And if the sheikhs were not heading your way with silly money, there was also the possibility of going to them. In 1976, British dockers were being recruited for the Saudi port of Dammam at four times their previous pay. Go east, young man, and be discreet about the home-brew hooch or else. Several Britons were caned by the Saudis after being caught selling alcohol. 'Just like a school caning,' said one gamely, after receiving 300 of the best. It was not so much decline, more a new world order.

With the creative tastelessness that was becoming its hallmark, *The Sun* led its front page on 18 October 1973 with the headline END OF THE WORLD. This referred to the fact that the England football team had, against all expectations, only drawn with Poland at Wembley and had thus failed to qualify for the World Cup finals for the first time since they had deigned to take part in this foreigners' gimmick in 1950.

It was assuredly the end for Sir Alf Ramsey, who seemed to forget the new-fangled rule permitting substitutes. He was followed in the job by Don Revie, a highly successful club manager at Leeds whose teams were never accused of being dainty. Even before England failed to make the finals a second time, Revie suddenly reinvented himself as the manager of the United Arab Emirates for a reported £85,000 a year tax-free – a staggering amount. It was not so much the resignation that made everyone so angry, it was *where* he was going.

In sport, where relative performance compared to other countries really does matter, British – and specifically English – national teams were beset by declinism. The England rugby team were persistent losers between 1963 and 1980: Wales, with a team for the ages, won the Five Nations title five times in the 1970s.

The England cricket team was massacred by the Australian fast bowlers in the definitive Ashes series of the era 1974–75, and their administrators were massacred in court by the Australian tycoon Kerry Packer when he bought up the world's leading players to put on his own show in 1977. In trying to stop the uncouth Packer, the gents of Lord's found themselves on the wrong end of restraint of trade legislation. At the eleven summer Olympics from 1928 to 1976, Britain won a total of thirty-nine gold medals – one less than Communist East Germany won at Montreal in 1976 alone. Given the obscene use of mass doping, it was a tribute to the British spirit of amateurism.

In one sporting event the white flag was actually raised. After half a century of playing and almost always losing to the US in the

Ryder Cup, the Britain and Ireland golf team was expanded to include the rest of Europe. This is said to have been a polite suggestion from the American star Jack Nicklaus (subtext: this is getting boring).

For its first ninety years, English league football was played almost wholly by tough working-class Anglo-Saxons with a leavening of even tougher Celts. Into the 1970s foreigners were exotics; a double-barrelled name like Ian Storey-Moore very rare; university men likewise, though Liverpool actually had two, Steve Heighway and Brian Hall.* The first home-grown black players were coming through, which was not an easy process. Then in 1978, something much more dramatic happened.

Harry Haslam, the manager of Second Division Sheffield United, had an Argentinian assistant, Oscar Arce, who helped Tottenham Hotspur sign two of Argentina's World Cup-winning team, Osvaldo Ardiles and Ricardo Villa. On the back of that, United themselves tried to sign a promising teenager called Diego Maradona, but had to content themselves with a fringe international called Alejandro Sabella. English football's demographics and, in due course, its quality would never be the same again.†

Sometimes the intimations of decline were more hurtful. The traditional boltholes of British escape, the old dominions, were closing. About a quarter of Britons fantasized about emigration, said the *Daily Telegraph*, and in 1974 emigrants far outnumbered immigrants. Indeed, the fancy touched both main party leaders: Jim Callaghan, before he got the job, told colleagues: 'If I were a younger man, I'd emigrate,' and Thatcher told Kingsley Amis that if she did not win the next election, she would fix her twins up with jobs in Canada.

But the top three countries of choice, Canada, Australia and

---

* Bamber Gascoigne, host of *University Challenge*, was the obvious source of inspiration, so Heighway became 'Big Bamber' and Hall 'Little Bamber'.

† Contemporary joke – Haslam (pointing to blackboard): 'Ball . . . kick . . . goal.' Player: 'You don't need to speak like that, boss. Sabella understands English.' Haslam: 'I'm not talking to him, I'm talking to you lot.' When Maradona died in 2020, the *Sheffield Star* called him 'Argentina World Cup winner and one-time Sheffield United transfer target'.

New Zealand, were all getting pickier as far as the British were concerned. The White Australia policy, which originally meant taking only the British and Irish, had gradually been softened, until by 1977 they wanted skills – and increasingly only the skills they were short of. All three countries said few British applicants met their criteria. So South Africa, less picky where whites were concerned, became the most popular destination in the mid-seventies, which suggested the newcomers might not be bringing the skill of political foresight.

Even Greenwich Mean Time was being abandoned globally to be replaced by UTC, which was a compromise: standing for either Coordinated Universal Time or *Temps Universel Coordonné* and swerving the French suggestion that it should be called TUC.

Out of sight and mostly out of mind, amid the stormy North Sea, something was bubbling. In November 1975, the Queen, wearing BP green, pressed a gold button to let the oil gush forth along a 130-mile pipeline and inaugurated what Harold Wilson called 'a day of outstanding significance' and 'a new industrial revolution'. Two years later, North Sea oil was already meeting almost half of Britain's needs. Here was hope. Here was a reason not to go to South Africa. Here was a way to buy back the Dorchester Hotel. Oh, joy!

11

ANARCHY ON THE KING'S ROAD

BY THE 1970S, HETEROSEXUAL SEX BETWEEN CONSENTING adults had become normalized, rather than being something fresh and exciting – like fridges and wall-to-wall carpeting. It became possible to imagine it was around in our parents' time. It almost seemed to have been around forever.

The term *living in sin*, meaning cohabitating outside marriage, began to disappear. It was now even feasible for young men and women to live together simply as flatmates or to be 'just good friends' without everyone assuming something else.* By 1978, the ITV comedy *Robin's Nest* centred on an unmarried couple living together; this was said to have been referred to the regulator, the IBA, for approval. Around the same time, *bastard* – previously regarded either as a technical term or a grave insult – lost most of its connection with illegitimacy and became routine abuse or even, as in Australia, a term of endearment.

The Sun's generally uninhibited approach led it to serialize Terry Garrity's *The Sensuous Woman*, 'the most outspoken sex manual ever written', as early as 1970. Its inhibitions did, however, kick in before allowing anything too outré. The *Mirror*, losing ground fast

---

* Although the phrase *let's just be friends* when that was not the plan was always a disastrous outcome to a night out.

in the circulation war, began running similar features, though with a more antiseptic whiff.

Yet consistency was not the 1970s' strong point. Despite all this, both papers shuddered with shock and refused to print a bland advert from the Health Education Council about contraception. Family planning ads were also banned from London's buses and tubes – and television. Yet sex as a commodity was everywhere.

'Pornography became industrialised,' wrote the historian of British sex Paul Ferris. After a few tentative moves in the late 1960s, the two standard masturbatory mags for males, *Playboy* and its (originally British) rival *Penthouse*, regularly revealed that women had pubic hair. *Penthouse*, as the newcomer, started it, and in 1971 *Playboy* felt obliged to join in. This became known as the 'Pubic Wars', and was mimicked a little more demurely in the upper-body wars waged by the British tabloids.

Rawer meat was readily available. One explanation for the appeal court rejecting the sentences imposed at the 1971 *Oz* trial was that one of the three judges, Mr Justice James, remarked to his colleagues that far more pornographic material was available in Soho. The other two were incredulous. James sent his clerk out with £20; he came back with an armful of hard porn and the case was over.

There was something even James might not have known: this was all officially sanctioned, in a manner of speaking. In 1967, an article in *The People* had noted that the twenty-eight Soho porn shops lasted longer if they got tipped off about police raids. It ultimately became clear to even the doziest judge that the tip-offs came from the police themselves, who had been running a racket on a spectacular scale with a fixed tariff for bribes: £60 a week for a sergeant up to £150 for a chief inspector, and £1,000 to open a new shop. Porn was lucrative enough to sustain this, and investment in new technology was helping the business expand – blue movies now lived up to their names by being in colour and professionally shot. Many were imported from anything-goes Denmark in 'fishing boats, bacon lorries and consignments of chicken offal'.

The facts became clearer when *The People* ran another story in

1972 revealing that James Humphreys, Soho's 'porn king', had been on holiday with Ken Drury, head of the Flying Squad, and their wives. Humphreys paid and kept records, just in case. Drury even signed the register of the hotel in Cyprus as 'Commander, Metropolitan Police'. By now the number of Soho shops had grown to fifty-nine. It still took five years before Drury was jailed for corruption. Ferris noted the decline in prostitution, and not just because they had become less visible after the 1959 Act drove them from the streets. 'The unheroic reason,' he suspected, 'was that men masturbated more.'

Meanwhile, out in the real world beyond Soho, it was more difficult. *Forum*, a mildly lubricious magazine offering sex advice to readers and edited by the psychotherapist Phillip Hodson, was intermittently harassed by less biddable coppers, especially around Manchester where a new, young and attention-seeking chief constable, James Anderton, was determined to take the city back to the early fifties. 'You can't even buy *Playboy* in Manchester any more,' lamented Hodson.

And in South London, on the quiet streets of Streatham, a delightful madam called Cynthia Payne ('Madam Cyn') operated an old-fashioned bawdy house with a varied menu and apparently no . complaints from either the neighbours or the clientele. The police marched in using Mancunian principles of policing rather than the Soho version. The public were delighted by the revelation that, as in-house currency, she used luncheon vouchers, which were designed to save poorly paid secretaries from starving themselves; Madame Cyn's business was aimed at stopping elderly males from being sex-starved. She refused to name her clients (some were rumoured to be famous, which is unlikely in Streatham) with the words: 'Me morals is low. But me ethics is high.' She went to jail and emerged as a popular character: one book, two films, two jolly election campaigns, but no whip-and-tell.

———•———

So the old Adam and Eve continued much as before, although Eve's requirements were still under-represented. The women's magazine

Over 21 ran an advert for a vibrator in 1977, but only once – the management took fright; its rivals had refused from the start. The newly legal pairing of Adam and Adam remained very fraught indeed. Although consensual homosexual acts in private were permissible for over-21s, privacy was being defined, according to the activist Peter Tatchell, as 'in a person's own home, behind locked doors and windows, with the curtains drawn and with no other person present in any part of the house'.* Beyond that, laws were more vigorously enforced than ever.

On a November night in 1970, Britain's first gay rights demo was held in Highbury Fields, Islington, demanding, among other things, the right to kiss and hold hands in public. If the police were looking to make arrests, it was dangerous to wink, smile or ask for a light. In 1972 came the first Gay Pride march, ending in a 2,000-strong mass kiss-in in Trafalgar Square.†

Outside London, the reception could be unpredictable. In Burnley an attempt to open a discreet gay club was thwarted by militant Christians. The Campaign for Homosexual Equality arranged their annual conference for Morecambe in 1973 only for the council's 'publicity, entertainments and baths committee' to fib that they did not have adequate facilities. The conference did go ahead on the privately owned pier, chaired by the broadcaster Ray Gosling, and made serious progress in refining its priorities – including getting more women members. Councillors did not respond to an invitation to attend a social night, drag act included. In 1974 the Court of Appeal ruled that it was still a slur to say someone was homosexual.

However, without anyone protesting, campaigning or even asking, someone began transforming the image of homosexuality. He did not come from Burnley or Morecambe; indeed, in more ways than one, he seemed to come from another planet. In 1972, after a few failed efforts to make the big time, David Bowie emerged at the Rainbow Theatre in London in the persona of Ziggy Stardust:

---

* And even the sealed-container exemption did not apply in Scotland or Northern Ireland.
† These events may be seen as the death knell for the old use of *gay* in Britain.

'sequinned, gleaming suits, spiky hair and high-heeled boots', along with 'a mime troupe, light show, film backdrop' plus 'an aura of camp: sparkling eye make-up, lipstick and sullen, butch looks at the audience whose own parade was a show in itself'.

This was the epitome of what became known as glam rock. In showbiz terms it was as if a sixties rock concert had met a Broadway musical. A few months earlier, the Rolling Stones had embarked on a tour of the US that started the revolution in how to stage a rock concert. Under Mick Jagger's direction they carted their stage set – spotlight, huge bank of speakers, a forty-foot-long overhead mirror – and his wardrobe of jumpsuits from state to state, as though this were Barnum & Bailey circus. Only the elephants were missing. It made The Beatles look like rank amateurs; no screamers would now drown out Mick. The tour was also infamous for the backstage bacchanal.

But Bowie had also broken fresh ground: he came out as gay, in an interview with *Melody Maker*. 'I'm gay and always have been,' he said, though he modified it under questioning to bisexual: he was already married and a father. This was certainly a pioneering declaration: previously in Britain this was usually admitted only in a courtroom. Elton John, also just making it big, was keeping very quiet and thought Bowie was committing career suicide.* Also, it was far from clear whether Bowie was making a genuine admission or betting that he was making himself more intriguing.

And to one group in particular, perhaps. In that era, especially in places in Burnley, many thousand boys were growing up, feeling ill at ease with the casual ribaldry of their mates, thinking they must be different, wondering if perhaps they might be, well, queer. Here was the first proof that, if so, they were not alone, and that they too could still be heroic. This was a huge moment, even if it was only for show.

Five years later Tom Robinson belted out the anthem '(Sing If You're) Glad to Be Gay' on ITV, to much public outrage – even

---

* Indeed, Bowie did not make it big in the States until four years later, when he junked the camp and reinvented himself as the Thin White Duke.

though the particularly provocative final verse was omitted. Robinson was light years ahead of Bowie's sly camp when it came to outness, though he did later lose a little authenticity and adulation when he went in the other direction and married a woman.

---·---

In the unusual case of Corbett v. Corbett in February 1970, Mr Justice Ormrod annulled the marriage between Arthur Corbett, a minor aristocrat, and the model April Ashley because it was not between a man and a woman. Before having a sex-change operation, as it was then always known, Ashley was physically male in all respects, if not psychologically, he concluded. The operation did not change that fact although, the judge declared, 'the pastiche of femininity was very convincing'. It was a devastating judgment for Ashley, which defined the law for more than thirty years and broke her financially.

In March 1974, the *Sunday Times* announced that the writer James Morris had also changed sex and was now Jan Morris. This was startling news from this previously little-known corner of life's rich tapestry. Morris was already well-known: a wartime officer in the Lancers, the man who had brought the news down from Everest in 1953, and had married and fathered five children, and a bestselling writer with a lush, imaginative style. She revealed that she had wanted to be a girl from about the age of three. As with Bowie and Robinson and gayness, this news and her book *Conundrum* must have encouraged some people with suppressed feelings along those lines to feel more comfortable about them. Some of Morris's friends thought, quietly, this was a triumph of her imagination over biological facts.

This case would not have impressed Mr Justice Ormrod, nor indeed Roberta Cowell, who had pioneered this journey twenty years earlier. In 1972 she had given a brief, rare interview and offered her advice on the subject: Don't. 'I was a freak,' she said. 'I had an operation and I'm not a freak any more. I had female chromosome make-up, XX. The people who have followed me have often been those with male chromosomes, XY. So they've been normal people who've turned themselves into freaks by means of the operation . . . Many people thought they could copy me. But it's like admiring someone without legs, like Douglas Bader, and having your legs off to be the same.'

————◆————

There were signs that slow progress was being made towards the normalization of gay life. One was that the Campaign for Homosexual Equality's annual conference no longer presented a united front to the outside world but bickered internally, just like the Labour Party. In 1975, the *Guardian* report said: 'Mr Keith Hose, a paedophile – one who is sexually attracted to children – persuaded the conference . . . to censure its committee . . .' Its offence was to relegate discussion of the paedophiles' wish list to a minor role in proceedings.

Note in particular the words between the dashes: readers were not expected to know what paedophiles were. Two days later the paper's diarist, John Torode, took up the theme: 'At what point do you climb off the trendy liberal bus? When do you ring the bell and tell the conductor "Thus far and no further?"' Torode also defined the word *paedophiles*: 'child molesters to you and me'. He was beset by angry letters, some from paedophiles and some from others who thought they deserved a hearing.

Hose and the other members of the previously unknown Paedophile Information Exchange (PIE) had reason to think they might be kicking at an open door. Outrageous cases of child abuse had long been treated with startling leniency by normally stern judges, as the case of Sir Ian Horobin in the sixties graphically illustrated,* and by the seventies this was morphing into the idea that the age of consent was too high because girls were maturing earlier and the law was simply being flouted. Before finally departing the Home Office, Roy Jenkins asked a committee to look into this, but the moment passed before anything could happen.

In some cases, the most unexpected institutions took a benign

———

* See p. 365.

attitude to liaisons between youngish men and teenage girls. At a Catholic school in Kent, a fifth-form girl became engaged to a 23-year-old teacher. The school was so delighted they called a special assembly to announce the news. When a teacher in County Durham became so obsessed with a pupil that he phoned her up to eighty times a day, he was fined £20. In the Appeal Court, Lord Justice Scarman freed a 19-year-old boy who got six months for having sex with a 13-year-old after a party. 'This happens almost every Saturday night all over the country,' he said. It was notable, said the historian Alwyn Turner, that in the rare cases involving older women and boys, the press were less sympathetic.

Meanwhile, a report from the Sexual Law Reform Society also proposed downgrading rape and incest to mere assaults. That pretty much left only bestiality on the taboo list, presumably because that was not what anyone had in mind when they said Britain was a nation of animal lovers. But actually the National Council for Civil Liberties trumped this by suggesting that incest should be legalized – and that paedophilia should at least be treated less seriously. It also proposed a sliding scale for consent: allowing, for instance, 14-year-olds to have sex with 10-year-olds. And hereabouts the trendy liberal bus finally did screech to a halt.

The bus was assailed by an unholy alliance comprising the *News of the World*, Mary Whitehouse and the National Union of Public Employees, who had Tom O'Carroll, by now the chairman of PIE, removed from a conference in Swansea with a strike threat. The *News of the World* infiltrated PIE and Whitehouse fastened on to the dangers of 'kiddie porn'; this got Margaret Thatcher, as opposition leader, involved – at which point Jim Callaghan had to respond as prime minister and ensure that the Protection of Children Act, banning indecent pictures of children, became law in 1978.

O'Carroll lost his job at the Open University, went to jail, and in 1984 fled the country. PIE folded, never to raise its head above the parapet again. Jimmy Savile did not leave the country. He had been called in by two senior officials at Radio 1 in 1973 to discuss 'serious' matters, had lightly dismissed the allegations of seducing underage girls knowing they had no proof, and carried on regardless.

The music of the 1970s was in many ways a reversion to that of the 1950s. Firstly, established artists were falling back on fifties stand-ards and turning them into big hits. Secondly, the fragmentation of taste meant a return to musical snobbery. Just as jazz looked down on pop, and classical had looked down on them both in the old days, smart-arse older brothers would listen to John Peel's pro-fundities late at night while snorting at the Eurovision pastiche, 'Chirpy Chirpy Cheep Cheep', by the Scottish group Middle of the Road, which sold 10 million copies worldwide and lingers as a particularly infuriating earworm.

The era of glam rock passed and there was a two-year run of success for the Bay City Rollers, which may constitute, despite the hot competition, the most baffling of all seventies phenomena. They were Scottish too, created by a Svengali called Tam Paton – son of a potato merchant from Prestonpans – using the Osmonds, the clean-cut Utah Mormon family band, as a model. He kitted the boys out with tartan trimmings, adding a touch of newly fashionable Scottish nationalism, and told the press their favourite drink was milk. They induced a lot of sixties-style screaming which helped disguise their fragile musicianship.

They had a string of hits, peaking – in keeping with the retro mood – with a remake of the Four Seasons' 'Bye, Bye, Baby'. This, according to the subculture expert Dick Hebdige, also had the distinction of being the first of their records the boys actually made themselves rather than session musicians. They even briefly made it big in the US. They were not, however, quite like the Osmonds, since they went on to drug overdoses, fatal car crashes and (in Paton's case) child abuse. There may have been some milk: band members later claimed Paton had milked them of up to £50 million in royalties.

In the opening days of the decade, a Liverpool road safety officer complained about girls wearing the new maxi-skirts as he was driving to work on dark winter mornings. They were much harder to see than those wearing minis and showing plenty of pale thigh, said Lionel Piper, 49. He would have been delighted by the next fashion: hot pants – tiny tailored shorts which took the hemline to the uppermost limit outside the Metropolitan Police-approved porn emporia, though not best suited to January mornings on Merseyside.

In the summer of 1970, women were allowed to wear trousers in the Royal Enclosure at Ascot, and as the decade developed women began to wear minis, maxis and midis as they saw fit, which was unheard of. There were a lot of Laura Ashley prints. Otherwise, men and women wore flared jeans and bell-bottoms, just after the Royal Navy modernized them away along with the rum ration. Men favoured kipper ties, sideburns and Zapata moustaches, gold medallions over hairy chests, and giant collars that looked like Concorde taking off. Those who got married in the 1970s may find their wedding pictures rather embarrassing, particularly if the photographer stayed on for the dancing. Ascot 1973 was notable for women in platform soles – inelegant, probably uncomfortable, but more practical than stilettos if it rained, which it did.

———◦———

The noun *punk* has been an unusually flexible one, meaning at various times in the past 450 years a prostitute (in Elizabethan England), a homosexual, a catamite, a petty criminal, a nobody, a coward, an amateur and a young circus animal. For most of its life, the word lived in America, and even as a musical genre it began life in the US in 1970. But punk reached its apotheosis when it returned to London halfway through the decade, when those too young to get the full flavour of the sixties found themselves living in a country mired in miserabilism.

Punk's attitudes were nurtured on London's football terraces. Its style was born in a rogue boutique on the King's Road run by Vivienne Westwood and her *amour* Malcolm McLaren, which, after various other incarnations, was called simply SEX. 'A chaos of quiffs and leather jackets, brothel creepers and winkle pickers,' wrote Hebdige, 'plimsolls and pacamacs, moddy crops and skinhead

strides, drainpipes and vivid socks, bum freezers and bovver boots
– all kept in place . . . by the spectacular adhesives: the safety pins
and plastic clothes pegs, the bondage straps and bits of string.'
Swastikas and fishnet stockings were optional accessories. Ripped
T-shirts cost £30 – a likely weekly wage for a working teenager.

Musically, it began in Britain at fetid London venues like the 100
Club on Oxford Street in September 1976, where 600 people
queued to watch 'the first ever' punk festival – including the Sex
Pistols, The Clash and The Damned. 'Indisputable evidence that a
new decade in rock is about to begin,' said *Melody Maker*.

As a national phenomenon and moral panic, it did not exist until
the December night when the Sex Pistols appeared on the early-
evening London regional show on ITV, *Today*, hosted by the gifted
but bibulous Bill Grundy. In a brief interview, eight group members
and hangers-on* plonked themselves round the studio like the
guests from hell, and added significantly to ITV's measly all-time
fuck count with three uses of the word in two minutes.

There was predictable fury – or at least the newspaper confection,
'fury'. This did not go the way one would normally expect. The
casualty was Grundy, who was deemed to have incited the Pistols;
he was banished from mainstream television and his career was
effectively over. McLaren, the group's manager, was ecstatic: 'Mr
Grundy's intention to expose the Sex Pistols as loud-mouthed yobs
was misdirected. They have never pretended to be anything else.'

The Pistols were banned from Preston and Bournemouth, and
two record companies, EMI and A&M, one after the other,
cancelled their contracts – which was a bonus, since both had to
pay compensation. The next move was for McLaren and the group's
lead singer, Johnny Rotten (né John Lydon), to axe the bassist, Glen
Matlock, who could actually play, and replace him with Sid Vicious
(né Simon Ritchie), who couldn't. This made it clear the Pistols
were essentially a novelty act trading in outrage. The kids lapped it
up. Other punk groups were playing seriously but they could not
compete with this.

---

*   Including Siouxsie Sioux, soon to be famous herself.

Rotten did have a sharp wit, and there was something compelling about his voice and his presence. On the other hand, the oeuvre had shock value but minimal artistic merit. It may have made sense after a few rum and cokes and a couple of uppers at the 100 Club.

The Establishment did have a kind of revenge: the Pistols' version of 'God Save the Queen' probably should have been No. 1 for the week of the Silver Jubilee in 1977, which would have been a huge and embarrassing story. Somehow Rod Stewart just beat them to it. Them that ask no questions isn't told a lie. Their album *Never Mind the Bollocks, Here's the Sex Pistols*, released that autumn, did reach No. 1.

'It was electrifying to a 15-year-old,' the future rock critic Tim de Lisle reminisced to me. 'It was this blast of energy and attitude that was like the first coming of rock and roll. It amplified all the complicated feelings of being a teenager. It was fast, catchy, shouty music and none of the grown-ups liked it.'

It was a moment in time. Then their fans grew a bit older and less angry, took more showers and began disco dancing instead.*

---

* Vicious became a heroin addict and was arrested for stabbing to death his even more outrageous girlfriend Nancy Spungen in New York in late 1978. On bail after a detox, he took a fatal overdose four months later. The others appeared to live contentedly ever after.

12

HEATWAVE AND HUMILIATION

O N MONDAY, 2 JUNE 1975, MUCH OF BRITAIN WOKE TO snowflakes. County cricket was snowed off at Buxton and Colchester. Gales flattened scoreboards and a refreshment tent at the Amateur Golf Championship at Hoylake. Vehicles were stranded in drifts all over the Highlands. The odd flurry was even sighted in London, where it was January-cold.

On the Thursday, the whole of Britain awoke to the duty of voting whether or not to stay in the Common Market. The sun appeared. In a fit of what might have been gratitude, Britain voted to remain in Europe, possibly to enjoy Continental drinking hours and weather.

And, lo, it came to pass, for two whole summers. The sun beat down. And even in the winter of 1975–76 there was little rain: the driest sixteen months since calculations began. In late June and July 1976, temperatures rose into the nineties Fahrenheit (above 32 Centigrade for young readers) day after day, over much of England. It was certainly the hottest summer in most of England since 1826 – maybe since the first primitive records were kept in 1659.

But this was Britain in the 1970s, when even the good times were bad. The summer of 1975, when the snows cleared, was very pleasant. 1976, however, began to seem unnerving, threatening, un-British.

A warm Easter and an agreeable May were followed by a long-range forecast for June of 'below average sunshine and above average rainfall'. Long-range meteorology at that stage was on a par with medieval medicine. The Met Office kept predicting rain. By June there was talk of water rationing. In East Anglia, people were being told to think twice about having a glass of water. Panic broke out on a Bakerloo line train stranded in a tunnel through signal failure. Overheating cars blocked the M4. Four hundred tennis-goers were overcome by heat at Wimbledon, not including the Egyptian diplomat arrested for bottom-pinching (he claimed diplomatic immunity). The House of Commons was described as 'a battlefield . . . people fainting all over the place'. In Hyde Park, there was a hundred-yard queue to swim in the Serpentine.

Some workers walked out because of the heat (air conditioning was still a rarity), while others walked out just because: a hundred British Leyland component delivery drivers complained they had not been included in a company raffle. The spring warmth brought forth aphids, which drew in billions of their predators, seven-spotted ladybirds – who, when the aphids had all gone, turned to nibbling the humans' ice creams, or failing that the humans themselves; their sweat helped the ladybirds rehydrate, it was said. Sharks, meanwhile, moved closer to shore, and thousands of acres of forest was destroyed.

The Met Office continued to do long-range predictions and continued to be bamboozled. 'Although the July weather was well forecast,' it announced blithely at the end of the month, 'it was warmer, sunnier and drier than forecast'. By August, the drought was getting serious. Bone-dry farms cried out for water for failing crops and starving stock, as if this were the outback. In Cardiff, the water was turned off for thirteen hours a day, then seventeen. Cricket grounds and golf courses were parched beige. Miscreants who watered their lawns were hauled before magistrates.

On 24 August, the Callaghan government appointed a Minister for Drought. The job went unexpectedly to Denis Howell, who was not a Cabinet minister and was best known as a football referee. But he was a popular figure with a breezy charm. 'The flowers are going to have to wilt,' he warned. 'The cars will have to remain dirty.' He also had a magic touch. Three days later, Lord Nugent, chairman of the National Water Council, was warned in advance of the long-range September weather forecast: the drought would go on. So that day the heavens opened, just in time for the August Bank Holiday. And then it rained and it rained and it rained.

The crisis was not over, the authorities insisted. Indeed, the threat that water would be completely shut off, forcing people to rely on standpipes in the street – the return of the old parish pump, as in the winter of '63 – finally came to pass, briefly, in parts of Devon in mid-September. That August, fallow deer in Lincolnshire had been culled because they were digging up potatoes in search of moisture. By November, Fenland farmers were inviting the public to dig up their own potatoes because the fields were too wet to be harvested by machinery.

As time passed, homeowners found large cracks in the walls of their houses, especially those built on clay. And the figures would come to show that in 1976 and 1977 more people died in England and Wales than were born. The heat did cause some excess deaths, but whether it also had a passion-killing effect on young couples was unclear: the birth rate had been falling for the past ten years.

The question about the weather that was never quite answered was *why?* The summer of '76 felt like something more than just an abnormally hot and dry one; it was as though the thermostat had broken, perhaps for ever. One explanation came from the World Meteorological Organization in Geneva, in response to a question from the *Daily Express*. It ascribed the heatwave to 'a layer of carbon dioxide formed by exhaust fumes from cars, domestic fires and factory furnaces'.

The paper quoted Kevin Myles of the Met Office, which had not otherwise had a good summer, to the effect the real change would come 'twenty or so years into the next century'. Well, there's a thing. But in the next forty-five years at least, Britain never again had such a summer, so this interesting theory did not make it into the nation's consciousness – until perhaps it was too late.

The combination of the heat and the general excitability of the times had its most unusual manifestation in Nottinghamshire. On the baked savannah, a lion was reported prowling through the undergrowth, presumably searching for a muddy waterhole or a juicy gazelle. It was spotted by two milkmen near Tollerton: 'We stood and watched it for a good two minutes.' A few days later, the county's deputy coroner, Dr John Chisholm, saw it in the undergrowth: 'I know a lion's tail when I see one.'

There were sixty-five sightings in all. Parents were told to keep children indoors. Helicopters, armed police and special marksmen were deployed. It was seen crossing an M1 bridge and swimming the Trent. Several docile golden Labradors came under suspicion. One of the last sightings – perhaps the one that spurred the police to decide there was no lion – turned out to be a large brown paper bag. It was all a nine-day wonder. Still, the feeling was that it was better to have looked and lost than never to have looked at all.

After the weather returned to normal, more routine hysteria took over. In October 1976, Lord Hailsham – the once and future Lord Chancellor – gave the Richard Dimbleby Lecture for the BBC, describing Britain's parliamentary system as an 'elective dictatorship' in which the executive could push anything it wished through the House of Commons: 'All other free nations impose limitations on their representative assemblies. We impose none on ours.' This was a very reasonable point, but it was a curious time to raise the issue.

Jim Callaghan was now prime minister, though at no point in his tenure did he have routine control of the legislative programme. By November his notional majority would be down to minus five, and in practice it was plus one. And even then he had dozens of bolshie left-wingers in his own ranks. Plus Britain, as we shall see, had to contend that autumn with what was almost an occupying power.

Hailsham was oblivious. He had already raised this point, less publicly, in both 1968 and 1969, when Labour were previously in power. Nothing was heard from him when he was Lord Chancellor in the Heath government, and certainly not during the eight years, from 1979 to 1987, when he held the same role in the government that came nearer to being an elective dictatorship than any peacetime regime before or since. He was like a football fan whose own team never commits a foul.

Once Harold Wilson left Downing Street, the tumult and shouting created by his secretary faded away and an air of calm descended. Jim Callaghan's father had died young and he had a hard childhood in distressed circumstances. Unable to afford university, he joined the Inland Revenue and became an active trade unionist, served in the Royal Navy (not very excitingly) and, like Wilson, became an MP in the 1945 landslide and was quickly spotted as a talent. When he became prime minister, he completed an unprecedented quadruple, having already held the other three Great Offices of State.* He had also been an MP for thirty years; in terms of varied experience of life, few other prime ministers could have matched him and perhaps only Ramsay MacDonald had known as much poverty.

Callaghan had also spent eight years observing Wilson and knew what not to do. He gave up alcohol for the duration of his premiership, and inside No. 10 ran a much tighter ship. It was not just the brandy that disappeared when Callaghan came in; so did the policy discussions between apparent equals that it washed down. The avuncular public image was misleading. As his speechwriter David Lipsey said: 'He was a man I greatly admired but struggled to love. It was a great privilege to be speechwriter for Callaghan, but not a constant pleasure.'

Callaghan was extremely proud that he had beaten five Oxonians in the contest to succeed a sixth, Wilson. But, like many of the most successful graduates of the University of Life, he was wary of men whose cleverness had been conventionally honed and validated and was not above making them squirm. Even Bernard Donoughue, the head of the policy unit and a great admirer, described Callaghan's

---

* Chancellor of the Exchequer, Home Secretary and Foreign Secretary.

in-house style as 'often authoritarian'. Against that, he was much more inclusive with the Cabinet than his predecessor, let alone his successor.

And from the start he brought an air of calm competence to the business of government – more like a Tory premier sedating the nation, as the long-time observer of Westminster, Norman Shrapnel, put it. Commentators found it a relief after the chaos that had enveloped both Wilson and Heath. There was, however, an interruption: Britain's economic issues had never gone away, and now they came back with a vengeance.

———◆———

Since crashing below the two-dollar mark just before Callaghan took over, the pound had continued to plummet, heading for parity with the Peruvian cocoa bean. A gentle decline might have had its plusses, but a selling frenzy did not – and that simmering summer, the government had to borrow to prevent a run on the pound. With Jack Jones acting as enforcer, wage inflation was calming down. The focus now was government overspending and the terrible balance of payments, and Callaghan and Healey, still the Chancellor, forced the Cabinet to swallow one large tranche of government cuts.

By the opening day of the Labour conference in rainy September, with Tony Benn calling for new and dramatic left-wing policies, sterling was down to $1.68. On Day 2 it was $1.63 and Healey, heading for routine conferences in the Far East, never boarded his plane. In Blackpool, Callaghan told the bewildered ranks that the old economic orthodoxy, sanctified by the prophet Maynard Keynes and maintained as religion by thirty years of post-war governments, was no longer valid.

'We used to think that you could just spend your way out of a recession and increase employment by cutting taxes and boosting government spending,' he said. 'I tell you in all candour that option no longer exists.' The effect would be to inject more inflation, he added, just as Britain was recovering from its worst inflation ever, to be followed by more unemployment. He also talked about balancing budgets and letting firms make large profits. John O'Sullivan, in the *Telegraph*, wondered whether it was Callaghan speaking or Sir Keith Joseph. 'Too stunned to hiss,' he added, 'the delegates simply sat and gaped.' Joseph was not speaking, but Peter Jay of *The Times*, then married to Callaghan's daughter, was involved in the drafting.

They did hiss Healey later when he said the existing cuts would stay. This came after the announcement that Britain was applying for more than £2 billion* from the International Monetary Fund. He did not say what else might have to be cut. That would be determined through the autumn, when modern Britain came as close as it ever has to occupation by a foreign power: in this case the IMF, setting up their HQ in Brown's Hotel to discuss surrender terms with the notional government. By the end of October sterling went below $1.60.

The appointed *gauleiter* was British himself: an ex-Bank of England high-up called Sir Alan Whittome. 'Objective and personable', in Healey's words, but now very much an international civil servant – and responsible to Johan Witteveen, a Dutch centre-right politician who had become the IMF's managing director. For now, these two had displaced even Jack Jones, never mind the prime minister, as the men in charge of Britain's destiny. Elective dictator? Callaghan? Huh!

'Cap in hand' was the cliché of the season. But Callaghan would not play the grovelling mendicant. He kept Whittome's team waiting for weeks at Brown's, which must have helped the balance of payments a little. In November, Callaghan allowed Whittome to meet Treasury officials; Whittome was flexible about the terms but his boss took a tougher line, calling for £2 billion of immediate cuts with £3 billion to follow. 'Tell him to take a running jump,' said Healey to Whittome.

Callaghan accused Witteveen of confronting Britain with mass unemployment and imperilling British democracy itself, and the IMF blinked. The amount came down to £2.5 billion in all. IMF

---

* Probably enough, at that time, to buy every house in Kensington.

made the loan. Healey only ever used half of it and paid that all back before leaving office. Sterling recovered. The economy stabilized – and so, for two whole years, did British politics. 'The foxy old peasant', as one Treasury official called Callaghan, had done it again. In that time Callaghan tried to lull the country into a sense of security; sadly for him, the person he lulled most completely was himself.

———•———

Twenty-eight years later, in 2004, a left-wing think tank, the New Economics Foundation, issued a report proclaiming that – on their index of 'national, economic and social well-being' – 1976 was Britain's best year since 1950. One historian of the era, Dominic Sandbrook, thought the findings 'peculiar'; another, Alwyn Turner, was more sympathetic. Me, I would say that all such surveys are nonsense and most are publicity gimmicks. An accurate survey of well-being might require questioning the entire nation on their job satisfaction, sex life, children's health, whether or not they have crippling arthritis or are currently providing 24-hour care to their demented mother-in-law, and the probability of being murdered by the next-door neighbour over a dispute about noise, parking or the height of the leylandii. And, in 1976, whether they enjoyed hot weather.

13

FLAPS, *SIR!*

O<small>N 18 JULY 1972, A TRAINEE PILOT CALLED ROB JENKINSON</small> was on a flight simulator in the British European Airways complex at Heston, near Heathrow. Suddenly he became aware of urgent whispering going on between the instructors and other officials. No one offered him a word of explanation – which, he later recalled, was typical of the way things worked. It was only when he got home and watched the news that he discovered a BEA Trident had crashed only a few miles away, near Staines, shortly after take-off from Heathrow for Brussels that afternoon. All 118 on board were killed.

This was the worst crash in BEA's history, and the last with passenger fatalities before it was merged into British Airways. But in commercial aviation every accident – every prang – is investigated, and lessons are learned. In the case of what became known in the trade as the Papa India crash, after the plane's call sign, human frailty was deemed the major cause.

Captain Stanley Key appeared in this history spotting bodies in the sea in 1954 after one of the Comet crashes. In 1972, aged 51 and with 15,000 flying hours behind him, he was still with BEA – one of the last of the wartime generation. He was known to have some longstanding heart problems. Now the pilots were, fashionably, contemplating strike action and Key was vociferously opposed, so much so that anti-Key graffiti had been scrawled in cabins including

Papa India's – and he had just had a row with another pilot (not on board) shortly before the fatal flight. 'Meticulous,' a manager at the inquiry said of him, 'but almost turbulent at times.'

No one knows exactly what happened because there was no voice recorder on board, something BEA would now be forced to remedy. But the post-mortem suggested that Key had a torn artery and became in some way incapacitated during the complex climb out of Heathrow, and the others were too slow and/or inexperienced or nervous to override him and remedy the situation. The plane stalled, with catastrophic consequences. It was a turning point: many safety recommendations were implemented, including improved health checks.

Jenkinson went on to have a long and successful career with the new merged airline. 'As I began I flew with many of the wartime pilots who had started flying by the seat of their pants,' he recalled. 'There were those from whom you learned a lot. But there were also those who weren't as talented but used their authority to bluster their way through. So you got this attitude that the captain was God.'

More people were killed in the air worldwide in 1972 than in any other post-war year. This does not mean flying had become more dangerous; there were many more people in the air than during the mad fifties.* But it was not yet safe enough. And there was a culture clash ahead with the merger of BOAC and BEA. BOAC had always felt itself superior: captains in silk scarves and white gloves who sneered at BEA as 'the local flying club'. There is a BOAC story about a captain and a new co-pilot separated by a gnarled old engineer. The captain gave the co-pilot the instruction to retract the flaps, and the co-pilot complied and responded, as he had been taught, 'Flaps!' The captain leaned over and yanked the flaps back.

'Flaps!' he called again. The young man repeated the action and the response; again the captain undid it. Then a third time. Now alarmed, the co-pilot looked at the engineer in bewilderment.

---

* Four of the ten crashes with most deaths in 1972 involved the Russian airline Aeroflot and a fifth was an East German plane.

'I think,' said the engineer, 'the cunt wants you to say "Flaps, *sir*!"'

'Interpersonal, communication and leadership skills' would become an important part of the training programme. Jenkinson and his fellow pilot Delphine Gray-Fisk agree that by the end of the 1970s flying was more collegiate – and safer.

————•————

One of the first moves of the Heath government's transport minister, John Peyton, was to float the idea of raising the 70-mph speed limit on motorways, introduced experimentally by Labour in 1965 and then made permanent by Barbara Castle – who, as a woman *and* a non-driver, was doubly suspect. Peyton declined to say what number he wanted, though the AA had been agitating for 80 mph. 'If eighty is not satisfactory, try a hundred,' said an RAC spokesman helpfully. 'After all, motorways were not built to play about on.' Eventually, Peyton settled on eighty but it never happened. Indeed, he ended his tenure having to reduce it to fifty in response to the 1973–74 fuel crisis.

Since motorists always understood that the measurement devices of the era were too primitive to record speed accurately, drivers could give themselves a 10 per cent margin without fear of being nicked – and more in towns where the 30-mph limit was almost wholly ignored. In any case, Peyton soon got diverted from this project by the need to start constructing metal barriers on Britain's motorways after twelve people were killed in eighteen days because of vehicles crossing the central reservation.

In 1970, households with cars overtook those without. This was probably the peak year for motor traffic in Britain, not in volume but in terms of its overweening dominance before the backlash set in. Cycling was at its lowest ebb since the penny-farthing: annual pedal-mileage had decreased in just fifteen years from 11 billion miles to 2.5 billion; railway travel was still falling and rail freight was plummeting; buses were beneath contempt.*

---

* There is no record of Margaret Thatcher ever saying that no one over 30 should be seen dead on a bus or anything like it – but millions of people thought just that.

The attitude was that roads were for cars, and anyone else was an interloper who took their chances. The breathalyser had proved its worth as a deterrent to drunken drivers but, as an offence, drink driving had not yet acquired a moral stigma unless you were insanely over the limit. Still, the road toll was now on a long-term downward trend. This had not yet reached the sport of motor racing, which continued as a licensed slaughterhouse. Nine Formula 1 drivers were killed in crashes associated with Grand Prix events in the 1970s.

That figure does not include the Swiss driver Jo Siffert, killed in a non-championship race at Brands Hatch where the fire extinguishers failed to work. Nor the New Zealander Bruce McLaren, who died testing a car at Goodwood, a death he himself foretold: 'I feel that life is measured in achievement, not in years alone,' he once wrote. Nor Niki Lauda, who narrowly survived a horrendous crash in the 1976 German Grand Prix and was rescued by other drivers. Notoriously, Lauda had failed to do the same when the Briton Roger Williamson was killed three years earlier. 'I'm paid to race, not to stop,' he said.

More years would pass before the efforts of Jackie Stewart and others would pay off and the sport started to take common-sense precautions.

———————

It is the instinct of every living creature that, all things being equal, it is better to live than die* – extreme pain, despair or heroism occasionally excepted. But in the 1970s, as the wartime generation aged and calmed down, the remaining daredevils found themselves increasingly hemmed in by new attitudes.

It was accepted that no one had the right to endanger others, and that children had to be protected. But did adults have the right to endanger themselves? Did they have the right to disagree with Albert Booth, a Callaghan Cabinet minister, who said people should

---

* Except, according to farmers, sheep.

not be free to do things that were 'silly and dangerous'. And who made that judgment?

The libertarian position was adopted most determinedly by a former maths teacher and keen motorcyclist called Fred Hill, who refused to obey the law – passed under the Tories in 1973 – making motorcycle helmets compulsory. Furthermore, he refused to pay the fines that accrued every time he was summonsed, for which he was regularly jailed.

'He believed that he was a safer motorcyclist without a helmet,' said one admirer, the columnist and former MP Matthew Parris. 'More importantly he held that, right or wrong, the decision was his to take and his alone.' Hill died in 1984, of a heart attack in Pentonville Prison, serving his thirty-first stint in jail, aged 74. He always served his time stoically and helped other prisoners write letters. There are still annual tribute rides in his honour. There is certainly an argument that helmets can slow up the reactions that might prevent an accident. And, in the three years after the law was passed, motorcyclists' fatalities increased quite sharply.

One Labour MP, George Strauss, argued in favour of the law on the grounds that helmetless motorcyclists diverted the resources of the health service. 'Of course we could enter into endless consideration of the reasons which brought patients to be treated under the NHS,' responded a former health minister. 'All manner of avoidable accidents, unwise courses of life, unwise behaviour of every kind. Are we to make all these criminal offences because the consequences might be to divert the use of resources inside the NHS?'

This was Enoch Powell, at his most forensic. He applied the same logic to the compulsory wearing of seat belts. Resistance to this was much more successful. New cars had had to have front seat belts fitted since 1965. Four times the Labour governments of the 1970s – the alleged elective dictatorship – tried to force people to wear them. And every time they were thwarted by an alliance of peers, MPs and the RAC (though not the AA), and people who just did not relish the police peering into their cars to see that everyone was following nanny's instructions. It was 1983 before the law finally got through.

14

THE LAND OF LOST CONTENT

I N 1970, WHEN USE OF BOTH HELMETS AND SEAT BELTS WERE novelty optional extras, there was no doubt who controlled the Queen's Highway. In its first issue of the decade, the AA magazine *Drive* blamed parents for road accidents involving children. It conducted a survey in the inner London district of Southwark which suggested that most of them happened between 4 and 6 p.m., and not on the way to and from school. There was no suggestion that drivers had any responsibility to note the presence of young children. The inference was that the role of kids was to stay indoors, watch TV and stay out of the way.

Professor Mathew Thomson sees the 1970s as a turning point in the decline of the liberty of the British child. In his book *Lost Freedom* he cites the work of the psychologists John and Elizabeth Newson on seven-year-olds in Nottingham in the early seventies. The Newsons found that many of the old ways persisted: nearly four-fifths walked home from school, and three-quarters were allowed to play in or roam the streets. In both cases, the figures for the middle class were lower than the working class.*

But now parents were experiencing the emotion their own parents had suppressed: *worry*. They wanted their children to grow

---

* Suburban schools might be further away, and some middle-class children would be privately educated.

up resourceful and independent – but. There were four types of concern: getting lost, 'strangers', non-traffic accidents and traffic accidents.

Three of these fears might have been overblown. Seven-year-olds normally had enough animal instinct to know their own territory. Molesters were perceived as a growing risk, on very flimsy evidence, though the paedophiles' failed bid for respectability had put them much more in the front of the parental mind. Mothers who themselves had played on the bomb sites now worried about the dangers of even purpose-built play areas: wayward swings and harsh asphalt. Manchester Royal Infirmary was said to admit up to a dozen children a day for such injuries. But this was no match for the fifties.

But the cars were a real, present and increasing danger – implacable enemies of an old-fashioned childhood. In 1971 the old kerb drill was abolished ('Look Right, Look Left, Look Right Again') on the grounds that kids would know the mantra but not the difference between right and left; it was replaced by the Green Cross Code, which was hard to remember at all.

There were places where the old ways persisted. The pioneering woman boxer Jane Couch grew up in Fleetwood in the seventies as its fishing declined. 'We had an amazing childhood, though we didn't have any money,' she recalled. 'Fleetwood was just like one big family. I could walk into any of the houses on our side of the street without knocking.' A tough childhood too, hence the boxing. But over most of Britain – especially the new estates and, heaven help us, the tower blocks – the communality that created ragged, rugged, resilient children was fading.

No childhood epitomized the old ways more than an Irish Catholic one. 'No one came in to steal anything, because we all had the same, that is, nothing,' an ex-boxer called Frankie Devlin told the chronicler of childhood Ysenda Maxtone Graham. 'All the doors were open all day . . . One day in 1971 – that was just after the first soldier had been killed – a policeman came down our street and said, "You must keep your front doors shut in the future." That changed our whole lives.'

Many of those families still had one important asset: enough kids to ensure that the older ones could keep an eye on the younger ones. And now they had new excitements: one group of children in Andersonstown, Belfast, found nine parcels of gelignite explosive in 1970. Elsewhere, some had no excitement at all. In the Central ward of Liverpool, *The Times* reported in 1971, there was nowhere to play except on the concrete between two tower blocks, and pre-schooling was available only for 60 under-fives out of 880. Further up the age scale, a new phrase emerged: 'latchkey kids', at least a million of them apparently, left to fend for themselves in empty homes as the number of working mothers rose.

For most, there were still elements that looked like a bygone childhood. In 1971 there was a proper old-fashioned craze: clackers – two small plastic balls on a string attached to a finger ring which made a terrific din when they crashed into each other. It was frightening enough, when a hijacker revealed himself and began clacking, to make an American pilot obey and fly his passengers to Cuba. The noise filled the streets as children left school that summer. Then, in the autumn, scare stories emerged of cheap imitations, bruised fingers and 'three girls in Thurnscoe, Yorkshire, who all broke bones in their wrists'. Sales plummeted. Within the week a clacker factory in Skelmersdale proclaimed itself 'practically ruined'.

Towards the end of the decade, skateboards arrived. Now the safety campaigners really did have something to worry them. David Larder from the Royal Society for the Prevention of Accidents (Rospa) was fuming: 'Skateboard promoters went ahead and launched in large numbers a vehicle without brakes, lights, steering and warning system, virtually on to British streets. They also put it into the hands of Britain's most inexperienced drivers.' Skateboard-related deaths were indeed running at about one a month. And the Society claimed in March 1978 that by the end of the year Britain's hospitals would have to deal with 100,000 extra injuries, and demanded the *immediate* provision of 20,000 skateboard parks with full first-aid facilities.*

---

*   Nearly fifty years later, there were about 1,600.

That same winter a Rospa survey showed that about a hundred children a year aged under six were being killed while crossing the road unaccompanied. Further research found that 13 per cent of mothers still thought two-year-olds could cross busy roads safely, and nearly half said five-year-olds could do so, whereas safety experts were suggesting the appropriate age was nine.

Something else arrived that year. It was called Pong, a feeble tennis simulation involving three white blobs on a dark screen, but one that could be played on an ordinary television. This was the ultimate answer to the dangers of childhood. Henceforth, no child need step outside ever again.

———•———

Tucked away close to Islington Town Hall in North London is the William Tyndale primary school, now one much like any of the other 21,000 in Britain that trumpet their selling points on their website. This school does not find space for a history section: nothing about the eponymous Tyndale, scholar and martyr; and certainly not about its more recent history, which involved several of the school's teachers being metaphorically burned at the stake for their defence of 'progressive education'.

Islington in the 1970s was becoming a hub of gentrification, attracting the young and trendy, who mostly applauded progressive principles – though not necessarily if those principles involved their children's education. In 1974, Tyndale acquired a new head, Terry Ellis – a pliable man, it was said – and he worked alongside a more dynamic figure, Brian Haddow, who believed that children should be taught 'not to be conditioned by society'.

In that he succeeded. The day was split between relatively traditional teaching and 'free option' learning on subjects ranging from maths (take-up on that not clear) to tie-dyeing. The children then began to add other subjects to the curriculum, including throwing stones and spitting at the infants in the school next door, swearing at the teachers, abusing the dinner ladies, gambling with their dinner money, and lobbing full milk bottles from upper windows into the infants' playground. Some of the kids proudly took their new behavioural standards home to impress their parents. They seemed to have learned little else.

Eventually, after the school roll had plummeted from 250 to less than a hundred inside eighteen months, a public inquiry held weeks of hearings that excoriated just about everyone but most particularly Ellis, Haddow and their supporters on the staff. But their careers were not the only casualty – their ideas were now discredited. The Tyndale clique were very old-fashioned: they refused to engage with parental opinion. That was fine in the days when home and school were different worlds, but the new generation of parents – especially in Islington – were more interested and keener to interfere.

From 1969 a proto-Thatcherite camp of educationists had coalesced around the Black Papers, a series of polemics favouring traditional methods, the Three Rs, grammar schools, clips round the ear'ole and non-bolshie undergraduates. And the Tyndale affair tainted even such moderate ideas as the 'child-centred learning' put forward by Lady Plowden, a Conservative, in her much-admired 1967 report on primary schools.

After Jim Callaghan's tell-it-like-it-is economics speech to the Labour conference on the economy, he decided to repeat the trick a month later with a speech on education in front of not very impressed educators at Ruskin College, Oxford. 'There is no virtue in producing socially well-adjusted members of society who are unemployed because they don't have the skills,' he said, and called for a great debate on improving education. He achieved what one assumes was his main objective – making sure Margaret Thatcher and her cheerleaders on the *Daily Mail* did not claim ownership of a promising-looking issue – then told the Education Secretary, Shirley Williams, to take charge of it.

There was not much of a debate and certainly no action, partly because Williams concluded the premise was faulty. The *Mail* was proclaiming the schools were falling apart and standards were declining. 'It actually wasn't true,' said Williams. 'Most of the inspectors' reports indicated the opposite.' And a series of other surveys indicated that the nature of teaching in most primary schools across Britain was pretty much the same as it had been a generation earlier.

———·———

Labour's return to government had killed nearly all the remaining grammar schools; only the most determined local authorities refused to surrender. In the now almost-ubiquitous comprehensives, some teachers were more worried about the threat to them personally. There was a general trend away from corporal punishment – starting with the primary schools. But many secondary teachers felt they needed a weapon in reserve for their protection.

Some called for the leaving age, raised from 15 to 16 in 1972, to be lowered again because of the disruptive effects of pupils who saw school as just one long detention. That year, delegates to the National Association of Schoolmasters' conference put down a succession of motions deploring the 'rising tide of violence, vandalism and tension'. The general secretary of the rival National Union of Teachers, Ted Britton, thought the fuss was overdone. 'The most lurid accounts look like a vicarage tea party compared with the nineteenth century,' he told his conference, 'when the militia were called out to quell the pupils of at least two public schools. And when in a third the pupils slowly roasted another one to death, the parents did not even complain to the authorities – presumably on the grounds that this was a normal childish prank.'

One unintended consequence of the extra year at school was the rise in the number of – another tabloid cliché of the times – 'gymslip mums'. Well, you wouldn't have wanted all those latchkey kids spending their time just watching TV, would you? And motherhood was certainly one way of bunking off school.

Another issue for comprehensives was that, gigantic though many of them were, they did not have the scope or resources to give sixth-formers sufficient choices (e.g. foreign languages) to be intellectually wide-ranging and stimulating. The quiet spread of sixth form colleges – the first opened in Luton in 1966 – was a genuine advance, creating a cane- and uniform-free zone between school and university, without the political poison that afflicted the rest of British education.

The best of these colleges slightly mitigated the self-inflicted disaster whereby Labour abolished the grammar schools and ignored the real class enemy, the public school. By 1971 the grammar schools were getting similar results with children *from the same background* (a big caveat) as the independent sector, and getting them into Oxbridge. 'They are giving us a terrific run for our money,' said one public school head. His costs were spiralling and so were the fees: Eton, £765 a year in 1970, hit £1,287 in 1975 with much more to come, just when the not-as-rich-as-all-that class was struggling with taxes high and shares at rock bottom.

Reform was one remedy: Jim Woodhouse, the young head of Rugby, admitted girls and abolished both the cane and the legalized slavery of fagging (though the more egalitarian system of 'chores' was substituted). He also allowed everyone at the annual leavers' party to hit him over the head with a rolled-up newspaper. Every little helped, but not as much as the decline of state-sponsored competition.

The prep schools who readied rich boys to progress to the public schools were not always designed to last long-term: the head was often the owner. Some of these places were perverts' playpens, though this is not mentioned as such in the autobiography of one of the most famous alumni of Heatherdown, near Ascot, which closed in 1982. 'At bath time we had to line up naked in front of a row of Victorian metal baths and wait for the headmaster, James Edwards, to blow a whistle before we got in,' he recalled. 'Another whistle would indicate that it was time to get out.' In between, the boys imbibed the delicate scent of the head's pipe.

'The food was spartan,' he added, 'I lost a stone in weight during a single term. There was one meal that consisted of curry, rice – and maggots.' It is a matter of opinion as to whether this regime benefited either the author or his contemporary Prince Edward. Asked to read the lesson at the carol service with Prince Edward's mother in the front row, the author forgot to say 'Thanks be to God' and, when he realized, said 'Oh shit' instead. It is not clear whether the

Queen recognized David Cameron thirty years later when he kissed hands as her prime minister.

The Queen had not led an entirely sheltered life. In 1970 she had a close encounter with a demo in front of the students' union at Warwick organized by women's activists, and was jostled by wine-swigging (there's posh) students at the University of Stirling who objected to the cost of her visit. These local difficulties were tapering off, although the University of Essex had a last hurrah in 1974 when ninety students were arrested during protests about alleged victimization.

But in a single week of 1975 there were signs that old-fashioned undergraduate indifference and frivolity were back. Students at the London School of Economics gave a majority on the union executive to moderates for the first time in seven years. And at the University of Surrey, a ginger tom called Orlando came third in union elections but was disqualified for not paying his fees.

15

MARK THE HERALD ANGELS SING

'L ONDON, GREATEST CITY IN THE WORLD AND HOME OF THE oldest democracy. A city whose worldwide reputation for honesty and integrity is firmly based on a thousand years of the rule of law – enforced and safeguarded by a police force as well known as London itself . . . Scotland Yard!'

Thus would begin the long-running series of fifties B-films showing fictionalized versions of real-life murders, narrated by a crime writer called Edgar Lustgarten with a sinister voice and a string of clichés ('a grizzly business'). The common theme was that the local plods would be confronted by some crime well beyond their bone-headed capacity and have to call in . . . Scotland Yard! And some star turn from the metropolis would turn up and solve it.

But the days had gone when the chief constable of Rutland presided over a force of twenty-eight men and one woman: the newly merged provincial forces had more resources and certainly their own opinions. And what they heard and saw of the Metropolitan Police appalled them. As Robert Mark, the ex-chief constable of Leicester parachuted into the Met by Roy Jenkins, put it: 'Though I had known wrongdoing, I had never experienced institutionalized wrongdoing, blindness, arrogance and prejudice on anything like the scale accepted as routine by the Met.' The CID, in particular, was out of control and riddled with corruption.

Mark spent five years as an assistant and then deputy

commissioner, kicking his heels, remembering snubs, snatching at lecture tours to break the monotony, and creating precious few alliances. It was not just the traditional frustrations of deputies everywhere; he was treated, he said, like a leper at a colonial garden party. Mark had turned down the post of commissioner once because he sensed too many obstacles to reform: the time was not ripe and a stopgap was appointed. In 1972, Commander Drury, the head of the Flying Squad, had just been exposed by the press and Chief Inspector Victor Kelaher, in charge of the drugs squad, was about to follow. This time, Mark accepted.

———◆———

The defining cop show on TV in the seventies was *The Sweeney* (Sweeney Todd = Flying Squad) starring John Thaw as Jack Regan, a rough corner-cutting detective inspector. It was broadcast against the background of the Drury case, and Regan fitted one of the three categories of wrongdoing Mark identified in real life: 'bent for the job', circumventing bureaucratic technicalities to ensure those who the police perceived as guilty got put away.

This was different from the backhanders to forget minor offences, as exacted by police forces in much of the world – and certainly by some bent beat coppers in London in the 1970s. And very different from the outrageous rackets run by senior officers in the capital at the time, especially among high-ups connected with drugs, porn and bank robberies – though even they justified themselves in their own minds as payback for inadequate pensions and London weighting.

Mark quickly ended the CID's long history of autonomy and, during his first few months of command, his enforcement operation – known as A10 – was averaging fifty suspensions a month, most of which ended in resignations. Few were actually jailed. It was still hard to get juries to believe that British bobbies lied.

Mark's tenure was dramatic, but cut short by the very inflexibility that made him so stout in defence of virtue: he left in a huff because he objected to having an independent element in the police complaints procedure. His retirement was long and anticlimactic, mainly distinguished by him taking part in a series of ads for Goodyear Tyres.

Part of the practice of being bent for the job was rounding up the usual suspects, and in March 1975 a Londoner called George Davis was given a twenty-year sentence for armed robbery in Ilford. He had not actually been involved, and his friends and family got very worked up about this.

Having crashed a car into the gates of Buckingham Palace and draped banners over St Paul's Cathedral to try to draw attention to his case, they went for the *coup de grâce*. The Test match between England and Australia at Leeds was excitingly poised, with a day to go. But before dawn broke, Davis's supporters got into the ground, gouged holes in the turf and poured on a gallon of oil for good measure. To avoid any doubts about their own guilt they painted the slogan GEORGE DAVIS IS INNOCENT – OK wherever they could. The match was abandoned, costing England any chance of regaining the Ashes.

The stunt worked. The Metropolitan Police took another look, and a year later Roy Jenkins, the Home Secretary, had Davis set free. However, not guilty though he was, he was not a holy innocent. The year after his release, he was caught red-handed robbing a bank: eleven years this time, and no protests. One of those really upset by the loss of the day's cricket had been Davis himself. With little else to do in his cell, he had been looking forward to the radio commentary.*

The best thing about the seventies was that comedy was never far away. These were not happy years for the Flying Squad, even when they really flew. One morning in January 1974, Chief Superintendent Jack Slipper knocked on the door of a hotel room in Rio de Janeiro, greeting the surprised occupant with a well-prepared 'Nice to see you, Ronnie. I think you'll remember me.'

Nine years after escaping from Wandsworth Prison, there was a suggestion that Biggs, tired and hard-up, wanted to come home –

---

* Actually, it rained most of the day so there would probably have been no play anyway.

even though he had served only fifteen months of his thirty-year sentence. He was hoping to surrender on his own terms after his story had appeared in the *Daily Express*. Slipper was not part of the deal. But even the good times were bad for the Met.

Brazil did not have an extradition treaty with the UK but would listen to a case to send him back. Except there was an obscure law that allowed the father of a Brazilian-born child to stay in the country if he had not committed a crime there. And lurking inside one of his charming local girlfriends, Raimunda, was Biggs's ticket not to ride. Now he had no need to hide and life in Rio was far more promising. Slipper flew home alone.

One effect of the train robbers' long sentences was not deterrence but a message to thieves that they might just as well carry guns, because the sentences could hardly be longer.

Bank robberies were fashionable, quintupling between 1972 and 1982 until there were up to five a day. Banks still carried a lot of cash and the security systems were primitive. If the banks were so vulnerable, what chance did anyone else have? Streetwise kids could open a car door with a coat hanger; the prize being the radio or new 8-track stereo or cassette players. And after he retired, Robert Mark said people should not expect the police to protect them from burglary. Alarms were not much help: they were set off by puffs of wind and so passers-by just ignored them.

More worryingly, mugging (the word imported from the US) became a perceived problem, especially on the London Underground. The *Sunday Telegraph* said 70 per cent of those responsible were believed to be British-born second-generation immigrants. Sociological theorists at Birmingham University saw the hysteria about mugging as a moral panic, as with mods and rockers a decade earlier, where the intensity of the reaction was 'at odds with the scale of the threat' – and obviously racist.

But white kids caused moral panics too. Skinheads first emerged in the late 1960s, with some moddish touches and, at first, an unexpected enthusiasm for reggae music. But the skinhead style mutated into what one academic, Professor Benjamin Bowling, called 'a severe and puritanical self-image . . . a formalised and very hard masculinity . . . and a strong sense of class and geographical location.' Their version of Neighbourhood Watch fed into football hooliganism and what became known as 'queer-bashing' and, particularly, 'Paki-bashing' – especially in the increasingly Bangladeshi East End of London, where there were 150 serious assaults reported in 1970 and one fatal stabbing.*

Even fiction could set off moral panic: the film *A Clockwork Orange* featuring Malcolm McDowell as a youth who enjoyed the unusual pairing of violence and Beethoven caused a controversy which was ended only when the director, Stanley Kubrick, banned the film himself. In better-balanced countries, it was seen as an art film or black comedy.

There was one great triumph for the police: Operation Julie, which in 1977 pretty much destroyed the market for the once-fashionable alternative-universe drug LSD. The skills that went into the creation of the illegal acid lab and supply chain, and the police work that broke it, were both very high-class. The culprits (the word *gang* does them scant justice) were mostly highly educated and at least partly idealistic.† The government should have merged the groups and put them in charge of British Leyland.

Overall, though – more than in most eras – things did seem to be somewhat out of control. Peter Coe of Bath was injured after being kicked in the bar of the Theatre Royal, where he was the manager. His assailants: two nine-year-old Brownies. The reason: he had run out of ice cream.

---

* The term *Paki-bashing*, which did not allow any distinction between different kinds of Asians, was thus particularly ironic, since in 1971 the East Pakistanis successfully extricated themselves from the dominance of West Pakistan, achieved independence as Bangladesh, and ceased to be any kind of 'Paki'.

† Stylish too. When one of them was confronted in his hallway by the policeman who had smashed down his door with a sledgehammer, he said: 'I suppose you've come about the television licence.' Another became a police scientist after his release.

16

THE GIRL THAT
I MARRY

SHORTLY AFTER JIM CALLAGHAN HAD REPLACED HAROLD
Wilson as prime minister, the pair of them were together in the
Members' Dining Room of the House of Commons when the
Labour backbencher Bryan Magee walked in. As an intellectual
with a TV following, he was a distinguished figure in his own right,
and they beckoned him to join them. They were discussing the
Queen, trying to crack the futile question about which party she
supported but also agreeing how good she was at the weekly
audiences – how she always wanted to hear what the PM's biggest
problem was and what was occupying his thoughts, and how sharp
she was at seeing the point.

'If she weren't the Queen she would make a good politician,'
said Jim.

'She IS a good politician,' said Harold.

——•——

The Queen's political skills kept her in position during the revolving
door premierships of the 1970s. She did not have much rapport
with awkward Ted Heath, especially because he was indifferent to
her beloved Commonwealth. But she extracted a pay rise out of

him, without having to make concessions.*

Her 1970 tour of Australia had something of the fresh delight that characterized the post-Coronation tour, and she kept well out of the 1975 political crisis there when the left-wing prime minister Gough Whitlam was sacked by her representative, the governor-general. Her senior staff were becoming more professional and no longer insisted on precedents from George V's reign. As her uncle the Duke of Windsor was dying, the Queen saw him in Paris and shed a tear. The ex-king's funeral was allowed, in Ben Pimlott's words, to 'err, but only a little, on the side of magnanimity'. Behind closed doors, the *froideur* between the Queen Mother and her sister-in-law the Duchess remained Arctic.

This was all good practice, because in 1978 the Queen had to endure the supreme trial of her diplomatic career: entertaining the Romanian dictator Nicolae Ceaușescu and his even more despicable wife, Elena. There was good reason. Ceaușescu really was a foxy old peasant – possibly to the extent of biting the heads off chickens. But in Britain's parlous state, even capricious megalomaniacs had their uses; he had made Romania a semi-detached member of the Soviet bloc, which was helpful. He was also interested in buying British aircraft.

It all went as well as could be expected: after many refusals, the Polytechnic of Central London agreed to make Elena, who had scientific pretensions, an honorary professor; Palace staff, having being warned that these kleptocrats were never off duty, removed the silver brushes from their Buckingham Palace bedroom. The morning after the banquet, the Queen, out with the dogs in the garden, saw them coming. She hid behind a bush.†

The Romanians did sign a contract to build twenty-two BAC 1-11 jets under licence, though only nine got built because Romania was running out of money. This was partly because

---

* She did, however, surrender her ancient prerogative right to all sturgeons and whales found in British waters or onshore.

† The 1973 visit of the Zairean tyrant President Mobutu was also trying: his wife smuggled a small dog through customs and then ordered him steak from the Palace kitchens.

Buckingham Palace had helped give Ceauşescu ideas. He spent his final decade, before he and Elena faced a firing squad, building himself a palace with 1,100 rooms rather than the Queen's pathetic 775.

Prince Philip now outdid both the Ceauşescus and his wife by becoming a god. He had been spotted by a tribal chieftain when he was on the deck of *Britannia* at anchor close to the island of Tanna, off the New Hebrides (later Vanuatu), on the royal tour of the South Pacific in 1974.

'I saw him standing on the deck in his white uniform,' said the local chief Jack Naiva. 'I knew then that he was the true messiah.' The prince appears to have handled the situation with great good taste and received a delegation from Tanna in 2007, a favour most gods ceased allowing to their adherents at least 2,000 years ago.

Other royals had to find their own route to heaven. And for the Queen's sister that was very hard indeed. In the 1970s, Princess Margaret was the undoubted star of the soap opera division of the family firm. Right at the start of the decade, an issue of the ultra-respectable US magazine *Ladies' Home Journal* carrying a piece about Margaret and Lord Snowdon's marital difficulties was taken off the shelves in Britain, by royal request. The family found the article 'distressing' and 'distasteful', i.e. all too true. The infidelities were mutual.

This was well enough known in certain circles, but not elsewhere, though it might have been inferred by the 7 million buyers of *Ladies' Home Journal*, whose most famous regular feature was entitled 'Can this marriage be saved?' No. In the summer of 1973, on the way to a house party hosted by her friends Colin and Anne Tennant – later Lord and Lady Glenconner – Margaret was met off the train in Edinburgh by their host, who also picked up another guest, one Roddy Llewellyn. They had never met, though the princess had known Roddy's father Harry, the Olympic equestrian champion. She was rising 43; he was 25. 'When the car pulled up,' Anne wrote later, 'there were Princess Margaret and Roddy in the back, more or less holding hands.'

It was discreet at first. But in February 1976 a brief gossip column item said: 'Princess Margaret flies off this weekend to her holiday pleasure island of Mustique. Coincidentally, also travelling to the sunny Caribbean plot will be friend Roddy Llewellyn . . .' Mustique was Tennant's privately owned tourist island, where the other guests included a young man purporting to be a teacher. He took a group picture which, carefully cropped by the *News of the World*, showed only the happy couple. The next month came the announcement that the Snowdons were separating.

Because that news followed so quickly after the revelation of the Llewellyn affair, it made Margaret look worse than she was. The public took against her; apart from the bogus notion that she had betrayed her husband, she was seen as a cradle-snatcher to boot. Snowdon's indiscretions had merely been more covert. And Margaret and Roddy was no fling: the relationship lasted eight years. After Margaret's funeral in 2002, the Queen went up to Anne Glenconner and thanked her for getting the couple together. Roddy had made her sister very happy.

Margaret may or may not have also spent a night in Mustique with John Bindon, well known as both an underworld thug and an occasional actor. His greatest claim to fame concerned his party trick, which was to hold a number of beer mugs with a part of his anatomy not designed for the purpose. The number, the size of the mugs and whether they were balanced or threaded varied in the telling; the part of the anatomy did not.

———•———

The media and the monarchy were also bedfellows, always uneasy; 150 years before Llewellyn and Bindon, *The Times* was savage about George IV's behaviour. But royalty needs the oxygen of publicity or it has no purpose. By the 1970s the Palace was getting more sophisticated in dealing with this, but the press was changing rapidly. In Britain it was entering a ruthlessly competitive phrase. This was mainly due to the success of *The Sun* under Rupert Murdoch, who could not be bought by Establishment baubles. This forced the *Mirror* to forget its old scruples. And then came the *Daily*

Star,* which made everything else look like *The Times Literary Supplement.*

The middle market had also had a shake-up, with the long-somnolent *Mail* turning itself tabloid (or, as it preferred to say, 'compact') under a skilful editor, David English, angling it towards women and slaughtering its old rival, the *Express*. Hungry and amoral freelance photographers used zoom lenses to sell pictures of any possible royal indiscretions to a worldwide market. And in Britain, amid the prevailing sense of decay, there was no story more welcome than the dalliances of the heir to the throne. And, boy, did he dally. And, boy, did people lap it up.[†]

On the Sunday after Christmas 1973, *ten thousand* people descended on Sandringham – defying government pleas not to drive unnecessarily because of the oil crisis – to watch Prince Charles emerge from church with Lady Jane Wellesley, daughter of the 8th Duke of Wellington, who was a guest of the royal family. And, through the decade, other contenders were paraded for public inspection likes fillies in the paddock: *inter alia* Davina, Sabrina, Georgina, Bettina, Henrietta, Fiona, Lucia, Anna, Cecily, Libby, Charlotte, Angela, Leonora, Sarah and Camilla. There was also Princess Marie-Astrid of Luxembourg, whose betrothal to Charles, the *Express* insisted over its entire front page, was to be announced the following Monday. This was indeed big news, especially to the non-happy non-couple. Charles apparently had no memory of meeting her.

Sarah was his skiing companion Lady Sarah Spencer, who was disqualified from the big race in 1978 after blabbing to *Woman's Own* about her anorexia and other issues. 'You've just done something incredibly stupid,' said Charles. Accounts vary as to how angry he actually was but, if Sarah was banished, the prohibition did not apply to her sister Diana, who was 16 at the time and not even in the starting stalls.

---

* And later the *Sunday Sport* and, for a while, the *Daily Sport* – which, had it been less repulsive, could have been really funny.

† This section on royal romance must be regarded with suspicion, like everything written on the subject – whether or not denied by the Palace. One can only try to synthesize what seems plausible from the mountain of gloop.

The Camilla mentioned in the press was Lady Camilla Fane, daughter of the Earl of Westmorland. Charles's association with the other Camilla (née Shand, later Parker-Bowles, later Duchess of Cornwall), had taken place largely in the privacy of the prince's paternal great-uncle Dickie's home, Broadlands, circa 1972. Lord Mountbatten was regarded highly by the public and was famously close to Charles, who felt support from him he did not find from his parents. Among those he had worked with, Mountbatten's reputation was more equivocal: he was widely regarded as vain and untrustworthy; his strategy as India's last viceroy may have caused millions of unnecessary deaths; and he was widely rumoured to be an enthusiastic pederast.*

The sexual advice he reputedly gave Charles did not turn out well. There were girls you wedded and those you bedded, said Uncle Dickie – according to the royal biographer Robert Lacey. He was happy enough to let Charles entertain Camilla Shand at Broadlands – but she was mere Sussex gentry and her great-great-grandmother was Alice Keppel, Edward VII's mistress, not queenly material. In any case, Mountbatten was very keen on steering him towards his own granddaughter Amanda Knatchbull. In the autumn of 1972 Charles and Camilla grew very fond of each other: she was affectionate, down-to-earth, funny and fun. They called each other Fred and Gladys. He told his biographer Jonathan Dimbleby he lost his heart to her 'almost at once'.

But Charles was in the Navy and had to join his ship for an eight-month tour. He could have proposed, but he was only 24 and the family response was uncertain. He dithered and didn't. Mountbatten had played the role of meddling Friar Laurence in this Romeo and Juliet story. Camilla went back to her old boyfriend Andrew Parker Bowles, an old flame of Princess Anne, and they were married before the prince returned. Hence many tears. Poor Charles, caught between desire and duty; old ways and new. He

---

* The famous remark on these subjects is attributed to Field Marshal Sir Gerald Templer: 'Dickie, you're so crooked, if you swallowed a nail, you'd shit a corkscrew.'

was *quite* fond of Amanda Knatchbull, and in 1979 he reportedly proposed. No fool, she said no.

Meanwhile, Anne had married Mark Phillips, known as 'Fog' (thick and wet). As a young woman she acquired a reputation for being grumpy, especially with the press.* But the couple were both skilful equestrians and Anne, having won the European Eventing Championships in 1971, was voted BBC Sports Personality of the Year in a fit of public sycophancy, ahead of George Best and Barry John, all-time greats in football and rugby.

Prince Andrew, aged 14, went to Toulouse on a Gordonstoun exchange visit and told questioners that his father was a farmer, his mother did no work and that his name was Edward. The real Edward was still blamelessly at Heatherdown, his bathtimes supervised by pipe-smoking James Edwards.†

In 1977, for the first time since 1935, there was a royal jubilee to celebrate. In advance, there was gloom; a morose and fractious nation seemed indifferent. By now Scottish separatism was starting to get serious. What with Princess Margaret and the Sex Pistols, the royal family seemed riper for ridicule than respect. Interest in street parties was patchy, especially in inner city areas. Talk of jubilee appeals was scorned even in bastions of loyalty: the mayor of Hereford said austerity meant many people thought them irrelevant. Suggestions to match George V's jubilee mugs included an amnesty on overdue library books, a moratorium on parking fines and the Queen selling the royal stamp collection. Polls suggested many people were not even sure what they were meant to be celebrating.

But on the chosen day in June, all traditions were observed and the nation responded. The weather was rubbish. Even so, a million were estimated to have been there to glimpse the state coach en route to and from the thanksgiving service at St Paul's. There were

---

* 'Naff orf!' she once told a colleague of mine.
† Not to be confused with cane-wielding Jimmy Edwards, headmaster of Chiselbury in the fifties BBC comedy *Whack-O!*

4,000 street parties in London alone, though fewer people now knew their neighbours. And millions more saw her on her jubilee journeys round the country and her realms across the sea, including Northern Ireland – to the alarm of the courtiers, if not Her stoic Majesty. But even that went smoothly. In Scotland, which had just swung hard to the SNP in local elections, the local press described the royal welcome as 'tumultuous' and 'rapturous'; the chaos in Dundee where the crowd control collapsed and the Queen was engulfed was put down to 'over-enthusiasm'.

Even one of HMQ's most infamous critics was more or less won round. Lord Altrincham, whose criticisms had caused such a hullabaloo twenty years earlier, had by now renounced his title to revert to being officially John Grigg, but he had become kinder, almost reverential: 'She has embodied a great tradition with remarkable dignity and consistency . . . Her bearing, is both simple and majestic – no actress could possibly match it . . . She never seems to lose her poise. These outward graces reflect the exceptionally steady character which is her most important quality . . . No breath of scandal has ever touched her . . . She behaves decently because she is decent.' Very mellow.

17

THE MADMAN OF KAMPALA

WITH THE EMPIRE LARGELY DISMEMBERED, IN THE 1970S the British were starting to run out of places to send out family members to lower the Union Jack. In 1970, Prince Charles was on duty in Fiji where he was given seventy-five slaughtered pigs and a dozen live turtles; and again in the Bahamas three years later, which was part of his post-Camilla tour of the Caribbean as a lieutenant on HMS *Minerva*. His gifts there included a string of bad-taste jokes from a stand-in commentator at a polo match, and a narrow escape from a heavy awning which collapsed on the distinguished guests.

Most of the new nations that followed were collections of dots and microdots in either the Caribbean or South Pacific – one of them being St Vincent and the Grenadines, which included the royalty-haunted isle of Mustique. There was also, notionally, Rhodesia, still under the control of its tiny white minority and its long-standing leader Ian Smith ('Good old Smithy'). The Rhodies had put up a spirited fight for their doomed cause: the right to live out the British dream on jacaranda-flanked avenues in a sparkling climate on stolen land with a servant or two, against the active or passive opposition of what was now about 97 per cent of the population.

But the death knell came from an event 4,000 miles away: the overthrow of the right-wing Portuguese dictatorship by rebel army officers in 1974. As the new Portugal took shape, Mozambique – landlocked Rhodesia's eastern neighbour – ceased to be a white-ruled colony and sympathetic buffer state. It had been the main conduit to get sanctions-busting oil in – and exports out. Instead, just after the huge leap in the oil price, it became a massive base for the main guerrilla army attacking Rhodesia. Far-sighted whites (a minority within the minority) headed for the exits.

This also changed the dynamic for another neighbour: the seemingly impregnable bastion of white supremacy, South Africa, without whose support Smith's Rhodesia would have been strangled at birth. Now the South Africans decided Rhodesia was a liability to its strategy of making nice to black Africa to ensure the survival of its own cruel system.

In September 1976, John Vorster, South Africa's prime minister – himself under pressure from the Americans – read Smith his bleak fortune: Rhodesia had to give way so South Africa could hold out. This was known to white Rhodesians as 'the surrender'. Britain, who notionally owned the place, was only tangentially involved in the arm-twisting – but the US allowed them to do the dirty work of negotiations, in which the Rhodesians kept trying to buy time by dealing with the black leaders they thought pliable rather than the ones they thought horrid. Meanwhile, bloody, self-inflicted war stained the path before another Prince Charles flag ceremony in 1980, when he handed what became Zimbabwe to the gracious mercy of Robert Mugabe.

———•———

In the affairs of another part of Africa, the UK may have played a much more significant role, though emphatically not one to boast about. In January 1971 the first-ever Commonwealth Heads of Government Meeting took place in Singapore. Ted Heath 'advised' the Queen not to attend – though she would sprinkle stardust on every subsequent get-together until she was almost 90. He knew Britain was going to be harangued because he had just resumed selling arms to South Africa. There was some risk of mass defections from the Commonwealth, especially with the Queen absent;

President Milton Obote of Uganda was especially vociferous and, indeed, the harangues were such that at one point Heath blurted out: 'I wonder how many of you will be allowed to return to your own countries from this conference.' Funny he should say that.

The coup took place when Obote was on his way home, and the journey back would actually take him more than eight years. Ugandan radio marked the occasion by playing not traditional martial music but 'My Boy Lollipop' and 'I Wonder Who's Kissing Her Now'. The new leader was one Idi Amin. 'General Amin, a beefy, soft-spoken man, sets an example of restraint,' said the *Daily Telegraph*. 'Completely reliable, a splendid man by any standards,' said O. G. Griffith, a Foreign Office official in London. Griffith did admit Amin was 'not very bright'. He appears to have omitted the word *psychopath*.

What made Amin different from most other mass murderers of history was his extraordinary sense of mischief and theatre. How we laughed at his antics: the day he made four British businessmen carry him into a meeting on a palanquin; how he offered to send Britain food during one of the miners' strikes; even how he forced Callaghan, as Foreign Secretary, to fly out and beg for the life of a British writer. Amin was parodied by the humorist Alan Coren, safely at home, and dramatized in blackface by John Bird. There was some regret about the laughter even before blackface went out of favour, as the extent of Amin's sadistic evil became understood. One can only guess how many died in his personal torture chamber next to the Iranian Embassy in Kampala.

The latest archival research discounts the idea of actual British involvement, and ascribes the coup to conflict between Obote and his generals. Israel, on this reading, gave some assistance for their own complex reasons, but the UK was more of 'a complicit bystander' that took 'opportunist pleasure' in the fall of the annoying Obote – and assumed that anyone else would be better. 'A good deal of our money is on him and in terms of face, HMG has a good deal to lose if Amin . . . fails or does not make a reasonably good job of governing Uganda,' wrote the head of the Foreign & Commonwealth Office's East Africa desk seven months after the coup. Whatever the truth, it's yet another candidate for not Britain's finest hour.

---·---

In 1978, the journalist Ian Jack visited what was then perhaps the least-known of all the remaining British outposts. It was a place of scudding rain half the size of Wales* and comprised 1,800 people – two-thirds of them men, forty-two of those Royal Marines – and maybe half a million sheep. The Upland Goose Hotel served 'packet onion soup and many intriguing ways with mutton'. The projector at Hardy's cinema had a persistent soundtrack fault, rendering much dialogue inaudible. The Falkland Islands Broadcasting Service had the unfortunate acronym FIBS, and in London, no word of a fib, the Foreign & Commonwealth Office was trying to find a way to persuade the Falklanders to accept a deal with their nearest neighbours, Argentina.

---

*   To use the traditional unit of measurement favoured by British journalists.

18

BUT THIS *IS* HOME

A YEAR AND A HALF AFTER TAKING POWER, IDI AMIN announced that all Asians holding British passports must leave the country within three months. By now it was understood that Amin's threats were not idle. It should not have been a shock. Gujarati Indians had constituted the trading and clerking classes across East Africa for generations; they were never popular with the black Africans (nor, in their day, the white imperialists), and the Kenyans had already started to chase them out. Obote, a vicious bastard in his own right,* might well have embarked on a similar course, but without Amin's grandstanding.

Just over half the 80,000 Asians in Uganda held British-issued passports, which had been offered as an alternative at independence. The rest were Ugandan citizens and theoretically exempt from the edict – but they didn't need a weatherman to know which way the wind blew. All the Asians were accused of illegally moving money out of Uganda, which was probably true and certainly wise.

The British passports did not mean much either; they were 'overseas passports' which did not necessarily allow settlement in Britain – it was like having associate membership of an exclusive club. But the government now did the right thing. 'I am sure the nation as a whole will see the clear duty which rests upon us,' said

---

* And even more vicious when he returned to power in 1980.

Sir Alec Douglas-Home, the Foreign Secretary. There may also have been a twinge of guilt about Amin from both him and Heath.

Enoch Powell, talking to the merry wives of the Merridale Ladies' Luncheon Club in his Wolverhampton constituency, denied Britain had any duty at all and talked of 'national catastrophe', the merry old soul. But the protest marches were damp squibs and the *Daily Express*, having run a banner headline NO NEED TO LET THEM IN!, then commissioned a poll on the subject which showed almost two-to-one in favour of doing just that. The British still understood a humanitarian emergency when they saw one. But it would have been much easier without the free-for-all of the fifties.

———·———

West Indian migrants were less vulnerable than Asians to attacks from white youths; their main problem was with the police. This was crystallized in the 1971 case immortalized as the trial of the Mangrove Nine, in which seven men and two women were charged with incitement to riot following a protest against police harassment of the Mangrove, a Caribbean restaurant and social centre in Notting Hill. The trial lasted fifty-five days and ended with the judge, Edward Clarke, saying there was 'racial hatred on both sides', which was a damning indictment of the police. The main charges were all thrown out, though four were given suspended sentences for lesser offences.

The 'sus' laws made it easy for police to pick on anyone without any evidence whatsoever, and in those days they still fussed about small amounts of soft drugs. 'A hippy might be stopped and searched on the street once every week or so,' according to the counterculture expert Barry Miles. 'One Trinidadian friend of mine was stopped seventeen times in one week in Notting Hill and said that was not abnormal.' Middle-aged white men in suits had less trouble.

Black kids were blighted by low expectations from teachers and then by discrimination – conscious or not – in a jobs market that was becoming increasingly difficult by the mid-seventies. With nowhere else to go, they haunted the streets. And given that the almost all-white police forces were not always scrupulous about getting the right black culprit, there were a lot of 'misunderstandings'. 'Loitering with intent' under the 1824 Vagrancy Act was a favourite weapon.

In 1976, a group of young West Indians gave written evidence to a parliamentary select committee citing police attitudes as their major grievance: insults, kickings, false arrests, magistrates automatically believing the police . . . 'It is as though we have reached a point of no return,' said one contributor. 'There are no further last straws. There is no hopefulness.'

'Trying does not make sense,' said another. 'We give up. Crime is exciting. Being unemployed is boring.'

That was at the start of the heatwave. And it was against this background that the long hot summer came to a fiery end at the Notting Hill Carnival. An estimated 150,000 were present on August Bank Holiday Monday for what had already become, in just ten years, the greatest free show in London. Then serious fighting broke out between police and some of the crowd.

The carnival organizers said the huge police presence was provocative: double the number of previous, more peaceable years. The police said they moved in to stop gangs of youths robbing and pickpocketing. The cost-effectiveness of this operation seemed questionable; on the Monday just eleven people were charged with actual stealing. And almost a year later, an Old Bailey jury spent fourteen weeks listening to – though sometimes, literally, snoring through – the evidence. They then spent a record 170 hours before convicting hardly any of the eighteen accused of events that actually occurred at the carnival. The jury were clearly troubled by allegations of police coercion.

And when the next carnival came round, a few weeks after the trial, there was further violence when the police came with stronger helmets and the novelty of riot shields. But this took place as the event was winding down, by the horrendous Westway flyover, where only gangs would dare to tread. By 1978 there was a smaller repetition and a risk that the Westway riot would become a permanent fringe event. But by now the police were getting cannier

and more diplomatic and talked about the 'good side' of carnival.
And in time the annual riot would fade into memory like the Teds,
mods and rockers.

————·————

The British still complained about immigrants, but immigration as
such was fading away. In 1971 the Heath government passed a new
Immigration Act which effectively ended the preferential treatment
of Commonwealth citizens and resurrected the long-lost word
patrial, which was defined as someone who was born or had a
parent or grandparent born in the UK and now had the right of
abode. 'Wretched and racialist and biased in favour of whites,' said
the Labour MP Arthur Bottomley – because more Australians
would qualify than Jamaicans. But it established the status of black
people born in the UK, which meant many of the carnival rioters.
Anyway, the main purpose of the legislation was to marginalize
Enoch Powell.

    But it did not stop the non-white population growing, which is
what bothered the Powellites. The primary immigration from the
West Indies and South Asia that had characterized the past twenty
years may have slowed to a trickle. But the earlier migrants had
families now and were extending their range.

    In addition to the Bengalis in East London and the Sikhs of
Southall, a growing Asian middle class – many of them refugees
from East Africa – spread out along the Betjeman-esque Metropolitan
line to Wembley and Harrow. Across the country, Asians took over
local stores, willing to work as many hours as it took to produce a
viable alternative to the supermarkets. At one point the Dewsbury
area reportedly had thirty-seven off-licences, all of them owned by
a handful of teetotal Pakistani families. Given that Dewsbury was
turning into a largely Muslim town, the off-licences might have had
to diversify.

    By 1976, 40 per cent of Britain's non-whites were British-born.
But less than a tenth of West Indians and Pakistanis had non-manual
jobs, against one-fifth of Indians and two-fifths of whites. This was
not just because they were less qualified. Nearly four-fifths of whites

with degrees had managerial or professional jobs compared to less than a third of non-whites. And so on.

Overt discrimination was now almost wholly outlawed. From 1976 there could be no more Goring Hotels or Smethwick Labour Clubs. But still there was little social integration, even among workmates of different colours. The indigenous British knew almost nothing about this new breed of Briton, and many of the new Britons knew little of the land they chose to call home. Some Muslim women never even mastered English. It was an unmelting pot.

And yet people were still desperate to come. There was a burst of known illegal immigration in 1973: three Asians were found in what was described as 'a coffin' in a lorry arriving at Folkestone; then a British trawler carrying two dozen more was cornered in a Dutch harbour. The racket had been long-standing; the captain got just five years. Thousands more must have been successfully smuggled in, to disappear into the burgeoning ghettoes and sweatshops of which the authorities knew little. The admission of family members could cover a multitude of relationships or none at all.

The extreme right-wing National Front had been making much noise – getting 16 per cent at the West Bromwich by-election in 1973. Powell was still banging on about huge bribes to make minorities 'go home'; but the kids *were* home, the only one they had ever known. By 1977 he was talking about civil war, with firearms or explosives 'so probable as to be predicted with virtual certainty'.

Having become an Ulster MP, Powell may have imbibed too much of the local irrationality. But his decade as the King Kong of British politics was to end abruptly, by what might be termed friendly fire. In January 1978, in an interview with ITV's *World in Action*, Margaret Thatcher noted the prediction of 4 million non-whites in Britain by 2000 and then added: 'Now that is an awful lot, and I think it means that people are really *rather* afraid that this country might be *rather swamped* by people of a different culture . . . if there is any fear that it might be *swamped*, people are going to react and be *rather* hostile to those coming in . . . We are a British nation with British characteristics.'

There was of course uproar, and not just from the you-mustn't-say-that brigade who had inhibited intelligent discussion of the subject all along. Labour, Liberals and the new predominantly white activists from the Anti-Nazi League and Rock Against Racism were of course shocked by the word *swamped* – but also many of her colleagues. In private, her deputy, Whitelaw, was also livid and talked of resignation. Fumed the future Tory star Chris Patten: 'Just imagine if she'd said we were being swamped by Jewish people.' But also note the repetition of *rather*, that very English word denoting tentativeness. She sounded sweetly reasonable. She did not promise to do anything (which Powell noticed, bitterly), but she expressed what was in the voters' minds. And, for the first time in her three years of leadership, it established that she was on their side. It was brilliant politics.

In a by-election two weeks later, the Tories gained the edge-of-Essex seat of Ilford North, which was not unexpected. But the National Front had been expecting a big show: they got 4 per cent. In the 1979 general election, fighting almost half the seats on offer, they got 0.6 per cent of the total vote. And the Powell threat was never the same again. For him, the rest was not silence but it was a descent towards irrelevance. The Right had a new and more plausible champion.

———◆———

For the inner-city working class, almost everything they knew was changing. And Britain was a tough, industrial country where mockery of otherness was the norm, especially among white males: the deaf, the disabled, the effeminate, the mentally ill, toffs, foreigners, black, brown, yellow – all were fair game. To be accepted, it was necessary to win respect. And that took time. Sport was one route. The world light-heavyweight champion John Conteh – half Sierra Leonean, half Irish, totally Scouse – was an early hero.

Football, with its crude partisanship, was always going to be tougher. Against Spurs in 1972 Ron Greenwood of West Ham picked three black players – Clyde Best, Clive Charles and Ade Coker – without fuss. The more ebullient Ron Atkinson matched that six years later by fielding Cyrille Regis, Brendon Batson and Laurie Cunningham at West Bromwich and christening them the Three Degrees.*

Clyde Best remembers a game at Goodison Park: 'The Everton crowd were on at me and I thought, "I've had enough of this." I picked the ball up from the halfway line and as the goalkeeper approached I sold him a dummy and he sat down on his backside and I dinked the ball over the top of his head . . . that was a way to silence them.' He also received a death threat before a home match: 'It was probably just one crackpot trying to spoil the day. I was frightened enough not to play badly.'

There were about fifty black professional footballers at the end of the seventies. They included Viv Anderson of Nottingham Forest, generally regarded as the first black England international, and Ces Podd, born in St Kitts, rejected sight unseen by big clubs so he signed for Bradford City, for whom he played 565 first-team games. 'I had bananas thrown at me and monkey chants,' he said. 'There were too many incidents to only pick one out. It wasn't even like it was isolated chants.' But he was and still is an absolute legend in Bradford.

And not far away, a generation earlier, another black footballer was making himself a legend in Doncaster. Apart from his Barbadian father, Charlie Williams couldn't have been more Yorkshire: thick accent, worked down the pit, and he was even eligible to play cricket for the county – had it been his sport – under their then-unyielding birth qualification rules. Instead he was Doncaster Rovers' centre-half in the late fifties before trying his luck as a singer on the northern club circuit. He found his jokes went down better than his songs, and in 1971 was signed up for *The Comedians*, a Granada TV programme that made huge stars of a dozen stand-up comics and had a terrible effect on others – since gags heard by millions instantly became stone-dead in the clubs.

Williams's shtick was self-deprecating, playing on his blackness:

---

* A black female trio of singers from Philadelphia (*When will I see you again?*). The lads were not female, American or singers, but what the heck?

'Man came to dinner and said "I don't like your mother-in-law." So I said: "Leave her on the side of the plate and just eat the chips and peas."' And again: 'When Enoch Powell said: "Go home, black man," I said: "I've got a hell of a long wait for a bus to Barnsley."' That humour is out of fashion; it did much to ease racial tensions at the time.

The ITV sitcom *Love Thy Neighbour* is now often abused as outright racist: it involved a black couple living next to a white couple, the wives great buddies, the men constantly bickering and slinging racial epithets. The black neighbour (played by Rudolph Walker) was a sophisticated Tory, the white a bigoted union official played by Jack Smethurst, who said he took the role only if he was the one in the wrong, which he was week after week. It drew audiences of 20 million, almost World Cup size, though it was helped by being on at 8 p.m. on Monday night, up against the BBC's worthy current-affairs flagship *Panorama*. It was robust and not very funny. In the context of the time, it almost certainly helped race relations far more than it hindered them.

The other seventies TV programme now regarded with retrospective contempt was *The Black and White Minstrel Show*, which involved the cast putting on blackface to perform dated song and dance routines. It also drew large audiences and few complaints at the time (though the black community leader Dr David Pitt protested). The BBC quietly gave way in 1978. Most mentions in *The Guardian* at the time were unfavourable, not because liberal opinion was outraged by the idea of blackface, but because it was 'bland, unadventurous and predictable' with a 'sagging old formula' or just 'banal'. The audience was elderly and most of them never glimpsed the twenty-first century, let alone imbibed its attitudes, though versions of the show continued touring seaside and provincial venues for several years to come.

19

WEIRDER STILL AND WEIRDER

W AS THERE EVER A DECADE LIKE THIS ONE FOR SENSATION? Perhaps it was the old Britain rubbing uncomfortably against the new and screaming before dying in agony.

No one represented the old (not least due to his Edwardian cad's moustache) more than the 7th Earl of Lucan. 'Lucky' Lucan was the great-great-grandson of the 3rd Earl who had contrived to lose the Light Brigade, and he himself lost – and sometimes won – fortunes in London's upmarket gambling dens. That was before the fateful night in 1974 when he apparently contrived to murder his children's nanny, mistaking her for his wife – the sort of mistake any chap might have made in a hurry. Lord Lucan in the kitchen with the lead piping.

Lucan then disappeared from London in a borrowed car. He stopped at a friend's house in Sussex, told his version (he surprised the real killer, who escaped), and went off and was not, so far as the world knows, seen again. The car was found at Newhaven. But his body was never found, and the ensuing mystery has tantalized theorists down the decades. Did he commit suicide, perhaps hurling himself off a ferry? Or was he spirited away by his Etonian friends?

Not everyone in his gambling coterie was perceived as helpful to the police. Among Lucan's alleged escape committee were the corporate raider and serial litigant James Goldsmith and John

Aspinall, original owner of Lucan's old haunt, the Clermont Club, and of two private zoos in Kent which did valuable conservation work, between the animals mauling their keepers. Such men were no strangers to sensation themselves, nor did they lack resourcefulness – or resources.

There was another group who had a vested interest in Lucan remaining elusive: the journalists who chased down each reported sighting across the globe. 'I regard not finding Lord Lucan as my most spectacular success in journalism,' said Garth Gibbs of the *Daily Mirror*. 'Of course, many of my colleagues have also been fairly successful in not finding Lord Lucan. But I have successfully not found him in more exotic spots than anybody else.'

After Lucan disappeared from view, he did play a role in thwarting another disappearance. The Labour MP John Stonehouse was the last person to be appointed Postmaster General, a Cabinet-level post dating back to 1691. He might have been vaguely remembered as the inventor of the two-tier postal service. Instead, he became the first incumbent of this historic office whose clothes were found on a beach in Miami with the owner missing, presumed drowned.

A month later he was arrested boarding a train 10,000 miles away, in the Melbourne suburbs, suspected of being another well-spoken English gentleman, Lucan. Stonehouse had presumably not swum there. Four years after leaving government, he had become embroiled in multiple sexual, financial and psychological complications, not to mention a total loss of moral compass in that he was travelling on passports in the name of dead constituents – and had probably been spying for Communist Czechoslovakia.

Lucan at least had the decency to keep quiet, living or dead. Stonehouse would not shut up. In the eighteen months it took to bring him to trial, he showboated from jail on two continents, on bail, in parliament and finally in court, exasperating anyone who might have sympathized. He got seven years for forgery, fraud and theft. His lasting fame came from doing a Reggie Perrin, as in the beloved TV series that also began with clothes on the beach and a fake suicide.*

Another seventies figure who fell from grace was Jim Slater, who was described in 1972 by one city editor as 'cleverer with money than anyone else in the world'. Statements like that are a guarantee that nemesis is imminent. Slater was the quintessential asset-stripper, surfing the sixties in partnership with his friend Peter Walker. Both were young thrusters and seen as infallible. 'The shares they bought shot up,' explained *The Independent*, 'especially when everyone else found out who was buying, and climbed on too. They took over sleepy companies, sold off their assets, then sold off the companies for more than they paid.'

Unfortunately, when the market crashed three years later, Slater Walker crashed with it. Walker's claim to have had little day-to-day involvement was supported by him being otherwise engaged as a Cabinet minister under Heath. Slater turned into a minus millionaire for a while but recovered, investing more quietly and writing children's books. No clothes on the beach.

————•————

Two women caused a sensation by landing in jail, one having fallen from much more grace than the other. And they could not have been more different without being reclassified as coming from separate species. One was Rose Dugdale, one of that final cohort of debutantes who curtseyed at the Palace in 1958: a reluctant deb and then an eccentric Oxford undergraduate. By the early seventies she had broken ranks with her family of Devon landowners and was distributing some of their wealth to North London's not necessarily deserving poor.

In 1973, the Dugdales' Devon home was burgled and the family silver disappeared along with their collection of paintings. Rose and her lover, not someone she met at a society ball, were both charged

---

* *The Fall and Rise of Reginald Perrin* was not shown on TV until 1976, just after Stonehouse was jailed. But the writer David Nobbs was writing the book on which the series was based before Stonehouse started his non-swim. So neither borrowed from the other.

with the crime. He got six years, she a two-year suspended sentence, which incensed her as inequitable. There were suspicions of IRA connections and she proclaimed herself a freedom fighter.

She was not kidding. The next year she tried and failed to bomb an Ulster police station by dropping milk churns containing high explosives from a hijacked helicopter, and then took part in a violent IRA raid on a mansion near Dublin and stole various art treasures – including the world's only privately owned Vermeer. She chose the works to steal by pointing to the valuable ones and using a fake French accent: 'Zis one!' They were found in a flat Rose had rented and this time she got nine years, though she served only a fraction of this before being released by the Irish government as a bargaining chip to save the life of a kidnapped Dutch businessman. She lived less adventurously thereafter but expressed no regrets, even after a stroke when confined to a nursing home run by the Poor Servants of the Mother of God. 'For a trained philosopher,' wrote Ben Macintyre of *The Times*, 'Dugdale's take on the complex situation in Northern Ireland was remarkably simplistic.'

Dugdale's polar opposite was called Joyce McKinney, Miss Wyoming 1973, who concocted perhaps the most bizarre romp of this or any other decade: the case of the Manacled Mormon. The Mormon was Kirk Anderson, an earnest young American missionary sent to Britain to god-bother the people of Surrey. The posting was intended to let him escape the voracious and un-Mormon attentions of his one-time girlfriend, the former Miss Wyoming.

Blinded by some combination of infatuation, publicity mania and barminess, McKinney, helped by a male accomplice called Keith May, flew to Britain in 1977 and allegedly kidnapped Anderson at fake gunpoint outside his church in Epsom and drove him to a remote cottage on Dartmoor. There he was given a bedroom in which Joyce appeared in her negligee and suggested sex, which they had certainly had before. On this occasion, he declined, whereupon Keith appeared with a bag full of shackles and allied accoutrements to prevent escape. In these circumstances, poor Kirk found that though the holy spirit was unwilling, the flesh was certainly up for it.

When justice caught up, the conspirators were charged with kidnap, assault and injurious imprisonment, just for starters. There followed a 'full committal' in front of Epsom magistrates – not the now-customary quick remand to comply with habeas corpus but a dress rehearsal for the trial to come. And what fun that was: with Joyce doing her full drama-queen act, it was like all Epsom's Derby Days at once. 'I loved Kirk so much,' she proclaimed, 'I would have skied down Mount Everest nude with a carnation up my nose.'

And then a strange thing happened: the two accused, having been refused bail several times, were let out pending the trial. And then, predictably, they vanished – disguised as the world's most improbable nuns – and reappeared in Atlanta, dealing with lucrative press offers. Another funny thing: Britain never asked the Americans to extradite them.

One man at least was livid: the future Labour MP Bob Marshall-Andrews – then a young barrister who had landed the brief to defend the accomplice Keith May – lost a very tasty payday. 'I am convinced a deliberate decision was made to let them go rather than have them sully the hallowed courts of the Old Bailey,' Marshall-Andrews told me. 'The higher authorities took the court very seriously and didn't want it turned into a laughing stock. It upset me no end.'

The very weekend the Mormon was manacled, the rest of Britain was otherwise preoccupied: a giraffe called Victor fell on the floor of his home at Marwell Zoo in Hampshire, did the splits and could not get up. It was never clear why: one suggestion was that he too was trying to get it together – with one of his three paramours, Domino, Dribbles and Arabesque. Or that he had been weakened by a contretemps with a waterbuck.

Early on, officials were pessimistic about Victor and talked of euthanasia, an idea they tried to resist – especially, perhaps, once they realized a previously little-known zoo suddenly had the most famous animal in Britain. After five days of headlines, scaffolding was erected so he could be winched to his feet. The operation was successful but, sadly, the patient died: Victor's heart gave out. In the nature of things, his death produced more tears in British homes than many distant famines, earthquakes and hurricanes.*

———•———

It was not a vintage decade for governmental sex scandals: the leading Labour politicians tend to be relatively staid in these matters and the Heath government was hit only once, when the air minister Lord Lambton was caught in a newspaper sting showing him smoking a joint while in bed with two prostitutes. The fallout also claimed the scalp of Lord Jellicoe, leader of the House of Lords and said to be the nicest man in politics.

However, there was one political scandal so bizarre that it still exercises a horrified fascination on the national imagination. Like the Profumo affair it began with sex, and it involved the death of an innocent party. But unlike Stephen Ward, not even a High Court judge could believe that the victim deserved his fate. It was a dog.

On a wild, in every sense of the word, October night in 1975, an incompetent hitman called Andrew 'Gino' Newton drove a curious figure called Norman Scott to a lonely spot on Exmoor and there, in the pitch-black and the pouring rain, he shot the other passenger: Rinka, Scott's Great Dane. Whereupon, as he turned to Scott, his intended target, his gun jammed and he scarpered, leaving the distraught Scott and his dead dog alone on the moor.

The trail led easily to the half-baked Newton, who was given two years for intent to endanger life, to run concurrently with six months for damaging property, i.e. Rinka. Newton claimed Scott had been blackmailing him over some compromising photos. But there was a far more important and infinitely more winding trail than that, and the signposts pointed to the leader of Britain's third-largest political party: Jeremy Thorpe of the Liberals.

More than fourteen years earlier, Scott, then 20, was introduced to Thorpe – charismatic, witty, an Etonian, an attention-seeker, and

———

* Victor did leave a legacy: nine months later Dribbles produced a daughter, Victoria. However, giraffes have a fifteen-month gestation period so it was not a dramatic farewell performance.

a rising political star in a potentially resurgent party. Scott was an unstable stable boy, uncertain of his sexuality and pretty much everything else. Thorpe was clear about his preference for men and very clear about the need to keep it secret, despite his penchant for risk-taking. He seduced/raped Scott and offered him help, which over time – as his mental and financial state wavered – Scott was inclined to take over-literally. Scott sensed betrayal; Thorpe, who became leader of his party in 1967, sensed possible blackmail.

The first hint of this in the public domain came three months after the shooting, when Scott was himself in court on a minor charge of social security fraud. This had attracted an improbably large press contingent to Barnstaple Magistrates Court to hear Scott's defence, which he duly offered: 'I am being hounded the whole time by people just because of my sexual relationship with Jeremy Thorpe.'

After the case, Thorpe issued an immediate but carefully worded denial, saying there was no truth in the 'wild allegations' and that he had not seen or spoken to Scott in twelve years. So there was *some* connection. Then the press repaired to Barnstaple's Imperial Hotel to file their copy and to glimpse Scott walking down the staircase performing Nat King Cole's 'You're the Cream in my Coffee' with the words changed to 'I'm the Queen in your Coffee'. Whatever the truth of his story he had something else in common with Thorpe: he was a show-off.

Ted Heath's sexuality was a topic of bar-room discussion in seventies Britain, even if he did not quite know what it was himself. Thorpe's inclinations did not attract much attention, even for most at Westminster. His marriage, fatherhood, and remarriage after the tragic death of his first wife were good enough cover even in a country where known homosexuals could still be hounded from public office. Harold Wilson was convinced that the whole Scott business was masterminded by South Africa's intelligence service to silence an implacable opponent of apartheid. Only a few at first knew otherwise.

Wilson's resignation as prime minister did not manage to keep Princess Margaret's marriage break-up off the front pages, but it did help downgrade the Newton trial, which came at the same time – with Scott's repetition of his allegation, but no clear indication of who might have hired Newton. But the press were now looking hard at the unthinkable candidate: the one man who had a motive to silence Scott. They were also knocking on the Californian door of the former Liberal MP Peter Bessell – an associate of Thorpe now fallen on hard times, concerned he might be a fall guy and willing to talk.

Bessell told the *Daily Mail* that he had lied to protect Thorpe, who retaliated by allowing the publication of two letters in the *Sunday Times* written showing his sympathy for Scott's difficulties. One, written in 1961, ended with the intriguing sentence: 'Bunnies can (and will) go to France.' Thorpe said he could not recall what that meant. What it implied to the readers was that his relationship with Scott was far more intimate than he had implied. In 1962, the government minister Sir Tam Galbraith had been forced to resign simply for beginning a letter to the homosexual spy John Vassall: 'My dear Vassall'.*

Bunnies? Within forty-eight hours Jeremy Thorpe was the ex-leader of the Liberal Party. And the saga was only just beginning.

---

* See pp. 218–9.

20

THE PEOPLE'S PLEASURES

I F VICTOR WAS ONE BRITISH HERO, THEN ONE OF HIS EXCEEDINGLY distant relatives among the ruminants was a more lasting one. The Grand National was a traditional British spectacle – the longest, toughest test in the racing calendar – that by the early seventies was on its knees; the Aintree course had been capriciously run for years, and developers licked their lips at this vast open space on the edge of Liverpool; at one stage the race seemed near certain to be moved to an alternative track, which would have wrecked its unique drawing power.

The saviour was eight years old when he began to work his miracle – without saying a word. Red Rum was a jobbing gelding who had been pottering round the lower reaches of jump racing for some time without uprooting any trees – but also not falling at any fences. He had finally been sold, pretty much lame, into Ginger McCain's stable near the beach at Southport. Sea water was the cure. The result was not just that Red Rum won the 1973 National, but also won it again the next year, came second the next two and then won it again. 'It's hats off and a tremendous reception, you've never heard one like it at Liverpool,' said the commentator Peter O'Sullevan when he won the third time. This in a race habitually described as a lottery. If it had been a lottery, Red Rum would have been arrested on suspicion of fraud.

And what's more, the race was on the BBC. It was an article of faith that the BBC's sports coverage and commentators were the best in the world – men* who had been through the war and understood both the importance of sport and its unimportance. They epitomized, give or take some of David Coleman's endearing foot-in-mouth comments, the excellence of British television. With hindsight one can see that, if British TV was the least worst in the world, the 1970s represented the pinnacle of its least-worstness.

Furthermore, not merely was it in glorious colour, but technology and attitudes were starting to change enough to wean TV companies off the habit of wiping old tapes. In the late 1970s the first clunky video recorders appeared on the market, making it possible to go out for the evening without missing the programme you fancied. This also made it almost certain that someone, somewhere, would have a copy of a lost classic. And it was the first hint of liberation from the twenty-five-year stranglehold that telly had had on British social life. You *could* always watch it later. And somehow, if you knew you could watch a programme anytime, the need to do so often faded. 'Reality TV' – which began in 1974 with *The Family*, a twelve-parter focused on the life of the Wilkins family of Reading, and turned rapidly into a ubiquitous and tedious genre – may have helped addicts decide they needed a little reality of their own.

The TV mania had indeed been extreme. In 1970, a survey of sixteen Western European countries showed that the average Briton watched eighteen hours of TV a week, far more than anyone else and more than double that of the Belgians, Swedes or Italians.† Yet more telling was a survey of (the overwhelmingly British) holiday-makers on the Isle of Man, which revealed that their favourite pastime while there was watching television.

Even the researchers were surprised by this. Their report suggested the establishment of indoor beaches for children and an undersea observatory, but above all TV halls. This implied a certain

---

* Inevitably, in that era.
† Northern Ireland, where there were good reasons to stay at home, had much higher viewing figures than any other region.

desperation to make up for the absence of the one amenity a damp island in the Irish Sea could never reliably offer: sunshine.

And, in the 1970s, sunshine was now more readily available than ever before. The restrictions on holiday spending had been swept away. The collapse of fascist rule in Spain and Portugal in mid-decade made them appealing even to the politically fastidious, and the Spanish resorts made themselves ever more attractive to the completely unfastidious – in the words of the classic Monty Python sketch – 'sweaty mindless oafs from Kettering and Coventry in their cloth caps and their cardigans and their transistor radios and their *Sunday Mirrors* . . . fish and chips and Watney's Red Barrel . . . there's no water in the pool, there's no water in the taps, there's no water in the bog and there's only a bleedin' lizard in the bidet'.

This was not meant to be the future of aviation. That was billed to be Concorde, the Anglo-French pride and joy, In November 1977, two Concordes, one from London and one from Paris, took off simultaneously and landed safely in New York in about three and a half hours – to the great delight of the newspapers, who had hailed the ill-fated early Comets.

But Concorde – super-fast, beautiful, uneconomic – turned into an expensive embarrassment. This was all well signalled in advance. Time and again, when government cuts were in season, Whitehall looked longingly at the figures and tried to scrap it. They were stopped by the French, with their adoration of *grand projets*, who pointed to the heavy penalties for cancellation. And also by Tony Benn, Labour's champion of the working class, who was in charge of Concorde for parts of both the sixties and the seventies. He was proud to claim credit for saving it when Labour returned to office in 1974. Yet it would only ever be for the very rich: the most famous regular was David Frost, satirist turned global TV star, who now commuted to New York as if to New Malden. It seated barely a hundred, people hated the noise, especially when it broke the sound barrier, and most of the world just shunned it. It was proof that just because something could be done, that did not mean it should.

The real future was travel for the masses. The jumbo jets, which in the early days were spaciously laid out even in what would later become cattle class, brought mass travel across the continents. Holidays in Australia became feasible for the un-rich. And two months before the Concordes touched down in New York came a development that should have appealed far more to an egalitarian like Benn.

Freddie Laker, an exuberant old-fashioned airline buccaneer, had just won a six-year battle against the established flag carriers in order to start selling tickets from London to New York for £59, a fraction of the previous price. Hundreds snuggled into sleeping bags at Gatwick for up to three days to catch the inaugural flight, bringing with them the spirit of the Harrods sale and the Wimbledon queue. Suddenly people (mostly young), for whom the US had been as distant as heaven, could be transported far from the culinary comfort zones being recreated for them on the Costas to a land where they could eat more bad food than they had ever imagined.

The following summer Laker was knighted and a makeshift, self-policed, shantytown with a population of 2,000 ('Lakerville') appeared near Victoria station to keep the queuers away from the airport. The shanties were to spare them torrential rain. Michael Bobseine, 21, from upstate New York, had been there for three days at the end of his trip to Britain but was expecting to catch a plane the next day. 'A once in a lifetime experience,' he said. 'I would not have missed it.' He meant the queue, not the holiday.

———◆———

Autumn was a good time to leave London because the football season was under way again. Attendances began falling sharply in the mid-seventies as the effect of winning the World Cup wore off; league football was getting ever more unpleasant, and the supposed spectators were getting more publicity than the players. Tuesday morning papers would have a regular round-up as magistrates used their choicest adjectives on the hooligans paraded before them. There was tough talk from politicians and officials, especially after the fatal stabbing of a Blackpool fan at Bolton. The players were also increasingly being outshone by the managers – once relatively shadowy, often lugubrious figures, now increasingly centre-stage and controversial: the likes of Brian Clough, Tommy Docherty and Malcolm Allison.

The state of the national game was another reason to stay in and watch telly. Of the best-remembered, best-loved TV comedies of the late twentieth century, almost all began or had their heyday in the 1970s: *Monty Python, Dad's Army, Porridge, Fawlty Towers, Steptoe and Son, Rising Damp* and many more. Above all, there was Morecambe and Wise, and on top of all that their Christmas edition, which in 1977 claimed 28.5 million viewers and was much more fun than England losing to West Germany.*

One thing bothers me, looking back after five decades. Over Christmas 2021, the BBC not only played one of the past Christmas shows but a long-lost tape from Morecambe and Wise's regular series in 1970. Eric and Ernie always closed with a song, most often their joyous theme tune 'Bring Me Sunshine' but they had alternatives. This time it was a number called 'Following You Around':

> *If you run, I'll run faster,*
> *Gonna stick, like a piece of plaster,*
> *Get my kicks, following you around*
> *Get my kicks, following you around.*

In those innocent days, no one batted an eyelid. And the words had no harmful intent. But in the 2020s, it sounds like a paean to stalking.

---

* Were Morecambe and Wise that good? All I can say is that I have just checked their Wikipedia page and even that had me crying tears of nostalgic laughter.

21

HEARTH AND HEALTH

IN 1971, JUST OVER A TENTH OF HOUSEHOLDS IN GREAT BRITAIN
still had an outside toilet – about a quarter in Scotland – and,
rather alarmingly, 1.2 per cent had no toilet at all. These figures
were diminishing all the time, but by now so were the number of
new homes. This was the obvious downside of the backlash against
both high-rise and urban sprawl. The last year in which more than
300,000 homes were completed in England was 1969, and that
figure has never been even remotely threatened since. By 1981 it
was below 200,000.

One twenty-four-storey tower block was built in the early
seventies. It was promoted by Kensington and Chelsea Council,
Conservative-run since its inception in 1964 and ever after, but
considered by some to have had an enlightened and paternalistic
view of its responsibility to the poor minority. The flats were
immediately offered to locally based immigrants and the building
became known unofficially as the Moroccan Tower. Its real name
was Grenfell.

What was far more typical of the housing trends of the era,
especially in London, derived from the new post-clearance policy
of improvement grants to do up decaying but salvageable old
houses. These were seized on – not by the poor as intended, but
by the middle classes who created their own, very conformist,
version of a Victorian or Edwardian artisan's terrace house.

The London historian Stephen Inwood summed it up: 'stripped pine doors, sanded floors, knocked-through living rooms, Habitat furniture, Laura Ashley wallpaper, fitted kitchens and gas-fired central heating'.

The most individual touch was often the coolly original downstairs loo. Gentrification was noticed as a phenomenon in 1964 but it reached its apogee in the decades after that.* The process drove the working class out to distant exurbs. But it increased the vibrancy and prosperity of London.

Yet not far away from this new dinner-party belt, much favoured by the leftish intellectuals whose party was in power for most of these years, was a new young underclass who came to find the streets of London paved with gold but were now afflicted by some combination of homelessness, unemployment, destitution, drug addiction, degeneration, crime and unwanted pregnancy. Beggars were on their way back. The major problem, the Bishop of Southwark told the Lords in 1973, was the decline in availability of the charity-run hostels. Those needing them could no longer afford them. And if left on the streets, they would be harried by the police.

The government wanted to do the right thing, and a 1977 Act had an unfunded provision obliging councils to offer housing to those most in want: the sick, the pregnant, the struggling. John Boughton, in his history of the subject, says this had a disastrous effect on the image of council housing. Homes fit for heroes were seen as becoming sink estates.

Perverse consequences were also at work in the health service. Before Barbara Castle fatuously kick-started the modern private health industry[†] there was Sir Keith Joseph, who reversed the stereotype of right-wingers in politics by being well-meaning but impractical. Put in charge of Health and Social Security by Ted

---

* It was in Islington, archetype of the newly fashionable district that I overheard, circa 1979, one builder telling another: 'All they said was they wanted to preserve the original. Well, you can always make the original again, can't you?' Islington's status earlier in the century can be gauged by its cheapness on the Monopoly board.

† See pp. 465–6.

Heath, he drew up a national pyramid of decision-making in the NHS that was a bonanza for bureaucrats. By the time Joseph realized he had created a monster, it could not be slain and to this day mention of his reorganization induces gasps of horror among health-service historians. Administrative and clerical staff rose by nearly a third for no obvious purpose.

Sir Keith was not quite the most unpopular figure of the decade in the NHS. Model Jo Moore posed for a nursing recruitment picture and was asked if she would like to be a nurse herself. 'Certainly not,' she replied. 'I can't stand people when they're sick.' The ministry promised to use a real nurse the next time.

In September 1978 came the last known death ever of the many millions worldwide caused by smallpox. But it did not happen as expected in Somalia, which the previous year had finally been able to follow the rest of the world and declare smallpox eradicated. It happened in Birmingham.

Ten years earlier, smallpox had been a widespread scourge across the Third World. Its eradication was an extraordinary effort led by the World Health Organization, in a huge tribute to the skills of the late twentieth century. Then, suddenly, Janet Parker fell ill. She worked as a medical photographer in Birmingham; her studio was just above the department of medical microbiology, one of the handful of labs allowed to hold stocks of the virus – including the most virulent.

By the time she died, horribly, Janet's mother had caught the disease but recovered, her father had died of a heart attack, and Professor Henry Bedson, head of the lab, had killed himself, though he was subsequently exonerated from any blame. But there was no epidemic and, touch wood, there has not been another anywhere else since. It is still not certain how the virus escaped. It was both a terrible tragedy and, in its way, a miracle.

22

THE EERIE QUIET,
THE BITTER HARVEST

HAVING SURVIVED ITS UNCOMFORTABLE EXPERIENCE WITH THE
International Monetary Fund, the Callaghan government
entered a contented middle age. The prime minister's biographer
Kenneth Morgan called 1977 an *annus mirabilis*, which is a stretch.
But both 1977 and 1978 were years when there was an unusual
absence of crisis.

The oil was flowing; the pound was rising, even as its role in
world trade kept diminishing. Jubilee Year and Britain's turn in the
Common Market presidency gave Sunny Jim excellent platforms
from which to spread his rather bogus bonhomie. England won
back the Ashes and Virginia Wade won Wimbledon, in front of the
Queen – who pretended for a day not to hate tennis.

The government did not actually *do* much. The Bullock
Report recommended that large companies should be obliged to
appoint worker directors but it just gathered dust. Labour's long-
held ambition to institute a wealth tax had sunk into the sands
of practicality. The firms building ships and aeroplanes had been
salvaged by the state, but there were no further ambitions to
nationalize anything. The main aims were to keep the sticking
plaster on the fragile agreement to maintain wage restraint,
and keep the promise to get the Scottish and Welsh assemblies

through the legislative bogs. The 1977 Queen's Speech was extremely feeble.*

There was not a lot the government *could* do. They lost four more strongholds to the Tories at by-elections in late 1976 and early 1977, forcing Labour and the Liberals – in even deeper trouble as the Thorpe scandal inched onwards – to cling together like orphans of the storm and make a parliamentary pact to restore a fragile majority and stop the whips having daily nervous breakdowns.

Although Labour were way behind in the polls, Callaghan was far more popular than Margaret Thatcher – an indicator that can be more telling in the long run. She was regarded as shrill and annoying by much of the public and not a few Tory MPs. Callaghan? The great American sage H. L. Mencken's grateful verdict on President Calvin Coolidge (1923–29) applied: 'He had no ideas and was not a nuisance.'

But things were happening deep underground which would point the way to a different future for industrial relations. And they came to the surface not in Westminster but Willesden. George Ward was an Anglo-Indian businessman who ran Grunwick, a film processing company that thrived in the age before digital cameras. His employees were mainly East African Asians, many of them women. It was not a sweatshop but Ward was a mean-spirited, inconsiderate employer and implacable with it. When his workers tried to join a union, he sacked them.

The strike leader was a tiny, bird-like Gujarati woman called Jayaben Desai, who exuded an almost Gandhian dignity. In the early stages, she drew support on the picket lines from ministers as moderate as Shirley Williams. But even in a country whose labour laws had been redrawn to the unions' specifications, Ward joined with allies on the hyperactive right wing and found cracks in the legislation.

The most hyper of all was John Gouriet, a retired major and leading light in the unfortunately named National Association for

---

* It was also blacked out by a BBC strike, in case anyone thought there was genuine industrial peace.

Freedom (NAFF). As the strike dragged on, post office workers blocked Grunwick's mail, which was crucial to their business. Gouriet ingeniously set up his own service to get round it. The law moved slowly, the strike went on and on and became mired in both aggressive picketing and aggressive policing that had little to do with the put-upon immigrants whose grievances were at stake.

The government sent for the famously fair-minded Lord Scarman, who said Ward's anti-union policy was 'within the letter but outside the spirit of the law'. Laws are written in letters. So Grunwick won and the poor got poorer, and Ward got richer for many years until technology overtook his business model. He became prominent in horse racing as an owner and sponsor but, noted one obituarist, 'he felt he was denied access to the establishment'. There is a world of meaning about Britishness in those few words.

There was a new type of Toryism emerging, and it was starting to attract converts from the Left including Kingsley Amis, the historian Hugh Thomas, the ideologue Alfred Sherman, the Labour MPs Brian Walden and Reg Prentice, and the journalist turned Labour minister, Lord Chalfont.*

Three were particularly influential. One was the scathing columnist Bernard Levin, who fell out with the always-Tory *Daily Mail* when it spiked a column of his urging people to vote Labour in 1970. He moved to the relatively unpartisan *Times* rather than the lefty *Guardian* because he wanted to 'write against the grain' of the newspaper. But soon enough he *was* the grain, his own leftiness forgotten.

Another was Paul Johnson, the former editor of Labour's intellectual sanctuary, the *New Statesman*. His old magazine sportingly

---

* Walden opted out of partisanship and became a forensic TV interviewer in the mould of Robin Day, though some thought him over-kind to Thatcher: at election time she appeared with Walden and avoided Day. Prentice, a Labour Cabinet minister until 1976, was deselected by his left-wing constituency party, switched to the Tories, found a rural haven and briefly served as a Thatcherite junior minister. It seemed a particularly self-serving defection.

published a series of punchy articles denouncing the unions, making his own transition to devout Thatcherism in public. In 1977 came the *coup de grâce* in which Johnson announced his resignation from the Labour Party. His sticking point was the closed shop, which was indeed an affront to libertarian theory – though one with practical advantages in an industrial setting. 'In a system of belief where conscience is collectivised,' he wrote, 'there is no dependable barrier along the highway which ultimately may lead to Auschwitz and Gulag.'

'When a man sees through the folly of one extreme and one-sided view of the world,' sighed Christopher Booker, 'there is no greater danger and no greater likelihood than that he will rush to another.' Alongside the angry letters in the next week's issue, there was a cartoon by Nicholas Garland showing Johnson walking out on to a pavement with Thatcher dolled up as Mae West: 'Come up and see me sometime,' she beckons.

Indeed, several of these middle-aged men seemed to be madly in love with Margaret Thatcher, whose sexual allure was lost on most others. And she was not above using this to political advantage, especially when it came to the most influential convert of all: Larry Lamb, of the soar-away *Sun*, by this time Britain's bestselling daily.

There would be late-night whisky-fuelled sessions with *Sun* executives in Lamb's office in which – contrary to her normal methods – she would ask, 'What do you think, Larry?' He would, according to a well-informed account, pompously give her his views; she would half listen and nod gravely before showering him with compliments: 'If only I had people like you who really know how to communicate. Absolutely marvellous.'

The Sun's embrace of Thatcher was not Lamb's decision alone; the paper's owner, Rupert Murdoch, who had sported a bust of Lenin in his room at Oxford, was turning into the personification of capitalism. And *The Sun* would help sustain Thatcher throughout her reign; she acknowledged the role of Lamb, son of a colliery blacksmith, with that so-hard-to-resist bauble: a knighthood.

The defectors had enough trade union excesses to moan about. The fire brigade staged a national strike in 1977–78 and the Army had to charge around in a thousand ancient trucks from the Ealing Comedy era known as Green Goddesses. The dispute lasted nine weeks in the depths of midwinter, and the union did not get the money they wanted – but did get a deal which lasted into the next century, promising that firemen* would always be in the 'upper quartile' (i.e. the top 25 per cent) of adult male manual wages. Terry Parry, the union general secretary, was so delighted he bought a greyhound and raced it under the name of Upper Quartile. The strike also had a most unexpected benefit for the nation: 194 people died due to fire while it lasted – compared to 228 in the same period a year earlier. Maybe the nervous public was more careful.

And there was always British Leyland. In 1978 and 1979, Derek Robinson – 'Red Robbo', the notorious Communist shop steward at the Longbridge plant – was single-handedly alleged to be responsible for 523 separate walkouts. But the clock was ticking for Robbo. And one sign was the government's appointment of Michael Edwardes, a small, Napoleonic figure with a clear plan, as chairman of British Leyland. 1977 had not been an *annus mirabilis* for the British motor industry, with 400,000 cars being lost to disputes – a quarter of the expected output – and most of those at BL.

In February 1978, Edwardes called a meeting of 650 shop stewards and managers in a Leamington hotel to outline his plans, which meant at least 12,500 job losses and maybe plant closures as well. He was greeted with prolonged applause. Boldly, he then asked for a vote on acceptance of his whole package. Only five hands were raised against. The show of hands was the traditional means of ensuring support for strike action; dubious workers were wary of being seen to break the solidarity. Edwardes turned that upside down: management could be intimidating too. 'It was a gamble which could have ended in disaster,' a union official said.

---

* The first woman firefighter in Britain qualified circa 1982.

'He chose to make an issue of our support, and he won.' Here was proof of the perversity of human nature, and it was fundamental to what was about to happen: a single human could simultaneously vote enthusiastically to go on strike, agree with the boss about the need for change, grumble about the unions to Her Indoors, and vote Tory in the privacy of the polling station.

———·———

Another pocket dynamo was put in charge of an even more benighted British liability. Callaghan put a chippy Yorkshireman, Roy Mason, in charge of Northern Ireland instead of the kindly, thoughtful Merlyn Rees. Mason had just been Minister of Defence, so he was well embedded into the military mindset and fitted easily into the nexus that linked the Army, the Royal Ulster Constabulary, the Protestant establishment and, more tenuously and clandestinely, the loyalist paramilitaries. Unlike Rees, he cared little about how confessions were obtained from suspects and rapidly alienated moderate Catholic opinion. Gerry Fitt, the SDLP leader at Westminster, called him 'that wee focker', and Mason's handling of Fitt would have fatal consequences for the Callaghan government.

There were no more plans for any political initiatives. 'Ulster has had enough of initiatives,' Mason told the 1976 Labour conference. He concentrated on security, with some success; was adamant (not unreasonably) about not allowing terrorists to have the status of political prisoner; and was almost certainly complicit in the brutal treatment of those arrested. He also tried to improve the Ulster economy; this involved handing over something like £100 million to an American called John DeLorean to build sports cars in Belfast. DeLorean was a confidence trickster who looked like a confidence trickster and the double bluff worked a treat.

Mason had arrived in September 1976. The previous month there had been a tragedy – one of many hundreds, but one that cut through the numb acceptance that now routinely greeted violent death in Ulster. It had not even been intentional. The Army were chasing a speeding car through West Belfast and shot dead the driver, IRA man Danny Lennon. The car then careered into a Catholic family out for a walk: a mother and four children. Anne Maguire's new baby, her toddler son and eight-year-old daughter were killed. Her seven-year-old son survived. Mrs Maguire was unconscious for days and woke to the news.

Her sister, Mairead Corrigan, and a housewife who witnessed the incident, Betty Williams, instigated a series of huge peace marches, three of them through areas at the heart of the Troubles – if *heart* was the word. The Peace People transfixed the world: plaudits and money poured in; in West Germany a third of the adult population signed the Peace People's declaration. A year later, Williams and Corrigan won the Nobel Peace Prize.

Long before that, *The Observer* reported, they were being viewed – especially among the Belfast Catholics – with 'increasing cynicism if not downright detestation'. The leaders' global gallivanting attracted much criticism: 'Have you heard that the Peace women are visiting Northern Ireland?' ran one sour joke. The organization was not geared up to handle the money. Nor was there an agreed philosophy or strategy, and it soon split into factions. The fact that the women kept the Nobel money was an easy weapon to their enemies. 'Sure it was the money they wanted,' said one Belfast woman. Its great success may have been making sentimental Irish-Americans think twice before handing over money to 'the boys'.

From the start, the boys, aka the IRA, sensed a dangerous enemy, and one that might encourage informers; the marchers were pelted with stones on the Falls Road. They were more respectfully received in the Protestant areas, but one vignette gave a clue to the failure. In the early days a group of 'Shankill peace women' from the Protestant Shankill Road were forming human barricades to stop loyalist paramilitaries hijacking buses. Journalists asked if they had invited Mairead and Betty to join them. 'We don't want any Fenians up here,' came the reply.*

---

* Anne Maguire committed suicide in 1980. Mairead Corrigan later married her widower, Jackie.

Whether or not the Peace People could take any credit, the second half of the seventies was much calmer then the first. The murders went on, but less regularly. And the IRA drew back a little from their campaign in England (Scotland and Wales were exempt). Random malevolence went out of fashion – a few more Birminghams and the Irish population in Britain would have been at risk – and became more targeted, usually aimed at representatives of the state, the plutocracy or the military. And fortunately, according to Callaghan's aide Bernard Donoughue, the failure rate of their bombing missions, the vast majority unknown to the public, was staggeringly high.

Within Ulster the death toll fell towards that horrible target identified by Reginald Maudling on his watch: 'an acceptable level of violence'. The Royal Ulster Constabulary was now more like a proper police force than a gang of partisans, and the Army could increasingly stand back. The squaddies had a taste of real soldiering, but not, on the whole, too much. The paramilitaries had plenty of nice rackets, not least the drugs trade. There was simply no imperative for peace.

Occasionally, the violence would veer out of control on one side or the other. One Protestant gang, the Shankill Butchers, picked up random Catholics at night and killed them with cleavers, axes and butcher's knives – sometimes with an hors d'oeuvre of torture. In 1978, the IRA killed twelve, mostly women, with a particularly fiendish device that burned the flesh like napalm, at the La Mon Hotel outside Belfast on the night of the Irish Collie Club's annual dinner-dance.

Such madness was becoming rarer, and being perceived as counterproductive. More common were the ritualized bombings along the lines of the Europa Hotel attacks. Almost every golf course in the province was bombed at one stage, but normally with warnings and only the clubhouses were attacked – it was considered unsporting to ruin the greens.

And in the midst of all this, the Northern Ireland football team was drawn in the same qualifying group as the Irish Republic for the 1980 European Championship. Ten thousand fans, nearly all Protestants (Catholics did not cheer for the North), travelled to Dublin for the first-ever match between the two. Everyone held their breath. There was much less trouble than on the average Saturday at Millwall.

———◆———

If 1977 and 1978 were good years for Callaghan, this did not apply to his temporary allies in the Liberal Party. In October 1977 Andrew Newton, now out of jail, told the press, for a lesser fee, that he had been hired to kill Norman Scott for £5,000. In August 1978 Jeremy Thorpe was taken to Minehead, on the edge of Exmoor, to be charged with incitement and conspiracy to murder. The unimaginable had become fact.

In September 1978, Jim Callaghan broke into song at the TUC annual conference at Brighton, doing a rendition ('tuneless' – *The Times*; 'off-key' – *The Guardian*) of the chorus of the music hall classic 'Waiting at the Church'. Then he added: 'I have promised nobody that I shall be at the altar in October.' Well, said the political commentators, he's just teasing. Of course he would hold an election. The polls, the economic indicators, the unions' growing impatience with wage restraint, the wearisome bargaining that went with having a minority government . . . everything was as good as it was likely to get and pointed to a quick election, even though he could cling on for another year.

Two days later, he told the nation that was just what he planned to do. The Cabinet was blindsided; even his closest aide, Tom McNally, was reduced to speculating that Callaghan thought three years as prime minister sounded more substantial than two. No one was crosser than his temporary ally, the Liberal leader David Steel, who was banking on getting the election over with quickly before his predecessor Thorpe went on trial. So that was the end of the Lib-Lab pact, and now the government was really a minority. Meanwhile, the Tories were ecstatic. Callaghan had also told the unions that he expected them to limit wage rises to 5 per cent, which was optimistic bordering on fantastical.

And so the quadrille began again – the ritual dance between the government, unions, employers and public. But this time it was a dance of death. In keeping with tradition, Ford was first on to the ballroom floor and the management caved at 17 per cent. Callaghan wanted to impose sanctions on Ford; that was scuppered by those friends of capitalism, the Labour Left. As Christmas approached, so did battalions of trade union leaders bearing demands. And the big two who had previously kept a semblance of order in the ranks, the austere Jack Jones and the jolly, golfing Hugh Scanlon, had both retired. Jones's successor as leader of the Transport and General Workers' Union, Moss Evans, took a narrower view of his responsibility.

In the bleak midwinter, there is nothing more cheering than the prospect of a tropical beach and, for a prime minister, a summit meeting: to leave behind the petty annoyances of the ungrateful populace and strut the big stage. In January 1979, Callaghan had both at once. The French had chosen a beachside resort on the Caribbean island of Guadeloupe, officially part of France, for a get-together with the leaders of Britain, the US and West Germany. Bliss!

It was not just a jolly. Much work was done, and Callaghan reached an important understanding with Jimmy Carter about replacing Polaris missiles with the new Trident on favourable terms. Even the Thatcher-loving *Telegraph* was impressed by the way he acted as a bridge between the Americans and Europeans.

But there was downtime, and the sea-dog prime minister sailed a dinghy into the distance with great élan. But then he returned in his trunks, to be snapped by a long-lens camera, sit down in his deckchair and be greeted by the head of his civil contingencies unit, Sir Clive Rose, with the latest news from home. 'Oh, Clive,' said the PM drowsily. 'Go away.' Perchance to dream about Reggie Perrin, or even John Stonehouse.

Rose had been trying to make him understand that the mood in Britain was taking a dark turn. But Callaghan went home (after a side trip to Barbados), brain still on the beach, and gave an impromptu press conference without stopping to calculate the national mood. When a journalist mentioned the 'mounting chaos' in Britain, he pooh-poohed it. Hence *The Sun*'s headline, not a quote but a masterful summary of his response: CRISIS? WHAT CRISIS? All those hours Margaret Thatcher had spent in Larry Lamb's office now reaped their dividend.

———•———

In the PM's absence, Britain had been part-snowbound and experiencing its nastiest weather since 1963. The lorry drivers had gone on strike and their pickets had closed most of the ports: shiploads of food were rotting by the quayside. Rail workers, postmen and even civil servants were threatening to join them. There was a fuel shortage, and schools were closing because there was no heat. In places, rubbish piled high. There were outbreaks of flu, and hundreds of coast-dwellers in North Devon had to be evacuated due to floods. And it was only just kicking off.

If Callaghan's public relations skills had failed him, that was nothing to the crassness of some of the strike leaders. The T&G agreed to make the lorry drivers' strike official: 'It's not my responsibility to manage the economy,' shrugged Moss Evans. 'We are concerned about getting the rate for the job.' 'No leadership qualities,' wrote a bitter Denis Healey later. Then London's public service workers joined in, including the paramedics. 'If it means lives lost, that is how it must be,' said their spokesman Bill Dunn, making himself sound like an IRA commander. There was more snow, even in London, and black ice, and freezing fog.

The threat to ignore 999 calls in the initial one-day strike was dropped, but selective action continued which included 'working without enthusiasm'. In this period, it happened that David Ennals, the Health and Social Services Secretary, was admitted to the Westminster Hospital for a recurring thrombosis. The public employees' branch leader announced that the minister would not receive newspapers, post, tea, soup or 'a single smile'.

The climax of this bonkers bonfire of all the Left's electoral hopes came when the Liverpool gravediggers downed tools. The strike lasted twelve days and spread to parts of Manchester, where the local union organizer, Michael Rawcliffe, refused to listen to entreaties. 'I am impervious to moral blackmail,' he said.

———————

The winter of discontent was far worse when magnified and megaphoned by the media. Many people suffered little, or nothing more than they would in any other cold winter. There were exceptions – like the population of Hull, whose geography made it easy for the picketing lorry drivers to cut off. And the bereaved of Liverpool. Many of the strikers had been underpaid for years and had watched others use militancy to milk the system. But it was a cataclysm for British trade unionism.

Later in February, the government and unions signed the latest incarnation of their old friend Solomon Binding – yet another promise to keep wage rises within sensible limits. This time it was called the 'concordat', normally an agreement involving the Holy See. No one can have imagined it working in this world.

It was not, however, any of this that actually finished off the Callaghan government. It was the Scots. All through this strange political decade there had been a drumbeat coming from Scotland (and a more muffled one from Wales) that their votes and loyalty could no longer be taken for granted. One by-election success in each country in the sixties lifted nationalism above joke status; then a huge swing from Labour in the Glasgow heartland seat of Govan in 1973 set off a panic not seen since Bonnie Prince Charlie marched on London.

By then, a Royal Commission – the classic device used by governments to outsource and defer tricky problems – had reported and recommended devolution. And in the October 1974 election, the Scottish National Party won eleven seats and 30 per cent of the votes. This was founded on a slogan of minimum idealism but maximum potency: 'It's Scotland's Oil'. Fortunately for the United Kingdom as an entity at that time, there was something no one knew outside government: the contents of a confidential report by the chief economist of the Scottish Office, Gavin McCrone.

McCrone told ministers that the nationalists' figures were wrong, as many of their opponents had claimed, trying to discredit the thesis that Scotland could prosper alone. However, what McCrone said was that their figures were far too pessimistic: 'There is a prospect of Government oil revenues in 1980 which could greatly exceed the present Government revenue in Scotland from all sources and could even be comparable in size to the whole of the Scottish national income in 1970 . . . Thus, for the first time since the Act of Union was passed, it can now be credibly argued that Scotland's economic advantage lies in its repeal.'

In other words, the independent Scots could be Europe's sheikhs, and the rest of the UK population might be allowed to an eke out a living as their stable lads and scullery maids. When the report emerged thirty years later there were allegations that it had been suppressed – Scotland betrayed *again* – which McCrone denied: it was a confidential briefing paper for ministers like any other, he said, never intended for publication. And by then the facts had changed.

Knowing what they did, the Callaghan government could not renege on the promise of devolution. But as the legislation meandered through parliament towards a pair of referendums, even the nationalists began to lose interest. 'The SNP didn't think the bill was in any way credible,' explained the Scottish historian Sir Tom Devine. 'In effect, all they were being offered was control of the Scottish Office and even the leading supporters of the bill thought the proposal was emaciated. The old Conservative side of Scotland was completely against it but it didn't have much attraction for either side. That's what created the apathy, along with the growing unpopularity of the Labour government.'

And the apathy mattered. One Labour anti-devolutionist, George Cunningham,* an unbiddable Scot who was MP for un-tartan Islington, pushed through an amendment requiring that 40 per cent

---

* Assisted by a young Welsh MP, Neil Kinnock.

of the entire Scots and Welsh electorate had to vote in favour of their assemblies, not just a simple majority. And by the time the referendums were held on St David's Day 1979 (to gee up the Welsh), with the winter of discontent barely over, everyone was just generally hacked off.

There was a feeble majority in Scotland for this feeble proposal: just over 51 per cent of the votes cast and, on a low poll, nowhere near the Cunningham threshold – but an injustice on normal democratic criteria, so yet one more betrayal. In Wales there was no such dispute: the Assembly was rejected by four to one. It is hard to know why they were quite so vehement. But an old remark attributed to that fine Welsh broadcaster Wynford Vaughan-Thomas comes to mind: 'If you stand on any Welsh street and shout "YESSSSS!", a hundred voices will come back shouting "NOOOOO!"'

The SNP had still not worked out what they were. Devolutionists or outright separatists? Left-of-centre or right-of-centre? Professionals or amateurs? In pique, they joined forces in a parliamentary vote of no confidence in the government, with both Margaret Thatcher, who had reneged on Ted Heath's support for devolution, and the desperate Liberals. Defeat for Callaghan meant an automatic election. He had great fun mocking that alliance in the debate where, by common consent, he outclassed Thatcher, as he usually did. But after much confusion, horse-trading and twinges of conscience, he lost the vote by one: 311 to 310. A tie would have been enough for the government to limp on a bit longer. The Belfast Catholic Gerry Fitt abstained rather than casting his usual vote with Labour; he could take the wee focker Mason no longer.

23

CHANGE AND ECHOES

At the height of the lorry drivers' strike in January 1979, there were fears that shops would run out of supplies. In North London, Gwendoline Johnson, 74, from the generation that had only just acquired fridges, now complained that people were bulk-buying for freezers and worsening the problem. 'All we need now is some power cuts, then those greedy shoppers would be in the same boat as me,' she said. This was around the time when there were reports from Somerset of cannibalism among starving pigs.

The old, sociable ways of shopping had pretty much gone now. The out-of-town hypermarket arrived in 1972, starting improbably with the French chain Carrefour arriving outside Caerphilly in South Wales, which caused such traffic jams that people were warned to stay away. Those who got in were very excited: 'In Caerphilly it costs 14p, it's three pence it's saved, isn't it?' a man who bought a pack of batteries told an ITV camera crew. But environmental constraints made expansion difficult and Carrefour soon retreated.

Green Shield stamps, given away free mainly by supermarkets and garages, also turned out to be something like a nine-year wonder. Perhaps the peak came in 1973 when a church congregation in Belfast clubbed together with stamps and spittle and acquired a new Ford Cortina. In 1977, Tesco pulled out and the business model began to crumble. Straitened times, Tesco concluded, meant shoppers preferred price cuts. Also, the Civil Service clamped down on employees who were being relocated (usually away from London) collecting stamps offered by the removal companies. It was estimated that the average family move would yield enough to buy a bread bin. Fortunately for him, Green Shield's boss Richard Tompkins had already started Argos as an alternative.

Stampless, Tesco thrived. In 1979, Ian MacLaurin, then the firm's managing director, showed the aged and ailing founder, Sir Jack Cohen, round a new superstore. The old man was awe-struck, and whispered: 'I never imagined that this was how it would be.' He died the next day. In rural Herefordshire, Michael and Maisie Griffith's handy village shop was still thriving throughout the seventies. But Jack Cohen's ghost would come to haunt them soon enough.

In 1976, Britain gained its first out-of-town (sort of) American-style indoor shopping centre at Brent Cross, the London end of the M1. This too would shape the future – a place for all the family to embrace corporatism and bad food, even in bad weather.

———•———

One pacifist leftie, Raymond Postgate, had handed over the *Good Food Guide* to another, Christopher Driver, who was far from pacific in his judgments. Twenty-seven years after Postgate's first slim volume, the post-war privations had faded and both the book and the diners had grown fatter. In his foreword, Driver admitted, 'It may be harder to get a strictly disgusting meal than it once was.' But, he went on: 'Meals are cooked with contempt by people whose minds are mainly on the cash register (if they own their own business) or on knocking-off time.'

Pizza Hut opened its first British outlet, in Islington, in 1973. And a year later came another American interloper, marked by a party for a thousand guests not at its own first outpost, in Woolwich, but at the Café Royal. There was also a threat from an unnamed executive: 'We are going to wipe Wimpy off the High Street.' Which it duly did. The *Daily Mail* was impressed from the start. Its correspondent thought that, unlike Wimpy, a McDonald's burger actually tasted like beef. This was probably incidental: McDonald's were selling the American experience. And, boy, did they sell it.

---·---

In October 1970, Sir George Godber issued his annual report on the nation's health – the tenth in his role as Britain's chief medical officer. As usual, he emphasized the dangers of tobacco: he now estimated smoking was causing 100,000 premature deaths across the UK. 'It seems incredible,' said Godber, 'that our country can go on accepting the lavish promotion . . . of a habit that is dangerous to all who indulge in it and offensive to many who do not.'

The British had already cut their consumption by half, but this was the era of bargaining with the tobacco dragon. The Ministry of Health solemnly began issuing league tables of tar and nicotine levels to enable smokers to switch to brands like table-topping Silk Cut Extra Mild and away from untipped Capstan Full Strength, which was far and away the strongest cigarette on sale and could probably kill you without being lit.

There were very minor curbs on the wherever-and-whenever tradition: smoking carriages on the Underground went down from half to a quarter, with similar cutbacks on British Rail. The BBC, whose Prom season – most unusually for classical concerts – did allow smoking, changed their mind in 1970.* But the balance of power had not shifted far enough to make more serious bans viable. Even Sir George Godber, who had not smoked since he was six, allowed visitors to do as they pleased in his office.

Indeed, though men were giving up – and male doctors in particular – more women than ever were now smoking, a by-product of liberation. But a single publican blazed a trail. Jack Showers, landlord of the New Inn at Appletreewick, in rural Yorkshire, imposed a ban after his much-loved chain-smoking barmaid died of lung cancer. He was far stricter than Sir George. Since he was an innovative businessman who usually had several other different

---

* Apparently, patrons were respectfully requested to use lighters not matches.

gimmicks on the go, he got away with it and thrived; the handful of other publicans who followed him voluntarily generally lost customers.*

The drinking culture was even more persistent, notably in Westminster and Fleet Street and most notably where the two met. Leading politicians routinely lunched with journalists (whose employers paid), with a large aperitif beforehand, wine with the meal and a brandy afterwards, before heading back to Westminster, sometimes to drink their way to the 10 p.m. division. Most of them still managed to function quite adequately. The Fleet Street lunch record was claimed by the foreign correspondents Philip Jacobson and Peter Pringle in Bogotá circa 1975: two people, eight hours, thirteen bottles.† There may be other contenders.

Even as most Britons reconciled themselves to buying cars made by their former enemies, not everything was forgotten or forgiven. At Reuters news agency in London, one of the senior editors, Peter Stewart, who had flown with the RAF, was reputedly introduced to a German delegation who were touring the building. 'Have you ever been to Germany, Mr Stewart?' one innocently asked. 'Only by night,' he replied. On the other hand, the younger generation had weaker memories. Shortly after Britain joined the Common Market, a young Reuters reporter is said to have started a story 'Relations between Britain and Germany fell to an all-time low today over potato quotas'.

There were some hints of the future that lay ahead. 1979 was the first year the British spent more on holidays abroad than at home. It was also the year when the Sony Walkman arrived, allowing portable private music via cassette tape. It was an immediate hit – not just for those who bought it but also for those in parks, beaches and the deep wilderness who were released from the

---

* Showers hoped to find a way of maintaining the ban after he retired. In that, he failed – in the short and medium term.
† There were casualties: two not-quite prime ministers, Reggie Maudling and George Brown, both died of cirrhosis. But my general observation is that men who had lived through the war mysteriously acquired an extra layer of iron in their constitution.

twenty-year tyranny of other peoples' transistor radios (though not from the headphones leaking on crowded trains).

In 1974, the BBC started their teletext service Ceefax, which gave people a taste for reading up-to-date news and other info from a screen *whenever they wanted*. It was much later in the decade before many people had sets capable of receiving it. Nearly half a century on, it may be hard to understand what a breakthrough this limited but lovable service was. Another one was just starting: under the Labour government, the Post Office gave up its monopoly on radio-telephones, allowing the embryonic market in car phones – 'some of them hardly bigger than an ordinary car radio', as an excited report explained – to begin taxiing down the runway towards take-off. And in February 1979 Trevor Francis was transferred from Birmingham to Nottingham Forest to become Britain's first million-pound footballer.*

The BBC had one other innovation, perhaps noticed only subconsciously by the vast majority of the population. It was a Radio 4 series aimed at people with disabilities, and its brilliance was in the title – *Does He Take Sugar?* – satirizing the common response of assuming that anyone in a wheelchair was too stupid to speak for themselves. The programme ran for twenty years from 1977, an effective champion for disabled rights in itself but perhaps even more effective for the title's subliminal effect on everyone else.

———·———

Five years after the teenage heiress Jayne Harries was barred from Royal Ascot for wearing trousers and then eloped with her hairdresser, she appeared in court for possessing cannabis. She was punished with a night in Holloway jail, a £350 fine and a pompous denunciation from an Old Bailey judge: 'The only contribution you have made to working life since you completed an expensive schooling was to act for a very short time as some sort of clothes peg, euphemistically known as a fashion model.' Her marriage had

---

* In 1952, the record was held by Jackie Sewell (Notts County to Sheffield Wednesday) at £34,500.

not lasted, and nor, alas, did she. Four years later she died, a heroin addict, evidently after injecting herself with a dirty needle in a public toilet. Her face and fortune had both long been ravaged.

In 1978, Keith Moon – the Who drummer and arguably the most extreme of all the sixties rock hellraisers – died after taking an overdose of a drug he used to combat his alcoholism. The man who had once driven his car through a hotel's glass doors to check in (and another into a swimming pool) checked out, aged 32. 'He had an incredible talent but was uncontrollable,' reflected his bandmate Roger Daltrey. 'Not just a little bit uncontrollable — completely uncontrollable.'

To the small extent that the 1960s represented one long party – and it was for Keith – the 1970s certainly represented the morning after. And for the upper crust, a single scribe emerged as chief chronicler of the resultant mess. Part of the *Daily Mail*'s revival in that era was a renewed emphasis on that old Fleet Street staple, the gossip column. And with Rupert Murdoch breaking old taboos every day in *The Sun*, a little old-fashioned scurrilousness was neither here nor there.

The charming posh rogue is a familiar figure in British journalism. And no one was quite as charming or as ruthless as Nigel Dempster. Hired as the No. 2 to Paul Callan, who had brought back the tradition of *Mail* gossip, Dempster hoarded a few juicy stories until Callan went off for a week to cover a party conference – and then fired them all off so they would appear under his own name. It was a *coup d'état* and it worked. Dempster thrived on the fact that people in the aristocracy/celebrity nexus were liable to have tangled private lives – and they were becoming keener to get their side of the story across. Dempster, said Princess Margaret's lover Roddy Llewellyn, 'was a charming slubberdegullion. No one can resist a cad.'

Well, a few could. For many years the *Guinness Book of Records* named Sir John Ellerman, who succeeded his father as chairman of Ellerman Shipping Lines, as the richest man in Britain. He gave no interviews, lived as a recluse, and when he travelled – always on his own ships – only selected officers could speak to him. He was mostly interested in rodents, and leased Brownsea Island in Poole Harbour from its equally reclusive owner so he could study its particularly interesting population of rats.* He secretly gave away much money, learned Braille so he could read to the blind with more empathy, and left no heir when he died in 1973.

Even less likely to appear in the Dempster column was Gerson Berger, who owned an estimated 11,000 properties through 400-odd companies while living in a ground-floor flat in then very unfashionable Hackney, where he died in 1977. Berger reputedly gave his money to the Sotmarers, a Hasidic Jewish sect as obscure as the man himself. Some of his tenants thought him less than charitable, and Ken Livingstone, the young vice-chairman of the Lambeth Housing Committee, talked of 'forcing the Berger Group out of the borough'.

One woman who had briefly become hugely famous for signposting the route to longevity surrendered in her mission. Dr Barbara Moore, who had walked the length of Britain and the width of the US seventeen years earlier, starved to death in 1977. She had once claimed that her diet could allow her to live to 150 but – worn down after failing in a complex court case about sewage pipes across her land – she stopped eating at all and chose to die, aged only 73 and not quite halfway.

And in the first decade since time immemorial when no one in Britain was executed for a crime they either did or did not commit, Laura Frank – on the very day she married Michael Spira – experienced a very disconcerting echo indeed. In the midst of the wedding celebrations at the Royal Majestic Rooms in Willesden, a white-clad figure appeared from the kitchens where he now worked and headed towards the top table.

It was, the bride eventually realized, James Hanratty senior, the dustman father of young James, who had built the Franks' garage before he was controversially hanged for murder. The father, who had fought with tireless dignity to prove his son's innocence, must

---

* *The Families and Genera of Living Rodents* by J. R. Ellerman was published in 1941.

have seen Laura's name on a list in the kitchen. 'My baby,' he always called her.

He did manage to have a few words with the bride's mother but it was all too confusing, especially for the bride. Weddings are like that. She thinks poor Mr Hanratty was hustled away, back to the kitchen. And the band played on.

24

THE WOMAN'S HOUR

ONCE JIM CALLAGHAN HAD LOST THE CENSURE VOTE, HE WAS almost totally constrained. With the Commons formally withdrawing support from him, he had to set an election in motion at once. Such a thing had not happened since 1924, but the precedents, conventions and gentlemanly principles of British politics also applied. He knew his duty.

Even without Gerry Fitt's vote, there might have been other ways of securing a majority that fateful night. There was Fitt's fellow Ulster Catholic Frank Maguire, who made a rare visit to the Commons but, according to Charles Moore, Margaret Thatcher's official biographer, was 'forbidden by Irish Republican heavies' – who were not gentlemen – from voting for Callaghan. There was a suggestion that Enoch Powell and some other unionists might be bought off with the promise of a gas pipeline to Ulster, but Callaghan rejected that.

And there was the even more delicate case of a desperately ill Labour MP, Sir Alfred Broughton, who could legitimately have been brought from his Yorkshire home by ambulance into the precincts of parliament to lie still and be counted. Broughton was keen to oblige; his wife was not. In the end, Walter Harrison, the deputy chief whip, decided against. Callaghan agreed. Sir Alfred died eight days later. Even politically, it was the right thing to do. These things say much about Callaghan's state of mind – 'he's lost his bottle,' the future leader John Smith said to Roy Hattersley – and also about the nature of Britain in 1979. What the constitutional expert Peter Hennessy called the good-chap theory of British democracy.

For such a consequential election, perhaps matched only by 1945, it was a very subdued campaign. The first reason was that, with parliament still tying up outstanding business ends before being dissolved, Airey Neave was killed by a car bomb – planted by a republican splinter group – as he drove out of his underground parking space beneath the Palace of Westminster. Neave, mastermind of Margaret Thatcher's defenestration of Ted Heath, was expected to become her Northern Ireland Secretary, and a very aggressively anti-republican one at that. Such events have an effect on politicians, making them focus on the values that unite them, but only briefly.

Secondly, the Conservatives were ahead in every poll bar one between the parliamentary vote and election day, and Thatcher's main tasks were to sound reasonable and to avoid arguments, errors and shrieking: Callaghan still led her in terms of personal popularity. Her manifesto was moderate in tone and traditionally Conservative in its promises. The Labour manifesto was thin.

And thirdly, as John Smith had foreshadowed, Callaghan had already reached the acceptance stage of grief. The old navy man talked privately about a 'sea-change' in favour of Thatcher, and in public he was variously described by reporters as being 'elegiac', 'half-hearted' and 'dignified'. He had effectively lost the election during that bitter January and he knew it. He was 67, had done it all and did not overdo the campaigning.

Thatcher, meanwhile, was up for anything and everything. She came under the aegis of Tim Bell, the adman responsible for the LABOUR ISN'T WORKING poster the previous year, which purported to show a long dole queue – implying that the Conservatives would cut unemployment.* And Bell liaised with Gordon Reece,

---

* Members of the Young Conservatives were invited along to be in the photograph of the snaking dole queue. The ad agency hoped for a hundred but only twenty turned up so different images had to be melded together to create the desired effect.

a TV producer and marketing man described as her 'Svengali', who improved her television technique and presentation, stopping her interrupting and banging on, at least when on camera. Unlike Ted Heath, she took note of presentational advice. She avoided hard-edged interviewers, preferring soft options with big audiences, like the women's magazines and the Jimmy Young show on Radio 2.

Above all, she gamely stooped to stunts and was shown doing ordinary things – the things Ted, Jim and indeed Elizabeth II would never pretend to do – like shopping. Ordinary, except for the presence of legions of cameramen. The Tory targets were the early-evening TV bulletins, which constituted family viewing. This reached a farcical apogee on a farm in Suffolk where Thatcher hugged a newborn calf – 'almost strangled,' said *The Guardian* – for thirteen minutes until the photographers had all had enough, never mind the poor calf. Her husband Denis, auditioning for the role of Prince Philip-style consort, muttered something about having 'a dead calf on our hands'.

These were not just home-based camera crews. The Thatcher show transcended Britain. A woman, housewife (sort of) and mother was on the brink of leading the mother of parliaments. It was a fitting way to conclude the decade of feminism, however contemptuous she was about that concept. She was a novelty in the way the radiant young Queen had been twenty-seven years earlier. The difference was that something like half the country already actively hated her.

———•———

A few weeks before the election, Sir Nicholas ('Nicko') Henderson, the ambassador to Paris, sent a valedictory despatch at the end of his posting, in keeping with longstanding Foreign Office tradition. It was addressed as usual to the Foreign Secretary – David Owen, who would himself shortly be leaving government for ever, though not voluntarily. Normally such letters would focus on the country the ambassador was leaving. But Henderson ranged far beyond France in his letter. It was a full-blown analysis of the failure of

Britain's attitude to Europe, with a strong overlay of declinism: 'We are not only no longer a world power, but we are not in the first rank even as a European one.'

He also offered three solutions. Firstly, he said, Britain – without giving up the right to assert itself – needed to act 'as though we were fully and irrevocably committed to Europe'. Secondly, the British people needed to be made much more conscious of the extent to which the country was falling behind. And thirdly, the government needed to stimulate a sense of national purpose – not in a Nazi sense, but learning from the way the French leaders since de Gaulle had played on patriotic sentiment.

Unusually, the despatch found its way into the public domain and, presumably, into the incoming prime minister's in-tray: Henderson, who was supposed to be retiring, was instead offered (and accepted) his profession's top prize – ambassador to Washington.

———•———

Were things really as bleak as Henderson thought? Obviously, his job meant he had to worry if the host government ignored him. But we come back to the question of whether other things mattered more. News, of its nature, concentrates on complaints and conflict. Yet when *The Times* sent their reporter John Young round Britain in the summer of 1977, he concluded: 'The British are less discontented, and more cheerful and tolerant, than most commentators proclaim. They work harder than is generally supposed, and for the most part enjoy it. They distrust politicians, and are sceptical of what they read in newspapers or see on television.'

This, he added, 'may simply confirm the view that the British are irredeemably complacent. Equally it may suggest a calmness, a refusal to be stampeded into believing that the world is collapsing around their ears, and a belief that life does not change all that much and will be much the same tomorrow.'

They were getting what they craved, a better life: by the late seventies, 96 per cent of homes had a TV, nine out of ten a vacuum cleaner and fridge, and four out of ten a food mixer. And quite suddenly, from hardly any in the winter of 1963 and a third in 1970, half of Britain's homes now had central heating.

Above all, there appeared what from this distance constitutes one of the most startling sentences ever published in a British newspaper. After analysing the latest figures on the distribution of wealth and income, Andreas Whittam Smith, then the city editor of the *Daily Telegraph*, concluded: 'The rich seem to get poorer and the poor get richer.' In November 1977 he reported that the top 20 per cent of Britain now accounted for just under 82 per cent of the nation's wealth, compared to almost 90 per cent in 1960. By this time, the slogan used successfully in the 1966 election – 'You know Labour Government works' – was a bad joke if remembered at all. But on this evidence it sort of did – if not for some of the *Telegraph*'s readers.

A few months later, it was reported that the top 1 per cent of the population received, after tax, less than four times the national average – *The Times* commented that the distribution of wealth in Britain was probably more even than in Communist countries.

Such statistics could be measured. Corrado Gini was an Italian statistician* who in 1912 devised the most common way of measuring inequality in a society. The Gini coefficient measures this on a scale in which 0 indicates that every citizen has the same amount of money and 1 indicates that one person has it all. So, very unequal societies like Brazil or South Africa have a much higher number than egalitarian ones like the Nordic nations.

In 1978, the UK's Gini coefficient touched its all-time low of 0.24, making it a more equal society than other comparable nations, as well as the Communist bloc. This was the product of the settlement of the post-1945 Attlee government, only tinkered with in the Tory years: very high top-end taxation matched by generous benefits for the poor, sick and elderly. Was this not perhaps the ideal to which Britain aspired: a slightly warmer Sweden?

From 1979 the coefficient began rising and rising. This was the choice the British people were about to make, knowingly or not:

---

* Tainted politically by his enthusiasm for eugenics.

everyone was unequal, after all, and henceforth some would be much more unequal than others.

————•————

It was not quite a triumphal progression for Mrs Thatcher. The polls did narrow, mainly because the Liberal vote ticked up. But there was little doubt about the result and the Tory-supporting press was full of enthusiasm for the leader – more enthusiastic indeed than some of Thatcher's own MPs. Her flirtatiousness with Larry Lamb, the editor of *The Sun*, continued to bear fruit. On election day the paper yelled:

VOTE TORY THIS TIME: *IT'S THE ONLY WAY TO STOP THE ROT**

Callaghan never had any doubt about the result: 'sea-change' was more than a cliché to an old naval man. Too late, he now sensed the storm clouds and the salt spray on the deck. Perhaps no prime minister has ever accepted the dying of the light with such fatalism, nor any sea captain gone down with the ship so stoically.

Even *The Archers* correctly predicted the result. The programme slipped a reference to a Tory win into the pre-recorded episode to be broadcast the evening after polling day. The primitive pre-digital technology was enough to allow a little light surgery to the tape had the prediction been wrong.

————•————

It was not wrong. Labour's vote stood still from the last election but the Tories increased theirs by 3 million. The most dramatic losers were the SNP, whose eleven seats slumped to two. As usual, the Liberals felt disappointed but they only lost three of their

---

* Mrs T was an enthusiastic *Sun* reader, and especially enjoyed the short, sharp leader columns published on page 2. Her aide Michael Dobbs told the story of her opening the paper during a pre-election discussion and pointing to page 2 approvingly. 'What do you think of those two, eh?' she said, oblivious to the fact that alongside them on page 3 were the two parts of the female anatomy for which the paper was more famous.

fourteen seats, and one of the casualties was the former leader, Jeremy Thorpe. His trial for conspiracy to murder Norman Scott now imminent, he was crushed by his Tory rival. Thorpe's face was a picture of desolation.

Thatcher's majority was forty-three, enough to govern cautiously but not quite enough for elective dictatorship. For Labour, it could have been much worse. Curiously, on such a day, the number of women MPs went down to its lowest level since 1951: 27 out of 635. None of the handful of non-white candidates had a winnable seat, but the closest, Narindar Saroop, the Conservative in Greenwich, polled in line with the national swing, which was a step forward.

Next day, the City of London was euphoric about the change of government: the pound shot up and the old FT30 index hit a new peak of 553.5. In mid-afternoon, Margaret Thatcher went to Buckingham Palace to see Elizabeth II. It would still be Elizabeth's Britain but would become a very different version of it.

The new prime minister was driven into Downing Street, through the traditional throng. A worldly aide advised her to sit in the right-hand back seat so her exit would be largely hidden from the camera crews and they would not focus on her legs. She then delivered a little homily she claimed was written by St Francis of Assisi, which it might have been had he still been alive in the early twentieth century, aged about 700.

> *Where there is discord, may we bring harmony.*
> *Where there is error, may we bring truth.*
> *Where there is doubt, may we bring faith.*
> *And where there is despair, may we bring hope.*

And with the alleged words of the saint who had devoted his life to poverty, peace, charity and the wonders of nature still ringing in the ears of the baffled nation, Margaret Thatcher went inside her new home to remake Britain – not necessarily to the prescription she had just outlined.

ACKNOWLEDGEMENTS

The book you have just finished (or, if you are expecting your name to be in this honours list, probably have not started yet) took four years to write. The research has involved dozens of interviews, hundreds of books and thousands of newspapers.

In the midst of this process came the global interruption of the Covid-19 epidemic, which I would like to blame for my slow progress. However, this is only partially true. The biggest minuses were that the interviewing was severely curtailed and library and archival access restricted. The plus was that there was a sudden absence of distractions.

Instead I sat in my study while my wife, daughter and the occasional passer-by regarded me as a combination of Rev. Casaubon, Mr Dick and the first Mrs Rochester, the madwoman in the attic.

When I did escape my garret and people asked what I was doing, they often became immediately engaged with the project. My own generation were very ready with their own thoughts about such matters as the nature of childhood in the fifties and sixties, the smell of an old-fashioned grocer and the changing pattern of dress codes. Some of their insights have indeed found their way into this book. Younger readers offered their experiences of change, which may yet surface in *The Reign* Part II. They all buoyed me up and strengthened my will to push on.

My first thanks go to the varied range of people – cabinet ministers and comedy writers, farmworkers and fishermen – who submitted to often lengthy face-to-face interviews about their varied experiences as both children and adults; many of them made far greater contributions to my understanding than would be obvious from the text:

Lord Armstrong of Ilminster; Neal Ascherson; Edward Barnes; Neil Barnes; Dr Denys Brierley; Dorothy Cooke; Rev. Victor de Waal; Nicholas Faith; Adam Fergusson; Sir Leslie Fielding; Mark and Renée Gerson; Revel Guest; Maisie and Michael Griffith; Joe Haines; Lord Hattersley; Lord Higgins; Marigold Johnson (née Hunt); Ken Knox; David McKie; Bryan Magee; Dr John Marks; Ian Mayes; Denis Norden; John O'Sullivan; Ruth Privett (née Patrick, later Borrill); Gillian Reynolds (née Morton); Barrie Rutter; Lord Tebbit; Sir Andreas Whittam Smith; Peter Wilby; Sam Williams; Douglas Wright; and Donald Zec.

Several of these – all sharp and lucid – were in their nineties when we spoke, and unsurprisingly a number have since died; I was honoured to have had the chance to meet them.

Once the Covid clampdown came, I carried on as best I could, asking questions on the phone and via email. One person led to another; experts world-famous in their fields patiently answered pathetically ignorant questions; only once did someone – a journalist of all people – knock me back rudely, which was a good thing, because it made me appreciate everyone else's kindness.

So for help of all kinds, I need to add:

Jonathan Agnew; Chris Arnot; Chris Aspin; Andrew Baker; Fiona Barnes; Simon Barnes; Professor Steve Barnett; Steve Bates; Mark Beswick; Edward Bevan; Steve Bierley; David Boardman; Robert Book; Chris Bowlby; Mike Brearley; Eileen Brown; Jeremy and Sue Bugler; Andy Bull; Professor Ed Bullmore; Jeremy Bullmore; Peter Burden and the Old Farts of Ludlow; Charlie Burgess; Professor Stefan Buczacki; Jeremy and Sue Bugler; Alistair Burt; Duncan Campbell; Bob Chesshyre; Andrew Cracknell; Stanley Challenger Graham; Dr Theo Chevallier; Professor John Clarke; Anna Coda and Steve Hancorn; Peter Cole; Anna Coote; Jason Cowley; James Coyne; Petra Cramsie; Ravi Das; Hunter Davies; Tim de Lisle; Professor Sir Tom Devine; Anne Dixey; Chris Douglas; Professor David Edgerton; Anthony and Sally Engel; James Engel; Richard and Liz Engel; Richard Evans; Stephen Fay; Stephen Fry; Alex Finer; Dr Clive Field; Neville Fleet; Stephen Frears; Professor Sir Lawrence Freedman; Right Rev. Richard Frith; Jane Gerson;

Delphine Gray-Fisk; Duncan Hamilton; Lady Hattersley; Petra (formerly Green) and Murray Hedgcock; Jon Henderson; John Hopkins; Steve Hopkins; Brian Hough; Richard Humphries; Keith James; Peter Jay; Rob Jenkinson; Peter Jinman; Daniel Johnson; Jane Keating; Chris Kitchen; Louisa Kuczinski; Helen Leadbeater; Ian Lee; Ruth Lesser (née Raven); Lesley Levene; Professor Michael Levi; Lord Lipsey; Bob Low; Steven Lynch; Alan McCardle; Don Macintyre; Rev. David Maclure; Robert Marshall-Andrews QC; Dr Paul Maslin; Andrew Medlock; Toby Murcott; Professor Philip Murphy; Andrew Nickolds; Philip Norman; Richard Norton-Taylor; Dr Peter Overstall; Matthew Parris; Nick Pitt; Chris Pond; Dr Siân Pooley; Philip Powell; Anthony Powers; Richard Price; Sir Tim Rice; Geoffrey Robertson QC; Prebendary Frank Rodgers; Rose Rouse (née Williams); John Segal; Paul Selfe; Alison Silver; Chris Smith; Professor Laura Spira; Marion and Clive Stainton; Inky Thomson; Professor Mathew Thomson; Geoffery Wansell; David Ward; Michael White; Des Wilson; Jonathan Wilson; Christian Wolmar; Martin Woollacott; Simon Worrall; and if I have forgotten anyone, please forgive me.

Without wanting to turn this into an Oscars speech, I must express my gratitude to Will Atkinson, James Nightingale and Derek Wyatt of Atlantic Books, who saw the possibilities of this project when other publishers shook their heads and who maintained faith and patience as my deadlines whooshed by. It was a pleasure to do business with such a pleasant and nimble company. They also provided me with an outstanding copy-editor in Gemma Wain.

For a while, I had the benefit of a brilliant polymathic research assistant in Matt Taylor, who brought a keen eye for both the factual and the quirky. Christopher Lane advised me with his customary skill and aplomb. And this book would never have been possible at all had not the London Library maintained a brilliant service to its members during Covid. I am grateful to all their staff, with special commendations to James Devine and Yvette Dickerson.

I am especially grateful to one of Britain's leading modern historians, David Kynaston, who welcomed me on to his territory, gave me much encouragement, and gently pointed out a bumper bundle of errors. My friends Hugh Chevallier and Geoffrey Wheatcroft also kindly read the proofs and saved me from many more mistakes between them. As Margaret Thatcher almost said (see page 589), 'Where there is error, bring me David, Hugh and Geoffrey.'

My wife Hilary and daughter Vika gave me reasons to keep working, even or perhaps especially when they thought I was going bonkers. And always in our hearts is our late son, Laurie, who, on the evidence we have, would by now have been far outshining his dad as a writer. As it is, I can only wish he could be here to be with us and to read this.

In a book so sprawling and eclectic, there are bound to be further mistakes. If you find any, please let me know via the website matthewengel.co.uk, so we can bring truth to later editions. I only ask that you do so civilly; to err is human. The website also contains the bibliography and, to save trees, all the reference material. For those intrigued by this book's jacket and can't quite identify everyone in Peter Quinnell's delightful montage, the answers to the puzzle are also there.

To find out what Maggie did next and the continuing drama of Elizabeth II's reign, please come back in due course.

ILLUSTRATIONS

p. 5: Queen Elizabeth II waves from the state coach while on her way to the House of Lords to open the first parliament of her reign, 5 November 1952 (*Bettman/Getty Images*)

p. 197: Elizabeth II talks to the Canadian prime minister as she makes the first call on the transatlantic telephone cable to Canada, 19 December 1961 (*Underwood Archives/Getty Images*)

p. 367: The Queen watches children folk dancing at the Pepys Estate, Deptford, June 1977 (*Trinity Mirror/Mirrorpix/Alamy Stock Photo*)

SECTION ONE: THE 1950S

George VI's coffin, Sandringham, February 1952 (*TopFoto*)

London street party for Elizabeth II's coronation, June 1953 (*Ernst Haas/Getty Images*)

Jamaican immigrants arriving in Britain, 1954 (© *Illustrated London News Ltd/ Mary Evans*)

Olga Noble-Mathews of *Good Housekeeping* learns how to use chopsticks, 1952 (*TopFoto/EUFD*)

Take Your Pick, 1955 (*TopFoto*)

Gilbert Harding (*Keystone Press/Alamy Stock Photo*)

Welsh family watches television, 1959 (*Bert Hardy Advertising Archive/Getty Images*)

Dai Rees plays in a tournament at Sunningdale, 1955 (*Central Press/Hulton Archive/Getty Images*)

Oxford University students, 1958 (*Bert Hardy Advertising Archive/Getty Images*)

John Cobb, 1952 (*Raymond Kleboe/Picture Post/Hulton Archive/Getty Images*)

Mike Hawthorn at the British Grand Prix, 1957 (*Bernard Cahier/Getty Images*)

Barbara Goalen, 1953 (*Waugh/Popperfoto via Getty Images*)

Lady Docker, 1954 (*Keystone Press/Alamy Stock Photo*)

Catching tiddlers in the River Wye, Hereford, 1955 (*Derek Evans*)

Children playing, 1954 (*Ken Russell/TopFoto*)

A grocer in Tottenham, 1958 (*Bert Hardy Advertising Archive/Getty Images*)

Farmer ploughing a field, 1952 (*Raymond Kleboe/Picture Post/Hulton Archive/ Getty Images*)

SECTION TWO: THE 1960S

Twiggy, 1966 (*Stan Meagher/Daily Express/Hulton Archive/Getty Images*)

John Stephen, 1967 (*Evening Standard/Hulton Archive/Getty Images*)

John 'Hoppy' Hopkins and Suzy Creamcheese, 1967 (*Victor Blackman/Daily Express/Getty Images*)

The Saddle Room, London's first discotheque, 1962 (*Trinity Mirror/Mirrorpix/Alamy Stock Photo*)

A teenage girl listens to a transistor radio, 1966 (*Terence Spencer/Getty Images*)

The cast of *That Was the Week That Was*, 1963 (*Don Smith/Radio Times/Getty Images*)

The Beatles before their performance at the Royal Variety Show, November 1963 (*Roy Illingworth/Mirrorpix/Getty Images*)

The Beatles at the launch of *Sergeant Pepper's Lonely Hearts Club Band*, June 1967 (*Keystone-France/Gamma-Keystone via Getty Images*)

John Profumo (*Hulton Archive/Getty Images*)

Christine Keeler (*Keystone Press/Alamy Stock Photo*)

Stephen Ward (*Victor Blackman/Daily Express/Hulton Archive/Getty Images*)

Mervyn Griffith-Jones (*George Freston/Fox Photos/Hulton Archive/Getty Images*)

The newly opened M1, 1960 (*Mary Evans Picture Library*)

Euston Arch, 1960 (*Eric de Maré/English Heritage/Heritage Images/Getty Images*)

Cleared terraced houses in Hulme, Manchester, 1962 (© *Estate of Shirley Baker/Mary Evans Picture Library*)

The last British Rail steam train leaves Liverpool Lime Street, August 1968 (*John H. Bird/ANISTR/Alamy Stock Photo*)

Jayne Harries at Ascot, June 1968 (*Trinity Mirror/Mirrorpix/Alamy Stock Photo*)

Jayne Harries in the Royal Enclosure at Ascot, June 1968 (*Fox Photos/Getty Images*)

Bruce Forsyth presents Vivian and Keith Nicholson with their winnings from the pools, 1961 (*Ron Case/Keystone/Hulton Archive/Getty Images*)

Don Thompson at the Rome Olympics, 1960 (*AP/Shutterstock*)

Pickles with his owner, 1966 (*Charlie Ley/Mirrorpix/Getty Images*)

PC Norwell Roberts, 1967 (*Douglas Miller/Keystone-France/Gamma-Keystone via Getty Images*)

Harry Roberts (*Keystone/Hulton Archive/Getty Images*)

INDEX

A NOTE ABOUT
THE AUTHOR

In fifty years of journalism, Matthew Engel has reported from all seven of the continents so far discovered, mostly for *The Guardian* and the *Financial Times*. He has covered war, elections, royal occasions and at least seventy different sports, including underwater hockey and tiddlywinks. For twelve years he edited *Wisden Cricketers' Almanack*, and has also written books on the counties of England, the railways, the press and the Americanization of the language.

He lives in Herefordshire and would have finished this book more quickly had he not been constantly distracted by the ever-changing view of the Black Mountains from his study window.

COPIERS
Coca-Cola
the Builder to watch!
TROLLOPE & COLLS
MONICO REDEVELOPMENT
TROLLOPE & COLLS
CIS
INSURANCE
19